See the Difference with LearningCurve!

learningcurveworks.com

LearningCurve is a winning solution for everyone: students come to class better prepared and instructors have more flexibility to go beyond the basic facts and concepts in class. LearningCurve's game-like quizzes are book-specific and link back to the textbook in LaunchPad so that students can brush up on the reading when they get stumped by a question. The reporting features help instructors track overall class trends and spot topics that are giving students trouble so that they can adjust lectures and class activities.

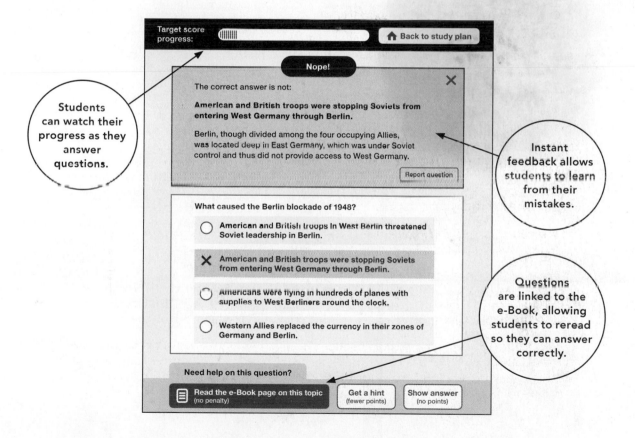

Students can watch their progress as they answer questions.

Instant feedback allows students to learn from their mistakes.

Questions are linked to the e-Book, allowing students to reread so they can answer correctly.

LearningCurve is easy to assign, easy to customize, and easy to complete. See the difference LearningCurve makes in teaching and learning history.

The American Promise

A Concise History

Volume 2: From 1865

SIXTH EDITION

James L. Roark
Emory University

Michael P. Johnson
Johns Hopkins University

Patricia Cline Cohen
University of California, Santa Barbara

Sarah Stage
Arizona State University

Susan M. Hartmann
The Ohio State University

bedford/st.martin's
Macmillan Learning
Boston | New York

FOR BEDFORD/ST. MARTIN'S

Vice President, Editorial, Macmillan Learning Humanities: Edwin Hill
Publisher for History: Michael Rosenberg
Senior Executive Editor for History: William J. Lombardo
Director of Development for History: Jane Knetzger
Developmental Editor: Robin Soule
Associate Editor: Tess Fletcher
Assistant Editor: Mary Posman
Editorial Assistant: Lexi DeConti
Senior Production Editor: Kendra LeFleur
Media Producer: Michelle Camisa
Media Editor: Jennifer Jovin
Production Manager: Joe Ford
History Marketing Manager: Melissa Famiglietti
Copy Editor: Lisa Wehrle
Indexer: Leoni McVey
Cartography: Mapping Specialists, Ltd.
Photo Editor: Cecilia Varas
Photo Researcher: Naomi Kornhauser
Permissions Editor: Eve Lehmann
Senior Art Director: Anna Palchik
Text Design: Cenveo Publisher Services
Cover Design: William Boardman
Cover Art/Cover Photo: Amelia Earhart in Cockpit (b/w photo)/UNIVERSAL IMAGES GROUP/Bridgeman Images.
Composition: Cenveo Publisher Services
Printing and Binding: LSC Communications

Manufactured in the United States of America.

1 0 9 8 7 6
f e d c b a

For information, write: Bedford/St. Martin's, 75 Arlington Street, Boston, MA 02116   (617-399-4000)

ISBN 978-1-319-04249-3 (Combined Edition)
ISBN 978-1-319-04273-8 (Volume 1)
ISBN 978-1-319-04274-5 (Volume 2)

Preface

Why This Book This Way

What is the best way to engage and teach students in their history survey course? From the beginning, *The American Promise* has been shaped by our firsthand knowledge that the survey course is one of the most difficult to teach and, for many, also the most difficult to take. From the outset we have met this challenge by providing a story students enjoy for its readability, clear chronology, and lively voices of ordinary Americans. *The American Promise: A Concise History* preserves the already-brief narrative and the full map program of the parent text, *The American Promise*, in a smaller, more affordable trim size with selected features and photos from the comprehensive edition. We remain committed to making the book the most teachable and readable introductory American history text available.

With **LaunchPad** we have made meeting the challenges of the survey course a great deal easier by providing an intuitive, interactive e-Book and course space with a wealth of primary sources. Ready to assign as is with key assessment resources built into each chapter, LaunchPad can also be edited and customized as instructors' imaginations and innovations dictate. Free when packaged with the print text, LaunchPad grants students and teachers access to a wealth of online tools and resources built specifically for our text to enhance reading comprehension and promote in-depth study. With LaunchPad, *Concise* users have access to the full art and feature program from the comprehensive book. LaunchPad is loaded with the full-color e-Book plus **LearningCurve,** an adaptive learning tool; the popular *Reading the American Past* primary documents collection; **additional primary sources**; special **skills-based assessment activities; videos; chapter summative quizzes**; and more.

What Makes *The American Promise* Special

Our experience as teachers and our frustrations with available textbooks inspired us to create a book that we could use effectively with our own students. Our knowledge of classroom realities has informed every aspect of each edition and version of *The American Promise*. We began with a **clear chronological, political framework**, as we have found that students need both the structure a political narrative provides *and* the insights gained from examining social and cultural experience. To write a comprehensive, balanced account of American history, we focus on the public arena — the place where politics intersects with social and cultural developments — to show how Americans confronted the major issues of their day and created far-reaching historical change.

The unique approach of our narrative is reflected in our title, *The American Promise*. We emphasize human agency and demonstrate our conviction that the essence of America has been its promise. For millions, the nation has held out the promise of a better life, unfettered worship, equality before the law, representative government, democratic politics, and other freedoms seldom found elsewhere. But none of these promises has come with guarantees. Throughout the narrative we demonstrate how much of American history is a continuing struggle over the definition and realization of the nation's promise.

To engage students in this American story and to portray fully the diversity of the American experience, we stitch into our narrative **the voices of hundreds of contemporaries**. We further animate this story with a **vivid art and map program**. **Visual and map activities in each chapter prompt students to think critically** about what they see. To help students of all levels understand American history, we provide the best in **primary sources** and **pedagogical aids**. To help instructors teach important skills and evaluate student learning, we provide a **rich assortment of assignments and assessments** in both the print and LaunchPad formats. While this edition rests solidly on our original goals and premises, it breaks new ground in addressing the specific needs of today's courses.

A New Skills Focus for the Special Features

For this revision we focused our attention on *The American Promise*'s acclaimed feature program by looking for ways to make the features more useful, skills-oriented assignments. In print, the features offer primary sources, visuals, essays, and discussion questions; in Launchpad, the feature program comes fully to life with both short-answer and multiple-choice questions that test students' critical reading skills. **Making Historical Arguments** (formerly **Historical Question**) now offers active, skills-based activities that demonstrate to students how historians make and support historical arguments. **Analyzing Historical Evidence** (formerly **Documenting the American Promise**) then gives students the opportunity to practice the skills introduced in **Making Historical Arguments** through analysis of text and visual sources. An enhanced **Beyond America's Borders** continues to offer students a global perspective on the narrative's themes with essays that connect U.S. history to developments around the globe. Those using LaunchPad will have access to **Experiencing the American Promise**, which offers essays that illuminate the stories of individuals who sought their dream in America, helping students evaluate to what extent individuals make history.

Collectively these features provide a range of new topics and content that includes a new focus on the weak opposition to the African slave trade in the eighteenth century; a nuanced look at reactions to the Boston Port Act outside Massachusetts; an examination of the nation's first formal declaration of war; attention to Ida B. Wells and her campaign to stop lynching; a spotlight on Franklin D. Roosevelt's use of New Deal programs to rebuild the navy during the 1930s; an exploration of the failure of the Equal Rights Amendment; and much more.

Evaluation of Primary Sources

Primary sources form the heart of historical study, and we are pleased to offer **the new Analyzing Historical Evidence feature, which asks students to use historical thinking skills to consider a range of documents**. Each feature juxtaposes two to four primary documents to reveal varying perspectives on a topic or issue and to provide students with opportunities to build and practice their skills of historical interpretation. Because students are so attuned to visuals and instructors deeply value their usefulness as primary sources, we have included both text and visual sources in this new feature. Images including artifacts of daily life in Chaco Canyon, examples of early photojournalism, political cartoons, and more show students how to mine visual documents for evidence about the past.

In **Analyzing Historical Evidence**, feature introductions and document head-notes contextualize the sources, and short-answer questions at the end of the feature promote critical thinking about primary sources. New topics have been added that are rich with human drama and include "The Nation's First Formal Declaration of War" and "Americans Encounter the New Deal." These features are available both in print and online and are easily assigned in LaunchPad, along with multiple-choice quizzes that measure student comprehension.

In addition, more than 150 documents in the accompanying collection *Reading the American Past* are available free to users who package the reader with the main print text, and they are automatically included in the LaunchPad e-Book. Not only can the short-answer questions be easily assigned from within LaunchPad, but multiple-choice questions are also available for assignment to measure comprehension and hold students accountable for their reading.

LaunchPad for *The American Promise* also comes with a collection of **more than 135 additional primary sources** that instructors can choose to assign. These sources include letters, memoirs, court records, government documents, and more, and they include items by or about such people as John Smith, William Penn, Anne Hutchinson, Jonathan Edwards, Mary Jemison, Black Hawk, John C. Calhoun, Frederick Douglass, Abraham Lincoln, Mary Elizabeth Lease, William Jennings Bryan, Theodore Roosevelt, Nicola Sacco and Bartolomeo Vanzetti, Huey P. Long, Franklin D. Roosevelt, Harry S. Truman, Paul Robeson, Richard Nixon, Ronald Reagan, and more.

To give students ample opportunity to practice thinking critically about primary source images, one picture in each chapter includes a special **visual activity caption** that reinforces this essential skill. One set of questions in these activities prompts analysis of the image, while a second set of questions helps students connect the image to main points in the narrative.

Distinctive Essay Features Practice Historical Thinking Skills

To demonstrate and engage students in various methods of historical thinking, our new **Making Historical Arguments** feature essays pose and interpret specific questions of continuing interest, such as "Why Did Cortés Win?," "Was the New United States a Christian Country?," "Did Westerners Really Build It All by Themselves?," and "Why Did the ERA Fail?"

Short-answer questions at the end of the features prompt students to consider things such as evidence, beliefs and values, and cause and effect as they relate to the historical question at hand. Available both in print and online, these features can be easily assigned in LaunchPad, along with multiple-choice quizzes that measure student comprehension.

Helping Students Understand the Narrative

Every instructor knows it can be a challenge to get students to complete assigned readings and then to fully understand what is important once they do the reading. *The American Promise* addresses these problems head-on with a suite of tools in LaunchPad that instructors can choose from.

To help students come to class prepared, instructors who adopt LaunchPad for *The American Promise* can assign the **LearningCurve** formative assessment activities. This online learning tool is popular with students because it helps them rehearse content at their own pace in a nonthreatening, game-like environment. Learning-Curve is also popular with instructors because the reporting features allow them to track overall class trends and spot topics that are giving their students trouble so they can adjust their lectures and class activities.

Encouraging active reading is another means for making content memorable and highlighting what is truly important. To help students read actively and understand the central idea of the chapter, instructors who use LaunchPad can also assign **Guided Reading Exercises**. These exercises appear at the start of each chapter, prompting students to collect information to be used to answer a broad analytic question central to the chapter as a whole.

To further encourage students to read and fully assimilate the text as well as measure how well they do this, instructors can assign the **multiple-choice summative quizzes** in LaunchPad, where they are automatically graded. These secure tests not only encourage students to study the book, they also can be assigned at specific intervals as higher-stakes testing and thus provide another means for analyzing class performance.

Another big challenge for survey instructors is meeting the needs of a range of students, particularly the students who need the most support. In addition to the formative assessment of LearningCurve, which adapts to the needs of students at any level, *The American Promise* offers a number of print and digital tools for the underprepared. Each chapter opener includes **Content Learning Objectives** to prepare students to read the chapter with purpose. Once into the heart of the chapter, students are reminded to think about main ideas through **Review Questions** placed at the end of every major section. In print and LaunchPad these questions can be assigned as a chapter review activity. **Key Terms** are defined in the margins, giving background on important ideas and events. Some students have trouble connecting events and ideas, particularly with special boxed features. To address this, we have added a **set of Questions for Analysis** to the end of each feature to help students understand the significance of the featured topic, its context, and how it might be viewed from different angles. These questions are also available in the print and LaunchPad versions of the book.

With this edition we also bring back two popular sets of end-of-chapter questions that help widen students' focus as they consider what they have read. **Making Connections** questions ask students to think about broad developments within the chapter, while **Linking to the Past** questions cross-reference developments in earlier chapters, encouraging students to draw connections to the modern world and consider how the issues addressed in the chapter are still relevant today. Both sets of questions are assignable from the print and LaunchPad versions.

Helping Instructors Teach with Digital Resources

With requests for clear and transparent learning outcomes coming from all quarters and with students who bring increasingly diverse levels of skills to class, even veteran teachers can find preparing for today's courses a trying matter. With LaunchPad we have reconceived the textbook as a suite of tools in multiple formats that allows each format do what it does best to capture students' interest and help instructors create meaningful lessons.

But one of the best benefits is that instructors using LaunchPad have a number of assessment tools that allow them to see what it is their students do and don't know and measure student achievement all in one convenient space. For example, **LearningCurve**, an adaptive learning tool that comes with LaunchPad, garners more than a 90 percent student satisfaction rate and helps students master book content. When Learning-Curve is assigned, the grade book results show instructors where the entire class or individual students may be struggling, and this information in turn allows instructors to adjust lectures and course activities accordingly — a benefit not only for traditional classes but invaluable for hybrid, online, and newer "flipped" classes as well. In addition, not only can instructors assign all of the questions that appear in the print book and view the responses in the grade book, but they also have the option to assign automatically graded multiple-choice questions for all of the book features.

With LaunchPad for *The American Promise* we make the tough job of teaching simpler by providing everything instructors need in one convenient space so they can set and achieve the learning outcomes they desire. To learn more about the benefits of LearningCurve and LaunchPad, see the "Versions and Supplements" section on page xiii.

Acknowledgments

We gratefully acknowledge all of the helpful suggestions from those who have read and taught from previous editions of *The American Promise: A Concise History,* and we hope that our many classroom collaborators will be pleased to see their influence in the sixth edition. In particular, we wish to thank the talented scholars and teachers who gave generously of their time and knowledge to review this book: Kirk R. Abendroth, *Vincennes University*; Donna J. Benson, *Winston-Salem State University*; Edward Black, *Jefferson State Community College*; David Burleson, *Doña Ana Community College*; Brian Casserly, *Bellevue College*; John W. Catron, *Santa Fe College*;

A. Glenn Crothers, *University of Louisville*; William J. Cuddihy, *Long Beach City College*; Andy DeRoche, *Front Range Community College*; Kimberly DesRoches, *Western Nevada College*; David Driscoll, *University of Massachusetts – Lowell*; Amy Drumb, *Polk State College*; Laura Dunn, *Eastern Florida State College*; Robert Elder, *Valparaiso University*; John Franklin, *Graceland University*; Mary Frederickson, *Miami University of Ohio*; Kirsten Gardner, *The University of Texas at San Antonio*; George Gerdow, *Northeastern Illinois University*; Nicki Gonzales, *Regis University*; Brian L. Hackett, *Northern Kentucky University*; Lindsey Hinds-Brown, *Middle Tennessee State University*; Caroline Hoefferle, *Wingate University*; Antoinnette Hudson, *Jacksonville State University*; Clifton Huffmaster, *Middle Tennessee State University*; Brian Ingrassia, *Middle Tennessee State University*; Kent Kaster III, *Eastern Florida State College*; Carey Kelley, *Missouri State University*; William J. Lipkin, *Union County College*; Matthew Loayza, *Minnesota State University, Mankato*; Stephanie A. L. Molholt, *The Community College of Baltimore County – Catonsville*; Wesley Moody, *Florida State College at Jacksonville*; Johnny S. Moore, *Radford University*; Steven Noll, *University of Florida*; Ellen Holmes Pearson, *University of North Carolina Asheville*; Robert D. Pittman, *Lindenwood University/St. Louis Community College*; Emily Rader, *El Camino College*; David B. Raymond, *Northern Maine Community College*; Daniel Rezny, *St. Charles Community College*; Leo Ribuffo, *George Washington University*; Tom Robertson, *The Community College of Baltimore County*; Thomas J. Rowland, *University of Wisconsin – Oshkosh*; George D. Salaita, *Eastern Tennessee University*; Christopher Staaf, *Georgia Gwinnett College*; Richard Trimble, *Ocean County College*; James H. Tuten, *Juniata College*; Christina A. Wilbur, *Lamar University*; Kathleen Williams, *Holy Names University*; Louis Williams, *St. Louis Community College – Forest Park*; and John Ralph Wilson, *Lone Star College North Harris*.

A project as complex as this requires the talents of many individuals. First, we would like to acknowledge our families for their support, forbearance, and toleration of our textbook responsibilities. Naomi Kornhauser contributed her vast knowledge, tireless energy, and diligent research to make possible the useful and attractive illustration program. We would also like to thank the many people at Bedford/St. Martin's and Macmillan Learning who have been crucial to this project. Thanks are due to Robin Soule, developmental editor; Edwin Hill, vice president; Michael Rosenberg, publisher; William J. Lombardo, senior executive editor for history; and Jane Knetzger, director of development for history, for their support and guidance. Thanks are also due to Heidi Hood, senior editor; Jennifer Jovin, media editor; Tess Fletcher, associate editor; Mary Posman, assistant editor; and Lexi DeConti, editorial assistant. For their imaginative and tireless efforts to promote the book, we want to thank history marketing manager Melissa Famiglietti and marketing assistant Morgan Ratner. With great skill and professionalism, senior production editor Kendra LeFleur pulled together the many pieces related to copyediting, design, and composition. Production manager Joe Ford oversaw the manufacturing of the book. Designer Jerilyn Bockorick, copy editor Lisa Wehrle, and proofreaders Arthur Johnson and Angela Morrison attended to the myriad details that help make the book shine. Leoni McVey provided an outstanding index. The covers for the book's many versions were researched and designed by William Boardman. Media producer Michelle Camisa oversaw the timely and complex production of digital components of *The American Promise*.

Versions and Supplements

Adopters of *The American Promise: A Concise History* and their students have access to abundant print and digital resources and tools, the acclaimed Bedford Series in History and Culture volumes, and much more. The LaunchPad course space for *The American Promise* provides access to the narrative as well as a wealth of primary sources and other features, along with assignment and assessment opportunities. See below for more information, visit the book's catalog site at **macmillanlearning.com**, or contact your local Bedford/St. Martin's sales representative.

Get the Right Version for Your Class

The American Promise franchise offers a variety of versions to best suit your course needs. The comprehensive *The American Promise* includes a full-color art program and a robust set of features. *Understanding the American Promise*, with a more modest feature program, enhances the full narrative with a question-driven approach and innovative active learning pedagogy. *The American Promise: A Concise History* also provides the full narrative, with a streamlined art and feature program, at a lower price. *The American Promise, Value Edition*, offers a trade-sized two-color option with the full narrative and selected art and maps at a steeper discount. The *Value Edition* is also offered at the lowest price point in loose-leaf, and all versions are available as low-priced PDF e-Books. For the best value of all, package a new print book with LaunchPad at no additional charge to get the best each format offers — a print version for easy portability, plus a LaunchPad interactive e-Book and course space with LearningCurve and loads of additional assignment and assessment options.

- **Combined Volume** (Chapters 1–31): available in the comprehensive, *Understanding*, Concise, Value, loose-leaf, and e-Book formats and in LaunchPad
- **Volume 1, To 1877** (Chapters 1–16): available in the comprehensive, *Understanding*, Concise, Value, loose-leaf, and e-Book formats and in LaunchPad
- **Volume 2, From 1865** (Chapters 16–31): available in the comprehensive, *Understanding*, Concise, Value, loose-leaf, and e-Book formats and in LaunchPad

As noted below, any of these volumes can be packaged with additional titles for a discount. To get ISBNs for discount packages, visit **macmillanlearning.com** or contact your Bedford/St. Martin's representative.

Assign LaunchPad — an Assessment-Ready Interactive e-Book and Course Space

Available for discount purchase on its own or for packaging with new books at no additional charge, LaunchPad is a breakthrough solution for history courses. Intuitive and easy-to-use for students and instructors alike, LaunchPad is ready to use as is, and can be edited, customized with your own material, and assigned quickly. LaunchPad for *The American Promise* includes Bedford/St. Martin's high-quality content all in one place, including the full interactive e-Book with all of the full-color maps and images and features of the comprehensive edition and the companion reader *Reading the American Past,* plus LearningCurve formative quizzing, guided reading activities designed to help students read actively for key concepts, auto-graded quizzes for each primary source, and chapter summative quizzes.

Through a wealth of formative and summative assessments, including the adaptive learning program of LearningCurve (see the full description ahead), students gain confidence and get into their reading *before* class. These features, plus additional primary source documents, video sources and tools for making video assignments, map activities, flashcards, and customizable test banks, make LaunchPad an invaluable asset for any instructor. For more information, visit **launchpadworks.com**, or to arrange a demo, contact us at **history@macmillan.com**.

Assign LearningCurve So Your Students Come to Class Prepared

Students using LaunchPad receive access to LearningCurve for *The American Promise*. Assigning LearningCurve in place of reading quizzes is easy for instructors, and the reporting features help instructors track overall class trends and spot topics that are giving students trouble so they can adjust their lectures and class activities. This online learning tool is popular with students because it was designed to help them comprehend content at their own pace in a nonthreatening, game-like environment. The feedback for wrong answers provides instructional coaching and sends students back to the book for review. Students answer as many questions as necessary to reach a target score, with repeated chances to revisit material they haven't mastered. When LearningCurve is assigned, students come to class better prepared.

Take Advantage of Instructor Resources

Bedford/St. Martin's has developed a rich array of teaching resources for this book and for this course. They range from lecture and presentation materials and assessment tools to course management options. Most can be found in LaunchPad or can be downloaded or ordered from the Instructor Resources tab of the book's catalog site at **macmillanlearning.com**.

Bedford Coursepack for Blackboard, Canvas, Brightspace by D2L, or Moodle. We can help you integrate our rich content into your course management system. Registered instructors can download coursepacks that include our popular free resources and book-specific content for *The American Promise*.

Instructor's Resource Manual. The instructor's manual offers both experienced and first-time instructors tools for presenting textbook materials in engaging ways. It includes chapter content learning objectives, annotated chapter outlines, and strategies for teaching with the textbook, plus suggestions on how to get the most out of LearningCurve, and a survival guide for first-time teaching assistants.

Guide to Changing Editions. Designed to facilitate an instructor's transition from the previous edition of *The American Promise: A Concise Edition* to this new edition, this guide presents an overview of major changes as well as of changes in each chapter.

Online Test Bank. The test bank includes a mix of fresh, carefully crafted multiple-choice, matching, short-answer, and essay questions for each chapter. Many of the multiple-choice questions feature a map, an image, or a primary-source excerpt as the prompt. All questions appear in easy-to-use test bank software that allows instructors to add, edit, resequence, filter by question type or learning objective, and print questions and answers. Instructors can also export questions into a variety of course management systems.

The Bedford Lecture Kit: Lecture Outlines, Maps, and Images. Look good and save time with *The Bedford Lecture Kit*. These presentation materials include fully customizable multimedia presentations built around chapter outlines that are embedded with maps, figures, and images from the textbook and are supplemented by more detailed instructor notes on key points and concepts.

America in Motion: Video Clips for U.S. History. Set history in motion with *America in Motion*, an instructor DVD containing dozens of short digital movie files of events in twentieth-century American history. From the wreckage of the battleship *Maine* to FDR's fireside chats to Ronald Reagan speaking before the Brandenburg Gate, *America in Motion* engages students with dynamic scenes from key events and challenges them to think critically. All files are classroom-ready, edited for brevity, and easily integrated with presentation slides or other software for electronic lectures or assignments. An accompanying guide provides each clip's historical context, ideas for use, and suggested questions.

Print, Digital, and Custom Options for More Choice and Value

For information on free packages and discounts up to 50 percent, contact your local Bedford/St. Martin's sales representative or visit **macmillanlearning.com**.

***Reading the American Past,* Fifth Edition.** Edited by Michael P. Johnson, one of the authors of *The American Promise*, and designed to complement the textbook, *Reading the American Past* provides a broad selection of more than 150 primary source documents, as well as editorial apparatus to help students understand the sources. Available free when packaged with the print text and included in the LaunchPad e-Book. Also available on its own as a downloadable PDF e-Book.

NEW Bedford Custom Tutorials for History. Designed to customize textbooks with resources relevant to individual courses, this collection of brief units, each sixteen pages long and loaded with examples, guides students through basic skills such as using historical evidence effectively, working with primary sources, taking effective notes, avoiding plagiarism and citing sources, and more. Up to two tutorials can be added to a Bedford/St. Martin's history survey title at no additional charge, freeing you to spend your class time focusing on content and interpretation. For more information, visit **macmillanlearning.com/historytutorials**.

NEW Bedford Digital Collections for U.S. History. This source collection provides a flexible and affordable online repository of discovery-oriented primary-source projects ready to assign. Each curated project — written by a historian about a favorite topic — poses a historical question and guides students step by step through analysis of primary sources. Examples include "What Caused the Civil War?," "The California Gold Rush: A Trans-Pacific Phenomenon," and "War Stories: Black Soldiers and the Long Civil Rights Movement." For more information, visit **macmillanlearning.com /bdc/ushistory/catalog**. Available free when packaged.

NEW Bedford Digital Collections Custom Print Modules. Choose one or two document projects from the collection (see above) and add them in print to a Bedford/St. Martin's title, or select several to be bound together in a custom reader created specifically for your course. Either way, the modules are affordably priced. For more information, visit **macmillanlearning.com/custombdc/ushistory** or contact your Bedford/St. Martin's representative.

The Bedford Series in History and Culture. More than 100 titles in this highly praised series combine first-rate scholarship, historical narrative, and important primary documents for undergraduate courses. Each book is brief, inexpensive, and focused on a specific topic or period. Revisions of several best-selling titles, such as *The Cherokee Removal: A Brief History with Documents* by Theda Perdue; *Narrative of the Life of Frederick Douglass*, edited by David Blight; and *The Triangle Fire: A Brief History with Documents* by Jo Ann Argersinger, are now available. For a complete list of titles, visit **macmillanlearning.com**. Package discounts are available.

Rand McNally Atlas of American History. This collection of more than eighty full-color maps illustrates key events and eras from early exploration, settlement, expansion, and immigration to U.S. involvement in wars abroad and on U.S. soil. Introductory pages for each section include a brief overview, timelines, graphs, and photos to quickly establish a historical context. Free when packaged.

The Bedford Glossary for U.S. History. This handy supplement for the survey course gives students historically contextualized definitions for hundreds of terms — from *abolitionism* to *zoot suit* — that they will encounter in lectures, reading, and exams. Free when packaged.

Trade Books. Titles published by sister companies Hill and Wang; Farrar, Straus and Giroux; Henry Holt and Company; St. Martin's Press; Picador; and Palgrave Macmillan are available at a 50 percent discount when packaged with Bedford/St. Martin's textbooks. For more information, visit **macmillanlearning.com/tradeup**.

A Pocket Guide to Writing in History. This portable and affordable reference tool by Mary Lynn Rampolla provides reading, writing, and research advice useful to students in all history courses. Concise yet comprehensive advice on approaching typical history assignments, developing critical reading skills, writing effective history papers, conducting research, using and documenting sources, and avoiding plagiarism — enhanced with practical tips and examples throughout — have made this slim reference a best seller. Package discounts are available.

A Student's Guide to History. This complete guide to success in any history course provides the practical help students need to be successful. In addition to introducing students to the nature of the discipline, author Jules Benjamin teaches a wide range of skills, from preparing for exams to approaching common writing assignments, and explains the research and documentation process with plentiful examples. Package discounts are available.

Going to the Source: The Bedford Reader in American History. Developed by Victoria Bissell Brown and Timothy J. Shannon, this reader combines a rich diversity of primary and secondary sources with in-depth instructions for how to use each type of source. Mirroring the chronology of the U.S. history survey, each of the main chapters familiarizes students with a single type of source — from personal letters to political cartoons — while focusing on an intriguing historical episode such as the Cherokee removal or the 1894 Pullman strike. The reader's wide variety of chapter topics and sources provokes students' interest as it teaches them the skills they need to successfully interrogate historical sources. Package discounts are available.

America Firsthand. With its distinctive focus on first-person accounts from ordinary people, this primary documents reader by Anthony Marcus, John M. Giggie, and David Burner offers a remarkable range of perspectives on America's history from those who lived it. Popular Points of View sections expose students to different perspectives on a specific event or topic. Package discounts are available.

Brief Contents

U.S. Political/Geographic Map   *ii*

Preface   *vii*

Versions and Supplements   *xiii*

Contents   *xx*

Maps, Figures, and Tables   *xxix*

Special Features   *xxxii*

16 Reconstruction, 1863–1877   *458*

17 The Contested West, 1865–1900   *488*

18 Railroads, Business, and Politics in the Gilded Age, 1865–1900   *518*

19 The City and Its Workers, 1870–1900   *548*

20 Dissent, Depression, and War, 1890–1900   *580*

21 Progressivism from the Grass Roots to the White House, 1890–1916   *610*

22 World War I: The Progressive Crusade at Home and Abroad, 1914–1920   *642*

23 From New Era to Great Depression, 1920–1932   *674*

24 The New Deal Experiment, 1932–1939   *706*

25 The United States and the Second World War, 1939–1945   *738*

26 Cold War Politics in the Truman Years, 1945–1953   *772*

27 The Politics and Culture of Abundance, 1952–1960   *798*

28 Reform, Rebellion, and Reaction, 1960–1974   *828*

29 Vietnam and the End of the Cold War Consensus, 1961–1975   *860*

30 America Moves to the Right, 1969–1989   *890*

31 The Promises and Challenges of Globalization, Since 1989   *922*

Appendices   *A-1*

Glossary   *G-1*

Index   *I-1*

About the Authors   *last book page*

Contents

U.S. Political/Geographic Map   *ii*

Preface   *vii*

Versions and Supplements   *xiii*

Brief Contents   *xix*

Maps, Figures, and Tables   *xxix*

Special Features   *xxxii*

CHAPTER 16

Reconstruction,
1863–1877   *458*

OPENING VIGNETTE: James T. Rapier emerges in the early 1870s as Alabama's most prominent black leader   *458*

Wartime Reconstruction   *460*

"To Bind Up the Nation's Wounds"   *460*

Land and Labor   *462*

The African American Quest for Autonomy   *463*

Presidential Reconstruction   *464*

Johnson's Program of Reconciliation   *465*

White Southern Resistance and Black Codes   *465*

Expansion of Federal Authority and Black Rights   *466*

Congressional Reconstruction   *467*

The Fourteenth Amendment and Escalating Violence   *467*

Radical Reconstruction and Military Rule   *469*

Impeaching a President   *470*

The Fifteenth Amendment and Women's Demands   *471*

The Struggle in the South   *472*

Freedmen, Yankees, and Yeomen   *472*

Republican Rule   *473*

White Landlords, Black Sharecroppers   *476*

BEYOND AMERICA'S BORDERS: The Slaveholder Exodus   *476*

Reconstruction Collapses   *480*

Grant's Troubled Presidency   *480*

Northern Resolve Withers   *481*

White Supremacy Triumphs   *482*

An Election and a Compromise   *484*

Conclusion: "A Revolution but Half Accomplished"   *485*

CHAPTER REVIEW   *486*

Photo: Elemental Studios/Alamy.

CHAPTER 17
The Contested West,
1865–1900 *488*

OPENING VIGNETTE: Frederick Jackson Turner delivers his "frontier thesis" *488*

Conquest and Empire in the West *490*
Indian Removal and the Reservation
System *491*
The Decimation of the Great Bison Herds *493*
Indian Wars and the Collapse of
Comanchería *494*
The Fight for the Black Hills *495*
**Forced Assimilation and Indian
Resistance** *496*
Indian Schools and the War on
Indian Culture *496*
The Dawes Act and Indian Land
Allotment *497*
Indian Resistance and Survival *498*
Mining the West *501*
Life on the Comstock Lode *501*
The Diverse Peoples of the West *504*
Land Fever *507*
Moving West: Homesteaders and
Speculators *507*
**MAKING HISTORICAL ARGUMENTS: Did
Westerners Really Build It All by
Themselves?** *508*
Tenants, Sharecroppers, and Migrants *512*
Commercial Farming and Industrial
Cowboys *513*
Territorial Government *515*
Conclusion: The West in the Gilded Age *515*

CHAPTER REVIEW *516*

CHAPTER 18
Railroads, Business, and Politics in the Gilded Age,
1865–1900 *518*

**OPENING VIGNETTE: Mark Twain and the
Gilded Age** *518*

Railroads and the Rise of New Industries *520*
Railroads: America's First Big Business *520*
Andrew Carnegie, Steel, and Vertical Integration *524*
John D. Rockefeller, Standard Oil, and the Trust *525*
New Inventions: The Telephone and the Telegraph *527*
From Competition to Consolidation *528*
J. P. Morgan and Finance Capitalism *529*
Social Darwinism, Laissez-Faire, and the
Supreme Court *530*
Politics and Culture *531*
Political Participation and Party Loyalty *531*
Sectionalism and the New South *532*
Gender, Race, and Politics *533*
**ANALYZING HISTORICAL EVIDENCE: Ida B. Wells
and Her Campaign to Stop Lynching** *534*
Women's Activism *536*
Presidential Politics *537*
Corruption and Party Strife *538*
Garfield's Assassination and Civil Service Reform *538*
Reform and Scandal: The Campaign of 1884 *539*
Economic Issues and Party Realignment *540*
The Tariff and the Politics of Protection *541*
Railroads, Trusts, and the Federal Government *542*
The Fight for Free Silver *543*
Panic and Depression *544*
Conclusion: Business Dominates an Era *545*

CHAPTER REVIEW *546*

CHAPTER 19
The City and Its Workers, 1870–1900 *548*

OPENING VIGNETTE: Workers build the Brooklyn Bridge *548*

The Rise of the City *550*
The Urban Explosion: A Global Migration *551*
Racism and the Cry for Immigration Restriction *555*
The Social Geography of the City *558*
At Work in Industrial America *560*
America's Diverse Workers *560*
The Family Economy: Women and Children *561*
White-Collar Workers: Managers, "Typewriters," and Salesclerks *562*
Workers Organize *563*
The Great Railroad Strike of 1877 *564*
The Knights of Labor and the American Federation of Labor *566*
Haymarket and the Specter of Labor Radicalism *567*
At Home and at Play *569*
Domesticity and "Domestics" *569*
Cheap Amusements *570*
City Growth and City Government *571*
Building Cities of Stone and Steel *571*
City Government and the "Bosses" *573*
BEYOND AMERICA'S BORDERS: The World's Columbian Exposition and Nineteenth-Century World's Fairs *574*
White City or City of Sin? *576*
Conclusion: Who Built the Cities? *577*

CHAPTER REVIEW *578*

CHAPTER 20
Dissent, Depression, and War, 1890–1900 *580*

OPENING VIGNETTE: Frances Willard participates in the creation of the Populist Party in 1892 *580*

The Farmers Unite *582*
The Farmers' Alliance *582*
The Populist Movement *584*
The Labor Wars *585*
The Homestead Lockout *585*
The Cripple Creek Miners' Strike of 1894 *587*
Eugene V. Debs and the Pullman Strike *588*
Women's Activism *590*
Frances Willard and the Woman's Christian Temperance Union *591*
Elizabeth Cady Stanton, Susan B. Anthony, and the Movement for Woman Suffrage *592*
Depression Politics *593*
Coxey's Army *594*
The People's Party and the Election of 1896 *595*
The United States and the World *597*
Markets and Missionaries *598*
The Monroe Doctrine and the Open Door Policy *600*
"A Splendid Little War" *601*
The Debate over American Imperialism *603*
MAKING HISTORICAL ARGUMENTS: Did Terrorists Sink the *Maine*? *604*
Conclusion: Rallying around the Flag *607*

CHAPTER REVIEW *608*

CHAPTER 21

Progressivism from the Grass Roots to the White House, 1890–1916 *610*

OPENING VIGNETTE: Jane Addams founds Hull House *610*

Grassroots Progressivism *612*
Civilizing the City *613*
Progressives and the Working Class *614*
Progressivism: Theory and Practice *616*
Reform Darwinism and Social Engineering *616*
Progressive Government: City and State *617*
Progressivism Finds a President: Theodore Roosevelt *618*
The Square Deal *619*
Roosevelt the Reformer *621*
Roosevelt and Conservation *622*
The Big Stick *623*
ANALYZING HISTORICAL EVIDENCE: **The Flash and the Birth of Photojournalism** *624*
The Troubled Presidency of William Howard Taft *629*
Woodrow Wilson and Progressivism at High Tide *631*
Progressive Insurgency and the Election of 1912 *631*
Wilson's Reforms: Tariff, Banking, and the Trusts *633*
Wilson, Reluctant Progressive *634*
The Limits of Progressive Reform *635*
Radical Alternatives *635*
Progressivism for White Men Only *636*
Conclusion: The Transformation of the Liberal State *639*

CHAPTER REVIEW *640*

CHAPTER 22

World War I: The Progressive Crusade at Home and Abroad, 1914–1920 *642*

OPENING VIGNETTE: Doughboy George "Brownie" Browne sees combat on the front lines in France *642*

Woodrow Wilson and the World *644*
Taming the Americas *645*
The European Crisis *646*
The Ordeal of American Neutrality *647*
The United States Enters the War *649*
"Over There" *650*
The Call to Arms *650*
The War in France *651*
The Crusade for Democracy at Home *654*
The Progressive Stake in the War *654*
Women, War, and the Battle for Suffrage *655*
Rally around the Flag — or Else *657*
A Compromised Peace *659*
Wilson's Fourteen Points *659*
The Paris Peace Conference *659*
The Fight for the Treaty *662*
Democracy at Risk *664*
Economic Hardship and Labor Upheaval *664*
The Red Scare *665*
BEYOND AMERICA'S BORDERS: **Bolshevism** *666*
The Great Migrations of African Americans and Mexicans *668*
Postwar Politics and the Election of 1920 *671*
Conclusion: Troubled Crusade *672*

CHAPTER REVIEW *672*

Photo: David J. & Janice L. Frent Collection/Corbis.

Photo: Collection of Colonel Stuart S. Corning Jr./Picture Research Consultants & Archives.

CHAPTER 23

From New Era to Great Depression, 1920–1932 *674*

OPENING VIGNETTE: Henry Ford puts America on wheels *674*

The New Era *677*
A Business Government *677*
Promoting Prosperity and Peace Abroad *678*
Automobiles, Mass Production, and Assembly-Line Progress *679*
Consumer Culture *680*
The Roaring Twenties *682*
Prohibition *682*
The New Woman *683*
The New Negro *685*
MAKING HISTORICAL ARGUMENTS: Was There a Sexual Revolution in the 1920s? *686*
Entertainment for the Masses *688*
The Lost Generation *690*
Resistance to Change *691*
Rejecting the Undesirables *691*
The Rebirth of the Ku Klux Klan *693*
The Scopes Trial *694*
Al Smith and the Election of 1928 *694*
The Great Crash *695*
Herbert Hoover: The Great Engineer *695*
The Distorted Economy *696*
The Crash of 1929 *697*
Hoover and the Limits of Individualism *697*
Life in the Depression *699*
The Human Toll *699*
Denial and Escape *701*
Working-Class Militancy *702*
Conclusion: Dazzle and Despair *703*

CHAPTER REVIEW *704*

CHAPTER 24

The New Deal Experiment, 1932–1939 *706*

OPENING VIGNETTE: "Migrant Mother" Florence Owens struggles to survive in the Great Depression *706*

Franklin D. Roosevelt: A Patrician in Government *708*
The Making of a Politician *708*
The Election of 1932 *710*
Launching the New Deal *712*
The New Dealers *712*
Banking and Finance Reform *713*
Relief and Conservation Programs *714*
Agricultural Initiatives *715*
Industrial Recovery *717*
Challenges to the New Deal *718*
Resistance to Business Reform *718*
Casualties in the Countryside *719*
Politics on the Fringes *720*
Toward a Welfare State *722*
Relief for the Unemployed *723*
Empowering Labor *724*
Social Security and Tax Reform *725*
ANALYZING HISTORICAL EVIDENCE: Americans Encounter the New Deal *726*
Neglected Americans and the New Deal *728*
The New Deal from Victory to Deadlock *730*
The Election of 1936 *731*
Court Packing *731*
Reaction and Recession *732*
The Last of the New Deal Reforms *733*
Conclusion: Achievements and Limitations of the New Deal *735*

CHAPTER REVIEW *736*

Photo: Division of Work & Industry, National Museum of American History, Smithsonian Institution.

Photo: David J. & Janice L. Frent Collection/Corbis.

CHAPTER 25
The United States and the Second World War,
1939–1945 738

OPENING VIGNETTE: Colonel Paul Tibbets drops the atomic bomb on Hiroshima, Japan 738

Peacetime Dilemmas 740
  Roosevelt and Reluctant Isolation 741
  The Good Neighbor Policy 741
  The Price of Noninvolvement 742
The Onset of War 743
  Nazi Aggression and War in Europe 743
  From Neutrality to the Arsenal of Democracy 745
  Japan Attacks America 747
Mobilizing for War 749
  Home-Front Security 749
  Building a Citizen Army 750
  Conversion to a War Economy 750
Fighting Back 753
  Turning the Tide in the Pacific 753
  The Campaign in Europe 754
The Wartime Home Front 756
  Women and Families, Guns and Butter 756
  The Double V Campaign 757
  Wartime Politics and the 1944 Election 758
  Reaction to the Holocaust 759
  BEYOND AMERICA'S BORDERS: Nazi Anti-Semitism and the Atomic Bomb 760
Toward Unconditional Surrender 762
  From Bombing Raids to Berlin 763
  The Defeat of Japan 765
  Atomic Warfare 768
Conclusion: Allied Victory and America's Emergence as a Superpower 769

CHAPTER REVIEW 770

CHAPTER 26
Cold War Politics in the Truman Years,
1945–1953 772

OPENING VIGNETTE: Helen Gahagan Douglas, congresswoman and loyal Truman ally, supports the Marshall Plan, the creation of NATO, and the war in Korea 772

From the Grand Alliance to Containment 774
  The Cold War Begins 774
  The Truman Doctrine and the Marshall Plan 777
  Building a National Security State 778
  MAKING HISTORICAL ARGUMENTS: Why Did the United States Launch the European Recovery Program? 780
  Superpower Rivalry around the Globe 782
Truman and the Fair Deal at Home 783
  Reconverting to a Peacetime Economy 784
  Blacks and Mexican Americans Push for Their Civil Rights 786
  The Fair Deal Flounders 788
  The Domestic Chill: McCarthyism 789
The Cold War Becomes Hot: Korea 791
  Korea and the Military Implementation of Containment 791
  From Containment to Rollback to Containment 793
  Korea, Communism, and the 1952 Election 794
  An Armistice and the War's Costs 795
Conclusion: The Cold War's Costs and Consequences 795

CHAPTER REVIEW 796

CHAPTER 27
The Politics and Culture of Abundance, 1952–1960 798

OPENING VIGNETTE: Vice President Richard Nixon debates Soviet premier Nikita Khrushchev 798

Eisenhower and the Politics of the "Middle Way" 800
Modern Republicanism 800
Termination and Relocation of Native Americans 801
The 1956 Election and the Second Term 803

Liberation Rhetoric and the Practice of Containment 804
The "New Look" in Foreign Policy 804
Applying Containment to Vietnam 805
Interventions in Latin America and the Middle East 806
The Nuclear Arms Race 808

New Work and Living Patterns in an Economy of Abundance 809
Technology Transforms Agriculture and Industry 810
Burgeoning Suburbs and Declining Cities 812
The Rise of the Sun Belt 812
The Democratization of Higher Education 815

The Culture of Abundance 815
Consumption Rules the Day 815
The Revival of Domesticity and Religion 816
Television Transforms Culture and Politics 817
Countercurrents 818

The Emergence of a Civil Rights Movement 819
African Americans Challenge the Supreme Court and the President 820
Montgomery and Mass Protest 821
ANALYZING HISTORICAL EVIDENCE:
   The *Brown* Decision 822

Conclusion: Peace and Prosperity Mask Unmet Challenges 825

CHAPTER REVIEW 826

Photo: Bill Philpot/Alamy Stock Photo.

CHAPTER 28
Reform, Rebellion, and Reaction, 1960–1974 828

OPENING VIGNETTE: Fannie Lou Hamer leads grassroots struggles of African Americans for voting rights and political empowerment 828

Liberalism at High Tide 830
The Unrealized Promise of Kennedy's New Frontier 831
Johnson Fulfills the Kennedy Promise 832
Policymaking for a Great Society 833
Assessing the Great Society 836
The Judicial Revolution 837

The Second Reconstruction 838
The Flowering of the Black Freedom Struggle 838
The Response in Washington 840
Black Power and Urban Rebellions 842

A Multitude of Movements 844
Native American Protest 845
Latino Struggles for Justice 846
Student Rebellion, the New Left, and the Counterculture 847
Gay Men and Lesbians Organize 848

The New Wave of Feminism 850
A Multifaceted Movement Emerges 850
Feminist Gains Spark a Countermovement 851
BEYOND AMERICA'S BORDERS: Transnational Feminisms 852

Liberal Reform in the Nixon Administration 854
Extending the Welfare State and Regulating the Economy 854
Responding to Environmental Concerns 855
Expanding Social Justice 856

Conclusion: Achievements and Limitations of Liberalism 857

CHAPTER REVIEW 858

Photo: Collection of Mark Hooper.

CHAPTER 29
Vietnam and the End of the Cold War Consensus,
1961–1975   860

OPENING VIGNETTE: Lieutenant Frederick Downs Jr. is wounded in Vietnam and returns home to a country divided over the war 860

New Frontiers in Foreign Policy 862
Meeting the "Hour of Maximum Danger" 862
New Approaches to the Third World 864
The Arms Race and the Nuclear Brink 865
A Growing War in Vietnam 866
Lyndon Johnson's War against Communism 868
An All-Out Commitment in Vietnam 868
Preventing Another Castro in Latin America 869
The Americanized War 870
Those Who Served 871
A Nation Polarized 873
The Widening War at Home 873
The Tet Offensive and Johnson's Move toward Peace 875
BEYOND AMERICA'S BORDERS: 1968: A Year of Protest 876
The Tumultuous Election of 1968 878
Nixon, Détente, and the Search for Peace in Vietnam 879
Moving toward Détente with the Soviet Union and China 880
Shoring Up U.S. Interests around the World 881
Vietnam Becomes Nixon's War 882
The Peace Accords 884
The Legacy of Defeat 885
Conclusion: An Unwinnable War 887

CHAPTER REVIEW 888

CHAPTER 30
America Moves to the Right, 1969–1989   890

OPENING VIGNETTE: Phyllis Schlafly promotes conservatism 890

Nixon, Conservatism, and Constitutional Crisis 892
Emergence of a Grassroots Movement 893
Nixon Courts the Right 895
The Election of 1972 896
Watergate 897
The Ford Presidency and the 1976 Election 898
The "Outsider" Presidency of Jimmy Carter 899
Retreat from Liberalism 900
Energy and Environmental Reform 901
Promoting Human Rights Abroad 904
The Cold War Intensifies 904
Ronald Reagan and the Conservative Ascendancy 906
Appealing to the New Right and Beyond 907
Unleashing Free Enterprise 908
Winners and Losers in a Flourishing Economy 910
Continuing Struggles over Rights 911
Battles in the Courts and Congress 911
Feminism on the Defensive 912
The Gay and Lesbian Rights Movement 912
MAKING HISTORICAL ARGUMENTS: Why Did the ERA Fail? 914
Ronald Reagan Confronts an "Evil Empire" 916
Militarization and Interventions Abroad 916
The Iran-Contra Scandal 917
A Thaw in Soviet-American Relations 918
Conclusion: Reversing the Course of Government 919

CHAPTER REVIEW 920

Photo: Political History, National Museum of American History, Smithsonian Institution.

Photo: Doug Steley B/Alamy.

CHAPTER 31
The Promises and Challenges of Globalization, Since 1989   922

OPENING VIGNETTE: Colin Powell adjusts to a post–Cold War world   922

Domestic Stalemate and Global Upheaval: The Presidency of George H. W. Bush   924
Gridlock in Government   924
The Cold War Ends   925
Going to War in Central America and the Persian Gulf   927
The 1992 Election   930

The Clinton Administration's Search for the Middle Ground   931
Clinton's Reforms   931
Accommodating the Right   932
Impeaching the President   934
The Booming Economy of the 1990s   934

The United States in a Globalizing World   935
Defining America's Place in a New World Order   935
Debates over Globalization   937
The Internationalization of the United States   938

President George W. Bush: Conservatism at Home and Radical Initiatives Abroad   940
The Disputed Election of 2000   940
The Domestic Policies of a "Compassionate Conservative"   940
The Globalization of Terrorism   942
Unilateralism, Preemption, and the Iraq War   944

The Obama Presidency: Reform and Backlash   946
Governing during Economic Crisis and Political Polarization   946
ANALYZING HISTORICAL EVIDENCE: Caricaturing the Candidates: Clinton and Obama in 2008   948
Redefining the War on Terror   950

Conclusion: Defining the Government's Role at Home and Abroad   951

CHAPTER REVIEW   952

APPENDICES
I. Documents   A-1
The Declaration of Independence   A-1
The Constitution of the United States   A-3
Amendments to the Constitution with Annotations (including the six unratified amendments)   A-10

II. Government and Demographics   A-26
Presidential Elections   A-26
Supreme Court Justices   A-31
Population Growth, 1630–2010   A-33
Major Trends in Immigration, 1820–2010   A-34

Glossary   G-1
Index   I-1
About the Authors   last book page

Maps, Figures, and Tables

CHAPTER 16

Spot Map Reconstruction Military Districts, 1867 *470*
Figure 16.1 Southern Congressional Delegations, 1865–1877 *474*
Map 16.1 A Southern Plantation in 1860 and 1881 *479*
Map 16.2 The Election of 1868 *480*
Map 16.3 The Reconstruction of the South *484*
Map 16.4 The Election of 1876 *485*

CHAPTER 17

Map 17.1 The Loss of Indian Lands, 1850–1890 *492*
Map 17.2 Western Mining, 1848–1890 *502*
Spot Map Midwestern Settlement before 1862 *510*
Map 17.3 Federal Land Grants to Railroads and the Development of the West, 1850–1900 *511*
Figure 17.1 Changes in Rural and Urban Populations, 1870–1900 *513*

CHAPTER 18

Map 18.1 Railroad Expansion, 1870–1890 *521*
Figure 18.1 Iron and Steel Production, 1870–1900 *525*
Map 18.2 The Election of 1884 *540*

CHAPTER 19

Map 19.1 Economic Regions of the World, 1890 *552*
Map 19.2 The Impact of Immigration, to 1910 *553*
Figure 19.1 Global Comparison: European Emigration, 1870–1890 *554*
Figure 19.2 European Emigration, 1870–1910 *554*
Figure 19.3 Women and Work, 1870–1890 *562*
Map 19.3 The Great Railroad Strike of 1877 *564*

CHAPTER 20

Figure 20.1 Consumer Prices and Farm Income, 1865–1910 *583*
Map 20.1 The Election of 1892 *595*
Map 20.2 The Election of 1896 *596*
Figure 20.2 Expansion in U.S. Trade, 1870–1910 *598*
Spot Map The Samoan Islands, 1889 *600*
Map 20.3 The Spanish-American War, 1898 *603*
Map 20.4 U.S. Overseas Expansion through 1900 *606*

CHAPTER 21

Map 21.1 National Parks and Forests *626*
Spot Map The Roosevelt Corollary in Action *627*

Map 21.2 The Panama Canal, 1914   *627*
Spot Map Taft's "Dollar Diplomacy"   *630*
Map 21.3 The Election of 1912   *633*

CHAPTER 22

Map 22.1 U.S. Involvement in Latin America and the Caribbean, 1895–1941   *645*
Spot Map U.S. Intervention in Mexico, 1916–1917   *646*
Map 22.2 European Alliances after the Outbreak of World War I   *647*
Spot Map Sinking of the *Lusitania*, 1915   *648*
Map 22.3 The American Expeditionary Force, 1918   *653*
Figure 22.1 Industrial Wages, 1912–1920   *655*
Map 22.4 Women's Voting Rights before the Nineteenth Amendment   *657*
Map 22.5 Europe after World War I   *661*
Map 22.6 The Election of 1920   *671*

CHAPTER 23

Map 23.1 Auto Manufacturing   *676*
Spot Map Detroit and the Automobile Industry in the 1920s   *679*
Figure 23.1 Production of Consumer Goods, 1921–1929   *681*
Map 23.2 The Shift from Rural to Urban Population, 1920–1930   *692*
Map 23.3 The Election of 1928   *695*
Figure 23.2 Manufacturing and Agricultural Income, 1920–1940   *699*
Spot Map Harlan County Coal Strike, 1931   *703*

CHAPTER 24

Map 24.1 The Election of 1932   *711*
Map 24.2 Electoral Shift, 1928–1932   *711*
Figure 24.1 Bank Failures and Farm Foreclosures, 1932–1942   *714*
Map 24.3 The Tennessee Valley Authority   *716*
Spot Map The Dust Bowl   *719*
Figure 24.2 Global Comparison: National Populations and Economies, ca. 1938   *734*

CHAPTER 25

Spot Map Spanish Civil War, 1936–1939   *743*
Map 25.1 Axis Aggression through 1941   *744*
Map 25.2 Japanese Aggression through 1941   *747*
Spot Map Bombing of Pearl Harbor, December 7, 1941   *748*
Map 25.3 Western Relocation Authority Centers   *750*
Figure 25.1 Global Comparison: Weapons Production by the Axis and Allied Powers during World War II   *752*
Spot Map The Holocaust, 1933–1945   *759*
Map 25.4 The European Theater of World War II, 1942–1945   *764*
Map 25.5 The Pacific Theater of World War II, 1941–1945   *766*

CHAPTER 26

Map 26.1 The Division of Europe after World War II   *776*
Spot Map Berlin Divided, 1948   *778*
Spot Map Israel, 1948   *783*
Figure 26.1 Women Workers in Selected Industries, 1940–1950   *785*

Map 26.2 The Election of 1948 *788*

Map 26.3 The Korean War, 1950–1953 *792*

CHAPTER 27

Map 27.1 The Interstate Highway System, 1930 and 1970 *802*

Spot Map Major Indian Relocations, 1950–1970 *803*

Spot Map Geneva Accords, 1954 *806*

Spot Map The Suez Crisis, 1956 *807*

Map 27.2 The Rise of the Sun Belt, 1940–1980 *813*

Figure 27.1 The Postwar Economic Boom: GNP and Per Capita Income, 1945–1970 *816*

CHAPTER 28

Map 28.1 The Election of 1960 *831*

Figure 28.1 Poverty in the United States, 1960–1974 *836*

Spot Map Civil Rights Freedom Rides, May 1961 *839*

Map 28.2 The Rise of the African American Vote, 1940–1976 *842*

Map 28.3 Urban Uprisings, 1965–1968 *843*

CHAPTER 29

Map 29.1 U.S. Involvement in Latin America and the Caribbean, 1954–1994 *863*

Spot Map Cuban Missile Crisis, 1962 *865*

Map 29.2 The Vietnam War, 1964–1975 *867*

Figure 29.1 U.S. Troops in Vietnam, 1962–1972 *869*

Map 29.3 The Election of 1968 *879*

Spot Map Chile *881*

Spot Map Israeli Territorial Gains in the Six-Day War, 1967 *882*

Spot Map U.S. Invasion of Cambodia, 1970 *882*

Table 29.1 Vietnam War Casualties *886*

CHAPTER 30

Spot Map Integration of Public Schools, 1968 *895*

Map 30.1 The Election of 1976 *899*

Figure 30.1 Global Comparison: Energy Consumption per Capita, 1980 *902*

Map 30.2 Worldwide Oil Reserves, 1980 *903*

Map 30.3 The Middle East, 1948–1989 *905*

Spot Map The Fight for the Equal Rights Amendment *912*

Spot Map El Salvador and Nicaragua *917*

CHAPTER 31

Map 31.1 Events in Eastern Europe, 1989–2002 *926*

Map 31.2 Events in the Middle East, 1989–2011 *929*

Figure 31.1 The Growth of Inequality: Changes in Family Income, 1969–1998 *935*

Figure 31.2 Global Comparison: Countries with the Highest Military Expenditures, 2005 *936*

Spot Map Breakup of Yugoslavia *937*

Spot Map Events in Israel since 1989 *937*

Map 31.3 The Election of 2000 *940*

Spot Map Afghanistan *944*

Spot Map Iraq *944*

Map 31.4 The Election of 2012 *951*

Special Features

Analyzing Historical Evidence

Ida B. Wells and Her Campaign to Stop Lynching   534
The Flash and the Birth of Photojournalism   624
Americans Encounter the New Deal   726
The *Brown* Decision   822
Caricaturing the Candidates: Clinton and Obama in 2008   948

Beyond America's Borders

The Slaveholder Exodus   476
The World's Columbian Exposition and Nineteenth-Century World's Fairs   574
Bolshevism   666
Nazi Anti-Semitism and the Atomic Bomb   760
Transnational Feminisms   852
1968: A Year of Protest   876

Making Historical Arguments

Did Westerners Really Build It All by Themselves?   508
Did Terrorists Sink the *Maine*?   604
Was There a Sexual Revolution in the 1920s?   686
Why Did the United States Launch the European Recovery Program?   778
Why Did the ERA Fail?   914

16

Reconstruction, 1863–1877

CONTENT LEARNING OBJECTIVES

After reading and studying this chapter, you should be able to:

- Identify the challenges facing reconstruction efforts.
- Describe President Johnson's reconstruction plan and the ways in which it aligned and differed from Lincoln's.
- Recount the significance of the Fourteenth Amendment and why President Johnson advised southern states to reject it. Explain the terms of radical reconstruction and how Johnson's interventions led some in Congress to seek his impeachment.
- Describe the provisions of the Fifteenth Amendment, and explain why some women's rights advocates were dissatisfied with it.
- Describe how congressional reconstruction altered life in the South. Explain why the North abandoned reconstruction, including the role of Grant's troubled presidency and the election of 1877 in this abandonment.

In 1856, John Rapier, a free black barber in Florence, Alabama, urged his four freeborn sons to flee the increasingly repressive and dangerous South. James T. Rapier chose Canada, where he went to live with his uncle in a largely black community and studied Greek and Latin in a log schoolhouse. In a letter to his father, he vowed, "I will endeavor to do my part in solving the problems [of African Americans] in my native land."

The Union victory in the Civil War gave James Rapier the opportunity to redeem his pledge. In 1865, after more than eight years of exile, the twenty-seven-year-old Rapier returned to Alabama, where he presided over the first political gathering of former slaves in the state. He soon discovered, however, that

CARPETBAG

A carpetbag was a suitcase made from carpet. "Carpetbagger" was a derogatory name for rootless adventurers, which critics of Republican administrations in the South hurled at white Northerners who moved south during Reconstruction. Elemental Studios/Alamy.

Alabama's whites found it agonizingly difficult to accept defeat and black freedom. They responded to the revolutionary changes under the banner "White Man — Right or Wrong — Still the White Man!"

During the elections of 1868, when Rapier and other Alabama blacks vigorously supported the Republican ticket, the recently organized Ku Klux Klan went on a bloody rampage. A mob of 150 outraged whites scoured Rapier's neighborhood seeking four black politicians they claimed were trying to "Africanize Alabama." They caught and hanged three, but the "nigger carpetbagger from Canada" escaped. After briefly considering fleeing the state, Rapier decided to stay and fight.

In 1872, Rapier won election to the House of Representatives, where he joined six other black congressmen in Washington, D.C. Defeated for reelection in 1874 in a campaign marked by ballot-box stuffing, Rapier turned to cotton farming. But persistent black poverty and unrelenting racial violence convinced him that blacks could never achieve equality and prosperity in the South. He purchased land in Kansas and urged Alabama's blacks to escape with him. In 1883, however, before he could leave Alabama, Rapier died of tuberculosis at the age of forty-five.

Union general Carl Schurz had foreseen many of the troubles Rapier encountered in the postwar South. In 1865, Schurz concluded that the Civil War was "a revolution but half accomplished." Northern victory had freed the slaves, he observed, but it had not changed former slaveholders' minds about blacks' unfitness for freedom. Left to themselves, whites would "introduce some new system of forced labor, not perhaps exactly slavery in its old form but something similar to it." To defend their freedom, Schurz concluded, blacks would need federal protection, land of their own, and voting rights. Until whites "cut loose from the past, it will be a dangerous experiment to put Southern society upon its own legs."

As Schurz understood, the end of the war did not mean peace. Indeed, the nation entered one of its most turbulent eras — Reconstruction. Answers to the era's central questions — about the defeated South's status within the Union and the meaning of freedom for ex-slaves — came not only from Washington, D.C., where the federal government played an active role, but also from the state legislatures and county seats of the South, where blacks eagerly participated in politics. The Fourteenth and Fifteenth Amendments to the Constitution strengthened the claim of African Americans to

CHRONOLOGY

1863	Proclamation of Amnesty and Reconstruction pardons most rebels.
1864	Lincoln refuses to sign Wade-Davis bill.
1865	Freedmen's Bureau established. Lincoln assassinated; Andrew Johnson becomes president. First black codes enacted. Thirteenth Amendment becomes part of Constitution.
1866	Congress approves Fourteenth Amendment. Civil Rights Act passes. American Equal Rights Association founded. Ku Klux Klan founded.
1867	Military Reconstruction Act passes. Tenure of Office Act passes.
1868	Impeachment trial of President Johnson held. Ulysses S. Grant elected president.
1869	Congress approves Fifteenth Amendment.
1871	Ku Klux Klan Act passes.
1872	Liberal Party formed. President Grant reelected.
1873	Economic depression sets in. Slaughterhouse cases decided. Colfax massacre kills more than eighty blacks.
1874	Democrats win majority in House of Representatives.
1875	Civil Rights Act passes.
1876	United States v. Cruikshank decided.
1877	Rutherford B. Hayes becomes president; Reconstruction era ends.

JAMES T. RAPIER

In 1874, when Representative James T. Rapier spoke before Congress on behalf of a civil rights bill, he described the humiliation of being denied service at inns all along his route from Montgomery to Washington. Elsewhere in the world, he said, class and religion were invoked to defend discrimination. But in America, "our distinction is color." Alabama Department of Archives and History, Montgomery, Alabama.

equal rights. The struggle also took place on the South's farms and plantations, where former slaves sought to become free workers while former slaveholders clung to the Old South. A small band of white women joined in the struggle for racial equality, and soon their crusade broadened to include gender equality. Their attempts to secure voting rights for women were thwarted, however, just as were the efforts of blacks and their allies to secure racial equality. In the contest to determine the consequences of Confederate defeat and emancipation, white Southerners prevailed.

Wartime Reconstruction

Reconstruction did not wait for the end of war. As the odds of a northern victory increased, thinking about reunification quickened. Immediately, a question arose: Who had authority to devise a plan for reconstructing the Union? President Abraham Lincoln firmly believed that reconstruction was a matter of executive responsibility. Congress just as firmly asserted its jurisdiction. Fueling the argument were significant differences about the terms of reconstruction.

In their eagerness to formulate a plan for political reunification, neither Lincoln nor Congress gave much attention to the South's land and labor problems. But as the war rapidly eroded slavery and traditional plantation agriculture, Yankee military commanders in the Union-occupied areas of the Confederacy had no choice but to oversee the emergence of a new labor system. Freedmen's aspirations played little role in the plans that emerged.

"To Bind Up the Nation's Wounds." As early as 1863, Lincoln began contemplating how "to bind up the nation's wounds" and achieve "a lasting peace." While deep compassion for the enemy guided his thinking about peace, his plan for reconstruction aimed primarily at shortening the war and ending slavery.

Lincoln's Proclamation of Amnesty and Reconstruction in December 1863 set out his terms. He offered a full pardon, restoring property (except slaves) and political rights, to most rebels willing to renounce secession and to accept emancipation. When 10 percent of a state's voting population had taken an oath of allegiance, the state could organize a new government and be readmitted into the Union. Lincoln's plan did not require ex-rebels to extend social or political rights to ex-slaves, nor did it anticipate a program of long-term federal assistance to freedmen. Clearly, the president looked forward to the rapid, forgiving restoration of the broken Union.

Lincoln's easy terms enraged abolitionists such as Wendell Phillips of Boston, who charged that the president "makes the negro's freedom a mere sham." He "is willing that the negro should be free but seeks nothing else for him." Comparing Lincoln to the Union's most passive general, Phillips declared, "What McClellan was on the battlefield — 'Do as little hurt as possible!' — Lincoln is in civil affairs — 'Make as little change as possible!'" Phillips and other northern Radicals called instead for a thorough overhaul of southern society. Their ideas proved to be too drastic for most Republicans during the war years, but Congress agreed that Lincoln's plan was inadequate.

In July 1864, Congress put forward a plan of its own. Congressman Henry Winter Davis of Maryland and Senator Benjamin Wade of Ohio jointly sponsored a bill that demanded that at least half of the voters in a conquered rebel state take the oath of allegiance before reconstruction could begin. The Wade-Davis bill also banned almost all ex-Confederates from participating in the drafting of new state constitutions. Finally, the bill guaranteed the equality of freedmen before the law. Congress's reconstruction would be neither as quick nor as forgiving as Lincoln's. When

WARTIME RECONSTRUCTION

This cartoon from the presidential campaign of 1864 shows the "Rail Splitter" Abraham Lincoln leveraging the broken nation back together while his running mate, Andrew Johnson, who once was a tailor by trade, stitches the Confederate states securely back into the Union. Optimism that the task of reconstructing the nation after the war would be both quick and easy shines through the cartoon. The Granger Collection, New York.

Lincoln refused to sign the bill and let it die, Wade and Davis charged the president with usurpation of power.

Undeterred, Lincoln continued to nurture the formation of loyal state governments under his own plan. Four states — Arkansas, Louisiana, Tennessee, and Virginia — fulfilled the president's requirements, but Congress refused to seat representatives from the "Lincoln states." Lincoln admitted that a government based on only 10 percent was not ideal, but he argued, "We shall sooner have the fowl by hatching the egg than by smashing it." Massachusetts senator Charles Sumner responded, "The eggs of crocodiles can produce only crocodiles." In his last public address in April 1865, Lincoln defended his plan but for the first time expressed publicly his endorsement of suffrage for southern blacks, at least "the very intelligent, and . . . those who serve our cause as soldiers." The announcement demonstrated that Lincoln's thinking about reconstruction was still evolving. Four days later, he was dead.

Land and Labor.

Of all the problems raised by the North's victory in the war, none proved more critical than the South's transition from slavery to free labor. As federal armies invaded and occupied the Confederacy, hundreds of thousands of slaves became free workers. In addition, Union armies controlled vast territories in the South where legal title to land had become unclear. The Confiscation Acts passed during the war punished "traitors" by taking away their property. The question of what to do with federally occupied land and how to organize labor on it engaged ex-slaves, ex-slaveholders, Union military commanders, and federal government officials long before the war ended.

In the Mississippi valley, occupying federal troops announced a new labor code. It required landholders to give up whipping, sign contracts with ex-slaves, pay wages, and provide food, housing, and medical care. The code required black laborers to enter into contracts, work diligently, and remain subordinate and obedient. Military leaders clearly had no intention of promoting a social or economic revolution. Instead, they sought to restore traditional plantation agriculture with wage labor. The effort resulted in a hybrid system that one contemporary called "compulsory free labor," something that satisfied no one.

Planters complained because the new system fell short of slavery. Blacks could not be "transformed by proclamation," a Louisiana sugar planter declared. Without the right to whip, he argued, the new labor system did not have a chance. Either Union soldiers must "*compel* the negroes to work," or the planters themselves must "be authorized and sustained in using force."

African Americans found the new regime too reminiscent of slavery to be called free labor. Its chief deficiency, they believed, was the failure to provide them with land of their own. Freedmen believed they had a moral right to land because they and their ancestors had worked it without compensation for centuries. "What's the use of being free if you don't own land enough to be buried in?" one man asked. Several wartime developments led freedmen to believe that the federal government planned to undergird black freedom with landownership.

In January 1865, General William Tecumseh Sherman set aside part of the coast south of Charleston for black settlement. By June 1865, some 40,000 freedmen sat on

400,000 acres of "Sherman land." In addition, in March 1865, Congress passed a bill establishing the Bureau of Refugees, Freedmen, and Abandoned Lands. The **Freedmen's Bureau**, as it was called, distributed food and clothing to destitute Southerners and eased the transition of blacks from slaves to free persons. Congress also authorized the agency to divide abandoned and confiscated land into 40-acre plots, to rent them to freedmen, and eventually to sell them "with such title as the United States can convey." By June 1865, the Bureau had situated nearly 10,000 black families on a half million acres abandoned by fleeing planters. Other ex-slaves eagerly anticipated farms of their own.

Despite the flurry of activity, wartime reconstruction failed to produce agreement about whether the president or Congress had the authority to devise policy or what proper policy should be.

Freedmen's Bureau
Government organization created in March 1865 to distribute food and clothing to destitute Southerners and to ease the transition of slaves to free persons. Early efforts by the Freedmen's Bureau to distribute land to the newly freed blacks were later overturned by President Andrew Johnson.

The African American Quest for Autonomy.
Ex-slaves never had any doubt about what they wanted from freedom. They had only to contemplate what they had been denied as slaves. Slaves had to remain on their plantations; freedom allowed blacks to see what was on the other side of the hill. Slaves had to be at work in the fields by dawn; freedom permitted blacks to sleep through a sunrise. Freedmen also tested the etiquette of racial subordination. "Lizzie's maid passed me today when I was coming from church *without speaking to me*," huffed one plantation mistress.

To whites, emancipation looked like pure anarchy. Blacks, they said, had reverted to their natural condition: lazy, irresponsible, and wild. Actually, former slaves were experimenting with freedom, but they could not long afford to roam the countryside, neglect work, and casually provoke whites. Soon, most were back at work in whites' kitchens and fields.

But they continued to dream of land and independence. "The way we can best take care of ourselves is to have land," one former slave declared in 1865, "and turn it and till it by our own labor." Another group of former slaves in South Carolina declared that they wanted land, "not a Master or owner[,] Neither a driver with his Whip."

Slavery had deliberately kept blacks illiterate, and freedmen emerged from bondage eager to learn to read and write. "I wishes the Childern all in School," one black veteran asserted, "It is beter for them then to be their Surveing a mistes [mistress]." Freemen looked on schools as "first proof of their *independence*."

The restoration of broken families was another persistent black aspiration. Thousands of freedmen took to the roads in 1865 to look for kin who had been sold away or to free those who were being held illegally as slaves. A black soldier from Missouri wrote his daughters that he was coming for them. "I will have you if it cost me my life," he declared. "Your Miss Kitty said that I tried to steal you," he told them. "But I'll let her know that god never intended for a man to steal his own flesh and blood." And he swore that "if she meets me with ten thousand soldiers, she [will] meet her enemy."

Independent worship was another continuing aspiration. African Americans greeted freedom with a mass exodus from white churches, where they had been required to worship when slaves. Some joined the newly established southern

HARRY STEPHENS AND FAMILY, 1866

The seven members of the Stephens family sit proudly for a photograph just after the Civil War ended. Many black families were not as fortunate as these Virginians. Separated by slavery or war, former slaves desperately sought news of missing family members through newspaper advertisements.

G. Gable, *Summer Scene*, 1866. Gilman Collection, Purchase, The Horace W. Goldsmith Foundation Gift, through Joyce and Robert Menschel, 2005 (2005.100.277). Image copyright © The Metropolitan Museum of Art. Image source: Art Resource, NY.

branches of all-black northern churches, such as the African Methodist Episcopal Church. Others formed black versions of the major southern denominations, Baptists and Methodists.

REVIEW To what extent did Lincoln's wartime plan for reconstruction reflect the concerns of newly freed slaves?

Presidential Reconstruction

Shot by john wilkes booth at fords theatre

Abraham Lincoln died on April 15, 1865, just hours after John Wilkes Booth shot him at a Washington, D.C., theater. Chief Justice Salmon P. Chase immediately administered the oath of office to Vice President Andrew Johnson of Tennessee. Congress had adjourned in March and would not reconvene until December. Throughout the summer and fall, Johnson drew up and executed a plan of reconstruction without congressional advice. ↪ *new pres.*

created a new program to make stricter reparations on south

Congress returned to the capital in December to find that, as far as the president and former Confederates were concerned, reconstruction was completed. Most Republicans, however, thought Johnson's plan made far too few demands of ex-rebels and made a mockery of the sacrifice of Union soldiers. They claimed that Johnson's leniency had acted as midwife to the rebirth of the Old South, that he had achieved political reunification at the cost of black freedom. Republicans in Congress then proceeded to dismantle Johnson's program and substitute a program of their own.

[handwritten: VP → P after lincoln death]

Johnson's Program of Reconciliation.
Born in 1808 in Raleigh, North Carolina, Andrew Johnson was the son of illiterate parents. Self-educated and ambitious, Johnson moved to Tennessee, where he worked as a tailor, accumulated a fortune in land, acquired five slaves, and built a career in politics championing the South's common white people and assailing its "illegitimate, swaggering, bastard, scrub aristocracy." The only senator from a Confederate state to remain loyal to the Union, Johnson held the planter class responsible for secession. Less than two weeks before he became president, he announced what he would do to planters if he ever had the chance: "I would arrest them — I would try them — I would convict them and I would hang them."

*[handwritten margin: * planter class; southern aristocracy]*

[handwritten margin: → hated planter class]

A Democrat all his life, Johnson occupied the White House only because the Republican Party in 1864 had needed a vice presidential candidate who would appeal to loyal, Union-supporting Democrats. Johnson vigorously defended states' rights (but not secession) and opposed Republican efforts to expand the power of the federal government. A steadfast supporter of slavery, Johnson had owned slaves until 1862, when Tennessee rebels, angry at his Unionism, confiscated them. When he grudgingly accepted emancipation, it was more because he hated planters than sympathized with slaves. "Damn the negroes," he said. "I am fighting those traitorous aristocrats, their masters." The new president harbored unshakable racist convictions. Africans, Johnson said, were "inferior to the white man in point of intellect — better calculated in physical structure to undergo drudgery and hardship."

*[handwritten margin: ** supporting liberalism]*

[handwritten margin: → confiscated slaves of Johns]

Like Lincoln, Johnson stressed the rapid restoration of civil government in the South. Like Lincoln, he promised to pardon most, but not all, ex-rebels. Johnson recognized the state governments created by Lincoln but set out his own requirements for restoring the other rebel states to the Union. All that the citizens of a state had to do was to renounce the right of secession, deny that the debts of the Confederacy were legal and binding, and ratify the Thirteenth Amendment abolishing slavery, which became part of the Constitution in December 1865.

[handwritten margin: → to re-enter union had to deny CS. renounce succession, ratify 13th A]

[handwritten margin: 13th Ammendment : abolish slavery]

Johnson also returned all confiscated and abandoned land to pardoned ex-Confederates, even if it was in the hands of freedmen. Reformers were shocked. Instead of punishing planters as he had promised, Johnson canceled the promising beginnings made by General Sherman and the Freedmen's Bureau to settle blacks on land of their own. As one freedman observed, "Things was hurt by Mr. Lincoln getting killed."

[handwritten margin: → returned land to ex-rebels. upset people]

White Southern Resistance and Black Codes.
In the summer of 1865, delegates across the South gathered to draw up the new state constitutions required by Johnson's plan of reconstruction. They refused to accept even the president's mild requirements. Refusing to renounce secession, the South Carolina and Georgia conventions merely "repudiated" their secession ordinances, preserving in principle their right to secede. South Carolina and Mississippi refused to disown their Confederate war debts. Mississippi rejected the Thirteenth Amendment, and Alabama rejected it in part. Despite this defiance, Johnson did nothing. White Southerners began to think that by standing up for themselves they could shape the terms of reconstruction.

[handwritten margin: → southern states rejected reform but Johnson did nothing.]

New state governments across the South adopted a series of laws known as black codes, which made a travesty of black freedom. The codes sought to keep ex-slaves subordinate to whites by subjecting them to every sort of discrimination.

[handwritten margin: → negative for blacks.]

black codes
Laws passed by state governments in the South in 1865 and 1866 that sought to keep ex-slaves subordinate to whites. At the core of the black codes lay the desire to force freedmen back to the plantations.

Vagrant: beggar, homeless

south refused to fully free blacks

aprentance shiplaws: black orphans as workers for planter "guardians"

eased punish on south and wanted white supremecy

thought black codes lead to slavery again

Several states made it illegal for blacks to own a gun. Mississippi made insulting gestures and language by blacks a criminal offense. The codes barred blacks from jury duty. Not a single southern state granted any black the right to vote.

At the core of the black codes, however, lay the matter of labor. Legislators sought to hustle freedmen back to the plantations. Whites were almost universally opposed to black landownership. Whitelaw Reid, a northern visitor to the South, found that the "man who should sell small tracts to them would be in actual personal danger." South Carolina attempted to limit blacks to either farmwork or domestic service by requiring them to pay annual taxes of $10 to $100 to work in any other occupation. Mississippi declared that blacks who did not possess written evidence of employment could be declared vagrants and be subject to involuntary plantation labor. Under so-called apprenticeship laws, courts bound thousands of black children — orphans and others whose parents they deemed unable to support them — to work for planter "guardians."

Johnson refused to intervene. A staunch defender of states' rights, he believed that citizens of every state should be free to write their own constitutions and laws. Moreover, Johnson was as eager as other white Southerners to restore white supremacy. "White men alone must manage the South," he declared.

Johnson also recognized that his do-nothing response offered him political advantage. A conservative Tennessee Democrat at the head of a northern Republican Party, he had begun to look southward for political allies. Despite tough talk about punishing traitors, he personally pardoned fourteen thousand wealthy or high-ranking ex-Confederates. By pardoning powerful whites, by accepting state governments even when they failed to satisfy his minimal demands, and by acquiescing in the black codes, he won useful southern friends.

In the fall elections of 1865, white Southerners dramatically expressed their mood. To represent them in Congress, they chose former Confederates. Of the eighty senators and representatives they sent to Washington, fifteen had served in the Confederate army, ten of them as generals. Another sixteen had served in civil and judicial posts in the Confederacy. Nine others had served in the Confederate Congress. One — Alexander Stephens — had been vice president of the Confederacy. As one Georgian remarked, "It looked as though Richmond had moved to Washington."

Expansion of Federal Authority and Black Rights.
Southerners had blundered monumentally. They had assumed that what Andrew Johnson was willing to accept, Republicans would accept as well. But southern intransigence compelled even moderates to conclude that ex-rebels were a "generation of vipers," still untrustworthy and dangerous. The black codes became a symbol of southern intentions to "restore all of slavery but its name." "We tell the white men of Mississippi," the *Chicago Tribune* roared, "that the men of the North will convert the State of Mississippi into a frog pond before they will allow such laws to disgrace one foot of the soil in which the bones of our soldiers sleep and over which the flag of freedom waves."

The moderate majority of the Republican Party wanted only assurance that slavery and treason were dead. They did not champion black equality, the confiscation of plantations, or black voting, as did the Radical minority within the party. But southern obstinacy had succeeded in forging unity (at least temporarily) among

Republican factions. In December 1865, Republicans refused to seat the southern representatives elected in the fall elections. Rather than accept Johnson's claim that the "work of restoration" was done, Congress challenged his executive power.

Republican senator Lyman Trumbull declared that the president's policy meant that an ex-slave would "be tyrannized over, abused, and virtually reenslaved without some legislation by the nation for his protection." Early in 1866, the moderates produced two bills that strengthened the federal shield. The first, the Freedmen's Bureau bill, prolonged the life of the agency established by the previous Congress. Arguing that the Constitution never contemplated a "system for the support of indigent persons," President Andrew Johnson vetoed the bill. Congress failed by a narrow margin to override the president's veto.

for blacks (handwritten annotation)

The moderates designed their second measure, what would become the **Civil Rights Act of 1866**, to nullify the black codes by affirming African Americans' rights to "full and equal benefit of all laws and proceedings for the security of person and property as is enjoyed by white citizens." The act boldly required the end of racial discrimination in state laws and represented an extraordinary expansion of black rights and federal authority. The president argued that the civil rights bill amounted to "unconstitutional invasion of states' rights" and vetoed it. In essence, he denied that the federal government possessed the authority to protect the civil rights of African Americans.

In April 1866, an incensed Republican Party again pushed the civil rights bill through Congress and overrode the presidential veto. In July, it passed another Freedmen's Bureau bill and overrode Johnson's veto. For the first time in American history, Congress had overridden presidential vetoes of major legislation. As a worried South Carolinian observed, Johnson had succeeded in uniting the Republicans and probably touched off "a fight this fall such as has never been seen."

> **REVIEW** When the southern states passed the black codes, how did the U.S. Congress respond?

→ erase black codes (handwritten annotation)

Civil Rights Act of 1866
Legislation passed by Congress in 1866 that nullified the black codes and affirmed that black Americans should have equal benefit of the law. President Andrew Johnson vetoed this expansion of black rights and federal authority, but Congress later overrode his veto.

Congressional Reconstruction

By the summer of 1866, President Andrew Johnson and Congress had dropped their gloves and stood toe-to-toe in a bare-knuckle contest unprecedented in American history. Johnson made it clear that he would not budge on either constitutional issues or policy. Moderate Republicans responded by amending the Constitution. But the obstinacy of Johnson and white Southerners pushed Republican moderates ever closer to the Radicals and to acceptance of additional federal intervention in the South. To end presidential interference, Congress voted to impeach the president for the first time since the nation was formed. Soon after, Congress also debated whether to make voting rights color-blind, while women sought to make voting sex-blind as well.

move voting equality (handwritten annotation)

The Fourteenth Amendment and Escalating Violence. In June 1866, Congress passed the **Fourteenth Amendment** to the Constitution, and two years later the states ratified it. The most important provisions of this complex

made blacks citizens (handwritten annotation)

Fourteenth Amendment
Constitutional amendment passed in 1866 that made all native-born or naturalized persons U.S. citizens and prohibited states from abridging the rights of national citizens. The amendment hoped to provide a guarantee of equality before the law for black citizens.

amendment made all native-born or naturalized persons American citizens and prohibited states from abridging the "privileges and immunities" of citizens, depriving them of "life, liberty, or property without due process of law," and denying them "equal protection of the laws." By making blacks national citizens, the amendment provided a national guarantee of equality before the law. In essence, it protected blacks against violation by southern state governments.

The Fourteenth Amendment also dealt with voting rights. It gave Congress the right to reduce the congressional representation of states that withheld suffrage from some of its adult male population. In other words, white Southerners could either allow black men to vote or see their representation in Washington slashed. Whatever happened, Republicans stood to benefit from the Fourteenth Amendment. If southern whites granted voting rights to freedmen, Republicans would gain valuable black votes. If whites refused, the number of southern Democrats in Congress would plunge.

The Fourteenth Amendment's suffrage provisions ignored the small band of women who had emerged from the war demanding "the ballot for the two disenfranchised classes, negroes and women." Founding the American Equal Rights Association in 1866, Susan B. Anthony and Elizabeth Cady Stanton lobbied for "a government by the people, and the whole people; for the people and the whole people." They felt betrayed when their old antislavery allies refused to work for their goals. "It was the Negro's hour," Frederick Douglass explained. Senator Charles Sumner suggested that woman suffrage could be "the great question of the future."

The Fourteenth Amendment provided for punishment of any state that excluded voters on the basis of race but not on the basis of sex. The amendment also introduced

Visual Activity

RECONSTRUCTION CARTOON

This 1865 cartoon pokes fun at two Richmond ladies as they pass by a Union officer on their way to receive free government rations. One says sourly to the other, "Don't you think that Yankee must feel like shrinking into his boots before such high-toned Southern ladies as we?" The New York Public Library/Art Resource, NY.

READING THE IMAGE: Just a step behind is a smiling black woman. What does her expression say about her impression of the scene taking place in front of her?

CONNECTIONS: What do these white women suggest about the white South's attitude toward defeat and reconstruction?

the word *male* into the Constitution when it referred to a citizen's right to vote. Stanton predicted that "if that word 'male' be inserted, it will take us a century at least to get it out."

Tennessee approved the Fourteenth Amendment in July, and Congress promptly welcomed the state's representatives and senators back. Had President Johnson counseled other southern states to ratify this relatively mild amendment, they might have listened. Instead, Johnson advised Southerners to reject the Fourteenth Amendment and to rely on him to trounce the Republicans in the fall congressional elections.

[handwritten margin note: Wanted to reject 14th]

Johnson had decided to make the Fourteenth Amendment the overriding issue of the 1866 elections and to gather its white opponents into a new conservative party, the National Union Party. The president's strategy suffered a setback when whites in several southern cities went on rampages against blacks. Mobs killed thirty-four blacks in New Orleans and forty-six blacks in Memphis. The slaughter shocked Northerners and renewed skepticism about Johnson's claim that southern whites could be trusted. "Who doubts that the Freedmen's Bureau ought to be abolished forthwith," a New Yorker observed sarcastically, "and the blacks remitted to the paternal care of their old masters, who 'understand the nigger, you know, a great deal better than the Yankees can.'"

[handwritten margin note: → new white party (conservative)]

[handwritten margin note: lead to white on black violence]

The 1866 elections resulted in an overwhelming Republican victory. Johnson had bet that Northerners would not support federal protection of black rights and that a racist backlash would blast the Republican Party. But the war was still fresh in northern minds, and as one Republican explained, southern whites "with all their intelligence were traitors, the blacks with all their ignorance were loyal."

Radical Reconstruction and Military Rule.

When Johnson continued to urge Southerners to reject the Fourteenth Amendment, every southern state except Tennessee voted it down. "The last one of the sinful ten," thundered Representative James A. Garfield of Ohio, "has flung back into our teeth the magnanimous offer of a

ELIZABETH CADY STANTON AND SUSAN B. ANTHONY

Stanton, seated, and Anthony, shown in their later years, were lifelong friends and veteran reformers who advocated, among other things, improved working conditions for labor, married women's property rights, liberalization of divorce laws, and women's admission into colleges and trade schools. Their broad agenda led some conservatives to oppose women's political rights because they equated the suffragist cause with radicalism in general. Library of Congress, 3a02558.

"THIS IS A WHITE MAN'S GOVERNMENT" (1868)

This Thomas Nast cartoon lambasts the Democratic Party's recent platform advocating white supremacy. Nast portrays the Democrats as a white Southerner with a knife, a stereotyped Irishman with a club, and a plutocrat lifting a wallet that reads, "capital for votes." They all rest a foot on the back of a prostrate African American soldier. Library of Congress, 3c21735.

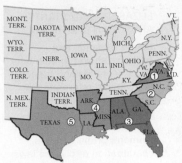

RECONSTRUCTION MILITARY DISTRICTS, 1867

Military Reconstruction Act

Congressional act of March 1867 that initiated military rule of the South. Congressional reconstruction divided the ten unreconstructed Confederate states into five military districts, each under the direction of a Union general. It also established the procedure by which unreconstructed states could reenter the Union.

wanted to have plantations confiscated and given to slaves

generous nation." After the South rejected the moderates' program, the Radicals seized the initiative.

Each act of defiance by southern whites had boosted the standing of the Radicals within the Republican Party. Except for freedmen themselves, no one did more to make freedom the "mighty moral question of the age." Radicals such as Massachusetts senator Charles Sumner and Pennsylvania representative Thaddeus Stevens united in demanding civil and political equality. Southern states were "like clay in the hands of the potter," Stevens declared in January 1867, and he called on Congress to begin reconstruction all over again.

In March 1867, Congress overturned the Johnson state governments and initiated military rule of the South. The **Military Reconstruction Act** (and three subsequent acts) divided the ten unreconstructed Confederate states into five military districts. Congress placed a Union general in charge of each district and instructed him to "suppress insurrection, disorder, and violence" and to begin political reform. After the military had completed voter registration, which would include black men, voters in each state would elect delegates to conventions that would draw up new state constitutions. Each constitution would guarantee black suffrage. When the voters of each state had approved the constitution and the state legislature had ratified the Fourteenth Amendment, the state could submit its work to Congress. If Congress approved, the state's senators and representatives could be seated, and political reunification would be accomplished.

Radicals proclaimed the provision for black suffrage "a prodigious triumph," for it extended far beyond the limited suffrage provisions of the Fourteenth Amendment. When combined with the disfranchisement of thousands of ex-rebels, it promised to cripple any neo-Confederate resurgence and guarantee Republican state governments in the South.

Despite its bold suffrage provision, the Military Reconstruction Act of 1867 disappointed those who also advocated the confiscation of southern plantations and their redistribution to ex-slaves. Thaddeus Stevens agreed with the freedman who said, "Give us our own land and we take care of ourselves, but without land, the old masters can hire us or starve us, as they please." But most Republicans believed they had provided blacks with what they needed: equal legal rights and the ballot. Besides, confiscation was too radical, even for some Radicals. Confiscating private property, declared the *New York Times*, "strikes at the root of all property rights in both sections. It concerns Massachusetts quite as much as Mississippi." If blacks were to get land, they would have to gain it themselves.

Johnson Against ↑

Declaring that he would rather sever his right arm than sign such a formula for "anarchy and chaos," Andrew Johnson vetoed the Military Reconstruction Act, but Congress overrode his veto. With the passage of the Reconstruction Acts of 1867, congressional reconstruction was virtually completed. Congress left whites owning most of the South's land but, in a departure that justified the term *radical reconstruction*, had given black men the ballot.

Impeaching a President. Despite his defeats, Andrew Johnson had no intention of yielding control of reconstruction. In a dozen ways, he sabotaged Congress's will and encouraged southern whites to resist. He issued a flood of pardons, waged war against the Freedmen's Bureau, and replaced Union generals eager to enforce Congress's Reconstruction Acts with conservative officers eager to block them. Johnson claimed that he was merely defending the "violated Constitution." At bottom, however, the president subverted congressional reconstruction to protect southern whites from what he considered the horrors of "Negro domination."

[handwritten: → tried to block Military recon. act]

Radicals argued that Johnson's abuse of constitutional powers and his failure to fulfill constitutional obligations to enforce the law were impeachable offenses. According to the Constitution, the House of Representatives can impeach and the Senate can try any federal official for "treason, bribery, or other high crimes and misdemeanors." But moderates interpreted the Constitution to mean violation of criminal statutes. As long as Johnson refrained from breaking the law, impeachment (the process of formal charges of wrongdoing against the president or other federal official) remained stalled.

Then in August 1867, Johnson suspended Secretary of War Edwin M. Stanton from office. As required by the Tenure of Office Act, which demanded the approval of the Senate for the removal of any government official who had been appointed with Senate approval, the president requested the Senate to consent to Stanton's dismissal. When the Senate balked, Johnson removed Stanton anyway. "Is the President crazy, or only drunk?" asked a dumbfounded Republican moderate. "I'm afraid his doings will make us all favor impeachment."

News of Johnson's open defiance of the law convinced every Republican in the House to vote for a resolution impeaching the president. Supreme Court chief justice Salmon Chase presided over the Senate trial, which lasted from March until May 1868. When the vote came, thirty-five senators voted guilty and nineteen not guilty. The impeachment forces fell one vote short of the two-thirds needed to convict.

[handwritten: failed because got less than 2/3]

After his trial, Johnson called a truce, and for the remaining ten months of his term, congressional reconstruction proceeded unhindered by presidential interference. Without interference from Johnson, Congress revisited the suffrage issue.

The Fifteenth Amendment and Women's Demands.
In February 1869, Republicans passed the **Fifteenth Amendment** to the Constitution, which prohibited states from depriving any citizen of the right to vote because of "race, color, or previous condition of servitude." The Reconstruction Acts of 1867 already required black suffrage in the South; the Fifteenth Amendment extended black voting nationwide.

Some Republicans, however, found the final wording of the Fifteenth Amendment "lame and halting." Rather than absolutely guaranteeing the right to vote, the amendment merely prohibited exclusion on grounds of race. The distinction would prove to be significant. In time, white Southerners would devise tests of literacy and property and other apparently nonracial measures that would effectively disfranchise blacks yet not violate the Fifteenth Amendment. But an amendment that fully guaranteed the right to vote courted defeat outside the South. Rising antiforeign sentiment — against the Chinese in California and European immigrants in the Northeast — caused states to resist giving up total control of suffrage requirements. In March 1870, after three-fourths of the states had ratified it, the Fifteenth Amendment became part of the Constitution.

Woman suffrage advocates, however, were sorely disappointed with the Fifteenth Amendment's failure to extend voting rights to women. Elizabeth Cady

Fifteenth Amendment
Constitutional amendment passed in February 1869 prohibiting states from depriving any citizen of the right to vote because of "race, color, or previous condition of servitude." It extended black suffrage nationwide. Woman suffrage advocates were disappointed that the amendment failed to extend voting rights to women.

women suffrage

Stanton and Susan B. Anthony condemned the Republicans' "negro first" strategy and pointed out that women remained "the only class of citizens wholly unrepresented in the government." Increasingly, activist women concluded that woman "must not put her trust in man." The Fifteenth Amendment severed the early feminist movement from its abolitionist roots. Over the next several decades, feminists established an independent suffrage crusade that drew millions of women into political life.

Republicans took enough satisfaction in the Fifteenth Amendment to conclude that black suffrage was the "last great point that remained to be settled of the issues of the war" and promptly scratched the "Negro question" from the agenda of national politics. Even that steadfast crusader for equality Wendell Phillips concluded that the black man now held "sufficient shield in his own hands. . . . Whatever he suffers will be largely now, and in future, his own fault." Northerners had no idea of the violent struggles that lay ahead.

> **REVIEW** Why did Congress impeach President Andrew Johnson?
>
> *removed secretary of war w/o senate aproval*

The Struggle in the South

Northerners believed they had discharged their responsibilities with the Reconstruction Acts and the amendments to the Constitution, but Southerners knew that the battle had just begun. Black suffrage had destroyed traditional southern politics and established the foundation for the rise of the Republican Party. Gathering outsiders and outcasts, southern Republicans won elections, wrote new state constitutions, and formed new state governments.

Challenging the established class for political control was dangerous business. Equally dangerous were the confrontations that took place on southern farms and plantations, where blacks sought to give fuller meaning to their newly won legal and political equality. Ex-masters had their own ideas about the labor system that should replace slavery, and freedom remained contested territory. Southerners fought pitched battles with one another to determine the contours of their new world.

Freedmen, Yankees, and Yeomen.
blacks = republicans

African Americans made up the majority of southern Republicans. After gaining voting rights in 1867, nearly all eligible black men registered to vote as Republicans, grateful to the party that had freed them and granted them the franchise. "It is the hardest thing in the world to keep a negro away from the polls," observed an Alabama white man. Southern blacks did not all have identical political priorities, but they united in their desire for education and equal treatment before the law.

Northern whites who made the South their home after the war were a second element of the South's Republican Party. Conservative white Southerners called them **carpetbaggers,** *opportunists who stuffed all their belongings in a single carpet-sided suitcase and headed south to "fatten on our misfortunes." But most

carpetbaggers
Southerners' pejorative term for northern migrants who sought opportunity in the South after the Civil War. Northern migrants formed an important part of the southern Republican Party.

★ northerners who moved south

Northerners who moved south were young men who looked upon the South as they did the West — as a promising place to make a living. Northerners in the southern Republican Party supported programs that encouraged vigorous economic development along the lines of the northern free-labor model.

Southern whites made up the third element of the South's Republican Party. Approximately one out of four white Southerners voted Republican. The other three condemned the one who did as a traitor to his region and his race and called him a **scalawag**, a term for runty horses and low-down, good-for-nothing rascals. Yeoman farmers accounted for the majority of southern white Republicans. Some were Unionists who emerged from the war with bitter memories of Confederate persecution. Others were small farmers who wanted to end state governments' favoritism toward plantation owners. Yeomen supported initiatives for public schools and for expanding economic opportunity in the South.

The South's Republican Party, then, was made up of freedmen, Yankees, and yeomen — an improbable coalition. The mix of races, regions, and classes inevitably meant friction as each group maneuvered to define the party. But Reconstruction represented an extraordinary moment in American politics: Blacks and whites joined together in the Republican Party to pursue political change. Formally, of course, only men participated in politics — casting ballots and holding offices — but white and black women also played a part in the political struggle by joining in parades and rallies, attending stump speeches, and even campaigning.

Most whites in the South condemned southern Republicans as illegitimate and felt justified in doing whatever they could to stamp them out. Violence against blacks — the "white terror" — took brutal institutional form in 1866 with the formation in Tennessee of the **Ku Klux Klan**, a social club of Confederate veterans that quickly developed into a paramilitary organization supporting Democrats. The Klan went on a rampage of whipping, hanging, shooting, burning, and throat-cutting to defeat Republicans and restore white supremacy. Rapid demobilization of the Union army after the war left only twenty thousand troops to patrol the entire South. Without effective military protection, southern Republicans had to take care of themselves.

Republican Rule. In the fall of 1867, southern states held elections for delegates to state constitutional conventions, as required by the Reconstruction Acts. About 40 percent of the white electorate stayed home because they had been disfranchised or because they had decided to boycott politics. Republicans won three-fourths of the seats. About 15 percent of the Republican delegates to the conventions were Northerners who had moved south, 25 percent were African Americans, and 60 percent were white Southerners. As a British visitor observed, the delegate elections reflected "the mighty revolution that had taken place in America."

The conventions brought together serious, purposeful men who hammered out the legal framework for a new order. The reconstruction constitutions introduced two broad categories of changes in the South: those that reduced aristocratic privilege and increased democratic equality and those that expanded the state's responsibility for the general welfare. In the first category, the constitutions adopted universal male suffrage, abolished property qualifications for holding office, and made more offices elective and fewer appointed. In the second category, they enacted

scalawag
A derogatory term that Southerners applied to southern white Republicans, who were seen as traitors to the South. Most were yeoman farmers.

Ku Klux Klan
A social club of Confederate veterans that quickly developed into a paramilitary organization supporting Democrats. With too few Union troops in the South to control the region, the Klan went on a rampage of violence to defeat Republicans and restore white supremacy.

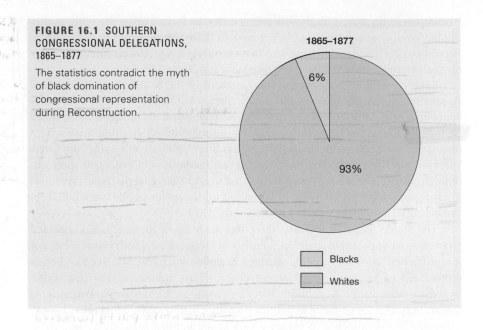

FIGURE 16.1 SOUTHERN CONGRESSIONAL DELEGATIONS, 1865–1877

The statistics contradict the myth of black domination of congressional representation during Reconstruction.

prison reform; made the state responsible for caring for orphans, the insane, and the deaf and mute; and exempted debtors' homes from seizure.

To Democrats, however, these progressive constitutions looked like wild revolution. They were blind to the fact that no constitution confiscated and redistributed land, as virtually every former slave wished, or disfranchised ex-rebels wholesale, as most southern Unionists advocated. And Democrats were convinced that the new constitutions initiated "Negro domination." In fact, although 80 percent of Republican voters were black men, only 6 percent of Southerners in Congress during Reconstruction were black (Figure 16.1). The sixteen black men in Congress included exceptional men, such as Representative James T. Rapier of Alabama (see pages 458–60). No state legislature experienced "Negro rule," despite black majorities in the populations of some states.

Southern voters ratified the new constitutions and swept Republicans into power. When the former Confederate states ratified the Fourteenth Amendment, Congress readmitted them. Southern Republicans then turned to a staggering array of problems. Wartime destruction littered the landscape. Making matters worse, racial harassment and reactionary violence dogged Southerners who sought reform. Democrats mocked Republican officeholders as ignorant field hands who had only "agricultural degrees" and "brick yard diplomas," but Republicans began a serious effort to rebuild and reform the region.

Activity focused on three areas — education, civil rights, and economic development. Every state inaugurated a system of public education. Before the Civil War, whites had deliberately kept slaves illiterate, and planter-dominated governments rarely spent tax money to educate the children of yeomen. By 1875, half of Mississippi's and South Carolina's eligible children were attending school. Although schools were underfunded, literacy rates rose sharply. Public schools were racially

STUDENTS AT A FREEDMEN'S SCHOOL IN VIRGINIA, CA. 1870S
"The people are hungry and thirsty after knowledge," a former slave observed immediately after the Civil War. African American leader Booker T. Washington remembered "a whole race trying to go to school." Students at this Virginia school stand in front of their log-cabin classroom reading books. For people long forbidden to learn to read and write, literacy symbolized freedom. Photo12/UIG/Getty Images.

segregated, but education remained for many blacks a tangible, deeply satisfying benefit of freedom and Republican rule.   *accessable but segregated*

State legislatures also attacked racial discrimination and defended civil rights.   *hard to enforce* Republicans especially resisted efforts to segregate blacks from whites in public transportation. Mississippi levied fines and jail terms for owners of railroads and steamboats that pushed blacks into "smoking cars" or to lower decks. But passing color-blind laws was one thing; enforcing them was another. A Mississippian complained: "Education amounts to nothing, good behavior counts for nothing, even money cannot buy for a colored man or woman decent treatment and the comforts that white people claim and can obtain." Despite the laws, segregation — later called Jim Crow — developed at white insistence. Determined to underscore the social inferiority of blacks, whites saw to it that separation by race became a feature of southern life long before the end of the Reconstruction era.

Republican governments also launched ambitious programs of economic development. They envisioned a South of diversified agriculture, roaring factories, and booming towns. State legislatures chartered scores of banks and industrial companies, appropriated funds to fix ruined levees and drain swamps, and went on a railroad-building binge. These efforts fell far short of solving the South's economic troubles, however. Republican spending to stimulate economic growth also meant rising taxes and enormous debt that siphoned funds from schools and other programs.

The southern Republicans' record, then, was mixed. To their credit, the biracial party adopted an ambitious agenda to change the South. But money was scarce, the

corruption ⌠ Democrats continued their harassment, and factionalism threatened the Republican
Party from within. Moreover, corruption infected Republican governments. Nonetheless, the Republican Party made headway in its efforts to purge the South of aristocratic
privilege and racist oppression. Republican governments had less success in overthrow-
⌡ ing the long-established white oppression of black farm laborers in the rural South.

White Landlords, Black Sharecroppers. Ex-slaves who wished to escape
slave labor and ex-masters who wanted to reinstitute old ways clashed repeatedly.
Except for having to pay subsistence wages, planters had not been required to offer

Beyond America's Borders

The Slaveholder Exodus

On the eve of the Civil War, southern slaveholders agreed that blacks were inferior, that without total subordination they were dangerous and destructive, and that without coercion they would not work. Voicing nearly universal sentiments, Henry Watson, an Alabama planter, declared that "if emancipation takes place," plantations "will be worth nothing." Mississippi planter James Kirkland asserted that he had rather "be exterminated" than live in the same society "with the slaves if freed." Faced with a Republican victory in the election of 1860, planters led the South out of the Union and fought a ferocious war to keep blacks in bondage.

Yankee victory meant abolition, but slaveholders ended the war much as they began it, still believing that without slavery the South "would be wholly worthless, a barren waste and desolate plain." Robert Barnwell Rhett Sr. of South Carolina reaffirmed the widespread conviction that "it is absurd to suppose that the African will work under a system of voluntary labor. . . . [T]he labor of the negro must be compulsory — he must be a slave."

Three months after Appomattox, an Alabama planter described the scene to his absent partner: "The Yankees have declared the Negroes all free. We have no authority to control them in any way, or even to defend ourselves . . . . Our country and town are filled with idle negroes, crops abandoned in many cases. On some plantations all the negroes have left. . . . The result will be that our whole country north and south will be impoverished and ruined. . . . The loss of our slaves, to a very great extent destroys the value of all other property. . . . All want to sell and get out of the country. Many expect to go to South [America]. . . . The idea is to get away from the free Negro."

Thousands of white Southerners, perhaps as many as ten thousand, fled after the Confederacy fell. They did not flee blindly; planters overwhelmingly chose Brazil. Because "it was the last resting place of slavery," they believed that it offered the best chance of resurrecting antebellum southern society. The ruler of Brazil, Dom Pedro II, personally encouraged Southerners to come settle. But planters had no intention of assimilating into local life. One emigrant remembered that southern planters in Brazil were "tenacious of their ideas, manners, & religion" and "laughed with scorn" at their "adopted land." They had to be, he said, "*masters.*"

Firsthand experience in Brazil pleased some Southerners. Charles G. Gunter of Marengo County, Alabama, loved Brazil's climate, people, land, and government, and he wrote to his son that he expected to soon buy a plantation with "fifty to a hundred slaves." Eight months later, he declared: "Dispose of, give away

many concessions to emancipation. They continued to believe that African Americans would not work without coercion. A Tennessee man declared two years after
the war ended that blacks were "a trifling set of lazy devils who will never make a
living without Masters." Whites moved quickly to restore as much of slavery as they
could get away with. (See "Beyond America's Borders" below.)

[handwritten margin note: stereotype of lazyness]

Ex-slaves resisted every effort to turn back the clock. They argued that if any
class could be described as "lazy," it was the planters, who, as one former slave noted,
"lived in idleness all their lives on stolen labor." Freedmen believed that land of their
own would anchor their economic independence and end planters' interference in
their personal lives. They could then, for example, make their own decisions about

and settle my affairs as if I were dead to the U.S. I shall never go there again." Now owner of a plot of six thousand acres and "enough negroes to work it," he concluded: "We shall be rich here." His only complaints were "ants and a spirit of democracy among the people — no great evils in comparison with free negro labor, radicalism and taxes."

But many more southern planters were shocked by Brazil. Andrew McCollam of Louisiana quickly concluded that "all is not gold that glitters here." He saw the "finger of decay" everywhere. Even more disturbing was the state of race relations. Everywhere he looked, he found "white men & negro women all together." But in the end it was the shaky status of slavery that ended his experiment as a Brazilian planter. The prevailing impression, he said, was that "slavery would be abolished in less than 20 years, perhaps . . . in ten years." McCollam was captivated by the beauty of the country and said wistfully that if only a hundred good "families from Louisiana could be located here and the institution of slavery insured I should think I had found a new land of promise." With that he boarded a steamer for Louisiana.

In the end, southern planters failed to recreate antebellum plantation society overseas. By 1870, most émigrés to Brazil had found their way back home, where they joined the vast majority of former slaveholders who had stayed put. Staying put, however, did not signal an acceptance of free black labor. Indeed, for every slaveholder who joined the exodus, several others longed to join him. Many had "the inclination," a Mississippi woman observed in 1866, but "not the means." Since both the emigrants and the stay-at-homes shared the same grim prediction for southern plantations with free black labor, they joined together to channel plantation affairs back into familiar antebellum ways.

QUESTIONS FOR ANALYSIS

Summarize the Argument What drove former slaveholders out of the South after the Civil War, and what specifically attracted them to Brazil?

Recognize Viewpoints What sustained slaveholders' proslavery ideas through the war, and why didn't the fact of emancipation change their minds about the necessity of slavery?

Consider the Context What were the consequences of the persistence of proslavery thinking for the South's transition from slavery to free labor during Reconstruction?

BLACK WOMAN IN COTTON FIELDS, THOMASVILLE, GEORGIA

Few images of everyday black women during the Reconstruction era survive. This 1895 photograph poignantly depicts the post–Civil War labor struggle, when white landlords wanted emancipated slaves to continue working in the fields. Freedom allowed some women to escape field labor, but not this Georgian. Her headdress protected her from the fierce heat, and her bare feet reveal the hardships of her life. Courtesy, Georgia Archives, Vanishing Georgia Collection tho096.

whether women and children would labor in the fields. Indeed, within months after the war, perhaps one-third of black women abandoned field labor to work on chores in their own cabins just as poor white women did. Black women also negotiated about work ex-mistresses wanted done in the big house. Hundreds of thousands of black children enrolled in school. But without their own land, ex-slaves had little choice but to work on plantations.

Although forced to return to the planters' fields, they resisted efforts to restore slavelike conditions. Instead of working for wages, a South Carolinian observed, "the negroes all seem disposed to rent land," which increased their independence from whites. Out of this tug-of-war between white landlords and black laborers emerged a new system of southern agriculture.

Sharecropping was a compromise that offered something to both ex-masters and ex-slaves but satisfied neither. Under the new system, planters divided their cotton plantations into small farms that freedmen rented, paying with a share of each year's crop, usually half. Sharecropping gave blacks more freedom than the system of wages and labor gangs and released them from day-to-day supervision by whites. Black families abandoned the old slave quarters and built separate cabins for themselves on the patches of land they rented (Map 16.1). Still, most black families remained dependent on white landlords, who had the power to evict them at the end of each growing season. For planters, sharecropping offered a way to resume agricultural production, but it did not allow them to restore the old slave plantation.

Sharecropping introduced the country merchant into the agricultural equation. Landlords supplied sharecroppers with land, mules, seeds, and tools, but blacks also needed credit to obtain essential food and clothing before they harvested their crops. Under an arrangement called a crop lien, a merchant would advance goods to a sharecropper in exchange for a *lien*, or legal claim, on the farmer's future crop. Some merchants charged exorbitant rates of interest, as much as 60 percent, on the goods they sold. At the end of the growing season, after the landlord had taken half of the farmer's crop for rent, the merchant took most of the rest.

deadly cycle ⟶ Sometimes, the farmer did not earn enough to repay the debt to the merchant, so he would have to borrow more from the merchant and begin the cycle again.

An experiment at first, sharecropping soon dominated the cotton South. Lien merchants forced tenants to plant cotton, which was easy to sell, instead of food crops. The result was excessive production of cotton and falling cotton prices, developments that cost thousands of small white farmers their land and pushed them into the great army of sharecroppers. The new sharecropping system of agriculture took shape just as the political power of Republicans in the South began to buckle under Democratic pressure.

> **REVIEW** How did politics and economic concerns shape reconstruction in the South?

sharecropping
Labor system that emerged in the South during Reconstruction. Under this system, planters divided their plantations into small farms that freedmen rented, paying with a share of each year's crop. Sharecropping gave blacks some freedom, but they remained dependent on white landlords and country merchants.

Map Activity

MAP 16.1   A SOUTHERN PLANTATION IN 1860 AND 1881

These maps of the Barrow plantation in Georgia illustrate some of the ways in which ex-slaves expressed their freedom. Freedmen and freedwomen deserted the clustered living quarters behind the master's house, scattered over the plantation, built family cabins, and farmed rented land. The former Barrow slaves also worked together to build a school and a church.

READING THE MAP: Compare the number and size of the slave quarters in 1860 with the homes of the former slaves in 1881. How do they differ? Which buildings were prominently located along the road in 1860, and which could be found along the road in 1881?

CONNECTIONS: How might the former master feel about the new configuration of buildings on the plantation in 1881? In what ways did the new system of sharecropping replicate the old system of plantation agriculture? In what ways was it different?

Reconstruction Collapses

redoing mem. in gov. general grant bad pres.

By 1870, after a decade of war and reconstruction, Northerners wanted to put "the southern problem" behind them. Practical business-minded men came to dominate the Republican Party, replacing the band of reformers and idealists who had been prominent in the 1860s. Civil War hero Ulysses S. Grant succeeded Andrew Johnson as president in 1869 and quickly became an issue himself, proving that brilliance on the battlefield does not necessarily translate into accomplishment in the White House. As northern commitment to defend black freedom eroded, southern commitment to white supremacy intensified. Without northern protection, southern Republicans were no match for the Democrats' economic coercion, political fraud, and bloody violence. One by one, Republican state governments fell in the South. The election of 1876 both confirmed and completed the collapse of reconstruction.

Grant's Troubled Presidency. In 1868, the Republican Party's presidential nomination went to Ulysses S. Grant, the North's favorite general. His Democratic opponent, Horatio Seymour of New York, ran on a platform that blasted reconstruction as "a flagrant usurpation of power . . . unconstitutional, revolutionary, and void." The Republicans answered by "waving the bloody shirt" — that is, they reminded voters that the Democrats were "the party of rebellion." Despite a reign of terror in the South, costing hundreds of Republicans their lives, Grant gained a narrow 309,000-vote margin in the popular vote and a substantial victory (214 votes to 80) in the electoral college (Map 16.2).

Grant was not as good a president as he was a general. The talents he had demonstrated on the battlefield — decisiveness, clarity, and resolution — were less obvious in the White House. Grant sought both justice for blacks and sectional reconciliation. But he surrounded himself with fumbling kinfolk and old friends from his army days and made a string of dubious appointments that led to a series of damaging scandals. Charges of corruption tainted his vice president, Schuyler Colfax, and brought down two of his cabinet officers. Though never personally implicated in any scandal, Grant was aggravatingly naive and blind to the rot that filled his administration. Republican congressman James A. Garfield declared: "His imperturbability is amazing. I am in doubt whether to call it greatness or stupidity."

In 1872, anti-Grant Republicans bolted and launched the Liberal Party. To clean up the graft and corruption, Liberals proposed ending the spoils system, by which victorious parties rewarded loyal workers with public office, and replacing it with a nonpartisan civil service commission that would oversee competitive examinations for appointment to office (as discussed in chapter 18). Liberals also demanded that the federal government remove its troops from the South and restore "home rule" (southern white control). Democrats

personal life in way

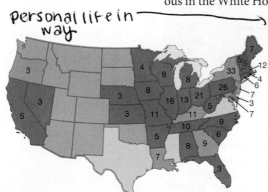

Candidate	Electoral Vote	Popular Vote	Percent of Popular Vote
Ulysses S. Grant (Republican)	214	3,012,833	52.7
Horatio Seymour (Democrat)	80	2,703,249	47.3
Nonvoting states (Reconstruction)			

MAP 16.2   THE ELECTION OF 1868

"I BEG TO REPEAT THAT THESE FRAUDS ON THE GOVERNMENT SHALL BE PROBED TO THE VERY BOTTOM."

GRANT AND SCANDAL

This anti-Grant cartoon by Thomas Nast, the nation's most celebrated political cartoonist, shows the president falling headfirst into the barrel of fraud and corruption that tainted his administration. During Grant's eight years in the White House, many members of his administration failed him. Sometimes duped, sometimes merely loyal, Grant stubbornly defended wrongdoers, even to the point of perjuring himself to keep an aide out of jail. Picture Research Consultants & Archives.

liked the Liberals' southern policy and endorsed the Liberal presidential candidate, Horace Greeley, the longtime editor of the *New York Tribune*. The nation, however, still felt enormous affection for the man who had saved the Union and reelected Grant with 56 percent of the popular vote.

Northern Resolve Withers. Although Grant genuinely wanted to see blacks' civil and political rights protected, he understood that most Northerners had grown weary of reconstruction and were increasingly willing to let southern whites manage their own affairs. Citizens wanted to shift their attention to other issues, especially after the nation slipped into a devastating economic depression in 1873. More than eighteen thousand businesses collapsed, leaving more than a million workers on the streets. Northern businessmen wanted to invest in the South but believed that recurrent federal intrusion was itself a major cause of instability in the region. Republican leaders began to question the wisdom of their party's alliance with the South's lower classes — its small farmers and sharecroppers. One member of Grant's administration proposed allying with the "thinking and influential native southerners . . . the intelligent, well-to-do, and controlling class."

Congress, too, wanted to leave reconstruction behind, but southern Republicans made that difficult. When the South's Republicans begged for federal protection *interfering w/ voting a felony*

outlawed racial discrimination in places

14th only protected rights of fed. gov

from increasing Klan violence, Congress enacted three laws in 1870 and 1871 that were intended to break the back of white terrorism. The severest of the three, the Ku Klux Klan Act (1871), made interference with voting rights a felony. Federal marshals arrested thousands of Klansmen and came close to destroying the Klan, but they did not end all terrorism against blacks. Congress also passed the Civil Rights Act of 1875, which boldly outlawed racial discrimination in transportation, public accommodations, and juries. But federal authorities never enforced the law aggressively, and segregation remained the rule throughout the South.

By the early 1870s, the Republican Party had lost its leading champions of African American rights to death or defeat at the polls. Other Republicans concluded that the quest for black equality was mistaken or hopelessly naive. In May 1872, Congress restored the right of officeholding to all but three hundred ex-rebels. Many Republicans had come to believe that traditional white leaders offered the best hope for honesty, order, and prosperity in the South.

Underlying the North's abandonment of reconstruction was unyielding racial prejudice. Northerners had learned to accept black freedom during the war, but deep-seated prejudice prevented many from accepting black equality. Even the actions they took on behalf of blacks often served partisan political advantage. Northerners generally supported Indiana senator Thomas A. Hendricks's harsh declaration that "this is a white man's Government, made by the white man for the white man."

The U.S. Supreme Court also did its part to undermine reconstruction. The Court issued a series of decisions that significantly weakened the federal government's ability to protect black Southerners. In the *Slaughterhouse* cases (1873), the Court distinguished between national and state citizenship and ruled that the Fourteenth Amendment protected only those rights that stemmed from the federal government, such as voting in federal elections and interstate travel. Since the Court decided that most rights derived from the states, it sharply curtailed the federal government's authority to defend black citizens. Even more devastating, the *United States v. Cruikshank* ruling (1876) said that the reconstruction amendments gave Congress the power to legislate against discrimination only by states, not by individuals. The "suppression of ordinary crime," such as assault, remained a state responsibility. The Supreme Court did not declare reconstruction unconstitutional but eroded its legal foundation.

The mood of the North found political expression in the election of 1874, when for the first time in eighteen years the Democrats gained control of the House of Representatives. As one Republican observed, the people had grown tired of the "negro question, with all its complications, and the reconstruction of Southern States, with all its interminable embroilments." Reconstruction had come apart. Rather than defend reconstruction from its southern enemies, Northerners steadily backed away from the challenge. By the early 1870s, southern Republicans faced the forces of reaction largely on their own.

White Supremacy Triumphs. Reconstruction was a massive humiliation to most white Southerners. Republican rule meant intolerable insults: Black militiamen patrolled town streets, black laborers negotiated contracts with former masters, black maids stood up to former mistresses, black voters cast ballots, and black legislators such as James T. Rapier enacted laws. Whites fought back by extolling the "great Confederate cause," or Lost Cause. They celebrated their soldiers, "the noblest

band of men who ever fought," and by making an idol of Robert E. Lee, the embodi-
ment of the southern gentleman.

But the most important way white Southerners responded to reconstruction was
their assault on Republican governments in the South. These Republican governments attracted more hatred than did any other political regimes in American history.
The northern retreat from reconstruction permitted southern Democrats to set things
right. Taking the name **Redeemers**, Democrats in the South promised to replace
"bayonet rule" (a few federal troops continued to be stationed in the South) with
"home rule." They promised that honest, thrifty Democrats would supplant corrupt
tax-and-spend Republicans. Above all, Redeemers swore to save southern civilization
from a descent into "African barbarism." As one man put it, "We must render this
either a white man's government, or convert the land into a Negro man's cemetery."

Southern Democrats adopted a multipronged strategy to overthrow Republican
governments. First, they sought to polarize the parties around race. They went about
gathering all the South's white voters into the Democratic Party, leaving the Republicans to depend on blacks, who made up a minority of the population in almost every
southern state. To dislodge whites from the Republican Party, Democrats fanned the
flames of racism. A South Carolina Democrat crowed that his party appealed to the
"proud Caucasian race, whose sovereignty on earth God has proclaimed." Ostracism
also proved effective. Local newspapers published the names of whites who kept
company with blacks. So complete was the ostracism that one of its victims said, "No
white man can live in the South in the future and act with any other than the Democratic party unless he is willing and prepared to live a life of social isolation."

Democrats also exploited the severe economic plight of small white farmers by
blaming it on Republican financial policy. Government spending soared during Reconstruction, and small farmers saw their tax burden skyrocket. "This is tax time," a South
Carolinian reported. "We are nearly all on our head about them. They are so high & so
little money to pay with" that farmers were "selling every egg and chicken they can get."
In 1871, Mississippi reported that one-seventh of the state's land — 3.3 million acres —
had been forfeited for nonpayment of taxes. The small farmers' economic distress had
a racial dimension. Because few freedmen succeeded in acquiring land, they rarely paid
taxes. In Georgia in 1874, blacks made up 45 percent of the population but paid only
2 percent of the taxes. From the perspective of a small white farmer, Republican rule
meant that he was paying more taxes and paying them to aid blacks.

If racial pride, social isolation, and financial hardship proved insufficient to
drive yeomen from the Republican Party, Democrats turned to terrorism. "Night
riders" targeted white Republicans as well as blacks for murder and assassination.
Whether white or black, a "dead Radical is very harmless," South Carolina Democratic leader Martin Gary told his followers.

But the primary victims of white violence were black Republicans. Violence
escalated to an unprecedented ferocity on Easter Sunday in 1873 in tiny Colfax, Louisiana. The black majority in the area had made Colfax a Republican stronghold
until 1872, when Democrats turned to intimidation and fraud to win the local election. Republicans refused to accept the result and occupied the courthouse in the
middle of the town. After three weeks, 165 white men attacked. They overran the
Republicans' defenses and set the courthouse on fire. When the blacks tried to surrender, the whites murdered them. At least 81 black men were slaughtered that day.

Redeemers
Name taken by southern
Democrats who harnessed
white rage in order to
overthrow Republican rule
and black political power
and thus, they believed,
save southern civilization.

Although the federal government indicted the attackers, the Supreme Court ruled that it did not have the right to prosecute. And since local whites would not prosecute neighbors who killed blacks, the defendants in the Colfax massacre went free.

Even before adopting the all-out white supremacist tactics of the 1870s, Democrats had taken control of the governments of Virginia, Tennessee, and North Carolina. The new campaign brought fresh gains. The Redeemers retook Georgia in 1871, Texas in 1873, and Arkansas and Alabama in 1874. As the state election approached in Mississippi in 1876, Governor Adelbert Ames appealed to Washington for federal troops to control the violence, only to hear from the attorney general that the "whole public are tired of these annual autumnal outbreaks in the South." Abandoned, Mississippi Republicans succumbed to the Democratic onslaught in the fall elections. By 1876, only three Republican state governments survived in the South (Map 16.3).

An Election and a Compromise. The year 1876 witnessed one of the most tumultuous elections in American history. The election took place in November, but not until March 2 of the following year did the nation know who would be inaugurated president on March 4. Sixteen years after Lincoln's election, Americans feared that a presidential election would again precipitate civil war.

Map Activity

MAP 16.3 THE RECONSTRUCTION OF THE SOUTH

Myth has it that Republican rule of the former Confederacy was not only harsh but long. In most states, however, conservative southern whites stormed back into power in months or just a few years. By the election of 1876, Republican governments could be found in only three states, and they soon fell.

READING THE MAP: List in chronological order the readmission of the former Confederate states to the Union. Which states reestablished conservative governments most quickly?

CONNECTIONS: What did the former Confederate states need to do to be readmitted to the Union? How did reestablished conservative governments react to reconstruction?

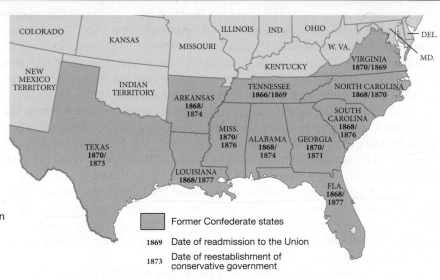

Former Confederate states

1869   Date of readmission to the Union

1873   Date of reestablishment of conservative government

The Democrats nominated New York's governor, Samuel J. Tilden, who immediately targeted the corruption of the Grant administration and the "despotism" of Republican reconstruction. The Republicans put forward Rutherford B. Hayes, governor of Ohio. Privately, Hayes considered "bayonet rule" a mistake but concluded that waving the bloody shirt remained the Republicans' best political strategy.

On election day, Tilden tallied 4,288,590 votes to Hayes's 4,036,298. But in the all-important electoral college, Tilden fell one vote short of the majority required for victory. The electoral votes of three states — South Carolina, Louisiana, and Florida, the only remaining Republican governments in the South — remained in doubt because both Republicans and Democrats in those states claimed victory. To win, Tilden needed only one of the nineteen contested votes. Hayes had to have all of them.

Congress had to decide who had actually won the elections in the three southern states and thus who would be president. The Constitution provided no guidance for this situation. Moreover, Democrats controlled the House, and Republicans controlled the Senate. Congress created a special electoral commission to arbitrate the disputed returns. All of the commissioners voted their party affiliation, giving every state to the Republican Hayes and putting him over the top in electoral votes (Map 16.4).

Some outraged Democrats vowed to resist Hayes's victory. Rumors flew of an impending coup and renewed civil war. But the impasse was broken when negotiations behind the scenes resulted in an informal understanding known as the **Compromise of 1877**. In exchange for a Democratic promise not to block Hayes's inauguration and to deal fairly with the freedmen, Hayes vowed to refrain from using the army to uphold the remaining Republican regimes in the South and to provide the South with substantial federal subsidies for railroads.

Stubborn Tilden supporters bemoaned the "stolen election" and damned "His Fraudulency," Rutherford B. Hayes. Old-guard Radicals such as William Lloyd Garrison denounced Hayes's bargain as a "policy of compromise, of credulity, of weakness, of subserviency, of surrender." But the nation as a whole celebrated, for the country had weathered a grave crisis. The last three Republican state governments in the South fell quickly once Hayes abandoned them and withdrew the U.S. Army. Reconstruction came to an end.

> **REVIEW** Why did northern support for Reconstruction collapse?

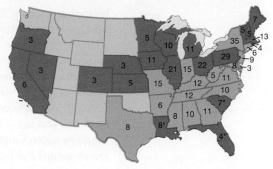

Candidate	Electoral Vote	Popular Vote	Percent of Popular Vote
Rutherford B. Hayes (Republican)	185*	4,036,298	47.9**
Samuel J. Tilden (Democrat)	184	4,288,590	51.0

*19 electoral votes were disputed.

**Percentages do not total 100 because some popular votes went to other parties.

MAP 16.4 THE ELECTION OF 1876

> **Compromise of 1877**
> Informal agreement in which Democrats agreed not to block Rutherford Hayes's inauguration and to deal fairly with freedmen; in return, Hayes vowed not to use the army to uphold the remaining Republican regimes in the South and to provide the South with substantial federal subsidies for railroads. The compromise brought the Reconstruction era to an end.

Conclusion: "A Revolution but Half Accomplished"

In 1865, when General Carl Schurz visited the South, he discovered "a revolution but half accomplished." White Southerners resisted the passage from slavery to free labor, from white racial despotism to equal justice, and from white political monopoly to biracial democracy. The old elite wanted to get "things back as near to slavery as possible," Schurz reported, while African Americans such as James T. Rapier and some whites were eager to exploit the revolutionary implications of defeat and emancipation.

Although the northern-dominated Republican Congress refused to provide for blacks' economic welfare, it employed constitutional amendments to require ex-Confederates to accept legal equality and share political power with black men. Congress was not willing to extend such power to women, however. Conservative southern whites fought ferociously to recover their power and privilege. When Democrats regained control of politics, whites used both state power and private violence to wipe out many of the gains of Reconstruction, leading one observer to conclude that the North had won the war but the South had won the peace.

The Redeemer counterrevolution, however, did not mean a return to slavery. Northern victory in the Civil War ensured that ex-slaves no longer faced the auction block and could send their children to school, worship in their own churches, and work independently on their own rented farms. Sharecropping, with all its hardships, provided more autonomy and economic welfare than bondage had. It was limited freedom, to be sure, but it was not slavery.

The Civil War and emancipation set in motion the most profound upheaval in the nation's history. War destroyed the largest slave society in the New World and gave birth to a modern nation-state. The world of masters and slaves gave way to that of landlords and sharecroppers. Washington increased its role in national affairs, and the victorious North set the nation's compass toward the expansion of industrial capitalism and the final conquest of the West.

Despite massive changes, however, the Civil War remained only a "half accomplished" revolution. By not fulfilling the promises the nation seemed to hold out to black Americans at war's end, Reconstruction represents a tragedy of enormous proportions. The failure to protect blacks and guarantee their rights had enduring consequences. It was the failure of the first reconstruction that made the modern civil rights movement necessary.

Chapter Review

KEY TERMS

Freedmen's Bureau (p. 463)	carpetbaggers (p. 472)
black codes (p. 465)	scalawag (p. 473)
Civil Rights Act of 1866 (p. 467)	Ku Klux Klan (p. 473)
Fourteenth Amendment (p. 467)	sharecropping (p. 478)
Military Reconstruction Act (p. 470)	Redeemers (p. 483)
Fifteenth Amendment (p. 471)	Compromise of 1877 (p. 485)

REVIEW QUESTIONS

1 To what extent did Lincoln's wartime plan for reconstruction reflect the concerns of newly freed slaves?   (pp. 460–64)

2 When the southern states passed the black codes, how did the U.S. Congress respond?   (pp. 464–67)

3 Why did Congress impeach President Andrew Johnson?   (pp. 467–72)

4 How did politics and economic concerns shape reconstruction in the South?   (pp. 472–79)

5 Why did northern support for reconstruction collapse?   (pp. 480–85)

MAKING CONNECTIONS

1 Why and how did the federal government retreat from defending African Americans' civil rights in the 1870s?

2 Why was distributing plantation land to former slaves such a controversial policy? Why did Congress reject redistribution as a general policy?

3 After emancipation, how did ex-slaves exercise their new freedoms, and how did white Southerners attempt to limit them?

4 How did the identification of the Republican Party with reconstruction policy affect the party's political fortunes in the 1870s?

LINKING TO THE PAST

1 In what ways did the attitudes and actions of President Johnson increase northern resolve to reconstruct the South and the South's resolve to resist reconstruction?

2 White women, abolitionists, and blacks all had hopes for a brighter future that were in some ways dashed during the turmoil of reconstruction. What specific goals of these groups slipped away? What political allies abandoned their causes, and why?

The Contested West, 1865–1900

CONTENT LEARNING OBJECTIVES

After reading and studying this chapter, you should be able to:

- Explain federal policies toward Native Americans during the last decades of the nineteenth century. Describe how Native Americans resisted these policies and how the government quashed these acts of resistance.
- Recount how the late-nineteenth-century frenzy for gold and silver in the West transformed the region and explain how the development of the western mining industry mirrored the processes of industrialization in other parts of the country.
- Identify who worked and settled in the West and why they were drawn there.
- Describe the ways in which farming became increasingly commercialized and ranching became increasingly industrialized.

To celebrate the 400th anniversary of Columbus's voyage to the New World, Chicago hosted the World's Columbian Exposition in 1893, creating a magical White City on the shores of Lake Michigan. Among the organizations vying to hold meetings at the fair was the American Historical Association, whose members gathered on a warm July evening to hear Frederick Jackson Turner deliver his landmark essay "The Significance of the Frontier in American History." Turner began by noting that the 1890 census no longer discerned a clear frontier line. His tone was elegiac: "The existence of an area of free land, its continuous recession, and the advance of settlement westward," he observed, "explained American development."

Of course, *west* has always been a comparative term in American history. Until the gold rush focused attention on California, the West for settlers lay beyond the Appalachians. But by the second half of the nineteenth century, the West stretched from Canada to Mexico, from the Mississippi River to the Pacific Ocean.

LAKOTA VEST

This late-nineteenth-century Lakota vest displays the American flag, which was a common design in Indian bead art and testifies to the great changes that took place in the American West. Private Collection, photograph American Hurrah Archive, NYC.

Frederick Jackson Turner

Turner, who originally studied the old frontier east of the Mississippi, viewed the West as a process as much as a place. The availability of land provided a "safety valve," releasing social tensions and providing opportunities for social mobility that worked to Americanize Americans. Turner's West demanded strength and nerve, fostered invention and adaptation, and produced self-confident, individualistic Americans. His frontier thesis underscored the exceptionalism of America's history, highlighting its difference from the rest of the world. His "frontier thesis" would earn him a professorship at Harvard and a permanent place in American history.

Yet the historians who applauded Turner in Chicago had short memories. That afternoon, many had crossed the midway to attend Buffalo Bill Cody's Wild West extravaganza — a cowboys-and-Indians shoot-'em-up. The historians cheering in the stands that hot afternoon no doubt dismissed Buffalo Bill's history as amateur, but he made a point that Turner's thesis ignored: The West was neither free nor open. It was the story of a fierce and violent contest for land and resources.

In the decades following the Civil War, the United States pursued empire in the American West in Indian wars that lasted until 1890. Pushed off their land and onto reservations, Native Americans resisted as they faced waves of miners and settlers as well as the degradation of the environment by railroads, mines, barbed wire, and mechanized agriculture. The pastoral agrarianism Turner celebrated in his frontier thesis clashed with the urban, industrial West emerging on the Comstock Lode in Nevada and in the commercial farms of California.

Buffalo Bill's mythic West, with its heroic cowboys and noble savages, also obscured the complex reality of the West as a fiercely contested terrain. Competing groups of Anglos, Hispanics, former slaves, Chinese, and a host of others arrived seeking the promise of land and riches, while the Indians struggled to preserve their cultural identities. Turner's rugged white "frontiersman" masked racial diversity and failed to acknowledge the role of women in community building.

Yet in the waning decade of the nineteenth century, as history blurred with nostalgia, Turner's evocation of the frontier as a crucible for American identity hit a nerve in a population facing rapid changes. A major depression started even before the Columbian

1851	First Treaty of Fort Laramie negotiated.
1862	Homestead Act passes. Great Sioux Uprising (Santee Uprising) kills 1,000 settlers.
1864	Sand Creek massacre kills several hundred Indians.
1867	Treaty of Medicine Lodge negotiated.
1868	Washita massacre led by Custer. Second Treaty of Fort Laramie negotiated.
1869	First transcontinental railroad completed.
1870s	Hunters begin to decimate bison herds.
1873	"Big Bonanza" discovered on Comstock Lode.
1874	Gold discovered in Black Hills.
1876	Battle of the Little Big Horn destroys Custer's army.
1877	Chief Joseph surrenders.
1879	Carlisle Indian School opens. Exodusters move to Kansas.
1881	Sitting Bull surrenders.
1882	Chinese Exclusion Act passes.
1886	Geronimo surrenders.
1886– 1887	Severe blizzards decimate cattle.
1887	Dawes Allotment Act passes.
1889	Ghost Dance spreads. Two million acres in Oklahoma opened for settlement.
1890	Sitting Bull killed. Massacre at Wounded Knee kills several hundred Indians.
1893	Last land rush occurs in Oklahoma Territory. Frederick Jackson Turner presents "frontier thesis."

BUFFALO BILL POSTER

William (Buffalo Bill) Cody used colorful posters to publicize his Wild West show during the 1880s and 1890s. This poster from 1899 shows Indians attacking a wagon train and a village of tepees in the background. By the 1870s, the era of the wagon train had ended with the coming of the transcontinental railroads. The mythic West Cody (featured on the right) recreated, was already part of the past. Library of Congress, LC-DIG-ppmsca-13514.

Exposition opened its doors. Americans worried about the economy, immigration, and urban industrialism found in Turner's message a new cause for concern. Would America continue to be America now that the frontier was closed? Were the problems confronting the United States at the turn of the twentieth century — the exploitation of land and labor, the consolidation of capital, and vicious ethnic and racial rivalries — destined to play out under western skies?

Conquest and Empire in the West

[handwritten: west instead of colonies]

*[handwritten: * being diff from other countries]*

While the European powers expanded their authority and wealth through imperialism and colonialism in far-flung empires abroad, the United States focused its attention on its own western lands. From the U.S. Army attack on the remainder of the Comanche empire to the conquest of the Black Hills, whites pushed Indians aside as they moved West. As posited by Frederick Jackson Turner, American exceptionalism stressed how the history of the United States differed from that of European nations, citing America's western frontier as a cause. Yet expansion in the trans-Mississippi West involved the conquest, displacement, and rule over native peoples — a process best understood in the global context of imperialism and colonialism.

The U.S. government, through trickery and conquest, pushed tribes off their lands (Map 17.1) and onto designated Indian territories or reservations. The Indian wars depleted the Native American population and handed most Indian land to white settlers. The decimation of the bison herds pushed the Plains Indians onto reservations, where they lived as wards of the state. Thus did the United States, committed to an imperialist, expansionist ideology, colonize the West.

[handwritten: took land from indians]

Indian Removal and the Reservation System.
Manifest destiny — the belief that the United States had a "God-given" right to aggressively spread the values of white civilization and expand the nation from ocean to ocean — dictated U.S. policy toward Indians and other nations. In the name of manifest destiny, Americans forced the removal of the Five Civilized Tribes of the South (the Cherokee, Choctaw, Chickasaw, Creek, and Seminole peoples) to Oklahoma in the 1830s; colonized Texas and won its independence from Mexico in 1836; conquered California, Arizona, New Mexico, and parts of Utah and Colorado in the Mexican-American War of 1846–1848; invaded Oregon in the mid-1840s; and paid Mexico for land in Arizona and New Mexico in the Gadsden Purchase of 1854.

[handwritten: moved tribes to oklahoma]

By midcentury, western lands no longer seemed inexhaustible. Hordes of settlers crossed the Great Plains on their way to the goldfields of California or the rich farmland of Washington and Oregon. In their path stood a solid wall of Indian land. To solve this "Indian problem," the U.S. government took Indian lands with the promise to pay annuities in return and put the Indians on lands reserved for their use — **reservations**. In 1851, some ten thousand Plains Indians came together at Fort Laramie in Wyoming to negotiate a treaty that ceded a wide swath of their land to allow passage to the West. In return, the government promised that the remaining Indian land would remain inviolate.

[handwritten: treaty w/ plains indians]

reservations
Land assigned by the federal government to American Indians beginning in the 1860s in an attempt to reduce tensions between Indians and western settlers. On reservations, Indians subsisted on meager government rations and faced a life of poverty and starvation.

The Indians who "touched the pen" to the 1851 Treaty of Fort Laramie hoped to preserve their land and culture in the face of the white onslaught. Settlers and miners cut down trees, polluted streams, and killed off the bison. Whites brought alcohol, guns, and something even more deadly — disease. Between 1780 and 1870, the population of the Plains tribes declined by half. "If I could see this thing, if I knew where it came from, I would go there and fight it," a Cheyenne warrior anguished. Disease shifted the power from Woodland agrarian tribes, whose proximity to whites meant they died at high rates, to the Lakota (Western) Sioux, who fled the contagion by pursuing an equestrian nomadic existence that displaced weaker tribes in the western plains.

In the Southwest, the Navajo people, in a removal similar to that of the Cherokee in the 1830s, endured a forced march called the "Long Walk" from their homeland to the desolate Bosque Redondo Reservation in New Mexico in 1864. "This ground we were brought on, it is not productive," complained the Navajo leader Barboncito. "All the stock we brought here have nearly all died."

Poverty and starvation stalked the reservations. Confined by armed force, the Indians eked out an existence on stingy government rations. Styled as stepping-stones to "civilization," Indian reservations closely resembled colonial societies where native populations, ruled by outside bureaucrats, saw their culture assaulted,

[handwritten: forced to stay]

their religious practices outlawed, their children sent away to school, and their way of life attacked in the name of progress.

attitude of superiority

To Americans raised on theories of racial superiority, the Indians, in the words of one Colorado militia major, constituted "an obstacle to civilization . . . [and] should be exterminated." This attitude pervaded the military. As a result, the massacre of Native American men, women, and children became commonplace in

Map Activity

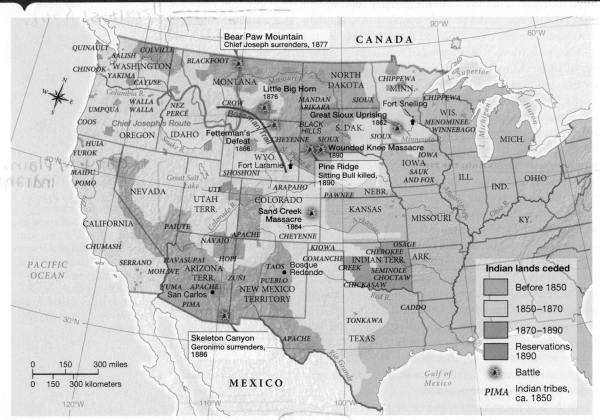

MAP 17.1   THE LOSS OF INDIAN LANDS, 1850–1890

By 1890, western Indians were isolated on small, scattered reservations. Native Americans had struggled to retain their land in major battles, from the Great Sioux Uprising in Minnesota in 1862 to the massacre at Wounded Knee, South Dakota, in 1890.

READING THE MAP: Where was the largest reservation located in 1890? Which states on this map show no reservations in 1890? Compare this map to Map 17.3.

CONNECTIONS: Why did the federal government force Native Americans onto reservations? What developments prompted these changes?

the West. In November 1864 at Sand Creek in Colorado Territory, Colonel John M. Chivington and his Colorado militia descended on a village of Cheyenne, mostly women and children. Their leader, Black Kettle raised a white flag and an American flag to signal surrender, but the charging cavalry ignored his signal and butchered 270 Indians. Chivington watched as his men scalped and mutilated their victims and later justified the killing of Indian children with the terse remark, "Nits make lice." The city of Denver treated Chivington and his men as heroes, but a congressional inquiry eventually castigated the soldiers for their "fiendish malignity" and condemned the "savage cruelty" of the massacre. Four years later, Black Kettle, who had survived Sand Creek, died in another massacre when George Armstrong Custer slaughtered more than one hundred people on the banks of the Washita River in Oklahoma.

[handwritten margin note: massacre after surrender]

The Decimation of the Great Bison Herds.

After the Civil War, the accelerating pace of industrial expansion brought about the near extinction of the American bison (buffalo). By 1850, the dynamic ecology of the Great Plains, with its droughts, fires, and blizzards, along with the demands of Indian buffalo-robe traders as well as whites and their cattle, had driven the bison herds onto the far western plains.

In the 1870s, industrial demand for heavy leather belting used in machinery and the development of larger, more accurate rifles combined to hasten the slaughter of the bison. The nation's transcontinental railroad systems cut the range in two and divided the dwindling herds. For the Sioux and other nomadic tribes of the plains, the buffalo constituted a way of life — a source of food, fuel, and shelter and a central part of religion and ritual. Railroad owners, however, considered bison a nuisance — at best a cheap source of meat for their workers and a target for sport.

Although the army took credit for the conquest of the Plains Indians, the decimation of the great bison herds was largely responsible for the Indians' fate. With their food supply gone, Indians had to choose between starvation and the reservation. "A cold wind blew across the prairie when the last buffalo fell," the great Sioux leader Sitting Bull lamented, "a death wind for my people."

On the southern plains in 1867, more than five thousand warring Comanches, Kiowas, and Southern Arapahos gathered at Medicine Lodge Creek in Kansas to negotiate the Treaty of Medicine Lodge, hoping to preserve limited land and hunting by moving the tribe

"SLAUGHTERED FOR THE HIDE"

In 1874, *Harper's Weekly* featured this illustration of a buffalo-hide hunter skinning a carcass on the southwestern plains. City father Colonel Richard Dodge wrote of the carnage, "The air was foul with sickening stench, and the vast plain, which only a short twelve-month before teemed with animal life, was a dead, solitary, putrid desert." Library of Congress, 3b03485.

[handwritten margin note: almost all bison gone]

to a reservation. Three years after the treaty became law, hide hunters poured into the region; within a decade, they had nearly exterminated the southern bison herds. Luther Standing Bear recounted the sight and stench: "I saw the bodies of hundreds of dead buffalo lying about, just wasting, and the odor was terrible. . . . They were letting our food lie on the plains to rot." Once an estimated 40 million bison roamed the West; by 1895, fewer than 1,000 remained. With the buffalo gone, the Indians faced starvation and reluctantly moved onto the reservations.

[handwritten margin note: Dakota tribe rose up r killed settlers]

Indian Wars and the Collapse of Comanchería. The Indian wars in the West marked the last resistance of a Native American population devastated by disease and demoralized by the federal government's reservation policy. The Dakota Sioux in Minnesota went to war in 1862. For years, under the leadership of Chief Little Crow, the Dakota — also known as the Santee — had pursued a policy of accommodation, ceding land in return for the promise of annuities. But with his people on the verge of starvation (the local Indian agent told the hungry Dakota, "Go and eat grass"), Little Crow led his angry warriors in a desperate campaign against the intruders, killing more than 1,000 settlers. American troops quelled the Great Sioux Uprising (also called the Santee Uprising) and marched 1,700 Sioux to Fort Snelling, where 400 Indians were put on trial for murder and 38 died in the largest mass execution in American history.

Comanchería
Indian empire based on trade in horses, hides, guns, and captives that stretched from the Canadian plains to Mexico in the eighteenth century. By 1865, fewer than five thousand Comanches lived in the empire, which ranged from west Texas north to Oklahoma.

Further west, the great Indian empire of **Comanchería** had once stretched from the Canadian plains to Mexico. By 1865, after two decades of what one historian has labeled "ethnic cleansing," fewer than five thousand Comanches remained in west Texas and Oklahoma. Through decades of dealings with the Spanish and French, the Comanche had built a complex empire based on trade in horses, hides, guns, and captives. Expert riders, the Comanche waged war in the saddle, giving the U.S. Cavalry reason to hate and fear them. *[handwritten: horse warfare]*

After the Civil War, President Ulysses S. Grant faced the prospect of protracted Indian war. Reluctant to spend more money and sacrifice more lives, Grant adopted a "peace policy" designed to segregate and control the Indians while opening up land to white settlers. This policy won the support of both friends of the Indians and those who coveted the Indians' land. The army herded the Indians onto reservations (Map 17.1), where the U.S. Bureau of Indian Affairs hired agents who, in the words of Paiute Sarah Winnemucca, did "nothing but fill their pockets." In 1871, Congress determined to no longer deal with Indians as sovereign nations but to eliminate treaties and treat Indians as wards of the state. Grant's peace policy in the West gave way to all-out warfare as the U.S. Army dispatched 3,000 soldiers to wipe out the remains of Comanchería. Raiding parties of Comanche virtually obliterated white settlements in west Texas. To defeat the Indians, the army adopted the practice of burning and destroying everything in its path, using the tactics that General William Tecumseh Sherman had perfected in his march through Georgia during the Civil War. At the decisive battle of Palo Duro Canyon in 1874, only three Comanche warriors died in battle, but U.S. soldiers took the Indians' camp; burned more than 200 tepees, hundreds of robes and blankets, and thousands of pounds of winter supplies; and shot more than 1,000 horses. Coupled with the decimation of the bison, the army's scorched-earth policy led to the final collapse of the Comanche people. The surviving Indians of Comanchería, now numbering fewer than 1,500, reluctantly retreated to the reservation at Fort Sill.

The Fight for the Black Hills. On the northern plains, the fever for gold ~2 tribes united~ fueled the conflict between Indians and Euro-Americans. In 1866, the Cheyenne united with the Sioux in Wyoming to protect their hunting grounds in the Powder River valley, which were threatened by the construction of the Bozeman Trail connecting Fort Laramie with the goldfields in Montana. Captain William Fetterman, who had boasted that with eighty men he could ride through the Sioux nation, died along with all of his troops at the hands of the Sioux. The Indians' impressive victories led to the second Treaty of Fort Laramie in 1868, in which the United States agreed to abandon the Bozeman Trail and guaranteed the Indians control of the Black Hills, land sacred to the Lakota Sioux.

The government's fork-tongued promises induced some of the tribes to accept the treaty. The great Sioux chief Red Cloud led many of his people onto the reservation. Red Cloud soon regretted his decision. "Think of it!" he told a visitor to the Pine Ridge Reservation. "I, who used to own . . . country so extensive that I could not ride through it in a week . . . must tell Washington when I am hungry. I must beg for that which I own." On a visit to Washington, D.C., in 1870, Red Cloud told the secretary of the interior, "We are melting like snow on the hillside, while you are grown like spring grass. . . . When the white man comes in my country he leaves a trail of blood behind him." As leadership of the Sioux passed to a new generation, younger chiefs, among them Crazy Horse and Sitting Bull, refused to sign the treaty and called for armed resistance. Crazy Horse later declared that he wanted no part of the "piecemeal penning" of his people.

In 1874, the discovery of gold in the Black Hills led the government to break its promise to Red Cloud. Miners began pouring into the Dakotas, and the Northern Pacific Railroad made plans to lay track. At first, the government offered to purchase the Black Hills. But the Lakota Sioux refused to sell. The army responded by issuing an ultimatum ordering all Lakota Sioux and Northern Cheyenne bands onto the Pine Ridge Reservation and threatening to hunt down those who refused.

In the summer of 1876, the army launched a three-pronged attack led by Lieutenant Colonel George Armstrong Custer, General George Crook, and Colonel John Gibbon. Crazy Horse stopped Crook at the Battle of the Rosebud. Custer, leading the second prong of the army's offensive, divided his troops and ordered an attack. On June 25, he spotted signs of the Indians' camp. Crying "Hurrah boys, we've got them," he led 265 men of the Seventh Cavalry into the largest gathering of Indians ever assembled on the Great Plains (more than 8,000) camped along the banks of the Greasy Grass River. Indian warriors led by Sitting Bull and Crazy Horse set upon Custer and his men and quickly annihilated them. "It took us about as long as a hungry man to eat his dinner," the Cheyenne chief Two Moons recalled.

"Custer's Last Stand," or the **Battle of the Little Big Horn,** soon became part of national mythology. But it proved to be the last stand for the Sioux. The nomadic

Black Hills
Mountains in western South Dakota and northeast Wyoming that are sacred to the Lakota Sioux. In the 1868 Treaty of Fort Laramie, the United States guaranteed Indians control of the Black Hills, but it broke its promise after gold was discovered there in 1874.

Battle of the Little Big Horn
1876 battle begun when American cavalry under George Armstrong Custer attacked an encampment of Indians who refused to remove to a reservation. Indian warriors led by Crazy Horse and Sitting Bull annihilated the American soldiers, but their victory was short-lived.

bands that had massed at the Little Big Horn scattered, and the army hunted them down. "Wherever we went," wrote the Oglala holy man Black Elk, "the soldiers came to kill us." In 1877, Crazy Horse was captured and killed. Four years later, Sitting Bull surrendered. The government took the Black Hills and confined the Lakota to the reservation. The Sioux never accepted the loss of the Black Hills. In 1923, they filed suit, demanding the return of the land illegally taken from them. After a protracted court battle lasting nearly sixty years, the U.S. Supreme Court ruled in 1980 that the government had illegally violated the Treaty of Fort Laramie. Declaring "a more ripe and rank case of dishonorable dealings will never, in all probability, be found in our history," the Court awarded the tribes $122.5 million. The Sioux refused the settlement and continue to press for the return of the Black Hills.

> **REVIEW** How did the slaughter of the bison contribute to the Plains Indians' removal to reservations?

Forced Assimilation and Indian Resistance

Imperialistic attitudes of whites toward Indians continued to evolve in the late nineteenth century. To "civilize" the Indians, the U.S. government sought to force assimilation on their children. Reservations became increasingly unpopular among whites who coveted Indian land and among friends of the Indians appalled by the conditions on the reservations. A new policy of allotment gained favor. It promised to put Indians on parcels of land, forcing them into farming, and then to redistribute the remaining land to settlers. In the face of this ongoing assault on their way of life, Indians actively resisted, contested, and adapted to colonial rule.

Indian Schools and the War on Indian Culture. Indian schools constituted the cultural battleground of the Indian wars in the West, their avowed purpose being, in the words of one of their fervent supporters, "To kill the Indian . . . and save the man." In 1877, Congress appropriated funds for Indian education, reasoning, in the words of one congressman, that it was less expensive to educate Indians than to kill them. That education effort focused on Native American boys and girls, from toddlers to teenagers. Virginia's Hampton Institute, created in 1868 to school newly freed slaves, accepted its first Indian students in 1878. Although many Indian schools operated on the reservations, authorities much preferred boarding facilities that isolated students from the "contamination" of tribal values.

Many Native American parents resisted sending their children away. When all else failed, the military kidnapped the children and sent them off to school. An agent at the Mescalero Apache Agency in Arizona Territory reported in 1886 that "it became necessary to visit the camps unexpectedly with a detachment of police, and seize such children as were proper and take them away to school, willing or unwilling." The parents put up a struggle. "Some hurried their children off to the mountains or hid them away in camp, and the police had to chase and capture them like so many wild rabbits," the agent observed. "This unusual proceeding created quite an outcry. The men were sullen and muttering, the women loud in their lamentations and the children almost out of their wits with fright."

Once at school, the children were stripped and scrubbed, their clothing and belongings confiscated, and their hair hacked off and doused with kerosene to kill lice. Issued stiff new uniforms, shoes, and what Luther Standing Bear recalled as the "torture" of woolen long underwear, the children often lost not only their possessions but also their names. Children were asked to stand at the blackboard, take a pointer, and select a proper English name, recalled Standing Bear, who immediately became Luther.

The **Carlisle Indian School** in Pennsylvania, founded in 1879, became the model for later institutions. To encourage assimilation, Carlisle pioneered the "outing system" — sending students to live with white families during summer vacations. The policy reflected the school's slogan: "To civilize the Indian, get him into civilization. To keep him civilized, let him stay." The curriculum featured agricultural and manual arts for boys and domestic skills for girls, training designed to eliminate Indians' dependence on government support.

Merrill Gates, a member of the Board of Indian Commissioners, summed up the goal of Indian education: "To get the Indian out of the blanket and into trousers, — and trousers with a pocket in them, *and with a pocket that aches to be filled with dollars!*" Gates's faith in the "civilizing" power of the dollar reflected the unabashed materialism of the age. But the cultural annihilation that Gates cheerfully predicted did not prove so easy.

Despite whites' efforts, Indians continued being Indians. Even in the "iron routine" of the "civilizing machine" at boarding school, Zitkala-Sa recounted how Indians retained their tribal loyalties and Indian identities. Luther Standing Bear, whose father enrolled him at Carlisle to learn white ways, confessed, "Though my hair had been cut and I wore civilian clothes, I never forsook the blanket." Students continued to speak tribal languages and attend tribal dances even though the punishment was whipping with a leather belt. The schools themselves ultimately subverted their goal by creating generations of Indians who shared a common language, English, and would later create a pan-Indian reform movement in the Progressive Era.

> **Carlisle Indian School**
> Institution established in Pennsylvania in 1879 to educate and assimilate American Indians. It pioneered the "outing system" in which Indian students were sent to live with white families in order to accelerate acculturation.

The Dawes Act and Indian Land Allotment.

In the 1880s, the practice of rounding up and herding Indians onto reservations lost momentum in favor of allotment — a new policy designed to encourage assimilation through farming and the ownership of private property. Americans vowing to avenge Custer's defeat urged the government to get tough with the Indians. Reservations, they argued, took up too much good land that white settlers coveted and forced Americans to support "lazy" reservation Indians. At the same time, people sympathetic to the Indians were appalled at the desperate poverty on the reservations and feared for the Indians' survival. Helen Hunt Jackson, in her classic work *A Century of Dishonor* (1881), convinced many readers that the Indians had been treated unfairly. "Our Indian policy," the *New York Times* concluded, "is usually spoliation behind the mask of benevolence."

The Indian Rights Association, a group of mainly white easterners formed in 1882, campaigned for the dismantling of the reservations, now viewed as obstacles to progress. To "cease to treat the Indian as a red man and treat him as a man" meant putting an end to tribal communalism and fostering individualism. "Selfishness," declared Senator Henry Dawes of Massachusetts, "is at the bottom of civilization." Dawes called for "allotment in severalty" — the institution of private property.

In 1887, Congress passed the **Dawes Allotment Act**, which divided up reservations and allotted parcels of land to individual Indians as private property. Each unmarried Indian man and woman as well as married men and children (married women were excluded) became eligible to receive 160 acres of land from reservation property. Indians who took allotments earned U.S. citizenship. This fostering of individualism through land distribution ultimately dealt a crippling blow to traditional tribal culture.

Dawes Allotment Act
1887 law that divided up reservations and allotted parcels of land to individual Indians as private property. In the end, the U.S. government sold almost two-thirds of "surplus" Indian land to white settlers. The Dawes Act dealt a crippling blow to traditional tribal culture.

To protect Indians from land speculators, the government held most of the allotted land in trust — Indians could not sell it for twenty-five years. Since Indian land far surpassed the acreage needed for allotments, the government reserved the right to sell the "surplus" to white settlers. Many Indians sold their allotments and moved to urban areas where they lost touch with tribal ways.

The Dawes Act effectively reduced Indian land from 138 million acres to a scant 48 million. The legislation, in the words of one critic, worked "to despoil the Indians of their lands and to make them vagabonds on the face of the earth." By 1890, the United States controlled 97.5 percent of the territory formerly occupied by Native Americans.

Indian Resistance and Survival.
Faced with the extinction of their entire way of life, different groups of Indians responded in different ways. In the 1870s, Comanche and Kiowa raiding parties frustrated the U.S. Army by brazenly using the reservations as a seasonal supply base during the winter months. When spring came they resumed their nomadic hunting as long as there were buffalo to hunt.

Some tribes, including the Crow and Shoshoni, chose to fight alongside the army against their old enemies, the Sioux. The Crow chief Plenty Coups explained why he allied with the United States: "Not because we loved the white man . . . or because we hated the Sioux . . . but because we plainly saw that this course was the only one which might save our beautiful country for us." The Crow and Shoshoni got to stay in their homelands and avoided the fate of other tribes shipped to reservations far away.

Indians who refused to stay on reservations risked being hunted down. The Nez Percé war is perhaps the most harrowing example of the army's policy. In 1863, the government dictated a treaty drastically reducing Nez Percé land. Most of the chiefs refused to sign the treaty and did not move to the reservation. When the army cracked down in 1877, some eight hundred Nez Percé people, many of them women and children, fled across the mountains of Idaho, Wyoming, and Montana, heading for the safety of Canada. After a 1,300-mile trek, 50 miles from freedom, they stopped in the Bear Paw Mountains to rest in the snow. The army caught up with them and attacked. Fewer than three hundred of the Indians eluded the army and made it to Canada. Yellow Wolf recalled the plight of those trapped: "Children crying with cold. No fire. There could be no light. Everywhere the crying, the death wail." After a five-day siege, the Nez Percé leader, Chief Joseph, surrendered. His speech, reported by a white soldier, would become famous. "I am tired of fighting," he said as he surrendered his rifle. "Our chiefs are killed. It is cold and we have no blankets. The little children are freezing to death. . . . I am tired. My heart is sick and sad. From where the sun now stands, I will fight no more forever."

In the Southwest, the Apaches resorted to armed resistance. They roamed the Sonoran Desert of southern Arizona and northern Mexico, perfecting a hit-and-run guerrilla warfare that terrorized white settlers and bedeviled the army in the 1870s and 1880s. General George Crook combined a policy of dogged pursuit with judicious diplomacy. Crook relied on Indian scouts to track the raiding parties, recruiting nearly two hundred Apaches, Navajos, and Paiutes. By 1882, Crook had succeeded in persuading most of the Apaches to settle on the San Carlos Reservation in Arizona Territory. A desolate piece of desert inhabited by scorpions and rattlesnakes, San Carlos, in the words of one Apache, was "the worst place in all the great territory stolen from the Apaches."

Geronimo, a respected shaman (medicine man) of the Chiricahua Apache, refused to stay at San Carlos and repeatedly led raiding parties in the early 1880s. His warriors attacked ranches to obtain ammunition and horses. Among Geronimo's band was Lozen, a woman who rode with the warriors, armed with a rifle and a cartridge belt. Lozen's brother, a great chief, described her as being as "strong as a man, braver than most, and cunning in strategy." In the spring of 1885, Geronimo and his followers, including Lozen, went on a ten-month offensive, moving from the Apache sanctuary in the Sierra Madre to raid and burn ranches and towns on both sides of the Mexican border. General Crook caught up with Geronimo in the fall and persuaded him to return to San Carlos, only to have him slip away on the way back to the reservation. Chagrined, Crook resigned his post. General Nelson Miles, Crook's replacement, adopted a policy of hunt and destroy.

Geronimo's band of thirty-three Apaches, including women and children, eluded Miles's troops for more than five months. The pursuit left Miles's cavalry ragged. Over time, Lieutenant Leonard Wood had discarded his horse and was reduced to wearing nothing "but a pair of canton flannel drawers, and an old blouse, a pair of moccasins and a hat without a crown." Eventually, Miles's scouts cornered Geronimo in 1886 at Skeleton Canyon where he agreed to march north and negotiate a settlement. "We have not slept for six months," he admitted, "and we are worn out." Although fewer than three dozen Apaches had been considered "hostile," when General Miles induced them to surrender, the government rounded up nearly five hundred Apaches and sent them as prisoners to the South. By 1889, more than a quarter of them had died, some as a result of illnesses contracted in the damp lowland climate of Florida and Alabama and some by suicide. Their plight roused public opinion, and in 1892 they were moved to Fort Sill in Oklahoma and later to New Mexico.

Geronimo lived to become something of a celebrity. He appeared at the St. Louis Exposition in 1904 and rode in President Theodore Roosevelt's inaugural parade in 1905. In a newspaper interview, he confessed, "I want to go to my old home before I die. . . . Want to go back to the mountains again. I asked the Great White Father to allow me to go back, but he said no." None of the Apaches were permitted to return to Arizona; when Geronimo died in 1909, he was buried in Oklahoma.

GHOST DANCERS, CA. 1893
Arapaho women participate in the Ghost Dance. Tribes performed variations of the dance, but generally dancers formed a circle and danced until they reached a trancelike state. Whites feared the dancers and demanded that the army dispatch troops. The result was the killing of Sitting Bull and the massacre at Wounded Knee. ©TopFoto/The Image Works.

Ghost Dance
Religion founded in 1889 by Paiute shaman Wovoka. It combined elements of Christianity and traditional Indian religion and served as a nonviolent form of resistance for Indians in the late nineteenth century. The Ghost Dance frightened whites and was violently suppressed.

On the plains, many tribes turned to a nonviolent form of resistance — a compelling new religion called the **Ghost Dance**. The Paiute shaman Wovoka, drawing on a cult that had developed in the 1870s, combined elements of Christianity and traditional Indian religion to found the Ghost Dance religion in 1889. Wovoka claimed that he had received a vision in which the Great Spirit spoke through him to all Indians, prophesying that if they would unite in the Ghost Dance ritual, whites would be destroyed in an apocalypse and the buffalo would return. His religion, born of despair and with a message of hope, spread like wildfire over the plains. The Ghost Dance was performed in Idaho, Montana, Utah, Wyoming, Colorado, Nebraska, Kansas, the Dakotas, and Indian Territory by tribes as diverse as the Sioux, Arapaho, Cheyenne, Pawnee, and Shoshoni. Dancers often went into hypnotic trances, dancing until they dropped from exhaustion.

The Ghost Dance was nonviolent, but it frightened whites, especially when the Sioux taught that wearing a white ghost shirt made Indians immune to soldiers' bullets. Soon whites began to fear an uprising. "Indians are dancing in the snow and are wild and crazy," wrote the Bureau of Indian Affairs agent at the Pine Ridge Reservation in South Dakota. Frantic, he pleaded for reinforcements. "We are at the mercy of these dancers. We need protection, and we need it now." President Benjamin Harrison dispatched several thousand federal troops to Sioux country to handle any outbreak.

Wounded Knee
1890 massacre of Sioux Indians by the Seventh Cavalry at Wounded Knee Creek, South Dakota. Sent to suppress the Ghost Dance, the soldiers opened fire on the Sioux as they attempted to surrender. More than two hundred Sioux men, women, and children were killed.

In December 1890, when Sitting Bull attempted to join the Ghost Dance, he was killed by Indian police as they tried to arrest him at his cabin on the Standing Rock Reservation. His people, fleeing the scene, joined with a larger group of Miniconjou Sioux, who were apprehended by the Seventh Cavalry, Custer's old regiment, near Wounded Knee Creek, South Dakota. As the Indians laid down their arms, a soldier attempted to take a rifle from a deaf Miniconjou man and the gun went off. The soldiers opened fire. In the ensuing melee, more than two hundred Indian men, women, and children were mowed down in minutes by the army's brutally efficient Hotchkiss rapid-fire guns. Settler Jules Sandoz surveyed the scene the day after the massacre at **Wounded Knee**. "Here in ten minutes an entire community was as the buffalo that bleached on the plains," he wrote. "There was something loose in the world that hated joy and happiness as it hated brightness and color, reducing everything to drab agony and gray."

It had taken Euro-Americans 250 years to wrest control of the eastern half of the United States from the Indians. It took them only 40 years to take the western half. The subjugation of the American Indians marked the first chapter in a national mission of empire that would anticipate overseas imperialistic adventures in Asia, Latin America, the Caribbean, and the Pacific islands.

> **REVIEW** In what ways did different Indian groups defy and resist colonial rule?

Mining the West

Mining stood at the center of the quest by the United States for empire in the West. *gold rush began* The California gold rush of 1849 touched off the frenzy. The four decades following witnessed equally frenetic rushes for gold and other metals, most notably on the **Comstock Lode** in Nevada and later in New Mexico, Colorado, the Dakotas, Montana, Idaho, Arizona, and Utah (Map 17.2). At first glance, the mining West may seem much different from the East, but by the 1870s the term *urban industrialism* described Virginia City, Nevada, as accurately as it did Pittsburgh or Cleveland. A close look at life on the Comstock Lode indicates some of the patterns and paradoxes of western mining. The diversity of peoples drawn to the West by the promise of mining riches and land made the region the most cosmopolitan in the nation, as well as the most contested. And although mining was often a tale of boom and bust, it was also a story of community building.

Comstock Lode
Silver ore deposit discovered in 1859 in Nevada. Discovery of the Comstock Lode touched off a mining rush that brought a diverse population into the region and led to the establishment of a number of boomtowns, including Virginia City, Nevada.

Life on the Comstock Lode. By 1859, refugees from California's played-out *from CA to NV* goldfields flocked to the Washoe basin in Nevada. While searching for gold, Washoe miners stumbled on the richest vein of silver ore on the continent — the legendary Comstock Lode named for prospector Henry Comstock. ——> *in Washoe*

To exploit even potentially valuable silver claims required capital and expensive *stock market* technology well beyond the means of the prospector. An active San Francisco stock market sprang up to finance operations on the Comstock. Shrewd businessmen soon recognized that the easiest way to get rich was to sell their claims or to form mining companies and sell shares of stock. The most unscrupulous mined the wallets of gullible investors by selling shares in bogus mines. Speculation, misrepresentation, and outright thievery ran rampant. In twenty years, more than $300 million poured from the earth in Nevada alone, most of it going to speculators in San Francisco.

The promise of gold and silver drew thousands to the mines of the West. As Mark Twain observed in Virginia City's *Territorial Enterprise,* "All the peoples of the earth had representative adventures in the Silverland." Irish, Chinese, Germans, English, Scots, Welsh, Canadians, Mexicans, Italians, Scandinavians, French, Swiss, Chileans, and other South and Central Americans came to share in the bonanza. With them came a sprinkling of Russians, Poles, Greeks, Japanese, Spaniards, Hungarians, Portuguese, Turks, Pacific Islanders, and Moroccans, as well as other North Americans, African Americans, and American Indians. This polyglot population,

MAP 17.2 WESTERN MINING, 1848–1890
Rich deposits of gold, silver, copper, lead, and iron larded the mountains of the West. Miners from all over the world flocked to the region. Few struck it rich, but many stayed on as paid workers in the increasingly mechanized corporate mines.

typical of mining boomtowns, made Virginia City in the 1870s more cosmopolitan than New York or Boston. In the part of Utah Territory that eventually became Nevada, as many as 30 percent of the people came from outside the United States, compared to 25 percent in New York and 21 percent in Massachusetts.

Irish immigrants formed the largest ethnic group in the mining district. In Virginia City, fully one-third of the population claimed at least one parent from Ireland. Irish women constituted the largest group of women on the Comstock.

As servants, boardinghouse owners, and washer-women, they made up a significant part of the workforce. In contrast, the Chinese community, numbering 642 in 1870, remained overwhelmingly male. Virulent anti-Chinese sentiment barred the men from work in the mines, but despite this, the mining community came to depend on Chinese labor.

The discovery of precious metals on the Comstock spelled disaster for the Indians. No sooner had the miners struck pay dirt than they demanded that army troops "hunt Indians" and establish forts to protect transportation to and from the diggings. This sudden and dramatic intrusion left Nevada's native tribes — the Northern Paiute and Bannock Shoshoni — exiles in their own land. At first they resisted, but over time they adapted and preserved their culture and identity despite the havoc wreaked by western mining and settlement.

In 1873, Comstock miners uncovered a new vein of ore, a veritable cavern of gold and silver. This "Big Bonanza" speeded the transition from small-scale industry to corporate oligopoly, creating a radically new social and economic environment. The Comstock became a laboratory for new mining technology. Huge stamping mills pulverized rock with pistonlike hammers driven by steam engines. Enormous Cornish pumps sucked water from the mine shafts, and huge ventilators circulated air in the underground chambers. No backwoods mining camp, Virginia City was an industrial center with more than 1,200 stamping mills working on average a ton of ore every day. Almost 400 men worked in milling, nearly 300 labored in manufacturing industries, and roughly 3,000 toiled in the mines. The Gould and Curry mine covered sixty acres. Most of the miners who came to the Comstock ended up as laborers for the big companies.

New technology eliminated some of the dangers of mining but often created new ones. In the hard-rock mines of the West, accidents in the 1870s disabled one out of every thirty miners and killed one in eighty. Ross Moudy, who worked as a miner in Cripple Creek, Colorado, recalled how a stockholder visiting the mine nearly fell to his death. The terrified visitor told the miner next to him that "instead of being paid $3 a day, they ought to have all the gold they could take out." On the Comstock Lode, because of the difficulty of obtaining skilled labor, the richness of the ore, and the need for a stable workforce, labor unions formed early and held considerable bargaining power. Comstock miners commanded $4 a day, the highest wage in the mining West.

The mining towns of the "Wild West" are often portrayed as lawless outposts, filled with saloons and rough gambling dens and populated almost exclusively by

MINING ON THE COMSTOCK

This photo of a miner at work shows the dangers faced on the Comstock Lode. Without a hardhat or miner's light, he is working with timbers to shore up the mine shaft. After the discovery of the "Big Bonanza" in 1873, eight years after this picture was taken, silver mines honeycombed the hills of Nevada. National Archives, photo no. 77-KS-1-15.

accidents/dangers

# of women increasing

men. The truth is more complex, as Virginia City's development attests. An established urban community built to serve an industrial giant, Virginia City in its first decade boasted churches, schools, theaters, an opera house, and hundreds of families. By 1870, women composed 30 percent of the population, and 75 percent of the women listed their occupation in the census as housekeeper. Mary McNair Mathews, a widow from Buffalo, New York, who lived on the Comstock in the 1870s, worked as a teacher, nurse, seamstress, laundress, and lodging-house operator. She later published a book on her adventures.

By 1875, Virginia City boasted a population of 25,000 people, making it one of the largest cities between St. Louis and San Francisco. The city, dubbed the "Queen of the Comstock," hosted American presidents as well as legions of lesser dignitaries. Virginia City represented, in the words of a recent chronicler, "the distilled essence of America's newly established course — urban, industrial, acquisitive, and materialistic, on the move, 'a living polyglot' of cultures that collided and converged."

The Diverse Peoples of the West.

The West of the late nineteenth century was a polyglot place, as much so as the big cities of the East. The sheer number of peoples who mingled in the West produced a complex blend of racism and prejudice. One historian has noted, not entirely facetiously, that there were at least eight oppressed "races" in the West — Indians, Latinos, Chinese, Japanese, blacks, Mormons, strikers, and radicals.

african americans couldnt go

African Americans who ventured out to the territories faced hostile settlers determined to keep the West "for whites only." In response, they formed all-black communities such as Nicodemus, Kansas. That settlement, founded by thirty black Kentuckians in 1877, grew to a community of seven hundred by 1880. Isolated and often separated by great distances, small black settlements grew up throughout the West, in Nevada, Utah, and the Pacific Northwest, as well as in Kansas. Black soldiers who served in the West during the Indian wars often stayed on as settlers. Called buffalo soldiers because Native Americans thought their hair resembled that of the bison, these black troops numbered up to 25,000. In the face of discrimination, poor treatment, and harsh conditions, the buffalo soldiers served with distinction and boasted the lowest desertion rate in the army.

Hispanic peoples had lived in Texas and the Southwest since Juan de Oñate led pioneer settlers up the Rio Grande in 1598. Hispanics had occupied the Pacific coast since San Diego was founded in 1769. Overnight, they were reduced to a "minority" after the United States annexed Texas in 1845 and took land stretching to California after the Mexican-American War ended in 1848. At first, the Hispanic owners of large *ranchos* in California, New Mexico, and Texas greeted conquest as an economic opportunity. But racial prejudice soon ended their optimism. *Californios* (Mexican residents of California), who had been granted American citizenship by the Treaty of Guadalupe Hidalgo (1848), faced discrimination by Anglos who sought to keep them out of California's mines and commerce. Whites illegally squatted on *rancho* land while protracted litigation over Spanish and Mexican land grants forced the Californios into court. Although the U.S. Supreme Court eventually validated most of their claims, it took so long — seventeen years on average — that many Californios sold their property to pay taxes and legal bills.

mexicans citizenship

Swindles, trickery, and intimidation dispossessed scores of Californios. Many ended up segregated in urban barrios (neighborhoods) in their own homeland. Their percentage of California's population declined from 82 percent in 1850 to 19 percent in 1880 as Anglos migrated to the state. In New Mexico and Texas, Mexicans remained a majority of the population but became increasingly impoverished as Anglos dominated business and took the best jobs. Skirmishes between Hispanics and whites in northern New Mexico over the fencing of the open range lasted for decades. Groups of Hispanics with names such as *Las Manos Negras* (the Black Hands) cut fences and burned barns. In Texas, violence along the Rio Grande pitted *Tejanos* (Mexican residents of Texas) against the Texas Rangers, who saw their role as "keeping Mexicans in their place."

Mormons, too, faced prejudice and hostility. The followers of Joseph Smith, the founder and prophet of the Church of Jesus Christ of Latter-Day Saints, fled west to Utah Territory in 1844 to avoid religious persecution. They believed they had a divine right to the land, and their messianic militancy made others distrust them. The Mormon practice of polygamy (church leader Brigham Young had twenty-three wives) also came under attack. To counter the criticism of polygamy, the Utah territorial legislature gave women the right to vote in 1870, the first universal woman suffrage act in the nation. (Wyoming had granted suffrage to white women in 1869.) Although women's rights advocates argued that the newly enfranchised women would "do away with the horrible institution of polygamy," it remained in force. Not until 1890 did the church hierarchy yield to pressure and renounce polygamy. The fierce controversy over polygamy postponed statehood for Utah until 1896.

[handwritten margin note: lead to womens right to vote]

The Chinese suffered the most brutal treatment of all the newcomers at the hands of employers and other laborers. Drawn by the promise of gold, more than 20,000 Chinese had joined the rush to California by 1852. Miners determined to

VAQUEROS IN A HORSE CORRAL, 1877

In this exciting scene, artist James Walker captures the skill of Hispanic *vaqueros* lassoing horses in a Texas corral. As Anglo settlers gradually displaced Hispanic landholders across the West, the domain of the rancho gradually declined, as did a way of life. Private Collection/ Peter Newark Pictures/Bridgeman Images.

CHINESE RAILROAD WORKER, CA. 1867

This photograph of a lone Chinese laborer carrying a shoulder pole illustrates the magnitude of the task workers faced in the Sierra Nevada. This worker stands in front of what would become Tunnel no. 8, one of the innumerable tunnels carved by hand through the granite. Six years of backbreaking work culminated in the epic achievement of the Central Pacific Railroad.

Library of Congress, 1s00553.

keep "California for Americans" succeeded in passing prohibitive foreign license laws to keep the Chinese out of the mines. But Chinese immigration continued. In the 1860s, when white workers moved on to find riches in the bonanza mines of Nevada, Chinese laborers took jobs abandoned by the whites. Railroad magnate Charles Crocker hired Chinese gangs to work on the Central Pacific, reasoning that "the race that built the Great Wall" could lay tracks across the treacherous Sierra Nevada. Some 10,000 Chinese, representing 90 percent of Crocker's workforce, completed America's first transcontinental railroad in 1869.

By 1870, more than 63,000 Chinese immigrants lived in America, 77 percent of them in California. A 1790 federal statute that limited naturalization to "white persons" was modified after the Civil War to extend naturalization to blacks ("persons of African descent"). But the Chinese and other Asians continued to be denied access to citizenship. As perpetual aliens, they constituted a reserve army of transnational laborers that many saw as a threat to American labor.

In 1876, the Workingmen's Party formed to fight for Chinese exclusion. Racial and cultural animosities stood at the heart of anti-Chinese agitation. Denis Kearney, the fiery San Francisco leader of the movement, made clear this racist bent when he urged legislation to "expel every one of the moon-eyed lepers."

Nor was California alone in its anti-immigrant nativism. As the country confronted growing ethnic and racial diversity with the rising tide of global immigration in the decades following the Civil War, many questioned the principle of racial equality at the same time they argued against the assimilation of "nonwhite" groups. In this climate, Congress passed the **Chinese Exclusion Act** in 1882, effectively barring Chinese immigration and setting a precedent for further immigration restrictions.

The Chinese Exclusion Act led to a sharp drop in the Chinese population — from 105,465 in 1880 to 89,863 in 1900 — because Chinese immigrants, overwhelmingly male, did not have families to sustain their population. Eventually, Japanese immigrants, including women as well as men, replaced the Chinese, particularly in agriculture. As "nonwhite" immigrants, they could not become naturalized citizens, but their children born in the United States claimed the rights of citizenship. Japanese parents, seeking to own land, purchased it in their children's names. Although anti-Asian prejudice remained strong in California and elsewhere in the West, Asian immigrants formed an important part of the economic fabric of the western United States.

Chinese Exclusion Act
1882 law that effectively barred Chinese immigration and set a precedent for further immigration restrictions. The Chinese population in America dropped sharply as a result of the passage of the act, which was fueled by racial and cultural animosities.

REVIEW What role did mining play in shaping the society and economy of the American West?

Land Fever

In the three decades following 1870, more land was settled than in all the previous history of the country. Americans by the hundreds of thousands packed up and moved west, goaded if not by the hope of striking gold, then by the promise of owning land to farm or ranch. The agrarian West shared with the mining West a persistent restlessness, an equally pervasive addiction to speculation, and a penchant for exploiting natural resources and labor.

Two factors stimulated the land rush in the trans-Mississippi West. The **Homestead Act of 1862** promised 160 acres free to any citizen or prospective citizen, male or female, who settled on the land for five years. Even more important, transcontinental railroads opened up new areas and actively recruited settlers. After the completion of the **first transcontinental railroad** in 1869, homesteaders abandoned the covered wagon, and by the 1880s rampant railroad overbuilding meant that settlers could choose from four competing rail lines and make the trip west in a matter of days. *improved transportation*

Although the country was rich in land and resources, not all who wanted to own land achieved their goal. During the transition from the family farm to large commercial farming, small farms and ranches gave way to vast spreads worked by migrant labor or paid farmworkers and cowhands. Just as industry corporatized and consolidated in the East, the period from 1870 to 1900 witnessed corporate consolidation in mining, ranching, and agriculture.

Moving West: Homesteaders and Speculators.

A Missouri homesteader remembered packing as her family pulled up stakes and headed west to Oklahoma in 1890. "We were going to God's Country," she wrote. "You had to work hard on that rocky country in Missouri. I was glad to be leaving it. . . . We were going to a new land and get rich."

Settlers who headed west in search of "God's Country" faced hardship, loneliness, and deprivation. To carve a farm from the raw prairie of Iowa, the plains of Nebraska, or the forests of the Pacific Northwest took more than fortitude and backbreaking toil. It took luck. Blizzards, tornadoes, grasshoppers, hailstorms, drought, prairie fires, accidental death, and disease were only a few of the catastrophes that could befall even the best farmer. Homesteaders on free land still needed as much as $1,000 for a house, a team of farm animals, a well, fencing, and seed. Poor farmers called "sodbusters" did without even these basics, living in houses made from sod (blocks of grass-covered earth) or dugouts carved into hillsides and using muscle instead of machinery. (See "Making Historical Arguments," page 508.)

"Father made a dugout and covered it with willows and grass," one Kansas girl recounted. When it rained, the dugout flooded, and "we carried the water out in buckets, then waded around in the mud until it dried." Rain wasn't the only problem. "Sometimes the bull snakes would get in the roof and now and then one would lose his hold and fall down on the bed. . . . Mother would grab the hoe . . . and after the fight was over Mr. Bull Snake was dragged outside."

For women on the frontier, obtaining simple daily necessities such as water and fuel meant backbreaking labor. Out on the plains, where water was scarce, women

hard to get started

Homestead Act of 1862
An act that promised 160 acres in the trans-Mississippi West free to any citizen or prospective citizen who settled on the land for five years. The act spurred American settlement of the West. Altogether, nearly one-tenth of the United States was granted to settlers.

first transcontinental railroad
Railroad completed in 1869 that was the first to span the North American continent. Built in large part by Chinese laborers, this railroad and others opened access to new areas, which fueled land speculation and actively recruited settlers.

Making Historical Arguments

Did Westerners Really Build It All by Themselves?

The myth of the American West goes something like this: In the mid-nineteenth century, torrents of gutsy pioneers began pouring into the vast empty space beyond the Mississippi. Abundant free land offered opportunity to anyone ambitious enough to claim it and tough enough to work it. Far from everything, entirely on his own, a man could rely only on his own will, grit, and muscle. In time, strong, self-reliant, can-do Americans made the harsh environment bloom and produce. The West offered limitless possibilities, as long as government kept out of the way.

While the myth is not wrong about the courage and endurance of the pioneer, it ignores a number of significant facts. The plains and prairies were not empty. Pioneer women were as important as men in conquering the West. And the celebration of self-reliance and individual responsibility ignores the heavy debt that pioneers owed the federal government for helping them settle and develop the West.

In countless ways, westerners depended on the government for access to the West's bountiful resources — land, minerals, grass, timber, and water. Through purchases, treaties, annexations, and war, the federal government acquired the land that would become the American West. Washington oversaw the territorial governments that controlled most of the West, sometimes well into the twentieth century. Federally appointed governors and judges meant political dependence, but they also provided access to federal funds for development. Government business brought jobs, contracts, and subsidies. And the federal presence offered access to policymakers. When westerners decided that Asian laborers were undesirable, Congress passed the 1882 Exclusion Act suspending Chinese immigration. When citizens objected to Mormon marriage practices, a federal law banned polygamy. Territorial status gave the national government increased power in the West, but westerners found that dependency had its rewards.

Westerners cheered when the U.S. Army swept away the Indians and Anglo law dispossessed the Hispanic inhabitants of the region, clearing the way for land-seeking settlers. The U.S. Geological Survey explored and mapped the region, and the General Land Office surveyed, sold, and registered the property it laid out. The federal government maintained public order until Congress judged settlers ready to take over their own affairs. Congress passed hundreds of laws granting Americans easy access to the public domain. The 1862 Homestead Act, for example, helped 1.4 million homesteaders gain land titles. The federal government's actions sometimes undercut its democratic land policy, but its openhanded distribution of public land drew countless numbers of settlers westward.

Farms without the means to transport crops to market were not worth much, and the second half of the nineteenth century became the great era of federal support for transportation. The federal government built roads, established stage and wagon lines, strung telegraph wires, and, most important, offered huge grants of public land to subsidize the construction of railroads. Federal initiatives built the communication and transportation networks that integrated the products of western farms into the markets of the nation and the world.

The mining industry also depended on the federal bounty. When the gold rush exploded in California in 1849, the federal government raced just to keep up. But by the time the Comstock Lode was discovered in 1859, federal law took control and framed the western mining enterprise. Federal laws helped mining companies beat back miner unions and collective bargaining. Mine owners won their fierce struggle with mine workers when the courts enforced the notion of individual responsibility and let mining corporations escape liability for injured miners. In 1874, when gold was discovered in the Black Hills, Congress promptly repealed the 1868 treaty that had granted the land to the Sioux, thereby opening new gold country to American citizens. Like farmers, miners celebrated their independence from government oversight while simultaneously reaping the benefits of government intervention.

Cattle ranchers also owed a debt to the federal government. The prosperous western cattle industry depended on cattle grazing on public lands and being shipped east on federally subsidized railroads. When nasty disputes between cattle owners threatened to disrupt the industry, Congress established the Bureau of Animal Husbandry to keep the peace. To protect ranchers from competition, Congress passed laws that banned foreign land purchases in the West. To protect vulnerable cattle, the U.S. Biological Survey and the Forest Service waged war on wolves and mountain lions, and to guard grazing land they took aim at elk, antelope, and prairie dogs. By 1884, with the crucial support of the government, 20 million cattle grazed the American West.

The last of the western territories became states early in the twentieth century, but statehood did not end the West's dependence on the federal government. Indeed, as the government undertook massive water projects, created subsidies for agriculture, opened scores of national parks, and increased its efforts to secure the nation's borders, Uncle Sam continued to expand his footprint. Today, the government makes resources available for private appropriation, investment, and development, as it did in the nineteenth century, and farmers, ranchers, miners, and lumber producers continue to need help in solving their problems.

QUESTIONS FOR ANALYSIS

Summarize the Argument   How did the federal government assist in the settlement and development of the West, and who were the major beneficiaries?

Analyze the Evidence   Does the evidence for federal assistance add up to a persuasive argument that the federal government played a crucial, even indispensable, role in the settlement and development of the West?

Consider the Context   What do you suppose were the origins of the myth of the American West? Can you identify other American beliefs and values that might have contributed to the myth? Why do you suppose the myth has been so persistent?

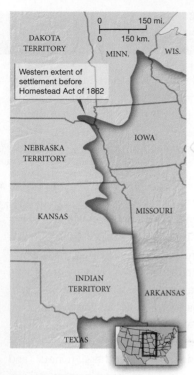

MIDWESTERN SETTLEMENT BEFORE 1862

often had to trudge to the nearest creek or spring. "A yoke was made to place across [Mother's] shoulders, so as to carry at each end a bucket of water," one daughter recollected, "and then water was brought a half mile from spring to house." Gathering fuel was another heavy chore. Without ready sources of coal or firewood, the most prevalent fuel was "chips" — chunks of dried cattle and buffalo dung, found in abundance on the plains.

Despite the hardships, some homesteaders succeeded in building comfortable lives. The dugout made way for the sod hut — a more substantial dwelling; the log cabin yielded to a white clapboard home with a porch and a rocking chair. For others, the promise of the West failed to materialize. Already by the 1870s, much of the best land had been taken. Too often, homesteaders found that only the least desirable tracts were left — poor land, far from markets, transportation, and society. "There is plenty of land for sale in California," one migrant complained in 1870, but "the majority of the available lands are held by speculators, at prices far beyond the reach of a poor man." The railroads, flush from land grants provided by the state and federal governments, owned huge swaths of land in the West and actively recruited buyers. Altogether, the land grants totaled approximately 180 million acres — an area almost one-tenth the size of the United States (Map 17.3). The vast majority of farmland sold for a profit.

As land grew scarce on the prairie in the 1870s, farmers began to push farther west, moving into western Kansas, Nebraska, and eastern Colorado — the region called the Great American Desert by settlers who had passed over

Visual Activity

NORWEGIAN IMMIGRANT AND SOD HOUSE

Norwegian immigrant Beret Olesdater sits in front of her sod house in Lac qui Parle, Minnesota, in 1896. On the plains, where trees were scarce, settlers carved dugouts into a hillside or built huts like the one here, carved from blocks of sod. Minnesota Historical Society/Corbis.

READING THE IMAGE: What do the woman's dress and the expression on her face tell us about the life of women on the plains?

CONNECTIONS: What expectations did homesteaders have for their lives on the plains, and how did this compare to the realities they faced?

it on their way to California and Oregon. Many agricultural experts warned that the semiarid land (where less than twenty inches of rain fell annually) would not support a farm on the 160 acres allotted to homesteaders. But their words of caution were drowned out by the extravagant claims of western promoters, many employed by the railroads to sell off land grants. "Rain follows the plow" became the slogan of

Map Activity

MAP 17.3   FEDERAL LAND GRANTS TO RAILROADS AND THE DEVELOPMENT OF THE WEST, 1850–1900

Railroads received more than 180 million acres, an area as large as Texas. Built well ahead of demand, the western railroads courted settlers, often onto land not fit for farming.

READING THE MAP: Which mining cities and towns were located directly on railroad lines? Which towns were located at the junction of more than one railroad line or branch?

CONNECTIONS: In what ways did the growth of the railroads affect the population of the West? What western goods and products did the railroads help bring east and to ports for shipping around the world?

western boosters, who insisted that cultivation would alter the climate of the region and bring more rainfall. Instead, drought followed the plow. Droughts were a cyclical fact of life on the Great Plains. Plowed up, the dry topsoil blew away in the wind. A period of relatively good rainfall in the early 1880s encouraged farming; then a protracted drought in the late 1880s and early 1890s forced thousands of starving farmers to leave, some in wagons carrying the slogan "In God we trusted, in Kansas we busted."

Fever for fertile land set off a series of spectacular land runs in Oklahoma. When two million acres of land in former Indian Territory opened for settlement in 1889, thousands of homesteaders massed on the border. At the opening pistol shot, "with a shout and a yell the swift riders shot out, then followed the light buggies or wagons," a reporter wrote. "Above all, a great cloud of dust hover[ed] like smoke over a battlefield." By nightfall, Oklahoma boasted two tent cities with more than ten thousand residents. In the last frenzied land rush on Oklahoma's Cherokee strip in 1893, several settlers were killed in the stampede, and nervous men guarded their claims with rifles. As public land grew scarce, the hunger for land grew fiercer for both farmers and ranchers.

Barbed wire, invented in 1874, revolutionized the cattle business and sounded the death knell for the open range. As the largest ranches in Texas began to fence, nasty fights broke out between big ranchers and "fence cutters," who resented the end of the open range. One old-timer observed, "Those persons, Mexicans and Americans, without land but who had cattle were put out of business by fencing." Fencing forced small-time ranchers who owned land but could not afford to buy barbed wire or sink wells to sell out for the best price they could get. The displaced ranchers, many of them Mexicans, ended up as wageworkers on the huge spreads owned by Anglos or by European syndicates.

On the range, the cowboy gave way to the cattle king and, like the miner, became a wage laborer. Many cowboys were African Americans (as many as five thousand in Texas alone). Writers of western literature chose to ignore the presence of black cowboys like Deadwood Dick (Nat Love), who was portrayed as a white man in the dime novels of the era.

By 1886, cattle overcrowded the range. Severe blizzards during the winter of 1886–87 decimated the herds. "A whole generation of cowmen," wrote one chronicler, "went dead broke." Fencing worsened the situation. During blizzards, cattle stayed alive by keeping on the move. But when they ran up against barbed wire fences, they froze to death. In the aftermath of the "Great Die Up," new labor-intensive forms of cattle ranching replaced the open-range model.

Tenants, Sharecroppers, and Migrants.
In the post–Civil War period, as agriculture became a big business tied by the railroads to national and global markets, an increasing number of laborers worked land that they would never own. In the southern United States, farmers labored under particularly heavy burdens. The Civil War wiped out much of the region's capital, which had been invested in slaves, and crippled the plantation economy. "The colored folks stayed with the old boss man and farmed and worked on the plantations," a black Alabama sharecropper observed bitterly. "They were still slaves, but they were free slaves." Some freed-people did

manage to pull together enough resources to go west. In 1879, more than fifteen thousand black Exodusters, as the black settlers were known, moved from Mississippi and Louisiana to take up land in Kansas.

California's Mexican cowboys, or *vaqueros*, commanded decent wages throughout the Southwest. But by 1880, as the coming of the railroads ended the long cattle drives and as large feedlots began to replace the open range, the value of their skills declined. Many vaqueros ended up as migrant laborers, often on land their families had once owned. Similarly, in Texas, Tejanos found themselves displaced. After the heyday of cattle ranching ended in the late 1880s, cotton production rose in the southeastern regions of the state. Ranchers turned their pastures into sharecroppers' plots and hired displaced cowboys, most of them Mexicans, as seasonal laborers for as little as seventy-five cents a day, thereby creating a growing army of agricultural wageworkers.

Land monopoly and large-scale farming fostered tenancy and migratory labor on the West Coast. By the 1870s, less than 1 percent of California's population owned half the state's available agricultural land. The rigid economics of large-scale commercial agriculture and the seasonal nature of the crops spawned a ragged army of migratory agricultural laborers. Derisively labeled "blanket men" or "bindle stiffs," these transients worked the fields in the growing season and wintered in the flophouses of San Francisco. After passage of the Chinese Exclusion Act of 1882, Mexicans, Filipinos, and Japanese immigrants filled the demand for migratory workers.

Commercial Farming and Industrial Cowboys.

In the late nineteenth century, the population of the United States remained overwhelmingly rural. The 1870 census showed that nearly 80 percent of the nation's people lived on farms and in villages of fewer than 8,000 inhabitants. By 1900, the figure had dropped to 60 percent (Figure 17.1). At the same time, the number of farms rose. Rapid growth in the West increased the number of farms from 2 million in 1860 to more than 5.7 million in 1900.

New technology and farming techniques revolutionized American farm life. Mechanized farm machinery halved the time and labor cost of production and made it possible to cultivate vast tracts of land. Meanwhile, urbanization provided farmers with expanding markets for their produce, and railroads carried crops to markets thousands of miles away. Even before the start of the twentieth century, American agriculture had entered the era of what would come to be called agribusiness — farming as a big business — with the advent of huge commercial farms.

As farming moved onto the prairies and plains, mechanization took command. Steel plows, reapers,

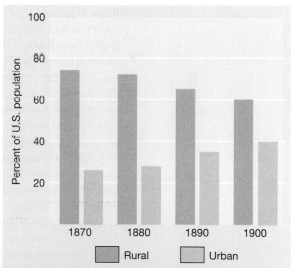

FIGURE 17.1 CHANGES IN RURAL AND URBAN POPULATIONS, 1870–1900

Between 1870 and 1900, both the number of urban dwellers and the number of farms increased, even as the number of rural inhabitants fell. Mechanization made it possible to farm with fewer hands, fueling the exodus from farm to city throughout the second half of the nineteenth century.

industrializ [mowers, harrows, seed drills, combines, and threshers replaced human muscle. Horse-drawn implements gave way to steam-powered machinery. By 1880, a single combine could do the work of twenty men, vastly increasing the acreage a farmer could cultivate. Mechanization spurred the growth of bonanza wheat farms, some more than 100,000 acres, in California and the Red River Valley of North Dakota and Minnesota. This agricultural revolution meant that Americans raised more than four times the corn, five times the hay, and seven times the wheat and oats they had before the Civil War.

Like cotton farmers in the South, western grain and livestock farmers increasingly depended on foreign markets for their livelihood. A fall in global market prices meant that a farmer's entire harvest went to pay off debts. In the depression that followed the panic of 1893, many heavily mortgaged farmers lost their land to creditors. As a Texas cotton farmer complained, "By the time the World Gets their Liveing out of the Farmer as we have to Feed the World, we the Farmer has nothing Left but a Bear Hard Liveing." Commercial farming, along with mining, represented another way in which the West developed its own brand of industrialism. The far West's industrial economy sprang initially from California gold and the vast territory that came under American control following the Mexican-American War. In the ensuing rush on land and resources, environmental factors interacted with economic and social forces to produce enterprises as vast in scale and scope as anything found in the East.

Two German immigrants, Henry Miller and Charles Lux, pioneered the West's mix of agriculture and industrialism. Beginning as meat wholesalers, Miller and Lux quickly expanded their business to encompass cattle, land, and land reclamation projects such as dams and irrigation systems. With a labor force of migrant workers, a highly coordinated corporate system, and large sums of investment capital, the firm of Miller & Lux became one of America's industrial behemoths. Eventually, these "industrial cowboys" grazed a herd of 100,000 cattle on 1.25 million acres of company land in California, Oregon, and Nevada and employed more than 1,200 migrant laborers on their corporate ranches. Miller & Lux dealt with the labor problem by offering free meals to migratory workers, thus keeping wages low while winning goodwill among an army of unemployed who competed for the work. When the company's Chinese cooks rebelled at washing all the dishes, the migrant laborers were forced to eat off dirty plates. By the 1890s, more than 800 migrants a year followed what came to be known as the "Dirty Plate Route" on Miller & Lux ranches throughout California.

Since the days of Thomas Jefferson, agrarian life had been linked with the highest ideals of a democratic society. Agrarianism had been transformed. The farmer was no longer a self-sufficient yeoman but often a businessman or a wage laborer tied to a global market. And even as farm production soared, industrialization outstripped it. More and more farmers left the fields for urban factories or found work in the "factories in the fields" of the new industrialized agribusinesses. Now that the future seemed to lie not with small farmers but with industrial enterprises, was democracy itself at risk? This question would ignite a farmers' revolt in the 1880s and dominate political debate in the 1890s.

Territorial Government. The federal government practiced a policy of benign neglect when it came to territorial government. A governor, a secretary, a few judges, an attorney, and a marshal held jurisdiction. In Nevada Territory, that meant a handful of officials governed an area the size of New England. Originally a part of the larger Utah Territory, Nevada, propelled by mining interests, moved on the fast track to statehood, entering the Union in 1864.

More typical were the territories extant in 1870 — New Mexico, Utah, Washington, Colorado, Dakota, Arizona, Idaho, Montana, and Wyoming. These areas remained territories for inordinately long periods ranging from twenty-three to sixty-two years. While awaiting statehood, they were subject to territorial governors, who won their posts due to party loyalty and who were largely underpaid, uninformed, often unqualified, and largely ignored by Washington. Wages rarely arrived on schedule, leading one cynic to observe, "Only the rich, or those having 'no visible means of support,' can afford to accept office." John C. Frémont, governor of Arizona Territory, complained he could not inspect the Grand Canyon because he was too poor to own a horse.

Western governors with fewer scruples accepted money from local interests — mine owners and big ranchers or lumber companies. Nearly all territorial appointees tried to maintain business connections in the East or take advantage of speculative opportunities in the West. Corruption ran rampant. Yet the distance from the nation's capital meant that few charges of corrupt dealings were investigated. Gun-toting westerners served as another deterrent. One judge sent to New Mexico Territory in 1871 to investigate fraud "stayed three days, made up his mind that it would be dangerous to do any investigating, . . . and returned to his home without action."

Underfunded and overlooked victims of cronyism and prey to special interests, territorial governments mirrored the self-serving political and economic values of the era.

> **REVIEW** How did the fight for land and resources unfold in the West?

Conclusion: The West in the Gilded Age

In 1871, author Mark Twain published *Roughing It*, a chronicle of his days spent in mining towns in California and Nevada. There he found the same corrupt politics, vulgar display, and mania for speculation that he later skewered in *The Gilded Age* (1873), his biting satire of greed and corruption in the nation's capital. Far from being an antidote to the tawdry values of the East — an innocent idyll out of place and time — the American West, with its get-rich-quick ethos, addiction to gambling and speculation, and virulent racism, helped set the tone for the Gilded Age.

Twain's view countered that of Frederick Jackson Turner and perhaps better suited a West that witnessed the reckless overbuilding of railroads; the consolidation of business in mining and ranching; the rise of commercial farming; corruption and a penchant for government handouts; racial animosity; the exploitation of labor and natural resources, which led to the decimation of the great bison herds, the pollution of rivers with mining wastes, and the overgrazing of the plains; and the beginnings of an imperial policy that would provide a template for U.S. adventures abroad. Turner, intent on promoting what was unique about the frontier, failed to note that the same issues that came to dominate debate east of the Mississippi — the growing power of big business, the exploitation of land and labor, corruption in politics, and ethnic and racial tensions exacerbated by colonial expansion and unparalleled immigration — took center stage in the West at the end of the nineteenth century.

Chapter Review

KEY TERMS

reservations (p. 491)

Comanchería (p. 494)

Black Hills (p. 495)

Battle of the Little Big Horn (p. 495)

Carlisle Indian School (p. 497)

Dawes Allotment Act (p. 498)

Ghost Dance (p. 500)

Wounded Knee (p. 500)

Comstock Lode (p. 501)

Chinese Exclusion Act (p. 506)

Homestead Act of 1862 (p. 507)

first transcontinental railroad (p. 507)

REVIEW QUESTIONS

❶ How did the slaughter of the bison contribute to the Plains Indians' removal to reservations?   (pp. 490–96)

❷ In what ways did different Indian groups defy and resist colonial rule?   (pp. 496–501)

❸ What role did mining play in shaping the society and economy of the American West?   (pp. 501–6)

❹ How did the fight for land and resources unfold in the West? (pp. 507–15)

MAKING CONNECTIONS

1 Westward migration brought settlers into conflict with Native Americans. What was the U.S. government's policy toward Indians in the West, and how did it evolve over time?

2 How did innovations in business and technology transform mining and agriculture in the West?

3 In competition for work and land in the American West, why did Anglo-American settlers usually have the upper hand over settlers from other countries? How did legal developments contribute to this circumstance?

4 What role did railroads play in western settlement, industrialization, and agriculture? How did railroads affect Indian populations in the West?

LINKING TO THE PAST

1 In what ways were the goals of migrants to the West similar to those of the Northerners who moved to the South after the Civil War? How did they differ? (See chapter 16.)

2 How did the racism of the West compare with the racist attitudes against African Americans in the Reconstruction South? (See chapter 16.)

18

Railroads, Business, and Politics in the Gilded Age, 1865–1900

CONTENT LEARNING OBJECTIVES

After reading and studying this chapter, you should be able to:

• Describe the ways in which industries were transformed in the late nineteenth century, including the railroad, steel, and oil industries.

• Explain the factors that led to business mergers and the rise of corporations and explain the role of finance capitalism. Describe the ideas of social Darwinism and the gospel of wealth.

• Describe how regional sectionalism, race, and gender affected political culture in the late nineteenth century.

• Describe the issues and personalities that drove national party politics during the Gilded Age and explain why the Republican Party divided into factions.

• Identify the key economic issues of the Gilded Age and how those issues led to party realignment in the 1890s.

One night over dinner, Mark Twain and Charles Dudley Warner teased their wives about the sentimental novels they read. When the two women challenged them to write something better, they set to work. Warner supplied the melodrama while Twain "hurled in the facts." The result, *The Gilded Age* (1873), was a runaway best seller, a savage satire of the "get-rich-quick" era that would forever carry the book's title.

Twain left no one unscathed in the novel — political hacks, Washington lobbyists, Wall Street financiers, small-town boosters, and the "great putty-hearted public." Underneath the glitter of the Gilded Age lurked vulgarity, crass materialism, and political

CAMPAIGN PINS

Presidential campaign pins from 1884 depict James G. Blaine thumbing his nose at rival Grover Cleveland. The gilt pins symbolize the lavish wealth and corruption and political strife of the Gilded Age. David J. & Janice L. Frent Collection/Corbis.

corruption. In Twain's satire, Congress is for sale to the highest bidder:

> Why the matter is simple enough. A Congressional appropriation costs money. . . . A majority of the House Committee, say $10,000 apiece — $40,000; a majority of the Senate Committee, the same each — say $40,000; a little extra to one or two chairmen of one or two such committees, say $10,000 each — $20,000; and there's $100,000 of the money gone, to begin with. Then, seven male lobbyists, at $3,000 each — $21,000; one female lobbyist, $3,000; a high moral Congressman or Senator here and there — the high moral ones cost more, because they give tone to a measure — say ten of these at $3,000 each, is $30,000; then a lot of small fry country members who won't vote for anything whatever without pay — say twenty at $500 apiece, is $10,000 altogether; lot of jimcracks for Congressmen's wives and children . . . well, those things cost in a lump, say $10,000 . . . and then comes your printed documents. . . . Well, never mind the details, the total in clean numbers foots up $118,254.42 thus far!

The Gilded Age seemed to tarnish many who lived under its reign. No one knew that better than Twain, who, even as he attacked it as an "era of incredible rottenness," fell prey to its enticements. Born Samuel Langhorne Clemens, he grew up in a rough Mississippi River town, where he became a riverboat pilot. Taking the pen name Mark Twain, he wrote and played to packed houses as an itinerant humorist. But his work was judged too vulgar for the genteel tastes of the time. Boston banned his masterpiece, *The Adventures of Huckleberry Finn*, when it appeared in 1884. Huck Finn's creator eventually stormed the citadels of polite society and hobnobbed with the wealthy. Succumbing to the money fever of his age, he plunged into a scheme in the hope of making millions. By the 1890s, he faced bankruptcy. Twain's tale was common in an age when the promise of wealth led as many to ruin as to riches. Wall Street panics in both 1873 and 1893 plunged the country into depression.

The rush to build railroads and other industries and the corrupt interplay of business and politics formed the key themes in the Gilded Age. The runaway growth of the railroads and the surge in new inventions and technologies like electricity, the telephone, and

CHRONOLOGY

1869	First transcontinental railroad completed. National Woman Suffrage Association founded.
1870	John D. Rockefeller incorporates Standard Oil Company.
1872	Andrew Carnegie builds world's largest steel plant.
1873	Wall Street panic leads to major economic depression.
1874	Woman's Christian Temperance Union founded.
1876	Alexander Graham Bell demonstrates telephone.
1877	Rutherford B. Hayes sworn in as president. *Munn v. Illinois* decided.
1880	James A. Garfield elected president.
1881	Garfield assassinated; Vice President Chester A. Arthur becomes president.
1882	John D. Rockefeller develops the trust.
1883	Pendleton Civil Service Act enacted.
1884	Grover Cleveland elected president.
1886	*Wabash v. Illinois* decided.
1887	Interstate Commerce Act enacted.
1888	Benjamin Harrison elected president.
1890	McKinley tariff passes. General Federation of Women's Clubs founded. Sherman Antitrust Act enacted.
1892	Ida B. Wells launches antilynching campaign.
1893	Wall Street panic touches off national depression.
1895	J. P. Morgan bails out U.S. Treasury.
1901	U.S. Steel incorporated and capitalized at $1.4 billion.

the telegraph encouraged the rise of big business and led to an age of industrial capitalism.

Such rapid growth had alarming social and political implications. Economic issues increasingly shaped party politics. Social Darwinism, with its insistence on the "survival of the fittest," supported the power of the wealthy, while the poor and middle classes championed antimonopoly measures to restore competition, currency reform to ease debt, and civil service to end corruption. As always, race, class, and gender influenced politics and policy.

The hopes and fears of the Gilded Age were most evident in the public's attitude toward the business moguls of the day. Men like Jay Gould, Andrew Carnegie, and John D. Rockefeller sparked the popular imagination as the heroes and villains of industrialization. And as concern grew over the power of big business and the growing chasm between rich and poor, many Americans, women as well as men, looked to the government for solutions.

Railroads and the Rise of New Industries

In the years following the Civil War, the American economy underwent a transformation. Where once wealth had been measured in tangible assets — property, livestock, buildings — the economy now ran on money and the new devices of business — paper currency, securities, and anonymous corporate entities. Wall Street, the heart of the country's financial system, increasingly affected Main Street. Driving the transition was the building of a transcontinental railroad system, which radically altered the scale and scope of American industry. Old industries like iron transformed into modern industries such as the behemoth U.S. Steel. Discovery and invention stimulated new industries, from oil refining to electric light and power. The overbuilding of the railroad in the decades after the Civil War played a key role in transforming the American economy as business came to rely on huge government subsidies, "friends" in Congress, and complicated financial transactions.

Gilded Age
A period of enormous economic growth and ostentatious displays of wealth during the last quarter of the nineteenth century. Industrialization dramatically changed U.S. society and created a newly dominant group of rich entrepreneurs and an impoverished working class.

Jay Gould in railroads, Andrew Carnegie in steel, and John D. Rockefeller in oil pioneered new strategies to seize markets and consolidate power. With keen senses of self-interest, these tycoons set the tone in the get-rich-quick era of freewheeling capitalism that came to be called the **Gilded Age**.

Railroads: America's First Big Business.
The military conquest of America's inland empire and the dispossession of Native Americans (see chapter 17) was fed by an elaborate new railroad system in the West built on speculation and government giveaways. Between 1870 and 1880, the amount of track in the country doubled, and it nearly doubled again in the following decade. By 1900, the nation

boasted more than 193,000 miles of railroad track — more than in all of Europe and Russia combined (Map 18.1). The railroads had become America's first big business. Credit fueled the railroad boom. Privately owned but publicly financed, and subsidized by enormous land grants from the federal government and the states, the railroads epitomized the insidious nexus of business and politics in the Gilded Age.

To understand how the railroads came to dominate American life, there is no better place to start than with the career of Jay Gould, the era's most notorious speculator. Jason "Jay" Gould bought his first railroad before he turned twenty-five. It was only sixty-two miles long, in bad repair, and on the brink of failure, but within two years he sold it at a profit of $130,000.

The secretive Gould operated in the stock market like a shark, looking for vulnerable railroads, buying enough stock to take control, and threatening to undercut his competitors until they bought him out at a high profit. The railroads that fell into his hands often went bankrupt. Gould's genius lay not in providing transportation, but in cleverly buying and selling railroad stock on Wall Street. Gould soon realized

Map Activity

MAP 18.1 RAILROAD EXPANSION, 1870–1890

Railroad mileage nearly quadrupled between 1870 and 1890, with the greatest growth occurring in the trans-Mississippi West. The western lines were completed in the 1880s. Fueled by speculation and built ahead of demand, the western railroads made fortunes for individual speculators. But they rarely paid for themselves and speeded the demise of Native Americans.

READING THE MAP: Where were most of the railroad lines located in 1870? What was the end point of the only western route? By 1890, how many railroads reached the West Coast?

CONNECTIONS: Why were so many rails laid between 1870 and 1890? How did the railroads affect the nation's economy?

Major railroads in 1870

Major railroads built between 1870 and 1890

that a corporate failure could still mean financial success. His strategy of expansion and consolidation encouraged overbuilding even as it stimulated a new national market.

The first transcontinental railway had been completed in 1869 at Promontory Summit, Utah. In the 1880s, Gould moved to put together a second transcontinental railroad. To defend their interests, his competitors had little choice but to adopt his strategy of expansion. The railroads built ahead of demand, regardless of the social and environmental costs. Soon more railroads trailed into the West — by 1893, Kansas alone had at least six competing lines.

The railroad moguls put up little of their own money to build the roads and instead relied on the largesse of government and the sale of railroad bonds and stock. Bondholders were creditors who required repayment at a specific time. Stockholders bought a share in the company and received dividends if the company prospered. Thus, railroad moguls received money from these sales of financial interests but did not need to pay out until later. If the railroad failed, a receiver was appointed to determine how many pennies on the dollar shareholders would receive. The owners, astutely using the market, came out ahead. Novelist Charles Dudley Warner described how wrecking a railroad could yield profits:

> [They fasten upon] some railway that is prosperous, . . . and has a surplus. They contrive to buy . . . a controlling interest in it. . . . Then they absorb its surplus; they let it run down so that it pays no dividends, and by-and-by cannot even pay

Visual Activity

JAY GOULD AS A SPIDER

In this 1885 political cartoon titled "Justice in the Web," artist Frederick Burr Opper portrays Jay Gould as a hideous spider whose web, formed by Western Union telegraph lines, has entrapped "Justice" through its monopoly of the telegraph industry. Gould made his fortune through speculation on railroads, which often ran with telegraph lines alongside the tracks. Images like this one fueled the public's hatred of Gould. The Granger Collection, New York.

READING THE IMAGE: By portraying Gould as a spider, what is the cartoonist trying to say about him?

CONNECTIONS: In what ways did wealthy industrialists use manipulative techniques for personal gain?

JUSTICE IN THE WEB.

its interest; then they squeeze the bondholders, who may be glad to accept any-thing that is offered out of the wreck, and perhaps they throw the property into the hands of a receiver, or consolidate it with some other road at a value far greater than it cost them in stealing it. Having one way or another sucked it dry, they look around for another road.

With help from railroad growth and speculation, the New York Stock Exchange expanded. The volume of stock increased sixfold between 1869 and 1901. The line between investment and speculation blurred, causing many Americans to question whether the manipulation of speculators fueled the boom and bust cycles that led to panic and depression in 1873 and again twenty years later. The dramatic growth of the railroads created the country's first big business. Before the Civil War, even the largest textile mill in New England employed no more than 800 workers. By con-trast, the Pennsylvania Railroad by the 1870s boasted a payroll of more than 55,000 workers. Capitalized at more than $400 million, the Pennsylvania Railroad consti-tuted the largest private enterprise in the world.

The big business of railroads bestowed enormous riches on a handful of tycoons. Both Gould and his competitor "Commodore" Cornelius Vanderbilt amassed for-tunes estimated at $100 million. Such staggering wealth eclipsed the power and influence of upper-class Americans from previous generations and created an abyss between the nation's rich and poor. In its wake it left a legacy of lavish spending for an elite crop of ultrarich heirs.

The Republican Party, firmly entrenched in Washington after the Civil War, worked closely with business interests, subsidizing the transcontinental railroad sys-tem. Significant amounts of money changed hands to move bills through Congress. Along with "friends," often on the railroads' payrolls, lobbyists worked to craft legis-lation favorable to railroad interests. Friends of the railroads in state legislatures and Congress lavished the new western roads with land grants of a staggering 100 million acres (mostly owned by the Indians) and $64 million in tax incentives and direct aid. States and local communities joined the railroad boom, betting that only those towns and villages along the tracks would grow and flourish. A revolution in com-munication accompanied and supported the growth of the railroads. The telegraph, developed by Samuel F. B. Morse, marched across the continent alongside the rail-road. By transmitting coded messages along electrical wire, the telegraph formed the "nervous system" of the new industrial order. Telegraph service quickly replaced Pony Express mail carriers in the West and transformed business by providing instantaneous communication. Again Jay Gould took the lead. In 1879, through stock manipulation, he seized control of Western Union, the company that monopo-lized the telegraph industry.

The railroads soon fell on hard times. Already by the 1870s, lack of planning led to overbuilding. Across the nation, railroads competed fiercely for business. Manu-facturers in areas served by competing railroads could get substantially reduced shipping rates in return for promises of steady business. Because railroad owners lost money through this kind of competition, they tried to set up agreements, or "pools," to divide up territory and set rates. But these informal gentlemen's agreements invar-iably failed because men like Gould, intent on undercutting all competitors, refused to play by the rules.

The public's alarm at the control wielded by the new railroad magnates and the tactics they employed came to light in the Crédit Mobilier scandal of 1872. Crédit Mobilier, a fiscal enterprise set up by partners including Thomas Durant, an executive of Union Pacific Railroad, would provide sole bids on construction work. Using money procured from investors and government bonds, the work was then subcontracted out, leaving profits in the hands of the financiers. With profits booming, senators clambered to profit as well. Charles Dana's *New York Sun* described the Crédit Mobilier money-making scheme as "The King of Frauds" and attempted to document the way the railroads controlled their friends in government with lavish gifts of stock. Although the press never got the financial dealings straight, the scandal and resulting investigation implicated the Union Pacific Railroad, the vice president, and numerous congressmen. The real revelation was how little the key players knew about how railroads were built or operated. The promoters knew little about building the roads; the investors had an even shakier grasp on what they were investing in; and the politicians who subsidized the roads, instead of overseeing them, remained vague on specifics and failed to provide governmental oversight. All that was clear was that the Union Pacific had sold stock below market prices to its friends. In the end, no one was punished and no money returned.

The Crédit Mobilier scandal increased public suspicion of the corrupt relationship between business and government and led to a strong antipathy toward speculators and a movement to end monopoly.

Andrew Carnegie, Steel, and Vertical Integration.
If Jay Gould was the man Americans loved to hate, Andrew Carnegie became one of America's heroes. Unlike Gould, Carnegie turned his back on speculation and worked to build something enduring — Carnegie Steel, the biggest steel business in the world during the Gilded Age.

The growth of the steel industry proceeded directly from railroad building. The first railroads ran on iron rails, which cracked and broke with alarming frequency. Steel, both stronger and more flexible than iron, remained too expensive for use in rails until Englishman Henry Bessemer developed a way to make steel more cheaply. Andrew Carnegie, among the first to champion the new "King Steel," came to dominate the emerging industry.

Carnegie, a Scottish immigrant, landed in New York in 1848 at the age of twelve. He rose from a job cleaning bobbins in a textile factory to become one of the richest men in America. Before he died, he gave away more than $300 million, most notably to public libraries. His generosity, combined with his own rise from poverty, burnished his public image.

While Carnegie was a teenager, his skill as a telegraph operator caught the attention of Tom Scott, superintendent of the Pennsylvania Railroad. Scott hired Carnegie, soon promoted him, and lent him the money for his first foray into Wall Street investment. As a result of this crony capitalism, Carnegie became a millionaire before his thirtieth birthday. At that point, Carnegie turned away from speculation. "My preference was always manufacturing," he wrote. "I wished to make something tangible." By applying the lessons of cost accounting and efficiency that he had learned with the Pennsylvania Railroad, Carnegie turned steel into the nation's first manufacturing big business.

In 1872, Andrew Carnegie built the world's largest, most up-to-date steel mill in Braddock, Pennsylvania. At that time, steelmakers produced about 70 tons a week. Within two decades, Carnegie's blast furnaces poured out an incredible 10,000 tons a week. His formula for success was simple: "Cut the prices, scoop the market, run the mills full; watch the costs and profits will take care of themselves." Carnegie pioneered a system of business organization called vertical integration in which all aspects of the business were under Carnegie's control — from the mining of iron ore, to its transport on the Great Lakes, to the production of steel. As one observer noted, "there was never a price, profit, or royalty paid to any outsider."

The great productivity Carnegie encouraged came at a high price. He deliberately pitted his managers against one another, firing the losers and rewarding the winners with a share in the company. Workers achieved the output Carnegie demanded by enduring low wages, dangerous working conditions, and twelve-hour days six days a week. One worker, observing the contradiction between Carnegie's generous endowment of public libraries and his labor policy, observed, "After working twelve hours, how can a man go to a library?"

By 1900, Andrew Carnegie had become the best-known manufacturer in the nation, and the age of iron had yielded to an age of steel (Figure 18.1). Steel from Carnegie's mills supported the elevated trains in New York and Chicago, formed the skeleton of the Washington Monument, supported the first steel bridge to span the Mississippi, and girded America's first skyscrapers. As a captain of industry, Carnegie's only rival was the titan of the oil industry, John D. Rockefeller.

John D. Rockefeller, Standard Oil, and the Trust.
In the days before the automobile and gasoline, crude oil was refined into lubricating oil for machinery and kerosene for lamps, the major source of lighting in the nineteenth century. The amount of capital needed to buy or build an oil refinery in the 1860s and 1870s

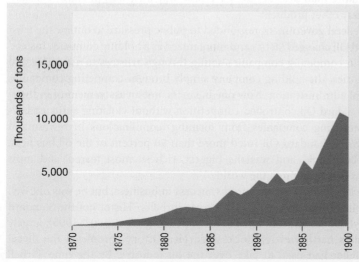

FIGURE 18.1 IRON AND STEEL PRODUCTION, 1870–1900

Iron and steel production in the United States grew from nearly none in 1870 to 10 million tons a year by 1900. The secrets to such a great increase were the use of the Bessemer process and vertical integration, pioneered by Andrew Carnegie. By 1900, Carnegie's mills alone produced more steel than all of Great Britain. With corporate consolidation after 1900, the rate of growth in steel proved even more spectacular.

remained relatively low — roughly what it cost to lay one mile of railroad track. As a result, the new petroleum industry experienced riotous competition. Ultimately, John D. Rockefeller and his Standard Oil Company succeeded in controlling nine-tenths of the oil-refining business.

Rockefeller grew up the son of a shrewd Yankee who peddled quack cures for cancer. Under his father's rough tutelage, Rockefeller learned how to drive a hard bargain. In 1865, at the age of twenty-five, he controlled the largest oil refinery in Cleveland. Like a growing number of business owners, Rockefeller abandoned partnership or single proprietorship to embrace the corporation as the business structure best suited to maximize profit and minimize personal liability. In 1870, he incorporated his oil business, founding the Standard Oil Company.

As the largest refiner in Cleveland, Rockefeller demanded illegal rebates from the railroads in exchange for his steady business. The secret rebates enabled Rockefeller to drive out his competitors through predatory pricing. The railroads needed Rockefeller's business so badly that they gave him a share of the rates that his competitors paid. A Pennsylvania Railroad official later confessed that Rockefeller extracted such huge rebates that the railroad, which could not risk losing his business, sometimes ended up paying him to transport Standard's oil. Rebates enabled Rockefeller to undercut his competitors and pressure competing refiners to sell out or face ruin.

trust
A system in which corporations give shares of their stock to trustees who hold the stocks "in trust" for their stockholders, thereby coordinating the industry to ensure profits to the participating corporations and to curb competition.

To gain legal standing for Standard Oil's secret deals, Rockefeller in 1882 pioneered a new form of corporate structure — the **trust**. The trust differed markedly from Carnegie's vertical approach in steel. Rockefeller used horizontal integration to control not the entire process, but only an aspect of oil production — refining. Several trustees held stock in various refinery companies "in trust" for Standard's stockholders. This elaborate stock swap allowed the trustees to coordinate policy among the refineries by gobbling up all the small, competing refineries. Often buyers did not know they were actually selling out to Standard. By the end of the century, Rockefeller enjoyed a virtual monopoly of the oil-refining business. The Standard Oil trust, valued at more than $70 million, paved the way for trusts in sugar, whiskey, matches, and many other products.

When the federal government responded to public pressure to outlaw the trust in 1890, Standard Oil changed tactics and reorganized as a holding company. Instead of stockholders in competing companies acting through trustees to set prices and determine territories, the holding company simply brought competing companies under one central administration. Now one business, not an assortment of individual refineries, Standard Oil controlled competition without violating antitrust laws that forbade competing companies from forming "combinations in restraint of trade." By the 1890s, Standard Oil ruled more than 90 percent of the oil business, employed 100,000 people, and was the biggest, richest, most feared, and most admired business organization in the world.

John D. Rockefeller enjoyed enormous success in business, but he was not well liked by the public. Editor and journalist Ida M. Tarbell's "History of the Standard Oil Company," which ran in serial form in *McClure's Magazine* (1902–1905), largely shaped the public's harsh view of Rockefeller. Her history chronicled the illegal methods Rockefeller had used to take over the oil industry. By the time Tarbell finished her story, Rockefeller slept with a loaded revolver by his bed. Standard Oil and the man who created it had become the symbol of heartless monopoly.

New Inventions: The Telephone and the Telegraph.

The second half of the nineteenth century was an age of invention. Men like Thomas Alva Edison and Alexander Graham Bell became folk heroes. But no matter how dramatic the inventors or the inventions, the new electric and telephone industries pioneered by Edison and Bell soon eclipsed their inventors and fell under the control of bankers and industrialists.

Alexander Graham Bell came to America from Scotland at the age of twenty-four with a passion to find a way to teach the deaf to speak (his wife and mother were deaf). Instead, he developed a way to transmit voice over wire — the telephone. Bell's invention astounded the world when he demonstrated it at the Philadelphia Centennial Exposition in 1876. In 1880, Bell's company, American Bell, pioneered "long lines" (long-distance telephone service), creating American Telephone and Telegraph (AT&T) as a subsidiary. In 1900, AT&T developed a complicated structure that enabled Americans to communicate not only locally but also across the country. And unlike a telegraph message, the telephone connected both parties immediately and privately. Bell's invention proved a boon to business, contributing to speed and efficiency. The number of telephones soared, reaching 310,000 in 1895 and more than 1.5 million in 1900.

Even more than Alexander Graham Bell, inventor Thomas Alva Edison embodied the old-fashioned virtues of Yankee ingenuity and rugged individualism that Americans most admired. A self-educated dynamo, he worked twenty hours a day in his laboratory in Menlo Park, New Jersey, vowing to turn out "a minor invention every

ALEXANDER GRAHAM BELL
Alexander Graham Bell sits at the New York end of the first long-distance telephone call to Chicago on October 18, 1892. Years earlier, Bell went to the Roosevelts for financial backing of his new invention. He hooked up a telephone so that young Theodore could talk from his desk to a room down the hall. Teddy concluded that while the device had potential as a toy, it had no real future. The Granger Collection, New York.

ten days and a big thing every six months or so." He almost made good on his promise. At the height of his career, he averaged a patent every eleven days and invented such "big things" as the phonograph, the motion picture camera, and the filament for the incandescent lightbulb.

Edison, in competition with George W. Westinghouse, pioneered the use of electricity as an energy source. By the late nineteenth century, electricity had become a part of American urban life. It powered trolley cars and lighted factories, homes, and office buildings. Indeed, electricity became so prevalent in urban life that it symbolized the city, whose bright lights contrasted with rural America, left largely in the dark.

The day of the inventor quietly yielded to the heyday of the corporation. In 1892, the electric industry consolidated. Reflecting a nationwide trend in business, Edison General Electric dropped the name of its inventor, becoming simply General Electric (GE). For years, an embittered Edison refused to set foot inside a GE building. GE, a prime example of the trend toward business consolidation, soon dominated the market.

> **REVIEW**   When, why, and how did the transcontinental railroad system develop, and what was its impact on American business?

From Competition to Consolidation

finance capitalism
Investment sponsored by banks and bankers that typified the American business scene at the end of the nineteenth century. After the panic of 1893, bankers stepped in and reorganized major industries to stabilize them, leaving power concentrated in the hands of a few influential capitalists.

Even as Rockefeller and Carnegie built their empires, the era of the "robber barons," as they were dubbed by their detractors, was drawing to a close. Increasingly, businesses replaced partnerships and sole proprietorships with the anonymous corporate structure that would come to dominate the twentieth century. At the same time, mergers led to the creation of huge new corporations.

Banks and financiers played key roles in this consolidation, so much so that the decades at the turn of the twentieth century can be characterized as a period of **finance capitalism** — investment sponsored by banks and bankers. When the depression that followed the panic of 1893 bankrupted many businesses, bankers stepped in to bring order and to reorganize major industries. During these years, a new social philosophy developed that helped to justify consolidation and to inhibit state or federal regulation of business. A conservative Supreme Court further frustrated attempts to control business by consistently declaring unconstitutional legislation designed to regulate railroads or to outlaw trusts and monopolies.

J. P. Morgan and Finance Capitalism.

John Pierpont Morgan, the preeminent finance capitalist of the late nineteenth century, loathed competition and sought whenever possible to eliminate it by substituting consolidation and central control. Morgan's passion for order made him the architect of business mergers. At the turn of the twentieth century, he dominated American banking, exerting an influence so powerful that his critics charged he controlled a vast "money trust" even more insidious than Rockefeller's Standard Oil.

Morgan acted as a power broker in the reorganization of the railroads and the creation of industrial giants such as General Electric. When the railroads collapsed, Morgan took over and eliminated competition by creating what he called "a community of interest." By the time he finished "Morganizing" the railroads, a handful of directors controlled two-thirds of the nation's track. Morgan's directors were bankers, not railroad men, and they saw the roads as little more than "a set of books." Their conservative approach aimed at short-term profit and discouraged the technological and organizational innovation necessary to run the railroads effectively.

In 1898, Morgan moved into the steel industry, directly challenging Andrew Carnegie. The pugnacious Carnegie cabled his partners in the summer of 1900: "Action essential: crisis has arrived . . . have no fear as to the result; victory certain." The press trumpeted news of the impending fight between the feisty Scot and the haughty Wall Street banker. But for all his belligerence, the sixty-six-year-old Carnegie yearned to retire to Scotland. Morgan, who disdained haggling, agreed to pay Carnegie's asking price, $480 million (the equivalent of about $10 billion in today's currency). According to legend, when Carnegie later teased Morgan, saying that he should have asked $100 million more, Morgan replied, "You would have got it if you had."

HOMESTEAD STEELWORKS

The Homestead steelworks, outside Pittsburgh, is pictured shortly after J. P. Morgan created U.S. Steel, the precursor of today's USX. Try to count the smokestacks in the picture. Air pollution on this scale posed a threat to the health of citizens and made for a dismal landscape. Workers complained that trees would not grow in Homestead. The Granger Collection, New York.

Morgan's acquisition of Carnegie Steel signaled the passing of the old entrepreneurial order personified by Andrew Carnegie and the arrival of a new anonymous corporate world. Morgan quickly moved to pull together Carnegie's chief competitors to form a huge new corporation, United States Steel, known today as USX. Created in 1901 and capitalized at $1.4 billion, U.S. Steel was the largest corporation in the world.

Even more than Carnegie or Rockefeller, Morgan left his stamp on the twentieth century and formed the model for corporate consolidation that economists and social scientists justified with a new social theory later called social Darwinism.

Social Darwinism, Laissez-Faire, and the Supreme Court.

John D. Rockefeller Jr., the son of the founder of Standard Oil, once remarked to his Baptist Bible class that the Standard Oil Company, like the American Beauty rose, resulted from "pruning the early buds that grew up around it." The elimination of competition, he declared, was "merely the working out of a law of nature and a law of God." The comparison of the business world to the natural world resembled the theory of evolution formulated by the British naturalist Charles Darwin. In his monumental work *On the Origin of Species* (1859), Darwin theorized that in the struggle for survival, adaptation to the environment triggered among species a natural selection process that led to evolution. Herbert Spencer in Britain and William Graham Sumner in the United States developed the theory of **social Darwinism**. The social Darwinists insisted that societal progress came about as a result of relentless competition in which the strong survived and the weak died out.

In social terms, the idea of the "survival of the fittest," coined by Spencer, had profound significance, as Sumner, a professor of political economy at Yale University, made clear in his book *What Social Classes Owe to Each Other* (1883). "The drunkard in the gutter is just where he ought to be, according to the fitness and tendency of things," Sumner insisted. Conversely, "millionaires are the product of natural selection," and although "they get high wages and live in luxury," Sumner claimed, "the bargain is a good one for society."

Social Darwinists equated wealth and power with "fitness" and believed that any efforts by the rich to aid the poor would only tamper with the laws of nature and slow down evolution. Social Darwinism acted to curb social reform while glorifying great wealth. In an age when Rockefeller and Carnegie amassed hundreds of millions of dollars (billions in today's currency) and the average worker earned $500 a year, social Darwinism justified economic inequality.

Carnegie softened some of the harshness of social Darwinism in his essay "The Gospel of Wealth," published in 1889. The millionaire, Carnegie wrote, acted as a "mere trustee and agent for his poorer brethren, bringing to their service his superior wisdom, experience, and ability to administer, doing for them better than they could or would do for themselves." Carnegie preached philanthropy and urged the rich to "live unostentatious lives" and "administer surplus wealth for the good of the people." His **gospel of wealth** earned much praise but won few converts. Most millionaires followed the lead of Morgan, who contributed to charity but hoarded private treasures in his marble library.

social Darwinism
A social theory popularized in the late nineteenth century by Herbert Spencer and William Graham Sumner. Proponents believed that only relentless competition could produce social progress and that wealth was a sign of "fitness" and poverty a sign of "unfitness" for survival.

gospel of wealth
The idea that the financially successful should use their wisdom, experience, and wealth to help the poor. Andrew Carnegie promoted this view in an 1889 essay in which he maintained that the wealthy should serve as stewards of society as a whole.

With its emphasis on the free play of competition and the survival of the fittest, social Darwinism encouraged the economic theory of laissez-faire (French for "let it alone"). Business leaders argued that government should not meddle in economic affairs, except to protect private property (or support high tariffs and government subsidies). A conservative Supreme Court agreed. During the 1880s and 1890s, the Court increasingly reinterpreted the Constitution, judging corporations to be "persons" in order to protect business from taxation, regulation, labor organization, and antitrust legislation.

Only in the arena of politics did Americans tackle the social issues raised by corporate capitalism.

> **REVIEW** Why did the ideas of social Darwinism appeal to many Americans in the late nineteenth century?

Politics and Culture

For many Americans, politics provided a source of identity, a means of livelihood, and a ready form of entertainment. No wonder voter turnout averaged a hefty 77 percent (compared to roughly 57.5 percent in the 2012 presidential election). A variety of factors contributed to the complicated interplay of politics and culture. Patronage provided an economic incentive for voter participation, but ethnicity, religion, sectional loyalty, race, and gender all influenced the political life of the period.

Political Participation and Party Loyalty. Political parties in power doled
out federal, state, and local government jobs to their loyal supporters. With hundreds of thousands of jobs to be filled, the choice of party affiliation could mean the difference between a paycheck and an empty pocket. Money greased the wheels of this system of patronage, dubbed the **spoils system** from the adage "To the victor go the spoils." With their livelihoods tied to their party identity, government employees had a powerful incentive to vote in great numbers.

spoils system
System in which politicians doled out government positions to their loyal supporters. This patronage system led to widespread corruption during the Gilded Age.

Political affiliation provided a sense of group identity for many voters proud of their loyalty to the Democrats or the Republicans. Democrats, who traced the party's roots back to Thomas Jefferson, called theirs "the party of the fathers." The Republican Party, founded in the 1850s, still claimed strong loyalties in the North as a result of its alignment with the Union during the Civil War. Republicans proved particularly adept at evoking Civil War loyalty, using a tactic called "waving the bloody shirt."

Religion and ethnicity also played a significant role in politics. In the North, Protestants from the old-line denominations, particularly Presbyterians and Methodists, flocked to the Republican Party, which championed a series of moral reforms, including local laws requiring businesses to close on Sunday in observance of the Sabbath. In the cities, the Democratic Party courted immigrants and working-class Catholic and Jewish voters and charged, rightly, that Republican moral crusades often masked attacks on immigrant culture.

Sectionalism and the New South. After the end of Reconstruction, most white voters in the former Confederate states remained loyal Democrats, creating the so-called solid South that lasted for the next seventy years. Labeling the Republican Party the agent of "Negro rule," Democrats urged white southerners to "vote the way you shot." Yet the South proved far from solid for the Democrats on the state and local levels, leading to shifting political alliances and to third-party movements that challenged Democratic attempts to define politics along race lines and maintain the Democrats as the white man's party.

The South's economy, devastated by the war, foundered at the same time the North experienced an unprecedented industrial boom. Soon an influential group of southerners called for a New South modeled on the industrial North. Henry Grady, the ebullient young editor of the *Atlanta Constitution*, used his paper's influence to exhort the South to use its natural advantages — cheap labor and abundant natural resources — to go head-to-head in competition with northern industry. And even as southern Democrats took back control of state governments, they embraced northern promoters who promised prosperity and profits.

The railroads came first, opening up the region for industrial development. Southern railroad mileage grew fourfold from 1865 to 1890. The number of cotton spindles also soared as textile mill owners abandoned New England in search of the cheap labor and proximity to raw materials promised in the South. By 1900, the South had become the nation's leading producer of cloth, and more than 100,000 southerners, many of them women and children, worked in the region's textile mills.

The New South prided itself most on its iron and steel industry, which grew up in the area surrounding Birmingham, Alabama. During this period, the smokestack replaced the white-pillared plantation as the symbol of the New South. Andrew Carnegie toured the region in 1889 and observed, "The South is Pennsylvania's most formidable industrial enemy." But southern industry remained controlled by northern investors, who had no intention of letting the South beat the North at its own game. Elaborate mechanisms rigged the price of southern steel, inflating it, as one northern insider confessed, "for the purpose of protecting the Pittsburgh mills and in turn the Pittsburgh steel users." Similarly, in the lumber and mining industries, investors in the North and abroad, not southerners, reaped the lion's share of the profits.

In only one industry did the South truly dominate — tobacco. Capitalizing on the invention of a machine for rolling cigarettes, the American Tobacco Company, founded by the Duke family of North Carolina, eventually dominated the industry. As cigarettes replaced chewing tobacco in popularity at the turn of the twentieth century, a booming market developed for Duke's "ready mades." Soon the company sold 400,000 cigarettes a day.

In practical terms, the industrialized New South proved an illusion. Much of the South remained agricultural, caught in the grip of the insidious crop lien system (see chapter 16). White southern farmers, desperate to get out of debt, sometimes joined African Americans to pursue mutual political goals. Between 1865 and 1900, voters in every southern state experimented with political alliances that crossed the color line and threatened the status quo.

Gender, Race, and Politics.

Gender — society's notion of what constitutes acceptable masculine or feminine behavior — influenced politics throughout the nineteenth century. From the early days of the Republic, citizenship had been defined in male terms. Citizenship and its prerogatives (voting and officeholding) served as a badge of manliness and rested on its corollary, patriarchy — the power and authority men exerted over their wives and families. With the advent of universal (white) male suffrage in the early nineteenth century, gender eclipsed class as the defining feature of citizenship; men's dominance over women provided the common thread that knit all white men together politically. The concept of separate spheres dictated political participation for men only. Once the public sphere of political participation became equated with manhood, women found themselves increasingly restricted to the private sphere of the home.

Women were not alone in their limited access to the public sphere. Blacks continued to face discrimination well after Reconstruction, especially in the New South. Segregation, commonly practiced through **Jim Crow** laws (as discussed in chapter 21), prevented ex-slaves from riding in the same train cars as whites, from eating in the same restaurants, or from using the same toilet facilities.

Amid the turmoil of the post-Reconstruction South, some groups struck cross-racial alliances. In Virginia, the "Readjusters," a coalition of blacks and whites determined to "readjust" (lower) the state debt and spend more money on public education, captured state offices from 1879 to 1883. Groups like the Readjusters believed universal political rights could be extended to black males while maintaining racial segregation in the private sphere. Democrats fought back by arguing that black voting would lead to racial mixing, and many whites returned to the Democratic fold to protect "white womanhood."

The notion that black men threatened white southern womanhood reached its most vicious form in the practice of lynching — the killing and mutilation of black men by white mobs. By 1892, the practice had become so prevalent that a courageous black editor, Ida B. Wells, launched an antilynching movement. That year, a white mob lynched a friend of Wells's whose grocery store competed too successfully with a white-owned store. Wells shrewdly concluded that lynching served "as an excuse to get rid of Negroes who were acquiring wealth and property and thus keep the race terrorized." (See "Analyzing Historical Evidence," page 534.) She began to collect data on lynching and discovered that in the decade between 1882 and 1892, lynching rose in the South by an overwhelming 200 percent, with more than 241 black people killed. The vast increase in lynching testified to the retreat of the federal government following Reconstruction and to white southerners' determination to maintain supremacy through terrorism and intimidation.

Wells articulated lynching as a problem of gender as well as race. She insisted that the myth of black attacks on white southern women masked the reality that mob violence had more to do with economics and the shifting social structure of the South than with rape. She demonstrated in a sophisticated way how the southern patriarchal system, having lost its control over blacks with the end of slavery, used its control over white women to circumscribe the liberty of black men.

Jim Crow
System of racial segregation in the South lasting from after the Civil War into the twentieth century. Jim Crow laws segregated African Americans in public facilities such as trains and streetcars, curtailed their voting rights, and denied other basic civil rights.

Analyzing Historical Evidence

Ida B. Wells and Her Campaign to Stop Lynching

Ida B. Wells fearlessly crusaded to stop lynching in the South by researching and reporting lynchings in detail and by comparing coverage from black and white sources.

DOCUMENT 1

Ida B. Wells, Editorial Protesting the Lynching of Friends in Memphis, 1892

The lynching in 1892 of three friends who ran a grocery store outside of Memphis touched Wells deeply. She wrote an outraged editorial in the Free Press. *Later she would repeat the details in her first pamphlet,* Southern Horrors: Lynch Law in All Its Phases *(1892).*

On March 9, 1892, there were lynched in this same city three of the best specimens of young since-the-war Afro-American manhood. They were peaceful, law-abiding citizens and energetic business men. . . . They owned a flourishing grocery business in a thickly populated suburb of Memphis, and a white man named Barrett had one on the opposite corner. After a personal difficulty which Barrett sought by going into the "People's Grocery" drawing a pistol and was thrashed by Calvin McDowell, he (Barrett) threatened to "clean them out." These men were a mile beyond the city limits and the police protection; hearing that Barrett's crowd was coming to attack them Saturday night, they mustered forces and prepared to defend themselves against the attack.

When Barrett came he led a posse of officers, twelve in number, who afterward claimed to be hunting a man for whom they had a warrant. That twelve men in citizen's clothes should think it necessary to go in the night to hunt one man who had never before been arrested, or made any record as a criminal has never been explained. When they entered the back door the young men thought the threatened attack was on, and

fired into them. Three of the officers were wounded, and when the defending party found it was officers of the law upon whom they had fired, they ceased and got away.

Thirty-one men were arrested and thrown in jail as "conspirators," although they all declared more than once they did not know they were firing on officers. Excitement was at fever heat until the morning papers, two days after, announced that the wounded deputy sheriffs were out of danger. This hindered rather than helped the plans of the whites. There was no law on the statute books which would execute an Afro-American for wounding a white man, but the "unwritten law" did. Three of these men, the president, the manager and the clerk of the grocery — "the leaders of the conspiracy" — were secretly taken from jail and lynched in a shockingly brutal manner. "The Negroes are getting too independent," they say, "we must teach them a lesson."

What lesson? The lesson of subordination. "Kill the leaders and it will cow the Negro who dares to shoot a white man, even in self-defense."

SOURCE: *Southern Horrors and Other Writings,* edited by Jacqueline Jones Royster (Boston: Bedford/St. Martin's, 1997), 64–65.

DOCUMENT 2

Ida B. Wells, On Lack of Justice and Due Process for Accused Blacks, 1894

In her 1894 pamphlet The Red Record, *Wells insisted that lynching assumed all black men were guilty, thus denying them the constitutional right to defend themselves in front of a judge and jury.*

In lynching, opportunity is not given the Negro to defend himself against the unsupported accusations of white men and women. The word of the accuser is held to be true and the excited blood-thirsty mob demands that the rule of law be reserved and instead of proving the accused to be guilty, the victim of their hate and revenge must prove himself innocent. No evidence he can offer will satisfy the mob; he is bound hand and foot and swung into eternity. Then to excuse its infamy, the mob almost invariably reports the monstrous falsehood that its victim made a full confession before he was hanged.

SOURCE: Royster, *Southern Horrors*, 153.

DOCUMENT 3

Ida B. Wells, On Mob Rule in New Orleans, 1900

In her last pamphlet, Mob Rule in New Orleans, *Wells describes the riot that occurred when a black man, Robert Charles, attacked by a police officer with a billy club, retaliated. This led to a duel that then brought on further violence.*

During the entire time the mob held the city in its hands and went about holding up street cars and searching them, taking from them colored men to assault, shoot and kill, chasing colored men upon the public square, through alleys and into houses of any body who would take them in, breaking into the homes of defenseless colored men and women and beating aged and decrepit men and women to death, the police and the legally-constituted authorities showed plainly where their sympathies were, for in no case reported through the daily papers does there appear the arrest, trial and conviction of one of the mob for any of the brutalities which occurred. The ringleaders of the mob were at no time disguised. Men were chased, beaten and killed by white brutes, who boasted of their crimes, and the murderers still walk the streets of New Orleans, well known and absolutely exempt from prosecution. Not only were they exempt from prosecution by the police while the town was in the hands of the mob, but even now that law and order is supposed to resume control, these men, well known, are not now, nor ever will be, called to account for the unspeakable brutalities of that terrible week. On the other hand, the colored men who were beaten by the police and dragged into the station for purposes of intimidation were quickly called before the courts and fined or sent to jail upon the statement of the police.

SOURCE: Royster, *Southern Horrors*, 181–82.

QUESTIONS FOR ANALYSIS

Analyze the Evidence   In her campaign to end lynching, how does Wells seek to generate sympathy for the victims and to build an outraged antilynching coalition that will end the practice?

Recognize Viewpoints   How did the white people involved in lynching defend their actions?

Consider the Context   In addition to lynching, what else did white southerners do to keep African Americans in subordinate positions?

IDA B. WELLS

Ida B. Wells began her antilynching campaign in 1892 after a friend's murder led her to examine lynching in the South. Through lectures and pamphlets, she brought the horror of lynching to national and international audiences and became a founding member of the National Association for the Advancement of Colored People (NAACP). Special Collections Research Center, University of Chicago Library.

Wells's outspoken stance immediately resulted in reprisal. While she was traveling in the North, vandals ransacked her office in Tennessee and destroyed her printing equipment. Yet the warning that she would be killed on sight if she ever returned to Memphis only stiffened her resolve. As she wrote in her autobiography, *Crusade for Justice* (1928), "Having lost my paper, had a price put on my life and been made an exile . . . , I felt that I owed it to myself and to my race to tell the whole truth now that I was where I could do so freely."

Lynching did not end during Wells's lifetime, but her forceful voice brought the issue to national and international prominence. At Wells's funeral in 1931, black leader W. E. B. Du Bois eulogized Wells as the woman who "began the awakening of the conscience of the nation." Wells's determined campaign against lynching provided just one example of women's political activism during the Gilded Age. The suffrage and temperance movements, along with the growing popularity of women's clubs, dramatized how women refused to be relegated to a separate sphere that kept them out of politics.

Women's Activism. In 1869, Elizabeth Cady Stanton and Susan B. Anthony formed the National Woman Suffrage Association (NWSA), the first independent women's rights organization in the United States, to fight for the vote for women. But women found ways to act politically long before they voted and cleverly used their moral authority as wives and mothers to move from the domestic sphere into the realm of politics.

The extraordinary activity of women's clubs in the period following the Civil War provides just one example. Women's clubs proliferated beginning in the 1860s. Newspaper reporter Jane Cunningham Croly (pen name Jennie June) founded the Sorosis Club in New York City in 1868, after the New York Press Club denied entry to women journalists wishing to attend a banquet honoring the British author Charles Dickens. In 1890, Croly brought state and local clubs together under the umbrella of the General Federation of Women's Clubs (GFWC). Not wishing to alienate southern women, the GFWC barred black women's clubs from joining, despite vehement objections. Women's clubs soon abandoned literary pursuits to devote themselves to "civic usefulness," endorsing an end to child labor, supporting the eight-hour workday, and helping pass pure food and drug legislation.

The temperance movement (the movement to end drunkenness) attracted by far the largest number of organized women in the late nineteenth century. By the late 1860s and the 1870s, the liquor business was flourishing, with about one saloon for every fifty males over the age of fifteen. During the winter of 1873–74, temperance women adopted a radical new tactic. Armed with Bibles and singing hymns, they marched on taverns and saloons and refused to leave until the proprietors signed a pledge to quit selling liquor. Known as the Woman's Crusade, the movement spread like a prairie fire through small towns in Ohio, Indiana, Michigan, and Illinois and soon moved east into New York, New England, and Pennsylvania. Before it was over, more than 100,000 women had marched in more than 450 cities and towns.

The women's tactics may have been new, but the temperance movement dated back to the 1820s. Originally, the movement was led by Protestant men who organized clubs to pledge voluntary abstinence from liquor. By the 1850s, temperance advocates won significant victories when states, starting with Maine, passed laws to prohibit the sale of liquor. The Woman's Crusade dramatically brought the issue of temperance back into the national spotlight and, in 1874, led to the formation of a new organization, the **Woman's Christian Temperance Union (WCTU)**. Composed entirely of women, the WCTU advocated total abstinence from alcohol.

Temperance provided women with a respectable outlet for their increasing resentment of women's inferior status and their growing recognition of women's capabilities. In its first five years, the WCTU relied on education and moral suasion, but when Frances Willard became president in 1879, she politicized the organization (as discussed in chapter 20). When the women of the WCTU joined with the Prohibition Party (formed in 1869 by a group of evangelical clergymen), one wag observed, "Politics is a man's game, an' women, childhern, and prohyibitionists do well to keep out iv it." By sharing power with women, the prohibitionist men violated the old political rules and risked attacks on their honor and manhood.

Even though women found ways to affect the political process, especially in third parties, it remained true that politics, particularly presidential politics, remained an exclusively male prerogative.

"WOMAN'S HOLY WAR"

This political cartoon styles the temperance campaign as "Woman's Holy War" and shows a woman knight in armor (demurely seated sidesaddle on her charger), wielding a battle-ax and trampling on barrels of liquor. The image of temperance women as ax-wielding Amazons proved a popular satiric image. The cartoon appeared in 1874, the year the Woman's Christian Temperance Union formed. Picture Research Consultants & Archives.

Woman's Christian Temperance Union (WCTU)
All-women organization founded in 1874 to advocate total abstinence from alcohol. The WCTU provided important political training for women, which many used in the suffrage movement.

> **REVIEW** How did race and gender influence politics?

Presidential Politics

The presidents of the Gilded Age, from Rutherford B. Hayes (1877–1881) to William McKinley (1897–1901), are largely forgotten men, primarily because so little was expected of them. The dominant creed of laissez-faire, coupled with the dictates of social Darwinism, warned the presidents and the government to leave business alone (except when they were working in its interests). Still, presidents in the Gilded Age grappled with corruption and party strife, and they struggled toward the creation of new political ethics designed to replace patronage with a civil service system that promised to award jobs on the basis of merit, not party loyalty.

Corruption and Party Strife. The political corruption and party factionalism that characterized the administration of Ulysses S. Grant (1869–1877) (see chapter 16) continued to trouble the nation in the 1880s. The spoils system remained the driving force in party politics at all levels of government. Pro-business Republicans generally held a firm grip on the White House, while Democrats had better luck in Congress. Both parties relied on patronage to cement party loyalty.

A small but determined group of reformers championed a new ethics that would preclude politicians from getting rich from public office. The selection of U.S. senators particularly concerned them. Under the Constitution, senators were selected by state legislatures, not directly elected by the voters. Powerful business interests often contrived to control state legislatures and through them U.S. senators. As journalist Henry Demarest Lloyd quipped, Standard Oil "had done everything to the Pennsylvania legislature except to refine it." In this climate, a constitutional amendment calling for the direct election of senators faced stiff opposition from entrenched interests.

Republican president Rutherford B. Hayes tried to steer a middle course between spoilsmen and reformers. Hayes proved a hardworking, well-informed executive who wanted peace, prosperity, and an end to party strife. Yet the Republican Party remained divided into factions led by strong party bosses who boasted that they could make or break any president.

Foremost among the Republican Senate bosses stood Roscoe Conkling of New York. He and his followers, who fiercely supported the patronage system, were known as "Stalwarts." Conkling's rival Senator James G. Blaine of Maine led the "Half Breeds," who were less openly corrupt yet still tainted by their involvement in the Crédit Mobilier scandal. A third group, called the "Mugwumps," consisted of reformers from Massachusetts and New York who deplored the spoils system and advocated civil service reform.

President Hayes's middle course pleased no one, and he soon managed to alienate all factions of his party. Few were surprised when he announced that he would not seek reelection in 1880. To avoid choosing among its factions, the Republican Party in 1880 nominated a dark-horse candidate, Representative James A. Garfield of Ohio. To foster party unity, they picked Stalwart Chester A. Arthur as the vice presidential candidate. The Democrats made an attempt to overcome sectionalism by selecting former Union general Winfield Scott Hancock. Hancock garnered only lukewarm support, receiving just 155 electoral votes to Garfield's 214, although the popular vote was less lopsided.

Garfield's Assassination and Civil Service Reform. "My God," Garfield swore after only a few months in office, "what is there in this place that a man

CIVIL SERVICE EXAMS

In this 1890 photograph, prospective police officers in Chicago take the written civil service exam. With the rise of a written exam, issues of class and status meant that many men, particularly immigrants and their sons, needed education and not simply connections to make the grade. © Chicago History Museum, USA/Bridgeman Images.

should ever want to get into it?" Garfield, like Hayes, faced the difficult task of remaining independent while pacifying the party bosses and placating the reformers. On July 2, 1881, less than four months after taking office, Garfield was shot and died two months later. His assailant, Charles Julius Guiteau, though clearly insane, turned out to be a disappointed office seeker, motivated by political partisanship. He told the police officer who arrested him, "I did it; I will go to jail for it: Arthur is president, and I am a Stalwart."

The press almost universally condemned Republican factionalism for creating the political climate that produced Guiteau. Attacks on the spoils system increased, and both parties claimed credit for passage of the Pendleton Civil Service Act of 1883, which established a permanent Civil Service Commission consisting of three members appointed by the president. Some fourteen thousand jobs came under a merit system that required examinations for office and made it impossible to remove jobholders for political reasons. The new law also prohibited federal jobholders from contributing to political campaigns, thus drying up the major source of the party bosses' revenue. Businesses soon stepped in as the nation's chief political contributors. Ironically, **civil service reform** gave business an even greater influence in political life.

civil service reform
Effort in the 1880s to end the spoils system and reduce government corruption. The Pendleton Civil Service Act of 1883 created the Civil Service Commission to award government jobs under a merit system that required examinations for office and made it impossible to remove jobholders for political reasons.

Reform and Scandal: The Campaign of 1884.

James G. Blaine assumed leadership of the Republican Party and at long last captured the presidential

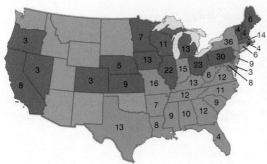

Candidate	Electoral Vote	Popular Vote	Percent of Popular Vote
Grover Cleveland (Democrat)	219	4,874,986	48.5*
James G. Blaine (Republican)	182	4,851,981	48.3

*Percentages do not total 100 because some popular votes went to other parties.

MAP 18.2   THE ELECTION OF 1884

nomination in 1884. A magnetic Irish American, Blaine inspired such devotion that his supporters called themselves Blainiacs. But Mugwump reformers bolted the party and embraced the Democrats' presidential nominee, Governor Grover Cleveland of New York. The burly, beer-drinking Cleveland distinguished himself from a generation of politicians by the simple motto "A public office is a public trust." First as mayor of Buffalo and later as governor of New York, he built a reputation for honesty, economy, and administrative efficiency. The Democrats, who had not won the presidency since 1856, had high hopes for his candidacy, especially after the Mugwumps threw their support to Cleveland, announcing, "The paramount issue this year is moral rather than political."

They soon regretted their words. In July, Cleveland's hometown paper, the *Buffalo Telegraph*, dropped the bombshell that the candidate had fathered an illegitimate child in an affair with a local widow. Cleveland, a bachelor, stoically accepted responsibility for the child. Crushed by the scandal, the Mugwumps lost much of their enthusiasm. At public rallies, Blaine's partisans taunted Cleveland, chanting, "Ma, Ma, where's my Pa?"

Blaine set a new campaign style by launching a whirlwind national tour. On a last-minute stop in New York City, the exhausted candidate committed a misstep that may have cost him the election. He overlooked a remark by a supporter, a local clergyman who cast a slur on Catholic voters by styling the Democrats as the party of "Rum, Romanism, and Rebellion." Linking drinking (rum) and Catholicism (Romanism) offended Irish Catholic voters, whom Blaine had counted on to desert the Democratic Party and support him because of his Irish background.

With less than a week to go until the election, Blaine had no chance to recover from the negative publicity. He lost New York State by fewer than 1,200 votes and with it the election. In the final tally, Cleveland defeated Blaine by a scant 23,005 votes nationwide but won with 219 electoral votes to Blaine's 182 (Map 18.2), ending twenty-four years of Republican control of the presidency. Cleveland's followers had the last word. To the chorus of "Ma, Ma, where's my Pa?" they retorted, "Going to the White House, ha, ha, ha."

> **REVIEW**   How did the question of civil service reform contribute to divisions within the Republican Party?

Economic Issues and Party Realignment

Four years later, in the election of 1888, fickle voters turned Cleveland out, electing Republican Benjamin Harrison, the grandson of President William Henry Harrison. Then, in the only instance in American history when a president once defeated at the polls returned to office, the voters brought Cleveland back in the election of 1892. What factors account for such a surprising turnaround? The 1880s witnessed a remarkable political realignment as a set of economic concerns replaced appeals to Civil War sectional loyalties. The tariff, federal regulation of the railroads and trusts, and the campaign for free silver restructured American politics. Then a Wall Street panic in 1893 set off a major depression that further fed political unrest.

The Tariff and the Politics of Protection.
The tariff became a potent political issue in the 1880s. The concept of a protective tariff to raise the price of imported goods and stimulate American industry dated back to the founding days of the Republic. Republicans turned the tariff to political ends in 1861 by enacting a measure that both raised revenues for the Civil War and rewarded their industrial supporters, who wanted protection from foreign competition. After the war, the pro-business Republicans continued to raise the tariff. Manufactured goods such as steel and textiles, and some agricultural products, including sugar and wool, benefited from protection. Most farm products, notably wheat and cotton, did not. By the 1880s, the tariff produced more than $2.1 billion in revenue. Not only did the high tariff pay off the nation's Civil War debt and fund pensions for Union soldiers, but it also created a huge surplus that sat idly in the Treasury's vaults while the government argued about how (or even whether) to spend it.

To many Americans, particularly southern and midwestern farmers who sold their crops in a world market but had to buy goods priced artificially high because of the protective tariff, the answer was simple: Reduce the tariff. But the Republican Party seized on the tariff question to forge a new national coalition. "Fold up the bloody shirt and lay it away," Blaine advised a colleague in 1880. "It's of no use to us. You want to shift the main issue to protection." By encouraging an alliance among industrialists, labor, and western producers of raw materials — groups seen to benefit from the tariff — Blaine hoped to solidify the North, Midwest, and West against the solidly Democratic South. Although the tactic failed for Blaine in the presidential election of 1884, it worked for the Republicans four years later.

Cleveland, who had straddled the tariff issue in the election of 1884, startled the nation in 1887 by calling for tariff reform. The president attacked the tariff as a tax levied on American consumers by powerful industries. And he pointed out that high tariffs impeded the expansion of American markets abroad at a time when American industries needed to expand. The Republicans countered by arguing that "tariff tinkering" would only unsettle prosperous industries, drive down wages, and shrink the farmers' home market. Republican Benjamin Harrison, who supported the high tariff, ousted Cleveland from the White House in 1888, carrying all the western and northern states except Connecticut and New Jersey.

Back in power, the Republicans brazenly passed the highest tariff in the nation's history in 1890. The new tariff, sponsored by Republican representative William McKinley of Ohio, stirred up a hornet's nest of protest across the United States. The American people had elected Harrison to preserve protection but not to enact a higher tariff. Democrats condemned the McKinley tariff and labeled the Republican Congress that passed it the "Billion Dollar Congress" for its carnival of spending, which depleted the nation's surplus by enacting a series of pork barrel programs shamelessly designed to bring federal money to congressmen's constituencies. In the congressional election of 1890, angry voters swept the hapless Republicans, including tariff sponsor McKinley, out of office. Two years later, Harrison himself was defeated, and Grover Cleveland returned to the White House. Such were the changes in the political winds whipped up by the tariff issue.

Controversy over the tariff masked deeper divisions in American society. Conflict between workers and farmers on the one side and bankers and corporate giants on the other erupted throughout the 1880s and came to a head in the 1890s. Both sides in the tariff debate spoke to concerns over class conflict when they insisted that their respective plans, whether McKinley's high tariff or Cleveland's tariff reform, would bring prosperity and harmony. For their part, many working people shared the sentiment voiced by one labor leader that the tariff was "only a scheme devised by the old parties to throw dust in the eyes of laboring men."

Railroads, Trusts, and the Federal Government.
American voters may have divided on the tariff, but increasingly they agreed on the need for federal regulation of the railroads and federal legislation to curb the power of the "trusts" (a term loosely applied to all large business combinations). As early as the 1870s, angry farmers in the Midwest who suffered from the unfair shipping practices of the railroads organized to fight for railroad regulation. The Patrons of Husbandry, or the Grange, founded in 1867 as a social and educational organization for farmers, soon became an independent political movement. By electing Grangers to state office, farmers made it possible for several midwestern states to pass laws in the 1870s and 1880s regulating the railroads. At first, the Supreme Court ruled in favor of state regulation (*Munn v. Illinois*, 1877). But in 1886, the Court reversed itself, ruling that because railroads crossed state boundaries, they fell outside state jurisdiction (*Wabash v. Illinois*). With more than three-fourths of railroads crossing state lines, the Supreme Court's decision effectively quashed the states' attempts at railroad regulation.

Anger at the *Wabash* decision finally led to the first federal law regulating the railroads, the Interstate Commerce Act, passed in 1887 during Cleveland's first administration. The act established the nation's first federal regulatory agency, the **Interstate Commerce Commission (ICC)**, to oversee the railroad industry. Railroad lobbyists worked furiously behind the scenes to make the new agency palatable to business leaders, many of whom felt a federal agency would be more lenient than state regulators. In its early years, the ICC was never strong enough to pose a serious threat to the railroads. For example, it could not end rebates to big shippers. In its early decades, the ICC proved more important as a precedent than effective as a watchdog.

Concern over the growing power of the trusts led Congress to pass the **Sherman Antitrust Act** in 1890. The act outlawed pools and trusts, ruling that businesses

---

Interstate Commerce Commission (ICC)
Federal regulatory agency designed to oversee the railroad industry. Congress created it through the 1887 Interstate Commerce Act after the Supreme Court decision in *Wabash v. Illinois* (1886) effectively denied states the right to regulate railroads. The ICC proved weak and did not immediately pose a threat to the industry.

Sherman Antitrust Act
1890 act that outlawed pools and trusts, ruling that businesses could no longer enter into agreements to restrict competition. Government inaction, combined with the Supreme Court's narrow reading of the act in the *United States v. E. C. Knight Company* decision, undermined the law's effectiveness.

could no longer enter into agreements to restrict competition. It did nothing to restrict huge holding companies such as Standard Oil, however, and proved to be a weak sword against the trusts. In the following decade, the government successfully struck down only six trusts but used the law four times against labor by outlawing unions as a "conspiracy in restraint of trade." In 1895, the conservative Supreme Court dealt the antitrust law a crippling blow in *United States v. E. C. Knight Company*. In its decision, the Court ruled that "manufacture" did not constitute "trade." This semantic quibble drastically narrowed the law, in this case allowing the American Sugar Refining Company, which had bought out a number of other sugar companies (including E. C. Knight) and controlled 98 percent of the production of sugar, to continue its virtual monopoly. Yet the Court insisted the law could be used against labor unions.

Both the ICC and the Sherman Antitrust Act testified to the nation's concern about corporate abuses of power and to a growing willingness to use federal measures to intervene on behalf of the public interest. As corporate capitalism became more and more powerful, public pressure toward government intervention grew. Yet not until the twentieth century would more active presidents sharpen and use these weapons effectively against the large corporations.

free silver
Term used in the late nineteenth century by those who advocated minting silver dollars in addition to supporting the gold standard and the paper currency backed by gold. Poor farmers from the West and South hoped this would result in inflation, effectively providing them with debt relief. Western silver barons wanted the government to buy silver and mint silver dollars, thereby raising the price of silver.

The Fight for Free Silver.
While the tariff and regulation of the trusts gained many backers, the silver issue stirred passions like no other issue of the day. On one side stood those who believed that gold constituted the only honest money. Many who supported the gold standard were eastern creditors who did not wish to be paid in devalued dollars. On the opposite side stood a coalition of western silver barons and poor farmers from the West and South who called for **free silver**. Farmers from the West and South hoped to increase the money supply with silver dollars and create inflation, which would give them some debt relief by enabling them to pay off their creditors with cheaper dollars. The mining interests, who had seen the silver bonanza in the West drive down the price of the precious metal, wanted the government to buy silver and mint silver dollars.

During the depression following the panic of 1873, critics of hard money organized the Greenback Labor Party, an alliance of farmers and urban wage laborers. The Greenbackers favored issuing paper currency not tied to the gold supply, citing the precedent of the greenbacks issued during the Civil War. The government had the right to define what constituted legal tender, the Greenbackers reasoned: "Paper is equally money, when . . . issued according to law." They proposed that the nation's currency be based on its wealth — land, labor, and capital — and not simply on its reserves of gold. The Greenback Labor Party captured more than a million votes and elected fourteen members to Congress in 1878. Although conservatives considered the

GREENBACK LABOR PARTY SEAL

The Greenback Labor Party, active in the 1870s, pushed for an inflationary currency that would give farmers and workers more money in circulation to help pay off debts. Its party seal is progressive for the era, focusing on the family by picturing a girl child and not a man or boy — a sign of how important women were in the organization. The Granger Collection, New York.

Greenbackers dangerous cranks, their views eventually prevailed in the 1930s, when the country abandoned the gold standard.

After the Greenback Labor Party collapsed, proponents of free silver came to dominate the monetary debate in the 1890s. Advocates of free silver pointed out that until 1873 the country had enjoyed a system of bimetallism — the minting of both silver and gold into coins. In that year, at the behest of those who favored gold, the Republican Congress had voted to stop buying and minting silver, an act silver supporters denounced as the "crime of '73." By sharply contracting the money supply at a time when the nation's economy was burgeoning, the Republicans had enriched bankers and investors at the expense of cotton and wheat farmers and industrial wageworkers. In 1878 and again in 1890, with the Sherman Silver Purchase Act, Congress took steps to ease the tight money policy and appease advocates of silver by passing legislation requiring the government to buy silver and issue silver certificates. Though good for the mining interests, the laws did little to promote the inflation desired by farmers. Soon monetary reformers began to call for "the free and unlimited coinage of silver," a plan whereby nearly all the silver mined in the West would be minted into coins circulated at the rate of sixteen ounces of silver — equal in value to one ounce of gold.

By the 1890s, the silver issue crossed party lines. The Democrats hoped to use it to achieve a union between western and southern voters. Unfortunately for them, Democratic president Grover Cleveland supported the gold standard as vehemently as any Republican. After a panic on Wall Street in the spring of 1893, Cleveland called a special session of Congress and bullied the legislature into repealing the Silver Purchase Act because he believed it threatened economic confidence. Repeal proved disastrous for Cleveland. It did nothing to bring prosperity and dangerously divided the country. Angry farmers warned Cleveland not to travel west of the Mississippi River if he valued his life.

Panic and Depression.

President Cleveland had scarcely begun his second term in 1893 when the country plunged into the worst depression it had yet seen. In the face of economic disaster, Cleveland clung to the economic orthodoxy of the gold standard. In the winter of 1894–95, the president walked the floor of the White House, sleepless over the prospect that the United States might go bankrupt. Individuals and investors, rushing to trade in their banknotes for gold, strained the country's monetary system. The Treasury's gold reserves dipped so low that unless they could be buttressed, the unthinkable might happen: The U.S. Treasury might not be able to meet its obligations.

At this juncture, J. P. Morgan stepped in. A group of bankers pledged to purchase millions in U.S. government bonds, paying in gold. Cleveland knew that such a scheme would unleash a thunder of protest, yet to save the gold standard, the president had no choice. But if President Cleveland's action managed to salvage the gold standard, it did not save the country from hardship. In the winter of 1894–95, people faced unemployment, cold, and hunger. Cleveland, a firm believer in limited government, insisted that nothing could be done to help: "I do not believe that the power and duty of the General Government ought to be extended to the relief of individual suffering which is in no manner properly related to the public service or benefit." Nor did it occur to Cleveland that his great faith in the gold standard prolonged the depression, favored creditors over debtors, and caused immense hardship for millions of Americans.

> **REVIEW** What role did economic issues play in party realignment?

Conclusion: Business Dominates an Era

The gold deal between J. P. Morgan and Grover Cleveland underscored a dangerous reality: The federal government was so weak that its solvency depended on a private banker. This lopsided power relationship signaled the dominance of business in the era Mark Twain satirically but accurately characterized as the Gilded Age. Birthed by the railroads, the new economy spawned greed, corruption, and vulgarity on a grand scale. Speculators like Jay Gould not only built but also wrecked railroads to turn paper profits; the get-rich-quick ethic of the gold rush infused the whole continent; and business boasted openly of buying politicians, who in turn lined their pockets at the public's expense.

Nevertheless, the Gilded Age was not without its share of solid achievements. Where dusty roads and cattle trails once sprawled across the continent, steel rails now bound the country together, creating a national market that enabled America to make the leap into the industrial age. Factories and refineries poured out American steel and oil at unprecedented rates. Businessmen like Carnegie, Rockefeller, and Morgan developed new strategies to consolidate American industry. New inventions, including the telephone and electric light and power, transformed Americans' everyday lives.

By the end of the nineteenth century, the United States had achieved industrial maturity. It boasted the largest, most innovative, most productive economy in the world. The rise of Gilded Age industry came at a cost, however. The rampant railway building changed the nature of politics in the United States, entwining the state and the corporations and making a mockery of a free market economy. And as one historian speculated, had railroad magnates waited to build western railroads to meet demand, their restraint might have resulted in less waste, less environmental degradation, and less human suffering for Native Americans and whites alike.

The effects of American industry worried many Americans and gave rise to the era's political turmoil. Race and gender profoundly influenced American politics, leading to new political alliances. Fearless activist Ida B. Wells fought racism in its most brutal form — lynching. Women's organizations championed causes, notably suffrage and temperance, and challenged prevailing views of woman's proper sphere. Reformers fought corruption by instituting civil service. And new issues — the tariff, the regulation of the trusts, and currency reform — restructured the nation's politics.

The Gilded Age witnessed a nation transformed. Fueled by railroad building and expanding industry, cities grew exponentially, bulging at the seams with new inhabitants from around the globe and bristling with new bridges, subways, and skyscrapers. The frenzied growth of urban America brought wealth and opportunity, but also the exploitation of labor, racism toward newcomers, and social upheaval that lent a new urgency to calls for social reform.

Chapter Review

KEY TERMS

Gilded Age (p. 520)

trust (p. 526)

finance capitalism (p. 528)

social Darwinism (p. 530)

gospel of wealth (p. 530)

spoils system (p. 531)

Jim Crow (p. 533)

Woman's Christian Temperance Union (WCTU) (p. 537)

civil service reform (p. 539)

Interstate Commerce Commission (ICC) (p. 542)

Sherman Antitrust Act (p. 542)

free silver (p. 543)

REVIEW QUESTIONS

1 When, why, and how did the transcontinental railroad system develop, and what was its impact on American business?   (pp. 520–28)

2 Why did the ideas of social Darwinism appeal to many Americans in the late nineteenth century?   (pp. 528–31)

3 How did race and gender influence politics?   (pp. 531–37)

4 How did the question of civil service reform contribute to divisions within the Republican Party?   (pp. 537–40)

5 What role did economic issues play in party realignment?   (pp. 540–45)

MAKING CONNECTIONS

❶ What were some of the key technology and business innovations in the late nineteenth century? How did they aid the maturation of American industry?

❷ By the 1870s, what new issues displaced slavery as the defining question of American politics, and how did they shape new regional, economic, and racial alliances and rivalries?

❸ How did the activism of women denied the vote contribute to Gilded Age electoral politics? Be sure to cite specific examples of political action.

❹ Citing specific policies and court decisions, discuss how government helped augment the power of big business in the late nineteenth century.

LINKING TO THE PAST

❶ In what ways did the military conquest of the trans-Mississippi West, with its dislocation of Native Americans, play a significant role in the industrial boom of the Gilded Age? (See chapter 17.)

❷ In what ways did the rampant get-rich-quick mentality of western miners and land speculators help set the tone for the Gilded Age? Is the West the herald of the Gilded Age, or must we look to New York and Washington? (See chapter 17.)

19

The City and Its Workers,
1870–1900

CONTENT LEARNING OBJECTIVES

After reading and studying this chapter, you should be able to:

- Identify the factors that led to rapid urbanization during the late nineteenth century. Describe how the social geography of the city changed and the reactions to those changes.
- Describe the diversity of American labor, including the role of women and children in the workforce.
- Understand why workers organized and how management responded to labor's demands. Analyze the impact of the Great Strike of 1877, the Knights of Labor, the American Federation of Labor, and the Haymarket bombing.
- Describe how notions of domesticity and everyday amusements reflected class divisions.
- Identify the nature of city government in the late nineteenth century and the growth of city amenities. Explain Americans' ambivalence toward cities.

"A town that crawled now stands erect, and we whose backs were bent above the hearths know how it got its spine," boasted a steelworker surveying New York City. Where once wooden buildings stood rooted in the mire of unpaved streets, cities of stone and steel sprang up in the last decades of the nineteenth century. The labor of millions of workers, many of them immigrants, laid the foundations for urban America.

No symbol better represented the new urban landscape than the Brooklyn Bridge, opened in May 1883. The great bridge soared over the East River in a single mile-long span. Building the Brooklyn Bridge took fourteen years and cost the lives of twenty-seven men. To sink the foundation in the riverbed, laborers tunneled through the mud and worked in

BROOKLYN BRIDGE FAN

This commemorative fan celebrates the opening of the bridge on May 24, 1883. It took fourteen years and cost the lives of twenty-seven men to complete the bridge.
© Museum of the City of New York, USA/Bridgeman Images.

boxes that were open at the bottom and pressurized to keep the water out. Before long workers experienced the malady they called "bends" because it left them doubled over in pain when they rose to the surface. (Scientists later learned that nitrogen bubbles trapped in the bloodstream caused the bends, which could be prevented by allowing for decompression.) The first death occurred when the foundation reached a depth of seventy-one feet. A German immigrant complained that he did not feel well. He collapsed and died on his way home. Eight days later, another man dropped dead, and the entire workforce went out on strike. Terrified workers demanded a higher wage for fewer hours of work.

A scrawny sixteen-year-old from Ireland, Frank Harris, remembered the fearful experience of going to work on the bridge a few days after landing in America:

> The six of us were working naked to the waist in the small iron chamber with the temperature of about 80 degrees Fahrenheit: In five minutes the sweat was pouring from us, and all the while we were standing in icy water that was only kept from rising by the terrific pressure. No wonder the headaches were blinding.

By his fifth day, Harris quit. Many immigrant workers walked off the job, often as many as a hundred a week. But a ready supply of immigrants meant that new workers took up the digging, where they could earn in a day more than they made in a week in Ireland or Italy.

Begun in 1869, the bridge was the dream of builder John Roebling, who died in a freak accident almost as soon as construction began. Washington Roebling took over as chief engineer after his father's death, routinely working twelve- to fourteen-hour days, six days a week. Soon he too fell victim to the bends. He directed the completion of the bridge through a telescope from his bedroom window in Brooklyn Heights. His wife, Emily Warren Roebling, acted as site superintendent and general engineer of the project.

At the end of the nineteenth century, the Brooklyn Bridge stood as a symbol of many things: the industrial might of the United States; the labor of the nation's immigrants; the ingenuity and genius of its engineers and inventors; the rise of iron and steel; and, most of all, the ascendancy of urban America. Poised on the brink of the twentieth century, the nation was shifting from a rural, agricultural society to an urban, industrial nation. The gap between rich

CHRONOLOGY

1869	Knights of Labor founded. Cincinnati mounts first paid baseball team.
1871	Boss Tweed's rule in New York City ends. Chicago's Great Fire breaks out.
1873	Panic on Wall Street touches off depression.
1877	Great Railroad Strike paralyzes nation.
1880s	Immigration from southern and eastern Europe rises.
1882	Chinese Exclusion Act enacted.
1883	Brooklyn Bridge opens.
1886	American Federation of Labor founded. Haymarket bombing occurs in Chicago.
1890	Jacob Riis publishes *How the Other Half Lives*.
1890s	African American migration from the South begins.
1892	Ellis Island opens.
1893	World's Columbian Exposition opens in Chicago. Panic on Wall Street touches off major economic depression.
1895	Boston Public Library opens in Copley Square.
1896	President Grover Cleveland vetoes immigrant literacy test.
1897	Steeplechase Park opens on Coney Island. Nation's first subway system opens in Boston.

WORKERS ON THE BROOKLYN BRIDGE
Illustrations show workers tunneling under the East River to lay the foundations for the Brooklyn Bridge. A cylindrical airlock took them down more than seventy feet. "What with the flaming lights, the deep shadows, the confusing noise of hammer, drills, and chains, the half-naked forms flitting about," wrote one reporter, the scene resembled hell.
Library of Congress, 3c24944.

and poor widened. In the burgeoning cities, tensions erupted into conflict as workers squared off to organize into labor unions and to demand safer working conditions, shorter hours, and better pay, sometimes with violent and bloody results. The explosive growth of the cities fostered political corruption as unscrupulous bosses and entrepreneurs cashed in on the building boom. Immigrants, political bosses, middle-class managers, poor laborers, and the very rich populated the nation's cities, crowding the streets, laboring in the stores and factories, and taking their leisure at the new ballparks, amusement parks, dance halls, and municipal parks. As the new century dawned, the city and its workers moved to center stage in American life.

The Rise of the City

"We cannot all live in cities, yet nearly all seem determined to do so," New York editor Horace Greeley complained. The last three decades of the nineteenth century witnessed an urban explosion. Cities and towns grew more than twice as rapidly as the total population. By 1900, the United States boasted three cities with more than a million inhabitants — New York, Chicago, and Philadelphia.

Patterns of **global migration** contributed to the rise of the city. In the port cities of the East Coast, more than fourteen million people arrived, many from southern and eastern Europe, and huddled together in dense urban ghettos. The word *slum* entered the American vocabulary along with a growing concern over the rising tide of newcomers. In the city, the widening gap between rich and poor became not just financial but physical. Changes in the city landscape brought about by advances in transportation and technology accentuated the great divide in wealth at the same time they put physical distance between rich and poor.

The Urban Explosion: A Global Migration.
The United States grew up in the country and moved to the city, or so it seemed by the end of the nineteenth century. Between 1870 and 1900, eleven million people moved into cities. Burgeoning industrial centers such as Pittsburgh, Chicago, New York, and Cleveland acted as giant magnets, attracting workers from the countryside. But rural Americans were not the only ones migrating to cities. Millions of immigrants moved from their native countries to America. Worldwide in scope, the movement from rural areas to urban industrial centers attracted millions of immigrants to American shores.

By the 1870s, the world could be conceptualized as three interconnected geographic regions (Map 19.1). At the center stood an industrial core that encompassed the eastern United States and western Europe. Surrounding this industrial core lay a vast agricultural domain from the Canadian wheat fields to the hinterlands of northern China. Capitalist development in the late nineteenth century shattered traditional patterns of economic activity in this rural periphery. As old patterns broke down, these rural areas exported, along with other raw materials, new recruits for the industrial labor force.

Beyond this second circle lay an even larger third world. Colonial ties between this part of the world and the industrial core strengthened in the late nineteenth century, but most of the people living there stayed put. They worked on plantations and railroads, and in mines and ports, as part of a huge export network managed by foreign powers that staked out spheres of influence and colonies in this vast region.

In the 1870s, railroad expansion and low steamship fares gave the world's peoples a newfound mobility, enabling industrialists to draw on a global population for cheap labor. When Andrew Carnegie opened his first steel mill in 1872, his superintendent hired workers he called "buckwheats" — young American boys just off the farm. By the 1890s, however, Carnegie's workforce was liberally sprinkled with other rural boys, Hungarians and Slavs who had migrated to the United States, willing to work for low wages.

Altogether, more than 25 million immigrants came to the United States between 1850 and 1920. They came from all directions: east from Asia, south from Canada, north from Latin America, and west from Europe (Map 19.2). Part of a worldwide migration, emigrants traveled to South America and Australia as well as to the United States. Yet more than 70 percent of all European emigrants chose North America as their destination.

Historically, the largest number of immigrants to the United States came from the British Isles and from German-speaking lands (Figure 19.1). The vast majority of immigrants were white; Asians accounted for fewer than one million immigrants,

global migration
Movement of populations across large distances such as oceans and continents. In the late nineteenth century, large-scale immigration from southern and eastern Europe into the United States contributed to the growth of cities and changes in American demographics.

and other people of color numbered even fewer. Yet ingrained racial prejudices increasingly influenced the country's perception of immigration patterns. One of the classic formulations of the history of European immigration divided immigrants into two distinct waves that have been called the "old" and the "new" immigration. According to this theory, before 1880 the majority of immigrants came from northern and western Europe, with Germans, Irish, English, and Scandinavians making up approximately 85 percent of the newcomers. After 1880, the pattern shifted, with more and more ships carrying passengers from southern and eastern Europe. Italians, Hungarians, eastern European Jews, Turks, Armenians, Poles, Russians, and

Map Activity

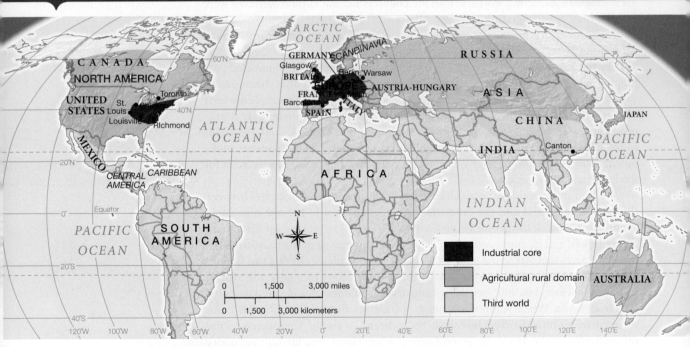

MAP 19.1 ECONOMIC REGIONS OF THE WORLD, 1890

The global nature of the world economy at the turn of the twentieth century is indicated by three interconnected geographic regions. At the center stands the industrial core — western Europe and the northeastern United States. The second region — the agricultural periphery — supplied immigrant laborers to the industries in the core. Beyond these two regions lay a vast area tied economically to the industrial core by colonialism.

READING THE MAP: What types of economic regions were contained in the United States in this period? Which continents held most of the industrial core? Which held most of the agricultural rural domain? Which held the greatest portion of the third world?

CONNECTIONS: Which of these three regions provided the bulk of immigrant workers to the United States? What major changes prompted the global migration at the end of the nineteenth century?

other Slavic peoples accounted for more than 80 percent of all immigrants by 1896 (Figure 19.2). Implicit in the distinction was an invidious comparison between "old" pioneer settlers and "new" unskilled laborers. Yet this sweeping generalization spoke more to perception than to reality. In fact, many of the earlier immigrants from Ireland, Germany, and Scandinavia came not as settlers or farmers, but as wage-workers, and they were met with much the same disdain as the Italians and Slavs who followed them.

During good financial times, the need for cheap, unskilled labor for America's industries stimulated demand for immigrant workers. In 1873 and again in 1893, when the United States experienced economic depressions, immigration slowed, only to pick up again when prosperity returned. Steamship companies courted immigrants — a highly profitable, self-loading cargo. By the 1880s, the price of a ticket from Liverpool had dropped to less than $25. Would-be immigrants eager for information about the United States relied on letters from friends and relatives, advertisements, and word of mouth — sources that were not always dependable or truthful. As one Italian immigrant recalled, "News was colored, success magnified, comforts and advantages exaggerated beyond all proportions." Even photographs proved deceptive: Workers dressed in their Sunday best looked more prosperous than they actually were to relatives in the old country, where only the very wealthy wore white collars or silk dresses. No wonder people left for the United States

Map Activity

MAP 19.2   THE IMPACT OF IMMIGRATION, TO 1910

Immigration flowed in all directions — south from Canada, north from Mexico and Latin America, east from Asia, and west from Europe.

READING THE MAP: Which states had the highest percentages of immigrants? Which cities attracted the most immigrants? Which cities attracted the fewest?

CONNECTIONS: Why did most immigrants gravitate toward the cities? Why do you think the South drew such a low percentage of immigrants?

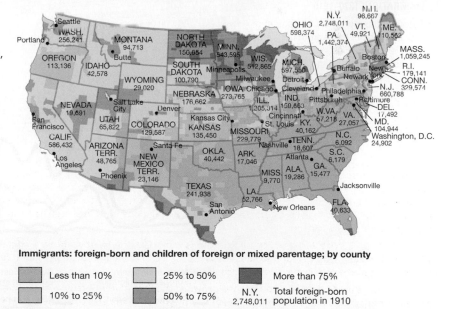

Immigrants: foreign-born and children of foreign or mixed parentage; by county

Less than 10%	25% to 50%	More than 75%
10% to 25%	50% to 75%	N.Y. 2,748,011 Total foreign-born population in 1910

FIGURE 19.1 GLOBAL COMPARISON: EUROPEAN EMIGRATION, 1870–1890

European emigration between 1870 and 1890 shows that people from Germany, Austria, and the British Isles formed the largest group of out-migrants. After 1890, the origin of European emigrants tilted south and east, with Italians and eastern European growing in number. The United States took in nearly two-thirds of the European emigrants. What factors account for the popularity of the United States?

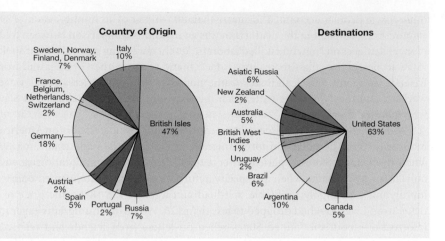

Country of Origin

Sweden, Norway, Finland, Denmark 7%
Italy 10%
France, Belgium, Netherlands, Switzerland 2%
Germany 18%
Austria 2%
Spain 5%
Portugal 2%
Russia 7%
British Isles 47%

Destinations

Asiatic Russia 6%
New Zealand 2%
Australia 5%
British West Indies 1%
Uruguay 2%
Brazil 6%
Argentina 10%
Canada 5%
United States 63%

believing, as one Italian immigrant observed, "that if they were ever fortunate enough to reach America, they would fall into a pile of manure and get up brushing the diamonds out of their hair."

Most of the newcomers stayed in the nation's cities. By 1900, almost two-thirds of the country's immigrant population resided in cities. Many of the immigrants

FIGURE 19.2 EUROPEAN EMIGRATION, 1870–1910

Before 1880, more than 85 percent of U.S. immigrants came from northern and western Europe — Germany, Ireland, England, and the Scandinavian countries. After 1880, 80 percent of the "new" immigrants came from Italy, Turkey, Hungary, Armenia, Poland, Russia, and other Slavic countries.

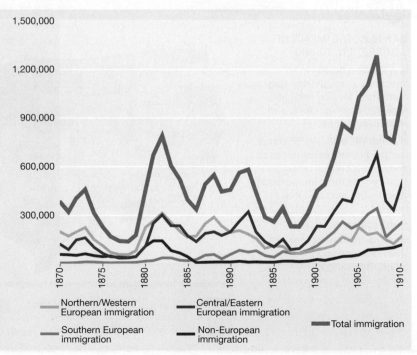

Northern/Western European immigration
Southern European immigration
Central/Eastern European immigration
Non-European immigration
Total immigration

were too poor to move on. (The average laborer immigrating to the United States carried only about $21.50.) Although the foreign-born rarely outnumbered the native-born population, taken together immigrants and their American-born children did constitute a majority in some areas, particularly in the nation's largest cities: Philadelphia, 55 percent; Boston, 66 percent; Chicago, 75 percent; and New York City, an amazing 80 percent in 1900.

Not all the newcomers came to stay. Perhaps eight million European immigrants — most of them young men — worked for a year or a season and then returned to their homelands. Immigration officers called these immigrants, many of them Italians, "birds of passage" because they followed a regular pattern of migration to and from the United States. By 1900, almost 75 percent of the new immigrants were young, single men. Willing to accept conditions other workers regarded as intolerable, these young migrants showed little interest in labor unions. They organized only when the dream of returning home faded, as it did for millions who ultimately remained in the United States.

Women generally had less access to funds for travel and faced tighter family control. Because the traditional sexual division of labor relied on women's unpaid domestic labor and care of the very young and the very old, women most often came to the United States as wives, mothers, or daughters, not as single wage laborers. Only among the Irish, where the great potato famine presented the grim choice of starve or leave, did women immigrants outnumber men by a small margin from 1871 to 1891.

Jews from eastern Europe and Russia most often came with their families and came to stay. Fear of conscription into the Russian army motivated many young men to leave Russia. In addition, beginning in the 1880s, a wave of violent pogroms, or persecutions, in Russia and Poland prompted the departure of more than a million Jews in the next two decades. Mary Antin, a Jew leaving Poland for America, recalled her excitement: "So, at last I was going to America! Really going at last! The boundaries burst. The arch of heaven soared. . . . America! America!" Most of the Jewish immigrants settled in the port cities of the East, creating distinct ethnic enclaves, like Hester Street in the heart of New York City's Lower East Side, which rang with the calls of pushcart peddlers and vendors hawking their wares, from pickles to feather beds.

Racism and the Cry for Immigration Restriction.
Ethnic diversity and racism played a role in dividing skilled workers (those with a craft or specialized ability) from the globe-hopping proletariat of unskilled workers (those who supplied muscle or tended machines). Skilled workers, frequently members of older immigrant groups, criticized the newcomers. One Irish worker complained, "There should be a law . . . to keep all the Italians from comin' in and takin' the bread out of the mouths of honest people."

The Irish worker's resentment brings into focus the impact racism had on America's immigrant laborers. Throughout the nineteenth century and into the twentieth, members of the educated elite as well as the uneducated viewed ethnic and even religious differences as racial characteristics, referring to the Polish or the Jewish "race." Americans judged immigrants of southern and eastern European

PUSHCART PEDDLERS IN LITTLE ITALY

This photo shows banana sellers working from a pushcart in a street in New York's Little Italy. Italian immigrants constituted the majority of banana importers at the turn of the twentieth century. Library of Congress, 3c31516.

"races" as inferior. Each wave of newcomers was deemed somehow inferior to the established residents. The Irish who criticized the Italians so harshly had themselves been stigmatized as a lesser "race" a generation earlier.

Immigrants not only brought their own religious and racial prejudices to the United States but also absorbed the popular prejudices of American culture. Social Darwinism, with its strongly racist overtones, decreed that whites stood at the top of the evolutionary ladder. But who was "white"? Skin color supposedly served as a marker for the "new" immigrants — "swarthy" Italians; dark-haired, olive-skinned Jews. But even blond, blue-eyed Poles were not considered "white." The social construction of race is nowhere more apparent than in the testimony of an Irish dockworker, who boasted that he hired only "white men," a category that he insisted excluded "Poles and Italians." For the new immigrants, Americanization and assimilation would prove inextricably part of becoming "white."

For African Americans, the cities of the North promised not just economic opportunity but an escape from institutionalized segregation and persecution. Throughout the South, Jim Crow laws — restrictions that segregated blacks — became common in the decades following reconstruction. Intimidation and lynching terrorized blacks. "To die from the bite of frost is far more glorious than at the hands of a mob," proclaimed the *Defender*, Chicago's largest African American newspaper. In the 1890s, many blacks moved north, settling for the most part in the growing cities. Racism relegated them to poor jobs and substandard living conditions, but by 1900 New York, Philadelphia, and Chicago had the largest black communities in the nation. Although the most significant African American migration out of the South would occur during and after World War I, the great exodus was already under way.

On the West Coast, Asian immigrants became scapegoats of the changing economy. Hard times in the 1870s made them a target for disgruntled workers, who dismissed them as "coolie" labor. Contract laborers recruited by employers, or later by prosperous members of their own race or ethnicity, represented the antithesis of free labor to the workers who competed with them. In the West, the issue became racialized, and while the Chinese were by no means the only contract laborers, the Sinophobia that produced the scapegoat of the "coolie" permeated the labor movement. Prohibited from owning land, the Chinese migrated to the cities. In 1870, San Francisco housed a Chinese population estimated at 12,022, and it continued to grow until passage of the Chinese Exclusion Act in 1882 (see chapter 17). For the first time in the nation's history, U.S. law excluded an immigrant group on the basis of race.

Some Chinese managed to come to America using a loophole in the exclusion law that allowed relatives to join their families. Meanwhile the number of Japanese immigrants rapidly grew until pressure to keep out all Asians led in 1910 to the creation of an immigration station at Angel Island in San Francisco Bay where immigrants were quarantined until judged fit to enter the United States.

On the East Coast, the volume of immigration from Europe in the last two decades of the century proved unprecedented. In 1888 alone, more than half a million Europeans landed in America, 75 percent of them in New York City. The Statue of Liberty, erected in 1886 as a gift from the people of France, stood sentinel in the harbor.

A young Jewish woman named Emma Lazarus penned the verse inscribed on Lady Liberty's base:

> Give me your tired, your poor,
> Your huddled masses yearning to breathe free,
> The wretched refuse of your teeming shore.
> Send these, the homeless, tempest-tost to me,
> I lift my lamp beside the golden door!

Lazarus's poem stood as both a promise and a warning. With increasing immigration, some Americans soon would question whether the country really wanted the "huddled masses" or the "wretched refuse" of the world.

The tide of immigrants to New York City soon swamped the immigration office in lower Manhattan. After the federal government took over immigration in 1890, it built a facility on **Ellis Island**, in New York harbor, which opened in 1892. After fire gutted the wooden building, a new brick edifice replaced it in 1900. Able to process 5,000 immigrants a day, it was already inadequate by the time it opened. Its overcrowded halls became the gateway to the United States for millions.

To many Americans the new southern and eastern European immigrants appeared backward, uneducated, and outlandish in appearance — impossible to assimilate. "These people are not Americans," editorialized the popular journal *Public Opinion*, "they are the very scum and offal of Europe." Terence V. Powderly, head of the broadly inclusive Knights of Labor, complained that the newcomers "herded together like animals and lived like beasts." Blue-blooded Yankees led by Senator Henry Cabot Lodge of Massachusetts formed an unlikely alliance with leaders of organized labor — who feared that immigrants would drive down wages — to press for immigration restrictions. In 1896, Congress approved a literacy test for

Ellis Island
Immigration facility opened in 1892 in New York harbor that processed new immigrants coming into New York City. In the late nineteenth century, some 75 percent of European immigrants to America came through New York.

immigrants, but President Grover Cleveland promptly vetoed it. "It is said," the president reminded Congress, "that the quality of recent immigration is undesirable. The time is quite within recent memory when the same thing was said of immigrants who, with their descendants, are now numbered among our best citizens."

The Social Geography of the City.

During the Gilded Age, the social geography of the city changed enormously. Cleveland, Ohio, provides a good example. In the 1870s, Cleveland was a small city in both population and area. Oil magnate John D. Rockefeller could, and often did, walk from his large brick house on Euclid Avenue to his office downtown. On his way, he passed the small homes of his clerks and other middle-class families. Behind these homes ran miles of alleys crowded with the dwellings of Cleveland's working class. Farther out, on the shores of Lake Erie, close to the factories and foundries, clustered the shanties of the city's poorest laborers.

Within two decades, the Cleveland that Rockefeller knew no longer existed. The coming of mass transit transformed the walking city. In its place emerged a central business district surrounded by concentric rings of residences organized by ethnicity and income. First the horsecar in the 1870s and then the electric streetcar in the 1880s made it possible for those who could afford the five-cent fare to work downtown and flee after work to the "cool green rim" of the city. Social segregation — the separation of rich and poor, and of ethnic and old-stock Americans — became one of the major social changes engendered by the rise of the industrial metropolis.

Race and ethnicity affected the way cities evolved. Newcomers to the nation's cities faced hostility and, not surprisingly, sought out their kin and countryfolk as

THE ARRIVAL OF THE ELECTRIC STREETCAR

The electric streetcar was part of the transformation of the cityscape in the late nineteenth century. This shiny new streetcar stands in front of Cincinnati's City Hall in 1890. Corbis.

they struggled to get ahead. Distinct ethnic neighborhoods often formed around a synagogue or church. African Americans typically experienced the greatest residential segregation, but every large city had its distinct ethnic neighborhoods — Little Italy, Chinatown, Bohemia Flats, Germantown — where English was rarely spoken.

Poverty, crowding, dirt, and disease constituted the daily reality of New York City's immigrant poor — a plight documented by photojournalist Jacob Riis in his best-selling book *How the Other Half Lives* (1890). By taking his camera into the hovels of the poor, Riis opened the nation's eyes to the filthy, overcrowded conditions in the city's slums (as discussed in chapter 21).

However, Riis's book, like his photographs, presented a world of black and white. There were many layers to the population Riis labeled "the other half" — distinctions deepened by ethnicity, religion, race, and gender. *How the Other Half Lives* must be read more as a reformer's call to action than as an entirely accurate portrayal of the varied and complex lives of "the other half." But it served its purpose. Tenement reform and city playgrounds grew out of Riis's exposé.

While Riis's audience shivered at his revelations about the "other half," many middle-class Americans worried equally about the excesses of the wealthy. They feared the class antagonism fueled by the growing chasm between rich and poor and shared Riis's view that "the real danger to society comes not only from the tenements, but from the ill-spent wealth which reared them."

The excesses of the Gilded Age's newly minted millionaires were nowhere more visible than in the lifestyle of the Vanderbilts. Cornelius "Commodore" Vanderbilt, the uncouth ferryman who built the New York Central Railroad, died in 1877. Today he still holds first place among the richest men in America (when adjusted for inflation). He left his son William $90 million. William doubled the sum, and his two sons proceeded to spend it on Fifth Avenue mansions and "cottages" in Newport, Rhode Island, that sought to rival the palaces of Europe. Alva Vanderbilt, looked down on by the old-money matrons of New York, launched herself into New York society in 1883 with a costume party so opulent that her detractors had to cave in and accept her invitation. Alice Vanderbilt, her sister, topped all the guests by appearing as that miraculous new invention, the electric light, resplendent in a white satin evening dress studded with diamonds. The *New York World* speculated that Alva's party cost more than a quarter of a million dollars, more than $5 million in today's dollars.

Such ostentatious displays of wealth became especially alarming when they were coupled with disdain for the well-being of ordinary people. When a reporter in 1882 asked William Vanderbilt whether he considered the public good when running his railroads, he shot back, "The public be damned." The fear that America had become a plutocracy — a society ruled by the rich — gained credence from the fact that the wealthiest 1 percent of the population owned more than half the real and personal property in the country. As the new century dawned, reformers would form a progressive movement to address the problems of urban industrialism and the substandard living and working conditions it produced.

REVIEW Why did American cities experience explosive growth in the late nineteenth century?

At Work in Industrial America

The number of industrial wageworkers in the United States exploded in the second half of the nineteenth century, more than tripling from 5.3 million in 1860 to 17.4 million in 1900. These workers toiled in a variety of settings. Many skilled workers and artisans still earned a living in small workshops. But with the rise of corporate capitalism, large factories, mills, and mines increasingly dotted the land-scape. Sweatshops and the contracting out of piecework, including finishing garments by hand, provided work experiences different from those of factory opera-tives and industrial workers. Pick-and-shovel labor constituted the lowest-paid labor, while managers, as well as women "typewriters" and salesclerks, formed a new white-collar segment of America's workforce. Children also worked in growing numbers in mills and mines across the country.

America's Diverse Workers. Common laborers formed the backbone of the American labor force. They built the railroads and subways, tunneled under New York's East River to anchor the Brooklyn Bridge, and helped lay the foundation of industrial America. These "human machines" generally came from the most recent immigrant groups. Initially, the Irish wielded the picks and shovels that built Ameri-can cities, but by the turn of the century, as the Irish bettered their lot, Slavs and Italians took up their tools.

At the opposite end of labor's hierarchy stood skilled craftsmen like iron pud-dler James J. Davis, a Welsh immigrant who worked in the Pennsylvania mills. Using brains along with brawn, puddlers earned good wages — Davis drew up to $7 a day at a time when streetcar fare was 3 cents — when there was work. But most industry and manufacturing work in the nineteenth century remained seasonal; few workers could count on year-round pay. In addition, two major depressions twenty years apart, beginning in 1873 and 1893, brought unemployment and hardship. With no social safety net, even the best worker could not guarantee security for his family. "The fear of ending in the poor-house is one of the terrors that dog a man through life," Davis confessed.

Employers attempted to replace people with machines, breaking down skilled work into ever-smaller tasks that could be performed by unskilled factory opera-tives. New England's textile mills provide a classic example. Mary, a weaver at the mills in Fall River, Massachusetts, went to work in the 1880s at the age of twelve. Mechanization of the looms had reduced the job of the weaver to watching for breaks in the thread. "At first the noise is fierce, and you have to breathe the cotton all the time, but you get used to it," Mary told a reporter from the *Independent* magazine. "When the bobbin flies out and a girl gets hurt, you can't hear her shout — not if she just screams, you can't. She's got to wait, 'till you see her. . . . Lots of us is deaf."

During the 1880s, the number of foreign-born mill workers almost doubled. At Fall River, Mary and her Scots-Irish family resented the new immigrants. "The Polaks learn weavin' quick," she remarked, using a common derogatory term to identify a rival group. "They just as soon live on nothin' and work like that. But it won't do 'em much good for all they'll make out of it." Employers encouraged racial and ethnic antagonism because it inhibited labor organization.

Mechanization transformed the garment industry as well. The introduction of the foot-pedaled sewing machine in the 1850s and the use of mechanical cloth-cutting knives drove out independent tailors, who were replaced by pieceworkers. Sadie Frowne, a sixteen-year-old Polish Jew, worked in a Brooklyn **sweatshop** in the 1890s. Frowne sewed for eleven hours a day in a 20-by-14-foot room containing fourteen machines. "The machines go like mad all day, because the faster you work the more money you get," she recalled. She earned about $4.50 a week and, by rigid economy, tried to save $2. Young and single, Frowne typified the woman wage earner in the late nineteenth century. In 1890, the average workingwoman was twenty-two and had been working since the age of fifteen, laboring twelve hours a day six days a week and earning less than $6 a week.

The Family Economy: Women and Children.

In 1900, the typical male worker in manufacturing earned $500 a year, about $12,000 in today's dollars. Many working-class families, whether native-born or immigrant, lived in or near poverty, their economic survival dependent on the contributions of all family members, regardless of sex or age. "Father," asked one young immigrant girl, "does everybody in America live like this? Go to work early, come home late, eat and go to sleep? And the next day again work, eat, and sleep?" Most workers did. The **family economy** meant that everyone contributed to maintain even the most meager household.

sweatshop
A small room used for clothing piecework beginning in the late nineteenth century. As mechanization transformed the garment industry with the introduction of foot-pedaled sewing machines and mechanical cloth-cutting knives, independent tailors were replaced with sweatshop workers hired by contractors to sew pieces into clothing.

family economy
Economic contributions of multiple members of a household that were necessary to the survival of the family. From the late nineteenth century into the twentieth, many working-class families depended on the wages of all family members, regardless of sex or age.

WOMEN AT WORK
Women workers labor under bright lights in this tenement hat shop in New York City. Often sweatshop workers labored in dim tenements belonging to the contractor who hired them. Garment workers frequently worked with highly combustible fabric in unsafe buildings. The Granger Collection, New York.

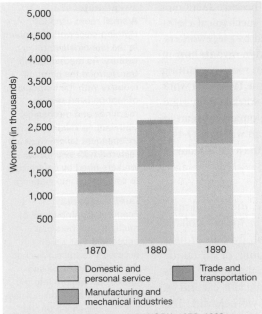

FIGURE 19.3 WOMEN AND WORK, 1870–1890

In 1870, close to 1.5 million women worked in nonagricultural occupations. By 1890, that number had more than doubled to 3.7 million. More and more women sought work in manufacturing and mechanical industries, although domestic service still constituted the largest employment arena for women.

In the cities, boys as young as six years old plied their trades as bootblacks and newsboys. Often working under an adult contractor, these children earned as little as fifty cents a day. Many of them were homeless — orphaned or cast off by their families. "We wuz six, and we ain't got no father," a child of twelve told reporter Jacob Riis. "Some of us had to go."

Child labor increased each decade after 1870. The percentage of children under fifteen engaged in paid labor did not drop until after World War I. The 1900 census estimated that 1,750,178 children ages ten to fifteen were employed, an increase of more than a million over thirty years. Children in this age range constituted more than 18 percent of the industrial labor force.

Women working for wages in nonagricultural occupations more than doubled in number between 1870 and 1900 (Figure 19.3). Yet white married women, even among the working class, rarely worked for wages outside the home. In 1890, only 3 percent were employed. Black women, married and unmarried, worked out of the home for wages in much greater numbers. The 1890 census showed that 25 percent of married African American women were employed, often as domestics in the houses of white families.

White-Collar Workers: Managers, "Typewriters," and Salesclerks. In the late nineteenth century, a managerial revolution created a new class of white-collar workers who worked in offices and stores. As skilled workers saw their crafts replaced by mechanization, some moved into management positions. "The middle class is becoming a salaried class," a writer for the *Independent* magazine observed, "and is rapidly losing the economic and moral independence of former days." As large business organizations consolidated, corporate development separated management from ownership, and the job of directing the firm became the province of salaried executives and managers, the majority of whom were white men drawn from the 8 percent of Americans who held high school diplomas.

Until late in the century, when engineering schools began to supply recruits, many skilled workers moved from the shop floor to positions of considerable responsibility. Captain William "Billy" Jones, son of a Welsh immigrant, grew up in the heat of the blast furnaces, where he worked as an apprentice at the age of ten. Jones, by all accounts the best steelman in the business, took as his motto "Good wages and good workmen." In 1872 Andrew Carnegie hired Jones as general superintendent of his new Pittsburgh steelworks. Although Carnegie constantly tried to force down workers' pay, Jones resisted, and he succeeded in shortening the shift from twelve to eight hours by convincing Carnegie that shorter hours reduced absenteeism and accidents. Jones demanded and received "a hell of a big salary" — $25,000, the same as the president of the United States.

The new white-collar workforce also included women **"typewriters"** and salesclerks. In the decades after the Civil War, as businesses became larger and more far-flung, the need for more elaborate and exact records, as well as the greater volume of correspondence, led to the hiring of more office workers. The adding machine, the cash register, and the typewriter came into general use in the 1880s. Employers seeking literate workers soon turned to nimble-fingered women. Educated men had many other career choices, but for middle-class white women, secretarial work constituted one of the very few areas where they could put their literacy to use for wages.

Sylvie Thygeson was typical of the young women who went to work as secretaries. Thygeson grew up in an Illinois prairie town and went to work as a country schoolteacher after graduating high school in 1884. Realizing that teaching school did not pay a living wage, she mastered typing and stenography and found work as a secretary to help support her family. According to her account, she made "a fabulous sum of money" (possibly $25 a month). Nevertheless, she gave up her job after a few years when she met and married her husband.

But by the 1890s, secretarial work was the overwhelming choice of native-born, single white women, who constituted more than 90 percent of the female clerical force. Not only considered more genteel than factory work or domestic labor, office work also meant more money for shorter hours. In 1883, Boston's clerical workers on average made more than $6 a week, compared with less than $5 for women working in manufacturing.

As a new consumer culture came to dominate American urban life in the late nineteenth century, department stores offered another employment opportunity for women in the cities. Boasting ornate facades, large plate-glass display windows, and marble and brass fixtures, stores such as Macy's in New York, Wanamaker's in Philadelphia, and Marshall Field in Chicago stood as monuments to the material promise of the era. Within these palaces of consumption, cash girls, stock clerks, and wrappers earned as little as $3 a week, while at the top of the scale, buyers like Belle Cushman of the fancy goods department at Macy's earned $25 a week, an unusually high salary for a woman in the 1870s. Salesclerks counted themselves a cut above factory workers. Their work was neither dirty nor dangerous, and even when they earned less than factory workers, they felt a sense of superiority.

> **REVIEW** How did business expansion and consolidation change workers' occupations in the late nineteenth century?

"typewriters"
Women who were hired by businesses in the decades after the Civil War to keep records and conduct correspondence, often using equipment such as typewriters. Secretarial work constituted one of the very few areas where middle-class women could use their literacy for wages.

Workers Organize

By the late nineteenth century, industrial workers were losing ground in the workplace. In the fierce competition to reduce prices and cut costs, industrialists invested heavily in new machinery that replaced skilled workers with unskilled labor. The erosion of skills and the redefinition of labor as mere "machine tending" left the worker with a growing sense of individual helplessness that spurred collective action.

The 1870s and 1880s witnessed the emergence of two labor unions — the Knights of Labor and the American Federation of Labor. In 1877, in the midst of a depression, labor flexed its muscle in the Great Railroad Strike. But unionism would suffer a major setback after the mysterious Haymarket bombing in 1886.

The Great Railroad Strike of 1877.

Economic depression following the panic of 1873 threw as many as three million people out of work. Those who were lucky enough to keep their jobs watched as pay cuts eroded wages until they could no longer feed their families. In the summer of 1877, the Baltimore and Ohio (B&O) Railroad announced a 10 percent wage cut at the same time it declared a 10 percent dividend to its stockholders. Angry brakemen in West Virginia, whose wages had already fallen from $70 to $30 a month, walked out on strike. One B&O worker described the hardship that drove him to take such desperate action: "We eat our hard bread and tainted meat two days old on the sooty cars up the road, and when we come home, find our wives complaining that they cannot even buy hominy and molasses for food."

The West Virginia brakemen's strike touched off the **Great Railroad Strike** of 1877, a nationwide uprising that spread rapidly to Pittsburgh and Chicago, St. Louis and San Francisco (Map 19.3). Within a few days, nearly 100,000 railroad workers had walked off the job. An estimated 500,000 sympathetic railway workers soon joined the strikers. In Reading, Pennsylvania, militiamen refused to fire on the strikers, saying, "We may be militiamen, but we are workmen first." Rail traffic ground to a halt; the nation lay paralyzed.

Violence erupted as the strike spread. In Pittsburgh, militia brought in from Philadelphia fired on the crowds, killing more than twenty people. Angry workers retaliated by reducing an area two miles long beside the tracks to rubble. Before the

Great Railroad Strike

A violent multicity strike that began in 1877 with West Virginia railroad brakemen who protested against sharp wage reductions and quickly spread to include roughly 600,000 workers. President Rutherford B. Hayes used federal troops to break the strike. Following the strike's failure, union membership surged.

MAP 19.3 THE GREAT RAILROAD STRIKE OF 1877

Starting in West Virginia and Pennsylvania, the strike spread as far north as Albany, New York, and as far west as San Francisco, bringing rail traffic to a standstill. Called the Great Uprising, the strike heralded the beginning of a new era of working-class protest and trade union organization.

✴ Strike activity

DESTRUCTION FROM THE GREAT RAILROAD STRIKE OF 1877
Pictures of the devastation caused in Pittsburgh during the strike shocked many Americans. When militiamen fired on striking workers, killing more than twenty strikers, the mob retaliated by destroying a two-mile area along the track, reducing it to a smoldering rubble. Property damage totaled $2 million. In the aftermath, the curious came out to view the destruction. Carnegie Library of Pittsburgh.

day ended, the militia shot twenty workers and the railroad sustained more than $2 million in property damage.

Within eight days, the governors of nine states, acting at the prompting of the railroad owners and managers, defined the strike as an "insurrection" and called for federal troops. President Rutherford B. Hayes, after hesitating briefly, called out the army. By the time the troops arrived, the violence had run its course. Federal troops did not shoot a single striker in 1877. But they struck a blow against labor by acting as strikebreakers — opening rail traffic, protecting nonstriking "scab" train crews, and maintaining peace along the line. In three weeks, the strike was over.

Middle-class Americans initially sympathized with the conditions that led to the strike. But they quickly condemned the strikers for the violence and property damage that occurred. The *New York Times* editorialized about the "dangerous classes," and the *Independent* magazine offered the following advice on how to deal with "rioters": "If the club of a policeman, knocking out the brains of the rioter, will answer then well and good; but if it does not promptly meet the exigency, then bullets and bayonets . . . constitutes the one remedy and one duty of the hour."

"The strikes have been put down by force," President Hayes noted in his diary on August 5. "But now for the real remedy. Can't something be done by education of the strikers, by judicious control of the capitalists, by wise general policy to end or diminish the evil? The railroad strikers, as a rule, are good men, sober, intelligent, and industrious." While Hayes acknowledged the workers' grievances, most businessmen condemned the idea of labor unions as agents of class warfare. For their part, workers quickly recognized that they held little power individually and flocked to join unions. As labor leader Samuel Gompers noted, the nation's first national strike dramatized the frustration and unity of the workers and served as an alarm bell to labor "that sounded a ringing message of hope to us all."

The Knights of Labor and the American Federation of Labor. The **Knights of Labor**, the first mass organization of America's working class, proved the chief beneficiary of labor's newfound consciousness. The Noble and Holy Order of the Knights of Labor had been founded in 1869 as a secret society of workers who envisioned a "universal brotherhood" of all workers, from common laborers to master craftsmen. Secrecy and ritual served to bind Knights together at the same time that they discouraged company spies and protected members from reprisals.

Although the Knights played no active role in the 1877 railroad strike, membership swelled as a result of the growing interest in labor organizing that followed the strike. In 1878, the Knights abandoned secrecy and launched an ambitious campaign to organize workers.

The Knights attempted to bridge the boundaries of ethnicity, gender, ideology, race, and occupation. Leonora Barry served as general investigator for women's work from 1886 to 1890, helping the Knights recruit teachers, waitresses, housewives, and domestics along with factory and sweatshop workers. Women composed perhaps 20 percent of the membership. The Knights also recruited more than 95,000 black workers. That the Knights of Labor often fell short of its goals to unify the working class proved less surprising than the scope of its efforts.

Under the direction of Grand Master Workman Terence V. Powderly, the Knights became the dominant force in labor during the 1880s. The organization advocated a kind of workers' democracy that embraced reforms including public ownership of the railroads, an income tax, equal pay for women workers, and the abolition of child labor. The Knights called for one big union to create a cooperative commonwealth that would supplant the wage system and remove class distinctions. Only the "parasitic" members of society — gamblers, stockbrokers, lawyers, bankers, and liquor dealers — were denied membership.

The Knights of Labor was not without rivals. Many skilled workers belonged to craft unions organized by trade. Among the largest and richest of these unions stood the Amalgamated Association of Iron and Steel Workers, founded in 1876 and counting twenty thousand skilled workers as members. Trade unionists spurned the broad reform goals of the Knights and focused on workplace issues. Samuel Gompers founded the Organized Trades and Labor Unions in 1881 and reorganized it in 1886 into the **American Federation of Labor (AFL)**, which coordinated the activities of craft unions throughout the United States. His plan was simple: Organize skilled workers such as machinists and locomotive engineers — those with the most bargaining power — and use strikes to gain immediate objectives such as higher pay and better working conditions. Gompers at first drew few converts. The AFL had only 138,000 members in 1886, compared with 730,000 for the Knights of Labor. But

---

Knights of Labor
The first mass organization of America's working class. Founded in 1869, the Knights of Labor attempted to bridge the boundaries of ethnicity, gender, ideology, race, and occupation to build a "universal brotherhood" of all workers.

American Federation of Labor (AFL)
Organization created by Samuel Gompers in 1886 that coordinated the activities of craft unions throughout the United States. The AFL worked to achieve immediate benefits for skilled workers. Its narrow goals for unionism became popular after the Haymarket bombing.

events soon brought down the Knights, and Gompers's brand of unionism came to prevail.

Haymarket and the Specter of Labor Radicalism.
While the AFL and the Knights of Labor competed for members, more radical labor groups, including socialists and anarchists, believed that reform was futile and called instead for social revolution. Both the socialists and the anarchists, sensitive to criticism that they preferred revolution in theory to improvements here and now, rallied around the popular issue of the eight-hour day.

Since the 1840s, labor had sought to end the twelve-hour workday, which was standard in industry and manufacturing. By the mid-1880s, it seemed clear to many workers that labor shared too little in the new prosperity of the decade, and pressure mounted for the eight-hour day. Labor championed the popular issue and launched major rallies in cities across the nation. Supporters of the movement set May 1, 1886, as the date for a nationwide general strike in support of the eight-hour workday.

All factions of the labor movement came together in Chicago on May Day. A group of labor radicals led by anarchist Albert Parsons, a *Mayflower* descendant, and August Spies, a German socialist, spearheaded the eight-hour movement in Chicago. Chicago's Knights of Labor rallied to the cause even though Powderly and the union's national leadership, worried about the increasing activism of the rank and file, refused to endorse the movement for shorter hours. Gompers was also on hand to lead the city's trade unionists, although he privately urged the AFL assemblies not to participate in the general strike.

The cautious labor leaders in their frock coats and starched shirts stood in sharp contrast to the dispossessed workers out on strike across town at Chicago's huge McCormick reaper works. There strikers watched helplessly as the company brought in strikebreakers to take their jobs and marched the "scabs" to work under the protection of the Chicago police and security guards supplied by the Pinkerton Detective Agency. Cyrus McCormick Jr., son of the inventor of the mechanical reaper, viewed labor organization as a threat to his power as well as to his profits; he was determined to smash the union.

During the May Day rally, 45,000 workers paraded peacefully down Michigan Avenue in support of the eight-hour day. Many sang what had become the movement's anthem:

> We want to feel the sunshine;
> We want to smell the flowers,
> We're sure that God has willed it,
> And we mean to have eight hours.
> Eight hours for work, eight hours for rest,
> Eight hours for what we will!

Trouble came two days later, when strikers attacked strikebreakers outside the McCormick works and police opened fire, killing or wounding six men. Angry radicals urged workers to "arm yourselves and appear in full force" at a rally in Haymarket Square.

On the evening of May 4, the turnout at Haymarket was disappointing. No more than two or three thousand gathered in the drizzle to hear Spies, Parsons, and the other speakers. Mayor Carter Harrison, known as a friend of labor, mingled conspicuously in the crowd, pronounced the meeting peaceable, and went home to bed. Sometime later, police captain John "Blackjack" Bonfield marched his men into the crowd, by now fewer than three hundred people, and demanded that it disperse. Suddenly, someone threw a bomb into the police ranks. After a moment of stunned silence, the police drew their revolvers. "Fire and kill all you can," shouted a police lieutenant. When the melee ended, seven policemen and an unknown number of others lay dead. An additional sixty policemen and thirty or forty civilians suffered injuries.

News of the "Haymarket riot" provoked a nationwide convulsion of fear, followed by blind rage directed at anarchists, labor unions, strikers, immigrants, and the working class in general. Eight men, including Parsons and Spies, went on trial in Chicago. "Convict these men," thundered the state's attorney, Julius S. Grinnell, "make examples of them, hang them, and you save our institutions." Although the state could not link any of the defendants to the **Haymarket bombing**, the jury

Haymarket bombing
May 4, 1886, conflict in which both workers and policemen were killed or wounded during a labor demonstration in Chicago. The violence began when someone threw a bomb into the ranks of police at the gathering. The incident created a backlash against labor activism.

Visual Activity

"THE CHICAGO RIOT"

Inflammatory pamphlets published in the wake of the Haymarket bombing aimed to scare the public. In this charged atmosphere, the anarchist speakers at the rally were tried and convicted for the bombing even though witnesses testified that none of them had thrown the bomb. Even today, the identity of the bomb thrower remains uncertain. © Chicago History Museum, USA/Bridgeman Images.

READING THE IMAGE: What does the cover suggest about the views of the author of the pamphlet?

CONNECTIONS: In what ways does this pamphlet reflect the public climate following the Haymarket bombing?

THE CHICAGO RIOT

A RECORD OF THE
Terrible Scenes of May 4, 1886.

Chicago and New York:
BELFORD, CLARKE & CO.,
1886.

nevertheless found them all guilty. Four men were hanged, one committed suicide, and three received prison sentences.

The bomb blast at Haymarket had lasting repercussions. To commemorate the death of the Haymarket martyrs, labor made May 1 an annual international celebration of the worker. But the Haymarket bomb, in the eyes of one observer, proved "a godsend to all enemies of the labor movement." It effectively scotched the eight-hour-day movement and dealt a blow to the Knights of Labor. With the labor movement everywhere under attack, many skilled workers turned to the AFL. Gompers's narrow economic strategy made sense at the time and enabled one segment of the workforce — the skilled — to organize effectively and achieve tangible gains.

> **REVIEW** Why did membership in the Knights of Labor rise in the late 1870s and decline in the 1890s?

At Home and at Play

The growth of urban industrialism not only dramatically altered the workplace but also transformed home and family life, and it gave rise to new forms of commercialized leisure. Industrialization redefined the very concepts of work and home. Increasingly, men went out to work for wages, while most white married women stayed home, either working in the home without pay — cleaning, cooking, and rearing children — or supervising paid domestic servants who did the housework.

Domesticity and "Domestics." The separation of the workplace and the home that marked the shift to industrial society led to a new ideology, one that sentimentalized the home and women's role in it. The cultural idea that dictated a woman's place was in the home, where she would create a haven for her family, began to develop in the early 1800s. It has been called the **cult of domesticity**, a phrase used to prescribe an ideal of middle-class, white womanhood that dominated the period from 1820 to the end of the nineteenth century.

The cult of domesticity and the elaboration of the middle-class home led to a major change in patterns of hiring household help. The live-in servant, or domestic, became a fixture in the North, replacing the hired girl of the previous century. In American cities by 1870, 15 to 30 percent of all households included live-in domestic servants, more than 90 percent of them women. Earlier in the mid-nineteenth century, native-born women increasingly took up other work and left domestic service to immigrants. In the East, the maid was so often Irish that "Bridget" became a generic term for female domestics. The South continued to rely on poorly paid black female "help."

Servants by all accounts resented the long hours and lack of privacy. "She is liable to be rung up at all hours," one study of domestics reported. "Her very meals are not secure from interruption, and even her sleep is not sacred." Domestic service became the occupation of last resort, a "hard and lonely life" in the words of one female servant.

cult of domesticity Nineteenth-century belief that women's place was in the home, where they should create havens for their families. This sentimentalized ideal led to an increase in the hiring of domestic servants and freed white middle-class women to spend time in pursuits outside the home.

For women of the white middle class, domestics were a boon, freeing them from household drudgery and giving them more time to spend with their children, to pursue club work, or to work for reforms. Thus, while domestic service supported the cult of domesticity, it created for those women who could afford it opportunities that expanded their horizons outside the home. They became involved in women's clubs as well as the temperance and suffrage movements.

Cheap Amusements. Growing class divisions manifested themselves in patterns of leisure as well as in work and home life. The poor and working class took their leisure, when they had any, not in the crowded tenements that housed their families but increasingly in the cities' new dance halls, music houses, ballparks, and amusement arcades, which by the 1890s formed a familiar part of the urban landscape.

Young workingwomen no longer met prospective husbands only through their families. Fleeing crowded tenements, the young sought each other's company in dance halls and other commercial retreats. Young workingwomen counted on being "treated" by men, a transaction that often implied sexual payback. Their behavior sometimes blurred the line between respectability and promiscuity. The dance halls became a favorite target of reformers who feared they lured teenage girls into prostitution.

For men, baseball became a national pastime in the 1870s — then, as now, one force in urban life capable of uniting a city across class lines. Cincinnati mounted the

BEACH SCENE AT CONEY ISLAND
Coney Island became a symbol of commercialized leisure and mechanical excitement at the turn of the century. This fanciful rendering of Coney Island captures men and women frolicking in the waves. Notice the modest woolen bathing outfits. Men box and play ball, a woman flies on a parachute, and a uniformed policeman wades into the fray, while the Ferris wheel dominates onshore. Library of Congress, var.2117.

first entirely paid team, the Red Stockings, in 1869. Soon professional teams proliferated in cities across the nation, and Mark Twain hailed baseball as "the very symbol, the outward and visible expression, of the drive and push and rush and struggle of the raging, tearing, booming nineteenth century."

The increasing commercialization of entertainment in the late-nineteenth-century city was best seen at Coney Island. A two-mile stretch of sand nine miles from Manhattan by trolley or steamship, Coney Island in the 1890s was transformed into the site of some of the largest and most elaborate amusement parks in the country. Promoter George Tilyou built Steeplechase Park in 1897, advertising "10 hours of fun for 10 cents." With its mechanical thrills and fun-house laughs, the amusement park encouraged behavior that one schoolteacher aptly described as "everyone with the brakes off." By 1900, as many as a million New Yorkers flocked to Coney Island on any given weekend, making the amusement park the unofficial capital of a new mass culture.

> **REVIEW** How did urban industrialism shape home life and the world of leisure?

City Growth and City Government

Private enterprise, not city planners, built the cities of the United States. With a few notable exceptions, cities simply mushroomed, formed by the dictates of profit and the exigencies of local politics. With the rise of the city came the need for public facilities, transportation, and services that would tax the imaginations of America's architects and engineers and set the scene for the rough-and-tumble of big-city government, politics, and bossism.

Building Cities of Stone and Steel.
Skyscrapers and mighty bridges dominated the imagination and the urban landscape. Less imposing but no less significant were the paved streets, the parks and public libraries, and the subways and sewers. In the late nineteenth century, Americans rushed to embrace new technology of all kinds, making their cities the most modern in the world.

Structural steel made enormous advances in building possible. A decade after the completion of the Brooklyn Bridge, engineers used the new technology to construct the Williamsburg Bridge. More prosaic and utilitarian than its neighbor, the new bridge was never as acclaimed, but it was longer by four feet and completed in half the time. It became the model for future building as the age of steel supplanted the age of stone and iron.

Chicago, not New York, gave birth to the modern skyscraper. Rising from the ashes of the Great Fire of 1871, which destroyed three square miles and left eighteen thousand people homeless, Chicago offered a generation of skilled architects and engineers the chance to experiment. Commercial architecture became an art form at the hands of a skilled group of architects who together constituted the "Chicago

CHICAGO STREET

This lantern slide depicts State Street, a major commercial thoroughfare in Chicago about 1890. The modern skyscraper (center right) contrasts with the dirt road and horse-pulled wagons. The number of horses and people in the photo is about the same. Notice that rules of the road familiar today did not exist; wagons traveled any part of the road in any direction. Pedestrians crowded along the sidewalk, avoiding the danger and dirt of the street. Imagno/Getty Images.

school." Employing the dictum "Form follows function," they built startlingly modern structures.

Across the United States, municipal governments undertook public works on a scale never before seen. They paved streets, built sewers and water mains, replaced gas lamps with electric lights, ran trolley tracks on the old horsecar lines, and dug underground to build subways, tearing down the unsightly elevated tracks that had clogged city streets. Boston completed the nation's first subway system in 1897, and New York and Philadelphia soon followed.

Cities became more beautiful with the creation of urban public parks to complement the new buildings that quickly filled city lots. Much of the credit for America's greatest parks goes to one man — landscape architect Frederick Law Olmsted. New York City's Central Park, completed in 1873, became the first landscaped public park in the United States. Olmsted and his partner, Calvert Vaux, directed the planting of more than five million trees, shrubs, and vines to transform the eight hundred acres between 59th and 110th streets into an oasis for urban dwellers. "We want a place," he wrote, where people "may stroll for an hour, seeing, hearing, and feeling nothing of the bustle and jar of the streets."

American cities did not overlook the mind in their efforts at improvement. They created a comprehensive free public school system that educated everyone from the children of the middle class to the sons and daughters of immigrant workers. Yet the exploding urban population strained the system and led to crowded and inadequate facilities. In 1899, more than 544,000 pupils attended school in New York's five boroughs. Municipalities across the United States provided free secondary school education for all who wished to attend, even though only 8 percent of Americans completed high school.

To educate those who couldn't go to school, American cities created the most extensive free public library system in the world. In 1895, the Boston Public Library opened its bronze doors in its new Copley Square location under the inscription "Free to All." Designed in the style of a Renaissance palazzo, with more than 700,000 books on the shelves ready to be checked out, the library earned the description "a palace of the people."

Despite the Boston Public Library's legend "Free to All," the poor did not share equally in the advantages of city life. The parks, the libraries, and even the subways and sewers benefited some city dwellers more than others. Few library cards were held by Boston's laborers, who worked six days a week and found the library closed on Sunday. And in the 1890s, there was nothing central about New York's Central

Park. It was a four-mile walk from the tenements of Hester Street to the park's entrance at 59th Street and Fifth Avenue. Then, as now, the comfortable, not the indigent, reaped a disproportionate share of the benefits in the nation's big cities.

Any story of the American city, it seems, must be a tale of two cities — or, given the cities' great diversity, a tale of many cities within each metropolis. At the turn of the twentieth century, a central paradox emerged: The enduring monuments of America's cities — the bridges, skyscrapers, parks, and libraries — stood as the undeniable achievements of the same system of municipal government that reformers dismissed as boss-ridden, criminal, and corrupt.

City Government and the "Bosses." The physical growth of the cities required the expansion of public services and the creation of entirely new facilities: streets, subways, elevated trains, bridges, docks, sewers, and public utilities. There was work to be done and money to be made. The professional politician — the colorful big-city boss — became a phenomenon of urban growth and **bossism** a national phenomenon. Though corrupt and often criminal, the boss saw to the building of the city and provided needed social services for the new residents in return for their political support. Yet not even the big-city boss could be said to rule the unruly city. The governing of America's cities resembled more a tug-of-war than boss rule.

The most notorious of all the city bosses was William Marcy "Boss" Tweed of New York. At midcentury, Boss Tweed's Democratic Party "machine" held sway. A machine was really no more than a political party organized at the grassroots level. Its purpose was to win elections and reward its followers, often with jobs on the city's payroll. New York's citywide Democratic machine, Tammany Hall, commanded an army of party functionaries. They formed a shadow government more powerful than the city's elected officials.

As chairman of the Tammany general committee, Tweed kept the Democratic Party together and ran the city through the use of bribery and graft. "As long as I count the votes," he shamelessly boasted, "what are you going to do about it?" The excesses of the Tweed ring soon led to a clamor for reform and cries of "Throw the rascals out." Tweed's rule ended in 1871. Eventually, he was tried and convicted, and later died in jail. New York was not the only city to experience bossism and corruption. The British visitor James Bryce concluded in 1888, "There is no denying that the government of cities is the one conspicuous failure of the United States." More than 80 percent of the nation's thirty largest cities experienced some form of boss rule in the decades around the turn of the twentieth century. However, infighting among powerful ward bosses often meant that no single boss enjoyed exclusive power in the big cities.

Urban reformers and proponents of good government (derisively called "goo goos" by their rivals) challenged machine rule and sometimes succeeded in electing reform mayors. But the reformers rarely managed to stay in office for long. Their detractors called them "mornin' glories," observing that they "looked lovely in the mornin' and withered up in a short time." The bosses enjoyed continued success largely because the urban political machine helped the cities' immigrants and poor, who remained the bosses' staunchest allies. "What tells in holding your district," a Tammany ward boss observed, "is to go right down among the poor and help them

bossism
Pattern of urban political organization that arose in the late nineteenth century in which an often corrupt "boss" maintains an inordinate level of power through command of a political machine that distributes services to its constituents.

Beyond America's Borders

The World's Columbian Exposition and Nineteenth-Century World's Fairs

The 1893 World's Columbian Exposition in Chicago, like the other great world's fairs of the nineteenth and twentieth centuries, represented a unique outgrowth of industrial capitalism and a testament to the expanding global market economy. The Chicago fair, named to celebrate the 400th anniversary of Columbus's arrival in the New World (the organizers missed the deadline by a year), offered a cornucopia of international exhibits, testifying to growing international influences ranging from cultural to technological exchange.

Great cities vied to host the fairs, as much to promote commercial growth as to demonstrate cultural refinement. Each successive fair sought to outdo its predecessor. Chicago's fair followed on the great success of the 1889 Universal Exposition in Paris, crowned by the 900-foot steel tower constructed by Alexandre-Gustave Eiffel. How could Chicago, a prairie upstart, top that?

The answer was to create from scratch an ideal White City with monumental architecture, landscaped grounds, and the world's first Ferris wheel. The White City celebrated the classicism of the French Beaux Arts school, with massive geometric styling and elaborate detailing borrowed from Greek, Roman, and Renaissance architecture. Prairie architects Louis Sullivan and Frank Lloyd Wright later complained the fair was a "virus" that held back modern architecture for decades.

But beneath its Renaissance facade, the White City acted as an enormous emporium dedicated to the unabashed materialism of the Gilded Age. Fairgoers could view virtually every kind of manufactured product in the world inside the imposing Manufactures and Liberal Arts Building. As suited an industrial age, manufactured products and heavy machinery drew the largest crowds. Displays introduced visitors to the latest innovations, many the result of international influences.

For five cents, fairgoers could put two hard rubber tubes into their ears and listen for the first time to a gramophone playing the popular tune "The Cat Came Back." The invention, the work of a German immigrant, Emile Berliner, signaled the beginning of the recorded music industry. Later Thomas Edison claimed credit for a similar invention, calling it the phonograph.

Such international influences were evident throughout the Columbian Exposition. At the Tiffany pavilion, Louis Comfort Tiffany displayed jewelry and objects influenced by Japanese art forms. The Colt firearms factory, known throughout the world for its revolver, was already international in scope, having opened a factory in England in 1851. At the fair Colt debuted its new automatic weapon, the machine gun — soon to play a major role on the world stage in both the Boxer uprising in China and the Spanish-American War.

All manner of foodstuffs tempted fairgoers — teas from India, whiskey from Ireland, and pastries and other confectionaries from Germany and France. American products such as Shredded Wheat, Aunt Jemima syrup, and Juicy Fruit gum debuted at the fair, where they competed for ribbons, like Pabst Blue Ribbon Beer. And the fair introduced two new foods — carbonated soda and the hamburger — destined to become America's best-known contributions to international cuisine.

By displaying technology in action, the White City tamed it and made it accessible to American and world consumers. The fair helped promote electric light and power, with its 90,000 electric lights, 5,100 arc lamps, electric fountains, an electric elevated railroad, and electric launches plying the lagoons. Fairgoers visited the Bell Telephone Company exhibit, marveled at General Electric's huge dynamo (electric generator), and gazed into the future at the all-electric home and model demonstration kitchen.

"ALL NATIONS ARE WELCOME"
Uncle Sam, flanked by the city of Chicago, welcomes representatives carrying the flags of many nations to the World's Columbian Exposition in 1893. In the background are the fairgrounds on the shores of Lake Michigan. More than one hundred nations participated in the fair by sending exhibits and mounting pavilions to showcase their cultures and products. © Chicago History Museum, USA/Bridgeman Images.

Consumer culture received its first major expression and celebration at the fair. Not only did this world's fair anticipate the mass marketing, packaging, and advertising of the twentieth century, but the vast array of products on display also cultivated the urge to consume. Thousands of concessionaires with products for sale sent a message that tied enjoyment inextricably to spending money and purchasing goods, both domestic and foreign. The Columbian Exposition encouraged the rise of a new middle-class consumer culture and made a powerful statement about the possibilities of urban life in an industrial age. As G. Brown Goode, head of the Smithsonian Institution observed, the Columbian Exposition was in many ways "an illustrated encyclopedia of civilization."

QUESTIONS FOR ANALYSIS

Summarize the Argument   To what extent was the Columbian Exposition simultaneously a commercial venture, a cultural display, and entertainment?

Consider the Context   How did the Columbian Exposition and the White City reflect changes in late-nineteenth-century America? How did the international flavor of the White City compare with the reality of global migration into America's fast-growing cities?

Ask Historical Questions   What role did the fair play in popularizing new technologies?

in the different ways they need help. It's philanthropy, but it's politics, too — mighty good politics."

The big-city boss, through the skillful orchestration of rewards, exerted powerful leverage and lined up support for his party from a broad range of constituents, from the urban poor to wealthy industrialists. In 1902, when journalist Lincoln Steffens began "The Shame of the Cities," a series of articles exposing city corruption, he found that business leaders who fastidiously refused to mingle socially with the bosses nevertheless struck deals with them. "He is a self-righteous fraud, this big businessman," Steffens concluded. "I found him buying boodlers [bribers] in St. Louis, defending grafters in Minneapolis, originating corruption in Pittsburgh, sharing with bosses in Philadelphia, deploring reform in Chicago, and beating good government with corruption funds in New York."

For all the color and flamboyance of the big-city boss, he was simply one of many actors in the drama of municipal government. Old-stock aristocrats, new professionals, saloonkeepers, pushcart peddlers, and politicians all fought for their interests in the hurly-burly of city government. They didn't much like each other, and they sometimes fought savagely. But they learned to live with one another. Compromise and accommodation — not boss rule — best characterized big-city government by the turn of the twentieth century, although the cities' reputation for corruption left an indelible mark on the consciousness of the American public.

White City or City of Sin?

Americans have always been of two minds about the city. They like to boast of its skyscrapers and bridges, its culture and sophistication, and they pride themselves on its bigness and bustle. At the same time, they fear it as the city of sin, the home of immigrant slums, the center of vice and crime. Nowhere did the divided view of the American city take form more graphically than in Chicago in 1893. In that year, Chicago hosted the **World's Columbian Exposition**, the grandest world's fair in the nation's history. (See "Beyond America's Borders," page 574.) The fairground, only five miles down the shore of Lake Michigan from downtown Chicago, offered a lesson in what Americans on the eve of the twentieth century imagined a city might be. Christened the "White City," it seemed light-years away from Chicago, with its stockyards, slums, and bustling terminals. Frederick Law Olmsted and architect Daniel Burnham supervised the transformation of a swampy wasteland into a pristine paradise of lagoons, fountains, wooded islands, gardens, and imposing white buildings.

"Sell the cookstove if necessary and come," novelist Hamlin Garland wrote to his parents on the farm. And come they did, in spite of the panic and depression that broke out only weeks after the fair opened in May 1893. In six months, fairgoers purchased more than 27 million tickets, turning a profit of nearly a half million dollars for promoters. Visitors from home and abroad strolled the elaborate grounds and visited the exhibits — everything from a model of the Brooklyn Bridge carved in soap to the latest goods and inventions. Half carnival, half culture, the great fair offered something for everyone. On the Midway Plaisance, crowds thrilled to the massive wheel built by Mr. Ferris and watched agog as Little Egypt danced the hootchy-kootchy.

World's Columbian Exposition
World's fair held in Chicago in 1893 that attracted millions of visitors. The elaborately designed pavilions of the "White City" included exhibits of technological innovation and of cultural exoticism. They embodied an urban ideal that contrasted with the realities of Chicago life.

In October, the fair closed its doors in the midst of the worst depression the country had yet seen. During that winter, Chicago's unemployed and homeless took over the grounds, vandalized the buildings, and frightened the city's comfortable citizens out of their wits. When reporters asked Daniel Burnham, its chief architect, what should be done with the moldering remains of the White City, he responded, "It should be torched." And it was. In July 1894, in a clash between federal troops and striking railway workers, incendiaries set fires that leveled the fairgrounds.

In the end, the White City remained what it had always been, a dreamscape. Buildings that looked like marble were actually constructed of staff, a plaster substance that began to crumble even before fire destroyed the fairgrounds. Perhaps it was not so strange, after all, that the legacy of the White City could be found on Coney Island, where two new amusement parks, Luna and Dreamland, sought to combine, albeit in a more tawdry form, the beauty of the White City and the thrill of the Midway Plaisance. More enduring than the White City itself was what it represented: the emergent industrial might of the United States, at home and abroad, with its inventions, manufactured goods, and growing consumer culture.

REVIEW How did municipal governments respond to the challenges of urban expansion?

Conclusion: Who Built the Cities?

As great a role as industrialists, financiers, and engineers played in building the nation's cities, common workers — most of them immigrants — provided the muscle. The unprecedented growth of urban, industrial America resulted from the labor of millions of men, women, and children who toiled in workshops and factories, in sweatshops and mines, and on railroads and construction sites across America.

America's cities in the late nineteenth century teemed with life. Townhouses and tenements jostled for space with skyscrapers and great department stores, while parks, ball fields, amusement arcades, and public libraries provided the city masses with recreation and entertainment. Municipal governments, straining to build the new cities, experienced the rough-and-tumble of machine politics as bosses and their constituents looked to profit from city growth.

For America's workers, urban industrialism along with the rise of big business and corporate consolidation drastically changed the workplace. Industrialists replaced skilled workers with new machines that could be operated by cheaper unskilled labor. And during hard times, employers did not hesitate to cut workers' already meager wages. As the Great Railroad Strike of 1877 demonstrated, when labor united, it could bring the nation to attention. Organization held out the best hope for the workers; first the Knights of Labor and later the AFL won converts among the nation's working class.

The rise of urban industrialism challenged the American promise, which for decades had been dominated by Jeffersonian agrarian ideals. Could such a promise exist in the changing world of cities, tenements, immigrants, and huge corporations? In the great depression that came in the 1890s, mounting anger and frustration would lead farmers and workers to join forces and create a grassroots movement to fight for change under the banner of a new People's Party.

Chapter Review

KEY TERMS

global migration (p. 551)
Ellis Island (p. 557)
sweatshop (p. 561)
family economy (p. 561)
"typewriters" (p. 563)
Great Railroad Strike (p. 564)
Knights of Labor (p. 566)

American Federation of Labor (AFL) (p. 566)
Haymarket bombing (p. 568)
cult of domesticity (p. 569)
bossism (p. 573)
World's Columbian Exposition (p. 576)

REVIEW QUESTIONS

1 Why did American cities experience explosive growth in the late nineteenth century?   (pp. 550–59)

2 How did business expansion and consolidation change workers' occupations in the late nineteenth century?   (pp. 560–63)

3 Why did membership in the Knights of Labor rise in the late 1870s and decline in the 1890s?   (pp. 563–69)

4 How did urban industrialism shape home life and the world of leisure? (pp. 569–71)

5 How did municipal governments respond to the challenges of urban expansion?   (pp. 571–77)

MAKING CONNECTIONS

❶ Americans expressed both wonder and concern at the nation's mush-rooming cities. Why did cities provoke such divergent responses?

❷ Why did patterns of immigration to the United States in the late nineteenth century change? How did Americans respond to the immigrants?

❸ How did urban industrialization affect Americans' lives outside of work?

❹ When workers began to embrace organization in the late 1870s, what did they hope to accomplish? Were they successful? Why or why not?

LINKING TO THE PAST

❶ Compare the lives of migrant workers and industrial cowboys in the West to workers in the nation's cities. What are the major similarities? (See chapter 17.)

❷ You have already looked at the development of America's industries in the nineteenth century from the vantage point of moguls such as Andrew Carnegie and John D. Rockefeller. How does your view of industrialism change when the focus is shifted to the nation's workers? (See chapter 18.)

20

Dissent, Depression, and War,
1890–1900

☐ = people/places
◯ = new word
— = details

CONTENT LEARNING OBJECTIVES

After studying this chapter, you should be able to:

- Identify the economic and social ills American farmers and laborers faced at the turn of the century and how Farmers' Alliances and the Populist movement aimed to address some of these problems.
- Explain the factors that led to the labor wars of the 1890s.
- Characterize the political activism of American women during the last decades of the nineteenth century.
- Describe the political climate during the depression of 1893 and identify the defining issues of the election of 1896.
- Explain American expansionism in the late nineteenth century, how the United States emerged as a world power, and the resulting debate over American imperialism.

Frances Willard traveled to St. Louis in February 1892 with high hopes. Political change was in the air, and Willard was there to help fashion a new reform party. As head of the Woman's Christian Temperance Union (WCTU), an organization with members in every state and territory in the nation, Willard wielded considerable clout. At her invitation, twenty-eight of the country's leading reformers met in Chicago to draft a set of principles to bring to St. Louis. No American woman before her had played such a central role in a political movement. At the height of her power, Willard took her place among the leaders onstage in St. Louis.

PEOPLE'S PARTY BANNER

This 1892 Populist convention banner promises to elect "Honest Men." The bison mascot was a poor choice for the new party, for just as the great herds were decimated, the People's Party was defeated in 1896. Nebraska State Historical Society, no. 7294-32, copy and reuse restrictions apply.

Exposition Music Hall presented a colorful spectacle. "The banners of the different states rose above the delegates throughout the hall, fluttering like the flags over an army encamped," wrote one reporter. The fiery orator Ignatius Donnelly attacked the money kings of Wall Street. Terence V. Powderly, head of the Knights of Labor, called on workers to join hands with farmers against the "nonproducing classes." And Frances Willard took the podium, urging the crowd to outlaw liquor and give women the vote.

Delegates hammered out a series of demands, breathtaking in their scope. They tackled the tough questions of the day — the regulation of business, the need for banking and currency reform, the right of labor to organize and bargain collectively, and the role of the federal government in regulating business, curbing monopoly, and giving the people greater voice. But the new party was determined to stick to economic issues and resisted endorsing either temperance or woman suffrage. As a member of the platform committee, Willard fought for both and complained of the "crooked methods . . . employed to scuttle these planks."

The convention ended its work amid a chorus of cheers. According to one eyewitness, "Hats, paper, handkerchiefs, etc., were thrown into the air; . . . cheer after cheer thundered and reverberated through the vast hall reaching the outside of the building where thousands who had been waiting the outcome joined in the applause till for blocks in every direction the exultation made the din indescribable."

What was all the shouting about? The crowd, fed up with the Democrats and the Republicans, celebrated the birth of a new political party, officially named the People's Party. The St. Louis gathering marked an early milestone in one of the most turbulent decades in U.S. history. An agrarian revolt, labor strikes, a severe depression, and a war shook the 1890s. As the decade opened, Americans flocked to organizations including the Farmers' Alliance, the American Federation of Labor, the Woman's Christian Temperance Union, and the National Woman's Suffrage Association. Their political alliance gave birth to the People's (or Populist) Party. In a decade of unrest and uncertainty, the Populists countered laissez-faire economics by insisting that the federal government play a more active role to ensure economic fairness in industrial America.

This challenge to the status quo culminated in 1896 in one of the most hotly contested presidential elections in the nation's history. At

CHRONOLOGY

1884 Frances Willard calls for woman suffrage.

1890 National American Woman Suffrage Association formed. Wyoming only state allowing women to vote in national elections. Southern Farmers' Alliance numbers three million members.

1892 People's (Populist) Party founded. Homestead lockout ends in violence.

1893 Stock market crash touches off economic depression. President Grover Cleveland nixes attempt to annex Hawai'i.

1894 Miners strike in Cripple Creek, Colorado. Coxey's army marches to Washington, D.C. Pullman boycott crushed.

1895 Cleveland enforces Monroe Doctrine in border dispute between British Guiana and Venezuela.

1896 Democrats and Populists support William Jennings Bryan for president. William McKinley elected president.

1898 USS *Maine* explodes in Havana harbor. Congress declares war on Spain. Admiral George Dewey destroys Spanish fleet in Manila Bay. U.S. troops defeat Spanish forces in Cuba. Treaty of Paris ends war with Spain. United States annexes Hawai'i.

1899– 1900 Secretary of State John Hay enunciates Open Door policy. Boxer uprising takes place in China.

1901 Boxer Protocol imposed on Chinese government.

the close of the tumultuous decade, the Spanish-American War brought the country together, with Americans rallying to support the troops. American imperialism and overseas expansion raised questions about the nation's role on the world stage as the United States stood poised to enter the twentieth century.

The Farmers Unite

Hard times in the 1880s and 1890s created a groundswell of agrarian revolt. A bitter farmer wrote from Minnesota, "I settled on this Land in good Faith Built House and Barn. Broken up Part of the Land. Spent years of hard Labor in grubbing fencing and Improving." About to lose his farm to foreclosure, he lamented, "Are they going to drive us out like trespassers . . . and give us away to the Corporations?"

Farm prices fell decade after decade, even as American farmers' share of the world market grew. In parts of Kansas, corn sold for as little as ten cents a bushel, and angry farmers burned their crops for fuel rather than sell them on the market. At the same time, consumer prices soared (Figure 20.1). In Kansas alone, almost half the farms had fallen into the hands of the banks by 1894 through foreclosure. Farmers soon banded together into Farmers' Alliances that gave birth to a broad political movement.

The Farmers' Alliance. At the heart of the farmers' problems stood a banking system dominated by eastern commercial banks committed to the gold standard, a railroad rate system both capricious and unfair, and rampant speculation that drove up the price of land. In the West, farmers rankled under a system that allowed railroads to charge them exorbitant freight rates while granting rebates to large shippers (see chapter 18). The practice of charging higher rates for short hauls than for long hauls meant that grain elevators could ship their wheat from Chicago to New York

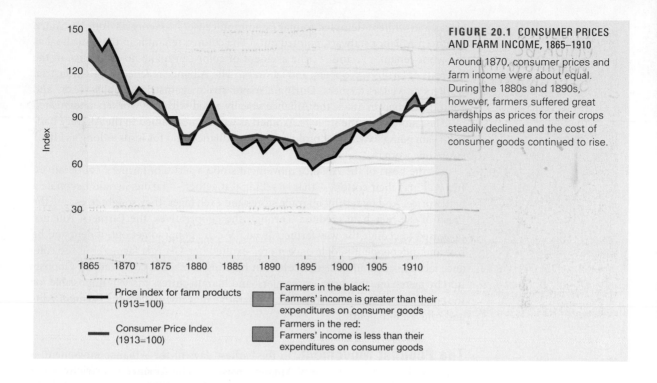

FIGURE 20.1 CONSUMER PRICES
AND FARM INCOME, 1865–1910

Around 1870, consumer prices and
farm income were about equal.
During the 1880s and 1890s,
however, farmers suffered great
hardships as prices for their crops
steadily declined and the cost of
consumer goods continued to rise.

Price index for farm products
(1913=100)

Consumer Price Index
(1913=100)

Farmers in the black:
Farmers' income is greater than their
expenditures on consumer goods

Farmers in the red:
Farmers' income is less than their
expenditures on consumer goods

and across the Atlantic for less than a Dakota farmer paid to send his crop to mills in
Minneapolis. In the South, lack of currency and credit drove farmers to the stopgap
credit system of the crop lien. To pay for seed and supplies, farmers pledged their
crops as collateral to local creditors (furnishing merchants). Determined to do
something, farmers banded together to fight for change.

Farm protest was not new. In the 1870s, farmers had supported the Grange
and the Greenback Labor Party. As the farmers' situation grew more desperate,
they organized, forming regional alliances. The first **Farmers' Alliance** came
together in Lampasas County, Texas, to fight "landsharks and horse thieves." In
frontier farmhouses in Texas, in log cabins in the backwoods of Arkansas, and in
the rural parishes of Louisiana, separate groups of farmers formed similar alliances for self-help.

As the movement grew in the 1880s, farmers' groups consolidated into two
regional alliances: the Northwestern Farmers' Alliance, active in Kansas, Nebraska,
and other midwestern Granger states; and the more radical Southern Farmers' Alliance. Traveling lecturers preached the Alliance message. Worn-out men and care-
worn women did not need to be convinced that something was wrong. By 1890, the
Southern Farmers' Alliance alone counted more than three million members.

Radical in its inclusiveness, the Southern Alliance reached out to African
Americans, women, and industrial workers. Through cooperation with the Colored
Farmers' Alliance, an African American group founded in Texas in the 1880s,

Farmers' Alliance
Movement to form local
organizations to advance
farmers' collective interests
that gained wide popularity
in the 1880s. Over time,
farmers' groups consolidated
into the Northwestern
Farmers' Alliance and the
Southern Farmers' Alliance.
In 1892, the Farmers'
Alliance gave birth to the
People's Party.

a mix of
people

blacks and whites attempted to make common cause. As Georgia's Tom Watson, a Southern Alliance stalwart, pointed out, "The colored tenant is in the same boat as the white tenant, . . . and . . . the accident of color can make no difference in the interests of farmers, croppers, and laborers." The Alliance reached out to industrial workers as well as farmers. During a major strike against Jay Gould's Texas and Pacific Railroad in 1886, the Alliance vocally sided with the workers and rushed food and supplies to the strikers. Women as well as men rallied to the Alliance banner. "I am going to work for prohibition, the Alliance, and for Jesus as long as I live," swore one woman.

At the heart of the Alliance movement stood a series of farmers' cooperatives. By "bulking" their cotton — that is, selling it together — farmers could negotiate a better price. And by setting up trade stores and exchanges, they sought to escape the grasp of the merchant/creditor. Through the cooperatives, the Farmers' Alliance promised to change the way farmers lived. "We are going to get out of debt and be free and independent people once more," exulted one Georgia farmer. But the Alliance faced insurmountable difficulties in running successful cooperatives. Opposition by merchants, bankers, wholesalers, and manufacturers made it impossible for the cooperatives to get credit. As the cooperative movement died, the Farmers' Alliance moved into politics.

The Populist Movement. In the earliest days of the Alliance movement, a leader of the Southern Farmers' Alliance insisted, "The Alliance is a strictly white man's nonpolitical, secret business association." But by 1892, it was none of those things. Advocates of a third party carried the day at the convention of laborers,

THE FARMERS' ALLIANCE AND THE POPULIST PARTY

Isaac Ware, from Southwest Custer County, Nebraska, proudly holds a copy of the *Alliance Independent*, a newspaper published in Lincoln, Nebraska. In 1892, before this picture was taken, Farmers' Alliance members came together in St. Louis to form the People's or Populist Party. Small local newspapers sprouted up all across the West and South to carry the message. Nebraska State Historical Society, no. 11188, copy and reuse restrictions apply.

farmers, and common folk in 1892 in St. Louis, where the Farmers' Alliance gave birth to the **People's Party (Populist Party)** and launched the Populist movement. The same spirit of religious revival that animated the Farmers' Alliance infused the People's Party. Convinced that the money and banking systems worked to the advantage of the wealthy few, Populists demanded economic democracy. To help farmers get the credit they needed at reasonable rates, southern farmers hit on the ingenious idea of a subtreasury — a plan that would allow farmers to store their nonperishable crops until prices rose and to receive commodity credit from the federal government to obtain needed supplies. To the western farmer, the Populists promised land reform, championing a plan to claim excessive land granted to railroads or sold to foreign investors. The Populists' boldest proposal called for government ownership of the railroads and the telegraph system to put an end to discriminatory rates.

The Populists solidly supported free silver, in the hope of increasing the nation's tight money supply. To empower the common people, the Populist platform called for the direct election of senators and for other electoral reforms, including the secret ballot and the right to initiate legislation, to recall elected officials, and to submit issues to the people by means of a referendum. In support of labor, the Populists supported the eight-hour workday.

The sweeping array of reforms enacted in the Populist platform changed the agenda of politics for decades to come. More than just a response to hard times, Populism presented an alternative vision of American economic democracy.

> **REVIEW** Why did American farmers organize alliances in the late nineteenth century?

People's Party (Populist Party)
Political party formed in 1892 by the Farmers' Alliance to advance the goals of the Populist movement. Populists sought economic democracy, promoting land, electoral, banking, and monetary reform. Republican victory in the presidential election of 1896 effectively destroyed the People's Party.

The Labor Wars

While farmers united to fight for change, industrial laborers fought their own battles in a series of bloody strikes historians have called the "labor wars." Industrial workers took a stand in the 1890s. At issue was the right of workers to organize and to speak through unions, to bargain collectively, and to fight for better working conditions, higher wages, shorter hours, and greater worker control in the face of increased mechanization. Three major conflicts — the lockout of steelworkers in Homestead, Pennsylvania, in 1892; the miners' strike in Cripple Creek, Colorado, in 1894; and the Pullman boycott that same year — raised fundamental questions about the rights of labor and the sanctity of private property.

The Homestead Lockout. In 1892, steelworkers in Pennsylvania squared off against Andrew Carnegie in a decisive struggle over the right to organize in the Homestead steel mills. Carnegie resolved to crush the Amalgamated Iron and Steel Workers, one of the largest and richest craft unions in the American Federation of Labor (AFL). When the Amalgamated attempted to renew its contract at Carnegie's Homestead mill, its leaders were told that since "the vast majority of

crushed union by not majority

our employees are Non union, the Firm has decided that the minority must give place to the majority." While it was true that only 800 skilled workers belonged to the elite Amalgamated, the union had long enjoyed the support of the plant's 3,000 non-union workers. Slavs, who did much of the unskilled work, made common cause with the Welsh, Scottish, and Irish skilled workers who belonged to the union.

Carnegie, who often praised labor unions, preferred not to be directly involved in the union busting, so that spring he sailed to Scotland and left Henry Clay Frick the toughest antilabor man in the industry, in charge. By summer, a strike looked inevitable. Frick prepared by erecting a fifteen-foot fence around the Homestead plant and topping it with barbed wire. Workers aptly dubbed it "Fort Frick." Frick then hired 316 mercenaries from the Pinkerton National Detective Agency at the rate of $5 per day, more than double the wage of the average Homestead worker.

On June 28, the **Homestead lockout** began when Frick locked the doors of the mills and prepared to bring in strikebreakers. Hugh O'Donnell, the young Irishman who led the union, vowed to prevent "scabs" from entering the plant. On July 6 at 4 a.m., a lookout spotted two barges moving up the Monongahela River in the fog. Frick was attempting to smuggle his Pinkertons into Homestead.

Workers sounded the alarm, and within minutes a crowd of more than a thousand, hastily armed with rifles, hoes, and fence posts, rushed to the riverbank. When the scabs attempted to come ashore, gunfire broke out, and more than a dozen Pinkertons and some thirty strikers fell, killed or wounded. The Pinkertons retreated to the barges. For twelve hours, the workers, joined by their family members, threw everything they had at the barges, from fireworks to dynamite. Finally, the Pinkertons hoisted a white flag and arranged with O'Donnell to surrender. With three workers dead and scores wounded, the crowd, numbering perhaps ten thousand, was in no mood for conciliation. As the hated "Pinks" came up the hill, they were forced to run a gantlet of screaming, cursing men, women, and children. When a young guard dropped to his knees, weeping for mercy, a woman used her umbrella to poke out his eye. One Pinkerton had been killed in the siege on the barges. In the grim rout that followed their surrender, not one avoided injury. The workers took control of the plant and elected a council to run the community. At first, public opinion favored

HOMESTEAD WORKERS ATTACK THE PINKERTONS
The nation's attention was riveted on labor strife at the Homestead steel mill in the summer of 1892. *Frank Leslie's Illustrated Weekly* ran a cover story on the violence that Pinkerton agents faced from an armed crowd of men, women, and children who were enraged that Frick had hired the Pinkertons to bring in strikebreakers. Beaten and overwhelmed by the strikers, the Pinkertons surrendered. The New York Society Library.

their cause. A congressman castigated Carnegie for "skulking in his castle in Scotland." Populists, meeting in St. Louis, condemned the use of "hireling armies."

The action of the Homestead workers struck at the heart of the capitalist system, pitting the workers' right to their jobs against the rights of private property. The workers' insistence that "we are not destroying the property of the company — merely protecting our rights" did not prove as compelling to the courts and the state as the property rights of the owners. Four days after the confrontation, Pennsylvania's governor, who sympathized with the workers, nonetheless yielded to pressure from Frick and ordered eight thousand National Guard troops into Homestead to protect Carnegie's property. The workers, thinking they had nothing to fear from the militia, welcomed the troops with a brass band. But the troops' occupation not only protected Carnegie's property but also enabled Frick to reopen the mills and bring in strikebreakers. "We have been deceived," one worker complained bitterly. "We have stood idly by and let the town be occupied by soldiers who come here, not as our protectors, but as the protectors of non-union men. . . . If we undertake to resist the seizure of our jobs, we will be shot down like dogs."

Then, in a misguided effort to ignite a general uprising, Alexander Berkman, a Russian immigrant and anarchist, attempted to assassinate Frick. Berkman bungled his attempt. Shot twice and stabbed with a dagger, Frick survived and showed considerable courage, allowing a doctor to remove the bullets but refusing to leave his desk until the day's work was completed. "I do not think that I shall die," Frick remarked coolly, "but whether I do or not, the Company will pursue the same policy and it will win."

After the assassination attempt, public opinion turned against the workers. Berkman was quickly tried and sentenced to prison. Although the Amalgamated and the AFL denounced his action, the incident linked anarchism and unionism. O'Donnell later wrote, "The bullet from Berkman's pistol, failing in its foul intent, went straight through the heart of the Homestead strike." The Homestead mill reopened in November, and the men returned to work, except for the union leaders, now blacklisted in every steel mill in the country. With the owners firmly in charge, the company slashed wages, reinstated the twelve-hour day, and eliminated five hundred jobs.

The workers at Homestead had been taught a lesson. They would never again, in the words of the National Guard commander, "believe the works are theirs quite as much as Carnegie's." Another forty-five years would pass before steelworkers, unskilled as well as skilled, successfully unionized. In the meantime, Carnegie's production tripled, even in the midst of a depression. "Ashamed to tell you profits these days," Carnegie wrote a friend in 1899. And no wonder: Carnegie's profits had grown from $4 million in 1892 to $40 million in 1900.

The Cripple Creek Miners' Strike of 1894.
Less than a year after the Homestead lockout, a panic on Wall Street in the spring of 1893 touched off a bitter economic depression. In the West, silver mines fell on hard times, leading to the Cripple Creek miners' strike of 1894. When mine owners moved to lengthen the workday from eight to ten hours, the newly formed Western Federation of Miners (WFM) vowed to hold the line in Cripple Creek, Colorado. In February 1894, the WFM threatened to strike all mines running more than eight-hour shifts.

8-10 hours

The mine owners divided: Some quickly settled with the WFM; others continued to demand ten hours, provoking a strike.

help from other miners

The striking miners received help from many quarters. Working miners paid $15 a month to a strike fund, and miners in neighboring districts sent substantial contributions. The miners enjoyed the support and assistance of local businesses and grocers, who provided credit to the strikers. With these advantages, the Cripple Creek strikers could afford to hold out for their demands.

Even more significant, Governor Davis H. Waite, a Populist elected in 1892, had strong ties to the miners and refused to use the power of the state against the strikers. Governor Waite asked the strikers to lay down their arms and demanded that the mine owners disperse their hired deputies. The miners agreed to arbitration and selected Waite as their sole arbitrator. By May, the recalcitrant mine owners capitulated, and the union won an eight-hour day.

Governor Waite's intervention demonstrated the pivotal power of the state in the nation's labor wars. Having a Populist in power made a difference. A decade later, in 1904, with Waite out of office, mine owners relied on state troops to take back control of the mines, defeating the WFM and blacklisting all of its members. In retrospect, the Cripple Creek miners' strike of 1894 proved the exception to the rule of state intervention on the side of private property.

Eugene V. Debs and the Pullman Strike.

1/2 pop unempl

The economic depression that began in 1893 swelled the ranks of the unemployed to three million, almost half of the working population. "A fearful crisis is upon us," wrote a labor publication. Nowhere were workers more demoralized than in the model town of Pullman, on the outskirts of Chicago.

In the wake of the Great Railroad Strike of 1877, George M. Pullman, the builder of Pullman railroad cars, moved his plant and workers nine miles south of Chicago and built a model town. The town of Pullman boasted parks, fountains, playgrounds, an auditorium, a library, a hotel, shops, and markets, along with 1,800 units of housing. Noticeably absent was a saloon. ?

The housing in Pullman was clearly superior to that in neighboring areas, but workers paid a high price to live there. Pullman's rents ran 10 to 20 percent higher than housing costs in nearby communities. In addition, George Pullman refused to "sell an acre under any circumstances." As long as he controlled the town absolutely, he held the powerful whip of eviction over his employees and could quickly get rid of "troublemakers." Although observers at first praised the beauty and orderliness of the town, critics by the 1890s compared Pullman's model town to a "gilded cage" for workers.

The depression brought hard times to Pullman. Workers saw their wages slashed five times between May and December 1893, with cuts totaling at least 28 percent. At the same time, Pullman refused to lower the rents in his model town, insisting that "the renting of the dwellings and the employment of workmen at Pullman are in no way tied together." When workers went to the bank to cash their paychecks, they found that the rent had been taken out. One worker discovered only forty-seven cents in his pay envelope for two weeks' work. When the bank teller asked him whether he wanted to apply it to his back rent, he retorted, "If Mr. Pullman needs that forty-seven cents worse than I do, let him have it." At the same time, Pullman continued to pay his stockholders an 8 percent dividend, and the company accumulated a $25 million surplus.

At the heart of the labor problems at Pullman lay not only economic inequity but also the company's attempt to control the work process, substituting piecework for day wages and undermining skilled craftsworkers. During the spring of 1894, Pullman's desperate workers, seeking help, flocked to the ranks of the American Railway Union (ARU), led by the charismatic Eugene V. Debs. The ARU, unlike the skilled craft unions of the AFL, pledged to organize all railway workers — from engineers to engine wipers.

George Pullman responded to union organization at his plant by firing three of the union's leaders the day after they protested wage cuts. Angry men and women walked off the job in disgust. What began as a spontaneous protest in May 1894 quickly blossomed into a strike that involved more than 90 percent of Pullman's 3,300 workers. Pullman countered by shutting down the plant. In June, the Pullman strikers appealed to the ARU to come to their aid. Debs pleaded with the workers to find another solution. But when George Pullman refused arbitration, the ARU membership voted to boycott all Pullman cars. Beginning on June 29, switchmen across the United States refused to handle any train that carried Pullman cars.

The conflict escalated quickly. The General Managers Association (GMA), an organization of managers from twenty-four different railroads, acted in concert to quash the **Pullman boycott.** They recruited strikebreakers and fired all the protesting switchmen. Their tactics set off a chain reaction. Entire train crews walked off the job in a show of solidarity with the Pullman workers. By July 2, rail lines from New York to California lay paralyzed. Even the GMA was forced to concede that the railroads had been "fought to a standstill."

The boycott remained surprisingly peaceful. In contrast to the Great Railroad Strike of 1877, no major riots broke out, and no serious property damage occurred. Debs fired off telegrams to all parts of the country advising his followers to avoid violence and respect law and order. But the nation's newspapers, fed press releases by the GMA, distorted the issues and misrepresented the strike. Across the country, papers ran headlines like "Wild Riot in Chicago" and "Mob Is in Control."

A PULLMAN CRAFTSWORKER

Pullman Palace cars were known for their luxurious details. Here, a painter working in the 1890s applies elaborate decoration to the exterior of a Pullman car. The Pullman workers' strike in 1894 stemmed in part from the company's efforts to undermine the status of craftsworkers by reducing them to low-paid piecework. The fight to control the workplace contributed to the labor wars of the 1890s. © Chicago History Museum, USA/Bridgeman Images.

Pullman boycott
Nationwide railroad workers' boycott of trains carrying Pullman cars in 1894 after Pullman workers, suffering radically reduced wages, joined the American Railway Union (ARU) and union leaders were fired in response. The boycott ended after the U.S. Army fired on strikers and ARU leader Eugene Debs was jailed.

In Washington, Attorney General Richard B. Olney, a lawyer with strong ties to the railroads, was determined to put down the strike. In his way stood the governor of Illinois, John Peter Altgeld, who, observing that the boycott remained peaceful, refused to call out troops. To get around Altgeld, Olney convinced President Grover Cleveland that federal troops had to intervene to protect the rails. To further cripple the boycott, two conservative Chicago judges issued an injunction so sweeping that it prohibited Debs from speaking in public. By issuing the injunction, the court made the boycott a crime punishable by a jail sentence for contempt of court, a civil process that did not require a jury trial. Even the conservative *Chicago Tribune* judged the injunction "a menace to liberty . . . a weapon ever ready for the capitalist." Furious, Debs risked jail by refusing to honor it.

Olney's strategy worked. President Grover Cleveland called out the army. On July 5, nearly 8,000 troops marched into Chicago. Violence immediately erupted. In one day, troops killed 25 workers and wounded more than 60. In the face of bullets and bayonets, the strikers held firm. "Troops cannot move trains," Debs reminded his followers, a fact that was borne out as the railroads remained paralyzed despite the military intervention. But if the army could not put down the boycott, the injunction did. Debs was arrested and imprisoned for contempt of court. With its leader in jail, its headquarters raided and ransacked, and its members demoralized, the ARU collapsed along with the boycott. Pullman reopened his factory, hiring new workers to replace many of the strikers and leaving 1,600 without jobs.

In the aftermath of the strike, a special commission investigated the events at Pullman, taking testimony from 107 witnesses, from the lowliest workers to George M. Pullman himself. Stubborn and self-righteous, Pullman spoke for the business orthodoxy of his era, steadfastly affirming the right of business to safeguard its interests through confederacies such as the GMA and at the same time denying labor's right to organize. "If we were to receive these men as representatives of the union," he stated, "they could probably force us to pay any wages which they saw fit."

From his jail cell, Eugene Debs reviewed the events of the Pullman strike. With the courts and the government ready to side with industrialists in defense of private property, strikes seemed futile, and unions remained helpless. Workers would have to take control of the state itself. Debs went into jail a trade unionist and came out six months later a socialist. At first, he turned to the Populist Party, but after its demise he formed the Socialist Party in 1900 and ran for president five times.

REVIEW What led to the labor wars of the 1890s?

Women's Activism

"Do everything," Frances Willard urged her followers in 1881. The new president of the Woman's Christian Temperance Union (WCTU) meant what she said. The WCTU followed a trajectory that was common for women in the late nineteenth century. As women organized to deal with issues that touched their homes and families, they moved into politics, lending new urgency to the cause of woman suffrage. Urban industrialism dislocated women's lives no less than men's. Like men, women sought political change and organized to promote issues central to their lives, campaigning for temperance and woman suffrage.

Frances Willard and the Woman's Christian Temperance Union.

A visionary leader, Frances Willard spoke for a group left almost entirely out of the U.S. electoral process. In 1890, only one state, Wyoming, allowed women to vote in national elections. But lack of the franchise did not mean that women were apolitical. The WCTU demonstrated the breadth of women's political activity in the late nineteenth century.

[margin note: Only state]

Women supported the temperance movement because they felt particularly vulnerable to the effects of drunkenness. Dependent on men's wages, married women and their children suffered when money went for drink. The drunken, abusive husband epitomized the evils of a nation in which women remained second-class citizens. The WCTU, composed entirely of women, viewed all women's interests as essentially the same and therefore did not hesitate to use the singular *woman* to emphasize gender solidarity. Although mostly white and middle-class, WCTU members resolved to speak for their entire sex.

When Willard became president in 1879, she radically changed the direction of the organization. Social action replaced prayer as women's answer to the threat of drunkenness. Viewing alcoholism as a disease rather than a sin and poverty as a cause rather than a result of drink, the WCTU became involved in labor issues, joining with the Knights of Labor to press for better working conditions for women workers. Describing workers in a textile mill, a WCTU member wrote in the organization's *Union Signal* magazine, "It is dreadful to see these girls, stripped almost to the skin . . . and running like racehorses from the beginning to the end of the day." She concluded, "The hard slavish work is drawing the girls into the saloon."

Willard capitalized on the cult of domesticity as a shrewd political tactic. Using "home protection" as her watchword, she argued as early as 1884 that women needed the vote to protect home and family. By the 1890s, the WCTU's grassroots network of local unions included 200,000 dues-paying members and had spread to all but the most isolated rural areas of the country.

Willard worked to create a broad reform coalition in the 1890s, embracing the Knights of Labor, the People's Party, and the Prohibition Party. Until her death in 1898, she led, if not a women's rights movement, then the first organized mass movement of women united around a women's issue. By 1900, thanks largely to the WCTU, women could claim a generation of experience in political action — speaking, lobbying, organizing, drafting legislation, and running private charitable institutions. As Willard observed, "All this work has tended more toward the liberation of women than it has toward the extinction of the saloon."

Elizabeth Cady Stanton, Susan B. Anthony, and the Movement for Woman Suffrage. Unlike the WCTU, the organized movement for woman suffrage remained small and relatively weak in the late nineteenth century. In 1869, Elizabeth Cady Stanton and her ally, Susan B. Anthony, launched the National Woman Suffrage Association (NWSA) demanding the vote for women (see chapter 18). A more conservative group, the American Woman Suffrage Association (AWSA) formed the same year. Composed of men as well as women, the AWSA believed that women should stick with the Republican Party and make suffrage the Sixteenth Amendment. Their optimism proved misplaced.

By 1890, the split had healed, and the newly united **National American Woman Suffrage Association (NAWSA)** launched campaigns on the state level to gain the vote for women. Twenty years had made a great change. Woman suffrage, though not yet generally supported, was no longer considered a crackpot idea, thanks in part to the WCTU's support of the "home protection" ballot. The NAWSA honored Elizabeth Cady Stanton by electing her its first president, but Susan B. Anthony, who took the helm in 1892, emerged as the leading figure in the new united organization.

Stanton and Anthony, both in their seventies, were coming to the end of their public careers. Since the days of the Seneca Falls woman's rights convention, they had worked for reforms for their sex, including property rights, custody rights, and the right to education and gainful employment. But the prize of woman suffrage still

National American Woman Suffrage Association (NAWSA) Organization formed in 1890 that united the National Woman Suffrage Association and the American Woman Suffrage Association. The NAWSA pursued state-level campaigns to gain the vote for women. With successes in Idaho, Colorado, and Utah, woman suffrage had become more accepted by the 1890s.

Visual Activity

WOMAN'S CHRISTIAN TEMPERANCE UNION POSTCARD

The WCTU distributed postcards like this to attack the liquor trade. Such cards are typical in their portrayal of saloon backers as traitors to the nation. Notice the man trampling on the American flag as he casts his ballot — a sly allusion to the need for woman suffrage. The History Center on Main Street, Mansfield, PA.

READING THE IMAGE: What do the images that surround the top slogan tell us about the abuses of alcohol?

CONNECTIONS: Why was temperance primarily a woman's movement?

eluded them. Suffragists won victories in Colorado in 1893 and Idaho in 1896. One more state joined the suffrage column in 1896 when Utah entered the Union. But women suffered a bitter defeat in a California referendum on woman suffrage that same year. Never losing faith, Anthony remarked in her last public appearance, in 1906, "Failure is impossible."

> **REVIEW** How did women's temperance activism contribute to the cause of woman suffrage?

Depression Politics

The depression that began in the spring of 1893 and lasted for more than four years put nearly half of the labor force out of work, a higher percentage than during the Great Depression of the 1930s. The human cost of the depression was staggering. "I Take my pen in hand to let you know that we are Starving to death," a Kansas farm woman wrote to the governor in 1894. "Last cent gone," wrote a young widow in her diary. "Children went to work without their breakfasts." Following the harsh dictates of social Darwinism and laissez-faire, the majority of America's elected officials believed that it was inappropriate for the government to intervene. But the scope of the depression made it impossible for churches and local agencies to supply sufficient relief, and increasingly Americans called on the federal government to take action. Armies of the unemployed marched on Washington to demand relief, and the Populist Party experienced a surge of support as the election of 1896 approached.

Coxey's Army.

Coxey's Army. Masses of unemployed Americans marched to Washington, D.C., in the spring of 1894 to call attention to their plight and to urge Congress to enact a public works program to end unemployment. Jacob S. Coxey of Massilon, Ohio, led the most publicized contingent. Convinced that men could be put to work building badly needed roads for the nation, Coxey proposed a scheme to finance public works through non-interest-bearing bonds. "What I am after," he maintained, "is to try to put this country in a condition so that no man who wants work shall be obliged to remain idle." His plan won support from the AFL and the Populists.

Starting out from Ohio with one hundred men, **Coxey's army**, as it was dubbed, swelled as it marched east through the spring snows of the Alleghenies. In Pennsylvania, Coxey recruited several hundred from the ranks of those left unemployed by the Homestead lockout.

On May 1, Coxey's army arrived in Washington. When Coxey defiantly marched his men onto the Capitol grounds, police set upon the demonstrators with nightsticks, cracking skulls and arresting Coxey and his lieutenants. Coxey went to jail for twenty days and was fined $5 for "walking on the grass." But other armies of the unemployed, totaling possibly as many as five thousand people, were still on their way. The more daring contingents commandeered entire trains, stirring fears of revolution. Journalists who covered the march did little to quiet the nation's fears. They delighted in military terminology, describing themselves as "war correspondents." To boost newspaper sales, they gave to the episode a tone of urgency and heightened the sense of a nation imperiled.

By August, the leaderless, tattered armies dissolved. Although the "On to Washington" movement proved ineffective in forcing federal relief legislation, Coxey's army dramatized the plight of the unemployed and acted, in the words of one participant, as a "living, moving object lesson." Like the Populists, Coxey's army

Coxey's army
Unemployed men who marched to Washington, D.C., in 1894 to urge Congress to enact a public works program to end unemployment. Jacob S. Coxey of Ohio led the most publicized contingent. The movement failed to force federal relief legislation.

COXEY'S ARMY

A contingent of Coxey's army stops to rest on its way to Washington, D.C. A "petition in boots," Coxey's followers were well dressed. Music was an important component of the march, including the anthem "Marching with Coxey." Band members are pictured on the right with their instruments. Despite their peaceful pose, the marchers stirred the fears of many Americans, who predicted an uprising of the unemployed. Courtesy of the Ohio Historical Connection, AL01139.

called into question the underlying values of the new industrial order and demonstrated how ordinary citizens turned to means outside the regular party system to influence politics in the 1890s.

The People's Party and the Election of 1896.
Even before the depression of 1893, the Populists had railed against the status quo. "We meet in the midst of a nation brought to the verge of moral, political, and material ruin," Ignatius Donnelly had declared in his keynote address at the creation of the People's Party in St. Louis in 1892. "The fruits of the toil of millions are boldly stolen to build up colossal fortunes for a few. . . . From the same prolific womb of governmental injustice we breed the two great classes — tramps and millionaires."

The fiery rhetoric frightened many who saw in the People's Party a call not to reform but to revolution. Throughout the country, the press denounced the Populists as "cranks, lunatics, and idiots." When one self-righteous editor dismissed them as "calamity howlers," Populist governor Lorenzo Lewelling of Kansas shot back, "If that is so I want to continue to howl until those conditions are improved."

The People's Party captured more than a million votes in the presidential election of 1892, a respectable showing for a new party (Map 20.1). But increasingly, sectional and racial animosities threatened its unity. Realizing that race prejudice obscured the common economic interests of black and white farmers, Populist Tom Watson of Georgia openly courted African Americans, appearing on platforms with black speakers and promising "to wipe out the color line." When angry Georgia whites threatened to lynch a black Populist preacher, Watson rallied two thousand gun-toting Populists to the man's defense. Although many Populists remained racist in their attitudes toward African Americans, the spectacle of white Georgians riding through the night to protect a black man from lynching was symbolic of the enormous changes the Populist Party promised in the South.

As the presidential election of 1896 approached, the depression intensified cries for reform not only from the Populists but also throughout the electorate. Depression worsened the tight money problem caused by the deflationary pressures of the gold standard. Once again, proponents of free silver stirred rebellion in the ranks of both the Democratic and the Republican parties. When the Republicans nominated Ohio governor William McKinley on a platform pledging the preservation of the gold standard, western advocates of free silver representing miners and farmers walked out of the convention. Open rebellion also split the Democratic Party as vast segments in the West and South repudiated President Grover Cleveland because of his support for gold. In South Carolina, Benjamin Tillman won his race for Congress by promising, "Send me to Washington and I'll stick my pitchfork into [Cleveland's] old ribs!"

The spirit of revolt animated the Democratic National Convention in Chicago in the summer of 1896. William

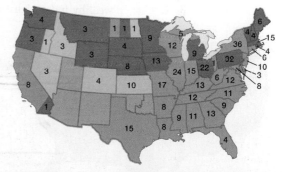

Candidate	Electoral Vote	Popular Vote	Percent of Popular Vote
Grover Cleveland (Democrat)	277	5,555,426	46.1
Benjamin Harrison (Republican)	145	5,182,690	43.0
James B. Weaver (People's)	22	1,029,846	8.5

MAP 20.1   THE ELECTION OF 1892

Jennings Bryan of Nebraska, the thirty-six-year-old "boy orator from the Platte," whipped the convention into a frenzy, calling passionately for free silver with a ringing exhortation: "Do not crucify mankind upon a cross of gold." Pandemonium broke loose as delegates stampeded to nominate Bryan, the youngest candidate ever to run for the presidency.

The juggernaut of free silver rolled out of Chicago and on to St. Louis, where the People's Party met a week after the Democrats adjourned. Many western Populists urged the party to ally with the Democrats and endorse Bryan. A major obstacle in the path of fusion, however, was Bryan's running mate, Arthur M. Sewall. A Maine railway director and bank president, Sewall, who had been placed on the ticket to appease conservative Democrats, embodied everything the Populists detested. Moreover, die-hard southern Populists wanted no part of fusion. Southern Democrats had resorted to fraud and violence to steal elections from the Populists in southern states, and support for a Democratic ticket proved hard to swallow.

Populists struggled to work out a compromise. To show that they remained true to their principles, delegates first voted to support all the planks of the 1892 platform, added to it a call for public works projects for the unemployed, and only narrowly defeated a plank for woman suffrage. To deal with the problem of fusion, the convention selected the vice presidential candidate first. The nomination of Tom Watson undercut opposition to Bryan's candidacy. And although Bryan quickly sent a telegram to protest that he would not drop Sewall as his running mate, mysteriously his message never reached the convention floor. Fusion triumphed. Bryan won nomination by a lopsided vote. The Populists did not know it, but their cheers for Bryan signaled the death knell for the People's Party.

Few contests in the nation's history have been as fiercely fought as the presidential election of 1896. On one side stood Republican William McKinley, backed by the wealthy industrialist and party boss Mark Hanna. Hanna played on the business community's fears of Populism to raise a Republican war chest more than double the amount of any previous campaign. On the other side, William Jennings Bryan, with few assets beyond his silver tongue, struggled to make up in energy and eloquence what his party lacked in campaign funds. He crisscrossed the country in a whirlwind tour, by his own reckoning visiting twenty-seven states and speaking to more than five million Americans.

On election day, four out of five voters went to the polls in an unprecedented turnout. The silver states of the Rocky Mountains lined up solidly for Bryan. The Northeast went for McKinley. The Midwest tipped the balance. In the end, the election hinged on between 100 and 1,000 votes in several key states, including Wisconsin, Iowa, and Minnesota. Although McKinley won twenty-three states to Bryan's twenty-two, the electoral vote showed a lopsided 271 to 176 in McKinley's favor (Map 20.2).

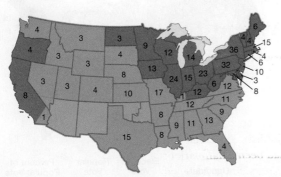

Candidate	Electoral Vote	Popular Vote	Percent of Popular Vote
William McKinley (Republican)	271	7,104,779	51.1
William J. Bryan (Democrat-People's)	176	6,502,925	47.7

MAP 20.2 THE ELECTION OF 1896

The biggest losers in 1896 turned out to be the Populists. On the national level, they polled fewer than 300,000 votes, a million less than in 1894. In the clamor to support Bryan, Populists in the South, determined to beat McKinley at any cost, swallowed their differences and drifted back to the Democratic Party.

> **REVIEW** Why was the People's Party unable to translate national support into victory in the 1896 election?

The United States and the World

Throughout much of the second half of the nineteenth century, U.S. interest in foreign policy took a backseat to territorial expansion in the American West. The United States fought the Indian wars while European nations carved empires in Asia, Africa, Latin America, and the Pacific.

At the turn of the twentieth century, the United States pursued a foreign policy consisting of two currents —isolationism and expansionism. Although the determination to remain detached from European politics had been a hallmark of U.S. foreign policy since the nation's founding, Americans simultaneously believed in manifest destiny— the "obvious" right to expand the nation from ocean to ocean. With its own inland empire secured, the United States looked outward. Determined to protect its sphere of influence in the Western Hemisphere and to expand its trading in Asia, the nation turned away from isolationism and toward a more active role on the world stage that led to intervention in China's Boxer uprising and war with Spain.

Markets and Missionaries. The depression of the 1890s provided a powerful impetus to American commercial expansion. As markets weakened at home, American businesses looked abroad for profits. As the depression deepened, one diplomat warned that Americans "must turn [their] eyes abroad, or they will soon look inward upon discontent."

Exports constituted a small but significant percentage of the profits of American business in the 1890s (Figure 20.2). And where American interests led, businessmen expected the government's power and influence to follow to protect their investments. Companies like Standard Oil actively sought to use the U.S. government as their agent, often putting foreign service employees on the payroll. "Our ambassadors and ministers and consuls," wrote John D. Rockefeller appreciatively, "have aided to push our way into new markets and to the utmost corners of the world."

America's foreign policy often appeared little more than a sidelight to business development. In Hawai'i (first called the Sandwich Islands), American sugar interests fomented a rebellion in 1893, toppling the increasingly independent Queen Lili'uokalani. They pushed Congress to annex the islands to avoid the high McKinley tariff on sugar. When President Cleveland learned that Hawai'ians opposed annexation, he withdrew the proposal from Congress. But expansionists still coveted the islands and looked for an opportunity to push through annexation.

Business interests alone did not account for the new expansionism that seized the nation during the 1890s. As Alfred Thayer Mahan, leader of a growing group of

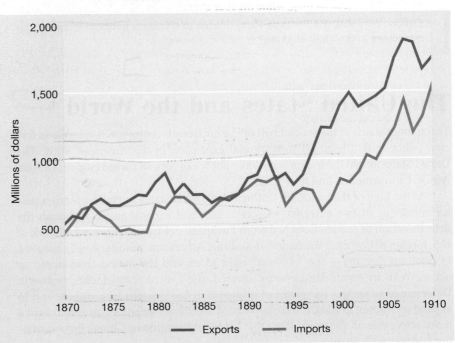

FIGURE 20.2 EXPANSION IN U.S. TRADE, 1870–1910

Between 1870 and 1910, American exports more than tripled. Imports generally rose, but they were held in check by the high protective tariffs championed by Republican presidents from Ulysses S. Grant to William Howard Taft. A decline in imports is particularly noticeable after the passage of the prohibitive McKinley tariff in 1890.

Millions of dollars

2,000
1,500
1,000
500

1870 1875 1880 1885 1890 1895 1900 1905 1910

—— Exports   —— Imports

American expansionists, confessed, "Even when material interests are the original exciting cause, it is the sentiment to which they give rise, the moral tone which emotion takes that constitutes the greater force." Much of that moral tone was set by American missionaries intent on spreading the gospel of Christianity to the "heathen." No area on the globe constituted a greater challenge than China.

An 1858 agreement, the Tianjin (Tientsin) treaty admitted foreign missionaries to China. Although Christians converted only 100,000 in a population of 400 million, the Chinese nevertheless resented the interference of missionaries in village life. Opposition to foreign missionaries took the form of antiforeign secret societies, most notably the Boxers, whose Chinese name translated to "Righteous Harmonious Fist." In 1899, the Boxers hunted down and killed Chinese Christians and missionaries in northwestern Shandong Province. With the tacit support of China's Dowager Empress, the Boxers, shouting "Uphold the Ch'ing Dynasty, Exterminate the Foreigners," marched on the cities. Their rampage eventually led to the massacre of some 30,000 Chinese converts and 250 foreign nuns, priests, and missionaries.

As the Boxers spread terror throughout northern China, some 800 Americans and Europeans sought refuge in the foreign diplomatic buildings in Peking (today's Beijing). Along with missionaries from the countryside came thousands of their Chinese converts. Unable to escape and cut off from outside aid and communication, the Americans and Europeans in Beijing mounted a defense to face the Boxer onslaught. One American described the scene as 20,000 Boxers stormed the walls in June 1900:

> Their yells were deafening, while the roar of gongs, drums, and horns sounded like thunder. . . . They waved their swords and stamped on the ground with their feet. They wore red turbans, sashes, and garters over blue cloth. . . . They were now only twenty yards from our gate. Three or four volleys from the Lebel rifles of our marines left more than fifty dead on the ground.

For two months the little group held out under siege, eating mule and horse meat and losing 76 men in battle. Sarah Conger, wife of the U.S. ambassador, wrote wearily, "[The siege] was exciting at first, but night after night of this firing, horn-blowing, and yelling, and the whizzing of bullets has hardened us to it."

In August 1900, 2,500 U.S. troops joined an international force sent to rescue the foreigners and put down the uprising in the Chinese capital. The European powers imposed the humiliating Boxer Protocol in 1901, giving themselves the right to maintain military forces in Beijing and requiring the Chinese government to pay an exorbitant indemnity of $333 million.

AMERICAN SOLDIERS AT THE CHINESE IMPERIAL PALACE

After helping suppress the Boxer uprising, these American soldiers stood alongside the road to the Chinese Imperial Palace to celebrate the conclusion of the fighting and the imposition of the Boxer Protocol. Strolling along the center of the road is a Christian missionary with his family, suggesting the triumph over the anti-Christian Boxers. Corbis.

Boxer uprising

Uprising in China led by the Boxers, an antiforeign society, in which 30,000 Chinese converts and 250 foreign Christians were killed. An international force rescued foreigners in Beijing and European powers imposed the humiliating Boxer Protocol on China in 1901.

Monroe Doctrine

President James Monroe's 1823 declaration that the Western Hemisphere was closed to further colonization or interference by European powers. In exchange, Monroe pledged that the United States would not become involved in European struggles. The United States strengthened the doctrine during the late nineteenth century.

THE SAMOAN ISLANDS, 1889

In the aftermath of the **Boxer uprising**, missionaries voiced no concern at the paradox of bringing Christianity to China at gunpoint. "It is worth any cost in money, worth any cost in bloodshed," argued one bishop, "if we can make millions of Chinese true and intelligent Christians." Merchants and missionaries alike shared such moralistic reasoning. Indeed, they worked hand in hand; trade and Christianity marched into Asia together. "Missionaries," admitted the American clergyman Charles Denby, "are the pioneers of trade and commerce. . . . The missionary, inspired by holy zeal, goes everywhere and by degrees foreign commerce and trade follow."

The Monroe Doctrine and the Open Door Policy. The emergence of the United States as a world power pitted the nation against other colonial powers, particularly Germany and Japan, which posed a threat to the twin pillars of America's expansionist foreign policy. The first, the **Monroe Doctrine**, came to be interpreted as establishing the Western Hemisphere as an American "sphere of influence" and warned European powers to stay away or risk war. The second, the Open Door, dealt with maintaining market access to China.

American diplomacy actively worked to buttress the Monroe Doctrine, with its assertion of American hegemony (domination) in the Western Hemisphere. In the 1880s, Republican secretary of state James G. Blaine promoted hemispheric peace and trade through Pan-American cooperation but, at the same time, used American troops to intervene in Latin American border disputes. In 1895, President Cleveland risked war with Great Britain to enforce the Monroe Doctrine when a conflict developed between Venezuela and British Guiana. After American saber rattling, the British backed down and accepted U.S. mediation in the area despite their territorial claims in Guiana.

In Central America, American business triumphed in a bloodless takeover that saw French and British interests routed. The United Fruit Company of Boston virtually dominated the Central American nations of Costa Rica and Guatemala, while an importer from New Orleans turned Honduras into a "banana republic" (a country run by U.S. business interests). Thus, by 1895, the United States, through business as well as diplomacy, had successfully achieved hegemony in Latin America and the Caribbean, forcing even the British to concur that "the infinite resources [of the United States] combined with its isolated position render it master of the situation and practically invulnerable as against any or all other powers."

At the same time that American foreign policy warned European powers to stay out of the Western Hemisphere, the United States competed for trade in the Eastern Hemisphere. As American interests in China grew, the United States became more aggressive in defending its presence in Asia and the Pacific. In 1889, it risked war with Germany to guarantee the U.S. Navy access to Pago Pago in the Samoan Islands, a port for refueling on the way to Asia. Germany, seeking dominance over the islands, sent warships to the region. But before fighting broke out, a typhoon destroyed the German and American ships. The potential combatants later divided the islands amicably in the 1899 Treaty of Berlin.

In the 1890s, China, weakened by years of internal warfare, was partitioned into spheres of influence by Britain, Japan, Germany, France, and Russia. Concerned about the integrity of China and no less about American trade, Secretary of State John Hay in 1899–1900 wrote a series of notes calling for an "open door" policy that would ensure trade access to all and maintain Chinese sovereignty. The notes were greeted by the major powers with polite evasion. Nevertheless, Hay skillfully managed to maneuver them into doing his bidding, and in 1900 he boldly announced the Open Door as international policy. The United States, by insisting on the **Open Door policy** managed to secure access to Chinese markets, expanding its economic power while avoiding the problems of maintaining a far-flung colonial empire on the Asian mainland. But as the Spanish-American War soon demonstrated, Americans found it hard to resist the temptations of overseas empire.

THE OPEN DOOR

The trade advantage the United States gained by its Open Door policy is depicted in this political cartoon. Uncle Sam stands in the doorway to China permitting access to representatives of Great Britain (left) and Russia (right) with the key of American diplomacy. In fact, the Open Door policy promised all foreign powers equal access to the China trade, not American control of access to the trade, as the cartoon suggests. The Granger Collection, New York.

"A Splendid Little War." The Spanish-American War began as a humanitarian effort to free Cuba from Spain's colonial grasp and ended with the United States itself acquiring territory overseas and fighting a dirty guerrilla war with Filipino nationalists who, like the Cubans, sought independence. Behind the contradiction stood the twin pillars of American foreign policy. The Monroe Doctrine made Spain's presence in Cuba unacceptable; and U.S. determination to keep open the door to Asia made the Philippines attractive. Precedent for the nation's imperial adventures also came from the recent Indian wars in the American West, which provided a template for the subjugation of native peoples in the name of civilization.

Looking back on the Spanish-American War of 1898, Secretary of State John Hay judged it "a splendid little war; begun with the highest motives, carried on with magnificent intelligence and spirit, favored by that fortune which loves the brave." At the close of a decade marred by bitter depression, social unrest, and political upheaval, the war offered Americans a chance to wave the flag and march in unison. War fever proved as infectious as the tune of a John Philip Sousa march. Few argued the merits of the conflict until it was over and the time came to divide the spoils.

The war began with moral outrage over the treatment of Cuban revolutionaries, who had launched a fight for independence against the Spanish colonial regime in 1895. In an attempt to isolate the guerrillas, the Spanish general Valeriano Weyler herded Cubans into crowded and unsanitary concentration camps, where thousands died of hunger, disease, and exposure. Starvation soon spread to the cities. By 1898, fully a quarter of the island's population had perished in the Cuban revolution.

Open Door policy
Policy successfully insisted upon by Secretary of State John Hay in 1899–1900 recommending that the major powers of the United States, Britain, Japan, Germany, France, and Russia all have access to trade with China and that Chinese sovereignty be maintained.

Spanish-American War
1898 war between Spain and the United States that began as an effort to free Cuba from Spain's colonial rule. This popular war left the United States an imperial power in control of Cuba and colonies in Puerto Rico, Guam, and the Philippines.

yellow journalism
Term first given to sensationalistic newspaper reporting and cartoon images rendered in yellow. A circulation war between two New York City papers provoked the tactics of yellow journalism that fueled popular support for the Spanish-American War in 1898.

As the Cuban rebellion dragged on, pressure for American intervention mounted. American newspapers fueled public outrage at Spain. A fierce circulation war raged in New York City between William Randolph Hearst's *Journal* and Joseph Pulitzer's *World*. Their competition provoked what came to be called **yellow journalism**, named for the colored ink used in a popular comic strip. The Cuban war provided a wealth of dramatic copy. Newspapers fed the American people a daily diet of "Butcher" Weyler and Spanish atrocities. Hearst sent artist Frederic Remington to document the horror, and when Remington wired home, "There is no trouble here. There will be no war," Hearst shot back, "You furnish the pictures and I'll furnish the war."

American interests in Cuba were, in the words of the U.S. minister to Spain, more than "merely theoretical or sentimental." American business had more than $50 million invested in Cuban sugar, and American trade with Cuba, a brisk $100 million a year before the rebellion, had dropped to near zero. Nevertheless, the business community balked, wary of a war with Spain. When industrialist Mark Hanna, the Republican kingmaker and senator from Ohio, urged restraint, a hotheaded Theodore Roosevelt exploded, "We will have this war for the freedom of Cuba, Senator Hanna, in spite of the timidity of commercial interests."

To expansionists like Roosevelt, more than Cuban independence was at stake. As assistant secretary of the navy, Roosevelt took the helm in the absence of his boss and, in the summer of 1897, audaciously ordered the U.S. fleet to be ready to steam to Manila in the Philippines. In the event of conflict with Spain, Roosevelt put the navy in a position to capture the islands and gain a stepping-stone to China.

President McKinley moved slowly toward intervention. In a show of American force, he dispatched the battleship *Maine* to Cuba. On the night of February 15, 1898, a mysterious explosion destroyed the *Maine*, killing 267 crew members. The source of the explosion remained unclear, but inflammatory stories in the press enraged Americans. (See "Making Historical Arguments," page 604.) Rallying to the cry "Remember the *Maine*," Congress declared war on Spain. In a surge of patriotism, more than a million men rushed to enlist. War brought with it a unity of purpose and national harmony that ended a decade of political dissent and strife. "In April, everywhere over this good fair land, flags were flying," wrote Kansas editor William Allen White. "At the stations, crowds gathered to hurrah for the soldiers, and to throw hats into the air, and to unfurl flags."

Five days after McKinley signed the war resolution, a U.S. Navy squadron destroyed the Spanish fleet in Manila Bay (Map 20.3). The stunning victory caught most Americans by surprise. Few had ever heard of the Philippines. Even McKinley confessed that he could not locate the archipelago on the map. Nevertheless he dispatched U.S. troops to secure the islands.

The war in Cuba ended almost as quickly as it began. The first troops landed on June 22, and after a handful of battles the Spanish forces surrendered on July 17. The war lasted just long enough to elevate Theodore Roosevelt to the status of bona fide war hero. Roosevelt resigned his navy post and formed the Rough Riders, a regiment composed of a sprinkling of Ivy League polo players and a number of western cowboys Roosevelt befriended during his stint as a cattle rancher in the Dakotas. The

Rough Riders' charge up Kettle Hill and Roosevelt's role in the decisive battle of San Juan Hill made front-page news. Overnight, Roosevelt became the most famous man in America. By the time he sailed home from Cuba, a coalition of independent Republicans was already plotting his political future.

The Debate over American Imperialism. After a few brief campaigns in Cuba and Puerto Rico brought the Spanish-American War to an end, the American people woke up in possession of an empire that stretched halfway around the globe. As part of the spoils of war, the United States acquired Cuba, Puerto Rico, Guam, and the Philippines. And Republicans quickly moved to annex Hawai'i in July 1898.

Contemptuous of the Cubans, whom General William Shafter declared "no more fit for self-government than gun-powder is for hell," the U.S. government imposed a Cuban constitution and refused to give up military control of the island until the Cubans accepted the so-called Platt Amendment — a series of provisions that granted the United States the right to intervene to protect Cuba's "independence,"

Map Activity

MAP 20.3 THE SPANISH-AMERICAN WAR, 1898

The Spanish-American War was fought in two theaters, the Philippine Islands and Cuba. Five days after President William McKinley called for a declaration of war, Admiral George Dewey captured Manila. The war lasted only eight months. Troops landed in Cuba in mid-June and by mid-July had destroyed the Spanish fleet.

READING THE MAP: Which countries held imperial control over countries and territories immediately surrounding the Philippine Islands and Cuba?

CONNECTIONS: What role did American newspapers play in the start of the war? How did the results of the war serve American aims in both Asia and the Western Hemisphere?

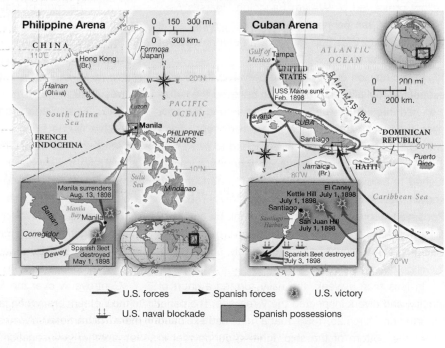

Making Historical Arguments

Did Terrorists Sink the *Maine*?

At 9:40 p.m. on the evening of February 15, 1898, the U.S. battleship *Maine* blew up in Havana harbor. "The shock threw us backward," reported one eyewitness. "From the deck forward of amidships shot a streak of fire as high as the tall buildings on Broadway. Then the glare of light widened out like a funnel at the top, and down through this bright circle fell showers of wreckage and mangled sailors." In all, 267 sailors drowned or burned to death in one of the worst naval catastrophes to occur during peacetime.

Captain Charles Dwight Sigsbee, the last man to leave the burning ship, filed a terse report saying that the *Maine* had blown up and "urging [that] public opinion should be suspended until further report." But the yellow press, led by William Randolph Hearst's *New York Journal*, ran banner headlines proclaiming, "The War Ship *Maine* Was Split in Two by an Enemy's Secret Infernal Machine!"

Public opinion quickly divided between those who suspected foul play and those who believed the explosion had been an accident. Foremost among the accident theorists was the Spanish government, along with U.S. business interests who hoped to avoid war. The "jingoes," as proponents of war were called, rushed to blame Spain. Even before the details were known, Assistant Secretary of the Navy Theodore Roosevelt wrote, "The *Maine* was sunk by an act of dirty treachery on the part of the Spaniards I believe; though we shall never find out definitely, and officially it will go down as an accident."

In less than a week, the navy formed a court of inquiry, and divers inspected the wreckage. The panel reported on March 25, 1898, that a mine had exploded under the bottom of the ship, igniting gunpowder in the forward magazine. The panel could not determine whether the mine had been planted by the Spanish government or by recalcitrant followers of Valeriano Weyler. The infamous Weyler had been ousted after

the American press dubbed him "the Butcher" for his harsh treatment of the Cubans.

As time passed, however, more people came to view the explosion of the *Maine* as an accident. European experts concluded that the *Maine* had exploded accidentally, from a fire in the coal bunker adjacent to the reserve gunpowder. Perhaps poor design, not treachery, had sunk the *Maine*.

In 1910, New York congressman William Sultzer put it succinctly: "The day after the ship was sunk, you could hardly find an American who did not believe that she had been foully done to death by a treacherous enemy. Today you can hardly find an American who believes Spain had anything to do with it." The *Maine* still lay in the mud of Havana harbor, a sunken tomb containing the remains of many sailors. The Cuban government asked for the removal of the wreck, and veterans demanded a decent burial for the sailors. So in March 1910, Congress voted to raise the *Maine* and reinvestigate.

The "Final Report on Removing the Wreck of Battleship *Maine* from the Harbor of Habana, Cuba" appeared in April 1913. This report confirmed that the original naval inquiry was in error, but it ruled out the accident theory by concluding that the nature of the initial explosion indicated a homemade bomb — once again casting suspicion on Weyler's fanatic followers. Following the investigation and removal of human remains, the wreckage of the *Maine* was towed out to sea and, with full funeral honors, sunk in six hundred fathoms of water.

Controversy over the *Maine* proved harder to sink. In the Vietnam era, when faith in the "military establishment" plummeted, Admiral Hyman Rickover launched yet another investigation. Viewing the 1913 "Final Report" as a cover-up, he complained that the ship had been sunk so deep "that there will be no chance of the true facts being revealed." Rickover, a maverick who held the naval brass in low esteem, blamed "the warlike

"MAINE EXPLOSION CAUSED BY BOMB OR TORPEDO?"

The front page of the *New York World* two days after the blast, trumpeted the news and graphically portrayed the destruction of the ship. The text insisted the explosion was not accidental, even though there was no evidence to back up the assertion. The extent of the destruction and the deaths of 267 sailors fueled war fever. © Collection of the New-York Historical Society, USA/Bridgeman Images.

atmosphere in Congress and the press, and the natural tendency to look for reasons for the loss that did not reflect on the Navy." Judging the sinking an accident, Rickover warned, "We must make sure that those in 'high places' do not without more careful consideration of the consequences, exert our prestige and might."

Two decades later, the pendulum swung back. A 1995 study of the *Maine* published by the Smithsonian Institution concluded that zealot followers of General Weyler sank the battleship: "They had the opportunity, the means, and the motivation, and they blew up the *Maine* with a small low-strength mine they made themselves." According to this theory, the terrorists' homemade bomb burst the *Maine*'s hull, triggering a massive explosion. And in

1998 *National Geographic* employed computer models to show that an external explosion (bomb) was capable of sinking the *Maine*.

QUESTIONS FOR ANALYSIS

Summarize the Argument   How have explanations for the sinking of the *Maine* changed over time? Has the evidence changed, or have interpretations of the evidence shifted?

Analyze the Evidence   Why were jingoists so quick to blame Spain for the sinking of the *Maine*?

Consider the Context   In 1995, the Smithsonian panel judged the sinking of the *Maine* a result of terrorism perpetrated by followers of the deposed General Weyler. Was their use of the word *terrorism* as inflammatory then as it is today?

as well as the power to oversee Cuban debt so that European creditors would not find an excuse for intervention. For good measure, the United States gave itself a ninety-nine-year lease on a naval base at Guantánamo. In return, McKinley promised to implement an extensive sanitation program to clean up the island, making it more attractive to American investors.

In the formal Treaty of Paris (1898), Spain ceded the Philippines to the United States along with the former Spanish colonies of Puerto Rico and Guam (Map 20.4). Empire did not come cheap. When Spain initially balked at these

Map Activity

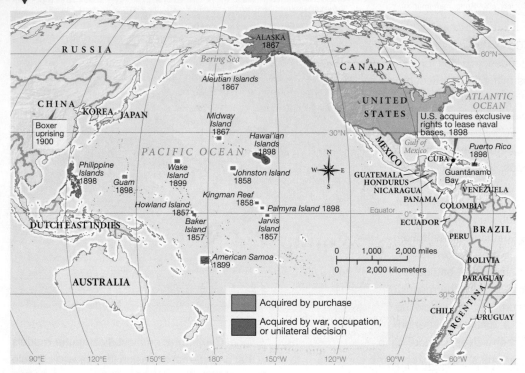

MAP 20.4   U.S. OVERSEAS EXPANSION THROUGH 1900

The United States extended its interests abroad with a series of territorial acquisitions. Although Cuba was granted independence, the Platt Amendment kept the new nation firmly under U.S. control. In the wake of the Spanish-American War, the United States woke up to find that it held an empire extending halfway around the globe.

READING THE MAP: Does the map indicate that more territory was acquired by purchase or by war, occupation, or unilateral decision? How many purchases of land outside the continental United States did the government make?

CONNECTIONS: What foreign policy developments occurred in the 1890s? How did American political leaders react to them? Where was U.S. expansion headed, and why?

terms, the United States agreed to pay an indemnity of $20 million for the islands. Nor was the cost measured in money alone. Filipino revolutionaries under Emilio Aguinaldo, who had greeted U.S. troops as liberators, bitterly fought the new masters. It would take seven years and 4,000 American dead — almost ten times the number killed in Cuba — not to mention an estimated 20,000 Filipino casualties, to defeat Aguinaldo and secure American control of the Philippines.

At home, a vocal minority, mostly Democrats and former Populists, resisted the country's foray into overseas empire, judging it unwise, immoral, and unconstitutional. William Jennings Bryan, who enlisted in the army but never saw action, concluded that American expansionism only distracted the nation from problems at home. Pointing to the central paradox of the war, Representative Bourke Cockran of New York admonished, "We who have been the destroyers of oppression are asked now to become its agents." But the expansionists won the day. As Senator Knute Nelson of Minnesota assured his colleagues, "We come as ministering angels, not as despots." Fresh from its conquest of Native Americans in the West, the nation largely embraced the heady mixture of racism and missionary zeal that fueled American adventurism abroad. The *Washington Post* trumpeted, "The taste of empire is in the mouth of the people," thrilled at the prospect of "an imperial policy, the Republic renascent, taking her place with the armed nations."

> **REVIEW** Why did the United States largely abandon its isolationist foreign policy in the 1890s?

Conclusion: Rallying around the Flag

A decade of domestic strife ended amid the blare of martial music and the waving of flags. The Spanish-American War drowned out the calls for social reform that had fueled the Populist politics of the 1890s. During that decade, angry farmers facing hard times looked to Farmers' Alliances to fight for their vision of economic democracy, workers staged bloody battles across the country to assert their rights, and women like Frances Willard preached temperance and suffrage. Together they formed a new People's Party to fight for change.

The bitter depression that began in 1893 led to increased labor strife. The Pullman boycott brutally dramatized the power of property and the conservatism of the laissez-faire state. But workers' willingness to confront capitalism on the streets of Chicago, Homestead, Cripple Creek, and a host of other sites across America eloquently testified to labor's growing determination, unity, and strength.

As the depression deepened, the sight of Coxey's army of unemployed marching on Washington to demand federal intervention in the economy signaled a growing shift in the public mind against the stand-pat politics of laissez-faire. The call for the government to take action to better the lives of workers, farmers, and the dispossessed manifested itself in the fiercely fought presidential campaign of William

Jennings Bryan in 1896. With the outbreak of the Spanish-American War in 1898, the decade ended on a harmonious note with patriotic Americans rallying around the flag. But even though Americans basked in patriotism and contemplated empire, old grievances had not been laid to rest. The People's Party had been beaten, but the Populist spirit lived on in the demands for greater government involvement in the economy, expanded opportunities for direct democracy, and a more equitable balance of profits and power between the people and the big corporations. A new generation of progressive reformers championed the unfinished reform agenda in the first decades of the twentieth century.

Chapter Review

KEY TERMS

Farmers' Alliance (p. 583)

People's Party (Populist Party) (p. 585)

Homestead lockout (p. 586)

Cripple Creek miners' strike of 1894 (p. 587)

Pullman boycott (p. 589)

National American Woman Suffrage Association (NAWSA) (p. 592)

Coxey's army (p. 594)

Boxer uprising (p. 600)

Monroe Doctrine (p. 600)

Open Door policy (p. 601)

Spanish-American War (p. 601)

yellow journalism (p. 602)

REVIEW QUESTIONS

❶ Why did American farmers organize alliances in the late nineteenth century?   (pp. 582–85)

❷ What led to the labor wars of the 1890s? (pp. 585–90)

❸ How did women's temperance activism contribute to the cause of woman suffrage?   (pp. 590–93)

❹ Why was the People's Party unable to translate national support into victory in the 1896 election?   (pp. 593–97)

❺ Why did the United States largely abandon its isolationist foreign policy in the 1890s?   (pp. 597–607)

MAKING CONNECTIONS

❶ Why did so many farmers and urban workers look to the government to help advance their visions of economic justice?

❷ What circumstances gave rise to labor protests in the 1890s? How did they differ from those triggering earlier strikes?

❸ How did women's activism in the late nineteenth century help advance the cause of woman suffrage?

LINKING TO THE PAST

❶ How did the conquest of Native Americans in the West foreshadow U.S. expansion abroad? In what ways did the assumptions of racial superiority evident in U.S. Indian policy affect the treatment of Cubans and Filipinos? (See chapter 17.)

❷ Why in the midst of burgeoning growth did the United States experience a major depression in the 1890s? Draw on your knowledge of the development of U.S. industries such as the railroads. (See chapter 18.)

Progressivism from the Grass Roots to the White House,
1890–1916

CONTENT LEARNING OBJECTIVES

After reading and studying this chapter, you should be able to:

- Explain how and why grassroots progressivism arose near the start of the twentieth century and why proponents like Jane Addams and Hull House served as a spearhead for reform.

- Identify how President Theodore Roosevelt put his progressive activism to work toward big business, conservation, and international affairs and how his successor William Howard Taft stalled the progressive reforms Roosevelt had begun.

- Explain why progressives led an insurgent campaign during the election of 1912 and the factors that led to Woodrow Wilson's victory.

- Describe how Wilson sought to enact his "New Freedom" once in office and explain how he became a reluctant progressive.

- Understand the limits of progressive reform, and identify the organizations that offered more radical visions of America's future.

I n the summer of 1889, Jane Addams leased two floors of a dilapidated mansion on Chicago's West Side. Her immigrant neighbors must have wondered why this well-dressed woman, who surely could afford better housing, chose to live on South Halsted Street. Yet the house, built by Charles Hull, precisely suited Addams's needs. For Addams, personal action marked the first step in her search for solutions to the

PROGRESSIVE PARTY SOUVENIR BANDANA

This red bandana is a campaign souvenir from 1912, the year Theodore Roosevelt's followers broke with Republicans to form the Progressive Party. Roosevelt challenged laissez-faire liberalism and argued for government action for social justice. David J. & Janice L. Frent Collection/Corbis.

social problems created by urban industrialism. She wanted to help her immigrant neighbors, and she wanted to offer meaningful work to educated women like herself. Addams's emphasis on the reciprocal relationship between the social classes made Hull House different from other philanthropic enterprises. She wished to do things with, not just for, Chicago's poor. *with not for*

In the next decade, Hull House expanded from two rented floors in the old brick mansion to some thirteen buildings housing a remarkable variety of activities. Addams provided public baths, opened a restaurant for working women too tired to cook after their long shifts, and sponsored a nursery and kindergarten. Hull House offered classes, lectures, art exhibits, musical instruction, and college extension courses. It boasted a gymnasium, a theater, a manual training workshop, a labor museum, and the first public playground in Chicago.

From the first, Hull House attracted an extraordinary set of reformers who pioneered the scientific investigation of urban ills. Armed with statistics, they launched campaigns to improve housing, end child labor, fund playgrounds, and lobby for laws to protect workers.

Addams quickly learned that it was impossible to deal with urban problems without becoming involved in politics. Piles of decaying garbage overflowed Halsted Street's wooden trash bins, breeding flies and disease. To rectify the problem, Addams got herself appointed garbage inspector. Out on the streets at six in the morning, she rode atop the garbage wagon to make sure it made its rounds. Eventually, her struggle to aid the urban poor led her on to the state capitol and to Washington, D.C.

Under Addams's leadership, Hull House became a "spearhead for reform," part of a broader movement that contemporaries called progressivism. The transition from personal action to political activism that Addams personified became one of the hallmarks of this reform period, which lasted from the 1890s to World War I. Classical liberalism, which opposed the tyranny of centralized government, did not address the enormous power of Gilded Age business giants. As the gap between rich and poor widened in the 1890s, progressive reformers demonstrated a willingness to use the government to counterbalance the power of private interests and, in doing so, redefined liberalism in the twentieth century.

Faith in activism united an otherwise diverse group of progressive reformers. A sense of Christian mission inspired some. Others,

CHRONOLOGY

1889	Jane Addams opens Hull House.
1896	*Plessy v. Ferguson* decided.
1900	Socialist Party founded.
1901	William McKinley assassinated; Theodore Roosevelt becomes president.
1902	Antitrust lawsuit filed against Northern Securities Company. Roosevelt mediates anthracite coal strike.
1903	Women's Trade Union League founded. Panama Canal construction begins.
1904	Roosevelt Corollary to Monroe Doctrine announced.
1905	Industrial Workers of the World founded.
1906	Pure Food and Drug Act and Meat Inspection Act enacted. Atlanta race riot kills several hundred blacks. Hepburn Act enacted.
1907	Panic on Wall Street causes economic downturn. "Gentlemen's Agreement" made with Japan.
1908	*Muller v. Oregon* decided. William Howard Taft elected president.
1909	Garment workers strike. National Association for the Advancement of Colored People formed.
1911	Triangle Shirtwaist Company fire kills workers.
1912	Roosevelt runs for president on Progressive Party ticket. Woodrow Wilson elected president.
1913	Suffragists march in Washington, D.C. Federal Reserve Act enacted.
1914	Federal Trade Commission created. Clayton Antitrust Act enacted.
1916	Margaret Sanger opens first U.S. birth control clinic.

JANE ADDAMS

Jane Addams was twenty-nine years old when she founded Hull House on South Halsted Street in Chicago. Her desire to live among the poor and her insistence that settlement house work benefited educated women such as her as well as her immigrant neighbors marked the distance from philanthropy to progressive reform. Her autobiographical *Twenty Years at Hull-House* was published in 1910. Photo: Jane Addams Memorial Collection (JAMC _8000_0005_0014), Special Collections, University of Illinois at Chicago, photographer: Max Platz; book: Newberry Library, Chicago, Illinois, USA/Bridgeman Images.

fearing social upheaval, sought to remove some of the worst evils of urban industrialism — tenements, child labor, and harsh working conditions. A belief in technical expertise and scientific management infused progressivism and made the cult of efficiency part of the movement.

Progressives shared a growing concern about the power of wealthy individuals and a distrust of the trusts, but they were not immune to the prejudices of their era. Although they called for greater democracy, many progressives sought to restrict the rights of African Americans, Asians, and even the women who formed the backbone of the movement.

Uplift and efficiency, social justice and social control, direct democracy and discrimination all came together in the Progressive Era at every level of politics and in the presidencies of Theodore Roosevelt and Woodrow Wilson. While in office, Roosevelt advocated conservation, pushed through antitrust reforms, and championed the nation as a world power. Roosevelt's successor, William Taft, failed to follow in Roosevelt's footsteps, and the resulting split in the Republican Party paved the way for Wilson's victory in 1912. A reluctant progressive, Wilson eventually presided over reforms in banking, business, and labor.

Grassroots Progressivism

Much of progressive reform began at the grassroots level and percolated upward into local, state, and eventually national politics as reformers attacked the social problems fostered by urban industrialism. Although **progressivism** flourished in many different settings across the country, urban problems inspired the progressives' greatest efforts. In their zeal to "civilize the city," reformers founded settlement houses, professed a new Christian social gospel, and campaigned against vice and crime in the name of "social purity." Allying with the working class, women progressives sought to better the lot of sweatshop garment workers and to end child labor. These local reform efforts often ended up being debated in state legislatures and in the U.S. Congress.

Civilizing the City. Progressives attacked the problems of the city on many fronts. **Settlement houses**, which began in England, spread in the United States. By 1893, the needs of poor urban neighborhoods that had motivated Jane Addams led Lillian Wald to recruit several other nurses to move to New York City's Lower East Side "to live in the neighborhood as nurses, identify ourselves with it socially, and . . . contribute to it our citizenship." Wald's Henry Street settlement pioneered public health nursing.

Women, particularly college-educated women like Addams and Wald, formed the backbone of the settlement house movement. Settlement houses gave college-educated women eager to use their knowledge a place to put their talents to work in the service of society and to champion progressive reform. Such reformers believed that only by living among the poor could they help bridge the growing class divide. Settlements like Hull House grew in number from six in 1891 to more than four hundred in 1911. In the process, settlement house women created a new profession — social work.

For their part, churches confronted urban social problems by enunciating a new **social gospel**, one that saw its mission as not simply to reform individuals but to reform society. The social gospel offered a powerful corrective to social Darwinism and the gospel of wealth, which fostered the belief that riches somehow signaled divine favor. Charles M. Sheldon's popular book *In His Steps* (1898) called on men and women to Christianize capitalism by asking the question "What would Jesus do?"

Ministers also played an active role in the social purity movement, the campaign to attack vice. To end the "social evil," as reformers delicately referred to prostitution, the social purity movement brought together ministers who wished to stamp out sin, doctors concerned about the spread of venereal disease, and women reformers. Advanced progressives linked prostitution to poverty and championed higher wages for women working in industrial or other jobs.

Attacks on alcohol went hand in hand with the push for social purity. The Anti-Saloon League, formed in 1895 under the leadership of Protestant clergy, added to the efforts of the Woman's Christian Temperance Union in campaigning to end the sale of liquor. Reformers pointed to links between drinking, prostitution, wife and child abuse, unemployment, and industrial accidents. The powerful liquor lobby fought back, spending liberally in election campaigns, fueling the charge that liquor corrupted the political process.

An element of nativism (dislike of foreigners) ran through the movement for prohibition, as it did in a number of progressive reforms. The Irish, the Italians, and the Germans were among the groups stigmatized by temperance reformers for their drinking. Progressives campaigned to enforce the Sunday closing of taverns, stores, and other commercial establishments and pushed for state legislation to outlaw the sale of liquor. By 1912, seven states were "dry."

progressivism
A reform movement that often advocated government activism to mitigate the problems created by urban industrialism. Progressivism reached its peak in 1912 with the creation of the Progressive Party. The term *progressivism* has come to mean any general effort advocating for social welfare programs.

settlement houses
Settlements established in poor neighborhoods beginning in the 1880s. Reformers like Jane Addams and Lillian Wald believed that only by living among the poor could they help bridge the growing class divide. College-educated women formed the backbone of the settlement house movement.

social gospel
A vision of Christianity that saw its mission as not simply to reform individuals but to reform society. Emerging in the early twentieth century, it offered a powerful corrective to social Darwinism and the gospel of wealth, which fostered the belief that riches signaled divine favor.

Progressives' efforts to civilize the city demonstrated their willingness to take action; their belief that environment, not heredity alone, determined human behavior; and their optimism that conditions could be corrected through government action without radically altering America's economy or institutions. All of these attitudes characterized the progressive movement.

Progressives and the Working Class. Day-to-day contact with their neighbors made settlement house workers particularly sympathetic to labor. When Mary Kenney O'Sullivan complained that her bookbinders' union met in a dirty, noisy saloon, Jane Addams invited them to meet at Hull House. And during the Pullman strike in 1894 (see chapter 20) Hull House residents organized strike relief. "Hull-House has been so unionized," grumbled one Chicago businessman, "that it has lost its usefulness and become a detriment and harm to the community." But to the working class, the support of middle-class reformers marked a significant gain.

Attempts to forge a cross-class alliance became institutionalized in 1903 with the creation of the Women's Trade Union League (WTUL). The WTUL brought together women workers and middle-class "allies." Its goal was to organize working women into unions under the auspices of the American Federation of Labor (AFL). Although the alliance between working women, primarily immigrants and daughters of immigrants, and their middle-class allies was not without tension, the WTUL helped working women achieve significant gains.

The WTUL's most notable success came in 1909 in the "uprising of the twenty thousand," when hundreds of women employees of the Triangle Shirtwaist Company in New York City went on strike to protest low wages, dangerous working conditions, and management's refusal to recognize their union, the International Ladies' Garment Workers Union. In support, an estimated twenty thousand garment workers, most of them teenage girls and many of them Jewish and Italian immigrants, stayed out on strike through the winter, picketing in the bitter cold. Police and hired thugs harassed the picketing strikers, beating them up and arresting more than six hundred of them for "street walking" (prostitution). When WTUL allies, including J. P. Morgan's daughter Anne, joined the picket line, the harassment quickly stopped. By the time the strike ended in February 1910, the workers had won important demands in many shops. The solidarity shown by the women workers proved to be the strike's greatest achievement. As Clara Lemlich, one of the strike's leaders, exclaimed, "They used to say that you couldn't even organize women. They wouldn't come to union meetings. They were 'temporary' workers. Well we showed them!"

But for all its success, the uprising of the twenty thousand failed fundamentally to change conditions for women workers, as the tragic Triangle fire dramatized in 1911. A little over a year after the shirtwaist makers' strike ended, fire alarms sounded at the Triangle Shirtwaist factory. The ramshackle building, full of lint and combustible cloth, burned to rubble in half an hour. A WTUL member described the scene below on the street: "Two young girls whom I knew to be working in the vicinity came rushing toward me, tears were running from their eyes and they were white and shaking as they caught me by the arm. 'Oh,' shrieked one of them, 'they are jumping. Jumping from ten stories up! They are going through the air like bundles of clothes.'"

IDENTIFYING THE DEAD

After the Triangle fire on March 26, 1911, New York City set up a makeshift morgue at the end of Manhattan's Charities Pier. There, the remains of more than a hundred young women and two dozen young men were laid out in coffins for their friends and relatives to identify. Often small personal items provided the only clues to the victim's identity.

Hadwin Collection, Kheel Center, Cornell University, Ithaca, NY.

14. Viewing the unfortunates at the Morgue

The terrified Triangle workers had little choice but to jump. Flames blocked one exit, and the other door had been locked to prevent workers from pilfering. The flimsy, rusted fire escape collapsed under the weight of fleeing workers, killing dozens. Trapped, 54 workers on the top floors jumped to their deaths. Of 500 workers, 146 died and scores of others were injured. The owners of the Triangle firm went to trial for negligence, but they avoided conviction when authorities determined that a careless smoker had started the fire. The Triangle Shirtwaist Company reopened in another firetrap within a matter of weeks.

Outrage and a sense of futility overwhelmed Rose Schneiderman, a leading WTUL organizer, who made a bitter speech at the memorial service for the dead Triangle workers. "I would be a traitor to those poor burned bodies if I came here to talk good fellowship," she told her audience. "We have tried you good people of the public and we have found you wanting. . . . I know from my experience it is up to the working people to save themselves . . . by a strong working class movement." The Triangle fire severely tested the bonds of the cross-class alliance. Schneiderman and other WTUL leaders determined that organizing and striking were no longer enough, particularly when the AFL paid so little attention to women workers. Increasingly, the WTUL turned its efforts to lobbying for protective legislation — laws that would limit hours and regulate women's working conditions.

The National Consumers League (NCL) also fostered cross-class alliance and advocated for protective legislation. When Florence Kelley took over the leadership of the NCL in 1899, she urged middle-class women to boycott stores and exert pressure for decent wages and working conditions for women employees. Frustrated by the reluctance of the private sector to reform, the NCL promoted protective legislation to better working conditions for women.

Advocates of protective legislation had won a major victory in 1908 when the U.S. Supreme Court, in *Muller v. Oregon*, reversed its previous rulings and upheld an Oregon law that limited to ten the number of hours women could work in a day. A mass of sociological evidence put together by Florence Kelley of the NCL and Josephine Goldmark of the WTUL convinced the Court that long hours endangered women and therefore the entire human race. The Court's ruling set a precedent, but one that separated the well-being of women workers from that of men by arguing that women's reproductive role justified special treatment. Later generations of women fighting for equality would question the effectiveness of this strategy and argue that it ultimately closed good jobs to women. The WTUL, however, greeted protective legislation as a first step in the attempt to ensure the safety of all workers.

Reform also fueled the fight for woman suffrage. For women like Jane Addams, involvement in social reform led inevitably to support for woman suffrage. These new suffragists emphasized the reforms that could be accomplished if women had the vote. Addams insisted that in an urban, industrial society, a good housekeeper could not be sure the food she fed her family, or the water and milk they drank, were pure unless she could vote.

> **REVIEW** What types of people were drawn to the progressive movement, and why?

Progressivism: Theory and Practice

Progressivism emphasized action and experimentation. Dismissing the view that humans should leave progress to the dictates of natural selection, a new group of reform Darwinists argued that evolution could be advanced more rapidly if men and women used their intellects to improve society. In their zeal for action, progressives often showed an unchecked admiration for speed and efficiency that promoted scientific management and a new cult to improve productivity. These varied strands of progressive theory found practical application in state and local politics, where reformers challenged traditional laissez-faire government.

reform Darwinism
Sociological theory developed in the 1880s that argued humans could speed up evolution by altering their environment. A challenge to the laissez-faire approach of social Darwinism, reform Darwinism insisted that the liberal state should play an active role in solving social problems.

Reform Darwinism and Social Engineering.
The active, interventionist approach of the progressives directly challenged social Darwinism, with its insistence on survival of the fittest. A new group of sociologists argued that progress could be advanced more rapidly if people used their intellects to alter their environment. The best statement of this reform Darwinism came from sociologist Lester Frank Ward in his book *Dynamic Sociology* (1883). Ward insisted the "blind natural forces in society must give way to human foresight." This theory condemned the laissez-faire approach, insisting that the liberal state should play a more active role in solving social problems.

Efficiency and *expertise* became progressives' watchwords. In *Drift and Mastery* (1914), journalist and critic Walter Lippmann called for skilled "technocrats" to use scientific techniques to control social change. Unlike the Populists, who advocated a greater voice for the masses, progressives, for all their interest in social justice, insisted that experts be put in charge. At its extreme, the application of expertise and social engineering took the form of scientific management.

Frederick Winslow Taylor pioneered "systematized shop management" in 1911. Obsessed with making humans and machines produce more and faster, he meticulously timed workers with a stopwatch and attempted to break down their work into its simplest components, one repetitive action after another. He won many converts among corporate managers, but workers hated the monotony of systematized shop management and argued that it led to speedup — pushing workers to produce more in less time and for less pay. Nevertheless many progressives applauded the increased productivity and efficiency of Taylor's system.

Progressive Government: City and State.

Progressivism burst forth at every level of government in 1900, but nowhere more forcefully than in Cleveland with the election of Democrat Thomas Loftin Johnson as mayor. A self-made millionaire by age forty, Johnson moved to Cleveland in 1899, where he began his career in politics. During his mayoral campaign, he pledged to reduce the streetcar fare from five cents to three cents. His election touched off a seven-year war between Johnson and the streetcar moguls. To get his three-cent fare, Johnson had Cleveland buy the streetcar system, a tactic of municipal ownership progressives called "gas and water socialism." Reelected four times, Johnson fought for fair taxation and championed greater democracy through the use of the initiative and referendum to let voters introduce legislation, and the recall to get rid of elected officials and judges. Under Johnson's administration, Cleveland became, in the words of journalist Lincoln Steffens, the "best governed city in America."

In Wisconsin, Republican Robert M. La Follette converted to the progressive cause early in the 1900s. La Follette capitalized on the grassroots movement for reform to launch his long political career as governor (1901–1905) and U.S. senator (1906–1925). La Follette brought scientists and professors into his administration and used the university, just down the street from the statehouse in Madison, as a resource. As governor, La Follette lowered railroad rates, raised railroad taxes, improved education, preached conservation, established factory regulation and workers' compensation, instituted the first direct primary in the country, and inaugurated the first state income tax. Under his leadership, Wisconsin earned the title "laboratory of democracy." A fiery orator, "Fighting Bob" La Follette united his supporters around issues that transcended party loyalties. Democrats and Republicans like Tom Johnson and Robert La Follette crossed party lines to work for reform.

West of the Rockies, progressivism arrived somewhat later and found a champion in Republican Hiram Johnson, who served as governor of California from 1911 to 1917 and later as U.S. senator. The Southern Pacific Railroad had dominated California politics since the 1870s. As governor, Johnson promised to "kick the Southern Pacific out of politics" and "return the government to the

TOM JOHNSON COLLAGE

Tom Johnson's greatest achievement as mayor of Cleveland is memorialized in this collage, which shows incidents from his successful fight to get a three-cent streetcar for Cleveland. To get this low fare, Johnson finally instituted municipal ownership of the transit system. In the picture on the bottom right, he takes the controls of the city's first streetcar in 1906.

Library of Congress, 3b16023.

TOM L. JOHNSON AND INCIDENTS IN THE BUILDING OF THE THREE CENT CAR LINE

people," winning support from progressive voters. During Johnson's governorship, California adopted the direct primary; supported initiative, referendum, and recall; strengthened the state's railroad commission; and enacted an employer's liability law.

> **REVIEW**   How did progressives justify their demand for more activist government?

Progressivism Finds a President: Theodore Roosevelt

On September 6, 1901, President William McKinley was shot by Leon Czolgosz, an anarchist, while attending the Pan-American Exposition in Buffalo, New York. Eight days later, McKinley died. When news of the assassination reached Republican boss Mark Hanna, he is said to have growled, "Now that damned cowboy is president." He was speaking of Vice President Theodore Roosevelt, the colorful hero of San Juan Hill, who had indeed cattle ranched in the Dakotas in the 1880s.

Roosevelt immediately reassured the shocked nation that he intended "to continue absolutely unbroken" the policies of McKinley. But Roosevelt was as different from McKinley as the nineteenth century from the twentieth. An activist and a moralist, imbued with the progressive spirit, Roosevelt would turn the Executive Mansion, which he insisted on calling the White House, into a "bully pulpit." Under his leadership, he achieved major reforms, advocated conservation and antitrust lawsuits, and championed the nation's emergence as a world power. In the process, Roosevelt would work to shift the nation's center of power from Wall Street to Washington.

After serving nearly two full terms as president, Roosevelt left office at the height of his powers. Any man would have found it difficult to follow in his footsteps, but his handpicked successor, William Howard Taft, proved poorly suited to the task. Taft's presidency was marked by vigorous trust-busting but would end with a progressive stalemate and a bitter break with Roosevelt that ultimately caused a schism in the Republican Party.

THEODORE ROOSEVELT

Aptly described by a contemporary observer as "a steam engine in trousers," Theodore Roosevelt, at forty-two, was the youngest president ever to occupy the White House. He brought to the office energy, intellect, and activism in equal measure. Roosevelt boasted that he used the presidency as a "bully pulpit" — a forum from which he advocated reforms ranging from trust-busting to conservation. Library of Congress, LC-DIG-ppmsca-37304.

The Square Deal.

At age forty-two, Theodore Roosevelt became the youngest man ever to move into the White House. A patrician by birth and an activist by temperament, Roosevelt brought to the job enormous talent and energy. Early in his career, he had determined that the path to power did not lie in the good government leagues formed by his well-bred New York friends. "If it is the muckers that govern," he wrote, "then I want to see if I cannot hold my own with them." He served his political apprenticeship under a Republican ward boss in a grubby meeting hall above a saloon on Morton Street. Roosevelt's rise in politics was swift and sure. He went from the New York assembly at the age of twenty-three to the presidency with time out as a cowboy in the Dakotas, police commissioner of New York City, assistant secretary of the navy, and a colonel of the Rough Riders. Elected governor of New York in 1898, he alienated the Republican boss, who finagled to get him "kicked upstairs" as a candidate for the vice presidency in 1900. The party bosses reasoned Roosevelt could do little harm as vice president. But one bullet proved the error of their logic.

Once president, Roosevelt would harness his explosive energy to strengthen the power of the federal government, putting business on notice that it could no longer count on a laissez-faire government to give it free rein. In Roosevelt's eyes, self-interested capitalists like John D. Rockefeller, whose Standard Oil trust monopolized the refinery business, constituted "the most dangerous members of the criminal class — the criminals of great wealth." The "absolutely vital question" facing the country, Roosevelt wrote to a friend in 1901, was "whether or not the government has the power to control the trusts." The Sherman Antitrust Act of 1890 had been badly weakened by a conservative Supreme Court and by attorneys general more willing to use it against labor unions than against monopolies. To determine whether the law had any teeth left, Roosevelt, in one of his first acts as president, ordered his attorney general to begin a secret antitrust investigation of the Northern Securities Company, a behemoth that monopolized railroad traffic in the Northwest.

Just five months after Roosevelt took office, Wall Street rocked with the news that the government had filed an antitrust suit against Northern Securities. As one newspaper editor sarcastically observed, "Wall Street is paralyzed at the thought that a President of the United States would sink so low as to try to enforce the law." Roosevelt's thunderbolt put Wall Street on notice that the new president expected to be treated as an equal and was willing to use government as a weapon to curb business excesses. Roosevelt later recounted how J. P. Morgan had come to him, one Harvard man to another, to suggest that "if we have done anything wrong, send your man to my man and they can fix it up." Roosevelt's attorney general responded, "We don't want to fix it up, we want to stop it." Roosevelt chortled over the exchange, noting "this is a most illuminating illustration of the Wall Street point of view. Mr. Morgan could not help regarding me as a big rival operator." And indeed he was. Perhaps sensing the new mood, the Supreme Court, in a significant turnaround, upheld the Sherman Act and called for the dissolution of Northern Securities in 1904.

"Hurrah for Teddy the Trustbuster," cheered the papers. Roosevelt went on to use the Sherman Act against forty-three trusts, including such giants as American Tobacco, Du Pont, and Standard Oil. Always the moralist, he insisted on a "rule of reason." He would punish "bad" trusts (those that broke the law) and leave "good" ones alone. In practice, he preferred regulation to antitrust suits. In 1903, he pressured Congress to pass the Elkins Act, outlawing railroad rebates. And he created the new cabinet-level Department of Commerce and Labor with the subsidiary Bureau of Corporations to act as a corporate watchdog.

In his handling of the anthracite coal strike in 1902, Roosevelt again demonstrated his willingness to assert the authority of the presidency, this time to mediate between labor and management. In May, 147,000 coal miners in Pennsylvania went on strike. The United Mine Workers (UMW) demanded a reduction in the workday from twelve to ten hours, an equitable system of weighing each miner's output, and a 10 percent wage increase, along with recognition of the union. When asked about the appalling conditions in the mines that led to the strike, George Baer, the mine operators' spokesman, scoffed, "The miners don't suffer, why they can't even speak English."

Realist author Stephen Crane had already investigated life "In the Depths of a Coal Mine." There he found a vicious circle. Children worked as "breaker boys" separating out pieces of slate from streams of coal speeding by on conveyor belts. Paid 55 cents a day, the boys moved up to become miners, where, "having survived gas, the floods, the 'squeezes' of falling rocks, the cars shooting through little tunnels, the precarious elevators," they had little to look forward to: "when old and decrepit, he finally returns to the breaker where he started as a child."

The strike dragged on through the summer and into the fall. Hoarding and profiteering more than doubled the price of coal. As winter approached, coal shortages touched off near riots in the nation's big cities. At this juncture, Roosevelt stepped in. Instead of sending in troops, he determined to mediate. His unprecedented intervention served notice that government counted itself an independent force in business and labor disputes. At the same time, it gave unionism a boost by granting the UMW a place at the table.

At the meeting, Baer and the mine owners refused to talk with the union representative — a move that angered the attorney general and insulted the president. Beside himself with rage over the "woodenheaded obstinacy and stupidity" of management, Roosevelt threatened to seize the mines and run them with federal troops. This quickly brought management to the table. In the end, the miners won a reduction in hours and a wage increase, but the owners succeeded in preventing formal recognition of the UMW.

Taken together, Roosevelt's actions in the Northern Securities case and the anthracite coal strike marked a dramatic departure from the presidential passivity of the Gilded Age. Roosevelt's actions demonstrated conclusively that government intended to act as a countervailing force to the power of the big corporations. Pleased with his role in the anthracite strike, Roosevelt announced that all he had tried to do was give labor and capital a "square deal."

The phrase "Square Deal" became Roosevelt's campaign slogan in the 1904 election. Roosevelt easily defeated the Democrats, who abandoned their former candidate, William Jennings Bryan, to support Judge Alton B. Parker, a "safe" choice they hoped would lure business votes away from Roosevelt. In the months before the election, the president prudently toned down his criticism of big business. Roosevelt swept into office with the largest popular majority — 57.9 percent — any candidate had polled up to that time.

Roosevelt the Reformer. "Tomorrow I shall come into my office in my own right," Roosevelt is said to have remarked on the eve of his election. "Then watch out for me!" Roosevelt's stunning victory gave him a mandate for reform. He would need all the popularity and political savvy he could muster, however, to guide his reform measures through Congress. The Senate remained controlled by a staunchly conservative Republican "Old Guard," with many senators on the payrolls of the corporations Roosevelt sought to curb. The *New York Times* suggested that "a millionaire could buy a Senate seat, just as he would buy an opera box, a yacht, or any other luxury."

Roosevelt's pet project remained railroad regulation. The Elkins Act prohibiting rebates had not worked. Roosevelt determined that the only solution lay in giving the Interstate Commerce Commission (ICC) real power to set rates and prevent discriminatory practices. But the right to determine the price of goods or services was an age-old prerogative of private enterprise, and one that business had no intention of yielding to government.

The Hepburn Act of 1906 marked the crowning legislative achievement of Roosevelt's presidency. It gave the ICC the power to set rates subject to court review. Committed progressives like La Follette judged the law a defeat for reform. Die-hard conservatives branded it a "piece of populism." Both sides exaggerated. The law left the courts too much power and failed to provide adequate means for the ICC to determine rates, but its passage proved a landmark in federal control of private industry. For the first time, a government commission had the power to investigate private business records and to set rates.

Always an apt reader of the public temper, Roosevelt witnessed a growing appetite for reform. Revelations of corporate and political wrongdoing as well as social injustice filled the papers and boosted the sales of popular magazines. Roosevelt counted many of the new investigative journalists among his friends. (See "Analyzing Historical Evidence," page 624.) But he warned them against going too far, citing the allegorical character in *Pilgrim's Progress* who was too busy raking muck to notice higher things. Roosevelt's criticism gave the American vocabulary a new word, *muckraker,* which journalists soon appropriated as a title of honor.

Muckraking, as Roosevelt well knew, provided enormous help in securing progressive legislation. In the spring of 1906, publicity generated by the muckrakers about poisons in patent medicines goaded the Senate, with Roosevelt's backing, into passing a pure food and drug bill. Opponents in the House of Representatives hoped to keep the legislation locked up in committee. There it would have died, were it not for the publication of Upton Sinclair's novel *The Jungle* (1906), with its sensational account of filthy conditions in meatpacking plants. Roosevelt, who read the book over breakfast, was sickened. He immediately invited Sinclair to the White House. Sinclair wanted socialism; Roosevelt wanted food inspection. But thanks to the publicity generated by *The Jungle,* a massive public outcry led to the passage of the Pure Food and Drug Act and the Meat Inspection Act in 1906.

In the waning years of his administration, Roosevelt allied with the more progressive elements of the Republican Party. In speech after speech, he attacked "malefactors of great wealth." Styling himself a "radical," he claimed credit for leading the "ultra conservative" party of McKinley to a position of "progressive conservatism and conservative radicalism."

When an economic panic developed in the fall of 1907, business interests quickly blamed the president. Once again, J. P. Morgan stepped in to avert disaster, this time switching funds from one bank to another to prop up weak institutions. For his services, Morgan dispatched his lieutenants to Washington, where they told Roosevelt that the sale of the Tennessee Coal and Iron Company would aid the economy "but little benefit" U.S. Steel. Willing to take the word of a gentleman, Roosevelt tacitly agreed not to institute antitrust proceedings against U.S. Steel over the acquisition. Roosevelt's promise would give rise to the charge that he acted as a tool of the Morgan interests.

The charge of collusion between business and government underscored the extent to which corporate leaders like Morgan found federal regulation preferable to unbridled competition or harsher state measures. During the Progressive Era, enlightened business leaders cooperated with government in the hope of avoiding antitrust prosecution. Convinced that regulation and not trust-busting offered the best way to deal with big business, Roosevelt never acknowledged that his regulatory policies fostered an alliance between business and government that today is called corporate liberalism.

Roosevelt and Conservation.

In the area of conservation, Roosevelt proved indisputably ahead of his time. When he took office, some 43 million acres of forestland remained as government reserves. He more than quadrupled that number to 194 million acres. To conserve natural resources, he fought western cattle barons, lumber kings, mining interests, and powerful leaders in Congress, including Speaker of the House Joseph Cannon, who vowed to spend "not one cent for scenery."

---

muckraking
Early-twentieth-century style of journalism that exposed the corruption of big business and government. Theodore Roosevelt coined the term after a character in *Pilgrim's Progress* who was too busy raking muck to notice higher things.

As the first president to have lived and worked in the West, Roosevelt came to the White House convinced of the need for better management of the nation's rivers and forests as well as the preservation of wildlife and wilderness. During his presidency, he placed the nation's conservation policy in the hands of scientifically trained experts like his chief forester, Gifford Pinchot. Pinchot preached conservation — the efficient use of natural resources. Willing to permit grazing, lumbering, and the development of hydroelectric power, conservationists fought private interests only when they felt business acted irresponsibly or threatened to monopolize water and electric power. Preservationists like John Muir, founder of the Sierra Club, believed that the wilderness needed to be protected. Roosevelt, a fervent Darwinian naturalist and an (overly) enthusiastic game hunter, a conservationist who built big dams and a preservationist who saved the redwoods, aimed to have it both ways.

In 1907, Congress attempted to put the brakes on Roosevelt's conservation program by passing a law limiting his power to create forest reserves in six western states. In the days leading up to the law's enactment, Roosevelt feverishly created twenty-one new reserves and enlarged eleven more, saving 16 million acres from development. Once again, Roosevelt had outwitted his adversaries. "Opponents of the forest service turned handsprings in their wrath," he wrote, "but the threats . . . were really only a tribute to the efficiency of our action." Worried that private utilities were gobbling up waterpower sites and creating a monopoly of hydroelectric power, he connived with Pinchot to withdraw 2,565 power sites from private use by designating them "ranger stations." Firm in his commitment to wild America, Roosevelt proved willing to stretch the law when it served his ends. His legacy is more than 234 million acres of American wilderness saved for posterity (Map 21.1).

The Big Stick. Roosevelt's activism extended to his foreign policy. A fierce proponent of America's interests abroad, he relied on executive power to pursue a vigorous foreign policy, sometimes stretching the powers of the presidency beyond legal limits. In his relations with the European powers, he relied on military strength and diplomacy, a combination he aptly described with the aphorism "Speak softly but carry a big stick."

A strong supporter of the Monroe Doctrine, Roosevelt jealously guarded the U.S. sphere of influence in the Western Hemisphere. His proprietary attitude toward the Caribbean became evident in the case of the Panama Canal. Roosevelt had long been a supporter of a canal linking the Caribbean and the Pacific. By enabling ships to move quickly from the Atlantic to the Pacific, a canal would trim 8,000 miles from a coast-to-coast voyage and effectively double the U.S. Navy's power. Having decided on a route across the Panamanian isthmus (a narrow strip of land connecting North and South America), then part of Colombia, Roosevelt in 1902 offered the Colombian government a one-time sum of $10 million and an annual rent of $250,000. When the government in Bogotá refused to accept the offer, Roosevelt became incensed at what he called the "homicidal corruptionists" in Colombia for trying to "blackmail" the United States. At the prompting of a group of New York investors, the Panamanians staged an uprising in 1903, and with unseemly haste the U.S. government recognized the new government within twenty-four hours. The Panamanians promptly accepted the $10 million, and the building got under way. The canal would take eleven years and $375 million to complete; it opened in 1914 (Map 21.2).

Analyzing Historical Evidence

The Flash and the Birth of Photojournalism

FIVE CENTS A SPOT
Widener Library, Harvard
University.

Photography changed the way Americans viewed their world. By the 1890s, any amateur could purchase the Kodak camera that George Eastman marketed with the slogan "You push the button, we do the rest." As the poet Oliver Wendell Holmes observed, the camera became not just "the mirror of reality" but "the mirror with a memory."

Yet for Jacob Riis, a progressive reformer wishing to document the grim horrors of tenement life, photography was useless because it required daylight or careful studio lighting. He could only crudely sketch the dim hovels, the criminal nightlife, and the windowless tenement rooms of New York. Then came the breakthrough: "One morning scanning my newspaper at my breakfast table, I put it down with an outcry. . . . There it was, the thing I had been looking for all these years. . . . A way had been discovered to take pictures by flashlight."

Riis set out to shine light in the dark corners of New York. "Our party carried terror wherever it went," Riis recalled. "The spectacle of strange men invading a house in the midnight hours armed with [flash] pistols which they shot off recklessly was hardly reassuring." But the results were a huge step forward for photojournalism.

Riis's book *How the Other Half Lives* (1890) made photographic history. Along with Riis's text and engravings of his drawings, it contained reproductions of seventeen photographs taken with his camera and flash. By looking at a line drawing side by side with the corresponding photograph, we can compare the impact of the two mediums.

DOCUMENT 1

In his early work, Riis had to rely on his own sketches of the conditions he encountered in New York's tenements. Riis is a careful draughtsman, but how much detail can you see in the line drawing (above)?

DOCUMENT 2

On a police raid to evict tenement lodgers, Riis describes the room as "not thirteen feet either way," in which "slept twelve men and women, two or three in bunks in a sort of alcove, the rest on the floor." Note how the flash catches the sleepy faces and tired bodies, the crowding, dirt, and disorder (right). Once Riis adopted the flash, he was able to show more graphically life in the tenements. What details are visible in the photograph that are missing in the line drawing?

DOCUMENT 3

Riis took his camera into Baxter Street Court and recorded these observations: "I counted the other day the little ones up to ten years old in a . . . tenement that for a yard has a . . . space in the center with sides fourteen or fifteen feet long, just enough for a row of ill-smelling closets [toilets] . . . and a hydrant. There was about as much light in the 'yard' as in the average cellar. . . . I counted one hundred twenty eight [children] in forty families." Riis's pioneering photojournalism shocked the nation and led not only to tenement reform but also to the development of city playgrounds, neighborhood parks, and child labor laws.

FIVE CENTS A SPOT
Library of Congress, 3a18572.

QUESTIONS FOR ANALYSIS

Summarize the Argument   How significant is the advent of flash photography? Compare the drawn image with the photograph. Why is the photo so much more dramatic?

Analyze the Evidence   Would you agree that Riis's photographs are "a mirror of reality," or did he interpret and frame the "reality" he photographed?

Ask Historical Questions   How do you think photography affected Americans' views of their society?

Map Activity

MAP 21.1   NATIONAL PARKS AND FORESTS

The national park system in the West began with Yellowstone in 1872. Grand Canyon, Yosemite, Kings Canyon, and Sequoia followed in the 1890s. During his presidency, Theodore Roosevelt added six parks — Crater Lake, Wind Cave, Petrified Forest, Lassen Volcanic, Mesa Verde, and Zion.

READING THE MAP: Collectively, do national parks or national forests encompass more land? According to the map, how many national parks were created before 1910? How many were created after 1910?

CONNECTIONS: How do conservation and preservation differ? Why did Roosevelt believe that saving land in the West was important? What principles guided the national land use policy of the Roosevelt administration?

In the wake of the Panama affair, a confrontation with Germany over Venezuela, and yet another default on a European debt, this time in the Dominican Republic, Roosevelt grew concerned that financial instability in Latin America would lead European powers to interfere. In 1904, he announced the **Roosevelt Corollary** to the Monroe Doctrine in which he declared the United States had a right to act as "an international police power" in the Western Hemisphere. Roosevelt stated the United States would not intervene in Latin America as long as nations there conducted their affairs with "decency," but it would step in to stop "brutal wrongdoing." The Roosevelt Corollary served notice to the European powers to keep out.

In Asia, Roosevelt inherited the Open Door policy initiated by Secretary of State John Hay in 1899, designed to ensure U.S. commercial entry into China. As European powers raced to secure Chinese trade and territory, Roosevelt was tempted to use force to gain economic or possibly territorial concessions. Realizing that Americans would not support an aggressive Asian policy, the president sensibly held back.

THE ROOSEVELT COROLLARY IN ACTION

Map Activity

MAP 21.2   THE PANAMA CANAL, 1914

The Panama Canal, completed in 1914, bisects the isthmus in a series of massive locks and dams. As Theodore Roosevelt had planned, the canal greatly strengthened the U.S. Navy by allowing ships to move from the Atlantic to the Pacific in a matter of days.

READING THE MAP: How long was the trip from New York to San Francisco before the Panama Canal was built? After it was built?

CONNECTIONS: How did Roosevelt's desire for a canal lead to independence for Panama? How did the canal benefit the U.S. Navy?

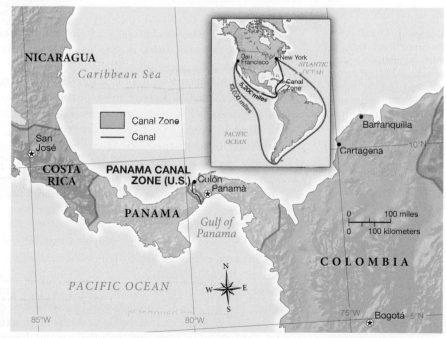

"THE WORLD'S CONSTABLE"

In this political cartoon from 1905, President Theodore Roosevelt, dressed as a constable, wields the club of "The New Diplomacy" in one hand with "Arbitration" tucked under his arm. The Roosevelt Corollary to the Monroe Doctrine made the United States the Western Hemisphere's policeman, a role Roosevelt relished.

The Granger Collection, New York.

THE WORLD'S CONSTABLE.

Roosevelt Corollary
Theodore Roosevelt's 1904 follow-up to the Monroe Doctrine in which he declared that the United States had the right to intervene in Latin America to stop "brutal wrongdoing" and protect American interests. The corollary warned European powers to keep out of the Western Hemisphere.

In his relations with Europe, Roosevelt sought to establish the United States as a rising force in world affairs. When tensions flared between France and Germany in Morocco in 1905, Roosevelt mediated at a conference in Algeciras, Spain, where he worked to maintain a balance of power that helped neutralize German ambitions. His skillful mediation gained him a reputation as an astute player on the world stage and demonstrated the nation's new presence in world affairs.

Roosevelt earned the Nobel Peace Prize in 1906 for his role in negotiating an end to the Russo-Japanese War, which had broken out when the Japanese invaded Chinese Manchuria, threatening Russia's sphere of influence in the area. Once again, Roosevelt sought to maintain a balance of power, in this case working to curb Japanese expansionism. Roosevelt admired the Japanese, judging them "the most dashing fighters in the world," but he did not want Japan to become too strong in Asia.

When good relations with Japan were jeopardized by discriminatory legislation in California calling for segregated public schools for Asians, Roosevelt smoothed over the incident and negotiated the "Gentlemen's Agreement" in 1907, which allowed the Japanese to save face by voluntarily restricting immigration to the United States. To demonstrate America's naval power and to counter Japan's growing bellicosity, Roosevelt dispatched the Great White Fleet, sixteen of the navy's most up-to-date battleships, on a "goodwill mission" around the world. U.S. relations with Japan improved, and in the 1908 Root-Takahira agreement the two nations pledged to maintain the Open Door and support the status quo in the Pacific. Roosevelt's show of American force constituted a classic example of his dictum "Speak softly but carry a big stick."

The Troubled Presidency of William Howard Taft.
Roosevelt promised on the eve of his election in 1904 that he would not seek another term. So he retired from the presidency in 1909 at age fifty and removed himself from the political scene by going on safari in Africa. He turned the White House over to his handpicked successor, William Howard Taft, a lawyer who had served as governor-general of the Philippines. Affectionately known as "Big Bill," Taft had served as Roosevelt's right-hand man in the cabinet. In the presidential election of 1908, Taft soundly defeated the perennial Democratic candidate William Jennings Bryan.

A genial man with a talent for law, Taft had no experience in elective office, no feel for politics, and no nerve for controversy. His ambitious wife coveted the office and urged him to seek it. He would have been better off listening to his mother, who warned, "Roosevelt is a good fighter and enjoys it, but the malice of politics would make you miserable." Sadly for Taft, his wife suffered a stroke in his first months in office, leaving him grieving and without his strongest ally.

Once in office, Taft proved a perfect tool in the hands of Republicans who yearned for a return to the days of a less active executive. A lawyer by training and instinct, Taft believed that it was up to the courts, not the president, to arbitrate social issues. Roosevelt had carried presidential power to a new level, often flouting the separation of powers and showing thinly veiled contempt for Congress and the courts. He believed that the president had the legal right to act as steward for the people, and to do anything necessary "unless

WILLIAM HOWARD TAFT

In this 1911 *Puck* cartoon, the hapless William Howard Taft veers out of control, losing power in the House of Representatives as he skis down the nomination slide for 1912. Taft had little aptitude for politics and quickly lost the support of progressives in his party. Library of Congress, LC-DIG-ppmsca-27702.

the Constitution or the laws explicitly forbid him to do it." Taft found such presidential activism difficult to condone. Although he pursued the trusts vigorously, he acted more like a judge than a steward. Wary of the progressive insurgents in Congress, Taft relied increasingly on conservatives in the Republican Party. As a progressive senator lamented, "Taft is a ponderous and amiable man completely surrounded by men who know exactly what they want."

Taft's troubles began on the eve of his inaugural, when he called a special session of Congress to deal with the tariff. Roosevelt had been too politically astute to tackle the troublesome tariff issue, even though he knew that rates needed to be lowered. Ida Tarbell, who lent her meticulous research skills to the tariff debate, concluded, "At a time when wealth is rolling up as never before, a vast number of hard-working people . . . are really having a more difficult time making ends meet than they have ever had before." Tarbell's articles proved a revelation to many, who had never understood the relationship between the tariff and the price of a pair of shoes.

taft did nothing

Taft struggled to transform growing public sentiment against the tariff into legislation. But Taft blundered into the fray. The Payne-Aldrich bill that emerged was amended in the Senate so that it actually raised the tariff, benefiting big business and the trusts at the expense of consumers. As if paralyzed, Taft neither fought for changes nor vetoed the measure. On a tour of the Midwest in 1909, he was greeted with jeers when he claimed, "I think the Payne bill is the best bill that the Republican Party ever passed." In the eyes of a growing number of Americans, Taft's praise of the tariff made him either a fool or a liar.

Taft's legalism soon got him into hot water in the area of conservation. He undid Roosevelt's work to preserve hydroelectric power sites when he learned that they had been improperly designated as ranger stations. And when Gifford Pinchot publicly denounced Taft's secretary of the interior as a tool of western land-grabbers, Taft fired Pinchot, touching off a storm of controversy that damaged Taft and alienated Roosevelt. When Roosevelt returned from Africa, Pinchot was among the first to greet him with a half dozen letters from progressives complaining of Taft's leadership.

Roosevelt returned to the United States in June 1910, where he received a hero's welcome and attracted a stream of visitors and reporters seeking his advice and opinions. Hurt, Taft kept his distance. By late summer, Roosevelt had taken sides with the progressive insurgents in his party. "Taft is utterly hopeless as a leader," Roosevelt confided to his son as he set out on a speaking tour of the West. Reading the mood of the country, Roosevelt began to sound more and more like a candidate.

With the Republican Party divided, the Democrats swept the congressional elections of 1910. Branding the Payne-Aldrich tariff "the mother of trusts," they captured a majority in the House of Representatives and won several key governorships. The revitalized Democratic Party could look to new leaders, among them the progressive governor of New Jersey, Woodrow Wilson.

The new Democratic majority in the House, working with progressive Republicans in the Senate, achieved a number of key reforms, including legislation to regulate railroad safety to create the Children's Bureau in the Department of Labor, and to establish an eight-hour day for federal workers and miners. Two significant constitutional amendments — the Sixteenth Amendment, which provided for a modest graduated income tax, and the Seventeenth Amendment, which called for the direct election of senators (formerly chosen by state legislatures) — went to the states, where they would win ratification in 1913. While Congress rode the high tide of progressive reform, Taft sat on the sidelines.

In foreign policy, Taft continued Roosevelt's policy of extending U.S. influence abroad, but here, too, Taft had a difficult time following Roosevelt. Taft's "dollar diplomacy" championed commercial goals rather than the strategic aims Roosevelt had pursued. Taft naively assumed he could substitute "dollars for bullets." In the Caribbean, he provoked anti-American feeling by dispatching U.S. Marines to Nicaragua and the Dominican Republic in 1912 pursuant to the Roosevelt Corollary. In Asia, he openly avowed his intent to promote "active intervention to secure for . . . our capitalists opportunity for

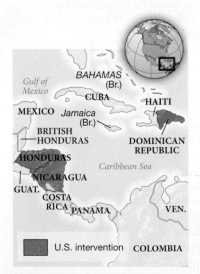

TAFT'S "DOLLAR DIPLOMACY"

profitable investment." Lacking Roosevelt's understanding of power politics, Taft failed to recognize that an aggressive commercial policy could not exist without the willingness to use military might to back it up.

Taft faced the limits of dollar diplomacy when revolution broke out in Mexico in 1911. Under pressure to protect American investments, he mobilized troops along the border. In the end, however, with no popular support for a war with Mexico, he had to fall back on diplomatic pressure to salvage American interests.

Taft's greatest dream was to encourage world peace through the use of a world court and arbitration. He unsuccessfully sponsored a series of arbitration treaties that Roosevelt, who prized national honor more than international law, vehemently opposed as weak and cowardly. By 1910, Roosevelt had become a vocal critic of Taft's foreign policy.

The final breach between Taft and Roosevelt came in 1911, when Taft's attorney general filed an antitrust suit against U.S. Steel. In its brief against the corporation, the government cited Roosevelt's agreement with the Morgan interests in the 1907 acquisition of Tennessee Coal and Iron. The incident greatly embarrassed Roosevelt. Either he had been hoodwinked or he had colluded with Morgan. Neither idea pleased him. Thoroughly enraged, he lambasted Taft's "archaic" antitrust policy and hinted that he might be persuaded to run for president again.

> **REVIEW** How did Theodore Roosevelt advance the progressive agenda?

Woodrow Wilson and Progressivism at High Tide

Disillusionment with Taft resulted in a split in the Republican Party and the creation of a new Progressive Party that rallied to Theodore Roosevelt. In the election of 1912, four candidates styled themselves "progressives," but it was Democrat Woodrow Wilson, with a minority of the popular vote, who won the presidency. He would continue Roosevelt's presidential power and help enact progressive legislation.

Progressive Insurgency and the Election of 1912. Convinced that Taft was inept, in February 1912, Roosevelt declared his candidacy for the Republican nomination announcing, "My hat is in the ring." Taft, with uncharacteristic strength, refused to step aside. Roosevelt took advantage of newly passed primary election laws and ran in thirteen states, winning 278 delegates to Taft's 48. But at the Chicago convention, Taft's bosses refused to seat the Roosevelt delegates. Fistfights broke out on the convention floor as Taft won nomination on the first ballot. Crying robbery, Roosevelt's supporters bolted the party.

Seven weeks later, in the same Chicago auditorium, the hastily organized Progressive Party met to nominate Roosevelt. Full of reforming zeal, the delegates chose Roosevelt and Hiram Johnson to head the new party. Jane Addams seconded Roosevelt's nomination. "I have been fighting for progressive principles for thirty years," she told the enthusiastic crowd. "This is the first time there has been a chance

WOODROW WILSON

Woodrow Wilson, the Democrats' presidential nominee in 1912, speaks to an outdoor campaign rally in New York City. Note the absence of a microphone. Wilson, a former professor of political science and president of Princeton University and recently elected governor of New Jersey, gave carefully phrased, logical, and clear speeches in a somewhat professorial style that contrasted with the charisma and bombast of the Bull Moose candidate, Theodore Roosevelt. Corbis.

to make them effective. This is the biggest day of my life." The new party lustily approved the most ambitious platform since that of the Populists. Planks called for woman suffrage, presidential primaries, conservation of natural resources, an end to child labor, workers' compensation, a living wage for both men and women workers, social security, health insurance, and a federal income tax.

Roosevelt arrived in Chicago to accept the nomination and announced that he felt "as fit as a bull moose," giving the new party a nickname and a mascot. With characteristic vigor, he launched his campaign with the exhortation, "We stand at Armageddon and do battle for the Lord!" But for all the excitement and the cheering, the new Progressive Party was doomed, and the candidate knew it. Privately he confessed to a friend, "I am under no illusion about it. It is a forlorn hope." The people may have supported the party, but the politicians, even progressives such as La Follette, refused to support the new party. The Democrats, delighted at the split in the Republican ranks, nominated Woodrow Wilson, the governor of New Jersey. After only eighteen months in office, the former professor of political science and president of Princeton University found himself running for president of the United States.

Voters in 1912 could choose among four candidates who claimed to be progressives. Taft, Roosevelt, and Wilson each embraced the label, and even the Socialist candidate, Eugene V. Debs, styled himself a progressive. That the term *progressive* could stretch to cover these diverse candidates underscored major disagreements in progressive thinking about the relationship between business and government. Taft, in spite of his trust-busting, was generally viewed as the candidate of the Republican Old Guard. Debs urged voters to support the Socialist Party as the true spirit of the working class. The real contest for the presidency came down to a fight between Roosevelt and Wilson and the two political philosophies summed up in their respective campaign slogans: "**The New Nationalism**" and "**The New Freedom**."

The New Nationalism expressed Roosevelt's belief in federal planning and regulation. He accepted the inevitability of big business but demanded that government act as "a steward of the people" to regulate the giant corporations. Wilson, schooled in the Democratic principles of limited government and states' rights, set a markedly different course with his New Freedom. Wilson promised to use antitrust legislation to get rid of big corporations and to give small businesses and farmers better opportunities in the marketplace.

The energy and enthusiasm of the Bull Moosers made the race seem closer than it was. In the end, the Republican vote split, while the Democrats remained united.

The New Nationalism
Theodore Roosevelt's 1912 campaign slogan, which reflected his commitment to federal planning and regulation. Roosevelt wanted to use the federal government to act as a "steward of the people" to regulate giant corporations.

The New Freedom
Woodrow Wilson's 1912 campaign slogan, which reflected his belief in limited government and states' rights. Wilson promised to use antitrust legislation to eliminate big corporations and to improve opportunities for small businesses and farmers.

No candidate claimed a majority in the race. Wilson captured a bare 42 percent of the popular vote. Roosevelt and his Bull Moose Party won 27 percent, an unprecedented tally for a new party. Taft came in third with 23 percent. The Socialist Party, led by Debs, captured a surprising 6 percent (Map 21.3). The Republican Party moved in a conservative direction, while the Progressive Party essentially collapsed after Roosevelt's defeat. It had always been, in the words of one astute observer, "a house divided against itself and already mortgaged."

Wilson's Reforms: Tariff, Banking, and the Trusts.
Born in Virginia and raised in Georgia, Woodrow Wilson became the first southerner elected president since 1844 and only the second Democrat to occupy the White House since Reconstruction. A believer in states' rights, Wilson nevertheless promised legislation to break the hold of the trusts. This lean, ascetic scholar was, as one biographer conceded, a man whose "political convictions were never as fixed as his ambition." Building on the base built by Roosevelt in strengthening presidential power, Wilson exerted leadership to achieve banking reform and worked through his party in Congress to accomplish the Democratic agenda. Before he was finished, Wilson lent his support to many of the Progressive Party's social reforms.

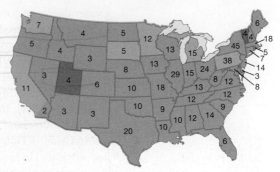

Candidate	Electoral Vote	Popular Vote	Percent of Popular Vote
Woodrow Wilson (Democrat)	435	6,293,454	41.9
Theodore Roosevelt (Progressive)	88	4,119,538	27.4
William H. Taft (Republican)	8	3,484,980	23.2
Eugene V. Debs (Socialist)	0	900,672	6.1

MAP 21.3   THE ELECTION OF 1912

With the Democrats thoroughly in control of Congress, Wilson immediately called for tariff reform. "The object of the tariff," Wilson told Congress, "must be effective competition." The Democratic House of Representatives hastily passed the Underwood tariff, which lowered rates by 15 percent. To compensate for lost revenue, the House approved a moderate federal income tax made possible by the ratification of the Sixteenth Amendment a month earlier. In the Senate, lobbyists for industries quietly went to work to get the tariff raised, but Wilson rallied public opinion by attacking the "industrious and insidious lobby." In the harsh glare of publicity, the Senate passed the Underwood tariff.

Wilson next turned his attention to banking. The panic of 1907 led the government to turn once again to J. P. Morgan to avoid economic catastrophe. But by the time Wilson came to office, Morgan's legendary power had come under close scrutiny. In 1913, a Senate committee investigated the "money trust," calling Morgan himself to testify. The committee uncovered an alarming concentration of banking power. J. P. Morgan and Company and its affiliates held 341 directorships in 112 corporations, controlling assets of more than $22 million (billions in today's dollars). The sensational findings led to reform.

The Federal Reserve Act of 1913 marked the most significant piece of domestic legislation of Wilson's presidency. It established a national banking system composed of twelve regional banks, privately controlled but regulated and supervised by the Federal Reserve Board, appointed by the president. It gave the United States its first efficient banking and currency system and, at the same time, provided for a greater degree of government control over banking. The new system made currency more elastic and credit adequate for the needs of business and agriculture.

Wilson, flush with success, tackled the trust issue next. When Congress reconvened in January 1914, he supported the introduction and passage of the Clayton Antitrust Act to outlaw "unfair competition" — practices such as price discrimination and interlocking directorates (directors from one corporation sitting on the board of another). In the midst of the successful fight for the Clayton Act, Wilson changed course and threw his support behind the creation of the Federal Trade Commission (FTC), precisely the kind of federal regulatory agency that Roosevelt had advocated in his New Nationalism. The FTC, created in 1914, had not only wide investigatory powers but also the authority to prosecute corporations for "unfair trade practices" and to enforce its judgments by issuing "cease and desist" orders. Despite his campaign promises, Wilson's antitrust program worked to regulate rather than to break up big business.

Wilson, Reluctant Progressive. By the fall of 1914, Wilson declared that the progressive movement had fulfilled its mission and that the country needed "a time of healing." Progressives watched in dismay as Wilson repeatedly obstructed or obstinately refused to endorse further reforms. He failed to support labor's demand for an end to court injunctions against labor unions. He twice threatened to veto legislation providing farm credits for nonperishable crops. He refused to support child labor legislation or woman suffrage. Wilson used the rhetoric of the New Freedom to justify his actions, claiming that his administration would condone "special privileges to none." But, in fact, his stance often reflected the interests of his small-business constituency.

In the face of Wilson's obstinacy, reform might have ended in 1913 had not politics intruded. In the congressional elections of 1914, the Republican Party, no longer split by Roosevelt's Bull Moose faction, won substantial gains. Democratic strategists recognized that Wilson needed to pick up support in the Midwest and the West by capturing votes from former Bull Moose progressives. Wilson responded belatedly by lending his support to reform in the months leading up to the election of 1916. In a sharp about-face, he cultivated union labor, farmers, and social reformers. To please labor, he appointed progressive Louis Brandeis to the Supreme Court. To woo farmers, he threw his support behind legislation to obtain rural credits. And he won praise from labor by supporting workers' compensation and the Keating-Owen child labor law (1916), which outlawed the regular employment of children younger than sixteen. When a railroad strike threatened in the months before the election, Wilson ordered Congress to establish an eight-hour day on the railroads. He had moved a long way from his New Freedom of 1912, and, as Wilson noted, the Democrats had "come very near to carrying out the platform of the Progressive Party." Wilson's shift toward reform, along with his claim that he had kept the United States out of the war in Europe (as discussed in chapter 22), helped him win reelection in 1916.

> **REVIEW** How and why did Woodrow Wilson's reform program evolve during his first term?

personal statement

The Limits of Progressive Reform

While progressivism called for a more active role for the liberal state, at heart it was a movement that sought reforms designed to preserve American institutions and stem the tide of more radical change. Its basic conservatism can be seen by comparing it with the more radical movements of socialism, radical labor, and birth control — and by looking at the groups progressive reform left behind, including women, Asians, and African Americans.

your personal rookie wopo 101 social media coach com 101,1201

Radical Alternatives. The year 1900 marked the birth of the Social Democratic Party in America, later called simply the **Socialist Party**. Like the progressives, the socialists were middle-class and native-born. They had broken with the older, more militant Socialist Labor Party precisely because of its dogmatic approach and immigrant constituency. The new group of socialists proved eager to appeal to a broad mass of disaffected Americans.

The Socialist Party chose as its presidential standard-bearer Eugene V. Debs, whose experience in the Pullman strike of 1894 (see chapter 20) convinced him that "there is no hope for the toiling masses of my countrymen, except by the pathways mapped out by Socialism." Debs would run for president five times, in every election (except 1916) from 1900 to 1920. The socialism Debs advocated preached cooperation over competition and urged men and women to liberate themselves from "the barbarism of private ownership and wage slavery." In the 1912 election, Debs indicted both old parties as each dedicated to the preservation of capitalism and the continuation of the wage system. Styling the Socialist Party the "revolutionary party of the working class," he urged voters to rally to his standard. Debs's best showing came in 1912, when his 6 percent of the popular vote totaled more than 900,000 votes.

Further to the left and more radical than the socialists stood the **Industrial Workers of the World (IWW)**, nicknamed the Wobblies. In 1905, Debs, along with Western Federation of Miners leader William Dudley "Big Bill" Haywood, created the IWW, "one big union" dedicated to organizing the most destitute segment of the workforce, the unskilled workers disdained by Samuel Gompers's AFL: western miners, migrant farmworkers, lumbermen, and immigrant textile workers. Haywood, a craggy-faced miner with one eye (he had lost the other in a childhood accident), was a charismatic leader and a proletarian intellectual. Seeing workers on the lowest rung of the social ladder as the victims of violent repression, the IWW advocated direct action, sabotage, and the general strike — tactics designed to trigger a workers' uprising and overthrow the capitalist state. The IWW claimed it had as many as 100,000 members. Although membership fluctuated greatly, the influence of the IWW extended far beyond its numbers (as discussed in chapter 22).

In contrast to political radicals like Debs and Haywood, Margaret Sanger promoted the **birth control movement** as a means of social change. Sanger, a nurse who had worked among the poor on New York's Lower East Side, coined the term *birth control* in 1915 and launched a movement with broad social implications.

◄ Socialist Party ►
Political party formed in 1900 that advocated cooperation over competition and promoted the breakdown of capitalism. Its members, who were largely middle-class and native-born, saw both the Republican and the Democratic parties as hopelessly beholden to capitalism. *SAT*

Industrial Workers of ► the World (IWW) ►
Umbrella union and radical political group founded in 1905 that was dedicated to organizing unskilled workers to oppose capitalism. Nicknamed the Wobblies, the IWW advocated direct action by workers, including sabotage and general strikes, in hopes of triggering a widespread workers' uprising. *pl WOPO*

◄ birth control movement ►
Movement launched in 1915 by Margaret Sanger in New York City's Lower East Side. Birth control advocates hoped that contraception would alter social and political power relationships: By having fewer babies, the working class could constrict the size of the workforce, thus making possible higher wages, and at the same time refuse to provide soldiers for the world's armies.

Sanger and her followers saw birth control not only as a sexual and medical reform but also as a means to alter social and political power relationships and to alleviate human misery. By having fewer babies, the working class could constrict the size of the workforce and make possible higher wages and at the same time refuse to provide "cannon fodder" for the world's armies.

The desire for family limitation was widespread, and in this sense birth control was nothing new. The birthrate in the United States had been falling consistently throughout the nineteenth century. The average number of children per family dropped from 7.0 in 1800 to 3.6 by 1900. But the open advocacy of contraception, the use of artificial means to prevent pregnancy, struck many people as both new and shocking. And it was illegal. Anthony Comstock, New York City's commissioner of vice, promoted laws in the 1870s making it a felony not only to sell contraceptive devices like condoms and cervical caps but also to publish information on how to prevent pregnancy.

When Sanger used her militant feminist paper, the *Woman Rebel,* to promote birth control, the Post Office confiscated Sanger's publication and brought charges of obscenity against her. Facing arrest, she fled to Europe, only to return in 1916 as something of a national celebrity. In her absence, birth control had become linked with free speech and had been taken up as a liberal cause. Under public pressure, the government dropped the charges against Sanger, who undertook a nationwide tour to publicize the birth control cause.

Sanger then took direct action, opening the nation's first birth control clinic in the Brownsville section of Brooklyn in October 1916. Located in the heart of a Jewish and Italian immigrant neighborhood, the clinic attracted 464 clients. On the tenth day, police shut down the clinic and threw Sanger in jail. By then, she had become a national figure, and the cause she championed had gained legitimacy, if not legality. Sanger soon reopened her clinic. After World War I, the birth control movement would become much less radical. Altering her tactics to suit the conservative temper of the times, Sanger sought support from medical doctors. She even jumped aboard the popular fad of eugenics, a racist genetic theory that warned against allowing the "unfit" to reproduce. But in its infancy, birth control was part of a radical vision for reforming the world that made common cause with the socialists and the IWW in challenging the limits of progressive reform.

Progressivism for White Men Only.
The day before President Woodrow Wilson's inauguration in March 1913, the largest mass march to that date in the nation's history took place as more than five thousand demonstrators took to the streets in Washington to demand the vote for women. A rowdy crowd on hand to celebrate the Democrats' triumph attacked the marchers. Men spat at the suffragists and threw lighted cigarettes and matches at their clothing. "If my wife were where you are," a burly cop told one suffragist, "I'd break her head." But for all the marching, Wilson pointedly ignored woman suffrage in his inaugural address the next day.

The march served as a reminder that the political gains of progressivism were not spread equally throughout the population. As the twentieth century dawned, women still could not vote in most states, although they had won major victories in the West. Increasingly, however, woman suffrage had become an international movement.

Alice Paul, a Quaker social worker who had visited England and participated in suffrage activism there, returned to the United States in 1910 in time to plan the mass march on the eve of Wilson's inauguration and to lobby for a federal amendment to give women the vote. Paul's dramatic tactics alienated many in the National American Woman Suffrage Association. In 1916, Paul founded the militant National Woman's Party, which became the radical voice of the suffrage movement.

Women weren't the only group left out in progressive reform. Progressivism, as it was practiced in the West and South, was tainted with racism by seeking to limit the rights of Asians and African Americans. Anti-Asian bigotry in the West led to a renewal of the Chinese Exclusion Act in 1902. At first, California governor Hiram Johnson stood against the strong anti-Asian prejudice of his state. But in 1913, he caved in to popular pressure and signed the Alien Land Law, which barred Japanese immigrants from purchasing land in California.

South of the Mason-Dixon line, the progressives' racism targeted African Americans. Progressives preached the disfranchisement of black voters as a "reform." During the bitter electoral fights that had pitted Populists against Democrats in the 1890s, the party of white supremacy held its power by votes purchased or coerced from African Americans. Southern progressives proposed to reform the electoral system by eliminating black voters. Beginning in 1890 with Mississippi, southern states curtailed the African American vote through devices such as poll taxes (fees required for voting) and literacy tests.

The Progressive Era also witnessed the rise of Jim Crow laws to segregate public facilities. The new railroads precipitated segregation in the South where it had rarely existed before, at least on paper. Soon, separate railcars, separate waiting rooms, separate bathrooms, and separate dining facilities for blacks sprang up across the South. In courtrooms in Mississippi, blacks were required to swear on a separate Bible.

In the face of this growing repression, Booker T. Washington, the preeminent black leader of the day, urged caution and restraint. A former slave, Washington opened the Tuskegee Institute in Alabama in 1881 to teach vocational skills to African Americans. He emphasized education and economic progress for his race and urged African Americans to put aside issues of political and social equality. In an 1895 speech in Atlanta that came to be known as the Atlanta Compromise, he stated, "In all things that are purely social we can be as separate as the fingers, yet one as the hand in all things essential to mutual progress." Washington's accommodationist policy appealed to whites and elevated "the wizard of Tuskegee" to the role of national spokesman for African Americans.

Plessy v. Ferguson
1896 Supreme Court ruling that upheld the legality of racial segregation. According to the ruling, blacks could be segregated in separate schools, restrooms, and other facilities as long as the facilities were "equal" to those provided for whites.

The year after Washington proclaimed the Atlanta Compromise, the Supreme Court upheld the legality of racial segregation, affirming in **Plessy v. Ferguson** (1896) the constitutionality of the doctrine of "separate but equal." Blacks could be segregated in separate schools, restrooms, and other facilities as long as the facilities were "equal" to those provided for whites. Of course, facilities for blacks rarely proved equal.

Woodrow Wilson brought to the White House southern attitudes toward race and racial segregation. He instituted segregation in the federal workforce, especially

Visual Activity

BOOKER T. WASHINGTON AND THEODORE ROOSEVELT DINE AT THE WHITE HOUSE

Theodore Roosevelt invited Booker T. Washington to the White House in 1901, stirring up a hornet's nest of controversy that continued into the election of 1904. The Republican campaign piece pictured shows Roosevelt and a light-skinned Washington sitting under a portrait of Abraham Lincoln. Democrats' campaign buttons pictured Washington with darker skin and implied that Roosevelt had "painted the White House black" and favored "race mingling." David J. & Janice L. Frent Collection/Corbis.

READING THE IMAGE: In this Republican image of the famous meeting of Booker T. Washington and Theodore Roosevelt at the White House, what role does skin color play in the depiction?

CONNECTIONS: Why did African Americans in the South continue to ally with the Republican Party?

DINNER GIVEN AT THE WHITE HOUSE BY PRESIDENT ROOSEVELT TO BOOKER T. WASHINGTON, OCTOBER 17th, 1901

the Post Office, and approved segregated drinking fountains and restrooms in the nation's capital. When critics attacked the policy, Wilson insisted that segregation was "in the interest of the Negro."

In 1906, a major race riot in Atlanta called into question Booker T. Washington's strategy of uplift and accommodation. For three days in September, the streets of Atlanta ran red with blood as angry white mobs chased and cornered any blacks they happened upon. An estimated 250 African Americans died in the riots — members of Atlanta's black middle class along with the poor and derelict. Professor William Crogman of Clark College noted the central irony of the riot: "Here we have worked and prayed and tried to make good men and women of our colored population," he observed, "and at our very doorstep the whites kill these good men." The riot caused many African Americans to question Washington's strategy of gradualism and accommodation.

Foremost among Washington's critics stood W. E. B. Du Bois, a Harvard graduate who urged African Americans to fight for civil rights and racial justice. In *The Souls of Black Folk* (1903), Du Bois attacked the "Tuskegee Machine," comparing Washington to a political boss who used his influence to silence his critics and reward his followers. Du Bois founded the Niagara movement in 1905, calling for universal male suffrage, civil rights, and leadership composed of a black intellectual elite. The Atlanta riot only bolstered his resolve. In 1909, the Niagara movement helped found the National Association for the Advancement of Colored People (NAACP), a coalition of blacks and whites that sought legal and political rights for African Americans through the courts. In the decades that followed, the NAACP came to represent the future for African Americans, while Booker T. Washington, who died in 1915, represented the past.

> **REVIEW** How did race, class, and gender shape the limits of progressive reform?

Conclusion: The Transformation of the Liberal State

Progressivism's goal was to reform the existing system — by government intervention if necessary — but without uprooting any of the traditional American political, economic, or social institutions. As Theodore Roosevelt, the bellwether of the movement, insisted, "The only true conservative is the man who resolutely sets his face toward the future." Roosevelt was such a man, and progressivism was such a movement. But although progressivism was never radical, progressives' willingness to use the power of government to regulate business and achieve a measure of social justice redefined liberalism in the twentieth century, tying it to the expanded power of the state.

Progressivism contained many paradoxes. A diverse coalition of individuals and interests, the progressive movement began at the grass roots but left as its legacy a stronger presidency and unprecedented federal involvement in the economy and social welfare. A movement that believed in social justice, progressivism often promoted social control. And while progressives called for greater democracy, they fostered elitism with their worship of experts and efficiency, and they often failed to champion equality for women and minorities.

Whatever its inconsistencies and limitations, progressivism took action to deal with the problems posed by urban industrialism. Progressivism saw grassroots activists address social problems on the local and state levels and search for national solutions. By increasing the power of the presidency and expanding the power of the state, progressives worked to bring about greater social justice and to achieve a better balance between government and business. Jane Addams and Theodore Roosevelt could lay equal claim to the movement that redefined liberalism and launched the liberal state of the twentieth century. War on a global scale would provide progressivism with yet another challenge even before it had completed its ambitious agenda.

Chapter Review

KEY TERMS

progressivism (p. 612)

settlement houses (p. 613)

social gospel (p. 613)

reform Darwinism (p. 616)

muckraking (p. 622)

Roosevelt Corollary (p. 627)

The New Nationalism (p. 632)

The New Freedom (p. 632)

Socialist Party (p. 635)

Industrial Workers of the World (IWW) (p. 635)

birth control movement (p. 635)

Plessy v. Ferguson (p. 638)

REVIEW QUESTIONS

❶ What types of people were drawn to the progressive movement, and why?   (pp. 612–16)

❷ How did progressives justify their demand for more activist government? (pp. 616–18)

❸ How did Theodore Roosevelt advance the progressive agenda? (pp. 618–31)

❹ How and why did Woodrow Wilson's reform program evolve during his first term?   (pp. 631–34)

❺ How did race, class, and gender shape the limits of progressive reform?   (pp. 635–39)

MAKING CONNECTIONS

❶ Roosevelt's foreign policy was summed up in the dictum "Speak softly but carry a big stick." Using two examples, describe how this policy worked.

❷ Compare the legislative programs of Roosevelt and Wilson and the evolution of their policies over time.

❸ What movements lay outside progressive reform? Why did progressivism coincide with the restriction of minority rights?

LINKING TO THE PAST

❶ In what ways did Populism and progressivism differ? In what ways were they similar? (See chapter 20.)

❷ During the Gilded Age, industrial capitalism concentrated power in the hands of corporations. How did Roosevelt respond to this problem? How did his approach differ from that of the Gilded Age presidents? Was his strategy effective? (See chapter 18.)

22

World War I: The Progressive Crusade at Home and Abroad, 1914–1920

CONTENT LEARNING OBJECTIVES

After reading and studying this chapter, you should be able to:

- Explain the origins of World War I, and why Woodrow Wilson advocated U.S. neutrality. List the events that prompted the United States to enter the war.
- Describe how America geared up domestically and militarily to fight a foreign war.
- Recognize how the war transformed policy at home and understand how women's rights activists used U.S. involvement to secure woman suffrage.
- Explain Wilson's vision for a postwar world, and how that vision was compromised at Versailles. Chronicle the fate of the Paris peace treaty in the U.S. Senate, and explain why it faced so much opposition.
- Understand what threats democracy faced in the immediate postwar period.

George "Brownie" Browne was one of two million soldiers who crossed the Atlantic during World War I to serve in the American Expeditionary Force in France. The twenty-three-year-old civil engineer from Waterbury, Connecticut, volunteered in July 1917, three months after the United States entered the war, serving with the 117th Engineers Regiment, 42nd Division. Two-thirds of the "doughboys" (American soldiers in Europe) saw action during the war, and few white troops saw more than Brownie did. *soldier in france ww*

GAS MASK

Both the Germans and Allies used poison gas during the First World War. Despite this gas mask's crude appearance, it proved highly effective. But many of those who were gassed and survived were left disabled. Collection of Colonel Stuart S. Corning Jr./Picture Research Consultants & Archives.

When the 42nd arrived at the front, veteran French troops taught Brownie's regiment of engineers how to build and maintain trenches, barbed-wire entanglements, and artillery and machine-gun positions. Although Brownie came under German fire each day, he wrote Martha Johnson, his girlfriend back home, "the longer I'm here the more spirit I have to 'stick it out' for the good of humanity and the U.S. which is the same thing."

Training ended in the spring of 1918 when the Germans launched a massive offensive in the Champagne region. The German bombardment made the night "as light as daytime, and the ground . . . was a mass of flames and whistling steel from the bursting shells." One doughboy from the 42nd remembered, "Dead bodies were all around me. Americans, French, Hun [Germans] in all phases and positions of death." Another declared that soon "the odor was something fierce. We had to put on our gas masks to keep from getting sick." Eight days of combat cost the 42nd nearly 6,500 dead, wounded, and missing, 20 percent of the division.

After only ten days' rest, Brownie and his unit joined in the first major American offensive, an attack against German defenses at Saint-Mihiel. On September 12, 3,000 American artillery launched more than a million rounds against German positions. This time the engineers preceded the advancing infantry, cutting through or blasting any barbed wire that remained. The battle cost the 42nd another 1,200 casualties, but Brownie was not among them.

At the end of September, the 42nd shifted to the Meuse-Argonne region, where it participated in the most brutal American fighting of the war. And it was there that Brownie's war ended. The Germans fired thousands of poison gas shells, and the gas, "so thick you could cut it with a knife," felled Brownie. When the war ended on November 11, 1918, he was recovering from his respiratory wounds at a camp behind the lines. Discharged from the army in February 1919, Brownie returned home, where he and Martha married. Like the rest of the country, they were eager to get on with their lives.

President Woodrow Wilson had never expected to lead the United States into the Great War, as the Europeans called it. When war erupted in 1914, he declared America's absolute neutrality. But trade and principle entangled the United States in Europe's troubles and gradually drew the nation into the conflict. Wilson

1914 U.S. Marines occupy Veracruz, Mexico.
Archduke Franz Ferdinand assassinated.
Austria-Hungary declares war on Serbia.
Germany attacks Russia and France.
Great Britain declares war on Germany.

1915 German U-boat sinks *Lusitania*.

1916 Pancho Villa attacks Americans in Mexico and New Mexico.
Wilson reelected.

1917 Zimmermann telegram intercepted.
United States declares war on Germany.
Committee on Public Information created.
Selective Service Act enacted.
Espionage Act and Trading with the Enemy Act enacted.

1918 Wilson gives Fourteen Points speech.
Russia arranges separate peace with Germany.
Sedition Act enacted.
U.S. Marines see first major combat.
Armistice signed ending World War I.

1919 Paris peace conference begins.
Treaty of Versailles signed.
Wave of labor strikes occurs.

1920 American Civil Liberties Union founded.
Prohibition begins.
Palmer raids ordered.
Senate votes against ratification of Treaty of Versailles.
American women get the vote.
Warren G. Harding elected president.

GEORGE "BROWNIE" BROWNE
Training at Fort Slocum, New York, Brownie complained about the army's red tape, bad food, shortage of equipment, inexperienced officers, lack of sleep, and physical exhaustion. Still, he enjoyed the camaraderie of the camp and was, as this photograph reveals, a happy soldier. When his unit arrived at Saint-Nazaire in October 1917, Brownie was proud to be one of the first doughboys in France. Courtesy of Janet W. Hansen.

claimed that America's participation would serve grand purposes and uplift both the United States and the entire world.

At home, the war helped progressives finally achieve their goals of national prohibition and woman suffrage, but it also promoted a vicious attack on Americans' civil liberties. Hyperpatriotism meant intolerance, repression, and vigilante violence. In 1919, Wilson sailed for Europe to secure a just peace. Unable to dictate terms to the victors, he accepted disappointing compromises. Upon his return to the United States, he met a crushing defeat that marked the end of Wilsonian internationalism abroad. Crackdowns on dissenters, immigrants, racial and ethnic minorities, and unions also signaled the end of the Progressive Era at home.

Woodrow Wilson and the World

Shortly after winning election to the presidency in 1912, Woodrow Wilson confided to a friend: "It would be an irony of fate if my administration had to deal with foreign affairs." Indeed, Wilson had focused his life and career on domestic concerns; in his campaign for the presidency, Wilson had hardly mentioned the world abroad.

Wilson, however, could not avoid the world and the rising tide of militarism, nationalism, and violence that beat against American shores. Economic interests compelled the nation outward. Moreover, Wilson was drawn abroad by his own progressive political principles. He believed that the United States had a moral duty to champion national self-determination, peaceful free trade, and political democracy. "We have no selfish ends to serve," he proclaimed. "We desire no conquest, no dominion. . . . We are but one of the champions of the rights of mankind." Yet as president, Wilson was as ready as any American president to apply military solutions to problems of foreign policy. This readiness led Wilson and the United States into military conflict in Mexico and then in Europe.

Taming the Americas.
When he took office, Wilson sought to distinguish his foreign policy from that of his Republican predecessors. To Wilson, Theodore Roosevelt's "big stick" and William Howard Taft's "dollar diplomacy" appeared as crude flexing of military and economic muscle. To signal a new direction, Wilson appointed William Jennings Bryan, a pacifist, as secretary of state.

But Wilson and Bryan, like Roosevelt and Taft, also believed that the Monroe Doctrine gave the United States special rights and responsibilities in the Western Hemisphere. Issued in 1823 to warn Europeans not to attempt to colonize the Americas again, the doctrine had become a cloak for U.S. domination. Wilson thus authorized U.S. military intervention in Nicaragua, Haiti, and the Dominican Republic, paving the way for U.S. banks and corporations to take financial control. All the while, Wilson believed that U.S. actions were promoting order and democracy. "I am going to teach the South American Republics to elect good men!" he declared (Map 22.1).

Wilson's most serious involvement in Latin America came in Mexico. When General Victoriano Huerta seized power by violent means in 1913, most European nations promptly recognized Mexico's new government, but Wilson refused, declaring that he would not support a "government of butchers." In April 1914, Wilson sent 800 Marines to seize the port of Veracruz to prevent the unloading of a large

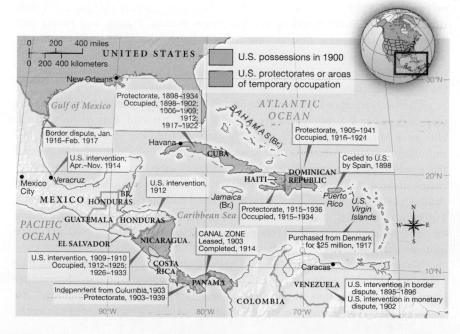

MAP 22.1 U.S. INVOLVEMENT IN LATIN AMERICA AND THE CARIBBEAN, 1895–1941

Victory against Spain in 1898 made Puerto Rico an American possession and Cuba a protectorate. The United States later gained control of the Panama Canal Zone. The nation protected its expanding economic interests with military force by propping up friendly, though not necessarily democratic, governments.

U.S. INTERVENTION IN MEXICO, 1916–1917

Map labels:
ARIZ. N. MEX. TEXAS MEXICO
Culberson's Ranch
El Paso
Columbus March 9
Ascensión
Colonia Dublán
Carrizal June 21
Casas Grandes
Galeana
Namiquipa
Guerrero March 29
Bachiniva
Chihuahua
Tomochic April 21
San Francisco de Borja
Parral April 12
Rio Grande

Legend:
✳ Raids and clashes
→ U.S. main force
→ U.S. cavalry

Triple Alliance

Early-twentieth-century alliance among Germany, Austria-Hungary, and Italy, which was formed as part of a complex network of military and diplomatic agreements intended to prevent war in Europe by balancing power. In actuality, such alliances made large-scale conflict more likely.

Triple Entente

Early-twentieth-century alliance among Great Britain, France, and Russia. The Triple Entente stood opposed to the Triple Alliance.

shipment of arms for Huerta. Huerta fled to Spain, and the United States welcomed a more compliant government.

But a rebellion erupted among desperately poor farmers who believed that the new government, aided by U.S. business interests, had betrayed the revolution's promise to help the common people. In January 1916 the rebel army, commanded by Francisco "Pancho" Villa, seized a train carrying gold to Texas from an American-owned mine in Mexico and killed the 17 American engineers aboard. In March, Villa's men crossed the border for a predawn raid on Columbus, New Mexico, where they killed 18 Americans. Wilson promptly dispatched 12,000 troops, led by Major General John J. Pershing. But Villa avoided capture, and in January 1917, Wilson recalled Pershing so that he might prepare the army for the possibility of fighting in the Great War.

killed americans

The European Crisis. Before 1914, Europe had enjoyed decades of peace, but just beneath the surface lay the potentially destructive forces of nationalism and imperialism. The consolidation of the German and Italian states into unified nations and the similar ambition of Russia to create a Pan-Slavic union initiated new rivalries throughout Europe. As the conviction spread that colonial possessions were a mark of national greatness, competition expanded onto the world stage. Most ominously, Germany's efforts under Kaiser Wilhelm II to challenge Great Britain's world supremacy by creating industrial muscle at home, an empire abroad, and a mighty navy threatened the balance of power and thus the peace.

European nations sought to avoid an explosion by developing a complex web of military and diplomatic alliances. By 1914, Germany, Austria-Hungary, and Italy (the **Triple Alliance**) stood opposed to Great Britain, France, and Russia (the **Triple Entente**, also known as "the Allies"). But in their effort to prevent war through a balance of power, Europeans had actually magnified the possibility of large-scale conflict (Map 22.2). Treaties, some of them secret, obligated members of the alliances to come to the aid of another member if attacked.

The fatal sequence began on June 28, 1914, in the city of Sarajevo, when a Bosnian Serb terrorist assassinated Archduke Franz Ferdinand, heir to the Austro-Hungarian throne. On July 18, Austria-Hungary declared war on Serbia. The elaborate alliance system meant that the war could not remain local. Russia announced that it would back the Serbs. Compelled by treaty to support Austria-Hungary, Germany on August 3 attacked Russia and France. In response, on August 4, Great Britain, upholding its pact with France, declared war on Germany. Within weeks, Europe was engulfed in war. The conflict became a world war when Japan, seeing an opportunity to rid itself of European competition in China, joined the cause against Germany.

The evenly matched alliances would fight a disastrous war lasting more than four years, at a cost of 8.5 million soldiers' lives. A war that started with a solitary murder proved impossible to stop. Britain's foreign secretary, Edward Grey, lamented: "The lamps are going out all over Europe. We shall not see them lit again in our lifetime."

MAP. 22.2 EUROPEAN ALLIANCES AFTER THE OUTBREAK OF WORLD WAR I

With Germany and Austria-Hungary wedged between their Entente rivals and all parties fully armed, Europe was poised for war when Archduke Franz Ferdinand of Austria-Hungary was assassinated in Sarajevo in June 1914.

The Ordeal of American Neutrality.

Woodrow Wilson promptly announced that because the war engaged no vital American interest and involved no significant principle, the United States would remain neutral. Neutrality entitled the United States to trade safely with all nations at war, he declared. Unfettered trade, Wilson believed, was not only a right under international law but also a necessity because in 1913 the U.S. economy had slipped into a recession that wartime disruption of European trade could drastically worsen.

Although Wilson proclaimed neutrality, his sympathies, like those of many Americans, lay with Great Britain and France. Americans gratefully remembered crucial French assistance in the American Revolution and shared with the British a language, a culture, and a commitment to liberty. Germany, by contrast, was a monarchy with strong militaristic traditions. Still, Wilson insisted on neutrality, in part because he feared the conflict's effects on the United States as a nation of immigrants. As he told the German ambassador, "We definitely have to be neutral, since otherwise our mixed populations would wage war on each other."

German submarine blockade

SINKING OF THE *LUSITANIA*, 1915

Lusitania
British passenger liner torpedoed by a German U-boat on May 7, 1915. The attack killed 1,198 passengers, including 128 Americans. The incident challenged American neutrality during World War I and moved the United States on a path toward entering the war.

Britain's powerful fleet controlled the seas and quickly set up an economic blockade of Germany. The United States vigorously protested, but Britain refused to give up its naval advantage. The blockade actually had little economic impact on the United States. Between 1914 and the spring of 1917, while trade with Germany evaporated, war-related exports to Britain — food, clothing, steel, and munitions — escalated by some 400 percent, enough to pull the American economy out of its slump. Although the British blockade violated American neutrality, the Wilson administration gradually acquiesced, thus beginning the fateful process of alienation from Germany.

Germany retaliated with a submarine blockade of British ports. German *Unterseebooten*, or U-boats, threatened notions of "civilized" warfare. Unlike surface warships that could harmlessly stop freighters and prevent them from entering a war zone, submarines relied on sinking their quarry. And once they sank a ship, the tiny U-boats could not pick up survivors. Nevertheless, in February 1915, Germany announced that it intended to sink on sight enemy ships en route to the British Isles. On May 7, 1915, a German U-boat torpedoed the British passenger liner *Lusitania*, killing 1,198 passengers, 128 of them U.S. citizens.

American newspapers featured drawings of drowning women and children, and some demanded war. Calmer voices pointed out that Germany had warned prospective passengers and that the *Lusitania* carried millions of rounds of ammunition and so was a legitimate target. Secretary of State Bryan resisted the hysteria and declared that a ship carrying war materiel "should not rely on passengers to protect her from attack — it would be like putting women and children in front of an army." He counseled Wilson to warn American citizens that they traveled on ships of belligerent countries at their own risk.

Wilson sought a middle course that would retain his commitment to peace and neutrality without condoning German attacks on passenger ships. On May 10, 1915, he announced that any further destruction of ships would be regarded as "deliberately unfriendly" and might lead the United States to break diplomatic relations with Germany. Wilson essentially demanded that Germany abandon unrestricted submarine warfare. Bryan resigned, predicting that the president had placed the United States on a collision course with Germany. Wilson replaced Bryan with Robert Lansing, who believed that Germany's antidemocratic character and goal of "world dominance" meant that it "must not be permitted to win this war."

After Germany apologized for the civilian deaths on the *Lusitania*, tensions subsided. And in 1916, Germany went further, promising no more submarine attacks without warning and without provisions for the safety of civilians. Wilson's supporters celebrated the success of his middle-of-the-road strategy.

Wilson's diplomacy proved helpful in his bid for reelection in 1916. In the contest against Republican Charles Evans Hughes, the Democratic Party ran Wilson under the slogan "He kept us out of war." Wilson felt uneasy with the claim, protesting that "they talk of me as though I were a god. Any little German lieutenant can push us into the war at any time by some calculated outrage." But the Democrats' case for Wilson's neutrality appealed to enough of those in favor of peace to eke out a majority. Wilson won, but only by the razor-thin margins of 600,000 popular and 23 electoral votes.

The United States Enters the War. Step by step, the United States backed away from "absolute neutrality." The consequence of protesting the German blockade of Great Britain but accepting the British blockade of Germany was that by 1916 the United States was supplying the Allies with 40 percent of their war materiel. When France and Britain ran short of money to pay for U.S. goods and asked for loans, Wilson argued that "loans by American bankers to any foreign government which is at war are inconsistent with the true spirit of neutrality." But rather than jeopardize America's wartime prosperity, Wilson allowed billions of dollars in loans that kept American goods flowing to Britain and France.

In January 1917, Germany decided that it could no longer afford to allow neutral shipping to reach Great Britain while Britain's blockade gradually starved Germany. It announced that its navy would resume unrestricted submarine warfare and sink without warning any ship, enemy or neutral, found in the waters off Great Britain. Germany understood that the decision would probably bring the United States into the war but gambled that its submarines would strangle the British economy and allow German armies to win a military victory in France before American troops arrived in Europe.

Resisting demands for war, Wilson continued to hope for a negotiated peace and only broke off diplomatic relations with Germany. Then, on February 25, 1917,

"CHUMS"

This American war poster from 1918 depicts the devil seated with his arm around Germany's Kaiser Wilhelm, a devil-like figure himself who holds a bloody sword. The devil is congratulating Wilhelm for sinking the *Lusitania* three years earlier. The poster left no doubt that America was on the side of the angels and did the right thing by going to war. Library of Congress, 3g07819.

British authorities informed Wilson of a secret telegram sent by the German foreign secretary, Arthur Zimmermann, to the German minister in Mexico. It promised that in the event of war between Germany and the United States, Germany would see that Mexico regained its "lost provinces" of Texas, New Mexico, and Arizona if Mexico would declare war against the United States. Wilson angrily responded to the Zimmermann telegram by asking Congress to approve a policy of "armed neutrality" that would allow merchant ships to fight back against attackers.

In March, German submarines sank five American vessels off Britain, killing 66 Americans. On April 2, the president asked Congress to issue a declaration of war. He accused Germany of "warfare against all mankind." Still, he called for a "war without hate" and declared that America fought only to "vindicate the principles of peace and justice." He promised a world made "safe for democracy." On April 6, 1917, by majorities of 373 to 50 in the House and 82 to 6 in the Senate, Congress voted to declare war.

Wilson feared what war would do at home. He said despairingly, "Once lead this people into war, and they'll forget there ever was such a thing as tolerance. To fight you must be brutal and ruthless, and the spirit of ruthless brutality will infect Congress, the courts, the policeman on the beat, the man in the street."

REVIEW Why did President Wilson fail to maintain U.S. neutrality during World War I?

"Over There"

American soldiers joined the fighting just after the Russians withdrew from the war, leaving France as the primary battleground. Americans sailed for France eager to do their part in making the world safe for democracy. Some doughboys, including George Browne, maintained their idealism to the end. Although black soldiers eventually won respect under the French command, they faced discrimination under American commanders. The majority of American soldiers found little that was noble in rats, lice, and poison gas and — despite the progressives' hopes — little to elevate the human soul in a landscape of utter destruction and death.

The Call to Arms. When America entered the war, Britain and France were nearly exhausted after almost three years of conflict. Millions of soldiers had perished; food and morale were dangerously low. Another Allied power, Russia, was in turmoil. In March 1917, a revolution had forced Czar Nicholas II to abdicate, and one year later, in a separate peace with Germany, the **Bolshevik** revolutionary government withdrew Russia from the war. Peace with Russia allowed Germany to withdraw hundreds of thousands of its soldiers from the eastern front and to deploy them against the Allies on the western front in France.

On May 18, 1917, Wilson signed a sweeping Selective Service Act, authorizing a draft of all young men into the armed forces. Conscription transformed a tiny volunteer armed force of 80,000 men into a vast army and navy. Draft boards

Bolshevik
Russian revolutionary. Bolsheviks forced Czar Nicholas II to abdicate and seized power in Russia in 1917. In a separate peace with Germany, the Bolshevik government withdrew Russia from World War I.

eventually inducted 2.8 million men into the armed services, in addition to the 2 million, including George Browne, who volunteered. Among the 4.8 million men under arms, 370,000 were black Americans. During training, black recruits suffered the same prejudices that they encountered in civilian life. One base in Virginia that trained blacks as cargo handlers quartered black recruits in tents without floors or stoves and provided no changes of clothes, no blankets for the winter, and no facilities for bathing. Only after several deaths from disease and exposure did the authorities move to make conditions even tolerable.

Training camps sought to transform raw white recruits into fighting men. Progressives in the government were also determined that the camps turn out soldiers with the highest moral and civic values. To provide recruits with "invisible armor," YMCA workers and veterans of the settlement house and playground movements led them in games, singing, and college extension courses. The army asked soldiers to stop thinking about sex, explaining that a "man who is thinking below the belt is not efficient." Wilson's choice to command the army on the battlefields of France, Major General John "Black Jack" Pershing, was as morally upright as he was militarily uncompromising. Described by one observer as "lean, clean, keen," he gave progressives perfect confidence.

The War in France.

At the front, the **American Expeditionary Force (AEF)** discovered a desperate situation. The war had degenerated into a stalemate of armies dug into hundreds of miles of trenches that stretched across France. Huddling in the mud among the corpses and rats, soldiers were separated from the enemy by only a few hundred yards of "no-man's-land." When ordered "over the top," troops raced desperately toward the enemy's trenches, only to be entangled in barbed wire, enveloped in poison gas, and mowed down by machine guns. The three-day battle of the Somme in 1916 cost the French and British forces 600,000 dead and wounded and the Germans 500,000. The deadliest battle of the war allowed the Allies to advance their trenches only a few meaningless miles.

Still, U.S. troops saw almost no combat in 1917. Troops continued to train and used much of their free time to explore places that most of them could otherwise never hope to see. True to the crusader image, American officials allowed only uplifting tourism. The temptations of Paris were off-limits. French premier Georges Clemenceau's offer to supply American troops with licensed prostitutes was declined with the half-serious remark that if Wilson found out he would stop the war.

Sightseeing ended abruptly in March 1918 when a million German soldiers punched a hole in the Allied lines. Pershing finally committed the AEF to combat. In May and June, at Cantigny and then at Château-Thierry, the eager but green Americans checked the German advance with a series of assaults (Map 22.3). Then they headed toward the forest stronghold of Belleau Wood, moving against streams of retreating Allied soldiers who cried defeat: "La guerre est finie!" (The war is over!). A French officer commanded the Americans to retreat with them, but the American commander replied sharply, "Retreat, hell. We just got here." After charging through a wheat field against withering machine-gun fire, the Marines plunged into hand-to-hand combat. Victory came hard, but a German report praised the enemy's spirit,

American Expeditionary Force (AEF)
U.S. armed forces under the command of General John Pershing who fought under a separate American command in Europe during World War I. They helped defeat Germany when they entered the conflict in full force in 1918.

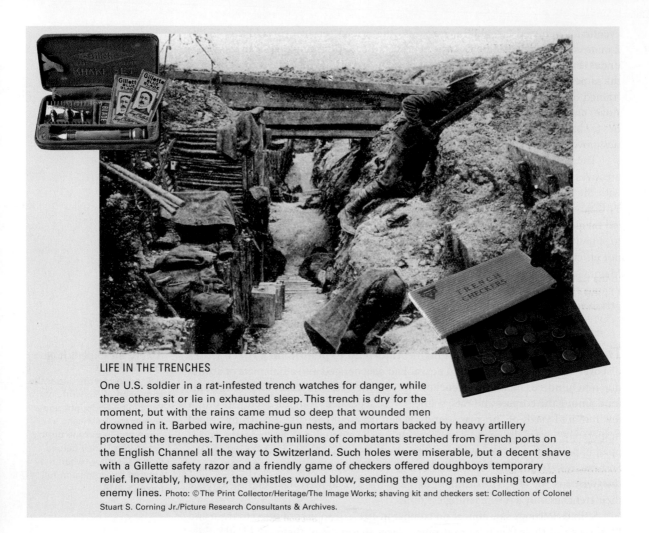

LIFE IN THE TRENCHES

One U.S. soldier in a rat-infested trench watches for danger, while three others sit or lie in exhausted sleep. This trench is dry for the moment, but with the rains came mud so deep that wounded men drowned in it. Barbed wire, machine-gun nests, and mortars backed by heavy artillery protected the trenches. Trenches with millions of combatants stretched from French ports on the English Channel all the way to Switzerland. Such holes were miserable, but a decent shave with a Gillette safety razor and a friendly game of checkers offered doughboys temporary relief. Inevitably, however, the whistles would blow, sending the young men rushing toward enemy lines. Photo: ©The Print Collector/Heritage/The Image Works; shaving kit and checkers set: Collection of Colonel Stuart S. Corning Jr./Picture Research Consultants & Archives.

noting that "the Americans' nerves are not yet worn out." Indeed, it was German morale that was on the verge of cracking.

In the summer of 1918, the Allies launched a massive counteroffensive that would end the war. A quarter of a million U.S. troops joined in the rout of German forces along the Marne River. In September, more than a million Americans took part in the assault that threw the Germans back from positions along the Meuse River. In four brutal days, the AEF sustained 45,000 casualties. In November, a revolt against the German government sent Kaiser Wilhelm II fleeing to Holland. On November 11, 1918, a delegation from the newly established German republic met with the French high command to sign an armistice that brought the fighting to an end.

The adventure of the AEF was brief, bloody, and victorious. When Germany had resumed unrestricted U-boat warfare in 1917, it had been gambling that it could defeat Britain and France before the Americans could raise and train an army and ship it to France. The German military had miscalculated badly. By the end, 112,000 AEF soldiers perished from wounds and disease, while another 230,000 Americans, including George Browne, suffered casualties but survived. Only the Civil War, which lasted much longer, had cost more American lives. European nations, however, suffered much greater losses: 2.2 million Germans, 1.9 million Russians,

Map Activity

MAP 22.3 THE AMERICAN EXPEDITIONARY FORCE, 1918

In the last year of the war, the AEF joined the French army on the western front to respond to the final German offensive and pursue the retreating enemy until surrender.

READING THE MAP: Across which rivers did the Germans advance in 1918? Where did the armistice line of November 11, 1918, lie in relation to the stabilized front of 1915–1917? Through which countries did the armistice line run?

CONNECTIONS: What events paved the way for the AEF to join the combat effort in 1918? What characteristic(s) differentiated American troops from other Allied forces and helped them achieve victory?

1.4 million French, and 900,000 Britons. Where they had fought, the landscape was as blasted and barren as the moon.

> **REVIEW** How did the AEF contribute to the defeat of Germany?

The Crusade for Democracy at Home

Many progressives hoped that the war would improve the quality of American life as well as free Europe from tyranny and militarism. Mobilization helped propel the crusades for woman suffrage and prohibition to success. Progressives enthusiastically channeled industrial and agricultural production into the vast war effort. Labor shortages caused by workers entering the military provided new opportunities for women in the booming wartime economy. With labor at a premium, unionized workers gained higher pay and shorter hours. To instill loyalty in Americans whose ancestry was rooted in the belligerent nations, Wilson launched a campaign to foster patriotism. But fanning patriotism led to suppressing dissent. When the government launched a harsh assault on civil liberties, mobs gained license to attack those whom they considered disloyal. As Wilson feared, democracy took a beating at home when the nation undertook its crusade for democracy abroad.

The Progressive Stake in the War.
Progressives embraced the idea that the war could be an agent of national improvement. The Wilson administration, realizing that the federal government would have to assert greater control to mobilize the nation's human and physical resources, created new agencies to manage the war effort. Bernard Baruch, a Wall Street stockbroker, headed the War Industries Board, charged with stimulating and directing industrial production. Baruch brought industrial management and labor together into a team that produced everything from boots to bullets and made U.S. troops the best-equipped soldiers in the world.

Herbert Hoover, a self-made millionaire engineer, headed the Food Administration. He led remarkably successful "Hooverizing" campaigns for "meatless" Mondays and "wheatless" Wednesdays and other ways of conserving resources. Guaranteed high prices, the American heartland not only supplied the needs of U.S. citizens and armed forces but also became the breadbasket of America's allies.

Wartime agencies multiplied: The Railroad Administration directed railroad traffic, the Fuel Administration coordinated the coal industry and other fuel suppliers, the Shipping Board organized the merchant marine, and the National War Labor Policies Board resolved labor disputes. Their successes gave most progressives reason to believe that, indeed, war and reform marched together. Still, skeptics like Wisconsin senator Robert La Follette declared that Wilson's promises of permanent peace and democracy were a case of "the blind leading the blind."

Industrial leaders found that wartime agencies enforced efficiency, which helped corporate profits triple. Some working people also had cause to celebrate. Mobilization meant high prices for farmers and plentiful jobs at high wages in the new war industries

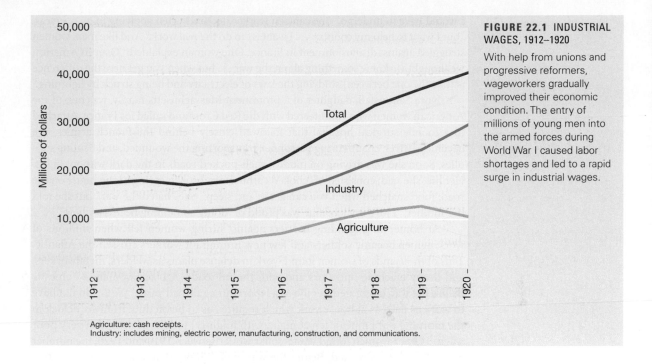

FIGURE 22.1 INDUSTRIAL
WAGES, 1912–1920

With help from unions and
progressive reformers,
wageworkers gradually
improved their economic
condition. The entry of
millions of young men into
the armed forces during
World War I caused labor
shortages and led to a rapid
surge in industrial wages.

Agriculture: cash receipts.
Industry: includes mining, electric power, manufacturing, construction, and communications.

(Figure 22.1). Because increased industrial production required peaceful labor relations, the National War Labor Policies Board enacted the eight-hour day, a living minimum wage, and collective bargaining rights in some industries. The American Federation of Labor (AFL) saw its membership soar from 2.7 million to more than 5 million.

The war also provided a huge boost to the crusade to ban alcohol. By 1917, prohibitionists had convinced nineteen states to go dry. Liquor's opponents now argued that banning alcohol would make the cause of democracy powerful and pure. At the same time, shutting down the distilleries would save millions of bushels of grain that could feed the United States and its allies. "Shall the many have food or the few drink?" the drys asked. Prohibition received an additional boost because many of the breweries had German names — Schlitz, Pabst, and Anheuser-Busch. In December 1917, Congress passed the **Eighteenth Amendment**, which banned the manufacture, transportation, and sale of alcohol. After swift ratification by the states, the prohibition amendment went into effect on January 1, 1920.

Women, War, and the Battle for Suffrage.
Women had made real strides during the Progressive Era, and war presented new opportunities. More than 25,000 women served in France. About half were nurses. The others drove ambulances; ran canteens for the Salvation Army, Red Cross, and YMCA; worked with French civilians in devastated areas; and acted as telephone operators and war correspondents. Like men who joined the war effort, they believed that they were taking part in a great national venture. "I am more than willing to live as a soldier and know of the hardships

**Eighteenth Amendment
(prohibition)**

Constitutional amendment
banning the manufacture,
transportation, and sale of
alcohol. Congress passed
the amendment in
December 1917, and it was
ratified in January 1920.
World War I provided a
huge boost to the crusade
to ban alcohol.

I would have to undergo," one canteen worker declared when applying to go overseas, "but I want to help my country. . . . I want . . . to do the *real* work." And like men, women struggled against disillusionment in France. One woman explained: "Over in America, we thought we knew something about the war . . . but when you get here the difference is [like the one between] studying the laws of electricity and being struck by lightning."

Nora Saltonstall, daughter of a prominent Massachusetts family, was one of the American women who volunteered with the Red Cross and sailed for France. Attached to a mobile surgical hospital that followed closely behind the French armies, she became a driver, chauffeuring personnel, transporting the wounded, and hauling supplies. Soon she was driving on muddy, shell-pocked roads in the dark without lights. Her life, she said, consisted of "choked carburetors, broken springs, long hours on the road, food snatched when you can get it, and sleep." She "hated the war," but she told her mother, "I love my job." She was proud of "doing something necessary here."

At home, long-standing barriers against hiring women fell when millions of workingmen became soldiers and few new immigrant workers crossed the Atlantic. Tens of thousands of women found work in defense plants as welders, metalworkers, and heavy machine operators and with the railroads. A black woman, a domestic before the war, celebrated her job as a laborer in a railroad yard: "We . . . do not have to work as hard as at housework which requires us to be on duty from six o'clock in the morning until nine or ten at night, with might[y] little time off and at very poor wages." Other women found white-collar work. Between 1910 and 1920, the number of women clerks doubled. Before the war ended, more than a million women had found work in war industries. One women's rights advocate exaggerated when she declared, "At last . . . women are coming into the labor and festival of life on equal terms with men," but women had made real economic strides.

The most dramatic advance for women came in the political arena. Adopting a state-by-state approach before the war, suffragists had achieved some success (Map 22.4). More commonly, voting rights for women met strong hostility and defeat. After 1910, suffrage leaders added a federal campaign to amend the Constitution to the traditional state-by-state strategy for suffrage.

The radical wing of the suffragists, led by Alice Paul, picketed the White House, where the marchers unfurled banners that proclaimed "America Is Not a Democracy. Twenty Million Women Are Denied the Right to Vote." They chained themselves to fences and went to jail, where many engaged in hunger strikes. "They seem bent on making their cause as obnoxious as possible," Woodrow Wilson declared. His wife, Edith, detested the idea of "masculinized" voting women. But membership in the mainstream organization, the National American Woman Suffrage Association (NAWSA), led by Carrie Chapman Catt, soared to some two million. Seeing the handwriting on the wall, the Republican and Progressive parties endorsed woman suffrage in 1916.

In 1918, Wilson finally gave his support to suffrage, calling the amendment "vital to the winning of the war." He conceded that it would be wrong not to reward the wartime "partnership of suffering and sacrifice" with a "partnership of privilege and right." By linking their cause to the wartime emphasis on national unity, the advocates of woman suffrage finally triumphed. In 1919, Congress passed the **Nineteenth Amendment**, granting women the vote, and by August 1920 the required two-thirds of the states had ratified it.

Nineteenth Amendment (woman suffrage)
Constitutional amendment granting women the vote. Congress passed the amendment in 1919, and it was ratified in August 1920. Like proponents of prohibition, the advocates of woman suffrage triumphed by linking their cause to the war.

Rally around the Flag — or Else.

When Congress committed the nation to war, only a handful of peace advocates resisted the tide of patriotism. A group of professional women, led by settlement house leader Jane Addams and economics professor Emily Greene Balch, denounced what Addams described as "the pathetic belief in the regenerative results of war." After America entered the conflict, advocates for peace were labeled cowards and traitors.

To suppress criticism of the war, Wilson stirred up patriotic fervor. In 1917, the president created the Committee on Public Information under the direction of George Creel, a journalist who became the nation's cheerleader for war. Creel sent "Four-Minute Men," a squad of 75,000 volunteers, around the country to give brief pep talks that celebrated successes on the battlefields and in the factories. Posters, pamphlets, and cartoons depicted brave American soldiers and sailors defending freedom and democracy against the evil "Huns," the derogatory nickname applied to German soldiers.

America rallied around Creel's campaign. The film industry cranked out pro-war melodramas and taught audiences to hiss at the German kaiser. Colleges and universities generated war propaganda in the guise of scholarship. When Professor James McKeen Cattell of Columbia University urged that America seek peace with Germany short of victory, university president Nicholas Murray Butler fired him on the grounds that "what had been folly is now treason."

Map Activity

MAP 22.4 WOMEN'S VOTING RIGHTS BEFORE THE NINETEENTH AMENDMENT

The long campaign for women's voting rights reversed the pioneer epic that moved from east to west. From its first successes in the new democratic West, suffrage rolled eastward toward the entrenched, male-dominated public life of the Northeast and South.

READING THE MAP: What was the first state to grant woman suffrage? How many states extended full voting rights to women before 1914? How many extended these rights during World War I (1914–1918)?

CONNECTIONS: Suffragists redirected their focus during the war. What strategies did they use then?

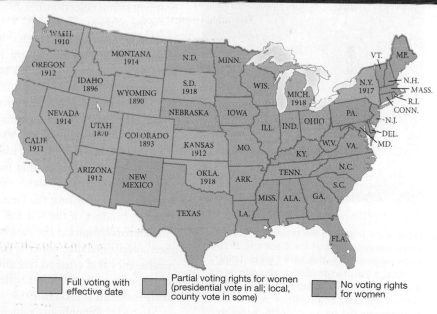

Full voting with effective date

Partial voting rights for women (presidential vote in all; local, county vote in some)

No voting rights for women

A firestorm of anti-German passion erupted. Across the nation, "100% American" campaigns enlisted ordinary people to sniff out disloyalty. German, the most widely taught foreign language in 1914, practically disappeared from the nation's schools. Targeting German-born Americans, the *Saturday Evening Post* declared that it was time to rid the country of "the scum of the melting pot." Anti-German action reached its extreme with the lynching of Robert Prager, a German-born baker with socialist leanings. Persuaded by the defense lawyer who praised what he called a "patriotic murder," the jury at the trial of the killers took only twenty-five minutes to acquit.

As hysteria increased, the campaign reached absurd levels. Menus across the nation changed German toast to French toast and sauerkraut to liberty cabbage. In Milwaukee, vigilantes mounted a machine gun outside the Pabst Theater to prevent the staging of Schiller's *Wilhelm Tell*, a powerful protest against tyranny. The fiancée of one of the war's leading critics, caught dancing on the dunes of Cape Cod, was held on suspicion of signaling to German submarines.

D. W. GRIFFITH'S *HEARTS OF THE WORLD*, 1918
Hollywood joined in the government's efforts to stir up rage against the Germans. In this poster announcing the 1918 film by D. W. Griffith, a German soldier is about to whip a defenseless farm woman (played by Lillian Gish). First Lady Edith Wilson, who sought to moderate the hate campaign, wrote to Griffith pleading with him to cut or soften the violent scene. Everett Collection.

The Wilson administration's zeal in suppressing dissent contrasted sharply with its war aims of defending democracy. In the name of self-defense, the Espionage Act (June 1917), the Trading with the Enemy Act (October 1917), and the Sedition Act (May 1918) gave the government sweeping powers to punish any opinion or activity it considered "disloyal, profane, scurrilous, or abusive." When Postmaster General Albert Burleson blocked mailing privileges for dissenting publications, dozens of journals were forced to close down. Of the 1,500 individuals eventually charged with sedition, all but a dozen had merely spoken words the government found objectionable.

One of them was Eugene V. Debs, the leader of the Socialist Party, who was convicted under the Espionage Act and sentenced to ten years. In a speech on June 16, 1918, Debs declared that the United States was not fighting a noble war to make the world safe for democracy but had joined greedy European imperialists seeking to conquer the globe. The government claimed that Debs had crossed the line between legitimate dissent and criminal speech. From the Atlanta penitentiary, Debs argued that he was just telling the truth, like hundreds of his friends who were also in jail.

The president hoped that national commitment to the war would silence partisan politics, but his Republican rivals used the war as a weapon against the Democrats. The trick was to oppose Wilson's conduct of the war but not the war itself. Republicans outshouted Wilson on the nation's need to mobilize for war but then complained that Wilson's War Industries Board was a tyrannical agency that crushed free enterprise. As the war progressed, Republicans gathered power against the Democrats, who had narrowly reelected Wilson in 1916.

In 1918, Republicans gained a narrow majority in both the House and the Senate. The end of Democratic control of Congress not only halted further domestic reform but also meant that the

United States would advance toward military victory in Europe with political power divided between a Democratic president and a Republican Congress likely to challenge Wilson's plans for international cooperation.

> **REVIEW** How did progressive ideals fare during wartime?

A Compromised Peace

Wilson decided to reaffirm his noble war ideals by announcing his peace aims before the end of hostilities. He hoped the victorious Allies would adopt his plan for international democracy, but he was sorely disappointed. America's allies understood that Wilson's principles jeopardized their own postwar plans for the acquisition of enemy territory, new colonial empires, and reparations. Wilson also faced strong opposition at home from those who feared that his enthusiasm for international cooperation would undermine American sovereignty.

Wilson's Fourteen Points.
On January 8, 1918, ten months before the armistice in Europe, President Wilson revealed to Congress his **Fourteen Points**, his blueprint for a new democratic world order. The first five points affirmed basic liberal ideals: an end to secret treaties, freedom of the seas, removal of economic barriers to free trade, reduction of weapons of war, and recognition of the rights of colonized peoples. The next eight points supported the right to self-determination of European peoples who had been dominated by Germany or its allies. Wilson's fourteenth point called for a "general association of nations" — a **League of Nations** to provide "mutual guarantees of political independence and territorial integrity to great and small states alike." A League of Nations reflected Wilson's lifelong dream of a "parliament of man." Only such an organization of "peace-loving nations," he believed, could justify the war and secure a lasting peace.

The Paris Peace Conference.
From January 18 to June 28, 1919, the eyes of the world focused on Paris. Wilson, inspired by his mission, decided to head the U.S. delegation. He said he owed it to the American soldiers. "It is now my duty," he announced, "to play my full part in making good what they gave their life's blood to obtain." A dubious British diplomat retorted that Wilson was drawn to Paris "as a debutante is entranced by the prospect of her first ball." The decision to leave the country at a time when his political opponents challenged his leadership was risky enough, but his stubborn refusal to include prominent Republicans in the delegation proved foolhardy and eventually cost him his dream of a new world order.

After four terrible years of war, the common people of Europe almost worshipped Wilson, believing that he would create a safer, more decent world. When the peace conference convened at Louis XIV's magnificent palace at Versailles, however, Wilson encountered a different reception. To the Allied leaders, Wilson appeared a naive and impractical moralist. His desire to gather former enemies within a new

Fourteen Points
Woodrow Wilson's plan, proposed in 1918, to create a new democratic world order with lasting peace. Wilson's plan affirmed basic liberal ideals, supported the right to self-determination, and called for the creation of a League of Nations. Wilson compromised on his plan at the 1919 Paris peace conference, and the U.S. Senate refused to ratify the resulting treaty.

League of Nations
International organization proposed in Woodrow Wilson's Fourteen Points that was designed to secure political independence and territorial integrity for all states and thus ensure enduring peace. The U.S. Senate refused to ratify the Treaty of Versailles, and the United States never became a member.

international democratic order showed how little he understood hard European realities. Georges Clemenceau, premier of France, claimed that Wilson "believed you could do everything by formulas" and "empty theory." Disparaging the Fourteen Points, he added, "God himself was content with ten commandments."

The Allies wanted to fasten blame for the war on Germany, totally disarm it, and make it pay so dearly that it would never threaten its neighbors again. The French demanded retribution in the form of territory containing Germany's richest mineral resources. The British made it clear that they were not about to give up the powerful weapon of naval blockade for the vague principle of freedom of the seas.

The Allies forced Wilson to make drastic compromises. In return for France's moderating its territorial claims, he agreed to support Article 231 of the peace treaty, assigning war guilt to Germany. Though saved from permanently losing Rhineland territory to the French, Germany was outraged at being singled out as the instigator of the war and being saddled with more than $33 billion in damages. Many Germans felt that their nation had been betrayed. After agreeing to an armistice in the belief that peace terms would be based in Wilson's generous Fourteen Points, they faced hardship and humiliation instead.

Wilson had better success in establishing the principle of self-determination. But from the beginning, Secretary of State Robert Lansing knew that the president's concept of self-determination was "simply loaded with dynamite." Lansing wondered, "What unit has he in mind? Does he mean a race, a territorial area, or a community?" Even Wilson was vague about what self-determination actually meant. "When I gave utterance to those words," he admitted, "I said them without the knowledge that nationalities existed, which are coming to us day after day." Lansing suspected that the notion "will raise hopes which can never be realized. It will, I fear, cost thousands of lives. In the end it is bound to be discredited, to be called the dream of an idealist who failed to realize the danger until it was too late."

Yet partly on the basis of self-determination, the conference redrew the map of Europe and parts of the rest of the world. Portions of Austria-Hungary were ceded to Italy, Poland, and Romania, and the remainder was reassembled into Austria, Hungary, Czechoslovakia, and Yugoslavia — independent republics whose boundaries were drawn with attention to concentrations of major ethnic groups. More arbitrarily, the Ottoman empire was carved up into small mandates (including Palestine) run by local leaders but under the control of France and Great Britain. The conference reserved the mandate system for those regions it deemed insufficiently "civilized" to have full independence. Thus, the reconstructed nations — each beset with ethnic and nationalist rivalries — faced the challenge of making a new democratic government work (Map 22.5). Many of today's bitterest disputes — in the Balkans and Iraq, between Greece and Turkey, between Arabs and Jews — have roots in the decisions made in Paris in 1919. *no attention to ethnicitys*

Wilson hoped that self-determination would also dictate the fate of Germany's colonies in Asia and Africa. But the Allies, who had taken over the colonies during the war, went no further than allowing the League of Nations a mandate to administer them. Technically, the mandate system rejected imperialism, but in reality it allowed the Allies to maintain control. Thus, while denying Germany its colonies, the Allies retained and added to their own empires.

MAP 22.5   EUROPE AFTER WORLD WAR I

The post–World War I settlement redrew boundaries to create new nations based on ethnic groupings. Within defeated Germany and Russia, this outcome left bitter peoples who resolved to recover the territory taken from them.

The cause of democratic equality suffered another setback when the peace conference rejected Japan's call for a statement of racial equality in the treaty. Wilson's belief in the superiority of whites, as well as his apprehension about how white Americans would respond to such a declaration, led him to oppose the clause. To soothe hurt feelings, Wilson agreed to grant Japan a mandate over the Shantung Peninsula in northern China, which had formerly been controlled by Germany. The gesture mollified Japan's moderate leaders, but the military faction preparing to take over the country used bitterness toward racist Western colonialism to build support for expanding Japanese power throughout Asia.

Closest to Wilson's heart was finding a new way to manage international relations. In Wilson's view, war had discredited the old strategy of balance of power. Instead, he proposed a League of Nations that would provide collective security. The league would establish rules of international conduct and resolve conflicts between nations through rational and peaceful means. When the Allies agreed to the league, Wilson was overjoyed. He believed that the league would rectify the errors his colleagues had forced on him in Paris.

Versailles treaty
Treaty signed on June 28, 1919, that ended World War I. The agreement redrew the map of the world and assigned Germany sole responsibility for the war, saddling it with a debt of $33 billion in war damages. Many Germans felt betrayed by the treaty.

To some Europeans and Americans, the Versailles treaty came as a bitter disappointment. Wilson's admirers were shocked that the president dealt in compromise like any other politician. But without Wilson's presence, the treaty that was signed on June 28, 1919, surely would have been more vindictive. Wilson returned home in July 1919 consoled that, despite his frustrations, he had gained what he most wanted — a League of Nations. In Wilson's judgment, "We have completed in the least time possible the greatest work that four men have ever done."

The Fight for the Treaty. The tumultuous reception Wilson received when he arrived home persuaded him, probably correctly, that the American people supported the treaty. When the president submitted the treaty to the Senate in July 1919, he warned that failure to ratify it would "break the heart of the world." By then,

THE SIGNING OF PEACE IN THE HALL OF MIRRORS, VERSAILLES, 28TH JUNE 1919, BY SIR WILLIAM ORPEN

Set in the dazzling Hall of Mirrors at Versailles, built for Louis XIV as a symbol of his power, this painting captures the moment when the treaty was signed in June 1919. The leaders in charge of putting the world back together after the Great War are gathered at the table. Wilson is seated fifth from the left, dignified but seemingly isolated, while the French premier Georges Clemenceau and the British prime minister David Lloyd George are huddled together at Wilson's left. Imperial War Museum, London, UK/Bridgeman Images.

however, criticism of the treaty was mounting, especially from Americans convinced that their countries of ethnic origin — Ireland, Italy, and Germany — had not been given fair treatment. Others worried that the president's concessions at Versailles had jeopardized the treaty's capacity to provide a workable plan for rebuilding Europe and to guarantee world peace.

In the Senate, Republican "irreconcilables" condemned the treaty for entangling the United States in world affairs. A larger group of Republicans did not object to American participation in world politics but feared that membership in the League of Nations would jeopardize the nation's ability to act independently. No Republican, in any case, was eager to hand Wilson and the Democrats a foreign policy victory with the 1920 presidential election little more than a year away.

At the center of Republican opposition was Wilson's archenemy, Senator Henry Cabot Lodge of Massachusetts. Lodge was no isolationist, but he thought that much of the Fourteen Points was a "general bleat about virtue being better than vice." Lodge expected the United States' economic and military power to propel the nation into a major role in world affairs. But he insisted that membership in the League of Nations, which would require collective action to maintain peace, threatened the nation's independence in foreign relations.

With Lodge as its chairman, the Senate Foreign Relations Committee produced several amendments, or "reservations," that sought to limit the consequences of American membership in the league. For example, several reservations required approval of both the House and the Senate before the United States could participate in league-sponsored economic sanctions or military action.

It gradually became clear that ratification of the treaty depended on acceptance of the Lodge reservations. Democratic senators, who overwhelmingly supported the treaty, urged Wilson to accept Lodge's terms, arguing that they left the essentials of the treaty intact. Wilson, however, insisted that the reservations cut "the very heart out of the treaty."

Wilson decided to take his case directly to the people. On September 3, 1919, still exhausted from the peace conference, he set out by train on the most ambitious speaking tour ever undertaken by a president. On September 25 in Pueblo, Colorado, Wilson collapsed and had to return to Washington. There, he suffered a massive stroke that partially paralyzed him. From his bedroom, Wilson sent messages instructing Democrats in the Senate to hold firm against any and all reservations. Wilson commanded enough loyalty to ensure a vote against the Lodge reservations. But when the treaty without reservations came before the Senate in March 1920, the combined opposition of the Republican irreconcilables and reservationists left Wilson six votes short of the two-thirds majority needed for passage.

CARTOON ABOUT THE LEAGUE OF NATIONS, 1919
This cartoon captures President Wilson's deep commitment to and personal sense of responsibility for the League of Nations. The failure of the United States to join the league broke Wilson's heart. The Granger Collection, New York.

The nations of Europe organized the League of Nations at Geneva, Switzerland. Although Woodrow Wilson received the Nobel Peace Prize in 1920 for his central role in creating the league, the United States never became a member. Whether American membership could have prevented the world war that would begin in Europe in 1939 is highly unlikely, but the United States' failure to join certainly weakened the league from the start. In refusing to accept relatively minor compromises with Senate moderates, Wilson lost his treaty and American membership in the league.

> **REVIEW** Why did the Senate fail to ratify the Versailles treaty?

Democracy at Risk

The defeat of Wilson's plan for international democracy proved the crowning blow to progressives who had hoped that the war could boost reform at home. When the war ended, Americans wanted to demobilize swiftly. In the process, servicemen, defense workers, and farmers lost their war-related jobs. The volatile combination — of unemployed veterans returning home, a stalled economy, and leftover wartime patriotism looking for a new cause — threatened to explode. Wartime anti-German passion was quickly succeeded by the Red scare, an antiradical campaign broad enough to ensnare unionists, socialists, dissenters, and African Americans and Mexicans who had committed no offense but to seek an escape from rural poverty as they moved north.

Economic Hardship and Labor Upheaval.
Americans demanded that the nation return to a peacetime economy. The government abruptly abandoned its wartime economic controls and canceled war contracts. In a matter of months, 3 million soldiers mustered out of the military and flooded the job market just as war production ceased. Unemployment soared. At the same time, consumers went on a postwar spending spree that drove inflation skyward. In 1919 alone, prices rose 75 percent over prewar levels.

Most of the gains workers had made during the war evaporated. Freed from government controls, business turned against the eight-hour day and attacked labor unions. With inflation eating up their paychecks, workers fought back. The year 1919 witnessed nearly 3,600 strikes involving 4 million workers. The most spectacular strike occurred in February 1919 in Seattle, where shipyard workers had been put out of work by demobilization. When a coalition of the radical Industrial Workers of the World (IWW, known as Wobblies) and the moderate American Federation of Labor (AFL) called a general strike, the largest work stoppage in American history shut down the city. Newspapers claimed that the walkout was "a Bolshevik effort to start a revolution." The suppression of the Seattle general strike by city officials cost the AFL many of its wartime gains and contributed to the destruction of the IWW soon afterward.

A strike by Boston policemen in the fall of 1919 underscored postwar hostility toward labor militancy. Although the police were paid less than pick-and-shovel laborers, they won little sympathy. Once the officers stopped walking their beats, looters sacked the city. Massachusetts governor Calvin Coolidge called in the National Guard to restore order and broke the Boston police strike. The public welcomed Coolidge's anti-union assurance that "there is no right to strike against the public safety by anybody, anywhere, any time."

Labor strife climaxed in the grim steel strike of 1919. Faced with the industry's plan to revert to seven-day weeks, twelve-hour days, and weekly wages of about $20, Samuel Gompers, head of the AFL, called for a strike. In September, 350,000 workers in fifteen states walked out. The steel industry hired 30,000 strikebreakers and convinced the public that the strikers were radicals bent on subverting democracy and capitalism. In January 1920, after 18 striking workers were killed, the strike collapsed. That devastating defeat initiated a sharp decline in the fortunes of the labor movement, a trend that would continue for almost twenty years.

The Red Scare.

Suppression of labor strikes was one response to the widespread fear of internal subversion that swept the nation in 1919. The **Red scare** ("Red" referred to the color of the Bolshevik flag) exceeded even the assault on civil liberties during the war. It had homegrown causes—the postwar recession, labor unrest, terrorist acts, and the difficulties of reintegrating millions of returning veterans. But unsettling events abroad also added to Americans' anxieties.

Two epidemics swept the globe in 1918. One was Spanish influenza, which brought on a lethal accumulation of fluid in the lungs. A nurse near the front lines in France observed that victims "run a high temperature, so high that we can't believe it's true. . . . It is accompanied by vomiting and dysentery. When they die, as about half of them do, they turn a ghastly dark gray and are taken out at once and cremated." Before the flu virus had run its course, 40 million people had died worldwide, including some 700,000 Americans.

The other epidemic was Russian bolshevism, which seemed to most Americans equally contagious and deadly. Bolshevism became even more menacing in March 1919, when the new Soviet leaders created the Comintern, a worldwide association of Communists sworn to revolution in capitalist countries. (See "Beyond America's Borders," page 666.) A Communist revolution in the United States was extremely unlikely, but edgy Americans, faced with a flurry of terrorist acts, believed otherwise. Dozens of prominent individuals had received bombs through the mail. On September 16, 1920, a wagon filled with dynamite and iron exploded on Wall Street, killing 38 and maiming 143 others. Authorities never caught the terrorists, and the successful attack on America's financial capital fed the nation's anger and fear.

Even before the Wall Street bombing, the government had initiated a hunt for domestic revolutionaries. Led by Attorney General A. Mitchell Palmer, who believed that "there could be no nice distinctions drawn between the theoretical ideals of the radicals and their actual violations of our national laws," the campaign targeted men and women for their ideas, not their illegal acts. In January 1920, Palmer ordered a series of raids that netted 6,000 alleged subversives. Finding no revolutionary conspiracies, Palmer nevertheless ordered 500 noncitizen suspects deported.

His action came in the wake of a campaign against the most notorious radical alien, Russian-born Emma Goldman. Before the war, Goldman's passionate support

Red scare
The widespread fear of internal subversion and Communist revolution that swept the United States in 1919 and resulted in suppression of dissent. Labor unrest, postwar recession, the difficult peacetime readjustment, and the Soviet establishment of the Comintern all contributed to the scare.

of labor strikes, women's rights, and birth control had made her a symbol of radicalism. In 1919, after she spent time in prison for denouncing military conscription, J. Edgar Hoover, the director of the Justice Department's Radical Division, ordered her deported. One observer remarked, "With Prohibition coming in and Emma Goldman goin' out, 'twill be a dull country."

The effort to rid the country of alien radicals was matched by efforts to crush troublesome citizens. Law enforcement officials and vigilante groups joined hands against so-called Reds. In November 1919 in the rugged lumber town of Centralia, Washington, a menacing crowd gathered in front of the IWW hall. Nervous Wobblies inside opened fire, killing three people. Three IWW members were arrested and later convicted of murder, but another, ex-soldier Wesley Everett, was carried off by the mob, which castrated him, hung him from a bridge, and then riddled his body with bullets. His death was officially ruled a suicide.

Public institutions joined the attack on civil liberties. Local libraries removed dissenting books. Schools fired unorthodox teachers. Police shut down radical newspapers. State legislatures refused to seat elected representatives who professed socialist ideas. And in 1919, Congress removed its lone socialist representative, Victor Berger, on the pretext that he was a threat to national safety.

That same year, the Supreme Court provided a formula for restricting free speech. In upholding the conviction of socialist Charles Schenck for publishing a pamphlet urging resistance to the draft during wartime (**Schenck v. United States**), the Court established a "clear and present danger" test. Such utterances as Schenck's during a time of national peril, Justice Oliver Wendell Holmes wrote, were equivalent to shouting "Fire!" in a crowded theater.

In 1920, the assault on civil liberties provoked the creation of the American Civil Liberties Union (ACLU), which was dedicated to defending an individual's constitutional rights. One of the ACLU's founders, Roger Baldwin, declared, "So long as we have enough people in this country willing to fight for their rights, we'll be called a democracy." The ACLU championed the targets of Attorney General Palmer's campaign — politically radical immigrants, trade unionists, socialists and Communists, and antiwar activists who still languished in jail.

The Red scare eventually collapsed because of its excesses. In particular, the antiradical campaign lost credibility after Palmer warned that radicals were planning to celebrate the Bolshevik Revolution with a nationwide wave of violence on May 1, 1920. Officials called out state militias, mobilized bomb squads, and even placed machine-gun nests at major city intersections. When May 1 came and went without a single disturbance, the public mood turned from fear to scorn.

Schenck v. United States
1919 Supreme Court decision that established a "clear and present danger" test for restricting free speech. The Court upheld the conviction of socialist Charles Schenck for urging resistance to the draft during wartime.

The Great Migrations of African Americans and Mexicans.
Before the Red scare lost steam, the government raised alarms about the loyalty of African Americans. A Justice Department investigation concluded that Reds were fomenting racial unrest among blacks. Although the report was wrong about Bolshevik influence, it was correct in noticing a new stirring among African Americans.

In 1900, nine of every ten blacks still lived in the South, where poverty, disfranchisement, segregation, and violence dominated their lives. A majority of black men worked as dirt-poor tenants or sharecroppers, while many black women worked in the homes of whites as domestics. Whites remained committed to keeping blacks down. "If we own a good farm or horse, or cow, or bird-dog, or yoke of oxen," a black sharecropper in Mississippi observed in 1913, "we are harassed until we are bound to sell, give away, or run away, before we can have any peace in our lives."

The First World War provided African Americans with the opportunity to escape the South's cotton fields and kitchens. When war channeled nearly 5 million

Visual Activity

If You are a Stranger in the City

If you want a job   If you want a place to live
If you are having trouble with your employer
If you want information or advice of any kind
CALL UPON
The CHICAGO LEAGUE ON URBAN
CONDITIONS AMONG NEGROES
3719 South State Street
Telephone Douglas 9098   T. ARNOLD HILL, Executive Secretary
No charges—no fees. We want to help Y O U

SELF HELP
1. Do not loaf. Get a job at once.
2. Do not live in crowded rooms. Others can be obtained.
3. Do not carry on loud conversations in street cars and public places.
4. Do not keep your children out of school.
5. Do not send for your family until you get a job.
6. Do not think you can hold your job unless you are industrious, sober, efficient and prompt.

Cleanliness and fresh air are necessary for good health. In case of sickness send immediately for a good physician. Become an active member in some church as soon as you reach the city.

Issued by _____

AFRICAN AMERICANS MIGRATE NORTH

Wearing their Sunday best and carrying the rest of what they owned in two suitcases, this southern family waits to board a northern-bound train in 1912. In Chicago, the League on Urban Conditions among Negroes, which became the Urban League, sought to ease the transition of southern blacks to life in the North by distributing cards such as the one shown here (front and back). Photo: Schomburg Center, NYPL/Art Resource, NY; cards: Arthur and Graham Aldis papers (APF_0001_0006a-01 a/b), Special Collections, The University Library, University of Illinois at Chicago.

READING THE IMAGE: This photograph captures the migration of a family. How many generations are represented?

CONNECTIONS: Why do you suppose the "Self-Help" card emphasizes hard work, cleanliness, and quiet?

American workers into military service and almost ended European immigration, northern industrialists turned to black labor. Black men found work in northern steel mills, shipyards, munitions plants, railroad yards, automobile factories, and mines. From 1915 to 1920, a half million blacks (approximately 10 percent of the South's black population) boarded trains bound for Philadelphia, Detroit, Cleveland, Chicago, St. Louis, and other industrial cities.

Thousands of migrants wrote home to tell family and friends about their experiences in the North. One man announced proudly that he had recently been promoted to "first assistant to the head carpenter." He added, "I should have been here twenty years ago. I just begin to feel like a man. . . . My children are going to the same school with the whites and I don't have to [h]umble to no one. I have registered — will vote the next election and there ain't any 'yes sir' — it's all yes and no and Sam and Bill."

MEXICAN WOMEN ARRIVING IN EL PASO, 1911
These Mexican women, carrying bundles and wearing traditional shawls, try to get their bearings upon arriving in El Paso, Texas — the Ellis Island for Mexican immigrants. They were part of the first modern wave of Mexican immigration to the United States. Women like them found work in the fields, canneries, and restaurants of the Southwest, as well as at home taking in sewing, laundry, and boarders. New Mexico State University Library, Archives and Special Collections.

But the North was not the promised land. Black men stood on the lowest rungs of the labor ladder. Jobs of any kind proved scarce for black women, and most worked as domestic servants as they did in the South. The existing black middle class sometimes shunned the less educated, less sophisticated rural southerners crowding into northern cities. Many whites, fearful of losing jobs and status, lashed out against the new migrants. Savage race riots ripped through two dozen northern cities. The worst occurred in July 1917 when a mob of whites invaded a section of East St. Louis, Illinois, and murdered 39 people. In 1918, the nation witnessed 96 lynchings of blacks, some of them decorated war veterans still in uniform.

Still, most black migrants stayed in the North and encouraged friends and family to follow. By 1940, more than one million blacks had left the South, profoundly changing their own lives and the course of the nation's history. Black enclaves such as Harlem in New York and the South Side of Chicago, "cities within cities," emerged in the North. These assertive communities provided a foundation for black protest and political organization in the years ahead.

At nearly the same time, another migration was under way in the American Southwest. Between 1910 and 1920, the Mexican-born population in the United States soared from 222,000 to 478,000. Mexican immigration resulted from developments on both sides of the border. When Mexicans revolted against dictator Porfirio Díaz in 1910, initiating a ten-year civil war, migrants flooded northward. In the United States, the Chinese Exclusion Act of 1882 and later the disruption of World War I cut off the supply of cheap foreign labor and caused western employers in the expanding rail, mining, construction, and agricultural industries to look south to Mexico for workers.

Like immigrants from Europe and black migrants from the South, Mexicans in the American Southwest dreamed of a better life. And like the others, they found both opportunity and disappointment. Wages were better than in Mexico, but life in the fields, mines, and factories was hard, and living conditions — in boxcars, labor camps, or urban barrios — were dismal. Signs warning "No Mexicans Allowed" increased rather than declined. Mexicans were considered excellent prospects for manual labor but not for citizenship. By 1920, ethnic Mexicans made up about three-fourths of California's farm laborers. 3/4 in CA

Among Mexican Americans, some of whom had lived in the Southwest for more than a century, *los recién llegados* (the recent arrivals) encountered mixed reactions. One Mexican American expressed this ambivalence: "We are all Mexicans anyway because the gueros [Anglos] treat us all alike." But he also called for immigration quotas because the recent arrivals drove down wages and incited white prejudice that affected all ethnic Mexicans.

Despite friction, large-scale immigration into the Southwest meant a resurgence of the Mexican cultural presence, which became the basis for greater solidarity and political action for the ethnic Mexican population. In 1929 in Texas, Mexican Americans formed the League of United Latin American Citizens.

Postwar Politics and the Election of 1920. A thousand miles away in Washington, D.C., President Woodrow Wilson, bedridden and paralyzed, ignored the mountain of domestic troubles — labor strikes, the Red scare, race riots, immigration backlash — and insisted that the 1920 election would be a "solemn referendum" on the League of Nations. Dutifully, the Democratic nominees for president, James M. Cox of Ohio, and for vice president, Franklin Delano Roosevelt of New York, campaigned on Wilson's international ideals. The Republican Party chose the handsome, gregarious Warren Gamaliel Harding, senator from Ohio.

Harding found the winning formula when he declared that "America's present need is not heroics, but healing; not nostrums [questionable remedies] but normalcy." But what was "normalcy"? Harding explained: "By 'normalcy' I don't mean the old order but a regular steady order of things. I mean normal procedure, the natural way, without excess." Eager to put wartime crusades and postwar strife behind them, voters responded by giving Harding the largest presidential victory ever: 60.5 percent of the popular vote and 404 out of 531 electoral votes (Map 22.6). Harding's election lifted the national pall, signaling a new, more easygoing era.

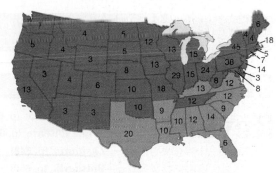

Candidate	Electoral Vote	Popular Vote	Percent of Popular Vote
Warren G. Harding (Republican)	404	16,143,407	60.5
James M. Cox (Democrat)	127	9,130,328	34.2
Eugene V. Debs (Socialist)	0	919,799	3.4

MAP 22.6   THE ELECTION OF 1920

REVIEW How did the Red scare contribute to the erosion of civil liberties after the war?

Conclusion: Troubled Crusade

America's experience in World War I was exceptional. For much of the world, the Great War produced great destruction — blackened fields, ruined factories, and millions of casualties. But in the United States, war and prosperity marched hand in hand. America emerged from the war with the strongest economy in the world and a position of international preeminence.

Still, the nation paid a heavy price both at home and abroad. American soldiers and sailors encountered unprecedented horrors — submarines, poison gas, machine guns — and more than 100,000 died. But rather than redeeming the sacrifice of George Browne and others as Woodrow Wilson promised, the peace that followed the armistice tarnished it.

At home, rather than permanently improving working conditions, advancing public health, and spreading educational opportunity, as progressives had hoped, the war threatened to undermine the achievements of the previous two decades. Moreover, rather than promoting democracy, the war bred fear, intolerance, and repression that led to a crackdown on dissent and a demand for conformity. Reformers could count only woman suffrage as a permanent victory.

Woodrow Wilson had promised more than anyone could deliver. Progressive hopes of extending democracy and liberal reform nationally and internationally were dashed. In 1920, a bruised and disillusioned society stumbled into a new decade. The era coming to an end had called on Americans to crusade and sacrifice. The new era promised peace, prosperity, and a good time.

Chapter Review

KEY TERMS

Triple Alliance (p. 646)

Triple Entente (p. 646)

Lusitania (p. 648)

Bolshevik (p. 650)

American Expeditionary Force (AEF) (p. 651)

Eighteenth Amendment (prohibition) (p. 655)

Nineteenth Amendment (woman suffrage) (p. 656)

Fourteen Points (p. 659)

League of Nations (p. 659)

Versailles treaty (p. 662)

Red scare (p. 665)

Schenck v. United States (p. 668)

REVIEW QUESTIONS

❶ Why did President Wilson fail to maintain U.S. neutrality during World War I? (pp. 644–50)

❷ How did the AEF contribute to the defeat of Germany? (pp. 650–54)

❸ How did progressive ideals fare during wartime? (pp. 654–59)

❹ Why did the Senate fail to ratify the Versailles treaty? (pp. 659–64)

❺ How did the Red scare contribute to the erosion of civil liberties after the war? (pp. 664–71)

MAKING CONNECTIONS

❶ Why did the United States at first resist intervening in World War I? Why did it later retreat from this policy and send troops?

❷ How did World War I contribute to progressive-influenced domestic developments? Did they endure in peacetime?

❸ After the war, what factors drove the conservative reaction in American politics, most vividly in the labor upheaval and Red scare that swept the nation? How did they shape the postwar political spectrum?

❹ What drove African American and Mexican migration north? How did the war facilitate these changes? How was this migration significant?

LINKING TO THE PAST

❶ How did America's experience in World War I compare with its experience during the Spanish-American War, its previous war abroad? Discuss the decision to go to war in each case, the military aspects, and the outcome. (See chapter 20.)

❷ How did the experience of America's workers during World War I compare with their experience in the previous three decades? Consider the composition of the workforce, wages, conditions, and labor's efforts to organize. (See chapters 20 and 21.)

23

From New Era to Great Depression, 1920–1932

CONTENT LEARNING OBJECTIVES

After reading and studying this chapter, you should be able to:

- Determine how business and industry contributed to a "New Era" and the growth of mass consumer and popular culture in the 1920s.
- Describe the effectiveness of prohibition in the 1920s.
- Explain how the "new woman" and the "New Negro" challenged social norms. Explain how some artists and intellectuals rejected America's mass culture.
- Evaluate ways in which social changes met with resistance, particularly in rural areas, and how this affected the presidential election of 1928.
- Describe the various factors that contributed to the Great Crash of 1929. Explain President Hoover's response and why it proved to be inadequate.
- Describe how the Great Depression affected the lives of ordinary Americans.

Americans in the 1920s cheered Henry Ford as an authentic American hero. When the decade began, he had already produced six million automobiles; by 1927, the figure reached fifteen million. In 1920, a Ford car cost $845; in 1928, the price was less than $300, within range of most of the country's skilled workingmen. Henry Ford put America on wheels, and in the eyes of most Americans he was an honest man who made an honest car: basic, inexpensive, and reliable.

Born in 1863 on a farm in Dearborn, Michigan, Ford at sixteen fled rural life for Detroit, where he

MODEL T FORD

When Henry Ford introduced the Model T in 1908, Americans thought of automobiles as toys of the rich. But by the 1920s, millions of Americans owned Fords, and their lives were never the same. Division of Work & Industry, National Museum of American History, Smithsonian Institution.

became a journeyman machinist. In 1893, he put together one of the first successful gasoline-driven carriages in the United States. His ambition, he said, was to "make something in quantity." The product he chose reflected American restlessness. "Everybody wants to be someplace he ain't," Ford declared. "As soon as he gets there he wants to go right back." In 1903, Ford gathered twelve workers in a 250-by-50-foot shed and created the Ford Motor Company.

Ford's early cars were custom-made one at a time. By 1914, his cars were being built along a continuously moving assembly line. Workers bolted on parts brought to them by cranes and conveyor belts. In 1920, one car rolled off the Ford assembly line every minute; in 1925, one appeared every ten seconds. Ford made only one kind of car, the Model T, which became synonymous with mass production. Throughout the rapid expansion of the automotive industry, the Ford Motor Company remained the industry leader, peaking in 1925, when it outsold all its rivals combined (Map 23.1).

When Ford began his rise, progressive critics condemned the industrial giants of the nineteenth century as "robber barons" who lived in luxury while reducing their workers to wage slaves. Ford, however, identified with the common folk and saw himself as the benefactor of average Americans. But like the age in which he lived, Ford was more complex and more contradictory than this simple image suggests.

A man of genius whose compelling vision of modern mass production led the way in the 1920s, Ford was also cranky, tightfisted, and mean-spirited. He hated Jews and Catholics, bankers and doctors, and liquor and tobacco, and his money allowed him to act on his prejudices. His automobile plants made him a billionaire, but their regimented assembly lines reduced workers to near robots. On the cutting edge of modern technology, Ford nevertheless remained nostalgic about rural values. He sought to revive the past in Greenfield Village, where he relocated buildings from a bygone era, including his parents' farmhouse. His museum contrasted sharply with the roaring Ford assembly plant at River Rouge. Yet if Americans remained true to their agrarian past and managed to be modern and scientific at the same time, Ford insisted, all would be well.

CHRONOLOGY

1920   Prohibition begins.
        Women get the vote.
        Warren G. Harding elected
        president.

1921   Sheppard-Towner Act
        enacted.
        Congress restricts
        immigration.

1922   Teapot Dome scandal breaks.
        Five-Power Naval Treaty
        signed.

1923   Equal Rights Amendment
        defeated in Congress.
        Harding dies; Vice President
        Calvin Coolidge becomes
        president.

1924   Dawes Plan effected.
        Coolidge elected president.
        Johnson-Reed Act enacted.
        Indian Citizenship Act
        enacted.

1925   Scopes trial held.

1927   Charles Lindbergh flies
        nonstop across Atlantic.
        Nicola Sacco and
        Bartolomeo Vanzetti
        executed.

1928   Kellogg-Briand pact signed.
        Herbert Hoover elected
        president.

1929   St. Valentine's Day murders
        occur.
        Agricultural Marketing Act
        enacted.
        Middletown published.
        Stock market collapses.

1930   Congress authorizes
        $420 million for public
        works projects.
        Hawley-Smoot tariff passed.

1931   Scottsboro Boys arrested.
        Harlan County, Kentucky,
        coal miners strike.

1932   River Rouge factory
        demonstration takes place.
        Reconstruction Finance
        Corporation established.
        National Farmers' Holiday
        Association formed.

Tension between traditional values and modern conditions lay at the heart of the conflicted 1920s. For the first time, more Americans lived in urban than in rural areas, and cities seemed to harbor everything rural people opposed. While millions admired urban America's sophisticated new style and consumer products, others condemned postwar society for its loose morals and vulgar materialism. The Ku Klux Klan and other champions of an older America resorted to violence as well as words when they chastised the era's "new woman," "New Negro," and surging immigrant populations. Those who sought to dam the tide of change proposed prohibition, Protestantism, and patriotism.

The public, disillusioned with the outcome of World War I, turned away from the Christian moralism and idealism of the Progressive Era. In the 1920s, Ford and businessmen like him replaced political reformers such as Theodore Roosevelt and Woodrow Wilson as the models of progress. The U.S. Chamber of Commerce crowed, "The American businessman is the most influential person in the nation." The fortunes of the era rose, then in 1929 crashed, according to the values and practices of the business community. When prosperity collapsed, the nation entered the most serious economic depression of all time.

Map Activity

MAP 23.1 AUTO MANUFACTURING

By the mid-1920s, the massive coal and steel industries of the Midwest had made that region the center of the new automobile industry. A major road-building program by the federal government carried the thousands of new cars produced each day to every corner of the country.

READING THE MAP: How many states had factories involved with the manufacture of automobiles? In what regions was auto manufacturing concentrated?

CONNECTIONS: On what related industries did auto manufacturing depend? How did the integration of the automobile into everyday life affect American society?

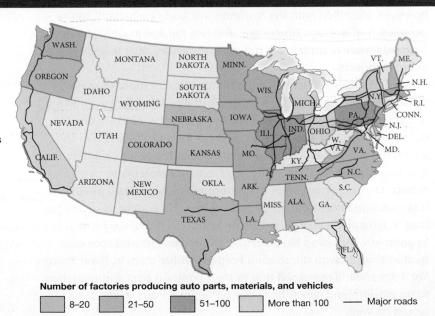

Number of factories producing auto parts, materials, and vehicles

8–20   21–50   51–100   More than 100   — Major roads

The New Era

Once Woodrow Wilson left the White House, energy flowed away from government activism and civic reform and toward private economic endeavor. The rise of a free-wheeling economy and a heightened sense of individualism caused Secretary of Commerce Herbert Hoover to declare that America had entered a "New Era," one of many labels used to describe the complex 1920s. Some terms focus on the decade's high-spirited energy and cultural change: Roaring Twenties, Jazz Age, Flaming Youth. Others echo the rising importance of money — Dollar Decade, Golden Twenties — or reflect the sinister side of gangster profiteering — Lawless Decade. Still others emphasize the lonely confusion of the Lost Generation and the stress and anxiety of the Aspirin Age.

America in the twenties was many things, but President Calvin Coolidge got at an essential truth when he declared: "The business of America is business." Politicians and diplomats proclaimed business the heart of American civilization as they promoted its products at home and abroad. Average men and women bought into the idea that business and its wonderful goods were what made America great, as they snatched up the flood of new consumer items American factories sent forth. Nothing caught Americans' fancy more powerfully than the automobile.

A Business Government. Republicans controlled the White House from 1921 to 1933. The first of the three Republican presidents was Warren Gamaliel Harding, *1st of 3* the Ohio senator who in his 1920 campaign called for a "return to normalcy," by which he meant the end of public crusades and a return to private pursuits. Harding appointed a few men of real stature to his cabinet. Herbert Hoover, for example, the former head of the wartime Food Administration, became secretary of commerce. But wealth and friendship also counted: Andrew Mellon, one of the richest men in America, became secretary of the treasury, and Harding handed out jobs to his friends, members of his old "Ohio gang." This curious combination of merit and cronyism made for a disjointed administration.

When Harding was elected in 1920 (see chapter 22, Map 22.6), the unemployment rate hit 20 percent, the highest ever up to that point. The bankruptcy rate of farmers increased tenfold. Harding pushed measures to regain national prosperity — high tariffs to protect American businesses, price supports for agriculture, and the dismantling of wartime government control over industry in favor of unregulated private business. "Never before, here or anywhere else," the U.S. Chamber of Commerce said proudly, "has a government been so completely fused with business."

Harding's policies to boost American enterprise made him very popular, but ultimately his small-town congeniality and trusting ways did him in. Some of his friends in the Ohio gang were up to their necks in lawbreaking. Three of Harding's appointees would go to jail. Interior Secretary Albert Fall was convicted of accepting bribes of more than $400,000 for leasing oil reserves on public land in Teapot Dome, Wyoming, and "**Teapot Dome**" became a synonym for political corruption.

On August 2, 1923, when Harding died from a heart attack, Vice President Calvin Coolidge became president. Coolidge, who once said that "the man who builds a factory builds a temple, the man who works there worships there," continued and

Teapot Dome
Nickname for the scandal in which Interior Secretary Albert Fall accepted $400,000 in bribes for leasing oil reserves on public land in Teapot Dome, Wyoming. It was part of a larger pattern of corruption that marred Warren G. Harding's presidency.

"TEAPOT DOME SCANDAL, 1924"

This cartoon shows Washington officials madly racing down the road to the White House in a desperate attempt to outrun the steamroller of scandal. Teapot Dome was only one example of the rampant corruption that tainted the Harding administration. The Granger Collection, New York.

extended Harding's policies of promoting business and limiting government. Secretary of the Treasury Andrew Mellon reduced the government's control over the economy and cut taxes for corporations and wealthy individuals. New rules for the Federal Trade Commission severely restricted its power to regulate business. Secretary of Commerce Herbert Hoover hedged government authority by encouraging trade associations that ideally would keep business honest and efficient through voluntary cooperation.

Coolidge found an ally in the Supreme Court. For years, the Court had opposed federal regulation of hours, wages, and working conditions on the grounds that such legislation was the proper concern of the states. In the 1920s, the Court found ways to curtail a state's ability to regulate business. It ruled against closed shops — businesses where only union members could be employed — while confirming the right of owners to form exclusive trade associations. In 1923, the Court declared unconstitutional the District of Columbia's minimum-wage law for women, asserting that the law interfered with the freedom of employer and employee to make labor contracts. The Court and the president attacked government intrusion in the free market, even when the prohibition of government regulation threatened the welfare of workers.

The election of 1924 confirmed the defeat of the progressive principle that the state should take a leading role in ensuring the general welfare. To oppose Coolidge, the Democrats nominated John W. Davis, a corporate lawyer whose conservative views differed little from Republican principles. Only the Progressive Party and its presidential nominee, Senator Robert La Follette of Wisconsin, offered a genuine alternative. When La Follette championed labor unions, regulation of business, and protection of civil liberties, Republicans coined the slogan "Coolidge or Chaos." Voters chose Coolidge in a landslide. Coolidge was right when he declared, "This is a business country, and it wants a business government." What was true of the government's relationship to business at home was also true abroad.

Promoting Prosperity and Peace Abroad. After orchestrating the Senate's successful effort to block U.S. membership in the League of Nations, Henry Cabot Lodge boasted, "We have torn Wilsonism up by the roots." But repudiation of Wilsonian internationalism and rejection of collective security through the League of Nations did not mean that the United States retreated into isolationism. The

United States emerged from World War I with its economy intact and enjoyed a decade of stunning growth. New York replaced London as the center of world finance, and the United States became the world's chief creditor. Economic involvement in the world and the continuing chaos in Europe made withdrawal impossible.

One of the Republicans' most ambitious foreign policy initiatives was the Washington Disarmament Conference, which convened in 1921 to establish a global balance of naval power. Secretary of State Charles Evans Hughes shaped the **Five-Power Naval Treaty of 1922** committing Britain, France, Japan, Italy, and the United States to a proportional reduction of naval forces. The treaty led to the scrapping of more than two million tons of warships, by far the world's greatest success in disarmament. By fostering international peace, Hughes also helped make the world a safer place for American trade.

A second major effort on behalf of world peace came in 1928, when Secretary of State Frank Kellogg joined French foreign minister Aristide Briand to produce the Kellogg-Briand pact. Nearly fifty nations signed the solemn pledge to renounce war and settle international disputes peacefully.

But Republican administrations preferred private-sector diplomacy to state action. With the blessing of the White House, a team of American financiers led by Charles Dawes swung into action when Germany suspended its war reparation payments in 1923. Impoverished, Germany was staggering under the massive bill of $33 billion presented by the victorious Allies in the Versailles treaty. When Germany failed to meet its annual payment, France occupied Germany's industrial Ruhr Valley, creating the worst international crisis since the war. In 1924, the Dawes Plan halved Germany's annual reparation payments, initiated fresh American loans to Germany, and caused the French to retreat from the Ruhr. Although the United States failed to join the League of Nations, it continued to exercise significant economic and diplomatic influence abroad. These Republican successes overseas helped fuel prosperity at home.

Five-Power Naval Treaty of 1922
Treaty that committed Britain, France, Japan, Italy, and the United States to a proportional reduction of naval forces, producing the world's greatest success in disarmament up to that time. Republicans orchestrated its development at the 1921 Washington Disarmament Conference.

Automobiles, Mass Production, and Assembly-Line
Progress. The automobile industry emerged as the largest single manufacturing industry in the nation. Henry Ford shrewdly located his company in Detroit, knowing that key materials for his automobiles were manufactured in nearby states (Map 23.1). Keystone of the American economy, the automobile industry not only employed hundreds of thousands of workers directly but also brought whole industries into being — filling stations, garages, fast-food restaurants, and "guest cottages" (motels). The need for tires, glass, steel, highways, oil, and refined gasoline for automobiles provided millions of related jobs. By 1929, one American in four found employment directly or indirectly in the automobile industry. "Give us our daily bread" was no longer addressed to the Almighty, one commentator quipped, but to Detroit.

Automobiles changed where people lived, what work they did, how they spent their leisure, even how they thought. Hundreds of small towns decayed because the automobile enabled rural people to bypass them in favor of more distant cities and towns. In cities, streetcars began to

DETROIT AND THE AUTOMOBILE INDUSTRY IN THE 1920S

AUTO ASSEMBLY LINE
This photograph of an automobile assembly line in Detroit in 1923 makes clear that workers stayed in one place while work came to them. Efficiency increased, but so, too, did boredom.
Library of Congress, 4a27966.

welfare capitalism
Industrial programs for workers that became popular in the 1920s. Some businesses improved safety and sanitation inside factories. They also instituted paid vacations and pension plans. This encouraged loyalty to companies and discouraged independent labor unions.

disappear as workers moved to the suburbs and commuted to work along crowded highways. Nothing shaped modern America more than the automobile, and efficient mass production made the automobile revolution possible.

Mass production by the assembly-line technique became standard in almost every factory, from automobiles to meatpacking to cigarettes. To improve efficiency, corporations reduced assembly-line work to the simplest, most repetitive tasks. Changes on the assembly line and in management, along with technological advances, significantly boosted overall efficiency. Between 1922 and 1929, productivity in manufacturing increased 32 percent. Average wages, however, increased only 8 percent.

Industries also developed programs for workers that came to be called **welfare capitalism**. Some businesses improved safety and sanitation inside factories. They also instituted paid vacations and pension plans. Welfare capitalism encouraged loyalty to the company and discouraged traditional labor unions. One labor organizer in the steel industry bemoaned the success of welfare capitalism. "So many workmen here had been lulled to sleep by the company union, the welfare plans, the social organizations fostered by the employer," he declared, "that they had come to look upon the employer as their protector, and had believed vigorous trade union organization unnecessary for their welfare."

Consumer Culture. Mass production fueled corporate profits and national economic prosperity. During the 1920s, per capita income increased by a third, the cost of living stayed the same, and unemployment remained low. But the rewards of the economic boom were not evenly distributed. Americans who labored with their hands inched ahead, while white-collar workers enjoyed significantly more money and more leisure time to spend it. Mass production of a broad range of new products — automobiles, radios, refrigerators, electric irons, washing machines — produced a consumer goods revolution.

In this new era of abundance, more people than ever conceived of the American dream in terms of the things they could acquire. *Middletown* (1929), a study of the inhabitants of Muncie, Indiana, revealed that Muncie had become, above all, "a culture in which everything hinges on money." Moreover, faced with technological and organizational change beyond their comprehension, many citizens had lost confidence in their ability to play an effective role in civic affairs. More and more they became passive consumers, deferring to the supposed expertise of leaders in politics and economics.

The rapidly expanding business of advertising stimulated the desire for new products and attacked the traditional values of thrift and saving. Advertising linked material goods to the fulfillment of every spiritual and emotional need. Americans increasingly defined and measured their social status, and indeed their personal worth, on the yardstick of material possessions. Happiness itself rode on owning a car and choosing the right cigarettes and toothpaste.

By the 1920s, the United States had achieved the physical capacity to satisfy Americans' material wants (Figure 23.1). The economic problem shifted from production to consumption: Who would buy the goods flying off American assembly lines? One solution was to expand America's markets in foreign countries, and government and business joined in that effort. Another solution to the problem of consumption was to expand the market at home.

Henry Ford realized early on that "mass production requires mass consumption." He understood that automobile workers not only produced cars but would also buy them if they made enough money. "One's own employees ought to be one's own

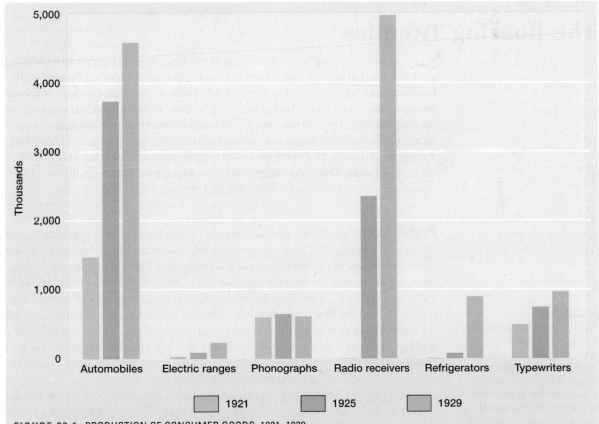

FIGURE 23.1 PRODUCTION OF CONSUMER GOODS, 1921–1929

Transportation, communications, and entertainment changed the lives of consumers in the 1920s. Laborsaving devices for the home were popular, but the vastly greater sales of automobiles and radios showed that consumerism was powerful in moving people's attention beyond their homes.

best customers," Ford said. In 1914, he raised wages in his factories to $5 a day, more than twice the going rate. High wages made for workers who were more loyal and more exploitable, and high wages returned as profits when workers bought Fords.

Many people's incomes, however, were too puny to satisfy the growing desire for consumer goods. The solution was installment buying — a little money down, a payment each month — which allowed people to purchase expensive items they could not otherwise afford or to purchase items before saving the necessary money. As one newspaper announced, "The first responsibility of an American to his country is no longer that of a citizen, but of a consumer." During the 1920s, America's motto became spend, not save. Old values — "Use it up, wear it out, make it do or do without" — seemed about as pertinent as a horse and buggy. American culture had shifted.

> **REVIEW** How did the spread of the automobile transform the United States?

The Roaring Twenties

A new ethic of personal freedom allowed many Americans to seek pleasure without guilt in a whirl of activity that earned the decade the name "Roaring Twenties." Prohibition made lawbreakers of millions of otherwise decent folk. Flappers and "new women" challenged traditional gender boundaries. Other Americans enjoyed the Roaring Twenties through the words and images of vastly expanded mass communication, especially radio and movies. In America's big cities, particularly New York, a burst of creativity produced the "New Negro," who confounded and disturbed white Americans. The "Lost Generation" of writers, profoundly disillusioned with mainstream America's cultural direction, fled the country.

Prohibition. Republicans generally sought to curb the powers of government, but the twenties witnessed a great exception to this rule when the federal government implemented one of the last reforms of the Progressive Era: the Eighteenth Amendment, which banned the manufacture and sale of alcohol and took effect in January 1920 (see chapter 22). Drying up the rivers of liquor that Americans consumed, supporters of **prohibition** claimed, would eliminate crime, boost production, and lift the nation's morality. Prohibition would destroy the saloon, which according to a leading "dry" was the "most fiendish, corrupt and hell-soaked institution that ever crawled out of the slime of the eternal pit." Instead, prohibition initiated a fourteen-year orgy of lawbreaking unparalleled in the nation's history.

The Treasury Department agents charged with enforcing prohibition faced a staggering task. Although they smashed more than 172,000 illegal stills in 1925 alone, loopholes in the law almost guaranteed failure. Sacramental wine was permitted, allowing fake clergy to party with bogus congregations. Farmers were allowed to ferment their own "fruit juices." Doctors and dentists could prescribe liquor for medicinal purposes.

prohibition
The ban on the manufacture and sale of alcohol that went into effect in January 1920 with the Eighteenth Amendment. Prohibition proved almost impossible to enforce. By the end of the 1920s, most Americans wished it to end, and it was finally repealed in 1933.

In 1929, a Treasury agent in Indiana reported intense local resistance to enforcement of prohibition. "Conditions in most important cities very bad," he declared. "Lax and corrupt public officials great handicap . . . prevalence of drinking among minor boys and the . . . middle or better classes of adults." The "speakeasy," an illegal nightclub, became a common feature of the urban landscape. Speakeasies' dance floors led to the sexual integration of the formerly all-male drinking culture, changing American social life forever. Detroit, probably America's wettest city, was home to more than 20,000 illegal drinking establishments, making the alcohol business the city's second-largest industry, behind automobile manufacturing.

PROHIBITION

In 1921, New York City deputy police commissioner John A. Leach watches as agents pour bootleg liquor that they have confiscated down the sewer. Successes like this were common during prohibition, but not even the criminalization of liquor could permanently defeat "Satan in a bottle." Library of Congress, 3c23257.

Eventually, serious criminals took over the liquor trade. During the first four years of prohibition, Chicago witnessed more than two hundred gang-related killings as rival mobs struggled for control of the lucrative liquor trade. The most notorious event came on St. Valentine's Day 1929, when Alphonse "Big Al" Capone's Italian-dominated mob machine-gunned seven members of a rival Irish gang. Capone's bootlegging empire brought in $95 million a year, when a chicken dinner cost 5 cents. Federal authorities finally sent Capone to prison for income tax evasion. "I violate the Prohibition law — sure," he told a reporter. "Who doesn't? The only difference is, I take more chances than the man who drinks a cocktail before dinner."

Americans overwhelmingly favored the repeal of the Eighteenth Amendment, the "noble experiment," as Herbert Hoover called prohibition. In 1931, a panel of distinguished experts reported that the experiment had failed. The social and political costs of prohibition outweighed the benefits. Prohibition fueled criminal activity, corrupted the police, demoralized the judiciary, and caused ordinary citizens to disrespect the law. In 1933, the nation ended prohibition, making the Eighteenth Amendment the only constitutional amendment to be repealed.

The New Woman. Of all the changes in American life in the 1920s, none sparked more heated debate than the alternatives offered to the traditional roles of women. Increasing numbers of women worked and went to college, defying older gender norms. Even mainstream magazines such as the *Saturday Evening Post* began publishing stories about young, college-educated women who drank gin cocktails, smoked cigarettes, and wore skimpy dresses and dangly necklaces. Before the Great War, the **new woman** dwelt in New York City's bohemian Greenwich Village, but afterward the mass media brought her into middle-class America's living rooms.

new woman
Alternative image of womanhood that came into the American mainstream in the 1920s. The mass media frequently portrayed young, college-educated women who drank, smoked, and wore skimpy dresses. New women also challenged American convictions about separate spheres for women and men and the sexual double standard.

When the Nineteenth Amendment, ratified in 1920, granted women the vote, feminists felt liberated and expected women to reshape the political landscape. A Kansas woman declared, "I went to bed last night a *slave*[;] I awoke this morning a *free woman*." Women began pressuring Congress to pass laws that especially concerned women, including measures to protect women in factories and grant federal aid to schools. Black women lobbied particularly for federal courts to assume jurisdiction over the crime of lynching. But women's only significant national legislative success came in 1921 when Congress enacted the Sheppard-Towner Act, which extended federal assistance to states seeking to reduce high infant mortality rates.

A number of factors helped thwart women's political influence. Male domination of both political parties, the rarity of female candidates, and lack of experience in voting, especially among recent immigrants, kept many women away from the polls. In some places, male-run election machines actually disfranchised women, despite the Nineteenth Amendment. In the South, poll taxes, literacy tests, and outright terrorism continued to decimate the vote of African Americans, men and women alike.

Most important, rather than forming a solid voting bloc, feminists divided. Some argued for women's right to special protection; others demanded equal protection. The radical National Woman's Party fought for an Equal Rights Amendment that stated flatly: "Men and women shall have equal rights throughout the United States." The more moderate League of Women Voters feared that the amendment's wording threatened state laws that provided women special protection, such as preventing them from working on certain machines. Put before Congress in 1923, the Equal Rights Amendment went down to defeat, and radical women were forced to work for the causes of birth control, legal equality for minorities, and the end of child labor through other means.

Economically, more women worked for pay — approximately one in four by 1930 — but they clustered in "women's jobs." The proportion of women working as secretaries, stenographers, and typists skyrocketed. Women almost monopolized the occupations of librarian, nurse, elementary school teacher, and telephone operator. Women also represented 40 percent of salesclerks by 1930. More female white-collar workers meant that fewer women were interested in protective legislation for women; new women wanted salaries and opportunities equal to men's.

Increased earnings gave working women more buying power in the new consumer culture. A stereotype soon emerged of the flapper, so called because of the short-lived fad of wearing unbuckled galoshes. The flapper had short "bobbed" hair and wore lipstick and rouge. She spent freely on the latest styles — dresses with short skirts, drop waists, bare arms, and no petticoats — and she danced all night to wild jazz. As F. Scott Fitzgerald described her in his novel *This Side of Paradise* (1920), she was "lovely and expensive and about nineteen."

The new woman both reflected and propelled the modern birth control movement. Margaret Sanger, the crusading pioneer for contraception during the Progressive Era (see chapter 21), restated her principal conviction in 1920: "No woman can call herself free until she can choose consciously whether she will or will not be a mother." Shifting strategy in the twenties, Sanger courted the conservative American Medical Association and linked birth control with the eugenics movement, which advocated limiting reproduction among "undesirable" groups. Thus, she made contraception a respectable subject for discussion.

Flapper style and values spread from coast to coast through films, novels, magazines, and advertisements. New women challenged American convictions about separate spheres for women and men, the double standard of sexual conduct, and Victorian ideas of proper female appearance and behavior. (See "Making Historical Arguments," page 686.) Although only a minority of American women became flappers, all women, even those who remained at home, heard about girls gone wild and felt the great changes of the era.

The New Negro. The 1920s witnessed the emergence not only of the "new woman" but also of the "New Negro." African Americans who challenged the caste system that confined dark-skinned Americans to the lowest levels of society confronted whites who insisted that race relations would not change. As cheers for black soldiers faded after their return from World War I, African Americans faced grim days of economic hardship and race riots.

The prominent African American intellectual W. E. B. Du Bois and the National Association for the Advancement of Colored People (NAACP) aggressively pursued the passage of a federal antilynching law to counter mob violence against blacks in

Visual Activity

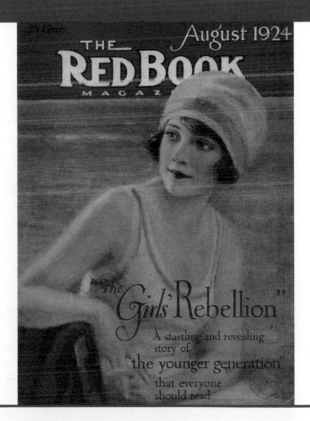

"THE GIRLS' REBELLION"

The August 1924 cover of *Redbook*, a popular women's magazine, portrays the kind of postadolescent girl who was making respectable families frantic. Flappers scandalized their middle-class parents by flouting the old moral code. This young woman sports the "badges of flapperhood," including what one critic called an "intoxication of rouge." Fictionalized, emotion-packed stories such as this brought the new woman into every woman's home. Picture Research Consultants & Archives.

READING THE IMAGE: In addition to the rouge, what else identifies this young woman as a flapper?

CONNECTIONS: In addition to flappers, what other developments in the 1920s challenged America's traditional values?

Making Historical Arguments

Was There a Sexual Revolution in the 1920s?

"Cigarette in hand, shimmying to the music of the masses, the New Woman and the New Morality have made their theatric debut upon the modern scene," lamented one commentator in 1926. The *Atlantic* magazine declared that a moral chasm had opened between the generations, and the old and young in America "were as far apart in point of view, codes, and standards as if they belonged to different races." Charlotte Perkins Gilman represented many older feminists who were disappointed with the outcome of recent advances for women: "It is sickening to see so many of the newly freed abusing that freedom in a mere imitation of masculine weakness and vice." Older Americans wholeheartedly agreed that the younger generation was in full-fledged revolt against traditional standards of morality, and that America was in danger of going to hell in a handbasket.

Critics had, it seemed, plenty of evidence. Between newspapers, movies, and magazines, even the small towns of America were "literally saturated with sex," one observer complained. Flappers and college coeds claimed the privileges of men, smoking cigarettes, drinking from hip flasks, and staying out all night. When eight hundred college women met to discuss life on campus and what "nice girls" should do, they concluded, "Learn temperance in petting, not abstinence." Anxious observers counseled intervention. The Ohio legislature debated whether to prohibit any "female over fourteen years of age" from wearing a "skirt which does not reach to that part of the foot known as the instep." The *Ladies' Home Journal* urged "legal prohibition" of jazz dancing.

But were the concerned observers correct? Was there really a sexual revolution in the 1920s? The principal movers of the new morality were youths, and without a doubt, young middle-class men and women felt freer than ever to openly express their feelings about sex. But we must separate the new candor from actual sexual behavior. Although solid evidence is difficult to come by, correspondence, diaries, and other personal documents; physicians' records; divorce proceedings; advice literature; and a few early sex surveys provide important clues.

A good place to begin the investigation is where youth congregated: college campuses. Campus life included a self-conscious ethos of experimentation and innovation, but as students demolished old rules, they also created new ones. One major innovation was "dating" — that is, going out unsupervised rather than receiving callers at home or meeting at church socials. Dating was encouraged by the automobile, that "house of prostitution on wheels," as one juvenile judge in Indiana labeled it. Dating led to a second innovation: "petting," or any sexual activity short of intercourse. One examination of coed behavior at the end of the 1920s found that 92 percent of women admitted engaging in petting.

Like dating, petting represented a significant change in female behavior. But it was not a total rejection of traditional morality because it took place within the search for the ideal marriage partner. There was also a modest increase in premarital sexual intercourse, made possible by the widespread acceptance of contraceptives. But sexual intercourse usually took place between partners who assumed they would marry. The new woman of the 1920s, though freer sexually, continued to focus on romance, marriage, and family.

Did the new sexual behavior mark a drastic change from the past? Evidence of sexual habits before World War I is even more difficult to come by than for the 1920s, but it appears that changes in attitudes and behaviors had been under way for decades. Nineteenth-century Victorian notions of sexless women who felt little or no passion had been eroding since at least the 1890s. A small survey of the sexual practices of middle-class women in the 1890s conducted by Dr. Clelia Duel Mosher, a physician at Stanford University, found that women were enthusiastic about sex and often found

satisfaction. The primary ideo-
logues of the sexual revolution, Havelock Ellis, who celebrated female passion, and
Sigmund Freud, who stressed
the centrality of sex in human
endeavor, reached large
American audiences before
World War I.

Changes in sexual moral-
ity, therefore, were evolutionary rather than revolutionary.
Still, liberal attitudes and
behaviors had their greatest
impact in the 1920s. American
culture was being remade,
and young people, especially
women, were on the cutting
edge. Now equal at the polling
booth, women were also
growing more economically
independent. Changes in
women's political and economic lives were reflected in
their sexual attitudes and

HEROES AND HEROINES

Two kinds of women look up adoringly at two kinds of 1920s heroes. A wholesome
image is seen on the left in a 1927 cover of *People's Popular Monthly* magazine. The
outdoor girl, smartly turned out in her raccoon coat and pennant, flatters a naive
college football hero. On the right, Vilma Banky kneels imploringly before the
hypnotic gaze of the movies' greatest heartthrob, Rudolph Valentino. Magazine: Picture
Research Consultants & Archives; poster: Mary Evans/FEATURE PICTURES INC/Ronald Grant/Everett
Collection.

behaviors. In place of the idea that women were natu-
rally pure, the new morality proclaimed the equality of
desire. Only the boldest women publicly rejected a
"double standard" (the notion that the sexual behavior
of women should be more circumscribed than that of

men), but many jettisoned notions of female
submission, obedience, and endless childbearing.
Charges that the giddy flapper and her partner were
bringing down American civilization were overblown,
but young women certainly were changing the culture.

QUESTIONS FOR ANALYSIS

Summarize the Argument   What is the evidence for the contention that changes in sexual
behavior in the 1920s were more evolutionary than revolutionary?

Analyze the Evidence   How did changes in women's political and economic lives affect their
sexual behaviors?

Consider the Context   What was the relationship of the emergence of the "new woman" in
the 1920s and the sexual habits of young women?

the South. At the same time, however, many disillusioned poor urban blacks turned to the new leadership of the Jamaican-born visionary Marcus Garvey, who urged African Americans to rediscover the heritage of Africa, take pride in their own achievements, and maintain racial purity by avoiding miscegenation. In 1917, Garvey launched the Universal Negro Improvement Association (UNIA) to help African Americans gain economic and political independence entirely outside white society. In 1919, the UNIA created its own shipping company, the Black Star Line, to support the "Back to Africa" movement among black Americans. In 1927, the federal government pinned charges of illegal practices on Garvey and deported him to Jamaica. Nevertheless, the issues Garvey raised about racial pride, black identity, and the search for equality persisted, and his legacy remains at the center of black nationalist thought.

Still, most African Americans maintained hope in the American promise. In New York City, hope and talent came together. The city's black population jumped 115 percent (from 152,000 to 327,000) in the 1920s. In Harlem in uptown Manhattan, an extraordinary mix of black artists, sculptors, novelists, musicians, and poets set out to create a distinctive African American culture that drew on their identities as Americans and Africans. As scholar Alain Locke put it in 1925, they introduced to the world the "**New Negro**," who rose from the ashes of slavery and segregation to proclaim African Americans' creative genius.

New Negro
Term referring to African Americans who, through the arts, challenged American racial hierarchy. The New Negro emerged in New York City in the 1920s in what became known as the Harlem Renaissance, which produced dazzling literary, musical, and artistic talent.

The emergence of the New Negro came to be known as the Harlem Renaissance. Building on the independence and pride displayed by black soldiers during the war, black artists sought to defeat the fresh onslaught of racial discrimination and violence with poems, paintings, and plays. "We younger Negro artists . . . intend to express our individual dark-skinned selves without fear or shame," poet Langston Hughes said of the Harlem Renaissance. "If white people are pleased, we are glad. If they are not, it doesn't matter. We know we are beautiful. And ugly, too."

The Harlem Renaissance produced dazzling talent. Black writer James Weldon Johnson, who in 1903 had written the Negro national anthem, "Lift Every Voice," wrote *God's Trombones* (1927), in which he expressed the wisdom and beauty of black folktales from the South. The poetry of Langston Hughes, Claude McKay, and Countee Cullen celebrated the vitality of life in Harlem. Zora Neale Hurston's novel *Their Eyes Were Watching God* (1937) explored the complex passions of black people in a southern community. Black painters, led by Aaron Douglas, linked African art, which had recently inspired European modernist artists, to the concept of the New Negro.

Despite such vibrancy, Harlem for most whites remained a separate black ghetto known only for its lively nightlife. Fashionable whites crowded into Harlem's segregated nightclubs, the most famous of which was the Cotton Club, where they believed they could hear "real" jazz, a relatively new musical form, in its "natural" surroundings. The vigor of the Harlem Renaissance left a powerful legacy for black Americans, but the creative burst did little in the short run to dissolve the prejudice of white society.

Entertainment for the Masses.
In the 1920s, popular culture, like consumer goods, was mass-produced and mass-consumed. The proliferation of movies, radios,

DUKE ELLINGTON LEADS HIS JAZZ BAND

From 1927 to 1931, the Duke Ellington Orchestra was the house band at the Cotton Club in Harlem, where black performers played for white audiences. The photograph captures something of the energy and exuberance that helped make Ellington America's greatest jazz composer and bandleader. © Bettmann/Corbis.

music, and sports meant that Americans found plenty to do, and in doing the same things, they helped create a national culture.

Nothing offered escapist delights like the movies. Hollywood, California, discovered the successful formula of combining opulence, sex, and adventure. Admission was cheap, and by 1929 the movies were drawing more than 80 million people in a single week. Hollywood created "movie stars," glamorous beings whose every move was tracked by fan magazines. Rudolph Valentino, described as "catnip to women," and Clara Bow, the "It Girl" (everyone knew what *it* was), became household names. Most loved of all was the comic Charlie Chaplin, whose famous character, the wistful Little Tramp, showed an endearing inability to cope with the rules and complexities of modern life.

Americans also found heroes in sports. Baseball solidified its place as the national pastime in the 1920s. It remained essentially a game played by and for the working class. In George Herman "Babe" Ruth, baseball had the most cherished free spirit of the time. The rowdy escapades of the "Sultan of Swat" demonstrated that sports offered a way to break out of the ordinariness of everyday life. By "his sheer exuberance," one sportswriter declared, Ruth "has lightened the cares of the world."

The public also fell in love with a young boxer from the grim mining districts of Colorado. As a teenager, Jack Dempsey had made his living hanging around saloons betting he could beat anyone in the house. When he took the heavyweight crown just after World War I, he was revered as the people's champ, a stand-in for the average American who felt increasingly confined by bureaucracy and machine-made culture. In Philadelphia in 1926, a crowd of 125,000 fans saw challenger Gene Tunney pummel and defeat the people's champ.

Football, essentially a college sport, held greater sway with the upper classes. The most famous coach, Knute Rockne of Notre Dame, celebrated football for its life lessons of hard work and teamwork. Let the professors make learning as exciting as football, Rockne advised, and the problem of getting young people to learn would disappear. But in keeping with the times, football moved toward a more commercial spectacle. Harold "Red" Grange, "the Galloping Ghost," led the way by going from stardom at the University of Illinois to the Chicago Bears in the new professional football league.

The decade's hero worship reached its zenith in the celebration of Charles Lindbergh, a young pilot who set out on May 20, 1927, to become the first person to fly solo nonstop across the Atlantic. Newspapers tagged Lindbergh "the Lone Eagle" — the perfect hero for an age that celebrated individual accomplishment. "Charles Lindbergh," one journalist proclaimed, "is the stuff out of which have been made the pioneers that opened up the wilderness. His are the qualities which we, as a people, must nourish." Lindbergh realized, however, that technical and organizational complexity was fast reducing chances for solitary achievement. Consequently, he titled his book about the flight *We* (1927) to include the machine that had made it all possible.

Another machine — the radio — became crucial to mass culture in the 1920s. The nation's first licensed radio station, KDKA in Pittsburgh, began broadcasting in 1920, and soon American airwaves buzzed with news, sermons, soap operas, sports, comedy, and music. Because they could now reach prospective customers in their own homes, advertisers bankrolled radio's rapid growth. Between 1922 and 1929, the number of radio stations in the United States increased from 30 to 606. In just seven years, homes with radios jumped from 60,000 to a staggering 10.25 million.

The Lost Generation. Some writers and artists felt alienated from America's mass-culture society, which they found shallow, anti-intellectual, and materialistic. Silly movie stars disgusted them. They believed that business culture blighted American life. In their minds, Henry Ford made a poor hero. Young, white, and mostly college educated, these expatriates, as they came to be called, felt embittered by the war and renounced the progressives who had promoted it as a crusade. For them, Europe — not Hollywood or Harlem — seemed the place to seek their potential.

The American-born writer Gertrude Stein, long established in Paris, remarked famously as the young exiles gathered around her, "They are the lost generation." Most of the expatriates, however, believed to the contrary that they had finally found themselves. The Lost Generation helped launch the most creative period in American art and literature in the twentieth century. The novelist whose spare, clean style best exemplified the expatriate efforts to make art mirror basic reality was Ernest Hemingway. Admirers found the terse language and hard lessons of his novel *The Sun Also Rises* (1926) to be perfect expressions of a world stripped of illusions.

Many writers who remained in America were exiles in spirit. Before the war, intellectuals had eagerly joined progressive reform movements. Afterward, they were more likely critics of American cultural vulgarity. Novelist Sinclair Lewis in *Main Street* (1920) and *Babbitt* (1922) satirized his native Midwest as a cultural wasteland. Humorists such as James Thurber created outlandish characters to poke fun at American stupidity and inhibitions. And southern writers, led by William Faulkner, explored the South's grim class and race heritage. Worries about alienation surfaced as well. F. Scott Fitzgerald spoke sadly in *This Side of Paradise* (1920) of a disillusioned generation "grown up to find all Gods dead, all wars fought, all faiths in man shaken."

> **REVIEW** How did the new freedoms of the 1920s challenge older conceptions of gender and race?

Resistance to Change

Large areas of the country did not share in the wealth of the 1920s. By the end of the decade, 40 percent of the nation's farmers were landless, and 90 percent of rural homes lacked indoor plumbing, gas, or electricity. Rural America's traditional distrust of urban America turned to despair in the 1920s when the census reported that the majority of the population had shifted to the city (Map 23.2). Once the "backbone of the republic," rural Americans had become poor country cousins. Urban domination over the nation's political and cultural life and sharply rising economic disparity drove rural Americans in often ugly, reactionary directions.

Cities seemed to stand for everything rural areas stood against. Rural America imagined itself as solidly Anglo-Saxon (despite the presence of millions of African Americans in the South and Mexican Americans, Native Americans, and Asian Americans in the West), and the cities seemed to be filled with undesirable immigrants. Rural America was the home of old-time Protestant religion, and the cities teemed with Catholics, Jews, liberal Protestants, and atheists. Rural America championed old-fashioned moral standards — abstinence and self-denial — while the cities spawned every imaginable vice. In the 1920s, frustrated rural people sought to recapture their country by helping to push through prohibition, dam the flow of immigrants, revive the Ku Klux Klan, defend the Bible as literal truth, and defeat an urban Roman Catholic for president.

Rejecting the Undesirables. Before the war, when about a million immigrants arrived each year, some Americans warned that unassimilable foreigners were drowning the nation. War against Germany and its allies expanded nativist and anti-radical sentiment. After the war, large-scale immigration resumed (another 800,000 immigrants arrived in 1921) at a moment when industrialists no longer needed new factory laborers. Returning veterans, as well as African American and Mexican migration, had relieved labor shortages. Moreover, union leaders feared that millions of poor immigrants would undercut their efforts to organize American workers. Rural America's God-fearing Protestants were particularly alarmed that most of the immigrants were Catholic or Jewish. In 1921, Congress responded by severely restricting immigration.

Three years later, Congress very nearly slammed the door shut. The Johnson-Reed Act of 1924 limited the number of immigrants to no more than 161,000 a year and established quotas for each European nation. The act revealed the fear and bigotry that fueled anti-immigration legislation. While it cut immigration by more than 80 percent, it squeezed some nationalities far more than others. Backers of Johnson-Reed, who declared that America had become the "garbage can and the dumping ground of the world," manipulated quotas to ensure entry only to "good" immigrants from western Europe. The law, for example, allowed Great Britain 62,458 entries, but Russia could send only 1,992. Johnson-Reed effectively reversed the trend toward immigration from southern and eastern Europe, which by 1914 had amounted to 75 percent of the yearly total.

Johnson-Reed Act
1924 law that severely restricted immigration to the United States to no more than 161,000 a year, with quotas for each European nation. The racist restrictions were designed to staunch the flow of immigrants from southern and eastern Europe and from Asia.

GB = 1,000
R = 1

Map Activity

MAP 23.2 THE SHIFT FROM RURAL TO URBAN POPULATION, 1920–1930

The movement of whites and Hispanics toward urban and agricultural opportunity made Florida, the West, and the Southwest the regions of fastest population growth. By contrast, large numbers of blacks left the rural South to find a better life in the North. Almost all migrating blacks went from the countryside to cities in distant parts of the nation, while white and Hispanic migrants tended to move shorter distances toward familiar places.

READING THE MAP: Which states had the strongest growth? To which cities did southern blacks predominantly migrate?

CONNECTIONS: What conditions in the countryside made the migration to urban areas appealing to many rural Americans? In what social and cultural ways did rural America view itself as different from urban America?

Population Change, 1920–1930

Very strong growth
Moderate growth
Loss
• Urban areas of strong growth
◄ Migration of black population

Chinese exclusion act

The 1924 law also reaffirmed the 1880s legislation barring Chinese immigrants and added Japanese and other Asians to the list of the excluded. But it left open immigration from the Western Hemisphere because farmers in the Southwest demanded continued access to cheap agricultural labor. During the 1920s, some 500,000 Mexicans crossed the border legally. In addition, Congress in 1924 passed the Indian Citizenship Act, which extended suffrage and citizenship to all American Indians.

Rural Americans, who had most likely never laid eyes on a Polish packinghouse worker, a Slovak coal miner, an Armenian sewing machine operator, or a Chinese laundry worker, strongly supported immigration restriction, as did industrialists and labor leaders. The laws of the 1920s marked the end of the era symbolized by the Statue of Liberty's open-armed welcome to Europe's "huddled masses yearning to breathe free."

Antiforeign hysteria climaxed in the trial of two anarchist immigrants from Italy, Nicola Sacco and Bartolomeo Vanzetti. Arrested in 1920 for robbery and murder in South Braintree, Massachusetts, the men were sentenced to death by a judge who openly referred to them as "anarchist bastards." In response to doubts about the fairness of the verdict, a blue-ribbon review committee found the trial judge guilty of a "grave breach of official decorum" but refused to recommend a motion for retrial. When Massachusetts executed Sacco and Vanzetti on August 23, 1927, fifty thousand American mourners followed the caskets, convinced that the men had died because they were immigrants and radicals, not because they were murderers.

The Rebirth of the Ku Klux Klan.

The nation's sour antiforeign mood struck a responsive chord in members of the secret society the **Ku Klux Klan.** The Klan first appeared in the South during Reconstruction to thwart black freedom and expired with the reestablishment of white supremacy (see chapter 16). In 1915, the Klan was reborn at Stone Mountain, Georgia, but when the new Klan extended its targets beyond black Americans, it quickly spread beyond the South. Under a banner proclaiming "100 percent Americanism," the Klan promised to defend family, morality, and traditional American values against the threats posed by blacks, immigrants, radicals, feminists, Catholics, and Jews.

Building on the frustrations of rural America, the Klan in the 1920s spread throughout the nation, almost controlling Indiana and influencing politics in Illinois, California, Oregon, Texas, Louisiana, Oklahoma, and Kansas. In 1926, Klan imperial wizard Hiram Wesley Evans described the assault of modernity: "One by one all our traditional moral standards went by the boards or were so disregarded that they ceased to be binding," he explained. "The sacredness of our Sabbath, of our homes, of chastity, and finally even of our right to teach our own children in schools [represented] fundamental facts and truth torn away from us."

Eventually, social changes, along with lawless excess, crippled the Klan. Immigration restrictions eased the worry about invading foreigners, and sensational wrongdoing by Klan leaders cost it the support of traditional moralists. Grand Dragon David Stephenson of Indiana, for example, went to jail for the kidnapping

Ku Klux Klan
Secret society that first thwarted black freedom after the Civil War but was reborn in 1915 to fight against perceived threats posed by blacks, immigrants, radicals, feminists, Catholics, and Jews. The new Klan spread well beyond the South in the 1920s.

and rape of a woman who subsequently committed suicide. Yet the social grievances, economic problems, and religious anxieties of the countryside and small towns remained alive, ready to be ignited.

The Scopes Trial. In 1925 in a Tennessee courtroom, old-time religion and the new spirit of science went head-to-head. The confrontation occurred after several southern states passed legislation against the teaching of Charles Darwin's theory of evolution in the public schools. Scientists and civil liberties organizations clamored for a challenge to the law, and John Scopes, a young biology teacher in Dayton, Tennessee, offered to test his state's ban on teaching evolution. When Scopes came to trial, Clarence Darrow, a brilliant defense lawyer from Chicago, volunteered to defend him. Darrow, an avowed agnostic, took on the prosecution's William Jennings Bryan, three-time Democratic nominee for president, fervent fundamentalist, and symbol of rural America.

The **Scopes trial** quickly degenerated into a media circus. The first trial to be covered live on radio, it attracted a nationwide audience. When, under relentless questioning by Darrow, Bryan declared on the witness stand that he did indeed believe that the world had been created in six days and that Jonah had lived in the belly of a whale, his humiliation in the eyes of most urban observers was complete. Nevertheless, the Tennessee court upheld the law and punished Scopes with a $100 fine. Although fundamentalism won the battle, it lost the war. Baltimore journalist H. L. Mencken had the last word in a merciless obituary for Bryan, who died just a week after the trial ended. Portraying the "monkey trial" as a battle between the country and the city, Mencken flayed Bryan as a "charlatan, a mountebank, a zany without shame or dignity," motivated solely by "hatred of the city men who had laughed at him for so long."

As Mencken's acid prose indicated, Bryan's humiliation was not purely a victory of reason and science. It also revealed the disdain urban people felt for country people and the values they clung to. The Ku Klux Klan revival and the Scopes trial dramatized and inflamed divisions between city and country, intellectuals and the uneducated, the privileged and the poor, the scoffers and the faithful.

Al Smith and the Election of 1928. The presidential election of 1928 brought many of the developments of the 1920s — prohibition, immigration, religion, and the clash of rural and urban values — into sharp focus. Republicans emphasized the economic success of their party's pro-business government and turned to Herbert Hoover, the energetic secretary of commerce and leading public symbol of 1920s prosperity. But because both parties generally agreed that the American economy was basically sound, the campaign turned on social issues that divided Americans.

The Democrats nominated four-time governor of New York Alfred E. Smith. Smith adopted "The Sidewalk of New York" as a campaign theme song and seemed to represent all that rural Americans feared and resented. A child of immigrants, Smith got his start in politics with the help of New York City's Irish-dominated Tammany Hall political machine, to many the epitome of big-city corruption. He denounced immigration quotas, signed New York State's anti-Klan bill, and

Scopes trial
1925 trial of John Scopes, a biology teacher in Dayton, Tennessee, for violating his state's ban on teaching evolution. The trial created a nationwide media frenzy and came to be seen as a showdown between urban and rural values.

opposed prohibition, believing that it was a nativist attack on immigrant customs. When Smith supposedly asked reporters, "Wouldn't you like to have your foot on the rail and blow the foam off some suds?" prohibition forces dubbed him "Alcohol Al." But Smith's greatest vulnerability in the heartland was his religion. He was the first Catholic to run for president. A Methodist bishop in Virginia denounced Roman Catholicism as "the Mother of ignorance, superstition, intolerance and sin" and begged Protestants not to vote for a candidate who represented "the kind of dirty people that you find today on the sidewalks of New York."

Hoover, who neatly combined the images of morality, efficiency, service, and prosperity, won the election by a landslide (Map 23.3). He received nearly 58 percent of the vote and gained 444 electoral votes to Smith's 87. The only bright spot for Democrats was the nation's cities, which voted Democratic, indicating the rising strength of ethnic minorities, including Smith's fellow Catholics.

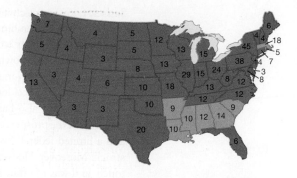

Candidate	Electoral Vote	Popular Vote	Percent of Popular Vote
Herbert Hoover (Republican)	444	21,391,381	57.4
Alfred E. Smith (Democrat)	87	15,016,443	40.3
Norman Thomas (Socialist)	0	881,951	2.3

MAP 23.3   THE ELECTION OF 1928

REVIEW How did some Americans resist cultural change?

The Great Crash

At his inauguration in 1929, Hoover told the American people, "Given a chance to go forward with the policies of the last eight years, we shall soon with the help of God be in sight of the day when poverty will be banished from this nation." Those words came back to haunt Hoover when eight months later the prosperity he touted collapsed in the stock market crash of 1929. The nation ended nearly three decades of barely interrupted economic growth. Like much of the world, the United States fell into the most serious economic depression of all time. Hoover's reputation was among the first casualties, along with the reverence for business that had been the hallmark of the New Era.

Herbert Hoover: The Great Engineer. When Hoover became president in 1929, he seemed the perfect choice to lead a prosperous business nation. His rise from poor Iowa orphan to one of the world's most celebrated mining engineers by the time he was thirty personified America's rags-to-riches ideal. His success in managing efforts to feed civilian victims of the fighting during World War I won him acclaim as "the Great Humanitarian" and led Woodrow Wilson to name him head of the Food Administration once the United States entered the war. Hoover's reputation soared even higher as secretary of commerce in the Harding and Coolidge administrations.

Hoover belonged to the progressive wing of his party. "The time when the employer could ride roughshod over his labor[ers] is disappearing with the doctrine of 'laissez-faire' on which it is founded," he declared in 1909. He urged a limited business-government partnership that would manage the sweeping changes Americans were experiencing. Hoover brought a reform agenda to the White House: "We want to see a nation built of home owners and farm owners. We want to see their savings protected. We want to see them in steady jobs. We want to see more and more of them insured against death and accident, unemployment and old age. We want them all secure."

But Hoover also had ideological and political liabilities. Principles that appeared strengths in the prosperous 1920s — individual self-reliance, industrial self-management, and a limited federal government — became straitjackets when economic catastrophe struck. Moreover, Hoover had never held an elected public office, had a poor political touch, and was too thin-skinned to be an effective politician. Even so, most Americans considered him "a sort of superman" able to solve any problem. Prophetically, he confided to a friend his fear that "if some unprecedented calamity should come upon the nation . . . I would be sacrificed to the unreasoning disappointment of a people who expected too much." The distorted national economy set the stage for the calamity Hoover so feared.

The Distorted Economy. In the spring of 1929, the United States enjoyed a fragile prosperity. Although America had become the world's leading economy, it had done little to help rebuild Europe's shattered economy after World War I. Instead, the Republican administrations demanded that Allied nations repay their war loans, creating a tangled web of debts and reparations that sapped Europe's economic vitality.

HOOVER CAMPAIGN POSTER

This poster effectively illustrates Herbert Hoover's 1928 campaign message: Republican administrations in the 1920s had produced middle-class prosperity, complete with a house in the suburbs and the latest automobile. David J. & Janice L. Frent Collection/Corbis.

Moreover, to boost American business, the United States enacted tariffs that prevented other nations from selling their goods to Americans. Fewer sales meant that foreign nations had less money to buy American goods. American banks propped up the nation's export trade by extending credit to foreign customers, deepening their debt.

America's domestic economy was also in trouble. Wealth was badly distributed. Farmers continued to suffer from low prices and chronic indebtedness; the average income of farm families was only $240 per year. The wages of industrial workers, though rising during the decade, failed to keep up with productivity and corporate profits. Overall, nearly two-thirds of all American families lived on less than the $2,000 per year that economists estimated would "supply only basic necessities." In sharp contrast, the wealthiest 1 percent of the population received 15 percent of the nation's income — the amount received by the poorest 42 percent. The Coolidge administration worsened the deepening inequality by cutting taxes on the wealthy.

By 1929, the inequality of wealth produced a serious problem in consumption. The rich, brilliantly portrayed in F. Scott Fitzgerald's novel *The Great Gatsby* (1925), spent lavishly, but they could absorb only a tiny fraction of the nation's output. For a time, the new device of installment buying — buying on credit — kept consumer demand up. By the end of the decade, four out of five cars and two out of three radios were bought on credit.

Signs of economic trouble began to appear at mid-decade. New construction slowed down. Automobile sales faltered. Companies began cutting back production and laying off workers. Between 1921 and 1928, as investment and loan opportunities faded, five thousand banks failed, wiping out the life savings of hundreds of thousands.

The Crash of 1929. Even as the economy faltered, Americans remained upbeat. Hoping for even bigger slices of the economic pie, Americans speculated wildly in the stock market on Wall Street. Between 1924 and 1929, the values of stocks listed on the New York Stock Exchange increased by more than 400 percent. Buying stocks on margin — that is, putting up only part of the money at the time of purchase — accelerated. Some people got rich this way, but those who bought on credit could finance their loans only if their stocks increased in value. A Yale economist assured doubters that stock prices had reached "a permanently high plateau." Former president Calvin Coolidge declared that, at current prices, stocks were a bargain. But President Hoover observed, "The only trouble with capitalism is capitalists. They're too damned greedy."

Finally, in the autumn of 1929, the market hesitated. Investors nervously began to sell their overvalued stocks. The dip quickly became a panic on October 24, the day that came to be known as Black Thursday. More panic selling came on Black Tuesday, October 29, the day the market suffered a greater fall than ever before. In the next six months, the stock market lost six-sevenths of its total value.

It was once thought that the crash alone caused the Great Depression. It did not. In 1929, the national and international economies were already riddled with severe problems. But the dramatic losses in the stock market crash and the fear of risking what was left acted as a great brake on economic activity. The collapse on Wall Street shattered the New Era's confidence that America would enjoy perpetually expanding prosperity.

Hoover and the Limits of Individualism. When the bubble broke, Americans expressed relief that Hoover resided in the White House. Not surprisingly for a man who had been such an active secretary of commerce, Hoover acted quickly to arrest the decline. In November 1929, to keep the stock market collapse from ravaging the entire economy, Hoover called a White House conference of business and labor leaders. He urged them to join in a voluntary plan for recovery: Businesses would maintain production and keep their workers on the job; labor would accept existing wages, hours, and conditions. Within a few months, however, the bargain fell apart. As demand for their products declined, industrialists cut production, sliced wages, and laid off workers. Poorly paid or unemployed workers could not buy much, and their decreased spending led to further cuts in production and further loss of jobs. Thus began the terrible spiral of economic decline.

To deal with the problems of rural America, Hoover got Congress to pass the Agricultural Marketing Act in 1929. The act created the Farm Board, which used its budget of $500 million to buy up agricultural surpluses and thus, it was hoped, raise prices. But prices continued to fall. To help end the decline, Hoover joined conservatives in urging protective tariffs on agricultural goods, and the Hawley-Smoot tariff of 1930 established the highest rates in history. The same year, Congress also authorized $420 million for public works projects to give the unemployed jobs and create more purchasing power. In three years, the Hoover administration nearly doubled federal public works expenditures.

But with each year of Hoover's term, the economy weakened. Tariffs did not end the suffering of farmers because foreign nations retaliated with increased tariffs of their own that crippled American farmers' ability to sell abroad. In 1932, Hoover hoped to help hard-pressed industry with the **Reconstruction Finance Corporation (RFC)**, a federal agency empowered to lend government funds to endangered banks and corporations. The theory was trickle-down economics: Pump money into the economy at the top, and in the long run the people at the bottom would benefit. Or, as one wag put it, "Feed the sparrows by feeding the horses." In the end, very little of what critics of the RFC called a "millionaires' dole" trickled down to the poor.

Meanwhile, hundreds of thousands of workers lost their jobs each month. By 1932, an astounding one-quarter of the American workforce — nearly thirteen million people — were unemployed. There was no direct federal assistance, and state services and private charities were swamped. The depression that began in 1929 devastated much of the world, but no other industrialized nation provided such feeble support to the jobless. Cries grew louder for the federal government to give hurting people relief.

Hoover was no do-nothing president, but there were limits to his conception of the government's proper role in fighting the economic disaster. He compared direct federal aid to the needy to the "dole" in Britain, which he thought destroyed the moral fiber of the chronically unemployed. "Prosperity cannot be restored by raids on the public Treasury," Hoover declared. Besides, he said, the poor could rely on their neighbors to protect them "from hunger and cold." In 1931, he allowed the Red Cross to distribute government-owned agricultural surpluses to the hungry. In 1932, he relaxed his principles further to offer small federal loans, not gifts, to the states to help them in their relief efforts. But Hoover's restricted notions of legitimate government action proved vastly inadequate to address the problems of restarting the economy and ending human suffering.

Reconstruction Finance Corporation (RFC)
Federal agency established by Herbert Hoover in 1932 to help American industry by lending government funds to endangered banks and corporations, which Hoover hoped would benefit people at the bottom through trickle-down economics. In practice, this strategy provided little help to the poor.

REVIEW Why did the American economy collapse in 1929?

Life in the Depression

In 1930, suffering on a massive scale set in. Men and women hollow-eyed with hunger grew increasingly bewildered and angry in the face of cruel contradictions. They saw agricultural surpluses pile up in the countryside and knew that their children were going to bed hungry. They saw factories standing idle, yet they knew that they and millions of others were willing to work. The gap between the American people and leaders who failed to resolve these contradictions widened as the depression deepened. By 1932, America's economic problems had created a dangerous social and political crisis.

The Human Toll. Statistics only hint at the human tragedy of the Great Depression. When Hoover took office in 1929, the American economy stood at its peak. When he left in 1933, it had reached its twentieth-century low (Figure 23.2). In 1929, national income was $88 billion. By 1933, it had declined to $40 billion. In 1929, unemployment was 3.1 percent, or 1.5 million workers. By 1933, unemployment stood at 25 percent, almost 13 million workers. In Cleveland, Ohio, 50 percent of the workforce was jobless, and in Toledo, 80 percent. By 1932, more than 9,000 banks had shut their doors, wiping out millions of savings accounts.

Jobless, homeless victims wandered in search of work, and the tramp, or hobo, became one of the most visible figures of the decade. Riding the rails or hitchhiking,

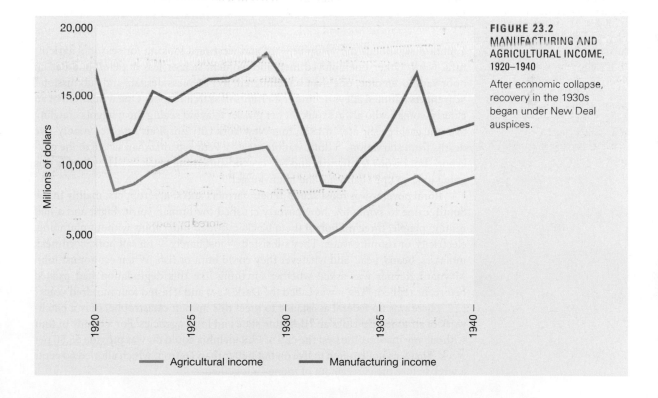

FIGURE 23.2
MANUFACTURING AND AGRICULTURAL INCOME, 1920–1940

After economic collapse, recovery in the 1930s began under New Deal auspices.

HOBOES, 1920s

Out-of-work men gather around a fire in front of the train that may have brought them to this unnamed place in the Midwest. With no work at home, many decided to "ride the rails" for free in search of a job. Hoboing was dangerous because of accidents and the violence of the railroad security staffs, nicknamed "bulls." The Granger Collection, New York.

a million vagabonds moved southward and westward looking for seasonal agricultural work. Other unemployed men and women, sick or less hopeful, huddled in doorways, overcome, one man remembered, by "helpless despair and submission." Scavengers haunted alleys behind restaurants in search of food. One writer told of an elderly woman who always took off her glasses to avoid seeing the maggots crawling over the garbage she ate. In 1931, four New York City hospitals reported ninety-five deaths from starvation. "I don't want to steal," a Pennsylvania man wrote to the governor, "but I won't let my wife and boy cry for something to eat. . . . How long is this going to keep up? I cannot stand it any longer."

Rural poverty was most acute. Tenant farmers and sharecroppers, mainly in the South, came to symbolize how poverty crushed the human spirit. Eight and a half million people, three million of them black, crowded into cabins without plumbing, electricity, or running water. They subsisted — just barely — on salt pork, cornmeal, molasses, beans, peas, and whatever they could hunt or fish. When economist John Maynard Keynes was asked whether anything like this degradation had existed before, he replied, "Yes, it was called the Dark Ages and it lasted four hundred years."

There was no federal assistance to meet this human catastrophe, only a patchwork of strapped charities and destitute state and local agencies. For a family of four without any income, the best the city of Philadelphia could do was provide $5.50 per week. That was not enough to live on but better than Detroit, which allotted 60 cents a week before the city ran out of money altogether.

The deepening crisis roused old fears and caused some Americans to look for scapegoats. Among the most thoroughly scapegoated were Mexican Americans. During the 1920s, cheap agricultural labor from Mexico flowed legally across the U.S. border, welcomed by the large farmers. In the 1930s, however, the public denounced the newcomers as dangerous aliens who took jobs from Americans. Government officials, most prominently those in Los Angeles County, targeted Mexican residents for deportation regardless of citizenship status. As many as half a million Mexicans and Mexican Americans were deported or fled to Mexico.

The depression deeply affected the American family. Young people postponed marriage. When they did marry, they produced few children. White women, who generally worked in low-paying service areas, did not lose their jobs as often as men who worked in steel, automobile, and other heavy industries. Idle husbands suffered a loss of self-esteem. "Before the depression," one unemployed man reported, "I wore the pants in this family, and rightly so." Jobless, he lost "self-respect" and also "the respect of my children, and I am afraid that I am losing my wife." Employers discriminated against married women workers, but necessity continued to drive women into the marketplace. As a result, by 1940 some 25 percent more women were employed for wages than in 1930.

Denial and Escape. President Hoover assured the American nation that economic recovery was on its way, but the president's optimism was contradicted by makeshift shantytowns, called "Hoovervilles," that sprang up on the edges of America's cities. Newspapers used as cover by those sleeping on the streets were "Hoover blankets." An empty pocket turned inside out was a "Hoover flag," and jackrabbits caught for food were "Hoover hogs." Bitter jokes circulated about the increasingly unpopular president. One told of Hoover asking for a nickel to telephone a friend. Flipping him a dime, an aide said, "Here, call them both."

While Hoover practiced denial, other Americans sought refuge from reality at the movies. Throughout the depression, between 60 million and 75 million people (nearly two-thirds of the nation) scraped together enough change to fill the movie palaces every week. Box office hits such as *42nd Street* and *Gold Diggers of 1933* capitalized on the hope that prosperity lay just around the corner. But a few filmmakers grappled with realities rather than escape them. *The Public Enemy* (1931) taught hard lessons about gangsters' ill-gotten gains. Indeed, under the new production code of 1930, designed to protect public morals, all movies had to find some way to show that crime did not pay.

Despite Hollywood's efforts to keep Americans on the right side of the law, crime increased. In the countryside, the plight of people who had lost their farms to bank foreclosures led to the romantic idea that bank robbers were only getting back what banks had stolen from the poor. Woody Guthrie, the populist folksinger from Oklahoma, captured the public's tolerance for outlaws in his tribute to a murderous bank robber with a choirboy face, "The Ballad of Pretty Boy Floyd." Guthrie sang that there were two kinds of robbers, those who used guns and those who used pens, and he observed that robbers with guns, like Pretty Boy Floyd, never drove families from their homes. Named Public Enemy No. 1, Floyd was shot and killed by police in 1934. His funeral in Oklahoma was attended by between 20,000 and 40,000 people, many of whom viewed Floyd as a tragic figure, a victim of the hard times.

Working-Class Militancy.

The nation's working class bore the brunt of the economic collapse. By 1931, William Green, head of the American Federation of Labor (AFL), had turned militant. "I warn the people who are exploiting the workers," he shouted, "that they can drive them only so far before they will turn on them and destroy them. They are taking no account of the history of nations in which governments have been overturned. Revolutions grow out of the depths of hunger."

The American people were slow to anger, but on March 7, 1932, several thousand unemployed autoworkers massed at the gates of Henry Ford's River Rouge factory in Dearborn, Michigan, to demand work. Pelted with rocks, Ford's private security forces responded with gunfire, killing four demonstrators. Forty thousand outraged citizens turned out for the unemployed men's funerals.

Farmers mounted uprisings of their own. When Congress refused to guarantee farm prices, several thousand farmers created the National Farmers' Holiday Association in 1932, so named because its members planned to take a "holiday" from shipping crops to market. Farm militants also resorted to what they called "penny sales." When banks foreclosed and put farms up for auction, neighbors warned others not to bid, bought the foreclosed property for a few pennies, and returned it to the bankrupt owners. Militancy won farmers little in the way of long-term solutions,

SCOTTSBORO BOYS

Nine black youths, ranging in age from thirteen to twenty-one, were convicted of the rape of two white women and sentenced to death by an all-white jury in March 1931. None was executed, and eventually the state dropped the charges against the youngest four and granted paroles to the others. The last "Scottsboro Boy" left jail in 1950. © Bettmann/Corbis.

but one individual observed that "the biggest and finest crop of revolutions you ever saw is sprouting all over the country right now."

Even those who had proved their patriotism by serving in World War I rose up in protest against the government. In 1932, tens of thousands of unemployed veterans traveled to Washington, D.C., to petition Congress for the immediate payment of the pension (known as a "bonus") that Congress had promised them in 1924. Hoover feared that the veterans would spark a riot and ordered the U.S. Army to evict the **Bonus Marchers** from their camp on the outskirts of the city. Tanks destroyed the squatters' encampments while five hundred soldiers wielding bayonets and tear gas sent the protesters fleeing. The spectacle of the army driving peaceful, petitioning veterans from the nation's capital further undermined public support for the beleaguered Hoover.

The Great Depression — the massive failure of capitalism — catapulted the Communist Party to its greatest size and influence in American history. Some 100,000 Americans — workers, intellectuals, college students — joined the Communist Party in the belief that only an overthrow of the capitalist system could save the victims of the depression. In 1931, the party, through its National Miners Union, moved into Harlan County, Kentucky, to support a strike by brutalized coal miners. Mine owners unleashed thugs against the strikers and eventually beat the miners down. But the Communist Party gained a reputation as the most dedicated and fearless champion of the union cause.

The left also led the fight against racism. While both major parties refused to challenge segregation in the South, the Socialist Party, led by Norman Thomas, attacked the system of sharecropping that left many African Americans in near servitude. The Communist Party also took action. When nine young black men in Scottsboro, Alabama (the **Scottsboro Boys**), were arrested on trumped-up rape charges in 1931, a team of lawyers sent by the party saved the defendants from the electric chair.

Radicals on the left often sparked action, but protests by moderate workers and farmers occurred on a far greater scale. Breadlines, soup kitchens, foreclosures, unemployment, government violence, and cold despair drove patriotic men and women to question American capitalism. "I am as conservative as any man could be," a Wisconsin farmer explained, "but any economic system that has in its power to set me and my wife in the streets, at my age — what can I see but red?"

REVIEW How did the depression reshape American politics?

HARLAN COUNTY COAL STRIKE, 1931

Bonus Marchers
World War I veterans who marched on Washington, D.C., in 1932 to lobby for immediate payment of the pension ("bonus") promised them in 1924. President Herbert Hoover believed the bonuses would bankrupt the government and sent the U.S. Army to evict the veterans from the city.

Scottsboro Boys
Nine African American youths who were arrested for the alleged rape of two white women in Scottsboro, Alabama, in 1931. After an all-white jury sentenced the young men to death, the Communist Party took action that saved them from the electric chair.

Conclusion: Dazzle and Despair

In the aftermath of World War I, America turned its back on progressive crusades and embraced conservative Republican politics, the growing influence of corporate leaders, and business values. Changes in the nation's economy — Henry Ford's automobile revolution, mass production, advertising — propelled fundamental change throughout society. Living standards rose, economic opportunity increased, and Americans threw themselves into private pleasures — gobbling up the latest household goods and fashions, attending baseball and football games and boxing matches, gathering around the radio, and going to the movies. As big cities came to dominate American life, the culture of youth and flappers became the leading edge of what one observer called a "revolution in manners and morals." At home in Harlem and abroad in Paris, American literature, art, and music flourished.

For many Americans, however, none of the glamour and vitality had much meaning. Instead of seeking thrills at the speakeasies, plunging into speculation on Wall Street, or escaping abroad, the vast majority struggled to earn a decent living. Blue-collar America did not participate fully in white-collar prosperity. Rural America was almost entirely left out of the Roaring Twenties. Country folk, deeply suspicious and profoundly discontented, championed prohibition, revived the Klan, attacked immigration, and defended old-time Protestant religion.

The crash of 1929 and the depression that followed starkly revealed the economy's crises of international trade and consumption. Hard times swept high living off the front pages of the nation's newspapers. Different images emerged: hoboes hopping freight trains, strikers confronting police, malnourished sharecroppers staring blankly into the distance, empty apartment buildings alongside cardboard shantytowns, and mountains of food rotting in the sun while guards with shotguns chased away the hungry.

The depression hurt everyone, but the poor were hurt most. As farmers and workers sank into aching hardship, businessmen rallied around Herbert Hoover to proclaim that private enterprise would get the country moving again. But things fell apart, and Hoover faced increasingly radical opposition. Membership in the Socialist and Communist parties surged, and more and more Americans contemplated desperate measures. By 1932, the depression had nearly brought the nation to its knees. America faced its greatest crisis since the Civil War, and citizens demanded new leaders who would save them from the "Hoover Depression."

Chapter Review

KEY TERMS

Teapot Dome (p. 677)

Five-Power Naval Treaty of 1922 (p. 679)

welfare capitalism (p. 680)

prohibition (p. 682)

new woman (p. 683)

New Negro (p. 688)

Johnson-Reed Act (p. 692)

Ku Klux Klan (p. 693)

Scopes trial (p. 694)

Reconstruction Finance Corporation (RFC) (p. 698)

Bonus Marchers (p. 703)

Scottsboro Boys (p. 703)

REVIEW QUESTIONS

❶ How did the spread of the automobile transform the United States? (pp. 677–82)

❷ How did the new freedoms of the 1920s challenge older conceptions of gender and race? (pp. 682–91)

❸ How did some Americans resist cultural change? (pp. 691–95)

❹ Why did the American economy collapse in 1929? (pp. 695–98)

❺ How did the depression reshape American politics? (pp. 699–703)

MAKING CONNECTIONS

❶ What drove popular opinion in the 1920s to unrestrained confidence in American business? How did it influence Republicans' approach to governance and the development of the American economy in the 1920s?

❷ Americans' encounters with the wealth and increased personal freedom characteristic of the 1920s varied greatly. Why did some embrace the era's changes, while others resisted them?

❸ How did shifting government policy contribute to both the boom of the 1920s and the bust of 1929?

❹ How did Americans attempt to lessen the impact of the Great Depression?

LINKING TO THE PAST

❶ How did America's experience in World War I — both at home and abroad — help shape the 1920s? (See chapter 22.)

❷ How did attitudes toward government in the Progressive Era differ from those in the 1920s? (See chapter 21.)

24

The New Deal Experiment,
1932–1939

○ : people
□ : words/places
— : info

CONTENT LEARNING OBJECTIVES

After reading and studying this chapter, you should be able to:

• Explain which issues shaped the presidential campaign of 1932 and how the candidates' strategies differed. Determine the significance of Roosevelt's victory.

• Analyze which factors united New Deal reformers and what kinds of policies they endorsed. Describe the initial reforms enacted during Roosevelt's first one hundred days in office.

• Recount why critics resisted the New Deal.

• Explain how the Second New Deal moved the country toward a welfare state and describe the kinds of programs reformers proposed. Evaluate why some Americans were left out of the New Deal.

• Identify the final phase of the New Deal and why it ultimately reached a deadlock.

I n March 1936, Florence Owens piled her seven children into her old Hudson. They had been picking beets in southern California, near the Mexican border, but the harvest was over now. Owens headed north, where she hoped to find work picking lettuce. About halfway there, her car broke down. She coasted into a labor camp of more than two thousand migrant workers who were hungry and out of work. They had been attracted by advertisements of work in the pea fields, only to find the crop ruined by a heavy frost. Owens set up a lean-to shelter and prepared food for her family while two of her sons worked on the car. They ate half-frozen peas from the field and small birds the children killed. Owens recalled

NEW DEAL PRESIDENTIAL CAMPAIGN POSTER

This 1936 poster proclaims President Franklin D. Roosevelt "A Real Depression Buster," without mentioning his name. The acronyms on the poster refer to the New Deal programs that exemplified Roosevelt's commitment to an activist government. David J. & Janice L. Frent Collection/Corbis.

later, "I started to cook dinner for my kids, and all the little kids around the camp came in. 'Can I have a bite? . . .' And they was hungry, them people was."

Florence Owens was born in 1903 in Oklahoma, then Indian Territory. Both of Florence's parents were Cherokee. When she was seventeen, Florence married Cleo Owens, a farmer who moved his growing family to California, where he worked in sawmills. Cleo died of tuberculosis in 1931, leaving Florence a widow with six young children.

Florence began to work as a farm laborer in California's Central Valley to support herself and her children. She picked cotton, earning about $2 a day. "I'd leave home before daylight and come in after dark," she explained. "We just existed!" To survive, she worked nights as a waitress, making "50-cents a day and the leftovers." Sometimes, she remembered, "I'd carry home two water buckets full" of leftovers to feed her children.

Like tens of thousands of other migrant laborers, Owens followed the crops, planting, cultivating, and harvesting as jobs opened up in the fields along the West Coast from California to Oregon and Washington. Joining Owens and other migrants — many of whom were Mexicans and Filipinos — were Okie refugees from the Dust Bowl, the large swath of Great Plains states that suffered drought, failed crops, and foreclosed mortgages during the 1930s.

Soon after Florence Owens fed her children at the pea pickers' camp, a car pulled up, and a woman with a camera got out and began to take photographs of Owens. The woman was Dorothea Lange, a photographer employed by a New Deal agency to document conditions among farmworkers in California. Lange snapped six photos of Owens, and climbed back in her car and headed to Berkeley. Owens and her family, their car now repaired, drove off to look for work in the lettuce fields.

Lange's last photograph of Owens, subsequently known as *Migrant Mother*, became an icon of the desperation among Americans that President Franklin Roosevelt's New Deal sought to alleviate. While *Migrant Mother* became Dorothea Lange's most famous photograph, Florence Owens continued to work in the fields, "ragged, hungry, and broke," as a San Francisco newspaper noted.

Unlike Owens, her children, and other migrant workers, many Americans received government help from Roosevelt's New Deal

1933   Franklin D. Roosevelt becomes president.
Roosevelt's "Hundred Days" launches the New Deal.
Roosevelt declares four-day "bank holiday."
Federal Emergency Relief Administration created.

1934   Securities and Exchange Commission created.
Upton Sinclair loses California governorship bid.
American Liberty League founded.
Dr. Francis Townsend devises Old Age Revolving Pension scheme.
Indian Reorganization Act enacted.

1935   Works Progress Administration created.
Wagner Act enacted.
Committee for Industrial Organization founded.
Social Security Act enacted.
Father Charles Coughlin begins National Union for Social Justice.

1936   Franklin Roosevelt reelected by a landslide.

1937   Sit-down strike organized at General Motors plant in Flint, Michigan.
Roosevelt's court-packing legislation defeated.
Economic recession deepens.

1938   Second Agricultural Adjustment Act enacted.
Fair Labor Standards Act enacted.
Congress rejects antilynching bill.

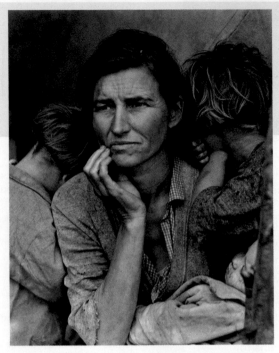

FLORENCE OWENS AND CHILDREN

This classic photograph of migrant farm laborer Florence Owens and her children was taken in 1936 in the labor camp of a pea field in California by New Deal photographer Dorothea Lange. The photo depicts the privations common among working people during the depression, but it also evokes a mother's leadership, dignity, and affection, qualities that helped shelter her family from poverty and joblessness. Library of Congress, 8b29516.

initiatives to provide relief for the needy, to speed economic recovery, and to reform basic economic and governmental institutions. Roosevelt's New Deal elicited bitter opposition from critics on the right and the left, and it failed to satisfy fully its own goals of relief, recovery, and reform. But within the Democratic Party, the New Deal energized a powerful political coalition that helped millions of Americans withstand the privations of the Great Depression. In the process, the federal government became a major presence in the daily lives of most American citizens.

Franklin D. Roosevelt: A Patrician in Government

Unlike the millions of impoverished Americans, Franklin Roosevelt came from a wealthy and privileged background that contributed to his optimism, self-confidence, and vitality. He drew on these personal qualities in his political career to bridge the economic, social, and cultural chasm that separated him from the struggles of ordinary people like Florence Owens. During the twelve years he served as president (1933–1945), many elites came to hate him as a traitor to his class, while millions more Americans in his New Deal coalition, especially the hardworking poor and dispossessed, revered him because he cared about them and their problems.

The Making of a Politician. Born in 1882, Franklin Delano Roosevelt grew up on his father's leafy estate at Hyde Park on the Hudson River, north of New York City. Roosevelt prepared for a career in politics, hoping to follow in the political footsteps of his fifth cousin, Theodore Roosevelt. In 1905 Franklin married his distant cousin, Eleanor Roosevelt, and Theodore Roosevelt — the current president of the United States and Eleanor's uncle — gave the bride away. Unlike cousin Teddy, Franklin Roosevelt sought his political fortune in the Democratic Party. In 1920, he catapulted to the second spot on the national Democratic ticket as the vice presidential candidate of presidential nominee James M. Cox. Although Cox lost the election (see chapter 22), Roosevelt's energetic campaigning convinced Democratic leaders that he had a bright future.

In the summer of 1921, at the age of thirty-nine, Roosevelt caught polio, which paralyzed both his legs. For the rest of his life, he wore heavy steel braces, and he could walk a few steps only by leaning on another person. Tireless physical therapy helped him regain his vitality and intense desire for high political office, although he carefully avoided being photographed in the wheelchair he used routinely.

After his polio attack, Roosevelt frequented a polio therapy facility at Warm Springs, Georgia. There, he got to know southern Democrats, which helped make him a rare political creature: a New Yorker from the Democratic Party's urban and immigrant wing who got along with whites from the party's entrenched southern wing.

By 1928, Roosevelt had recovered sufficiently to campaign for governor of New York, and he squeaked out a victory. As governor of the nation's most populous state, Roosevelt showcased his activist policies, which became a dress rehearsal for his presidency.

Visual Activity

ROOSEVELT CAMPAIGNING

This photo of Franklin Roosevelt on the campaign trail in rural Georgia in October 1932 displays the candidate's support for ordinary Americans. The carefully posed photo illustrates Roosevelt's attempt to reach across the class divide that separated his patrician upbringing and lifestyle from the experience of the vast majority of Americans who lacked his privileges. Hulton-Deutsch/Corbis.

READING THE IMAGE: How does the photo contrast the lives of rural people with that of the presidential candidate? What is the significance of Roosevelt sitting atop the seat back in the car to shake hands?

CONNECTIONS: Why was it important in the 1932 election for the presidential candidates to seek the support of rural Americans?

As the Great Depression spread hard times throughout the nation, Governor Roosevelt believed that government should intervene to protect citizens from economic hardships rather than wait for the law of supply and demand to improve the economy. According to the laissez-faire views of many conservatives — especially Republicans, but also numerous Democrats — the depression simply represented market forces separating strong survivors from weak losers. Unlike Roosevelt, conservatives believed that government help for the needy sapped individual initiative and impeded the self-correcting forces of the market by rewarding people for losing the economic struggle to survive. Roosevelt lacked a full-fledged counterargument to these conservative claims, but he sympathized with the plight of poor people. "To these unfortunate citizens," he proclaimed, "aid must be extended by governments, not as a matter of charity but as a matter of social duty. . . . [No one should go] unfed, unclothed, or unsheltered."

To his supporters, Roosevelt seemed to be a leader determined to attack the economic crisis without deviating from democracy — unlike the fascist parties gaining strength in Europe — or from capitalism — unlike the Communists in power in the Soviet Union. Roosevelt's ideas about how to revive the economy were vague. A prominent journalist described Roosevelt in 1931 as "a kind of amiable boy scout . . . who, without any important qualifications for the office, would very much like to be president." Roosevelt's many supporters appreciated his energy and his conviction that government should do something to help Americans climb out of the economic abyss, and they propelled him into the front ranks of the national Democratic Party.

The Election of 1932. Democrats knew that Herbert Hoover's unpopularity gave them a historic opportunity to recapture the White House in 1932. Since Abraham Lincoln's election, Republicans had occupied the White House three-fourths of the time, a trend Democrats hoped to reverse. Democrats, however, had to overcome warring factions that divided the party by region, religion, culture, and commitment to the status quo. The southern, native-born, white, rural, Protestant, conservative wing of the Democratic Party found little common ground with the northern, immigrant, urban, disproportionately Catholic, liberal wing. Eastern-establishment Democratic dignitaries shared few goals with angry farmers and factory workers. Still, this unruly coalition managed to agree on Franklin Roosevelt as its presidential candidate.

In his acceptance speech, Roosevelt vowed to help "the forgotten man at the bottom of the pyramid" with "bold, persistent experimentation." Highlighting his differences with Hoover and the Republicans, he pledged "a new deal" for the American people." Few details about what Roosevelt meant by "a new deal" emerged in the presidential campaign. He declared that "the people of America want more than anything else . . . two things: work . . . and a reasonable measure of security . . . for themselves and for their wives and children." Voters decided that whatever Roosevelt's new deal might be, it was better than reelecting Hoover.

Roosevelt won the 1932 presidential election in a historic landslide. He received 57 percent of the nation's votes, the first time a Democrat had won a majority of the popular vote since 1852 (Map 24.1). He amassed 472 electoral votes to Hoover's 59,

New Deal coalition

Political coalition that supported Franklin D. Roosevelt's New Deal and the Democratic Party, including farmers, factory workers, immigrants, city dwellers, women, African Americans, and progressive intellectuals. The coalition dominated American politics during and long after Roosevelt's presidency.

carrying state after state that had voted Republican for years (Map 24.2). Roosevelt's coattails swept Democrats into control of Congress by large margins. The popular mandate for change was loud and clear.

Roosevelt's victory represented the emergence of what came to be known as the **New Deal coalition**. Attracting support from farmers, factory workers, immigrants, city folk, African Americans, women, and progressive intellectuals, Roosevelt launched a realignment of the nation's political loyalties. The New Deal coalition dominated American politics throughout Roosevelt's presidency and remained powerful long after his death in 1945. United less by their ideologies or support for specific policies, voters in the New Deal coalition instead expressed faith in Roosevelt's promise of a government that would somehow change things for the better. Nobody, including Roosevelt, knew exactly what the New Deal would change or whether the changes would revive the nation's ailing economy and improve Americans' lives. But as he said during the presidential campaign, "It is

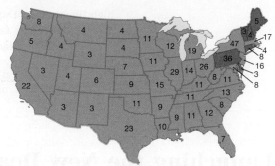

Candidate	Electoral Vote	Popular Vote	Percent of Popular Vote
Franklin D. Roosevelt (Democrat)	472	22,821,857	57.4
Herbert C. Hoover (Republican)	59	15,761,841	39.7
Norman Thomas (Socialist)	0	881,951	2.2
William Z. Foster (Communist)	0	102,991	0.3

MAP 24.1 THE ELECTION OF 1932

Map Activity

MAP 24.2 ELECTORAL SHIFT, 1920–1932

The Democratic victory in 1932 signaled the rise of a New Deal coalition in which women and minorities, many of them new voters, made the Democrats the majority party for the first time in the twentieth century.

READING THE MAP: How many states voted Democratic in 1928? How many states voted Republican in 1932? How many states shifted from Republican to Democratic between 1928 and 1932?

CONNECTIONS: What factions within the Democratic Party opposed Franklin Roosevelt's candidacy in 1932, and why did they do so? To what do you attribute his landslide victory?

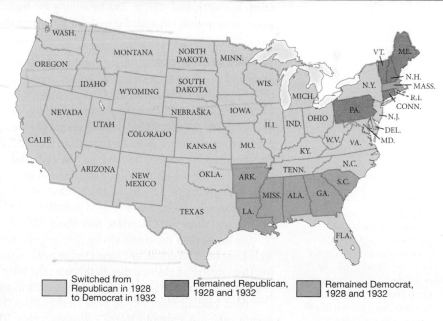

Switched from Republican in 1928 to Democrat in 1932 | Remained Republican, 1928 and 1932 | Remained Democrat, 1928 and 1932

high time to admit with courage that we are in the midst of an emergency at least equal to that of war. Let us mobilize to meet it." Roosevelt and many others knew that the future of American capitalism and democracy was at stake.

> **REVIEW** Why did Franklin D. Roosevelt win the 1932 presidential election by such a large margin?

Launching the New Deal

At noon on March 4, 1933, Americans gathered around their radios to hear the inaugural address of the newly elected president. Roosevelt began by asserting his "firm belief that the only thing we have to fear is fear itself — nameless, unreasoning, unjustified terror which paralyzes needed efforts to convert retreat into advance." He promised "direct, vigorous action," and the first months of his administration, termed "the Hundred Days," fulfilled that promise in a whirlwind of government initiatives that launched the New Deal.

Roosevelt and his advisers had three interrelated objectives: to provide relief to the destitute, especially the one out of four Americans who were unemployed; to foster the economic recovery of farms and businesses, thereby creating jobs and reducing the need for relief; and to reform the government and economy in ways that would reduce the risk of devastating consequences in future economic slumps and thereby strengthen capitalism. The New Deal never fully achieved these goals of relief, recovery, and reform. But by aiming for them, Roosevelt's experimental programs enormously expanded government's role in the nation's economy and society.

The New Dealers. To design and implement the New Deal, Roosevelt needed ideas and people. He convened a "Brains Trust" of economists and other leaders to offer suggestions and advice about the problems facing the nation. No New Dealers were more important than the president and his wife, Eleanor. The gregarious president radiated charm and good cheer, giving the New Deal's bureaucratic regulations a benevolent human face. Eleanor Roosevelt became the New Deal's unofficial ambassador. She served, she said, as "the eyes and ears of the New Deal," traveling throughout the nation meeting Americans of all colors and creeds. A North Carolina women's rights activist recalled, "One of my greatest pleasures was meeting Mrs. Roosevelt. . . . She was so free of prejudice . . . and she was always willing to take a stand, and there were stands to take about blacks and women."

As Roosevelt's programs swung into action, the millions of beneficiaries of the New Deal became grassroots New Dealers who expressed their appreciation by voting Democratic on election day. In this way, the New Deal created a durable political coalition of Democrats that reelected Roosevelt in 1936, 1940, and 1944.

Four guiding ideas shaped New Deal policies. First, Roosevelt and his advisers sought capitalist solutions to the economic crisis. They had no desire to eliminate private property or impose socialist programs, such as public ownership of productive resources. Instead, they hoped to save the capitalist economy by remedying its flaws.

Second, Roosevelt's Brains Trust persuaded him that the greatest flaw of America's capitalist economy was **underconsumption**, the root cause of the current economic paralysis. Underconsumption, New Dealers argued, resulted from the gigantic productive success of capitalism. Factories and farms produced more than they could sell to consumers, causing factories to lay off workers and farmers to lose money on bumper crops. Workers without wages and farmers without profits shrank consumption and choked the economy. Somehow, the balance between consumption and production needed to be restored.

Third, New Dealers believed that the immense size and economic power of American corporations needed to be counterbalanced by government and by organization among workers and small producers. Unlike progressive trustbusters, New Dealers did not seek to splinter big businesses. Roosevelt and his advisers hoped to counterbalance big economic institutions with government programs focused on protecting individuals and the public interest.

Fourth, New Dealers believed that government must somehow moderate the imbalance of wealth created by American capitalism. Wealth concentrated in a few hands reduced consumption by most Americans and thereby contributed to the current economic gridlock. Government needed to find a way to permit ordinary working people to share more fully in the fruits of the economy. "Our task now," Roosevelt declared during the presidential campaign, "is . . . meeting the problem of underconsumption, . . . adjusting production to consumption, . . . [and] distributing wealth and products more equitably."

Banking and Finance Reform.
Roosevelt wasted no time making good on his inaugural pledge for "action now." As he took the oath of office on March 4, the nation's banking system was on the brink of collapse. Roosevelt immediately devised a plan to shore up banks and restore depositors' confidence. Working round the clock, New Dealers drafted the Emergency Banking Act, propped up the private banking system with federal funds, and subjected banks to federal regulation and oversight. To secure the confidence of depositors, Congress passed the Glass-Steagall Banking Act, setting up the **Federal Deposit Insurance Corporation (FDIC)**, which guaranteed bank customers that the federal government would reimburse them for deposits if their banks failed. In addition, the act required the separation of commercial banks (which accept deposits and make loans to individuals and small businesses) and investment banks (which make speculative investments with their funds), in an effort to insulate the finances of Main Street America from the risky speculations of Wall Street wheeler-dealers.

On Sunday night, March 12, while the banks were still closed, Roosevelt broadcast the first of a series of **fireside chats**. Speaking in a friendly, informal manner, he explained the new banking legislation that, he said, made it "safer to keep your money in a reopened bank than under the mattress." With such plain talk, Roosevelt translated complex matters into common sense. This and subsequent fireside chats forged a direct connection — via radio — between Roosevelt and millions of Americans, a connection felt by a man from Paris, Texas, who wrote to Roosevelt, "You are the one & only President that ever helped a Working Class of People. . . . Please help us some way I Pray to God for relief."

underconsumption
A situation in which factories and farms produce more than consumers buy, causing factories to lay off workers and farmers to lose money. New Dealers believed that underconsumption was the root cause of the country's economic paralysis. Workers without wages and farmers without profits shrank consumption and choked the economy. The only way to increase consumption, New Dealers believed, was to provide jobs that put wages in consumers' pockets.

Federal Deposit Insurance Corporation (FDIC)
Regulatory body established by the Glass-Steagall Banking Act that guaranteed the federal government would reimburse bank depositors if their banks failed. This key feature of the New Deal restored depositors' confidence in the banking system during the Great Depression.

fireside chats
Series of informal radio addresses Franklin Roosevelt made to the nation in which he explained New Deal initiatives. The chats helped bolster Roosevelt's popularity and secured popular support for his reforms.

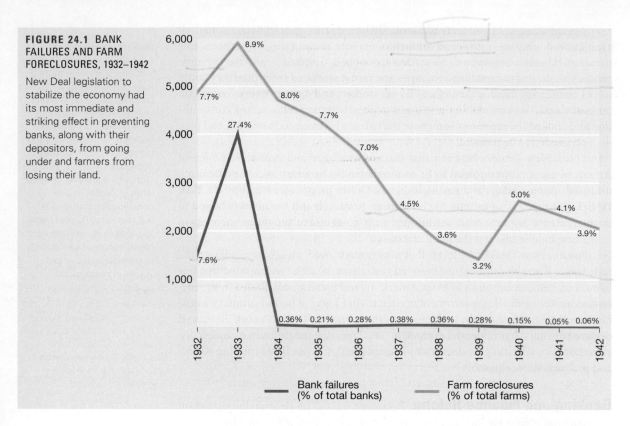

FIGURE 24.1 BANK FAILURES AND FARM FORECLOSURES, 1932–1942

New Deal legislation to stabilize the economy had its most immediate and striking effect in preventing banks, along with their depositors, from going under and farmers from losing their land.

Bank failures (% of total banks)   Farm foreclosures (% of total farms)

The banking legislation and fireside chat worked. Within a few days, most of the nation's major banks reopened, and they remained solvent as reassured depositors switched funds from their mattresses to their bank accounts (Figure 24.1). One New Dealer boasted, "Capitalism was saved in eight days." The rescue of the banking system took much longer to succeed, though.

In his inaugural address, Roosevelt criticized financiers for their greed and incompetence. To prevent the fraud, corruption, and insider trading that had tainted Wall Street and contributed to the crash of 1929, New Dealers created the Securities and Exchange Commission (SEC) in 1934 to oversee financial markets by licensing investment dealers, monitoring all stock transactions, and requiring corporate officers to make full disclosures about their companies. To head the SEC, Roosevelt appointed an ambitious Wall Street financier, Joseph P. Kennedy (father of the future president John F. Kennedy), who had a shady reputation for stock manipulation. Under Kennedy's leadership, the SEC helped clean up and regulate Wall Street, which slowly recovered.

Relief and Conservation Programs. Patching the nation's financial structure provided little relief for the hungry and unemployed. A poor man from Nebraska asked Eleanor Roosevelt "if the folk who was borned here in America . . . are this Forgotten Man, the President had in mind, [and] if we are this Forgotten Man then we are still Forgotten." The federal government had never assumed responsibility for needy people, except in moments of natural disaster or emergencies such as the Civil War. Instead, churches, private charities, county and municipal governments, and occasionally states assumed the burden of poor relief, usually with meager payments. The depression necessitated unprecedented federal relief efforts, according to New Dealers. As a New Yorker who still had a job wrote the government, "We work, ten hours a day for six days. In the grime and dirt of a nation [for] . . . low pay [making us] . . . slaves — slaves of the depression!"

The Federal Emergency Relief Administration (FERA) established in May 1933, supported four million to five million households with $20 or $30 a month. FERA also created jobs for the unemployed on thousands of public works projects, organized into the Civil Works Administration (CWA), which put paychecks worth more than $800 million into the hands of previously jobless workers. Earning wages between 40 and 60 cents an hour, laborers renovated schools, dug sewers, and rebuilt roads and bridges.

The most popular work relief program was the **Civilian Conservation Corps** **(CCC)**, established in March 1933. It offered unemployed young men a chance to earn wages while working to conserve natural resources, a long-standing interest of Roosevelt. Women were excluded from working in the CCC until Eleanor Roosevelt demanded that a token number of young women be hired. By the end of the program in 1942, three million CCC workers had left a legacy of vast new recreation areas, along with roads that made those areas accessible to millions of Americans. Just as important, the CCC, CWA, and other work relief efforts replaced the stigma of welfare with the dignity of jobs. As one woman said about her husband's work relief job, "We aren't on relief anymore. My husband is working for the Government."

The New Deal's most ambitious and controversial natural resources development project was the Tennessee Valley Authority (TVA), created in May 1933 to build dams along the Tennessee River to supply impoverished rural communities with cheap electricity (Map 24.3). The TVA set out to demonstrate that a partnership between the federal government and local residents could overcome the barriers of state governments and private enterprises to make efficient use of abundant natural resources and break the ancient cycle of poverty. The TVA improved the lives of millions in the region with electric power, flood protection, soil reclamation, and jobs, although it raised the hackles of many Americans who thought it trespassed unforgivably on free enterprise.

New sources of hydroelectric power helped the New Deal bring the wonders of electricity to country folk, fulfilling an old progressive dream. When Roosevelt became president, 90 percent of rural Americans lacked electricity. Private electric companies refused to build transmission lines into the sparsely settled countryside when they had a profitable market in more accessible and densely populated urban areas. Beginning in 1935, the Rural Electrification Administration (REA) made low-cost loans available to local cooperatives for power plants and transmission lines to serve rural communities. Within ten years, the REA delivered electricity to nine out of ten farms, giving rural Americans access for the first time to modern conveniences that urban people had enjoyed for decades.

Agricultural Initiatives. Farmers had been mired in a depression since the end of World War I. New Dealers diagnosed the farmers' plight as a classic case of overproduction and underconsumption. Following age-old practices, farmers tried to compensate for low crop prices by growing more crops. Of course, producing

Civilian Conservation Corps (CCC)
Federal relief program established in March 1933 that provided assistance in the form of jobs to millions of unemployed young men and a token number of women. CCC workers worked on conservation projects throughout the nation.

more crops pushed prices lower still. Farm families' income sank to $167 a year, barely one-tenth of the national average in 1932.

New Dealers sought to cut agricultural production, thereby raising crop prices and farmers' income. With more money in their pockets, farm families — who made up one-third of all Americans — would then buy more goods and lift consumption in the entire economy. To reduce production, the **Agricultural Adjustment Act (AAA)** passed in May 1933 authorized the "domestic allotment plan," which paid farmers not to grow crops. Individual farmers who agreed not to plant crops on a portion of their fields (their "allotment") would receive a government payment compensating them for the crops they did not plant. While millions of Americans like Florence Owens and her children went to bed hungry, farmers slaughtered livestock and destroyed crops to qualify for their allotment payments.

With the formation of the Commodity Credit Corporation, the federal government allowed farmers to hold their harvested crops off the market and wait for a higher price. New Dealers also sponsored the Farm Credit Act (FCA) to provide long-term credit on mortgaged farm property, allowing debt-ridden farmers to avoid foreclosures that were driving thousands off their land (Figure 24.1).

Crop allotments, commodity loans, and mortgage credit made farmers major beneficiaries of the New Deal. Crop prices rose impressively, farm income jumped

Agricultural Adjustment Act (AAA)

New Deal legislation passed in May 1933 aimed at cutting agricultural production and raising crop prices and, consequently, farmers' income. Through the "domestic allotment plan," the AAA paid farmers to not grow crops.

Map Activity

MAP 24.3 THE TENNESSEE VALLEY AUTHORITY

The New Deal created the Tennessee Valley Authority to modernize a vast impoverished region with hydroelectric power dams and, at the same time, to reclaim eroded land and preserve old folkways.

READING THE MAP: How many states were affected by the TVA? How many miles of rivers (approximately) were affected?

CONNECTIONS: What kinds of benefits — economic as well as social and cultural — did TVA programs bring to the region? How might the lives of a poor farming family in Alabama or Tennessee have changed after the mid-1930s owing to these programs?

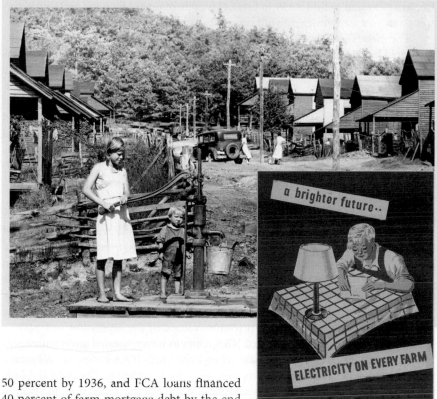

50 percent by 1936, and FCA loans financed 40 percent of farm mortgage debt by the end of the decade. These gains were distributed fairly equally among farmers in the corn, hog, and wheat region of the Midwest. In the South's cotton belt, however, landlords controlled the distribution of New Deal agricultural benefits and shamelessly rewarded themselves while denying benefits to many sharecroppers and tenant farmers — blacks and whites — by taking the land they worked out of production and assigning it to the allotment program. As the president of the Oklahoma Tenant Farmers' Union explained, large farmers who got "Triple-A" payments often used the money to buy tractors and then "forced their tenants and [share]croppers off the land," causing these "Americans to be starved and dispossessed of their homes in our land of plenty."

Industrial Recovery. Unlike farmers, industrialists cut production with the onset of the depression. Between 1929 and 1933, industrial production fell more than 40 percent in an effort to balance low demand with low supply and thereby maintain prices. But falling industrial production meant that millions of working people lost their jobs. Unlike farmers, most working people needed jobs to eat. Mass unemployment also reduced consumer demand for industrial products, contributing to a downward spiral in both production and jobs, with no end in sight. Industries responded by reducing wages for employees who still had jobs, further reducing demand — a trend made worse by competition among industrial producers. New

National Recovery Administration (NRA)
Federal agency established in June 1933 to promote industrial recovery. The NRA encouraged industrialists to voluntarily adopt codes that defined fair working conditions, set prices, and minimized competition. In practice, large corporations developed codes that served primarily their own interests rather than those of workers or the economy.

Dealers struggled to find a way to break this cycle of unemployment and underconsumption — a way consistent with corporate profits and capitalism.

The New Deal's National Industrial Recovery Act opted for a government-sponsored form of industrial self-government through the **National Recovery Administration (NRA)**, established in June 1933. The NRA encouraged industrialists to agree on rules, known as "codes", to define fair working conditions, to set prices, and to minimize competition. The idea behind codes was to stabilize existing industries and maintain their workforces. Industry after industry wrote elaborate codes addressing detailed features of production, pricing, and competition. In exchange for the relaxation of federal antitrust regulations that prohibited such business agreements, the participating businesses promised to recognize the right of working people to organize and engage in collective bargaining. To encourage consumers to patronize businesses with NRA codes, posters with the NRA's Blue Eagle appeared in shop windows throughout the nation.

New Dealers hoped that NRA codes would yield businesses with a social conscience, ensuring fair treatment of workers and consumers as well as promotion of the general economic welfare. Instead, NRA codes tended to strengthen conventional business practices. Large corporations wrote codes that served primarily their own interests rather than the needs of workers or the welfare of the national economy. The failure of codes to cover domestic workers or agricultural laborers like Florence Owens led one woman to complain to Roosevelt that the NRA "never mentioned the robbery of the Housewives" by the privations caused by the depression.

Many business leaders criticized NRA codes as heavy-handed government regulation of private enterprise. In reality, compliance with NRA codes was voluntary, and government enforcement efforts were weak to nonexistent. The NRA did little to reduce unemployment, raise consumption, or relieve the depression. In effect, it represented a peace offering to business leaders by Roosevelt and his advisers, conveying the message that the New Deal did not intend to wage war against profits or private enterprise. The peace offering failed, however. Most corporate leaders became bitter opponents of Roosevelt and the New Deal.

> **REVIEW** How did the New Dealers try to steer the nation toward recovery from the Great Depression?

Challenges to the New Deal

The first New Deal initiatives engendered fierce criticism and political opposition. From the right, Republicans and businesspeople charged that New Deal programs were too radical, undermining private property, economic stability, and democracy. Critics on the left faulted the New Deal for its failure to allay the human suffering caused by the depression and for its timidity in attacking corporate power and greed.

Resistance to Business Reform. New Deal programs rescued capitalism, but business leaders lambasted Roosevelt, even though their economic prospects improved more than those of most other Americans during the depression.

Republicans and business leaders denounced New Deal efforts to regulate or reform what they considered their private enterprises.

By 1935, two major business organizations, the National Association of Manufacturers and the Chamber of Commerce, had become openly anti–New Deal. Their critiques were amplified by the American Liberty League, founded in 1934, which blamed the New Deal for betraying basic constitutional guarantees of freedom and individualism. A League spokesman declared, "This administration has copied the autocratic tactics of fascism, Hitlerism and communism at their worst."

Economists who favored rational planning in the public interest and labor leaders who sought to influence wages and working conditions by organizing unions attacked the New Deal from the left. In their view, the NRA stifled enterprise by permitting monopolistic practices. They pointed out that industrial trade associations twisted NRA codes to suit their aims, thwarted competition, and engaged in price gouging. Labor leaders especially resented the NRA's willingness to allow businesses to form company-controlled unions while blocking workers from organizing genuine grassroots unions to bargain for themselves.

The Supreme Court stepped into this cross fire of criticisms in May 1935 and declared that the NRA unconstitutionally conferred powers reserved to Congress on an administrative agency. The NRA codes soon lost the little authority they had. The failure of the NRA demonstrated the depth of many Americans' resistance to economic planning and the stubborn refusal of business leaders to yield to government regulations or reforms.

Casualties in the Countryside.
The AAA weathered critical battering by champions of the old order better than the NRA. Allotment checks for keeping land fallow and crop prices high created loyalty among farmers with enough acreage to participate. As a white farmer in North Carolina declared, "I stand for the New Deal and Roosevelt . . . , the AAA . . . and crop control."

Protests stirred, however, among those who did not qualify for allotments. The Southern Farm Tenants Union argued passionately that the AAA enriched large farmers while it impoverished small farmers who rented rather than owned their land. One black sharecropper explained why only $75 a year from New Deal agricultural subsidies trickled down to her: "De landlord is landlord, de politicians is landlord, de judge is landlord, de shurf [sheriff] is landlord, ever'body is landlord, en we [sharecroppers] ain' got nothin'!" Like the NRA, the AAA tended to help most those who least needed help. Roosevelt's political dependence on southern Democrats caused him to avoid confronting economic and racial inequities in the South.

Displaced tenants often joined the army of migrant workers like Florence Owens who straggled across rural America during the 1930s, some to flee Great Plains dust storms. Many migrants came from Mexico to work Texas cotton, Michigan beans, Idaho sugar beets, and California crops of all kinds. But since the number of people willing to take agricultural jobs usually exceeded the number of jobs available, wages fell and native-born white migrants fought to reserve even these low-wage jobs for themselves. Hundreds of thousands of "Okies" streamed out of the Dust Bowl of Oklahoma, Kansas,

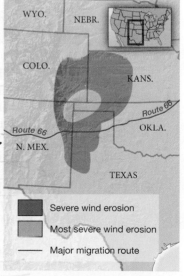

THE DUST BOWL

- Severe wind erosion
- Most severe wind erosion
- Major migration route

EVICTED SHARECROPPERS
The New Deal's Agricultural Adjustment Administration that maintained farm prices by reducing acreage in production often resulted in the eviction of tenant farmers when the land they worked was left idle. These African American sharecroppers protested AAA policies that caused cotton farmers to evict them from their homes. They were among the many rural laborers whose lives were made worse by New Deal agricultural policies. Bettmann/Corbis.

Texas, and Colorado, where chronic drought and harmful agricultural practices blasted crops and hopes. Parched, poor, and windblown, Okies — like the Joad family immortalized in John Steinbeck's novel *The Grapes of Wrath* (1939) — migrated to the lush fields and orchards of California, congregating in labor camps and hoping to find work and a future. But migrant laborers seldom found steady or secure work. As one Okie said, "When they need us they call us migrants, and when we've picked their crop, we're bums and we got to get out."

Politics on the Fringes. Politically, the New Deal's staunchest opponents were in the Republican Party — organized, well-heeled, mainstream, and determined to challenge Roosevelt at every turn. But the New Deal also faced challenges from the political fringes, fueled by the hardship of the depression and the hope for a cure-all. Socialists and Communists accused the New Deal of being the handmaiden of business elites and of rescuing capitalism from its self-inflicted crisis. Socialist author Upton Sinclair ran for governor of California in 1934 on a plan that the state take ownership of idle factories and unused land and then give them to cooperatives of working people, a first step toward putting the needs of people above profits. Sinclair lost the election, ending the most serious socialist electoral challenge to the New Deal.

Some intellectuals and artists sought to advance the cause of more radical change by joining left-wing organizations, including the American Communist Party. At its high point in the 1930s, the party had only about thirty thousand members, the large majority of them immigrants, especially Scandinavians in the upper

Midwest and eastern European Jews in major cities. Individual Communists worked to organize labor unions, protect the civil rights of black people, and help the destitute, but the party preached the overthrow of "bourgeois democracy" and the destruction of capitalism in favor of Soviet-style communism. Such talk attracted few followers among the nation's millions of poor and unemployed. They wanted jobs and economic security within American capitalism and democracy, not violent revolution to establish a dictatorship of the Communist Party.

More powerful radical challenges to the New Deal sprouted from homegrown roots. Many Americans felt overlooked by New Deal programs that concentrated on finance, agriculture, and industry but did little to produce jobs or aid the poor. The merciless reality of the depression also continued to erode the security of people who still had jobs but worried constantly that they, too, might be pushed into the legions of the unemployed and penniless.

A Catholic priest in Detroit named Charles Coughlin spoke to and for many worried Americans in his weekly radio broadcasts, which reached a nationwide audience of 40 million. Father Coughlin expressed outrage at the suffering and inequities that he blamed on Communists, bankers, and "predatory capitalists" who, he claimed, appealing to widespread anti-Semitic sentiments, were mostly Jews. At first, Coughlin championed the New Deal, proclaiming, "I will never change my philosophy that the New Deal is Christ's deal." When Coughlin became frustrated by Roosevelt's refusal to grant him influence, he turned against the New Deal and in 1935 founded the National Union for Social Justice, or Union Party, to challenge Roosevelt in the 1936 presidential election.

Dr. Francis Townsend of Long Beach, California, also criticized the timidity of the New Deal. Angry that many of his retired patients lived in misery, Townsend proposed in 1934 the creation of the Old Age Revolving Pension, which would pay every American over age sixty a pension of $200 a month. To receive the pension, senior citizens had to agree to spend the entire amount within thirty days, thereby stimulating the economy.

Townsend organized pension clubs and petitioned the federal government to enact his scheme. When the major political parties ignored his impractical plan, Townsend merged his forces with Coughlin's Union Party in time for the 1936 election.

A more formidable challenge to the New Deal came from the powerful southern wing of the Democratic Party. Huey Long, son of a backcountry Louisiana farmer, was elected governor of the state in 1928 with his slogan "Every man a king, but no one wears a crown." Unlike nearly all other southern white politicians who harped on white supremacy, Long championed the poor over the rich, country people over city folk, and the humble over elites. As governor, "the Kingfish" — as he liked to call himself — delivered on his promises to provide jobs and build roads, schools, and hospitals, but he also behaved ruthlessly to achieve his goals. Long delighted his supporters, who elected him to the U.S. Senate in 1932, where he introduced a sweeping "soak the rich" tax bill that would outlaw personal incomes of more than $1 million and inheritances of more than $5 million. When the Senate rejected his proposal, Long decided to run for president, mobilizing more than five million Americans behind his "Share Our Wealth" plan. "Is that right," Long asked, "when . . . more [is] owned by 12 men than . . . by 120,000,000 people? . . . They own the banks, they own the steel mills, they own the railroads, they own the bonds, they own the mortgages, they own the stores, and they have chained the country from one end to the other." Like Townsend's

HUEY LONG

Huey Long, U.S. senator and former governor of Louisiana, pressured delegates at the 1932 Democratic convention into supporting Franklin Roosevelt, as depicted here. After Roosevelt's election, Long challenged the president from the left with his Share Our Wealth plan and, until he was assassinated in 1935, campaigned to replace Roosevelt on the Democratic ticket in the next presidential election. NY Daily News via Getty Images.

scheme, Long's program promised far more than it could deliver. The Share Our Wealth campaign died when Long was assassinated in 1935, but his constituency and the wide appeal of a more equitable distribution of wealth persisted.

The challenges to the New Deal from both right and left stirred Democrats to solidify their winning coalition. In the midterm congressional elections of 1934 — normally a time when a president loses support — voters gave New Dealers a landslide victory. Democrats increased their majority in the House of Representatives and gained a two-thirds majority in the Senate.

> **REVIEW** Why did groups at both ends of the political spectrum criticize the New Deal?

Toward a Welfare State

The popular mandate for the New Deal revealed by the congressional elections persuaded Roosevelt to press ahead with bold new efforts to achieve relief, recovery, and reform. Despite the initiatives of the Hundred Days, the depression still strangled the economy. In 1935, Roosevelt capitalized on his congressional majorities to enact major new programs that signaled the emergence of an American welfare state.

Taken together, these New Deal efforts stretched a safety net under the lives of ordinary Americans, including such landmark initiatives as Social Security, which provided modest pensions for the elderly, and the Wagner Act which encouraged the organization of labor unions. Although many citizens remained unprotected, New Deal programs helped millions with jobs, relief, and government support. Knitting together the safety net was the idea that, when individual Americans suffered because of forces beyond their control, the federal government had the responsibility to support and protect them. The safety net of welfare programs tied the political loyalty of working people to the New Deal and the Democratic Party. As a North Carolina mill worker said, "Mr. Roosevelt is the only man we ever had in the White House who would understand that my boss is a sonofabitch." *haha*

Relief for the Unemployed.
First and foremost, Americans still needed jobs. Since the private economy left eight million people jobless by 1935, Roosevelt and his advisers launched a massive work relief program. Roosevelt believed that direct government handouts crippled recipients with "spiritual and moral disintegration . . . destructive to the human spirit." Jobs, by contrast, bolstered individuals' "self-respect, . . . self-reliance and courage and determination." With a congressional appropriation of nearly $5 billion — more than all government revenues in 1934 — the New Deal created the **Works Progress Administration (WPA)** to give unemployed Americans government funded jobs on public works projects. The WPA put millions of jobless citizens to work on roads, bridges, parks, public buildings, and more. In addition, Congress passed, over Roosevelt's veto, the bonus long sought by Bonus Marchers, giving veterans an average of $580 and further stimulating the economy.

Works Progress Administration (WPA)
Federal New Deal program established in 1935 that provided government-funded public works jobs to millions of unemployed Americans during the Great Depression, in areas ranging from construction to the arts.

CITY ACTIVITIES MURAL
During the 1930s, artists — many of them employed by New Deal agencies — painted thousands of murals depicting the variety of American life. These murals often appeared in public buildings. The mural shown here, by Missouri-born artist Thomas Hart Benton, illustrates the seductive pleasures and the spirit found in American cities. The Metropolitan Museum of Art. Gift of AXA Equitable, 2012 (2012 478a-j). © The Metropolitan Museum of Art. Image Source: Art Resource, NY.

By 1936, WPA funds provided jobs for 7 percent of the nation's labor force. In effect, the WPA made the federal government the employer of last resort, creating useful jobs when the capitalist economy failed to do so. In hiring, WPA officials tended to discriminate in favor of white men and against women and racial minorities. Still, the WPA made major contributions to both relief and recovery, putting thirteen million men and women to work earning paychecks worth $10 billion. (See "Analyzing Historical Evidence," page 726.)

3/4 construction

About three out of four WPA jobs involved construction and renovation of the nation's physical infrastructure. WPA workers built 572,000 miles of roads, 78,000 bridges, 67,000 miles of city streets, 40,000 public buildings, and much else. In addition, the WPA gave jobs to thousands of artists, musicians, actors, journalists, poets, and novelists. The WPA also organized sewing rooms for jobless women, giving them work and wages. These sewing rooms produced more than 100 million pieces of clothing that were donated to the needy. Throughout the nation, WPA projects displayed tangible evidence of the New Deal's commitment to public welfare.

Empowering Labor. During the Great Depression, factory workers who managed to keep their jobs worried constantly about being laid off while their wages and working hours were cut. When workers tried to organize labor unions to protect themselves, municipal and state governments usually sided with employers. Since the Gilded Age, state and federal governments had been far more effective at busting unions than at busting trusts. The New Deal dramatically reversed the federal government's stance toward unions. With legislation and political support, the New Deal encouraged an unprecedented wave of union organizing among the nation's working people. When the head of the United Mine Workers, John L. Lewis, told coal miners that "the President wants you to join a union," he exaggerated only a little. New Dealers believed that unions would counterbalance the organized might of big corporations by defending working people, maintaining wages, and replacing the bloody violence that often accompanied strikes with economic peace and commercial stability.

Violent battles on the nation's streets and docks showed the determination of militant labor leaders to organize unions that would protect jobs as well as wages. In 1934, striking workers in Toledo, Minneapolis, San Francisco, and elsewhere were beaten and shot by police and the National Guard. In Congress, labor leaders lobbied for the National Labor Relations Act, a bill sponsored by Senator Robert Wagner of New York that authorized the federal government to intervene in labor disputes and supervise the organization of labor unions. The **Wagner Act**, as it came to be called, guaranteed industrial workers the right to organize unions, putting the might of federal law behind the appeals of labor leaders. If the majority of workers at a company voted for a union, the union became the sole bargaining agent for the entire workplace, and the employer was required to negotiate with the elected union leaders. Roosevelt signed the Wagner Act in July 1935, for the first time providing federal support for labor organization — the most important New Deal reform of the industrial order.

The achievements that flowed from the Wagner Act and renewed labor militancy were impressive. When Roosevelt became president in 1933, union membership — composed almost entirely of skilled workers in trade unions affiliated with the American Federation of Labor (AFL) — stood at three million. With the support

Wagner Act

1935 law that guaranteed industrial workers the right to organize into unions; also known as the National Labor Relations Act. Following passage of the act, union membership skyrocketed to 30 percent of the workforce, the highest in American history.

of the Wagner Act, union membership expanded to fourteen million by 1945. By then, 30 percent of the workforce was unionized, the highest in American history.

Most of the new union members were factory workers and unskilled laborers, many of them immigrants, women, and African Americans. For decades, established AFL unions had no desire to organize factory and unskilled workers. In 1935, under the aggressive leadership of the mine workers' John L. Lewis and the head of the Amalgamated Clothing Workers, Sidney Hillman, a coalition of unskilled workers formed the **Committee for Industrial Organization (CIO)**; later the Congress of Industrial Organizations. The CIO, helped by the Wagner Act, mobilized organizing drives in major industries, including the bitterly anti-union automobile and steel industries.

The bloody struggle by the CIO-affiliated United Auto Workers (UAW) to organize workers at General Motors climaxed in January 1937. Striking workers occupied the main assembly plant in Flint, Michigan, in a sit-down strike that slashed the plant's production of 15,000 cars a week to a mere 150. Stymied, General Motors eventually surrendered and agreed to make the UAW the sole bargaining agent for all the company's workers and to refrain from interfering with union activity. The UAW expanded its campaign until, after much violence, the entire industry was unionized by 1941.

The CIO hoped to ride organizing success in auto plants to victory in the steel mills. But after unionizing the giant U.S. Steel, the CIO ran up against determined opposition from smaller steel firms. Following a police attack that killed ten strikers at Republic Steel outside Chicago in May 1937, the battered steelworkers halted their organizing campaign. In steel and other major industries, such as the stridently anti-union southern textile mills, organizing efforts stalled until after 1941, when military mobilization created labor shortages that gave workers greater bargaining power.

Social Security and Tax Reform.

The single most important feature of the New Deal's emerging welfare state was Social Security. An ambitious, far-reaching, and permanent reform, Social Security was designed to provide a modest income to relieve the poverty of elderly people. Only about 15 percent of older Americans had private pension plans, and during the depression corporations and banks often failed to pay the meager pensions they had promised. Corporations routinely fired or demoted employees to avoid or reduce pension payments. Prompted by the popular but impractical panaceas of Dr. Townsend, Father Coughlin, and Huey Long, Roosevelt told Congress that "it is our plain duty to provide for that security upon which welfare depends . . . and undertake the great task of furthering the security of the citizen and his family through social insurance."

The political struggle for Social Security highlighted class differences among Americans. Support for the measure came from a coalition of advocacy groups for the elderly and the poor, traditional progressives, leftists, social workers, and labor unions. Arrayed against them were economic conservatives, including the American Liberty League, the National Association of Manufacturers, the Chamber of Commerce, and the American Medical Association. Enact the Social Security system, these conservatives and other Republicans warned, and the government will ruin private property, destroy initiative, and reduce proud individuals to spineless loafers.

The large New Deal majority in Congress passed the Social Security Act in August 1935. The act provided that contributions from workers and their employers

Committee for Industrial Organization (CIO)
Coalition (later called the Congress of Industrial Organizations) of mostly unskilled workers formed in 1935 that mobilized massive union organizing drives in major industries. By 1941, through the CIO-affiliated United Auto Workers, organizers had overcome violent resistance to unionize the entire automobile industry.

Social Security
New Deal program created in August 1935 that was designed to provide a modest income for elderly people. The act also created unemployment insurance with modest benefits. Social Security provoked sharp opposition from conservatives and the wealthy.

Analyzing Historical Evidence

Americans Encounter the New Deal

Americans in all walks of life encountered New Deal measures in their daily lives. In 1938 and 1939, the Federal Writers Project, a part of the WPA, interviewed thousands of ordinary citizens throughout the nation, and many expressed their opinions about the New Deal. A sample of their views of the depression, Franklin Roosevelt, the WPA, and the CIO, as well as of political and economic power, can be found in the following excerpts from three interviews.

DOCUMENT 1

Charles Fusco, On the Value of Relief Work during the Depression, December 6, 1938

An Italian American machinist in a munitions plant in Hampden, Connecticut, explained the value of the relief work provided by the WPA.

I can get a job today even if we got a depression. I don't mean that I wasn't on relief when things got tough because there was a time when everything was shut down and I had to get on relief for a job. It isn't so long ago I was working on WPA. Believe me it was a big help. But it wasn't the kind of a job I should have had because this town is Republican and I am a Republican and I was a good worker for the party — making voters and helping a lot of people out. . . . Getting jobs for them. When it came my turn that I needed help the politicians told me that I had to go on relief — well, when I did I was handed a shovel and pick. . . . Roosevelt is a damn good man. . . . You know there shouldn't be a depression in this country . . . the Democrats are in power and the Republicans won't let loose with the money. Well I say that the money men started this thing and I believe the government should make laws to force these capitalists to bring back prosperity. They can do it if they wanted to.

SOURCE: Interview with Charles Fusco. Manuscript. U.S. Works Progress Administration, Federal Writers Project. From Library of Congress, *Folklore Project, Life Histories, 1936–39*, GIF. http://www.loc.gov/resource /wpalh0.09030115/seq-1#seq-1 (accessed December 3, 2013).

DOCUMENT 2

Myron Buxton, The Benefits of WPA Projects, July 25, 1939

A native-born draftsman and assistant to an engineer working on WPA building projects in Newburyport, Massachusetts, illuminated the WPA's benefits to the community and to the individual workers.

One reason people here don't like WPA is because they don't understand it's not all bums and drunks and aliens! Nobody ever explains to them that they'd never have had the new High School they're so goddam proud of if it hadn't been for WPA. They don't stop to figure that new brick sidewalks wouldn't be there, the shade trees wouldn't be all dressed up to look at along High Street and all around town, if it weren't for WPA projects. To most in this town, and I guess it's not much different in this, than any other New England place, WPA's just a racket, set up to give a bunch of loafers and drunks steady pay to indulge in their vices! They don't stop to consider that on WPA are men and women who have traveled places and seen things, been educated and found their jobs folded up and nothing to replace them with. . . . The working guy in this country never had such a swell chance to get a toe-hold as he's had in the last four years! The louder the Republicans yell, the more of a toe-hold you can figure the ordinary guy's got!

SOURCE: Seymour D. Buck. Interview with Myron Buxton. Manuscript. U.S. Works Progress Administration, Federal Writers Project. From Library of Congress, *Folklore Project, Life Histories, 1936–39*, GIF. http://www.loc.gov /resource/wpalh1.14030415/#seq-1 (accessed December 3, 2013).

DOCUMENT 3

Jim Cole, Overcoming Racism in the Unions, May 18, 1939

An African American packinghouse worker near Chicago, Illinois, explained how the CIO united workers from different racial and ethnic backgrounds when other unions turned them away.

I'm working in the Beef Kill section. Butcher on the chain. Been in the place twenty years, I believe. You got to have a certain amount of skill to do the job I'm doing. Long ago, I wanted to join the AFL union, the Amalgamated Butchers and Meat Cutters, they called it and wouldn't take me. Wouldn't let me in the union. Never said it to my face, but reason of it was plain. Negro. That's it. Just didn't want a Negro man to have what he should. That's wrong. You know that's wrong. Long about 1937 the CIO come. Well, I tell you, we Negroes was glad to see it come. Well, you know, sometimes the bosses, or either the company stooges try to keep the white boys from joining the union. They say, "you don't want to belong to a black man's organization. That's all the CIO is." Don't fool nobody, but they got to lie, spread lyin' words around. There's a many different people, talkin' different speech, can't understand English very well, we have to have us union interpreters for lots of our members, but that don't make no mind, they all friends in the union, even if they can't say nothin' except "Brother", an' shake hands. Well, my own local, we elected our officers and it's the same all over. We try to get every people represented. President of the local, he's Negro. First V[ice] President, he's Polish. Second V. President, he's Irish. Other officers, Scotchman, Lithuanian, Negro, German. . . . I don't care if the union don't do another lick of work raisin' our pay, or settling grievances about anything, I'll always believe they done the greatest thing in the world gettin' everybody who works in the yards together, and breakin' up the hate and bad feelings that used to be held against the Negro.

SOURCE: Betty Burke. Interview with Jim Cole. Manuscript. U.S. Works Progress Administration, Federal Writers Project. From Library of Congress, *Folklore Project, Life Histories, 1936–39*, GIF. http://www.loc.gov/resource /wpalh0.0/050602/seq-1#seq-1 (accessed December 3, 2013).

QUESTIONS FOR ANALYSIS

Analyze the Evidence   What did Fusco, Buxton, and Cole see as successes and shortcomings of the New Deal? According to these men, how did New Deal programs influence the lives of ordinary American citizens?

Consider the Context   Who did these men identify as opponents of New Deal measures, and why?

Recognize Viewpoints   What attitudes did these men believe other Americans had about the WPA, the CIO, and the New Deal in general?

would fund pensions for the elderly, giving contributing workers a personal stake in the system and making it politically invulnerable. When eligible workers reached retirement age, they were not subject to a means test to prove that they were needy. Instead, they had earned benefits based on their contributions and years of work. Social Security also created unemployment insurance that provided modest benefits for workers who lost their jobs.

Not all workers benefited from the Social Security Act. It excluded domestic and agricultural workers like Florence Owens, thereby making ineligible about half of all African Americans and more than half of all employed women — about five million people in all. The law also excluded employees of religious and nonprofit organizations, such as schools and hospitals, thereby rendering even more women and minorities ineligible.

Social Security provided states with multimillion-dollar grants to help them support dependent children, blind people, and public health services. After the Supreme Court upheld Social Security in 1937, the program was expanded to include benefits for dependent survivors of deceased recipients. Although the first Social Security check (for $41.30) was not issued until 1940, the system gave millions of working people the assurance that, when they became too old to work, they would receive a modest income from the federal government. This safety net protected many ordinary working people from fears of a penniless and insecure old age.

Fervent opposition to Social Security struck New Dealers as evidence that the rich had learned little from the depression. Roosevelt had long felt contempt for the moneyed elite who ignored the suffering of the poor. He looked for a way to redistribute wealth that would weaken conservative opposition, advance the cause of social equity, and defuse political challenges from Huey Long and Father Coughlin. Roosevelt charged in 1935 that large fortunes put "great and undesirable concentration of control in [the hands of] relatively few individuals." He urged a graduated tax on corporations, an inheritance tax, and an increase in maximum personal income taxes. Congress endorsed Roosevelt's basic principle by taxing those with higher incomes at a somewhat higher rate.

Neglected Americans and the New Deal. The patchwork of New Deal reforms erected a two-tier welfare state. In the top tier farmers and organized workers in major industries were the greatest beneficiaries of New Deal initiatives. In the bottom tier, millions of neglected Americans — women, children, and old folks, along with the unorganized, unskilled, uneducated, and unemployed — often fell through the New Deal safety net. Many working people remained more or less untouched by New Deal benefits. The average unemployment rate for the 1930s stayed high — 17 percent. Workers in industries that resisted unions received little help from the Wagner Act or the WPA. Tens of thousands of women in southern textile mills, for example, commonly received wages of less than ten cents an hour and were fired if they protested. Domestic workers, almost all of them women, and agricultural workers — many of them African, Hispanic, or Asian Americans — were neither unionized nor eligible for Social Security.

The New Deal neglected few citizens more than African Americans. About half of black Americans in cities were jobless, more than double the unemployment rate among whites. In the rural South, where the vast majority of African Americans lived, conditions were worse, given the New Deal agricultural policies such as the AAA that favored landowners, who often pushed blacks off the land they farmed. Only 11 of more than 10,000 WPA supervisors in the South were black, even though African Americans accounted for a third of the region's population. Disfranchisement by intimidation and legal subterfuge prevented southern blacks from protesting their plight at the ballot box. Protesters risked vicious retaliation from local whites. Bitter critics charged that the New Deal's NRA stood for "Negro Run Around" or "Negroes Ruined Again."

Roosevelt responded to such criticisms with great caution since New Deal reforms required the political support of powerful conservative, segregationist, southern white Democrats who would be alienated by programs that aided blacks. A white Georgia relief worker expressed the common view that "any Nigger who gets over $8 a week is a spoiled Nigger, that's all." Stymied by the political clout of entrenched white racism, New Dealers still attracted support from black voters. Roosevelt's overtures to African Americans prompted northern black voters in the 1934 congressional elections to shift from the Republican to the Democratic Party, helping elect New Deal Democrats.

Eleanor Roosevelt sponsored the appointment of Mary McLeod Bethune — the energetic cofounder of the National Council of Negro Women — as head of the Division of Negro Affairs in the National Youth Administration. The highest-ranking black official in Roosevelt's administration, Bethune used her position to guide a small number of black professionals and civil rights activists to posts within New Deal agencies. Ultimately, about one in four African Americans got access to New Deal relief programs.

Despite these gains, by 1940 African Americans still suffered severe handicaps. Most of the thirteen million black workers toiled at low-paying menial jobs, unprotected by the New Deal safety net. Segregated and unequal schools were the norm, and only 1 percent of black students earned college degrees. In southern states, vigilante violence against blacks went unpunished. For these problems of black Americans, the New Deal offered few remedies.

Hispanic Americans fared no better. About a million Mexican Americans lived in the United States in the 1930s, most of them first- or second-generation immigrants who worked crops throughout the West. During the depression, field workers saw their low wages plunge lower still to about a dime an hour. Ten thousand Mexican American pecan shellers in San Antonio, Texas, earned only a nickel an hour. To preserve scarce jobs for U.S. citizens, the federal government choked off immigration from Mexico, while state and local officials deported tens of thousands of

ANTILYNCHING PROTESTERS

These Howard University students protested the New Deal's refusal to support antilynching legislation by standing outside the Washington, D.C., building of the Daughters of the American Revolution in 1935 with nooses around their necks and placards naming recent lynching victims. Roosevelt and his advisers never made federal antilynching laws a priority since they feared alienating white southerners whose votes were needed to pass other New Deal measures. Corbis.

Mexican Americans, many with their American-born children. New Deal programs throughout the West often discriminated against Hispanics and other people of color. A New Deal study concluded that "the Mexican is . . . segregated from the rest of the community as effectively as the Negro . . . [by] poverty and low wages."

Asian Americans had similar experiences. Asian immigrants were still excluded from U.S. citizenship and in many states were not permitted to own land. By 1930, more than half of Japanese Americans had been born in the United States, but they were still liable to discrimination. One young Asian American expressed the frustration felt by many others: "I am a fruit-stand worker. I would much rather it were doctor or lawyer . . . but my aspirations [were] frustrated long ago by circumstances. . . . I am only what I am, a professional carrot washer."

Native Americans also suffered neglect from New Deal agencies. As a group, they remained the poorest of the poor. Since the Dawes Act of 1887 (see chapter 17), the federal government had encouraged Native Americans to assimilate — to abandon their Indian identities and adopt the cultural norms of the majority society. Under the leadership of the New Deal's commissioner of Indian affairs, John Collier, the New Deal's Indian Reorganization Act (IRA) of 1934 largely reversed that policy. Collier claimed that "the most interesting and important fact about Indians" was that they "do not expect much, often they expect nothing at all; yet they are able to be happy." Given such views, the IRA provided little economic aid to Native Americans, but it did restore their right to own land communally and to have greater control over their own affairs. The IRA brought little immediate benefit to Native Americans, but it provided an important foundation for Indians' economic, cultural, and political resurgence a generation later.

Voicing common experiences among Americans neglected by the New Deal, singer and songwriter Woody Guthrie traveled the nation for eight years during the 1930s and heard other rambling men tell him "the story of their life": "how the home went to pieces, how . . . the crops got to where they wouldn't bring nothing, work in factories would kill a dog . . . and — always, always [you] have to fight and argue and cuss and swear . . . to try to get a nickel more out of the rich bosses."

> **REVIEW** What features of a welfare state did the New Deal create, and why?

The New Deal from Victory to Deadlock

To accelerate the sputtering economic recovery, Roosevelt shifted the emphasis of the New Deal in the mid-1930s. Instead of seeking cooperation from conservative business leaders, he decided to rely on the growing New Deal coalition to enact reforms over the strident opposition of the Supreme Court, Republicans, and corporate interests. Roosevelt's conservative opponents reacted to the massing of New Deal forces by intensifying their opposition to the welfare state.

While he continued to lose conservatives' support, Roosevelt added new allies on the left in farm states and big cities. Throughout Roosevelt's first term, socialists and Communists denounced the slow pace of change and accused the New Deal of failing to serve the interests of the workers who produced the nation's wealth. But in 1935, the Soviet Union, worried about the threat of fascism in Europe, instructed Communists throughout the world to join hands with non-Communist progressives in a "Popular Front" to advance the fortunes of the working class. Many radicals soon switched from opposing the New Deal to supporting its relief programs and support for labor unions.

Roosevelt won reelection in 1936 in a landslide and soon concluded that the economy was improving. He reduced government spending in 1937, triggering a sharp recession that undermined economic recovery and prolonged the depression.

The Election of 1936.
Roosevelt believed that the presidential election of 1936 would test his leadership and progressive ideals. The depression still had a stranglehold on the economy. Conservative leaders believed that the New Deal's failure to lift the nation out of the depression indicated that Americans were ready for a change. Left-wing critics insisted that the New Deal had missed the opportunity to displace capitalism with a socialist economy and that voters would embrace candidates who recommended more radical remedies.

Republicans turned to Kansas governor Alfred (Alf) Landon as their presidential nominee, a moderate who stressed mainstream Republican proposals to achieve a balanced federal budget and less government bureaucracy. Landon recommended that the perils of sickness and old age should be eased by old-fashioned neighborliness instead of a government program like Social Security.

Roosevelt put his faith in the growing New Deal coalition, whose members shared his conviction that the New Deal promised to liberate the nation from the long era of privilege and wealth for a few and "economic slavery" for the rest. He proclaimed that "the forces of selfishness and lust for power met their match" in his first term as president, and he hoped it would be said about his second term that "these forces met their master."

Roosevelt triumphed spectacularly. He won 60.8 percent of the popular vote, making it the widest margin of victory in a presidential election to date. Third parties — including the Socialist and Communist parties — fell pitifully short of the support they expected and never again mounted a significant challenge to the New Deal. Congressional results were equally lopsided, with Democrats outnumbering Republicans more than three to one in both houses. In his inaugural address, Roosevelt announced, "I see one third of a nation ill-housed, ill-clad, [and] ill-nourished," and he promised to devote his second term to alleviating their hardship.

Court Packing.
In the afterglow of his reelection triumph, Roosevelt pondered how to remove the remaining obstacles to New Deal reforms. He decided to target the Supreme Court. Conservative justices appointed by Republican presidents had invalidated eleven New Deal measures as unconstitutional interferences with free enterprise. Now, Social Security, the Wagner Act, the Securities and Exchange Commission, and other New Deal innovations were about to be considered by the justices.

To ensure that the Supreme Court did not dismantle the New Deal, Roosevelt proposed a **court-packing plan** that added one new justice for each existing judge who had served for ten years and was over the age of seventy. In effect, the proposed

court-packing plan
Law proposed by Franklin Roosevelt to add one new Supreme Court justice for each existing judge who had served for ten years and who was over the age of seventy. Roosevelt wanted to pack the Court with up to six New Dealers who could protect New Deal legislation, but the Senate defeated the bill in 1937.

law would give Roosevelt the power to pack the Court with up to six New Dealers who could outvote the elderly, conservative, Republican justices.

But the president had not reckoned with Americans' deeply rooted deference to the independent authority of the Supreme Court. More than two-thirds of Americans believed that the Court should be free from political interference. Even New Deal supporters were disturbed by the court-packing scheme. The suggestion that individuals over age seventy had diminished mental capacity offended many elderly members of Congress, which defeated Roosevelt's plan in 1937.

Supreme Court justices still got the message. The four most conservative of the elderly justices — the "four horsemen of reaction," according to one New Dealer — retired. Roosevelt eventually named eight justices to the Court — more than any other president — ultimately giving New Deal laws safe passage through the Court.

Reaction and Recession. Emboldened by their defeat of the court-packing plan, Republicans and southern Democrats rallied around their common conservatism to obstruct additional reforms. Former president Herbert Hoover proclaimed that the New Deal was the "repudiation of Democracy" and that "the Republican Party alone [was] the guardian of . . . the charter of freedom." Democrats' arguments over whether the New Deal needed to be expanded — and if so, how — undermined the consensus among reformers and sparked antagonism between Congress and the White House. The ominous rise of belligerent regimes in Germany, Italy, and Japan also slowed reform as some Americans began to worry more about defending the nation than changing it.

Roosevelt himself favored slowing the pace of the New Deal. He believed that existing New Deal measures had steadily boosted the economy and largely eliminated the depression crisis. In fact, the gross national product in 1937 briefly equaled the 1929 level before dropping lower for the rest of the decade. Unemployment declined to 14 percent in 1937 but quickly spiked upward and stayed higher until 1940. Roosevelt's unwarranted optimism about the economic recovery persuaded him that additional deficit spending by the federal government was no longer necessary.

Roosevelt's optimism failed to consider the stubborn realities of unemployment and poverty, and the reduction in deficit spending reversed the improving economy. Even at the high-water mark of recovery in the summer of 1937, seven million people lacked jobs. In the next few months, national income and production slipped so steeply that almost two-thirds of the economic gains since 1933 were lost by June 1938.

This economic reversal hurt the New Deal politically. Conservatives argued that this recession proved that New Deal measures produced only an illusion of progress. The way to weather the recession was to tax and spend less as well as to wait for the natural laws of supply and demand to restore prosperity. Many New Dealers insisted instead that the continuing depression demanded that Roosevelt revive federal spending and redouble efforts to stimulate the economy. In 1938, Congress heeded such pleas and enacted a massive new program of federal spending.

The recession scare of 1937–1938 taught the president the lesson that economic growth had to be carefully nurtured. The English economist John Maynard Keynes argued that only government intervention could pump enough money into the economy to restore prosperity, a concept that became known as Keynesian economics. Roosevelt never had the inclination or time to master Keynesian thought. But in a

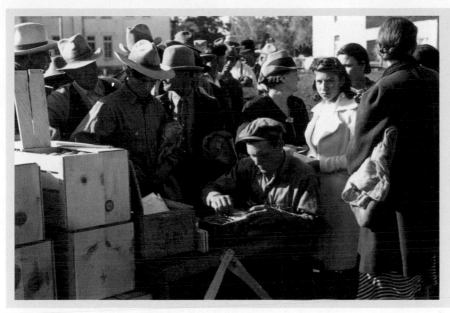

DISTRIBUTING SURPLUS FOOD TO THE NEEDY

When bountiful harvests produced surplus crops that would depress prices if they were sent to market, the New Deal arranged to distribute some of the surplus to needy Americans. Here, farmworkers in east-central Arizona near the New Mexico border line up to receive a ration of potatoes authorized by the New Deal agent checking the box of index cards. Library of Congress, 1a34185.

commonsense way, he understood that escape from the depression required a plan for large-scale spending to alleviate distress and stimulate economic growth (Figure 24.2).

The Last of the New Deal Reforms. From the moment he was sworn in, Roosevelt sought to expand the powers of the presidency. He believed that the president needed more authority to meet emergencies such as the depression and to administer the sprawling federal bureaucracy. Combined with a Democratic majority in Congress, a now-friendly Supreme Court, and the revival of deficit spending, the newly empowered White House seemed to be in a good position to move ahead with a revitalized New Deal.

Resistance to further reform was also on the rise, however. Conservatives argued that the New Deal had pressed government centralization too far. Even the New Deal's friends became weary of one emergency program after another while economic woes continued to shadow New Deal achievements. By the midpoint of Roosevelt's second term, restive members of Congress balked at new initiatives. But enough support remained for one last burst of reform.

Agriculture still had strong claims on New Deal attention in the face of drought, declining crop prices, and impoverished sharecroppers and tenants. In 1937, the Agriculture Department created the Farm Security Administration (FSA) to provide housing and loans to help tenant farmers become independent. A black tenant farmer in North Carolina who received an FSA loan told a New Deal interviewer, "I wake up in the night sometimes and think I must be half-dead and gone to heaven." For those who owned farms, the New Deal offered renewed prosperity with a second Agricultural Adjustment Act (AAA) in 1938, which placed production quotas on

FIGURE 24.2 GLOBAL COMPARISON: NATIONAL POPULATIONS AND ECONOMIES, CA. 1938

Throughout the Great Depression, the United States remained more productive than any other nation in the world. By 1938, the United States produced more than twice as much as its closest competitors, Germany and the USSR. If Germany had gained control of the other European nations listed here, it would have become the biggest economy in the world. What do these data suggest about the relationship between population and product?

	Population (millions)	Gross Domestic Product (millions of dollars)
United States		
Britain		
British Colonies		
France		
French Colonies		
Italy		
Italian Colonies		
Netherlands		
Dutch Colonies		
USSR		
Japan		
Japanese Colonies		
Germany		
Austria		
Czechoslovakia		
Poland		
Hungary		
Yugoslavia		
Romania		

= 10 million people
= 10 million dollars

cotton, tobacco, wheat, corn, and rice while issuing food stamps to allow poor people to obtain surplus food. The AAA of 1938 brought stability to American agriculture and ample food to most — but not all — tables.

Advocates for the urban poor also made modest gains after decades of neglect. New York senator Robert Wagner convinced Congress to pass the National Housing Act in 1937. By 1941, some 160,000 residences had been made available to poor people at affordable rents. The program did not come close to meeting the need for affordable housing, but for the first time the federal government took an active role in providing decent urban housing.

The last major piece of New Deal labor legislation, the Fair Labor Standards Act of June 1938, reiterated the New Deal pledge to provide workers with a decent standard of living. The new law set wage and hours standards and at long last curbed the use of child labor. The minimum-wage level was twenty-five cents an hour for a maximum of forty-four hours a week. To critics of the minimum wage law who said it was "government interference," one New Dealer responded, "It was. It interfered with the fellow running that pecan shelling plant . . . [and] told him he couldn't pay that little widow seven cents an hour." To attract enough conservative votes, the act exempted domestic help and farm laborers — relegating most women and African Americans to lower wages. Enforcement of the minimum-wage standards was weak and haphazard. Nevertheless, the Fair Labor Standards Act slowly advanced Roosevelt's inaugural promise to improve the living standards of the poorest Americans.

The final New Deal reform effort failed to make much headway against the hidebound system of racial injustice. Although Roosevelt denounced lynching as murder, he would not jeopardize his vital base of southern political support by demanding antilynching legislation, and Congress voted down attempts to make lynching a federal crime. Laws to eliminate the poll tax — used to deny blacks the opportunity to vote — encountered the same overwhelming resistance. The New Deal refused to confront racial injustice with the same vigor it brought to bear on economic hardship.

By the end of 1938, the New Deal had lost steam and encountered stiff opposition. In the congressional elections of 1938, Republicans made gains that gave them more congressional influence than they had enjoyed since 1932. New Dealers could claim unprecedented achievements since 1933, but nobody needed reminding that those achievements had not ended the depression. In his annual message to Congress in January 1939, Roosevelt signaled a halt to New Deal reforms by speaking about preserving the progress already achieved rather than extending it. Roosevelt pointed to the ominous threats posed by fascist aggressors in Germany and Japan, and he proposed defense expenditures that surpassed New Deal appropriations for relief and economic recovery.

REVIEW Why did political support for New Deal reforms decline?

Conclusion: Achievements and Limitations of the New Deal

The New Deal demonstrated that a growing majority of Americans agreed with Roosevelt that the federal government should help those in need. Through programs that sought relief, recovery, and reform, the New Deal vastly expanded the size and influence of the federal government and changed the way many Americans viewed Washington. New Dealers achieved significant victories, such as Social Security, labor's right to organize, and guarantees that farm prices would be maintained through controls on production and marketing. New Deal measures marked the emergence of a welfare state, but its limits left millions of needy Americans like Florence Owens and her children with little aid.

Full-scale relief, recovery, and reform eluded the New Deal. Even though millions of Americans benefited from New Deal initiatives, both relief and recovery were limited and temporary. In 1940, the depression still plagued the economy. Perhaps the most impressive achievement of the New Deal was what did not happen. Although authoritarian governments and anticapitalist policies were common outside the United States during the 1930s, they were shunned by the New Deal. The greatest economic crisis the nation had ever faced did not cause Americans to abandon democracy, as happened in Germany, where Adolf Hitler seized dictatorial power. Nor did the nation turn to radical alternatives such as socialism or communism.

Republicans and other conservatives claimed that the New Deal amounted to a form of socialism that threatened democracy and capitalism. But rather than attack capitalism, Franklin Roosevelt sought to save it. And he succeeded. That success also marked the limits of the New Deal's achievements. Franklin Roosevelt believed that a shift of authority toward the federal government would allow capitalist enterprises to be balanced by the nation's democratic tradition. The New Deal stopped far short of challenging capitalism either by undermining private property or by imposing strict national planning.

New Dealers repeatedly described their programs as a kind of warfare against the depression of the 1930s. In the next decade, the Roosevelt administration had to turn from the economic crisis at home to participate in a worldwide conflagration to defeat the enemies of democracy abroad.

Nonetheless, many New Deal reforms continued for decades to structure the basic institutions of banking, the stock market, union organizations, agricultural markets, Social Security, minimum-wage standards, and more. Opponents of these measures and of the basic New Deal notion of an activist government remained powerful, especially in the Republican Party. They claimed that government was the problem, not the solution — a slogan that Republicans championed during and after the 1980s and that led, with the cooperation of some Democrats, to the dismantling of a number of New Deal programs, including the regulation of banking. The deregulation of banking played a large role in the financial meltdown that began in 2008.

Chapter Review

KEY TERMS

New Deal coalition (p. 711)
underconsumption (p. 713)
Federal Deposit Insurance Corporation (FDIC) (p. 713)
fireside chats (p. 713)
Civilian Conservation Corps (CCC) (p. 715)
Agricultural Adjustment Act (AAA) (p. 716)

National Recovery Administration (NRA) (p. 718)
Works Progress Administration (WPA) (p. 723)
Wagner Act (p. 724)
Committee for Industrial Organization (CIO) (p. 725)
Social Security (p. 725)
court-packing plan (p. 731)

REVIEW QUESTIONS

❶ Why did Franklin D. Roosevelt win the 1932 presidential election by such a large margin?   (pp. 708–12)

❷ How did the New Dealers try to steer the nation toward recovery from the Great Depression?   (pp. 712–18)

❸ Why did groups at both ends of the political spectrum criticize the New Deal?   (pp. 718–22)

❹ What features of a welfare state did the New Deal create, and why? (pp. 722–30)

❺ Why did political support for New Deal reforms decline?   (pp. 730–35)

MAKING CONNECTIONS

❶ How did Roosevelt build an effective interregional political coalition for the Democratic Party? How did the coalition shape the policies of the New Deal?

❷ How effective were reform efforts targeting rural and industrial America?

❸ Were any of Roosevelt's critics able to influence the New Deal? If so, how?

❹ Who was in need of New Deal assistance but did not receive it? Why?

LINKING TO THE PAST

❶ To what degree did the New Deal reflect a continuation of the progressive movement of the late nineteenth and early twentieth centuries? In what ways did the New Deal depart from progressive ideals? In general, how new was the New Deal? (See chapters 21 and 22.)

❷ How did the New Deal coalition compare to the long-standing political coalition that had elected Republicans to the presidency since 1920? What accounted for the differences and similarities? (See chapter 23.)

25

The United States and the Second World War, 1939–1945

CONTENT LEARNING OBJECTIVES

After reading and studying this chapter, you should be able to:

- Describe the foreign policy dilemmas that confronted the United States during the interwar years.
- Explain which events led to the onset of war and why the United States became involved. Describe the United States' war mobilization efforts.
- Outline the crucial military and diplomatic events of 1941 through 1943, demonstrating how the United States turned the tide in the Pacific and explaining its prime military objectives in the European theater.
- Analyze the impact of the war on American society, including the effects it had on women and families, African Americans, and the 1944 presidential campaign.
- Assess which military and diplomatic events during 1943 to 1945 contributed to Allied victory in Europe and over Japan.

O n a sun-drenched Florida afternoon in 1927, twelve-year-old Paul Tibbets clambered into the front seat of the open cockpit of a biplane for his first airplane ride. While the pilot brought the plane in low over the Hialeah racetrack in Miami, Florida, Tibbets pitched Baby Ruth candy bars tethered to small paper parachutes to racing fans in the grandstands below. After repeating this stunt, sales of Baby Ruths soared, and Tibbets was hooked on flying.

In 1937, Tibbets joined the Army Air Corps and became a military pilot. Shortly after the Japanese attack on Pearl Harbor in December 1941 immediately

GI MAIL

Soldiers who engaged in deadly combat also stayed in touch with family and friends. The soldier who drew on this envelope emphasized that Uncle Sam was crushing the leaders of Germany and Japan. National Museum of American History, Smithsonian Institution, USA/Bridgeman Images.

overcame American isolationism and brought the United States into World War II, Tibbets flew antisubmarine patrols against German U-boats lurking along the East Coast. When heavily armored B-17 Flying Fortress bombers became available early in 1942, he took a squadron of the new planes to England. In August 1942, he led the first American daytime bombing raid on German-occupied Europe, releasing on railroad yards in northern France the first of some 700,000 tons of explosives dropped by American bombers during the air war in Europe.

After numerous raids over Europe, Tibbets was reassigned to the North African campaign. After eight months of combat missions, Tibbets returned to the United States and was ordered to test the new B-29 Super Fortress being built in Wichita, Kansas. The B-29 was much bigger than the B-17 and could fly higher and faster, making it ideal for the campaign against Japan. Tibbets's mastery of the B-29 caused him to be singled out in September 1944 to command a top-secret unit training for a special mission.

The mission was to be ready to drop on Japan a bomb so powerful that it might end the war. No such bomb yet existed, but American scientists and engineers were working around the clock to build one. In May 1945, Tibbets and his men went to Tinian Island in the Pacific, where they trained for their secret mission by flying raids over Japanese cities and dropping ordinary bombs. The atomic bomb arrived on Tinian on July 26, just ten days after a successful test explosion in the New Mexico desert. Nicknamed "Little Boy," the bomb packed the equivalent of 40 million pounds of TNT, or 200,000 of the 200-pound bombs Tibbets and other American airmen had dropped on Europe.

On August 6, 1945, Tibbets, his crew, and their atomic payload took off in the B-29 bomber *Enola Gay* and headed for Japan. Less than seven hours later, over the city of Hiroshima, Tibbets and his men released Little Boy from the *Enola Gay*'s bomb bay. Three days later, airmen from Tibbets's command dropped a second atomic bomb on Nagasaki, and within five days Japan surrendered.

Paul Tibbets's experiences traced an arc followed by millions of Americans during World War II. Like Tibbets, Americans joined their allies to fight the Axis powers in Europe and Asia. Like his *Enola Gay* crewmen — who hailed from New York, Texas, California,

CHRONOLOGY

1935–1937	Neutrality acts passed.
1936	Nazi Germany occupies Rhineland. Italian armies conquer Ethiopia. Spanish civil war begins.
1937	Japanese troops capture Nanjing.
1938	Hitler annexes Austria.
1939	German troops occupy Czechoslovakia. Nazi-Soviet nonaggression pact formed. Germany's attack on Poland begins World War II.
1940	Germany invades Denmark, Norway, France, Belgium, Luxembourg, and the Netherlands. British and French troops evacuate from Dunkirk. Battle of Britain fought. Tripartite Pact formed.
1941	Lend-Lease Act passes. Germany invades Soviet Union. Japanese attack Pearl Harbor.
1942	Japanese Americans moved to internment camps. Japan captures the Philippines. Congress of Racial Equality founded. Battles of Coral Sea and Midway fought. Manhattan Project begins. U.S. forces invade North Africa.
1943	Allied leaders demand unconditional surrender of Axis powers. U.S. and British forces invade Sicily.
1944	D Day executed.
1945	Yalta Conference held. Roosevelt dies; Vice President Harry Truman becomes president. Germany surrenders. United States joins United Nations. United States drops atomic bombs on Hiroshima and Nagasaki. Japan surrenders, ending World War II.

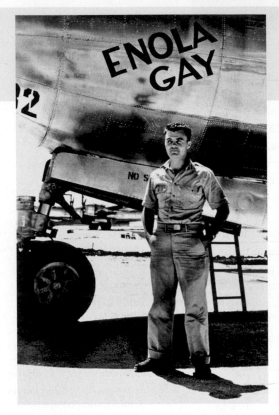

New Jersey, New Mexico, Maryland, North Carolina, Pennsylvania, Michigan, and Nevada — Americans from all regions united to help defeat the fascist aggressors in Asia and Europe. American industries mobilized to produce advanced bombers along with enough other military equipment to supply the American armed forces and their allies. At enormous cost in human life and suffering — including millions of civilians killed in military actions and millions more exterminated in the Holocaust of the Nazis' racist death camps — the war resulted in employment and prosperity to most Americans at home, ending the depression, providing new opportunities for women and African Americans, and ushering the nation into the postwar world as a triumphant economic and atomic superpower.

Peacetime Dilemmas

The First World War left a dangerous and ultimately deadly legacy. The victors — especially Britain, France, and the United States — sought to avoid future wars at almost any cost. The defeated nation, Germany, aspired to reassert its power and avenge its losses by means of renewed warfare. Italy and Japan felt humiliated by the Versailles peace settlement and saw war as a legitimate way to increase their global power. Japan invaded the northern Chinese province of Manchuria in 1931 with ambitions to expand throughout Asia. Italy, led by the fascist Benito Mussolini since 1922, hungered for an empire in Africa. In Germany, National Socialist Adolf Hitler rose to power in 1933 in a quest to dominate Europe and the world. These aggressive, militaristic, antidemocratic regimes seemed a smaller threat to most people in the United States during the 1930s than did the economic crisis at home. Shielded from external threats by the Atlantic and Pacific oceans, Americans hoped to avoid entanglement in foreign woes and to concentrate on climbing out of the nation's economic abyss.

Roosevelt and Reluctant Isolation. Like most Americans during the 1930s, Franklin Roosevelt believed that the nation's highest priority was to attack the domestic causes and consequences of the depression. But unlike most Americans, Roosevelt had long advocated an active role for the United States in international affairs.

The depression forced Roosevelt to retreat from his previous internationalism. He came to believe that energetic involvement in foreign affairs diverted resources and political support from domestic recovery. Once in office, Roosevelt sought to combine domestic economic recovery with a low-profile foreign policy that encouraged free trade and disarmament.

Roosevelt's pursuit of international amity was constrained by economic circumstances and American popular opinion. After an opinion poll demonstrated popular support for recognizing the Soviet Union — an international pariah since the Bolshevik Revolution in 1917 — Roosevelt established formal diplomatic relations in 1933. But when the League of Nations condemned Japanese and German aggression, Roosevelt did not support the league's attempts to keep the peace because he feared jeopardizing isolationists' support for New Deal measures in Congress. America watched from the sidelines when Japan withdrew from the league and ignored the limitations on its navy imposed after World War I. The United States also looked the other way when Hitler rearmed Germany and recalled its representative to the league in 1933. Roosevelt worried that German and Japanese actions threatened world peace, but he reassured Americans that the nation would not "use its armed forces for the settlement of any [international] dispute anywhere."

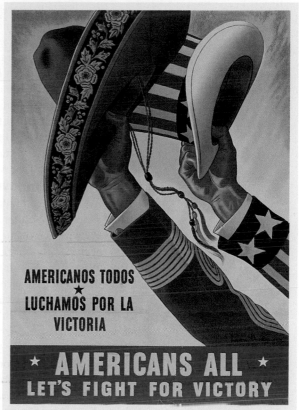

AMERICANOS TODOS
★
LUCHAMOS POR LA
VICTORIA

★ **AMERICANS ALL** ★
LET'S FIGHT FOR VICTORY

AMERICANS ALL
The good neighbor policy emphasized the common interests of the United States and its Latin American neighbors. One consequence of the policy is illustrated by this World War II poster, which asserts the shared goal of Uncle Sam and sombrero-wearing Latin Americans to defeat the Axis powers. Above all, the United States sought to prevent Latin American nations from allying with Germany or Japan. National Archives photo no. 513803.

The Good Neighbor Policy. In 1933, Roosevelt announced that the United States would pursue "the policy of the good neighbor" in international relations, which meant that no nation had the right to intervene in the internal or external affairs of another. He emphasized that this policy applied specifically to Latin America, where U.S. military forces had often intervened. The good neighbor policy did not indicate a U.S. retreat from empire in Latin America, though. Instead, it declared that, unlike in past decades, the United States would not depend on military force to exercise its influence in the region. Roosevelt refrained from sending troops to defend the interests of American corporations when Mexico nationalized American oil properties and revolution boiled over in Nicaragua, Guatemala, and Cuba during the 1930s. In 1934, Roosevelt withdrew American Marines from Haiti, where they had been stationed

good neighbor policy
Foreign policy announced by Franklin Roosevelt in 1933 that promised the United States would not interfere in the internal or external affairs of another country, thereby ending U.S. military interventions in Latin America.

since 1916. While Roosevelt's hands-off policy honored the principle of national self-determination, it also permitted the rise of dictators in Nicaragua, Cuba, and elsewhere, who exploited and terrorized their nations with private support from U.S. businesses.

Military nonintervention also did not prevent the United States from exerting its economic influence in Latin America. In 1934, Congress gave the president the power to reduce tariffs on goods imported into the United States from nations that agreed to lower their own tariffs on U.S. exports. By 1940, twenty-two nations had agreed to such reciprocal tariff reductions, helping to double U.S. exports to Latin America, contributing to the New Deal's goal of boosting the domestic economy through free trade, and planting seeds of friendship and hemispheric solidarity.

The Price of Noninvolvement. In Europe, fascist governments in Italy and Germany threatened military aggression. Britain and France made only verbal protests. Emboldened, Hitler plotted to avenge defeat in World War I by recapturing territories with German inhabitants, all the while accusing Jews of polluting the purity of the Aryan master race. The virulent anti-Semitism of Hitler and his Nazi Party unified non-Jewish Germans and attracted sympathizers among many other Europeans, even in France and Britain.

In Japan, a stridently militaristic government planned to follow the invasion of Manchuria in 1931 with conquests extending throughout Southeast Asia. The Manchurian invasion bogged down in a long and vicious war when Chinese Nationalists rallied around their leader, Jiang Jieshi (Chiang Kai-shek), to fight against the Japanese. Preparations for new Japanese conquests continued, however. In 1936, Japan openly violated naval limitation treaties and began to build a battle-ready fleet to seek naval superiority in the Pacific.

In the United States, the hostilities in Asia and Europe reinforced isolationist sentiments. Popular disillusionment with the failure of Woodrow Wilson's idealistic goals caused many Americans to question the nation's participation in World War I. In 1933, Gerald Nye, a Republican from North Dakota, chaired a Senate committee that concluded that greedy "merchants of death" — American weapons makers, bankers, and financiers — dragged the nation into the war to line their own pockets. International tensions and the Nye committee report prompted Congress to pass a series of **neutrality acts** between 1935 and 1937 designed to avoid entanglement in foreign wars. The neutrality acts prohibited making loans and selling arms to nations at war.

By 1937, the growing conflicts overseas caused some Americans to call for a total embargo on all trade with warring countries. The Neutrality Act of 1937 attempted to reconcile the nation's desire for both peace and foreign trade with a "cash-and-carry" policy that required warring nations to pay cash for nonmilitary goods and to transport them in their own ships. This policy benefited the nation's economy, but it also helped foreign aggressors by supplying them with goods and thereby undermining peace.

The desire for peace in France, Britain, and the United States led Germany, Italy, and Japan to launch offensives on the assumption that the Western democracies lacked the will to oppose them. In March 1936, Nazi troops marched into the industry-rich Rhineland on Germany's western border, in blatant violation of the Treaty of Versailles. One month later, Italian armies completed their conquest of Ethiopia, projecting fascist power into Africa. In December 1937, Japanese

neutrality acts
Legislation passed in 1935 and 1937 that sought to avoid entanglement in foreign wars while protecting trade. The 1937 act prohibited selling arms to nations at war and required nations to pay cash for nonmilitary goods and to transport them in their own ships.

invaders captured Nanjing (Nanking) and celebrated their triumph in the "Rape of Nanking," a deadly rampage that killed 200,000 Chinese civilians.

In Spain, a bitter civil war broke out in July 1936 when the Nationalists — fascist rebels led by General Francisco Franco — attacked the democratically elected Republican government. Both Germany and Italy reinforced Franco, while the Soviet Union provided much less aid to the Republican Loyalists. The Spanish civil war did not cause European democracies or the U.S. government to help the Loyalists, but more than 3,000 individual Americans enlisted in the Russian-sponsored Abraham Lincoln Brigade to fight alongside the Republicans. Abandoned by the Western nations, the Republican Loyalists were defeated in 1939, and Franco built a fascist bulwark in Spain.

Hostilities in Europe, Africa, and Asia alarmed Roosevelt and some Americans. The president sought to persuade most Americans to moderate their isolationism and find a way to support the victims of fascist aggression. He warned that an "epidemic of world lawlessness is spreading" and pointed out that "mere isolation or neutrality" offered no remedy. The popularity of isolationist sentiment caused Roosevelt to remark, "It's a terrible thing to look over your shoulder when you are trying to lead and find no one there." Roosevelt understood that he needed to maneuver carefully if the United States were to help prevent fascist aggressors from conquering Europe and Asia, leaving the United States an isolated island of democracy.

SPANISH CIVIL WAR, 1936–1939

> **REVIEW** Why did isolationism during the 1930s concern Roosevelt?

The Onset of War

Between 1939 and 1941, fascist victories overseas eventually eroded American isolationism. At first, U.S. intervention was limited to providing material support to the enemies of Germany and Japan, principally Britain, China, and the Soviet Union. But Japan's surprise attack on Pearl Harbor eliminated that restraint, and the nation began to mobilize for an all-out assault on foreign foes.

Nazi Aggression and War in Europe

Under the spell of isolationism, Americans passively watched Hitler's relentless campaign to dominate Europe (Map 25.1). In 1938, Hitler incorporated Austria into Germany and turned his attention to the Sudetenland, which had been granted to Czechoslovakia by the World War I peace settlement. Hoping to avoid war, British prime minister Neville Chamberlain offered Hitler terms of appeasement that would give the Sudetenland to Germany if Hitler agreed to leave the rest of Czechoslovakia alone. Hitler accepted the terms but did not keep his promise. By 1939, Hitler had annexed Czechoslovakia and demanded that Poland return the German territory it had gained after World War I. Recognizing that appeasement of Hitler had failed, Britain and France assured Poland that they would go to war with Germany if Hitler attacked. In turn, Hitler negotiated with his

appeasement
British strategy aimed at avoiding a war with Germany in the late 1930s by not objecting to Hitler's policy of territorial expansion.

MAP 25.1   AXIS AGGRESSION THROUGH 1941

Through a series of surprise strikes before 1942, Mussolini sought to re-create the Roman empire in the Mediterranean while Hitler aimed to annex Austria and reclaim German territories occupied by France after World War I. World War II broke out when the German dictator attacked Poland.

bitter enemy, Soviet premier Joseph Stalin, offering him concessions to prevent the Soviet Union from joining Britain and France in opposing a German attack on Poland. Despite the enduring hatred between fascist Germany and the Communist Soviet Union, the two powers signed the Nazi-Soviet treaty of nonaggression in August 1939, exposing Poland to an onslaught by both the German and Soviet armies.

At dawn on September 1, 1939, Hitler unleashed his *blitzkrieg* (literally, "lightning war") on Poland. "Act brutally!" Hitler exhorted his generals. "Send [every] man, woman, and child of Polish descent and language to their deaths, pitilessly and remorselessly." The attack triggered Soviet attacks on eastern Poland and declarations of war from France and Britain two days later, igniting a conflagration that raced around the globe. In September 1939, Germany seemed invincible, causing many people to fear that all of Europe would soon share Poland's fate.

After the Nazis overran Poland, Hitler soon launched a westward blitzkrieg. In the first six months of 1940, German forces smashed through Denmark, Norway, the Netherlands, Belgium, and France. The speed of the German attack trapped more than 300,000 British and French soldiers, who retreated to the port of Dunkirk, where an improvised armada of British vessels ferried them to safety across the English Channel. By mid-June 1940, France had surrendered the largest army in the world, signed an armistice that gave Germany control of nearly two-thirds of the countryside, and installed a collaborationist government at Vichy. With an empire that stretched across Europe from Poland to France, Hitler seemed poised to attack Britain.

The new British prime minister, Winston Churchill, vowed that Britain, unlike France, would never surrender to Hitler. "We shall fight on the seas and oceans [and] . . . in the air," he proclaimed, "whatever the cost may be, we shall fight on the beaches, . . . and in the fields and in the streets." Churchill's defiance stiffened British resolve against Hitler's attack, which began in mid-June 1940 when wave after wave of German bombers targeted British military installations and cities, killing tens of thousands of civilians. The outgunned Royal Air Force fought as doggedly as Churchill had predicted and finally won the Battle of Britain by November, clearing German bombers from British skies and handing Hitler his first defeat. Churchill praised the valiant British pilots, declaring that "never . . . was so much owed by so many to so few." Advance knowledge of German plans aided British pilots, who had access to the new technology of radar and to decoded top-secret German military communications. Battered and exhausted by German attacks, Britain needed American help to continue to fight, as Churchill repeatedly wrote Roosevelt in private.

From Neutrality to the Arsenal of Democracy. Most Americans condemned German aggression and favored Britain and France, but isolationism remained powerful. Roosevelt feared that if Congress did not repeal the arms embargo mandated by the Neutrality Act of 1937, France and Britain would soon succumb to the Nazi onslaught. "What worries me," Roosevelt wrote a friend, "is that public opinion . . . is patting itself on the back every morning and thanking God for the Atlantic Ocean (and the Pacific Ocean)" and underestimating "the serious implications" of the European war "for our own future." Congress agreed in November 1939 to allow belligerent nations to buy arms, as well as nonmilitary supplies, on a cash-and-carry basis.

In practice, the revised neutrality law permitted Britain and France to purchase American war materiel and carry it across the Atlantic in their own ships, thereby shielding American vessels from attack by German submarines lurking in the Atlantic. Roosevelt searched for a way to aid Britain short of entering a formal alliance or declaring war against Germany. Churchill pleaded for American destroyers, aircraft, and munitions, but he had no money to buy them under the prevailing cash-and-carry neutrality law. By late summer in 1940, as the Battle of Britain raged, Roosevelt concocted a scheme to deliver fifty old destroyers to Britain in exchange for American access to British bases in the Western Hemisphere, the first steps toward building a firm Anglo-American alliance against Hitler.

While German Luftwaffe (air force) pilots bombed Britain, Roosevelt decided to run for an unprecedented third term as president in 1940. But the presidential election, which Roosevelt won handily, provided no clear mandate for American involvement in the European war. The Republican candidate, Wendell Willkie, ridiculed by New Dealers as a "simple, barefoot Wall Street lawyer," attacked Roosevelt as a warmonger. Willkie's accusations caused the president to promise voters, "Your boys are not going to be sent into any foreign wars," a pledge counterbalanced by his repeated warnings about the threats to America posed by Nazi aggression.

Once reelected, Roosevelt maneuvered to support Britain in every way short of war. In a fireside chat shortly after Christmas 1940, he proclaimed that it was incumbent on the United States to become "the great arsenal of democracy" and send "every ounce and every ton of munitions and supplies that we can possibly spare to help the defenders who are in the front lines."

Lend-Lease Act
Legislation in 1941 that enabled Britain to obtain arms from the United States without cash but with the promise to reimburse the United States when the war ended. The act reflected Roosevelt's desire to assist the British in any way possible, short of war.

In January 1941, Roosevelt proposed the **Lend-Lease Act**, which allowed the British to obtain arms from the United States without paying cash but with the promise to reimburse the United States when the war ended. The purpose of Lend-Lease, Roosevelt proclaimed, was to defend democracy and human rights throughout the world, specifically the Four Freedoms: "freedom of speech and expression . . . freedom of every person to worship God in his own way . . . freedom from want . . . [and] freedom from fear." Isolationist opponents accused Roosevelt of concocting a "Triple A foreign policy" that would lead to war and "plow under every fourth American boy." Fiercely debated but approved by Congress, Lend-Lease started a flow of support to Britain that totaled more than $50 billion during the war, far more than all federal expenditures combined since Roosevelt had become president in 1933.

Stymied in his plans for an invasion of England, Hitler turned his massive army eastward and on June 22, 1941, sprang a surprise attack on the Soviet Union, his ally in the 1939 Nazi-Soviet nonaggression pact. Neither Roosevelt nor Churchill had any love for Joseph Stalin or communism, but they both welcomed the Soviet Union to the anti-Nazi cause. Both Western leaders understood that Hitler's attack on Russia would provide relief for the hard-pressed British. Roosevelt quickly persuaded Congress to extend Lend-Lease to the Soviet Union, beginning the shipment of millions of tons of trucks, jeeps, and other equipment that, in all, supplied about 10 percent of Russian war materiel.

As Hitler's Wehrmacht raced across the Russian plains and Nazi U-boats tried to choke off supplies to Britain and the Soviet Union, Roosevelt met with Churchill aboard a ship near Newfoundland to cement the Anglo-American alliance. In August 1941, the two leaders issued the Atlantic Charter, pledging the two nations to freedom of the seas and free trade as well as the right of national self-determination.

Japan Attacks America. Although the likelihood of war with Germany preoccupied Roosevelt, Hitler exercised a measure of restraint in directly provoking America. Japanese ambitions in Asia clashed more openly with American interests and commitments, especially in China and the Philippines. And unlike Hitler, the Japanese high command planned to attack the United States in order to pursue Japan's aspirations to rule an Asian empire it termed the Greater East Asia Co-Prosperity Sphere. Appealing to widespread Asian bitterness toward such white colonial powers as the British in India and Burma, the French in Indochina (now Vietnam), and the Dutch in the East Indies (now Indonesia), the Japanese campaigned to preserve "Asia for the Asians." Japan's invasion of China — which had lasted for ten years by 1941 — proved that its true goal was Asia for the Japanese (Map 25.2). Japan coveted the raw materials available from China and

MAP 25.2   JAPANESE AGGRESSION THROUGH 1941

Beginning with the invasion of Manchuria in 1931, Japan sought to extend its imperialist control over most of East Asia. Japanese aggression was driven by the need for raw materials for the country's expanding industries and by the military government's devotion to martial honor.

BOMBING OF PEARL
HARBOR, DECEMBER 7, 1941

Southeast Asia, and it ignored American demands to stop its campaign of aggression.

In 1940, Japan signaled a new phase of its imperial designs by entering a defensive alliance with Germany and Italy — the Tripartite Pact. To thwart Japanese plans to invade the Dutch East Indies, in July 1941 Roosevelt announced a trade embargo that denied Japan access to oil, scrap iron, and other goods essential for its war machines. Roosevelt hoped the embargo would strengthen factions within Japan that opposed the militarists.

Instead, the American embargo played into the hands of Japanese militarists headed by General Hideki Tojo, who seized control of the government in October 1941 and persuaded other leaders, including Emperor Hirohito, that swift destruction of American naval bases in the Pacific would leave Japan free to follow its destiny. On December 7, 1941, 183 aircraft lifted off six Japanese carriers and attacked the U.S. Pacific Fleet at Pearl Harbor on the Hawai'ian island of Oahu. The devastating surprise attack sank all of the fleet's battleships, killed more than 2,400 Americans, and almost crippled U.S. war-making capacity in the Pacific. Luckily for the United States, Japanese pilots failed to destroy oil storage facilities at Pearl Harbor or any of the nation's aircraft carriers, which happened to be at sea during the attack.

The Japanese scored a stunning tactical victory at Pearl Harbor, but in the long run the attack proved a colossal blunder. The victory made many Japanese commanders overconfident about their military prowess. Worse for the Japanese, Americans instantly united in their desire to fight and avenge the attack. Roosevelt vowed that "this form of treachery shall never endanger us again." On December 8,

PEARL HARBOR ATTACK

A Japanese photographer took this picture just as the attack on Pearl Harbor began. A torpedo has exploded into the American battleship *West Virginia*, causing the huge plume of water and smoke. Other ships have already been torpedoed and are listing. Two Japanese aircraft can be seen in the upper right quadrant of the picture, while Japanese submarines are invisible beneath the surface of the water. U.S. Naval History and Heritage Command Photograph.

Congress endorsed the president's call for a declaration of war. Both Hitler and Mussolini declared war against America on December 11, bringing the United States into all-out war with the Axis powers in both Europe and Asia.

> **REVIEW** How did Roosevelt attempt to balance American isolationism with the military aggression of Germany and Japan in the late 1930s and early 1940s?

Mobilizing for War

The time had come, Roosevelt announced, for the prescriptions of "Dr. New Deal" to be replaced by the stronger medicines of "Dr. Win-the-War." Military and civilian leaders rushed to secure the nation against possible attacks, causing Americans with Japanese ancestry to be stigmatized and sent to internment camps. Roosevelt and his advisers lost no time enlisting millions of Americans in the armed forces to bring the isolationist-era military to fighting strength for a two-front war. The war emergency also required economic mobilization unparalleled in the nation's history. As Dr. Win-the-War, Roosevelt set aside the New Deal goal of reform and plunged headlong into transforming the American economy into the world's greatest military machine, thereby achieving full employment and economic recovery, goals that had eluded the New Deal.

Home-Front Security. Shortly after declaring war against the United States, Hitler dispatched German submarines to hunt American ships along the Atlantic coast, where Paul Tibbets and other American pilots tried to destroy them. The U-boats had devastating success for about eight months, sinking hundreds of U.S. ships and threatening to disrupt the Lend-Lease lifeline to Britain and the Soviet Union. But by mid-1942, the U.S. Navy had chased German submarines into the mid-Atlantic.

Within the continental United States, Americans remained sheltered from the chaos and destruction the war brought to hundreds of millions in Europe and Asia. Nevertheless, the government worried constantly about espionage and internal subversion. Posters warned Americans that "Loose lips sink ships" and "Enemy agents are always near; if you don't talk, they won't hear." The campaign for patriotic vigilance focused on German and Japanese foes, but Americans of Japanese descent became targets of official and popular persecution because of Pearl Harbor and long-standing racial prejudice against people of Asian descent.

About 320,000 people of Japanese ancestry lived in U.S. territory in 1941, two-thirds of them in Hawai'i, where they largely escaped wartime persecution because they were essential and valued members of society. On the mainland, however, Japanese Americans were a tiny minority — even along the West Coast, where most of them worked on farms and in small businesses. Although an official military survey concluded that Japanese Americans posed no danger, popular hostility fueled a campaign to round up all mainland Japanese Americans — two-thirds of them U.S. citizens. "A Jap's a Jap. . . . It makes no difference whether he is an American citizen or not," one official declared.

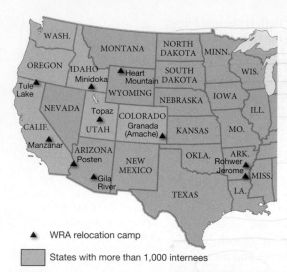

▲ WRA relocation camp

States with more than 1,000 internees

MAP 25.3 WESTERN RELOCATION AUTHORITY CENTERS

Responding to prejudice and fear of sabotage, President Roosevelt authorized the relocation of all Americans of Japanese descent in 1942. Taken from their homes in the cities and farmland of the far West, more than 120,000 Japanese Americans were confined in camps scattered as far east as the Mississippi River.

internment camps
Makeshift prison camps, to which Americans of Japanese descent were sent as a result of Roosevelt's Executive Order 9066, issued in February 1942. In 1944, the Supreme Court upheld this blatant violation of constitutional rights as a "military necessity."

Selective Service Act
Law enacted in 1940 requiring all men who would be eligible for a military draft to register in preparation for the possibility of a future conflict. The act also prohibited discrimination based on "race or color."

On February 19, 1942, Roosevelt issued Executive Order 9066, which authorized sending all Americans of Japanese descent to ten makeshift **internment camps** located in remote areas of the West and South (Map 25.3). Allowed little time to sell or secure their properties, Japanese Americans lost homes and businesses worth about $400 million and lived out the war penned in by barbed wire and armed guards. Although several thousand Japanese Americans served with distinction in the U.S. armed forces and no case of subversion by a Japanese American was ever uncovered, the Supreme Court, in its 1944 *Korematsu* decision, upheld Executive Order 9066's blatant violation of constitutional rights as justified by "military necessity."

Building a Citizen Army. In 1940, Roosevelt encouraged Congress to pass the **Selective Service Act** to register men of military age who would be subject to a draft if the need arose. More than 6,000 local draft boards registered more than 30 million men and, when the war came, rapidly inducted them into military service. In all, more than 16 million men and women served in uniform during the war, two-thirds of them draftees, mostly young men. Women were barred from combat duty, but they worked at nearly every noncombatant task, eroding traditional barriers to women's military service.

The Selective Service Act prohibited discrimination "on account of race or color," and almost a million African American men and women donned uniforms, as did half a million Mexican Americans, 25,000 Native Americans, and 13,000 Chinese Americans. The racial insults and discrimination suffered by all people of color made some soldiers ask, as a Mexican American GI did on his way to the European front, "Why fight for America when you have not been treated as an American?" Only black Americans were trained in segregated camps, confined in segregated barracks, and assigned to segregated units.

Most black Americans were consigned to manual labor, and relatively few served in combat until late in 1944, when the need for military manpower in Europe intensified. Then, as General George Patton told black soldiers in a tank unit in Normandy, "I don't care what color you are, so long as you go up there and kill those Kraut sonsabitches."

Homosexuals also served in the armed forces, although in much smaller numbers than black Americans. Allowed to serve as long as their sexual preferences remained covert, gay Americans, like other minorities, sought to demonstrate their worth under fire. "I was superpatriotic," a gay combat veteran recalled. Another gay GI remarked, "Who in the hell is going to worry about [homosexuality]" in the midst of the life-or-death realities of war?

Conversion to a War Economy. In 1940, the American economy remained mired in the depression. Nearly one worker in seven was still unemployed, factories operated far below their productive capacity, and the total federal budget was less than $10 billion. Shortly after the attack on Pearl Harbor, Roosevelt announced the goal of converting the economy to produce "overwhelming . . . , crushing superiority of equipment in any theater of the world war." Factories were converted to assembling tanks and airplanes, and production soared to record levels. By the end of the war, jobs exceeded workers, plants operated at full capacity, and the federal budget topped $100 billion.

To organize and oversee this tidal wave of military production, Roosevelt called upon business leaders to come to Washington and, for the token payment of a dollar a year, head new government agencies such as the War Production Board, which set production priorities and pushed for maximum output. Contracts flowed to large corporations, often on a basis that guaranteed their profits. During the first half of 1942, the government issued contracts worth more than the entire gross national product in 1941.

Booming wartime employment swelled union membership. To speed production, the government asked unions to pledge not to strike. Despite the relentless pace of work, union members mostly kept their no-strike pledge, with the important exception of members of the United Mine Workers, who walked out of the coal mines in 1943, demanding a pay hike and earning the enmity of many Americans.

Overall, conversion to war production achieved Roosevelt's ambitious goal of "crushing superiority" in military goods. At a total cost of $304 billion (equivalent to about $4 trillion today) during the war, the nation produced an avalanche of military equipment, more than double the combined production of Germany, Japan, and

FIGURE 25.1 GLOBAL COMPARISON: WEAPONS PRODUCTION BY THE AXIS AND ALLIED POWERS DURING WORLD WAR II

U.S. weapons dominated the air and the sea during World War II. Together, the three Allied powers produced about three times as many aircraft and five to eight times as many warships as the two Axis powers. The Soviet Union led the other Allies in the production of tanks and artillery. What does the chronology of weapons production suggest about the kind of warfare emphasized by each belligerent nation and the course of the war?

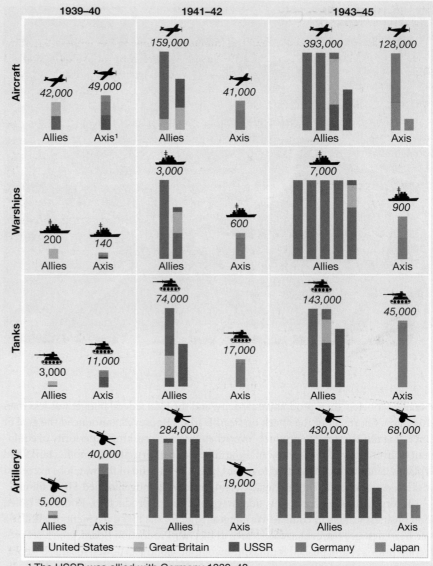

¹ The USSR was allied with Germany 1939–40.
² No reliable data exist for Japan.

Italy (Figure 25.1). This outpouring of military goods supplied not only U.S. forces but also America's allies, giving tangible meaning to Roosevelt's pledge to make America the "arsenal of democracy."

REVIEW How did the Roosevelt administration mobilize the human and industrial resources necessary to fight a two-front war?

Fighting Back

The United States confronted a daunting military challenge in December 1941. The attack on Pearl Harbor destroyed much of its Pacific Fleet. In the Atlantic, Hitler's U-boats sank American ships, while German armies occupied most of western Europe and relentlessly advanced eastward into the Soviet Union. Roosevelt and his military advisers believed that defeating Germany took top priority. To achieve that victory required preventing Hitler from defeating America's allies, Britain and the Soviet Union. If they fell, Hitler would command all the resources of Europe in a probable assault on the United States. To fight back effectively against Germany and Japan, the United States had to coordinate military and political strategy with its allies and muster all its human and economic assets. Victory over the Japanese fleet at the Battle of Midway, the successful elimination of Germany's menace to Allied shipping in the prolonged Battle of the Atlantic, and the Allied assault on North Africa and then Italy established Allied naval superiority in the Atlantic and Pacific and began to challenge German domination of southern Europe.

Turning the Tide in the Pacific. In the Pacific theater, Japan's leading military strategist, Admiral Isoroku Yamamoto, believed that if his forces did not quickly conquer and secure the territories they targeted, Japan would eventually lose the war because of America's far greater resources. Swiftly, the Japanese assaulted American airfields in the Philippines and captured U.S. outposts on Guam and Wake Island. After capturing Singapore and Burma, Japan sought to complete its domination of the southern Pacific with an attack in January 1942 on the American stronghold in the Philippines (Map 25.5). American defenders surrendered to the Japanese in May. The Japanese victors sent captured American and Filipino soldiers on the infamous Bataan Death March to a concentration camp, causing thousands to die. By the summer of 1942, the Japanese had conquered the Dutch East Indies and were poised to strike Australia and New Zealand.

In the spring of 1942, U.S. forces launched a major two-pronged counteroffensive that military officials hoped would reverse Japanese advances. Forces led by General Douglas MacArthur, commander of the U.S. armed forces in the Pacific theater, moved north from Australia and eventually attacked the Japanese in the Philippines. Far more decisively, Admiral Chester W. Nimitz sailed his battle fleet west from Hawai'i to retake Japanese-held islands in the southern and mid-Pacific. On May 7–8, 1942, in the Coral Sea just north of Australia, the American fleet and carrier-based warplanes defeated a Japanese armada that was sailing around the coast of New Guinea.

Nimitz then learned from an intelligence intercept that the Japanese were massing an invasion force aimed at Midway Island, an outpost guarding the Hawai'ian Islands. Nimitz maneuvered his carriers and cruisers to surprise the Japanese at the Battle of Midway. In a furious battle that raged on June 3–6, American ships and planes delivered a devastating blow to the Japanese navy. The **Battle of Midway** reversed the balance of naval power in the Pacific and put the Japanese at a disadvantage for the rest of the war. Japan managed to build only six more large aircraft carriers during the war, while the United States launched dozens, proving the wisdom of Yamamoto's prediction. But the Japanese still occupied and defended the many places they had conquered.

Battle of Midway
June 3–6, 1942, naval battle in the Central Pacific in which American forces surprised and defeated the Japanese who had been massing an invasion force aimed at Midway Island. The battle put the Japanese at a disadvantage for the rest of the war.

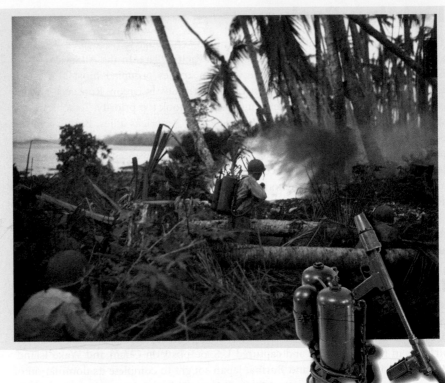

FLAMETHROWER IN COMBAT IN THE SOLOMON ISLANDS

American soldiers used flamethrowers in both the Pacific and European theaters. They were especially effective against enemy soldiers dug into bunkers that were difficult to penetrate by rifle or machine-gun fire. The Marine shown here, fighting in the Solomon Islands in 1943, carried on his back canisters of jellied gasoline and compressed air that were combined and projected through the gunlike machine. Soldiers: National Archives photo no. 111-SC-233458; flamethrower: National Museum of American History, Smithsonian Institution, USA/Bridgeman Images.

The Campaign in Europe. After Pearl Harbor, Hitler's eastern-front armies marched ever deeper into the Soviet Union while his western-front forces prepared to invade Britain. As in World War I, the Germans attempted to starve the British into submission by destroying their seaborne lifeline. In 1941 and 1942, they sank Allied ships faster than new ones could be built. Overall, the U-boat campaign sank 4,700 merchant vessels and almost 200 warships and killed 40,000 Allied seamen.

Until mid-1943, the outcome of the war in the Atlantic remained in doubt. Then, newly invented radar detectors and production of sufficient destroyer escorts for merchant vessels allowed the Allies to prey upon the lurking U-boats. After suffering a 75 percent casualty rate among U-boat crews, Hitler withdrew German submarines from the North Atlantic in late May 1943, allowing thousands of American supply ships to cross the Atlantic unimpeded. Winning the Battle of the Atlantic allowed the United States to continue to supply its British and Soviet allies for the duration of the war and to reduce the imminent threat of a German invasion of Britain.

The most important strategic questions confronting the United States and its allies were when and where to open a second front against the Nazis. Stalin demanded that America and Britain mount an immediate and massive assault across the English Channel into western France to force Hitler to divert his armies from the eastern front and relieve the pressure on the Soviet Union. Churchill and Roosevelt instead delayed opening a second front, allowing the Germans and the Soviets to slug it out. This drawn-out conflict weakened both the Nazis and the Communists and made an eventual Allied attack on western France more likely to succeed. Churchill and Roosevelt decided to strike first in North Africa to help secure Allied control of the Mediterranean.

In October and November 1942, British forces at El-Alamein in Egypt halted German general Erwin Rommel's drive to capture the Suez Canal, Britain's lifeline to the oil of the Middle East and to British colonies in India and South Asia (Map 25.4). In November, an American army under General Dwight D. Eisenhower landed far to the west, in French Morocco. Propelled by American tank units commanded by General George Patton, the Allied armies defeated the Germans in North Africa in

NORTH AFRICAN CAMPAIGN

The Allied campaign to clear Axis forces from North Africa involved highly mobile tanks on both sides. Here relatively fast-moving American M-10 tank destroyers — widely used during World War II — roll through a Tunisian village in 1943. The open tops gave crewmen excellent visibility to spot enemy forces but also made them vulnerable to attack. Corbis.

May 1943. The North African campaign pushed the Germans out of Africa, made the Mediterranean safe for Allied shipping, and opened the door for an Allied invasion of Italy.

In January 1943, while the North African campaign was still under way, Roosevelt and Churchill met in Casablanca and announced that they would accept nothing less than the "unconditional surrender" of the Axis powers, ruling out peace negotiations. They concluded that they should capitalize on their success in North Africa and strike against Italy, consigning the Soviet Union to continue to bear the brunt of the Nazi war machine.

In July 1943, American and British forces landed in Sicily. Soon afterward, Mussolini was deposed in Italy, ending the reign of Italian fascism. Quickly, the Allies invaded the mainland, and the Italian government surrendered unconditionally. The Germans responded by rushing reinforcements to Italy, turning the Allies' Italian campaign into a series of battles to liberate Italy from German occupation.

German troops dug into strong fortifications and fought to defend every inch of Italy's rugged terrain. Allied forces continued to battle against stubborn German defenses for the remainder of the war, making the Italian campaign the war's deadliest for American infantrymen. One soldier wrote that his buddies "died like butchered swine."

REVIEW How did the United States seek to counter the Japanese in the Pacific and the Germans in Europe?

The Wartime Home Front

The war effort mobilized Americans as never before. Factories churned out ever more bombs, bullets, tanks, ships, and airplanes, which workers rushed to assemble, leaving their farms and small towns and congregating in cities. Women took jobs with wrenches and welding torches, boosting the nation's workforce and violating traditional notions that a woman's place was in the home rather than on the assembly line. Despite rationing and shortages, unprecedented government expenditures for war production brought prosperity to many Americans after years of depression-era poverty. Although Americans in uniform risked their lives on battlefields in Europe and Asia, Americans on the U.S. mainland enjoyed complete immunity from foreign attack — in sharp contrast to their Soviet and British allies. The wartime ideology that contrasted Allied support for human rights with Axis tyranny provided justification for the many sacrifices Americans were required to make in support of the military effort. It also established a standard of basic human equality that became a potent weapon in the campaign for equal rights at home and in condemning atrocities such as the Holocaust perpetrated by the Nazis.

Women and Families, Guns and Butter. Millions of American women gladly took their places on assembly lines in defense industries. At the start of the war, about a quarter of adult women worked outside the home, but few women worked in factories, except for textile mills and sewing industries. But wartime mobilization of the economy and the enlistment of millions of men in the armed forces left factories begging for women workers.

Government advertisements urged women to take industrial jobs by assuring them that their household chores had prepared them for work on the "Victory Line." One billboard proclaimed, "If you've sewed buttons, or made buttonholes, on a [sewing] machine, you can learn to do spot welding on airplane parts." Millions of women responded. Advertisers often referred to a woman who worked in a war industry as "Rosie the Riveter," a popular wartime term. By the end of the war, women working outside the home numbered 50 percent more than in 1939. Contributing to the war effort also paid off in wages. A Kentucky woman remembered her job at a munitions plant, where she earned "the fabulous sum of $32 a week. To us it was an absolute miracle. Before that we made nothing." Although men were paid an average of $54 for comparable wartime work, women accepted the pay differential and welcomed their chance to earn wages and help win the war at the same time.

The majority of married women remained at home, occupied with domestic chores and child care. But they, too, supported the war effort, planting Victory Gardens, saving tin cans and newspapers for recycling into war materiel, and buying war bonds. Many families scrimped to cope with the 30 percent inflation during the war, but men and women in manufacturing industries enjoyed wages that grew twice as fast as inflation.

The war influenced how all families spent their earnings. Buying a new washing machine or car was out of the question since factories that formerly built them now made military goods. Many other consumer goods — such as tires, gasoline, shoes, and meat — were rationed at home to meet military needs overseas. But most

Americans readily found things to buy, including movie tickets, cosmetics, and music recordings.

The wartime prosperity and abundance enjoyed by most Americans contrasted with the experiences of their hard-pressed allies. Personal consumption fell by 22 percent in Britain, and food output plummeted to just one-third of prewar levels in the Soviet Union, creating widespread hunger and even starvation. Few went hungry in the United States as farm output grew 25 percent annually during the war, providing a cornucopia of food for export to the Allies.

The Double V Campaign.

Fighting against Nazi Germany and its ideology of Aryan racial supremacy, Americans confronted extensive racial prejudice in their own country. The *Pittsburgh Courier*, a leading black newspaper, asserted that the

Visual Activity

RIVETING ROSIES

Dora Miles (left) and Dorothy Johnson (right) were among the millions of women (nicknamed "Rosie the Riveter") who flocked to work in war industries at jobs formerly held by men. Like many other women war workers, Miles and Johnson helped build airplanes. Here they are depicted riveting the frame of an aircraft at a plant in Long Beach, California. Library of Congress, 8e01288.

READING THE IMAGE: How does the work Miles and Johnson are doing compare to the conventional work routines of women before the war? What does the photo suggest about the relationship between Miles (driving the rivet into a hole) and Johnson (smashing the end of the rivet snug against the airframe)?

CONNECTIONS: What contributions did American women make to the war effort?

Double V campaign

World War II campaign in America to attack racism at home and abroad. The campaign pushed the federal government to require defense contractors to integrate their workforces. In response, Franklin Roosevelt authorized a committee to investigate and prevent racial discrimination in employment.

wartime emergency called for a **Double V campaign** seeking "victory over our enemies at home and victory over our enemies on the battlefields abroad." As a Mississippi-born African American combat veteran of the Pacific theater recalled, "We had two wars to fight: prejudice . . . and those Japs."

In 1941, black organizations demanded that the federal government require companies receiving defense contracts to integrate their workforces. A. Philip Randolph, head of the Brotherhood of Sleeping Car Porters, promised that 100,000 African American marchers would descend on Washington if the president did not eliminate discrimination in defense industries. Roosevelt decided to risk offending his white allies in the South and in unions, and he issued Executive Order 8802 in mid-1941. It authorized the Committee on Fair Employment Practices to investigate and prevent racial discrimination in employment.

Progress came slowly, however. In 1940, nine out of ten black Americans lived below the federal poverty line, and those who worked earned an average of just 39 percent of whites' wages. In search of better jobs and living conditions, 5.5 million black Americans migrated from the South to centers of industrial production in the North and West, making a majority of African Americans city dwellers for the first time in U.S. history. Severe labor shortages and government fair employment standards opened assembly-line jobs in defense plants to African Americans, causing black unemployment to drop by 80 percent during the war. But more jobs did not mean equal pay for blacks. The average income of black families rose during the war, but by the end of the conflict it still stood at only half of what white families earned.

Blacks' migration to defense jobs intensified racial antagonisms, which boiled over in the hot summer of 1943, when 242 race riots erupted in 47 cities. The worst mayhem occurred in Detroit, where a long-simmering conflict between whites and blacks over racially segregated housing ignited into a race war. In two days of violence, twenty-five blacks and nine whites were killed, and scores more were injured.

Racial violence created the impetus for the Double V campaign, officially supported by the National Association for the Advancement of Colored People (NAACP), which asserted black Americans' demands for the rights and privileges enjoyed by all other Americans — demands reinforced by the Allies' wartime ideology of freedom and democracy. While the NAACP focused on court challenges to segregation, a new organization founded in 1942, the Congress of Racial Equality, organized picketing and sit-ins against racially segregated restaurants and theaters. Still, the Double V campaign achieved only limited success against racial discrimination during the war.

GI Bill of Rights

Legislation passed in 1944 authorizing the government to provide World War II veterans with funds for education, housing, and health care, as well as loans to start businesses and buy homes.

Wartime Politics and the 1944 Election.
Americans rallied around the war effort in unprecedented unity. In June 1944, Congress recognized the sacrifices made by millions of veterans and unanimously passed the landmark **GI Bill of Rights,** which gave military veterans government funds for education, housing, and health care, as well as providing loans to start businesses and buy homes. The GI Bill put the financial resources of the federal government behind the abstract goals of

freedom and democracy for which veterans were fighting, and it empowered millions of GIs to better themselves and their families after the war.

After twelve turbulent years in the White House, Roosevelt was exhausted and gravely ill with heart disease, but he was determined to remain president until the war ended. His poor health made the selection of a vice presidential candidate unusually important. Convinced that many Americans had soured on liberal reform, Roosevelt chose Senator Harry S. Truman of Missouri as his running mate. A reliable party man from a southern border state, Truman satisfied urban Democratic leaders while not worrying white southerners who were nervous about challenges to racial segregation.

R WON

The Republicans, confident of a strong conservative upsurge in the nation, nominated as their presidential candidate the governor of New York, Thomas E. Dewey, who had made his reputation as a tough crime fighter. In the 1944 presidential campaign, Roosevelt's failing health alarmed many observers, but his frailty was outweighed by Americans' unwillingness to change presidents in the midst of the war and by Dewey's failure to persuade most voters that the New Deal was a creeping socialist menace. Voters gave Roosevelt a 53.5 percent majority, his narrowest presidential victory, ensuring his continued leadership as Dr. Win-the-War.

Reaction to the Holocaust. Since the 1930s, the Nazis had persecuted Jews in Germany and every German-occupied territory, causing many Jews to seek asylum beyond Hitler's reach. (See "Beyond America's Borders," page 760.) Thousands of Jews sought to immigrate to the United States, but 82 percent of Americans opposed admitting them, and they were turned away. In 1942, numerous reports reached the United States that Hitler was sending Jews, Gypsies, religious and political dissenters, homosexuals, and others to concentration camps, where old people, children, and others deemed too weak to work were systematically killed and cremated, while the able-bodied were put to work at slave labor until they died of starvation and abuse. Other camps were devoted almost exclusively to murdering and cremating Jews. Despite reports of the brutal slave labor and death camps, U.S. officials refused to grant asylum to Jewish refugees. Most Americans, including top officials, believed that reports were exaggerated. Only 152,000 of Europe's millions of Jews managed to gain refuge in the United States before America's entry into the war. Afterward, the number of Jewish refugees dropped to just 2,400 by 1944.

Desperate to stem the killing, the World Jewish Congress appealed to the Allies to bomb the death camps and the railroad tracks leading to them in order to hamper the killing and block further shipments of victims. Intent on achieving military victory as soon as possible, the Allies repeatedly turned down such bombing requests, arguing that the air forces could not spare resources from their military missions.

The nightmare of the **Holocaust** was all too real. When Russian troops arrived at Auschwitz in Poland in January 1945, they found emaciated prisoners, skeletal corpses, gas chambers, pits filled with human ashes, and loot the Nazis had stripped from the dead, including hair, gold fillings, and false teeth.

Holocaust
German effort during World War II to murder Europe's Jews, along with other groups the Nazis deemed "undesirable." Despite reports of the ongoing genocide, the Allies did almost nothing to interfere. In all, some 11 million people were killed in the Holocaust, most of them Jews.

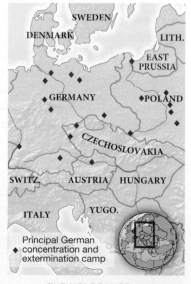

THE HOLOCAUST, 1933–1945

Principal German
♦ concentration and
extermination camp

Beyond America's Borders

Nazi Anti-Semitism and the Atomic Bomb

During the 1930s, Jewish physicists fled Adolf Hitler's fanatical anti-Semitic persecutions and came to the United States, where they played a leading role in the research and development of the atomic bomb. In this way, Nazi anti-Semitism contributed to making the United States the first atomic power.

One of Germany's greatest scientists, Albert Einstein, won the Nobel Prize for physics in 1921. Among other things, Einstein's work demonstrated that the nuclei of atoms of physical matter stored almost inconceivable quantities of energy. A fellow scientist praised Einstein's discoveries as "the greatest achievements in the history of human thought." But Einstein was a Jew, and his ideas were ridiculed by German anti-Semites. A German physicist who had won the Nobel Prize in 1905 attacked Einstein for his "Jewish nonsense," which was "hostile to the German spirit." Einstein wrote to a friend, "Anti-Semitism is strong here [in Berlin] and political reaction is violent." Einstein's associates warned him that the anti-Semites had targeted him for assassination.

In his manifesto, *Mein Kampf*, Hitler proclaimed that Jews were "a foreign people," "inferior beings," the "personification of the devil," "a race of dialectical liars," "parasites," and "eternal bloodsuckers," who had the "clear aim of ruining the . . . white race." Hitler's rantings attracted a huge audience in Germany, and his personal Nazi army, which numbered 400,000 by 1933, terrorized and murdered anyone who got in the way.

In January 1933, just weeks before Franklin Roosevelt's inauguration as president of the United States, Hitler became chancellor of Germany on a tidal wave of popular support for his Nazi Party. Within months, he abolished freedom of speech and assembly, outlawed all political opposition, and exercised absolute dictatorial power. On April 7, Hitler announced the Law for the Restoration of the Professional Civil Service, which stipulated that "civil servants of non-Aryan descent must retire." A non-Aryan was defined as any person "descended from non-Aryan, especially Jewish, parents or grandparents." The law meant that scientists of Jewish descent who worked for state institutions, including universities, no longer had jobs. About 1,600 intellectuals in Germany immediately lost their livelihood and their future in Hitler's Reich. Among them were about a quarter of the physicists in Germany, including Einstein and ten other Nobel Prize winners. The Nazis' anti-Semitism laws forced many leading scientists to leave Germany. Between 1933 and 1941, Einstein and about 100 other Jewish physicists joined hundreds of Jewish intellectuals in an exodus from Nazi Germany to the safety of the United States.

The refugee physicists scrambled to find positions at American universities and research institutes that would allow them to continue their studies. The accelerating pace of research in physics during the 1930s raised the possibility that a way might exist to release the phenomenal energy bottled up in atomic nuclei, perhaps even to create a superbomb. Einstein and other scientists considered that possibility remote. But many worried that if scientists loyal to Germany discovered a way to harness nuclear energy, Hitler would have the power to spread Nazi terror throughout the world. The refugee physicists asked Einstein to write a letter to President Roosevelt explaining the military and political threats posed by the latest research in nuclear physics.

In early October 1939, as Hitler's blitzkrieg swept through Poland, Roosevelt received Einstein's letter and immediately grasped the central point, exclaiming, "What you are after is to see that the Nazis don't blow us up." Roosevelt quickly convened a small group of distinguished American scientists, who convinced the president to mount an all-out effort to learn whether an atomic bomb could be built and, if so, to build it. Only weeks before the Japanese attack on Pearl Harbor, Roosevelt decided to launch the Manhattan Project, the top-secret atomic bomb program.

Leading scientists from the United States and Britain responded to the government's appeal: "No matter what you do with the rest of your life, nothing will be as important to the future of the World as your work on this Project right now." Many of the most creative, productive, and irreplaceable scientists involved in the Manhattan Project were physicists who had fled Nazi Germany. Their efforts had brought the possibility of an atomic bomb to Roosevelt's attention. Having personally experienced Nazi anti-Semitism, they understood what was at stake — a world in which either Hitler had the atomic bomb or his enemies did.

In the end, Hitler's scientists failed to develop an atomic bomb, and Germany surrendered before the American bomb was ready to be used. But the Manhattan Project succeeded, as Paul Tibbets proved over Hiroshima, Japan, on August 6, 1945. After the war, Leo Szilard, a leader among the

EINSTEIN BECOMES A U.S. CITIZEN

Nazi anti-Semitism caused Albert Einstein to renounce his German citizenship, immigrate to the United States, and — in the 1940 naturalization ceremony recorded in this photo — officially become an American citizen. He is joined here by his secretary, Helen Dukas (right), and his stepdaughter, Margot Einstein (left). American Stock Archive/Getty Images.

refugee physicists, remarked, "If Congress knew the true history of the atomic energy project . . . it would create a special medal to be given to meddling foreigners for distinguished services."

QUESTIONS FOR ANALYSIS

Summarize the Argument How did German anti-Semitism contribute to the United States' willingness to build and employ the atomic bomb?

Analyze the Evidence Why did Jewish physicists leave Germany for the United States?

Consider the Context Why were German Jewish scientists accepted into American society at a time when Japanese Americans were isolated in internment camps?

Ask Historical Questions In what ways were the United States' development and use of the atomic bomb "important to the future of the World"?

MASS EXECUTION OF JEWISH WOMEN AND CHILDREN

On October 14, 1942, Jewish women and children from the village of Mizocz in present-day Ukraine were herded into a ravine, forced to undress and lie facedown, and then shot at point-blank range by German officials. To centralize such executions, the Nazis built death camps, where they systematically slaughtered millions of Jews and other "undesirables." United States Holocaust Memorial Museum.

At last, the truth about the Holocaust began to be known beyond the Germans who had perpetrated and tolerated these atrocities and the men, women, and children who had succumbed to the genocide. By then, it was too late for the 11 million civilian victims — mostly Jews — of the Nazis' crimes against humanity.

> **REVIEW** How did the war influence American society?

Toward Unconditional Surrender

By February 1943, Soviet defenders had finally defeated the massive German offensive against Stalingrad, turning the tide of the war in Europe. After gargantuan sacrifices in fighting that had lasted for eighteen months, the Red Army forced Hitler's Wehrmacht to turn back toward the west. In the Pacific, the Allies had halted the expansion of the Japanese empire but now had the deadly task of dislodging Japanese defenders from the outposts they still occupied. Allied military planners devised a strategy to annihilate Axis resistance by taking advantage of America's industrial superiority. A secret plan to develop a superbomb harnessing atomic power came to fruition too late to use against Germany. But when the atomic bomb devastated the cities of Hiroshima and Nagasaki, Japan finally surrendered, canceling the planned assault on the Japanese homeland by hundreds of thousands of American soldiers and sailors and their allies.

From Bombing Raids to Berlin. While the Allied campaigns in North Africa and Italy were under way, British and American pilots flew bombing missions from England to German-occupied territories and to Germany itself as an airborne substitute for the delayed second front on the ground. During night raids, British bombers targeted general areas, hoping to hit civilians, create terror, and undermine morale. Beginning with Paul Tibbets's flight in August 1942, American pilots flew heavily armored B-17s from English airfields in daytime raids on industrial targets vital for the German war machine.

German air defenses took a fearsome toll on Allied pilots and aircraft. In 1943, *⅔ died* two-thirds of American airmen did not survive to complete their twenty-five-mission tours of duty. In all, 85,000 American airmen were killed in the skies over Europe. Many others were shot down and held as prisoners of war. In February 1944, the arrival of America's durable and deadly P-51 Mustang fighter gave Allied bombers superior protection. The Mustangs slowly began to sweep the Luftwaffe from the skies, allowing bombers to penetrate deep into Germany and pound civilian and military targets around the clock.

In November 1943, Churchill, Roosevelt, and Stalin met in Tehran to discuss wartime strategy and the second front. Roosevelt conceded to Stalin that the Soviet Union would exercise de facto control of the Eastern European countries that the Red Army occupied as it rolled back the still-potent German Wehrmacht. Stalin agreed to enter the war against Japan once Germany finally surrendered, in effect promising to open a second front in the Pacific theater. Roosevelt and Churchill promised that they would at last launch a massive second-front assault in northern France, code-named Overlord, scheduled for May 1944.

General Eisenhower was assigned overall command of Allied forces, and mountains of military supplies were stockpiled in England. The huge deployment of Hitler's armies in the east, which were trying to halt the Red Army's westward offensive, left too few German troops to stop the millions of Allied soldiers waiting to attack France. More decisive, years of Allied air raids had decimated the German Luftwaffe, which could send aloft only 300 fighter planes against 12,000 Allied aircraft.

After frustrating delays caused by stormy weather, Eisenhower launched the largest amphibious assault in world history on **D Day**, June 6, 1944 (Map 25.4). Allied soldiers finally succeeded in securing the beachhead. An officer told his men, "The only people on this beach are the dead and those that are going to die — now let's get the hell out of here." And they did, finally surmounting the cliffs that loomed over the beach and destroying the German defenses. One GI who made the landing recalled the soldiers "were exhausted and we were exultant. We had survived D Day!"

Within a week, a flood of soldiers, tanks, and other military equipment propelled Allied forces toward Germany. On August 25, the Allies liberated Paris from four years of Nazi occupation. As the giant pincers of the Allied and Soviet armies closed on Germany in December 1944, Hitler ordered a counterattack to capture the Allies' essential supply port at Antwerp, Belgium. In the Battle of the Bulge

D Day
June 6, 1944, the date of the Allied invasion of northern France. D Day was the largest amphibious assault in world history. The invasion opened a second front against the Germans and moved the Allies closer to victory in Europe.

Map Activity

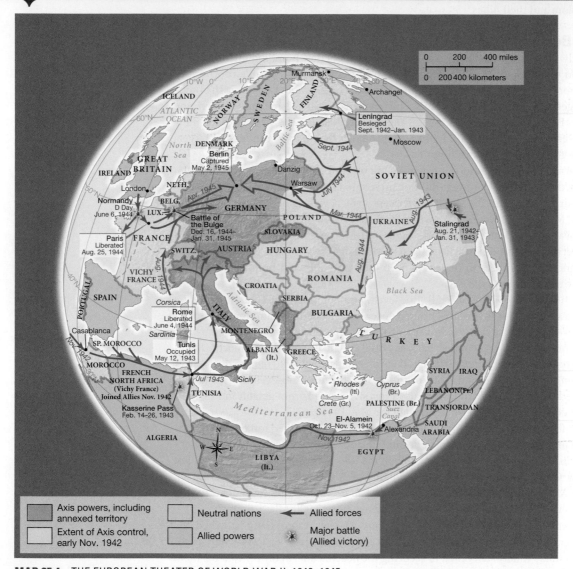

MAP 25.4 THE EUROPEAN THEATER OF WORLD WAR II, 1942–1945

The Russian reversal of the German offensive at Stalingrad and Leningrad, combined with Allied landings in North Africa and Normandy, trapped Germany in a closing vise of Allied armies on all sides.

READING THE MAP: By November 1942, which nations or parts of nations in the European theater were under Axis control? Which had been absorbed by the Axis powers before the war? Which nations remained neutral? Which ones were affiliated with the Allies?

CONNECTIONS: What were the three fronts in the European theater? When did the Allies initiate actions on each front, and why did Churchill, Stalin, and Roosevelt disagree on the timing of the opening of these fronts?

(December 16, 1944, to January 31, 1945), as the Allies termed it, German forces drove fifty-five miles into Allied lines before being stopped at Bastogne. The battle caused nearly 90,000 American casualties, more than in any other battle of the war. An American lieutenant recalled the macabre scene of "all the bodies . . . frozen stiff . . . many dead Americans and Germans . . . [many with] the ring finger . . . cut off in order to get the ring." The battle cost the Nazis hundreds of tanks and more than 100,000 men, fatally depleting Hitler's reserves.

In February 1945, while Allied armies relentlessly pushed German forces backward, Churchill, Stalin, and Roosevelt met secretly at the Yalta Conference (named for the Russian resort town where it was held) to discuss their plans for the postwar world. Roosevelt managed to secure Stalin's promise to permit votes of self-determination in the Eastern European countries occupied by the Red Army. The Allies pledged to support Jiang Jieshi (Chiang Kai-shek) as the leader of China. The Soviet Union obtained a role in the postwar governments of Korea and Manchuria in exchange for entering the war against Japan after the defeat of Germany.

The "Big Three" also agreed on the creation of a new international peacekeeping organization, the United Nations (UN). All nations would have a place in the UN General Assembly, but the Security Council would wield decisive power, and its permanent representatives from the Allied powers — China, France, Great Britain, the Soviet Union, and the United States — would possess a veto over UN actions. The Senate ratified the United Nations Charter in July 1945 by a vote of 89 to 2, reflecting the triumph of internationalism during the nation's mobilization for war.

While Allied armies sped toward Berlin, Allied warplanes dropped more bombs after D Day than in all the previous European bombing raids combined. By April 11, Allied armies reached the banks of the Elbe River and paused while the Soviets smashed into Berlin. The Red Army captured Berlin on May 2. Hitler had committed suicide on April 30, and the provisional German government surrendered unconditionally on May 7. The war in Europe was finally over, with the sacrifice of 135,576 American soldiers, nearly 250,000 British troops, and 9 million Russian combatants.

Roosevelt did not live to witness the end of the war. On April 12, he suffered a fatal stroke. Americans grieved for the man who had led them through years of depression and world war, and they worried about his untested successor, Vice President Harry Truman.

The Defeat of Japan.

After punishing defeats in the Coral Sea and at Midway, Japan had to fend off Allied naval and air attacks. In 1943, British and American forces, along with Indian and Chinese allies, launched an offensive against Japanese outposts in southern Asia, pushing through Burma and into China, where Jiang's armies continued to resist conquest. In the Pacific, Americans and their allies attacked Japanese strongholds by sea, air, and land, moving island by island toward the Japanese homeland (Map 25.5).

The island-hopping campaign began in August 1942, when American Marines landed on Guadalcanal in the southern Pacific. For the next six months, a savage battle raged for control of the strategic area. Finally, during the night of February 8,

Map Activity

MAP 25.5   THE PACIFIC THEATER OF WORLD WAR II, 1941–1945

To drive the Japanese from their far-flung empire, the Allies launched two combined naval and military offensives — one to recapture the Philippines and then attack Japanese forces in China, the other to hop from island to island in the Central Pacific toward the Japanese mainland.

READING THE MAP: What was the extent of Japanese control up until August 1942? Which nations in the Pacific theater sided with the Allies? Which nations remained neutral?

CONNECTIONS: Describe the economic and military motivations behind Japanese domination of the region. How and when did they achieve this dominance? Judging from this map, what strategic and geographic concerns might have prompted Truman and his advisers to consider using the atomic bomb against Japan?

THE ALLIED WAR EFFORT

The Russian poster shown here illustrates the combined efforts of the Allies, declaring, "We won't let the evil enemy escape the noose. He will not evade it." Museum of World War II, Natick, MA, www.museumofworldwarii.com.

1943, Japanese forces withdrew. The terrible losses on both sides indicated to the Marines how costly it would be to defeat Japan. After the battle, Joseph Steinbacher, a twenty-one-year-old from Alabama, sailed from San Francisco to New Guinea, where, he recalled, "all the cannon fodder waited to be assigned" to replace the killed and wounded.

In mid-1943, Allied forces launched offensives in New Guinea and the Solomon Islands that gradually secured the South Pacific. In the Central Pacific, amphibious forces conquered the Gilbert and Marshall islands, which served as forward bases for air assaults on the Japanese home islands. As the Allies attacked island after island, Japanese soldiers were ordered to refuse to surrender no matter how hopeless their plight.

While the island-hopping campaign kept pressure on Japanese forces, the Allies invaded the Philippines in the fall of 1944. In the four-day Battle of Leyte Gulf, one of the greatest naval battles in world history, the American fleet crushed the Japanese armada, clearing the way for Allied victory in the Philippines. While the Philippine campaign was under way, American forces captured two crucial islands — Iwo Jima and Okinawa — from which they planned to launch an attack on the Japanese homeland. To defend Okinawa, Japanese leaders ordered thousands of suicide pilots, known as *kamikaze*, to crash their bomb-laden planes into Allied ships. But instead of destroying the American fleet, they demolished the last vestige of the Japanese air force. By June 1945, the Japanese were nearly defenseless on the sea and in the air. Still, their leaders prepared to fight to the death for their homeland.

Joseph Steinbacher and other GIs who had suffered "horrendous" casualties in the Philippines were now told by their commanding officer, "Men, in a few short months we are going to invade [Japan]. . . . We will be going in on the first wave and are expecting ninety percent casualties the first day. . . . For the few of us left alive the war will be over." Steinbacher later recalled his mental attitude at that moment: "I know that I am now a walking dead man and will not have a snowball's chance in hell of making it through the last great battle to conquer the home islands of Japan."

Atomic Warfare. In mid-July 1945, as Allied forces prepared for the final assault on Japan, American scientists tested a secret weapon at an isolated desert site near Los Alamos, New Mexico. In 1942, Roosevelt had authorized the top-secret **Manhattan Project** to find a way to convert nuclear energy into a superbomb before the Germans added such a weapon to their arsenal. More than 100,000 Americans, led by scientists, engineers, and military officers at Los Alamos, worked frantically to win the race for an atomic bomb. Germany surrendered two and a half months before the test on July 16, 1945, when scientists first witnessed an atomic explosion that sent a mushroom cloud of debris eight miles into the atmosphere. After watching the successful test of the bomb, J. Robert Oppenheimer, the head scientist at Los Alamos, remarked soberly, "Lots of boys not grown up yet will owe their life to it."

President Truman saw no reason not to use the atomic bomb against Japan if doing so would save American lives. Despite numerous defeats, Japan still had more than 6 million reserves at home for a last-ditch defense against the anticipated Allied assault, which U.S. military advisers estimated would kill at least 250,000 Americans. But first Truman issued an ultimatum: Japan must surrender unconditionally or face utter ruin. When the Japanese failed to respond by the deadline, Truman ordered that an atomic bomb be dropped on a Japanese city. The bomb that Colonel Paul Tibbets and his crew released over Hiroshima on August 6 leveled the city and incinerated about 80,000 people, and many thousands more died later from injuries and

Manhattan Project

Top-secret project authorized by Franklin Roosevelt in 1942 to develop an atomic bomb ahead of the Germans. The thousands of Americans who worked on the project at Los Alamos, New Mexico, succeeded in producing a successful atomic bomb by July 1945.

HIROSHIMA

This photo shows part of Hiroshima shortly after the atomic bomb dropped from the *Enola Gay*, leveling the densely populated city. Deadly radiation from the bomb maimed and killed Japanese civilians for years afterward. Bettmann/Corbis.

radiation. Three days later, after the Japanese government still refused to surrender, the second atomic bomb killed nearly as many civilians at Nagasaki.

With American assurance that the emperor could retain his throne after the Allies took over, Japan surrendered on August 14. On a troopship departing from Europe for what would have been the final assault on Japan, an American soldier spoke for millions of others when he heard the wonderful news that the killing was over: "We are going to grow to adulthood after all."

While all Americans welcomed peace, some worried about the consequences of unleashing atomic power. Almost every American believed that the atomic bomb had brought peace in 1945, but nobody knew what it would bring in the future.

> **REVIEW** Why did Truman elect to use the atomic bomb against Japan?

Conclusion: Allied Victory and America's Emergence as a Superpower

At a cost of 405,399 American lives, the nation united with its allies to crush the Axis aggressors into unconditional surrender. Almost all Americans believed they had won a "good war" against totalitarian evil. The Allies saved Asia and Europe from enslavement and finally halted the Nazis' genocidal campaign against Jews and many others whom the Nazis considered inferior. To secure human rights and protect the world against future wars, the Roosevelt administration took the lead in creating the United Nations.

Wartime production lifted the nation out of the Great Depression. The gross national product soared to four times what it had been when Roosevelt became president in 1933. Jobs in defense industries eliminated chronic unemployment, provided wages for millions of women workers and African American migrants from southern farms, and boosted Americans' prosperity. Ahead stretched the challenge of maintaining that prosperity while reintegrating millions of uniformed men and women, with help from the benefits of the GI Bill.

By the end of the war, the United States had emerged as a global superpower. Wartime mobilization made the American economy the strongest in the world, buttressed by the military clout of the nation's nuclear monopoly. Although the war left much of the world a rubble-strewn wasteland, the American mainland had enjoyed immunity from attack. The Japanese occupation of China had left 50 million people without homes and millions more dead, maimed, and orphaned. The German offensive against the Soviet Union had killed more than 20 million Russian soldiers and civilians. Germany and Japan lay in ruins, their economies and societies as shattered as their military forces. But in the gruesome balance sheet of war, the Axis powers had inflicted far more grief, misery, and destruction on the global victims of their aggression than they had suffered in return.

As the dominant Western nation in the postwar world, the United States asserted its leadership in the reconstruction of Europe while occupying Japan and overseeing its economic and political recovery. America soon confronted new challenges in the tense aftermath of the war, as the Soviets seized political control of Eastern Europe, a Communist revolution swept China, and national liberation movements emerged in the colonial empires of Britain and France. The forces unleashed by World War II would shape the United States and the rest of the world for decades to come. Before the ashes of World War II had cooled, America's wartime alliance with the Soviet Union fractured, igniting a Cold War between the superpowers. To resist global communism, the United States became, in effect, the policeman of the free world, repudiating the pre–World War II legacy of isolationism.

Chapter Review

KEY TERMS

good neighbor policy (p. 741)

neutrality acts (p. 742)

appeasement (p. 743)

Lend-Lease Act (p. 746)

internment camps (p. 750)

Selective Service Act (p. 750)

Battle of Midway (p. 753)

Double V campaign (p. 758)

GI Bill of Rights (p. 758)

Holocaust (p. 759)

D Day (p. 763)

Manhattan Project (p. 768)

REVIEW QUESTIONS

❶ Why did isolationism during the 1930s concern Roosevelt? (pp. 740–43)

❷ How did Roosevelt attempt to balance American isolationism with the military aggression of Germany and Japan in the late 1930s and early 1940s? (pp. 743–49)

❸ How did the Roosevelt administration mobilize the human and industrial resources necessary to fight a two-front war? (pp. 749–52)

❹ How did the United States seek to counter the Japanese in the Pacific and the Germans in Europe? (pp. 753–55)

❺ How did the war influence American society? (pp. 756–62)

❻ Why did Truman elect to use the atomic bomb against Japan? (pp. 762–69)

MAKING CONNECTIONS

❶ Did isolationism bolster or undermine national security and national economic interests? Discuss Roosevelt's evolving answer to this question.

❷ Who benefited most from the wartime economy? What financial limitations did various members of society face, and why?

❸ How did the United States play a decisive role in the Allies' victory?

❹ How did minorities' contributions to the war effort draw attention to domestic racism? What were the political implications of these developments?

LINKING TO THE PAST

❶ How did America's involvement in World War II differ from its participation in World War I? Consider diplomacy, allies and enemies, wartime military and economic policies, and social and cultural changes. (See chapter 22.)

❷ Why did World War II succeed in creating the full economic recovery that remained elusive during the New Deal? Consider specifically the scope and limits of New Deal economic reforms and how they changed, if at all, during World War II. (See chapter 24.)

Cold War Politics in the Truman Years, 1945–1953

CONTENT LEARNING OBJECTIVES

After reading and studying this chapter, you should be able to:

• Explain the origins of the Cold War, and describe where and how the containment policy was implemented.
• Describe President Truman's Fair Deal domestic agenda, and explain its accomplishments and failures.
• Explain why the United States went to war in Korea and how military objectives changed. Identify the war's costs and consequences.

H eads turned when congresswoman Helen Gahagan Douglas walked through the U.S. Capitol. She was one of only ten female representatives in the 435-seat body, and she also drew attention as an attractive former Broadway star and opera singer. Douglas served in Congress from 1945 to 1951 when the fate of the New Deal hung in the balance and the nation charted an unprecedented course in foreign policy.

Born in 1900, Helen Gahagan grew up in Brooklyn, New York, and left college early for the stage. She quickly won fame on Broadway, starring in show after show until she fell in love with one of her leading men, Melvyn Douglas. They married in 1931, and she followed him to Hollywood, where he hoped to advance his movie career and where she bore two children.

Helen Gahagan Douglas admired Franklin D. Roosevelt's leadership during the depression, and the Douglases joined Hollywood's liberal political circles. Douglas visited migrant camps where she saw "faces

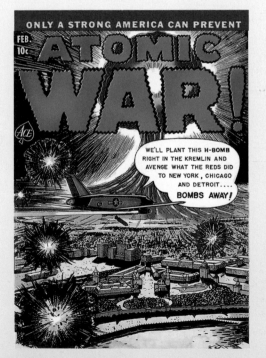

ONLY A STRONG AMERICA CAN PREVENT

FEB. 10¢

ATOMIC WAR!

ACE

WE'LL PLANT THIS H-BOMB RIGHT IN THE KREMLIN AND AVENGE WHAT THE REDS DID TO NEW YORK, CHICAGO AND DETROIT....
BOMBS AWAY!

COLD WAR COMIC BOOK
After World War II, fear of communism pervaded American politics and popular culture. This comic book series showed the United States winning victories over the Soviet Union with nuclear weapons. Image Courtesy of The Advertising Archives.

772-779
782-783

stamped with poverty and despair." Her work on behalf of poor migrant farmworkers led her to testify before Congress and become a friend of the Roosevelts. In 1944, she won election to Congress, representing not the posh Hollywood district where she lived but a multiracial district in downtown Los Angeles, which cemented her dedication to progressive politics.

Like many liberals, Douglas was devastated by Roosevelt's death and unsure of his successor. "Who was Harry Truman anyway?" she asked. A compromise choice for the vice presidency, this "accidental president" lacked the charisma and political skills with which Roosevelt had transformed foreign and domestic policy, won four presidential elections, and forged a Democratic Party coalition that dominated national politics. Besides confronting domestic problems that the New Deal had not solved — how to avoid another depression without the war to fuel the economy — Truman faced new international challenges that threatened to undermine the nation's security.

By 1947, a new term described the hostility that had emerged between the United States and its wartime ally, the Soviet Union: Cold War. Truman and his advisers insisted that the Soviet Union posed a major threat to the United States, and they gradually shaped a policy to contain Soviet power wherever it threatened to spread. As a member of the House Foreign Affairs Committee, Douglas urged cooperation with the Soviet Union and initially opposed aid to Greece and Turkey, the first step in the new containment policy. Yet thereafter, Douglas was Truman's loyal ally, supporting the Marshall Plan, the creation of the North Atlantic Treaty Organization, and the war in Korea. The containment policy achieved its goals in Europe, but communism spread in Asia, and at home a wave of anti-Communist hysteria — a second Red scare — harmed many Americans and stifled dissent and debate.

Douglas's earlier links with leftist groups and her advocacy of civil rights and social welfare programs made her and other liberals easy targets for conservative politicians exploiting the anti-Communist fervor that accompanied the Cold War. Running for the U.S. Senate in 1950, she faced Republican Richard M. Nixon, who had gained national attention for his efforts to expose Communists in government. Nixon's campaign labeled Douglas as "pink right down to her underwear" and sent thousands of voters the

CHRONOLOGY

1945	Roosevelt dies; Truman becomes president.
1946	Postwar labor unrest affects major industries. President's Committee on Civil Rights created. George F. Kennan drafts containment policy. United States grants independence to Philippines. Employment Act passes. Republicans gain control of Congress.
1947	National Security Act passes. Truman announces Truman Doctrine. United States sends aid to Greece and Turkey. Truman establishes loyalty program. *Mendez v. Westminster* decided.
1948	Marshall Plan approved. Truman orders desegregation of military. American GI Forum founded. United States recognizes Israel. Truman elected president.
1948–1949	Berlin crisis precipitates airlift drops.
1949	Communists take over China. North Atlantic Treaty Organization formed. Soviet Union explodes atomic bomb. Truman approves hydrogen bomb.
1950	Senator Joseph McCarthy claims U.S. government harbors Communists. Korean War begins.
1951	Truman fires General Douglas MacArthur. U.S. occupation of Japan ends.
1952	Dwight D. Eisenhower elected president.
1953	Korean War ends.

anonymous message, "I think you should know Helen Douglas is a Communist." Douglas's political career ended in defeat, just as much of Truman's domestic agenda fell victim to the Red scare.

From the Grand Alliance to Containment

With Japan's surrender in August 1945, Americans besieged the government to bring their loved ones home. They looked forward to the end of international crises and the dismantling of the large military establishment. Postwar realities quickly shattered these hopes. The wartime alliance of the United States, Great Britain, and the Soviet Union crumbled, giving birth to a Cold War. The United States began to develop the means for containing the spread of Soviet power around the globe, including a military buildup and an enormous aid program for Europe, known as the Marshall Plan.

The Cold War Begins.
"The guys who came out of World War II were idealistic," reported Harold Russell, a young paratrooper who had lost both hands in a training accident. "We felt the day had come when the wars were all over." But such hopes were quickly dashed. Once the Allies had overcome a common enemy, the prewar mistrust and antagonism between the Soviet Union and the West resurfaced over their very different visions of the postwar world.

The Western Allies' delay in opening a second front in Western Europe aroused Soviet suspicions during the war. The Soviet Union had made supreme wartime sacrifices, losing more than twenty million citizens and vast portions of its agricultural and industrial capacity. Soviet leader Joseph Stalin wanted to make Germany pay for Soviet economic reconstruction and to expand Soviet influence in the world. Above all, he wanted friendly governments on the Soviet Union's borders in Eastern Europe, through which his nation had been attacked twice in the past twenty-five years. A ruthless dictator, Stalin also wanted to maintain his own power.

In contrast to the Soviet devastation, American losses were light, and the United States emerged from the war as the most powerful nation on the planet, with a vastly expanded economy and a monopoly on atomic weapons. That sheer power, along with U.S. economic interests and a belief in the superiority of American institutions and intentions, all affected how American leaders approached the Soviet Union.

With the depression still fresh in their minds, American officials believed that a healthy economy depended on opportunities abroad. American companies needed access to raw materials, markets for their goods, and security for their investments overseas, needs best met in countries with similar economic and political systems. As President Harry S. Truman put it in 1947, "The American system can survive in America only if it becomes a world system." Yet leaders and citizens alike regarded their foreign policy not as a self-interested campaign for economic advantage, but as the means to preserve national security and bring freedom, democracy, and capitalism to the rest of the world. Laura Briggs, a woman from Idaho, spoke for many Americans who believed "it was our destiny to prove that we were the children of God and that our way was right for the world."

Recent history also shaped postwar foreign policy. Americans believed that World War II might have been avoided had Britain and France resisted rather than appeased Hitler's initial aggression. Navy Secretary James V. Forrestal opposed trying to "buy [the Soviets'] understanding and sympathy. We tried that once with Hitler." The man with ultimate responsibility for U.S. policy was a keen student of history but had little international experience beyond his service in World War I. Harry S. Truman expected Soviet-American cooperation, as long as the Soviet Union conformed to U.S. plans for the postwar world. Proud of his ability to make quick decisions, Truman was determined to take a firm hand if the Soviets tried to expand, confident that America's nuclear monopoly gave him the upper hand.

The **Cold War** first emerged over clashing Soviet and American interests in Eastern Europe. Stalin insisted that wartime agreements gave him a free hand in the countries defeated or liberated by the Red Army, just as the United States was unilaterally reconstructing governments in Italy and Japan. The Soviet dictator used harsh methods to install Communist governments in neighboring Poland and Bulgaria but initially tolerated non-Communist governments in Hungary and Czechoslovakia. In early 1946, he responded to Western pressure and removed troops from Iran on the Soviet Union's southwest border, allowing U.S. access to the rich oil fields there.

Stalin saw hypocrisy when U.S. officials demanded democratic elections in Eastern Europe while supporting dictatorships friendly to U.S. interests in Latin America. But the Western Allies were unwilling to match tough words with military force against the largest army in the world. Their sharp protests failed to prevent the Soviet Union from establishing satellite countries throughout Eastern Europe (Map 26.1).

In 1946, the wartime Allies contended over Germany's future. Both sides wanted to demilitarize Germany, but U.S. policymakers sought rapid industrial revival there to foster European economic recovery. By contrast, the Soviet Union wanted Germany weak both militarily and economically, and Stalin demanded heavy reparations from Germany to help rebuild the devastated Soviet economy. Unable to settle their differences, the Allies divided Germany. The Soviet Union installed a puppet Communist government in the eastern section, and Britain, France, and the United States began to unify their occupation zones, eventually establishing the Federal Republic of Germany — West Germany — in 1949.

The war of words escalated early in 1946. Boasting of the superiority of the Soviet system, Stalin told a Moscow audience in February that capitalism inevitably produced war. One month later, Truman sat beside Winston Churchill, the former prime minister, who denounced Soviet interference in Eastern Europe. "From Stettin in the Baltic to Trieste in the Adriatic, an **iron curtain** has descended across the Continent," Churchill said. Stalin saw Churchill's proposal for joint British-American action to combat Soviet aggression as "a call to war against the USSR."

In February 1946, George F. Kennan, a career diplomat and expert on Russia, wrote a comprehensive rationale for what came to be called the policy of **containment**. Downplaying the influence of Communist ideology, he instead stressed Soviet insecurity and Stalin's need to maintain authority at home as the prime forces

Cold War
Term given to the tense and hostile relationship between the United States and the Soviet Union from 1947 to 1989. The term *cold* was apt because the hostility stopped short of direct armed conflict.

iron curtain
Metaphor coined by Winston Churchill in 1946 to demark the line dividing Soviet-controlled countries in Eastern Europe from democratic nations in Western Europe following World War II.

containment
The post–World War II foreign policy strategy that committed the United States to resisting the influence and expansion of the Soviet Union and communism. The strategy of containment shaped American foreign policy throughout the Cold War.

behind efforts to expand Soviet power abroad. Kennan believed that the Soviet Union would retreat if the United States would respond with "unalterable counterforce." This approach, he predicted, would eventually end in "either the breakup or the gradual mellowing of Soviet power."

Not all public figures agreed. In September 1946, Secretary of Commerce Henry A. Wallace urged greater understanding of the Soviets' national security concerns, insisting that "we have no more business in the political affairs of Eastern Europe than Russia has in the political affairs of Latin America." State Department officials were furious at Wallace for challenging the administration's hard line against the Soviet Union, and Truman fired Wallace.

Map Activity

MAP 26.1 THE DIVISION OF EUROPE AFTER WORLD WAR II

The "iron curtain," a term coined by Winston Churchill to refer to the Soviet grip on Eastern Europe, divided the continent for nearly fifty years. Communist governments controlled the countries along the Soviet Union's western border, except for Finland, which remained neutral.

READING THE MAP: Is the division of Europe among NATO, Communist, and neutral countries about equal? Why would the location of Berlin pose a problem for the Western Allies?

CONNECTIONS: When was NATO founded, and what was its purpose? How did the postwar division of Europe compare with the wartime alliances?

The Truman Doctrine and the Marshall Plan.
In 1947, the United States began to implement the doctrine of containment that would guide foreign policy for the next four decades. It was not an easy transition; Americans approved of taking a hard line against the Soviet Union but wanted to keep their soldiers and tax dollars at home. In addition to selling containment to the public, Truman had to gain the support of a Republican-controlled Congress, which included those staunchly opposed to a strong U.S. presence in Europe.

Crises in two Mediterranean countries triggered the implementation of containment. In February 1947, Britain informed the United States that its crippled economy could no longer sustain military assistance to Greece, where the autocratic government faced economic disaster and a leftist uprising, and to Turkey, which was trying to resist Soviet pressures. Unaware that the Soviet Union had deliberately avoided aiding the Greek Communists, Truman promptly sought congressional authority to send both countries military and economic aid. Meeting with congressional leaders, Undersecretary of State Dean Acheson predicted that if Greece and Turkey fell, communism would soon consume three-fourths of the world. After a stunned silence, Michigan senator Arthur Vandenberg, the Republican foreign policy leader, warned that to get approval, Truman would have to "scare hell out of the country." Scare country

Truman did just that. He warned that if Greece fell to the rebels, "confusion and disorder might well spread throughout the entire Middle East" and then create instability in Europe. According to what came to be called the **Truman Doctrine**, the United States must not only resist Soviet military power but also "support free peoples who are resisting attempted subjugation by armed minorities or by outside pressures." The president failed to convince Helen Gahagan Douglas and some of her congressional colleagues, who wanted the United States to work through the United Nations and opposed propping up the authoritarian Greek government. But the administration won the day, setting a precedent for forty years of Cold War interventions that would aid any kind of government if the only alternative appeared to be communism.

A much larger assistance program for Europe followed aid to Greece and Turkey. In May 1947, Acheson described a war-ravaged Western Europe, with "factories destroyed, fields impoverished, transportation systems wrecked, populations scattered and on the borderline of starvation." American citizens were sending generous amounts of private aid, but Europe needed large-scale assistance to keep desperate citizens from turning to socialism or communism.

In March 1948, Congress approved such assistance, which came to be called the **Marshall Plan**, after Secretary of State George C. Marshall, who proposed what a British official called "a lifeline to a sinking man." Over the next five years, the United States spent $13 billion ($117 billion in 2010 dollars) to restore the economies of sixteen Western European nations. Marshall invited all European nations and the Soviet Union to cooperate in a request for aid, but the Soviets objected to the American insistence on free trade and financial disclosure. As U.S. officials had expected, the Soviets rejected the offer and ordered their Eastern European satellites to do the same.

Humanitarian impulses as well as the goal of keeping Western Europe free of communism drove the adoption of this enormous aid program. The Marshall Plan

Truman Doctrine
President Harry S. Truman's commitment to "support free peoples who are resisting attempted subjugation by armed minorities or by outside pressures." First applied to Greece and Turkey in 1947, it became the justification for U.S. intervention into many countries during the Cold War.

Marshall Plan
Aid program begun in 1948 to help European economies recover from World War II. Between 1948 and 1953, the United States provided $13 billion to seventeen western European nations in a project that helped its own economy as well.

BERLIN DIVIDED, 1948

also helped boost the U.S. economy; the European recipients used the aid to buy American products, and Europe's economic recovery created new markets and opportunities for American investment. By insisting that the recipient nations work together, the Marshall Plan marked the first step toward the European Union. (See "Making Historical Arguments," page 780.)

While Congress was debating the Marshall Plan, in February 1948 the Soviets brutally installed a Communist regime in Czechoslovakia, the last democracy left in Eastern Europe. Next, Stalin threatened Western access to Berlin. That former capital of Germany lay within Soviet-controlled East Germany, but all four Allies jointly occupied it. As the Western Allies moved to organize West Germany as a separate nation, the Soviets retaliated by blocking roads and rail lines between West Germany and the Western-held sections of Berlin, cutting off food, fuel, and other essentials to two million inhabitants (see Map 26.1).

"We stay in Berlin, period," Truman vowed. To avoid a confrontation with Soviet troops, for nearly a year U.S. and British pilots airlifted 2.3 million tons of goods to sustain the West Berliners. Stalin hesitated to shoot down these cargo planes, and in 1949 he lifted the blockade. The city was then divided into East Berlin, under Soviet control, and West Berlin, which became part of West Germany.

Building a National Security State. During the Truman years, advocates of the new containment policy fashioned a six-pronged defense strategy: (1) development of atomic weapons, (2) strengthening traditional military power, (3) military alliances with other nations, (4) military and economic aid to friendly nations, (5) an espionage network and secret means to subvert Communist expansion, and (6) a propaganda offensive to win friends around the world.

In September 1949, the Soviet Union detonated its own atomic bomb, ending the U.S. monopoly on atomic weapons. Truman then approved the development of

THE BERLIN AIRLIFT

At the peak of the Berlin airlift in 1948, U.S. or British planes landed every three minutes twenty-four hours a day. These children, on top of a mountain of wartime rubble, may have been watching for air force pilot Gail S. Halvorsen, who, after meeting hungry schoolchildren, began to drop candy and gum as his plane approached the landing strip. picture-alliance/dpa/AP Images.

(1) a hydrogen bomb — equivalent to five hundred atomic bombs — rejecting the counterarguments of several scientists who had worked on the atomic bomb and of George Kennan, who warned of an endless arms race. The "superbomb" was ready by 1954, but the U.S. advantage was brief. In November 1955, the Soviets exploded their own hydrogen bomb.

From the 1950s through the 1980s, deterrence formed the basis of American nuclear strategy. To deter a Soviet attack, the United States strove to maintain a nuclear force more powerful than that of the Soviets. Because the Russians pursued a similar policy, the superpowers became locked in an ever-escalating nuclear arms race amassing weapons that could destroy the earth many times over. Albert Einstein, whose mathematical discoveries had laid the foundations for nuclear weapons, commented grimly that the war that came after World War III would "be fought with sticks and stones."

(2) Implementing the second component of containment, the United States beefed up its conventional military power to deter Soviet threats that might not warrant nuclear retaliation. The National Security Act of 1947 united the military branches under a single secretary of defense and created the National Security Council (NSC) to advise the president. During the Berlin crisis in 1948, Congress hiked military appropriations and enacted a peacetime draft. In addition, Congress granted permanent status to the women's military branches, though it limited the number of women, the jobs they could do, and the rank they could attain. With 1.5 million men and women in uniform in 1950, the military strength of the United States had quadrupled since the 1930s, and defense expenditures claimed one-third of the federal budget.

(3) Collective security, the third prong of containment strategy, marked a sharp reversal of the nation's traditional foreign policy. In 1949, the United States joined Canada and Western European nations in its first peacetime military alliance, the **North Atlantic Treaty Organization (NATO)**, designed to counter a Soviet threat to Western Europe (Map 26.1). For the first time in its history, the United States pledged to go to war if one of its allies was attacked.

(4) The fourth element of defense strategy provided foreign assistance programs to strengthen friendly countries, such as aid to Greece and Turkey and the Marshall Plan. In addition, in 1949 Congress approved $1 billion of military aid to its NATO allies, and the government began economic assistance to nations in other parts of the world.

(5) The fifth ingredient of containment improved the government's capacity to thwart communism through espionage and covert activities. The National Security Act of 1947 created the **Central Intelligence Agency (CIA)** to gather information and to perform any activities "related to intelligence affecting the national security" that the NSC might authorize. Such functions included propaganda, sabotage, economic warfare, and support for "anti-communist elements in threatened countries of the free world." In 1948, secret CIA operations helped defeat Italy's Communist Party. Subsequently, CIA agents would intervene even more actively, helping to topple legitimate foreign governments and violating the rights of U.S. citizens.

(6) Finally, the U.S. government created cultural exchanges and propaganda to win "hearts and minds" throughout the world. The Voice of America, established during World War II to broadcast U.S. propaganda abroad, expanded, and the State Department sent books, exhibits, jazz musicians, and other performers to foreign countries as "cultural ambassadors."

North Atlantic Treaty Organization (NATO) Military alliance formed in 1949 among the United States, Canada, and Western European nations to counter any possible Soviet threat. It represented an unprecedented commitment by the United States to go to war if any of its allies were attacked.

Central Intelligence Agency (CIA) Agency created by the National Security Act of 1947 to expand the government's espionage capacities and ability to thwart communism through covert activities, including propaganda, sabotage, economic warfare, and support for anti-Communist forces around the world.

Why Did the United States Launch the European Recovery Program?

When Secretary of State George Marshall proposed a program of massive economic aid to Europe in June 1947, the United States was still recovering from World War II, the national debt had skyrocketed, and most Americans ranked foreign events low among their concerns. The Truman administration insisted that $17 billion was needed over the next four years and asked specifically for $6.8 billion for the first 15 months, a staggering amount when the total annual federal budget was around $40 billion. The $13 billion that was ultimately spent amounted to more than $100 billion in current dollars. So why did the administration believe it was necessary to launch such an enormous program, and why did Congress consent?

The objective conditions in Europe were plain for anyone to see. World War II had left behind utter devastation. Thirty percent of Britain's housing stock lay in rubble, and three-fourths of Berlin's buildings were uninhabitable. Destroyed roads, railroads, and bridges littered the landscape. Thirteen million people had been displaced from their homes, and millions of Europeans subsisted on the borderline of starvation. Then, in January 1947, a brutal winter descended, freezing to a stop what factories and railroads had survived the war and destroying three million acres of wheat. The snowmelt from that winter produced ravaging floods.

When Marshall proposed what came to be called the European Recovery Program (ERP), he declared, "Our policy is directed not against any country or doctrine but against hunger, poverty, desperation and chaos." Indeed, the U.S. government had already sent millions of dollars of aid and huge loans to individual countries, and the American people sent some $2 billion of private aid in the six years following World War II. British foreign secretary Ernest Bevin spoke of the Marshall Plan as "generosity beyond my belief."

But motives beyond humanitarianism were also at work. With the Soviet Union in control of Eastern Europe, U.S. policymakers feared the spread of communism to Western nations. In most of Europe, Communist parties enjoyed popular support, in part because Communists had led the resistance to Nazism. After the war, they were elected to coalition governments in several Western countries, including Italy, where a Communist coalition had won 40 percent of the vote, and France. U.S. leaders feared that persistent economic desperation could send Western European countries into the arms of the Soviets without a shot being fired.

If U.S. policy leaders were alarmed by the security threat posed by a Soviet-dominated Europe, they also recognized how closely European recovery was tied to the health of the American economy. A prosperous and stable continent meant markets for American products and investment opportunities for American businesses. But in the postwar years, European nations were importing much more from the United States than they could export, resulting in a mounting "dollar gap." If not contained, this dollar deficit would leave Europeans without the means to trade with the United States. Marshall Plan advocates also pointed out that American businesses would benefit in the short run because Europeans would use the assistance to purchase American goods — ranging from milk to tractors to industrial equipment — carried on American ships and loaded by American dockworkers.

Finally, the ERP helped to solve the problem of how to promote German reindustrialization, deemed necessary for the recovery of the rest of Western Europe, while also containing Germany's ability to wage war. To this end, the United States required nations receiving aid to take the initiative, cooperate with one another, and lower trade restrictions among themselves. Encouraged by Marshall Plan aid, European leaders knit their countries together, eventually leading to the creation of the European Union in 1993.

The multitude of interests that lay behind the Marshall Plan proposal gave the Truman administration a broad platform on which to appeal for congressional support. It launched a full-scale publicity campaign of ads, brochures, and speakers to appeal to every segment of the American public. Marshall himself compared his strenuous speaking tour to "running for the

WIR BAUEN

EIN NEUES EUROPA

ERP

"WE BUILD A NEW EUROPE"

In 1950, the ERP launched a poster contest on the subject "Intra-European Cooperation for a Better Standard of Living" and received more than 10,000 submissions from artists throughout Europe. One of the finalists, "We Build a New Europe," submitted by Austrian Kurt Krapeik, shows the wartime devastation in a burned tree and the promise of recovery in new shoots. The European nations, represented by flags, fit tightly together in the nest, which is being supplied by doves, symbols of peace. Library of Congress, 3b49410.

In the end, security interests carried the day. Senator Arthur Vandenberg, a leading Republican spokesman on foreign policy and an advocate for the Marshall Plan, opened the debate on the ERP bill with the warning, "The exposed frontiers of hazard move almost hourly to the west." Other members of Congress echoed their support for the Marshall Plan in terms that emphasized the Soviet threat, such as Oklahoma senator Elmer Thomas's argument that European aid would "enable the free countries of Europe to prepare themselves to resist the aggression of Russia over their territories." A CIA report asserted in April 1947 that "the greatest danger to the security of the United States is the possibility of economic collapse in western Europe and the consequent accession to power of Communist elements." Created to serve strategic interests, the Marshall Plan simultaneously helped the U.S. economy and highlighted values of generosity and humanitarianism.

Senate or the presidency." Truman allowed the program to be popularly named after the revered, nonpartisan general, making it more palatable to Republicans who controlled Congress.

The Soviet Union made its own contributions to the enactment of the Marshall Plan. Not wanting to be judged responsible for the division of Europe, U.S. officials had extended the invitation to develop a recovery plan to every European nation. Foreign ministers from the Soviet Union, Britain, and France met to discuss a response, but Stalin balked at sharing economic information with other participants, and he wanted German industry used for reparations rather than for European recovery. The Soviet representative walked out of the meeting, and Stalin ordered the Eastern European satellites not to participate. Consequently, no U.S. aid would be going to Communist countries. Further solidifying public and congressional support for the Marshall Plan, the iron curtain moved westward in February 1948, when Communists in Czechoslovakia staged a coup and took over the government.

QUESTIONS FOR ANALYSIS

Summarize the Argument   What does the author conclude were the U.S. government's primary motivations for launching the ERP?

Analyze the Evidence   What specific risks did the U.S. government hope to avoid by implementing the ERP? What conditions enabled the ERP to gain the support of the Republican-controlled Congress?

Consider the Context   How did external events that occurred during the period between Marshall's proposal for European aid in June 1947 and its enactment into law in April 1948 influence the passage of the ERP? What specific events were significant in the passage of the ERP?

COLD WAR SPYING

"Intelligence," the gathering of information about the enemy, took on new importance with the Cold War and creation of the Central Intelligence Agency (CIA) in 1947. While much intelligence work took place in Washington, where analysts combed through Communist newspapers, official reports, and speeches, secret agents gathered information behind the iron curtain with bugs and devices such as these cameras hidden in cigarette packs. Jack Naylor Collection/ Picture Research Consultants & Archives.

By 1950, the United States had abandoned age-old tenets of foreign policy. Isolationism and neutrality gave way to a peacetime military alliance and efforts to control events far beyond U.S. borders. Short of war, the United States could not stop the descent of the iron curtain, but it aggressively and successfully promoted economic recovery and a military shield for the rest of Europe.

Superpower Rivalry around the Globe.

Efforts to implement containment moved beyond Europe. In Africa, Asia, and the Middle East, World War II accelerated a tide of national liberation movements against war-weakened imperial powers. By 1960, forty countries had won their independence. These nations, along with Latin America, came to be referred to collectively as the third world.

Like Woodrow Wilson during World War I, Roosevelt and Truman promoted the ideal of self-determination. The United States granted independence to the Philippines in 1946 and applauded the British withdrawal from India. As the Cold War intensified, however, the ideal of self-determination gave way to concern when new governments supplanting the old empires failed to emulate the American model. U.S. policymakers encouraged democracy and capitalism in emerging nations and sought to preserve opportunities for American trade, while U.S. corporations coveted the vast oil reserves in the Middle East. Yet leaders of many liberation movements, impressed with Russia's rapid economic growth, adopted socialist or Communist ideas. Although few of these movements had formal ties with the Soviet Union, American leaders saw them as a threatening extension of Soviet power. Seeking to hold communism at bay by fostering economic development and political stability, in 1949 the Truman administration began a small program of aid to developing nations.

Meanwhile civil war raged in China, where the Communists, led by Mao Zedong (Mao Tsetung) fought the official Nationalist government under Jiang Jieshi (Chiang Kai-shek). While the Communists gained popular support for their land reforms, Jiang's corrupt, incompetent government alienated much of the population, and his military forces had been devastated by the Japanese. Failing to achieve a settlement between Jiang and Mao, the United States provided $3 billion in aid to the

Nationalists. Yet, recognizing the ineptness of Jiang's government, Truman refused to divert further resources from Europe to China.

In October 1949, Mao established the People's Republic of China (PRC), and the Nationalists fled to the island of Taiwan. Fearing a U.S.-supported invasion to recapture China for the Nationalists, Mao signed a mutual defense treaty with the Soviet Union. The United States refused to recognize the PRC, blocked its admission to the United Nations, and supported the Nationalist government in Taiwan. Only a massive U.S. military commitment could have stopped the Chinese Communists, yet some Republicans charged that Truman and "pro-Communists in the State Department" had "lost" China. China became a political albatross for the Democrats, who resolved never again to be vulnerable to charges of being soft on communism.

With China in turmoil, U.S. policy shifted to helping Japan rapidly reindustrialize. In a short time, the Japanese economy was flourishing, and the official military occupation ended when the two nations signed a peace treaty and a mutual security pact in September 1951. Like West Germany, Japan now sat squarely within the American orbit, ready to serve as an economic hub in a vital area.

The one place where Cold War considerations did not control American policy was Palestine. In 1943, then-senator Harry Truman spoke passionately about Nazi Germany's annihilation of the Jews, asserting, "This is not a Jewish problem, it is an American problem — and we must . . . face it squarely and honorably." As president, he made good on his words. Jews had been migrating to Palestine, their biblical homeland, since the nineteenth century, resulting in tension and hostilities with the Palestinian Arabs. After World War II, as hundreds of thousands of European Jews sought refuge and a national homeland in Palestine, fighting and terrorism escalated on both sides.

Truman's foreign policy experts sought American-Arab friendship to contain Soviet influence in the Middle East and to secure access to Arabian oil. Uncharacteristically defying his advisers, the president responded instead to pleas from Jewish organizations, his moral commitment to Holocaust survivors, and his interest in the American Jewish vote. When Jews in Palestine declared the state of Israel in May 1948, Truman quickly recognized the new country and made its defense the cornerstone of U.S. policy in the Middle East.

ISRAEL, 1948

> **REVIEW** What factors contributed to the emergence of the Cold War?

Truman and the Fair Deal at Home

Referring to the Civil War general who coined the phrase "War is hell," Truman said in December 1945, "Sherman was wrong. I'm telling you I find peace is hell." Challenged by crises abroad, Truman also faced shortages, strikes, and inflation as the economy shifted to peacetime production. At the same time, he tried to expand the New Deal with his own Fair Deal agenda of initiatives in civil rights, housing, education, and health care — efforts hindered by the wave of anti-Communist hysteria sweeping the country. In sharp contrast to the bipartisan support Truman won for his foreign policy, he achieved few domestic reforms.

Reconverting to a Peacetime Economy.
Despite scarcities and deprivations, World War II had brought most Americans a higher standard of living than ever before. Economic experts as well as ordinary citizens worried about sustaining that standard and providing jobs for millions of returning soldiers. To that end, Truman asked Congress for a twenty-one-point program of social and economic reforms. He wanted the government to continue regulating the economy while it adjusted to peacetime production, and he sought government programs to provide basic essentials such as housing and health care to those in need. "Not even President Roosevelt ever asked for as much at one sitting," exploded Republican leader Joseph W. Martin Jr.

Congress approved just one of Truman's key proposals — full-employment legislation — and then only after watering it down. The Employment Act of 1946 called on the federal government "to promote maximum employment, production, and purchasing power," thereby formalizing government's responsibility for maintaining a healthy economy. It created the Council of Economic Advisors to assist the president, but it authorized no new powers to translate the government's obligations into effective action.

Inflation, not unemployment, turned out to be the biggest problem. Consumers had $30 billion in wartime savings to spend, but shortages of meat, automobiles, housing, and other items persisted, thereby driving up prices. With a basket of groceries to dramatize rising costs, Helen Gahagan Douglas urged Congress to maintain price and rent controls. Those efforts, however, fell to pressures from business groups and others determined to trim government powers.

Labor relations were another thorn in Truman's side. Organized labor emerged from the war with its 14.5 million members making up 35 percent of the nonagricultural workforce. Yet union members feared the erosion of wartime gains and turned to the weapon they had surrendered during the war. Five million workers went out on strike in 1946, affecting nearly every major industry. Shortly before voting to strike, a former Marine and his coworkers calculated that an executive had spent more on a party than they would earn in a whole year at the steel mill. "That sort of stuff made us realize, hell we had to bite the bullet. . . . The bosses sure didn't give a damn for us." Although most Americans approved of unions in principle, they became fed up with strikes and blamed unions for shortages and rising prices. When the strikes subsided, workers had won wage increases of about 20 percent, but the loss of overtime pay and rising prices left their purchasing power only slightly higher than in 1942.

Women workers fared even worse. Polls indicated that 68 to 85 percent wanted to keep their wartime jobs, but most who remained in the workforce had to settle for relatively low-paying jobs in light industry or the service sector (Figure 26.1). Displaced from her shipyard work, Marie Schreiber took a cashier's job, lamenting, "You were back to women's wages, you know . . . practically in half." With the backing of women's organizations and union women, Congresswoman Douglas sponsored bills to require equal pay for equal work, provide child care for employed mothers, and create a government commission to study women's status. But at a time when women were viewed primarily as wives and mothers and opposition to further expansion of federal powers was strong, these initiatives got nowhere.

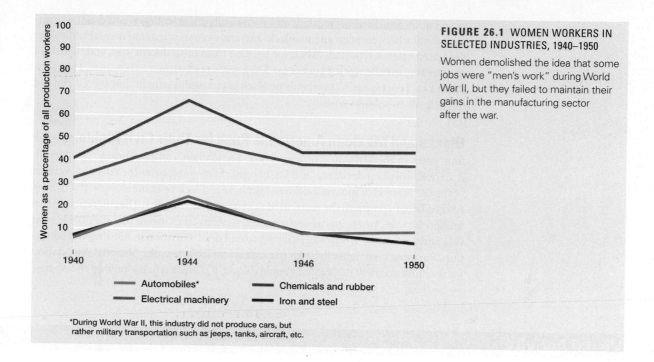

FIGURE 26.1 WOMEN WORKERS IN SELECTED INDUSTRIES, 1940–1950

Women demolished the idea that some jobs were "men's work" during World War II, but they failed to maintain their gains in the manufacturing sector after the war.

Legend:
— Automobiles*
— Electrical machinery
— Chemicals and rubber
— Iron and steel

*During World War II, this industry did not produce cars, but rather military transportation such as jeeps, tanks, aircraft, etc.

By 1947, the economy had stabilized, avoiding the postwar depression that so many had feared. Wartime profits enabled businesses to expand. Consumers could now spend their wartime savings on items that had lain beyond their reach during the depression and war. Defense spending and foreign aid that enabled war-stricken countries to purchase American products also stimulated the economy. A soaring birthrate further sustained consumer demand. Although prosperity was far from universal, the United States entered into a remarkable economic boom that lasted through the 1960s (see chapter 27).

Another economic boost came from the only large welfare measure passed after the New Deal. The Servicemen's Readjustment Act (GI Bill), enacted in 1944, offered 16 million veterans job training and education; unemployment compensation until they found jobs; and low-interest loans to purchase homes, farms, and small businesses. By 1948, some 1.3 million veterans had bought houses with government loans. Helping 2.2 million ex-soldiers attend college, the subsidies sparked a boom in higher education. A drugstore clerk before his military service, Don Condren was able to get an engineering degree and buy his first house. "I think the GI Bill gave the whole country an upward boost economically," he said.

Yet the impact of the GI Bill was uneven. As wives and daughters of veterans, women benefited indirectly from the GI subsidies, but few women qualified for the employment and educational preferences available to some 15 million men. Moreover, GI programs were administered at the state and local levels, which resulted in routine racial and ethnic discrimination, especially in the South. Southern universities remained segregated, and historically black colleges could not accommodate all who wanted to attend. Black veterans were shuttled into menial labor. One decorated veteran reported, "My color bars me from most decent jobs, and if, instead of accepting menial work, I collect my $20 a week readjustment allowance, I am classified as a 'lazy nigger.'" Thousands of black veterans did benefit, but the GI Bill did not help all ex-soldiers equally.

Blacks and Mexican Americans Push for Their Civil Rights.

"I spent four years in the army to free a bunch of Frenchmen and Dutchmen," an African American corporal declared, "and I'm hanged if I'm going to let the Alabama version of the Germans kick me around when I get home." Black veterans along with civilians resolved not to return to the racial injustices of prewar America. The migration of two million African Americans to northern and western cities meant that they could now vote and participate in ongoing struggles to end discrimination in housing and education. Pursuing civil rights through the courts and Congress, the National Association for the Advancement of Colored People (NAACP) counted half a million members.

Visual Activity

WOMEN'S ROLE IN PEACETIME

Like many manufacturers during World War II, Proctor Electric Company, which had shifted its focus from making appliances to producing bomb fuses, cartridges, and airplane wing flaps, hoped to profit after the war from pent-up consumer demand. Even before the company had fully reconverted its plants, ads tempted consumers with products soon to come, as in this 1946 ad. Picture Research Consultants & Archives.

READING THE IMAGE: Why do you think a woman is featured in this ad? Considering the scene in the background, what message is conveyed about women's employment during and after the war?

CONNECTIONS: How did the shortage of consumer goods affect the postwar economy? What role did consumer goods play in the economic revival?

In the postwar years, individual African Americans broke through the color barrier, achieving several "firsts." Jackie Robinson integrated major league baseball, playing for the Brooklyn Dodgers and braving abuse from fans and players to win the Rookie of the Year Award in 1947. In 1950, Ralph J. Bunche received the Nobel Peace Prize for his United Nations work, and Gwendolyn Brooks won the Pulitzer Prize for poetry. Some organizations, such as the American Medical Association in 1949, opened their doors to black members. Still, little had changed for most African Americans, especially in the South, where violence greeted their attempts to assert their rights. Armed white men prevented Medgar Evers (who would become a key civil rights leader in the 1960s) and four other veterans from voting in Mississippi. A mob lynched Isaac Nixon for voting in Georgia, and an all-white jury acquitted the men accused of his murder. Segregation and economic discrimination were widespread in the North as well.

INTEGRATION OF THE MILITARY

Truman's 1948 executive order integrating the armed services met steely resistance from parts of the military and took years to implement fully. The pressures of the Korean War forced the military to use African Americans where personnel were needed, placing black and white soldiers, such as these Marines, side by side. In 1954, the army dissolved its last all-black unit. Official Marine Corps Photo #A171810.

The Cold War heightened U.S. leaders' sensitivity to racial issues, as the superpowers vied for the allegiance of newly independent nations with nonwhite populations, and Soviet propaganda repeatedly highlighted racial injustice in the United States. Secretary of State Dean Acheson noted that systematic segregation and discrimination endangered "our moral leadership of the free and democratic nations of the world."

"My very stomach turned over when I learned that Negro soldiers just back from overseas were being dumped out of army trucks in Mississippi and beaten," wrote Truman. Risking support from southern white voters, Truman spoke more boldly on civil rights than any previous president had. In 1946, he created the President's Committee on Civil Rights, and in February 1948 he asked Congress to enact the committee's comprehensive recommendations. The first president to address the NAACP, Truman asserted that all Americans should have equal rights to housing, education, employment, and the ballot.

As with much of his domestic program, Truman failed to act aggressively on his bold words. Congress rejected his proposals for national civil rights legislation, although some non-Southern states did pass laws against discrimination in employment and public accommodations. Running for reelection in 1948 and hoping to appeal to northern black and liberal voters, Truman issued an executive order to desegregate the armed services, but it lay unimplemented until the Korean War, when the cost of segregation to military efficiency became apparent. Then officers gradually integrated their ranks, and by 1953 nearly all African Americans served in mixed units. Although actual accomplishments fell far short of Truman's proposals, desegregation of the military and the administration's support of civil rights cases in the Supreme Court contributed to far-reaching changes.

Discussion of race and civil rights usually focused on African Americans, but Mexican Americans fought similar injustices. In 1929, they had formed the League of United Latin American Citizens (LULAC) to combat discrimination and segregation in the Southwest. Like black soldiers, Mexican American veterans believed, as one insisted, that "we had earned our credentials as American citizens." Problems with getting their veterans' benefits spurred the formation of the American GI Forum in 1948 in Corpus Christi, Texas. Dr. Héctor Peréz García, president of the local LULAC and a Bronze Star combat surgeon, led the GI Forum, which became a national force for battling discrimination and electing sympathetic officials.

"Education is our freedom," read the GI Forum's motto, yet Mexican American children were routinely segregated in public schools. In 1945, with the help of LULAC, parents filed a class action suit in southern California, challenging school districts that barred their children from white schools. In the resulting decision, *Mendez v. Westminster* (1947), a federal court for the first time struck down school segregation. NAACP lawyer Thurgood Marshall filed a supporting brief in the case, which foreshadowed the landmark *Brown v. Board of Education* decision of 1954 (as discussed in chapter 27). Efforts to gain equal education, challenges to employment discrimination, and campaigns for political representation all demonstrated a growing mobilization of Mexican Americans in the Southwest.

Taft-Hartley Act
Law passed by the Republican-controlled Congress in 1947 that amended the Wagner Act and placed restrictions on organized labor that made it more difficult for unions to organize workers.

The Fair Deal Flounders.
Republicans capitalized on public frustrations with strikes and shortages in the 1946 congressional elections, accusing the Truman administration of "confusion, corruption, and communism." Helen Gahagan Douglas kept her seat, but the Republicans captured control of Congress for the first time in fourteen years. Many had campaigned against the New Deal, and in the Eightieth Congress they weakened some reform programs and enacted tax cuts favoring higher-income groups.

Organized labor took the most severe blow when Congress passed the **Taft-Hartley Act** over Truman's veto in 1947. Called a "slave labor" law by unions, the measure amended the Wagner Act (see chapter 24), putting restraints on unions that reduced their power to bargain with employers and made it more difficult to organize workers. States could now pass "right-to-work" laws, which banned the practice of requiring all workers to join a union once a majority had voted for it. Many states, especially in the South and West, rushed to enact such laws, encouraging industries to relocate there. Taft-Hartley maintained the New Deal principle of government protection for collective bargaining, but it tipped the balance of power more in favor of management.

In the 1948 elections, Truman faced not only a resurgent Republican Party headed by New York governor Thomas E. Dewey but also two revolts within his own party. On the left, Henry A. Wallace, whose foreign policy views had cost him his cabinet seat, led the new Progressive Party. On the right, South Carolina governor J. Strom Thurmond headed the States' Rights Party — the Dixiecrats — formed by southern Democrats who walked out of the 1948 Democratic Party convention when it passed a liberal civil rights plank.

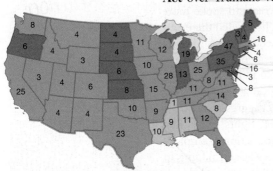

Candidate	Electoral Vote	Popular Vote	Percent of Popular Vote
Harry S. Truman (Democrat)	303	24,105,695	49.5
Thomas E. Dewey (Republican)	189	21,969,170	45.1
J. Strom Thurmond (States' Rights)	39	1,169,021	2.4
Henry A. Wallace (Progressive)	0	1,156,103	2.4

MAP 26.2   THE ELECTION OF 1948

Truman launched a vigorous campaign, yet his prospects were so bleak that on election night the *Chicago Daily Tribune* printed its next day's issue with the headline "Dewey Defeats Truman." But even though the Dixiecrats won four southern states, Truman took 303 electoral votes to Dewey's 189, and his party regained control of Congress (Map 26.2). His unexpected victory attested to the broad support for his foreign policy and the enduring popularity of New Deal reform.

While most New Deal programs survived Republican attacks, Truman failed to enact his Fair Deal agenda. Congress made modest improvements in Social Security and raised the minimum wage, but it passed only one significant reform measure. The **Housing Act of 1949** authorized 810,000 units of government-constructed housing over the next six years and represented a landmark commitment by the government to address the housing needs of the poor. Yet it fell far short of actual need, and slum clearance frequently displaced the poor without providing alternatives.

Housing Act of 1949
Law authorizing the construction of 810,000 units of government housing. This landmark effort marked the first significant commitment of the federal government to meet the housing needs of the poor.

With southern Democrats posing a primary obstacle, Congress rejected Truman's proposals for civil rights, a powerful medical lobby blocked plans for a universal health care program, and conflicts over race and religion thwarted federal aid to education. Truman's efforts to revise immigration policy were mixed. The McCarran-Walter Act of 1952 ended the outright ban on immigration and citizenship for Japanese and other Asians, but it authorized the government to bar suspected Communists and homosexuals and maintained the discriminatory quota system established in the 1920s.

Truman's concentration on foreign policy rather than domestic proposals contributed to the failure of his Fair Deal. By late 1950, the Korean War embroiled the president in controversy and depleted his power as a legislative leader (see pages 791–95). Truman's failure to make good on his domestic proposals set the United States apart from most European nations, which by the 1950s had in place comprehensive health, housing, and employment security programs to underwrite the material well-being of their populations.

The Domestic Chill: McCarthyism.
Truman's domestic agenda also suffered from a wave of anticommunism that weakened liberals. "Red-baiting" (attempting to link individuals or ideas with communism) and official retaliation against leftist critics of the government had flourished during the Red scare at the end of World War I (see chapter 22), and Republicans had attacked the New Deal as a plot of radicals. A second Red scare followed World War II, born of partisan politics, foreign policy setbacks, and disclosures of Soviet espionage.

Republicans jumped on events such as the Soviet takeover of Eastern Europe and the Communist triumph in China to accuse Democrats of fostering internal subversion. Wisconsin senator Joseph R. McCarthy

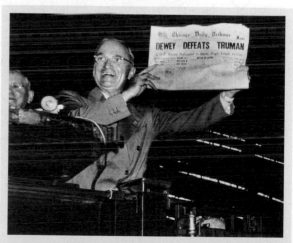

TRUMAN'S 1948 VICTORY
Although large crowds turned out for Truman's coast-to-coast "whistle-stop" campaign, most experts thought he had little chance to win the election, given the defections from his party on both the left and right. Polls predicted that Dewey would win about 50 percent of the popular vote and Truman around 45 percent, but the last one was taken two weeks before election day.
W. Eugene Smith/Getty Images.

avowed that "the Communists within our borders have been more responsible for the success of Communism abroad than Soviet Russia." McCarthy's charges — such as the allegation that retired general George C. Marshall belonged to a Communist conspiracy — were reckless and often ludicrous, but the press covered him avidly, and *McCarthyism* became a term synonymous with the anti-Communist crusade.

Revelations of Soviet espionage lent credibility to fears of internal communism. A number of ex-Communists, including Whittaker Chambers and Elizabeth Bentley, testified that they and others had provided secret documents to the Soviets. Most alarming of all, in 1950 a British physicist working on the atomic bomb project confessed that he was a spy and implicated several Americans, including Ethel and Julius Rosenberg. The Rosenbergs pleaded not guilty but were convicted of conspiracy to commit espionage and electrocuted in 1953.

THE RED SCARE

The celebrated editorial cartoonist for the *Washington Post*, Herbert Lawrence Block was a frequent critic of McCarthyism. In this 1949 cartoon, he addressed the intimidation of teachers, which occurred across the country in public schools and universities. Public officials demanded that teachers take loyalty oaths, grilled them about their past and present political associations, and fired those who refused to cooperate. A 1949 Herblock Cartoon, ©The Herb Block Foundation.

Records opened in the 1990s showed that the Soviet Union did receive secret documents from Americans that probably hastened its development of nuclear weapons by a year or two. Yet the vast majority of individuals hunted down in the Red scare had done nothing more than at one time joining the Communist Party, associating with Communists, or supporting radical causes. And nearly all the accusations related to activities that had taken place long before the Cold War had made the Soviet Union an enemy.

The hunt for subversives was conducted by both Congress and the executive branch. Stung by charges of communism in the 1946 midterm elections, Truman issued Executive Order 9835 in March 1947, establishing loyalty review boards to investigate every federal employee. "A nightmare from which there [was] no awakening" was how State Department employee Esther Brunauer described it when she and her husband, a chemist in the navy, both lost their jobs because he had joined a Communist youth organization in the 1920s and associated with suspected radicals. Government investigators allowed anonymous informers to make charges and placed the burden of proof on the accused. More than two thousand civil service employees lost their jobs, and another ten thousand resigned as Truman's loyalty program continued into the mid-1950s. Hundreds of homosexuals resigned or were fired over charges of "sexual perversion," which anti-Communist crusaders said could subject them to blackmail. Years later, Truman said privately that the loyalty program had been a mistake.

Congressional committees, such as the **House Un-American Activities Committee (HUAC)**, also investigated individuals' political associations. When those under scrutiny refused to name names, investigators charged that silence was tantamount to confession, and these "unfriendly witnesses" lost their jobs and suffered public ostracism. In 1947, HUAC investigated radical activity in Hollywood. Some actors and directors cooperated, but ten refused, citing their First Amendment rights. The "Hollywood Ten" served jail sentences for contempt of Congress — a punishment that Helen Gahagan Douglas fought — and then found themselves blacklisted in the movie industry. Popular crooner Frank Sinatra, a defender of the Hollywood Ten, wondered if someone called for "a square deal for the underdog, will they call you a Commie?"

The Truman administration went after the Communist Party directly, prosecuting its leaders under a 1940 law that made it a crime to "advocate the overthrow and destruction of the [government] by force and violence." Although civil libertarians argued that the guilty verdicts violated First Amendment freedoms of speech, press, and association, the Supreme Court ruled in 1951 that the Communist threat overrode constitutional guarantees.

The domestic Cold War spread beyond the nation's capital. State and local governments investigated citizens, demanded loyalty oaths, fired employees suspected of disloyalty, banned books from public libraries, and more. College professors and public school teachers lost their jobs in New York, California, and elsewhere. Because the Communist Party had helped organize unions and championed racial justice, labor and civil rights activists fell prey to McCarthyism as well. African American activist Jack O'Dell remembered that segregationists pinned the tag of Communist on "anybody who supported the right of blacks to have civil rights."

McCarthyism caused untold harm to thousands of innocent individuals. Anti-Communist crusaders humiliated and discredited law-abiding citizens, hounded them from their jobs, and in some cases even sent them to prison. The anti-Communist crusade violated fundamental constitutional rights of freedom of speech and association and stifled the expression of dissenting ideas or unpopular causes.

> **REVIEW** Why did Truman have limited success in implementing his domestic agenda?

The Cold War Becomes Hot: Korea

The Cold War erupted into a shooting war in June 1950 when troops from Communist North Korea invaded South Korea. For the first time, Americans went into battle to implement containment. Confirming the global reach of the Truman Doctrine, U.S. involvement in Korea also marked the militarization of American foreign policy. The United States, in concert with the United Nations, ultimately held the line in Korea, but at a great cost in lives, dollars, and domestic unity.

Korea and the Military Implementation of Containment. The **Korean War** grew out of the artificial division of Korea after World War II. Having expelled

---

House Un-American Activities Committee (HUAC)
Congressional committee especially prominent during the early years of the Cold War that investigated Americans who might be disloyal to the government or might have associated with Communists or other radicals. It was one of the key institutions that promoted the second Red scare.

Korean War
Conflict between North Korean forces supported by China and the Soviet Union and South Korean and U.S.-led United Nations forces over control of South Korea. Lasting from 1950 to 1953, the war represented the first time that the United States went to war to implement containment.

Am: syngman Rhee

the Japanese, the United States and the Soviet Union created two occupation zones separated by the thirty-eighth parallel (Map 26.3). With Moscow and Washington unable to agree on unification, the United Nations sponsored elections in South Korea in July 1948. The American-favored candidate, Syngman Rhee, was elected president, and the United States withdrew most of its troops. In the fall of 1948, the Soviets established the People's Republic of North Korea under Kim Il-sung and also withdrew. Although unsure whether Rhee's repressive government could sustain popular support, U.S. officials appreciated his anticommunism and provided economic and military aid to South Korea.

Skirmishes between North and South Korean troops at the thirty-eighth parallel began in 1948. Then, in June 1950, 90,000 North Koreans swept into South Korea. Truman's advisers assumed that the Soviet Union or China had instigated the attack (an assumption later proved incorrect), and the president quickly decided to intervene, viewing Korea as "the Greece of the Far East." With the Soviet Union absent

Map Activity

MAP 26.3   THE KOREAN WAR, 1950–1953

Although each side had plunged deep into enemy territory, the war ended in 1953 with the dividing line between North and South Korea nearly where it had been before the fighting began.

READING THE MAP: How far south did the North Korean forces progress at the height of their invasion? How far north did the UN forces get? What countries border Korea, and what was the significance of these particular countries' presence so close to the territory in dispute?

CONNECTIONS: What dangers did the forays of MacArthur's forces to within forty miles of the Korean-Chinese border pose? Why did Truman forbid MacArthur to approach that border? What political considerations on the home front influenced Truman's policy and military strategy regarding Korea?

International boundaries, 1950

UN offensive Sept.–Nov. 1950

North Korean invasion June–Sept. 1950

Communist Chinese offensive Nov. 1950–Jan. 1951

ON THE DEFENSIVE IN KOREA

After UN troops approached the Yalu River, the Chinese entered the Korean War, throwing UN forces on the defensive and pushing deep into the South. In this photo, taken in April 1951, infantrymen are protecting a pontoon bridge so that UN trucks and tanks on the other side can escape the advancing Chinese army. Eventually, UN forces recaptured this territory. AP Photo/James Martenhoff.

from the Security Council, the United States obtained UN sponsorship of a collective effort to repel the attack. Authorized to appoint a commander for the UN force, Truman named World War II hero General Douglas MacArthur *commander*

Sixteen nations sent troops to Korea, but the United States furnished most of the personnel and weapons, deploying almost 1.8 million troops and dictating strategy. By dispatching troops without asking Congress for a declaration of war, Truman violated the spirit if not the letter of the Constitution and contributed to the expansion of executive power that would characterize the Cold War.

The first American soldiers rushed to Korea unprepared and ill equipped: "I didn't even know how to dig a foxhole," recalled a nineteen-year-old army reservist, who was told by his sergeant to "Make it like a grave." As a result, U.S. forces suffered severe defeats early in the war. The North Koreans took the capital of Seoul and drove deep into South Korea, forcing UN troops to retreat to Pusan. Then, in September 1950, General MacArthur launched a bold counteroffensive at Inchon, 180 miles behind North Korean lines. By October, UN and South Korean forces had retaken Seoul and pushed the North Koreans back to the thirty-eighth parallel. Now Truman had to decide whether to invade North Korea and seek to unify the country.

From Containment to Rollback to Containment.
"Troops could not be expected . . . to march up to a surveyor's line and stop," remarked Secretary of State Dean Acheson, reflecting support for transforming the military objective from containment to elimination of the enemy and unification of Korea. Thus, for the only time during the Cold War, the United States tried to roll back communism by force. With UN approval,

on September 27, 1950, Truman authorized MacArthur to cross the thirty-eighth paral-lel. Concerned about possible intervention by China, the president directed him to keep UN troops away from the Korean-Chinese border. Disregarding the order, MacArthur sent them to within forty miles of China, whereupon 300,000 Chinese soldiers crossed into Korea. With Chinese help, the North Koreans recaptured Seoul.

After three months of grueling battle, UN forces fought their way back to the thirty-eighth parallel. At that point, Truman decided to seek a negotiated settlement. MacArthur was furious when the goal of the war reverted to containment, which to him represented defeat. Taking his case to the public, he challenged both the presi-dent's authority to conduct foreign policy and the principle of civilian control of the military. Fed up with MacArthur's insubordination, Truman fired him in April 1951. Many Americans sided with MacArthur, reflecting their frustration with contain-ment. Why should Americans die simply to preserve the status quo? Why not destroy the enemy once and for all? Those siding with MacArthur assumed that the United States was all-powerful and blamed the stalemate in Korea on the government's ineptitude or willingness to shelter subversives.

When Congress investigated MacArthur's dismissal, all of the top military lead-ers supported the president. According to the chairman of the Joint Chiefs of Staff, MacArthur wanted to wage "the wrong war, at the wrong place, at the wrong time, with the wrong enemy." Yet Truman never recovered from the political fallout. Nor was he able to end the war. Negotiations began in July 1951, but peace talks dragged on for two years while 12,000 more U.S. soldiers died.

Korea, Communism, and the 1952 Election.

Popular discontent with Truman's war boosted Republicans in the 1952 election. Their presidential nominee, General Dwight D. Eisenhower was a popular hero. As supreme commander in Europe, he won widespread acclaim for leading the Allied armies to victory over Germany in World War II, and in 1950 Truman appointed Eisenhower the first supreme commander of NATO forces.

Although Eisenhower believed that professional soldiers should stay out of poli-tics, he found compelling reasons to run in 1952. He largely agreed with Truman's foreign policy, but he deplored the Democrats' propensity to solve domestic problems with costly new federal programs. He also disliked the foreign policy views of leading Republican presidential contender Senator Robert A. Taft, who attacked containment and sought to cut defense spending. Eisenhower defeated Taft for the nomination, but the old guard prevailed on the party platform. It excoriated containment as "negative, futile, and immoral" and charged the Truman administration with shielding "traitors to the Nation in high places." By choosing thirty-nine-year-old Senator Richard M. Nixon for his running mate, Eisenhower helped to appease the right wing of the party.

Richard Milhous Nixon grew up in southern California, worked his way through college and law school, served in the navy, and briefly practiced law before winning election to Congress in 1946. Nixon quickly made a name for himself as a member of HUAC and a key anti-Communist, moving to the Senate with his victory over Helen Gahagan Douglas in 1950.

With his public approval ratings plummeting, Truman decided not to run for reelection. The Democrats nominated Adlai E. Stevenson the popular governor of

Illinois, but he could neither escape the domestic fallout from the Korean War or match Eisenhower's widespread appeal. Shortly before the election, Eisenhower announced dramatically, "I shall go to Korea," and voters registered their confidence in his ability to end the war. Cutting sharply into traditional Democratic territory, Eisenhower won several southern states and garnered 55 percent of the popular vote overall. His coattails carried a narrow Republican majority to Congress.

An Armistice and the War's Costs. Eisenhower made good on his pledge to end the Korean War. In July 1953, the two sides reached an armistice that left Korea divided, again roughly at the thirty-eighth parallel, with North and South separated by a two-and-a-half-mile-wide demilitarized zone (Map 26.3). The war fulfilled the objective of containment, since the United States had backed up its promise to help nations that were resisting communism. Both Truman and Eisenhower managed to contain what amounted to a world war — involving twenty nations altogether — within a single country and to avoid the use of nuclear weapons.

Yet the war took the lives of 36,000 Americans and wounded more than 100,000. Thousands of U.S. soldiers suffered as prisoners of war. South Korea lost more than a million people to war-related causes, and 1.8 million North Koreans and Chinese were killed or wounded.

Korea had an enormous effect on defense policy and spending. In April 1950, just before the war began, the National Security Council completed a top-secret report, known as **NSC 68**, on the United States' military strength, warning that national survival required a massive military buildup. The Korean War brought about nearly all of the military expansion called for in NSC 68, vastly increasing U.S. capacity to act as a global power. Military spending shot up from $14 billion in 1950 to $50 billion in 1953 and remained above $40 billion thereafter. By 1952, defense spending claimed nearly 70 percent of the federal budget, and the size of the armed forces had tripled.

To General Matthew Ridgway, MacArthur's successor as commander of the UN forces, Korea taught the lesson that U.S. forces should never again fight a land war in Asia. Eisenhower concurred. Nevertheless, during the Korean War the Truman administration had expanded its role in Asia by increasing aid to the French, who were fighting to hang on to their colonial empire in Indochina. As U.S. Marines retreated from a battle against Chinese soldiers in 1950, they sang, prophetically, "We're Harry's police force on call, / So put back your pack on, / The next step is Saigon."

> **NSC 68**
> Top-secret government report of April 1950 warning that national survival required a massive military buildup. The Korean War brought nearly all of the expansion called for in the report, and by 1952 defense spending claimed nearly 70 percent of the federal budget.

> **REVIEW** How did U.S. Cold War policy lead to the Korean War?

Conclusion: The Cold War's Costs and Consequences

Hoping for continued U.S.-Soviet cooperation rather than unilateral American intervention to resolve foreign crises, Helen Gahagan Douglas initially opposed the implementation of containment. By 1948, however, she was squarely behind

Truman's decision to fight communism throughout the world, a decision that marked the most momentous foreign policy initiative in the nation's history.

More than any development in the postwar world, the Cold War defined American politics and society for decades to come. It transformed the federal government, shifting its priorities from domestic to external affairs, greatly expanding its budget, and substantially increasing the power of the president. Military spending helped transform the nation itself, as defense contracts promoted economic and population booms in the West and Southwest. The nuclear arms race put the people of the world at risk, consumed resources that might have been used to improve living standards, and skewed the economy toward dependence on military projects.

In sharp contrast to foreign policy, the domestic policies of the postwar years reflected continuity with the 1930s. Douglas had come to Congress hoping to expand the New Deal, to help find "a way by which all people can live out their lives in dignity and decency." She avidly supported Truman's proposals for new programs in education, health, and civil rights, but a majority of her colleagues did not. Consequently, the poor and minorities suffered even while a majority of Americans enjoyed a higher standard of living in an economy boosted by Cold War spending and the reconstruction of Western Europe and Japan.

Another cost of the early Cold War years was the anti-Communist hysteria that swept the nation, denying Douglas a Senate seat, intimidating radicals and liberals, and narrowing the range of ideas acceptable for political discussion. Partisan politics and Truman's warnings about the Communist menace fueled McCarthyism, along with popular frustrations over the failure of containment to produce clear-cut victories. The Korean War, which ended in stalemate rather than the defeat of communism, exacerbated feelings of frustration. It would be a major challenge of the Eisenhower administration to restore national unity and confidence.

Chapter Review

KEY TERMS

Cold War (p. 775)
iron curtain (p. 775)
containment (p. 775)
Truman Doctrine (p. 777)
Marshall Plan (p. 777)
North Atlantic Treaty Organization (NATO) (p. 779)

Central Intelligence Agency (CIA) (p. 779)
Taft-Hartley Act (p. 788)
Housing Act of 1949 (p. 789)
House Un-American Activities Committee (HUAC) (p. 791)
Korean War (p. 791)
NSC 68 (p. 795)

REVIEW QUESTIONS

❶ What factors contributed to the emergence of the Cold War? (pp. 774–83)

❷ Why did Truman have limited success in implementing his domestic agenda?   (pp. 783–91)

❸ How did U.S. Cold War policy lead to the Korean War?   (pp. 791–95)

MAKING CONNECTIONS

❶ What was the containment policy, and how successful was it up to 1953? Discuss the views of both the supporters and the critics of the policy.

❷ How did returning American soldiers change postwar domestic life in the areas of education and civil rights? Discuss how wartime experiences influenced their demands.

❸ Why did anti-Communist hysteria sweep the country in the early 1950s? How did it shape domestic politics? Be sure to consider the influence of developments abroad and at home.

LINKING TO THE PAST

❶ What events and decisions during World War II contributed to the rise of the Cold War in the late 1940s? (See chapter 25.)

❷ What did the anti-Communist hysteria of the late 1940s and the 1950s have in common with the Red scare that followed World War I, and how did these two phenomena differ? (See chapter 22.)

The Politics and Culture of Abundance, 1952–1960

CONTENT LEARNING OBJECTIVES

After reading and studying this chapter, you should be able to:

- Explain the major issues of the Eisenhower administration and how Eisenhower's approach represented the politics of the "Middle Way."
- Describe how the Eisenhower administration practiced containment and explain how the "New Look" in foreign policy influenced its handling of world events.
- Explain the factors that led to an economy of abundance and how that abundance influenced Americans' lives.
- Analyze how the economy of abundance influenced consumption, religion, gender roles, and the media.
- Explain the origins of the modern civil rights movement and the strategies activists used to end racial segregation.

Trailed by reporters, Vice President Richard M. Nixon led Soviet premier Nikita Khrushchev through the American National Exhibition in Moscow in July 1959. The display of American consumer goods was part of a cultural exchange that reflected a slight thaw in the Cold War after Khrushchev replaced Stalin. In Moscow, both Khrushchev and Nixon seized on the propaganda potential of the moment. As they examined the display, they exchanged a slugfest of words and gestures that reporters dubbed the kitchen debate.

Showing off a new color television set, Nixon said that the Soviet Union "may be ahead of us . . . in the thrust of

1959 CADILLAC
The automobile reflected 1950s prosperity and generated one of every six jobs. This Cadillac was manufactured by General Motors, the biggest and richest corporation in the world. Bill Philpot/Alamy Stock Photo.

your rockets," but he insisted that the United States outstripped the Soviets in consumer goods. Nixon linked capitalism with democracy, asserting that the array of products represented "what freedom means to us . . . our right to choose." Moreover, Nixon boasted that "any steelworker could buy this house," as the two leaders walked through a model of a six-room ranch-style home. Khrushchev retorted that in the Soviet Union "you are entitled to housing," whereas in the United States the homeless slept on the pavement.

Nixon declared that the household appliances were "designed to make things easier for our women." Khrushchev disparaged "the capitalist attitude toward women," maintaining that the Soviets appreciated women's contributions to the economy, not their domesticity. Nixon got Khrushchev to agree that it was "far better to be talking about washing machines than machines of war," yet Cold War tensions surfaced when Khrushchev later blustered, "We too are giants. You want to threaten — we will answer threats with threats."

In fact, the Eisenhower administration (1953–1961) had begun with threats, and the two nations engaged in an intense arms race throughout the decade and beyond. During the 1952 campaign, Republicans had vowed to roll back communism and liberate "enslaved" peoples under Soviet rule. In practice, President Dwight D. Eisenhower pursued a containment policy much like that of his predecessor, Harry S. Truman, though Eisenhower relied more on nuclear weapons and on Central Intelligence Agency (CIA) secret operations against left-leaning governments. Yet as Nixon's visit to Moscow demonstrated, Eisenhower seized on political changes in the Soviet Union to reduce tensions in Soviet-American relations.

Continuity with the Truman administration also characterized domestic policy. Although Eisenhower favored corporations with tax cuts and resisted strong federal efforts in health care, education, and race relations, he did not try to demolish the New Deal. He even extended the reach of the federal government with a massive highway program.

Although poverty clung stubbornly to one of every five Americans, the Moscow display testified to the unheard-of material gains savored by many in the postwar era. Cold War weapons production spurred the economy, whose vitality stimulated suburban development, contributed to the growth of the South and Southwest (the Sun Belt), and enabled millions of Americans to buy a host of

CHRONOLOGY

1952 Dwight D. Eisenhower elected president.

1953 CIA organizes coup against Iranian government.

1954 CIA organizes coup against Guatemalan government. Geneva accords end French presence in Vietnam. United States begins aid to South Vietnam. Operation Wetback begins. *Hernandez v. Texas* decided. *Brown v. Board of Education* decided. Senate condemns Senator Joseph McCarthy.

1955 Eisenhower and Khrushchev meet in Geneva.

1955– Montgomery, Alabama,
1956 bus boycott carried out.

1956 Interstate Highway and Defense System Act becomes law. Eisenhower reelected.

1957 Southern Christian Leadership Conference (SCLC) founded. Soviets launch *Sputnik*. Civil Rights Act of 1957 passes.

1958 National Aeronautics and Space Administration (NASA) established. National Defense Education Act passes.

1959 Nixon and Khrushchev engage in kitchen debate.

1960 Soviets shoot down U.S. U-2 spy plane. One-quarter of Americans live in suburbs. Thirty-five percent of women work outside the home.

new products. As new homes, television sets, and household appliances transformed living patterns, Americans took part in a consumer culture that celebrated the family and traditional gender roles, even as more and more married women took jobs outside the home. Challenging the dominant norms were dissenting writers known as the Beats and an emerging youth culture.

The Cold War and the economic boom helped African Americans mount the most dramatic challenge of the 1950s, a struggle against the system of segregation and disfranchisement that had replaced slavery. Large numbers of African Americans took direct action against the institutions of injustice, developing the organizations, leadership, and strategies to mount a civil rights movement of unprecedented size and influence.

Eisenhower and the Politics of the "Middle Way"

Moderation was the guiding principle of Eisenhower's domestic agenda and leadership style. In 1953, he pledged a "middle way between untrammeled freedom of the individual and the demands for the welfare of the whole Nation," promising that his administration would "avoid government by bureaucracy as carefully as it avoids neglect of the helpless." Eisenhower generally resisted expanding the federal government's power, he acted reluctantly when the Supreme Court ordered schools to desegregate, and his administration terminated the federal trusteeship of dozens of Indian tribes. As a moderate Republican, however, Eisenhower supported the continuation of New Deal programs, and in some cases, such as in the creation of a national highway system, he expanded federal action. Nicknamed "Ike," the confident war hero remained popular, but he was not able to lift his party to national dominance.

Modern Republicanism. In contrast to the old guard conservatives in his party who criticized containment and wanted to repeal much of the New Deal, Dwight D. Eisenhower preached "modern Republicanism." This meant resisting additional federal intervention in economic and social life, but not turning the clock back to the 1920s. "Should any political party attempt to abolish social security and eliminate labor laws and farm programs," he wrote privately in 1954, "you would not hear of that party again in our political history." Democratic control of Congress after the elections of 1954 further contributed to Eisenhower's moderate approach.

The new president attempted to distance himself from the anti-Communist fervor that had plagued the Truman administration, even as he intensified Truman's loyalty program, allowing federal executives to dismiss thousands of employees on grounds of loyalty, security, or "suitability." Reflecting his inclination to avoid controversial issues, Eisenhower refused to denounce Senator Joseph McCarthy publicly. But, in 1954, McCarthy began to destroy himself when he hurled reckless charges of communism against military personnel during televised hearings. When the army's lawyer demanded of McCarthy, "Have you left no sense of decency?" those in the hearing room applauded. A Senate vote in 1954 to condemn him marked the end of his influence but not the end of harassing dissenters on the left.

Eisenhower sometimes echoed conservative Republicans' conviction that government was best left to the states and economic decisions to private business. Yet he signed laws bringing ten million more workers under Social Security, increasing the minimum wage, and creating a new Department of Health, Education, and Welfare. And when the spread of polio neared epidemic proportions, Eisenhower obtained funds from Congress to distribute a vaccine, even though conservatives wanted the states to bear that responsibility.

Eisenhower's greatest domestic initiative was the **Interstate Highway and Defense System Act of 1956** (Map 27.1). Promoted as essential to national defense and an impetus to economic growth, the act authorized construction of a national highway system, with the federal government paying most of the costs through increased fuel and vehicle taxes. The new highways accelerated the mobility of people and goods, spurred suburban expansion, and benefited the trucking, construction, and automobile industries that had lobbied hard for the law. Eventually, the monumental highway project exacted unforeseen costs in the form of air pollution, energy consumption, declining railroads and mass transportation, and decay of central cities.

In other areas, Eisenhower restrained federal activity in favor of state governments and private enterprise. His large tax cuts directed most benefits to business and the wealthy, and he resisted federal aid to primary and secondary education as well as strong White House leadership on behalf of civil rights. Eisenhower opposed national health insurance, preferring the growing practice of private insurance provided by employers. Although Democrats sought to keep nuclear power in government hands, Eisenhower signed legislation authorizing the private manufacture and sale of nuclear energy. The first commercial nuclear power plant opened in 1958 in northwest Pennsylvania.

Termination and Relocation of Native Americans.
Eisenhower's efforts to limit the federal government were consistent with a new direction in Indian policy, which reversed the New Deal emphasis on strengthening tribal governments and preserving Indian culture (see chapter 24). After World War II, when some 25,000 Indians had left their homes for military service and another 40,000 for work in defense industries, policymakers began to favor assimilating Native Americans and ending their special relationships with the government.

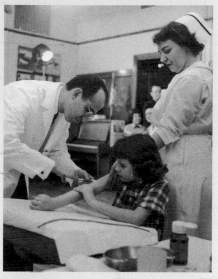

THE POLIO VACCINE

Building on the work of other scientists, Dr. Jonas Salk, a researcher at the University of Michigan and the University of Pittsburgh, was the first to develop a successful polio vaccine. In this 1953 photo, he injects a girl during the trials that established the drug's success. Salk became a national hero when the vaccine became available to millions of children in 1955. Hulton Archive/Getty Images.

Interstate Highway and Defense System Act of 1956
Law authorizing the construction of a national highway system. Promoted as essential to national defense and an impetus to economic growth, the national highway system accelerated the movement of people and goods and changed the nature of American communities.

To some officials, who reflected Cold War emphasis on conformity to dominant American values, the communal practices of Indians resembled socialism and stifled individual initiative. Eisenhower's commissioner of Indian affairs, Glenn Emmons, did not believe that tribal lands could produce income sufficient to eliminate poverty, but he also revealed the bias of policymakers when he insisted that Indians wanted to "work and live like Americans." Moreover, Indians still held rights to water, land, minerals, and other resources that were increasingly attractive to state governments and private entrepreneurs.

By 1960, the government had implemented a three-part program of compensation, termination, and relocation. In 1946, Congress established the Indian Claims Commission to hear outstanding claims by Native Americans for land taken by the government. When it closed in 1978, the commission had settled 285 cases, with compensation exceeding $800 million. Yet the awards were based on land values at the time the land was taken and did not include interest.

The second policy, termination, also originated in the Truman administration when Commissioner Dillon S. Myer asserted that his Bureau of Indian Affairs should do "nothing for Indians which Indians can do for themselves." Beginning in 1953, Eisenhower signed bills transferring jurisdiction over tribal land to state and local governments and ending the trusteeship relationship between Indians and the federal government. The loss of federal hospitals, schools, and other special arrangements

Map Activity

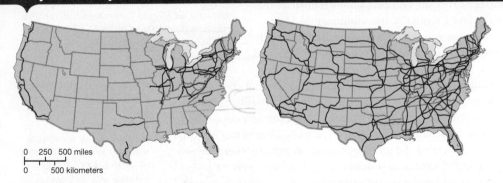

```
0   250  500 miles
0        500 kilometers
```

——— Main U.S. highways, 1930   ——— Interstate highways, 1970

MAP 27.1 THE INTERSTATE HIGHWAY SYSTEM, 1930 AND 1970

Built with federal funds authorized in the Interstate Highway and Defense System Act of 1956, superhighways soon crisscrossed the nation. Trucking, construction, gasoline, and travel were among the industries that prospered, but railroads suffered from the subsidized competition.

READING THE MAP: What regions of the United States had main highways in 1930? What regions did not? How had the situation changed by 1970?

CONNECTIONS: What impact did the growth of the interstate highway system have on migration patterns in the United States? What benefits did the new interstate highways bring to Americans, and at what costs?

devastated Indian tribes. As had happened after passage of the Dawes Act in 1887 (see chapter 17), corporate interests and individuals took advantage of the opportunity to purchase Indian land cheaply. The government abandoned termination in the 1960s after some 13,000 Indians and more than one million acres of their land had been affected.

The Indian Relocation Program, the third piece of Native American policy, began in 1948 and involved more than 100,000 Native Americans by 1973. The government encouraged Indians to move to cities, where relocation centers were supposed to help with housing, job training, and medical care. Even though Indians were moved far from their reservations, about one-third returned.

Most who stayed in cities faced racism, unemployment, poor housing, and the loss of their traditional culture. "I wish we had never left home," said one woman whose husband was out of work and drinking heavily. "It's dirty and noisy, and people all around, crowded. . . . It seems like I never see the sky or trees." Reflecting long-standing disagreements among Indians themselves, some who overcame these obstacles applauded the program. But most urban Indians remained poor, and even many who had welcomed relocation worried that "we would lose our identity as Indian people, lose our culture and our [way] of living." Within two decades, a national pan-Indian movement — a by-product of this urbanization — emerged to resist assimilation and to demand much more for Indians (as discussed in chapter 28).

MAJOR INDIAN RELOCATIONS, 1950–1970

The 1956 Election and the Second Term.
Eisenhower easily defeated Adlai Stevenson in 1956, doubling his victory margin of 1952. Yet Democrats kept control of Congress, and in the midterm elections two years later, they all but wiped out the Republican Party, gaining a 64–34 majority in the Senate and a 282–135 advantage in the House. Although Ike captured voters' hearts, a majority of Americans remained wedded to the programs and policies of the Democrats.

Eisenhower faced more serious leadership challenges in his second term. When the economy plunged into a recession in late 1957, he fought with Congress over the budget and vetoed bills to expand housing, urban development, and public works projects. The president and Congress did agree on the first, though largely symbolic, civil rights law in a century and on a larger federal role in education, largely in the interest of national security (as discussed on pages 808 and 821).

In the end, the first Republican administration after the New Deal left the functions of the federal government intact, though it tipped policy benefits somewhat toward corporate interests. Even with two recessions, unparalleled prosperity graced the Eisenhower years, and inflation was kept low. Eisenhower celebrated what he called the "wide diffusion of wealth and incomes" across the United States, yet amid the remarkable

INDIAN RELOCATION

As part of its new emphasis on assimilation, the Bureau of Indian Affairs urged Native Americans to move from their reservations to cities, and the percentage of Indians in urban areas grew from 13.4 in 1950 to 44 in 1970.
Jack Riddle/Getty Images.

abundance were some forty million impoverished Americans. Rural deprivation was particularly pronounced, as was poverty among the elderly, African Americans, and other minorities.

> **REVIEW** How did Eisenhower's domestic policies reflect his moderate political vision?

Liberation Rhetoric and the Practice of Containment

At his first inauguration, Eisenhower warned that "forces of good and evil are massed and armed and opposed as rarely before in history." Like Truman, he saw communism as a threat to the nation's security and economic interests, and he wanted to keep the United States the most powerful country in the world. Eisenhower's foreign policy differed, however, in three areas: its rhetoric, its means, and — after Stalin's death in 1953 — its movement toward accommodation with the Soviet Union.

Although some Republicans, such as Secretary of State John Foster Dulles, deplored containment as "negative, futile, and immoral," the Eisenhower administration did not attempt to roll back communism with force. Nuclear weapons and CIA secret operations took on a more prominent role in defense strategy, and the United States intervened at the margins of Communist power in Asia, Latin America, and the Middle East. Toward the end of his presidency, Eisenhower sought to ease tensions between the superpowers.

The "New Look" in Foreign Policy. Eisenhower was determined to control military expenditures in order to balance the budget and cut taxes. Reflecting American confidence in technology and opposition to a large peacetime army, Eisenhower's "New Look" in defense strategy concentrated U.S. military strength in nuclear weapons and missiles to deliver them. Instead of maintaining large ground forces of its own, the United States would arm friendly nations and back them up with an ominous nuclear arsenal, providing, according to one defense official, "more bang for the buck." Dulles believed that America's willingness to "go to the brink" of war with its intimidating nuclear weapons — a strategy called brinksmanship — would block any Soviet efforts to expand.

Nuclear weapons could not stop a Soviet nuclear attack, but in response to one, they could inflict enormous destruction. This certainty of "massive retaliation" was meant to deter the Soviets from launching an attack. Because the Soviet Union could respond similarly to an American first strike, this nuclear standoff became known as **mutually assured destruction**, or **MAD**. As leaders of both nations pursued an ever-escalating arms race, the United States stayed on top of the Soviet Union in nuclear warheads and delivery missiles.

Nuclear weapons could not roll back the iron curtain. When a revolt against the Soviet-controlled government began in Hungary in 1956, Dulles's liberation rhetoric proved to be empty. A radio plea from Hungarian freedom fighters cried, "SOS!

mutually assured destruction (MAD) Term for the standoff between the United States and Soviet Union based on the assumption that a nuclear first strike by either nation would result in massive retaliation and mutual destruction for both. Despite this, both countries pursued an ever-escalating arms race.

MISSILES IN THE NUCLEAR AGE

By the 1950s, both the United States and the Soviet Union were arming missiles with nuclear weapons, and the U.S. Air Force began to deploy those missiles in Europe before it developed the capability to strike Moscow from a launching site in the United States. This photograph shows the first Thor ballistic missile arriving at an RAF base in Norfolk, England, in 1958. © Mary Evans/The Image Works.

They just brought us a rumor that the American troops will be here within one or two hours." But help did not come. Eisenhower was unwilling to risk U.S. soldiers and possible nuclear war, and Soviet troops soon suppressed the insurrection, killing or wounding thousands of Hungarians.

Applying Containment to Vietnam. A major challenge to the containment policy came in Southeast Asia. During World War II, Ho Chi Minh and his nationalist coalition, the Vietminh, fought both the occupying Japanese forces and the French colonial rulers. In 1945, the Vietminh declared Vietnam's independence from France, and when France fought back, the area plunged into war. Because Ho declared himself a Communist, the Truman administration quietly began to provide aid to the French. American principles of national self-determination took a backseat to the battle against communism.

Eisenhower viewed communism in Vietnam much as Truman had regarded it in Greece and Turkey. In what became called the **domino theory**, Eisenhower explained, "You have a row of dominoes, you knock over the first one, and what will happen to the last one is the certainty that it will go over very quickly." A Communist victory in Southeast Asia, he warned, could trigger the fall of Japan, Taiwan, and the Philippines. By 1954, the United States was paying 75 percent of the cost of France's war, but Eisenhower resisted a larger role. When the French asked for American troops and planes to avert almost certain defeat in the battle for Dien Bien Phu, Eisenhower, remembering the Korean War, refused.

domino theory
Theory of containment articulated by President Eisenhower in the context of Vietnam. He warned that the fall of a non-Communist government to communism would trigger the spread of communism to neighboring countries.

GENEVA
ACCORDS, 1954

Dien Bien Phu fell to the Vietminh in May 1954, and two months later in Geneva a truce was signed. The Geneva accords recognized Vietnam's independence and temporarily partitioned it at the seventeenth parallel, separating the Vietminh in the north from the puppet government established by the French in the south. Within two years, the Vietnamese people were to vote in elections for a unified government. Some officials warned against U.S. involvement in Vietnam, envisioning "nothing but grief in store for us if we remained in that area." Eisenhower and Dulles nonetheless moved to prop up the dominoes with a new alliance and put the CIA to work infiltrating and destabilizing North Vietnam. Fearing a Communist victory in the elections mandated by the Geneva accords, they supported South Vietnamese prime minister Ngo Dinh Diem's refusal to hold the vote.

Between 1955 and 1961, the United States provided $800 million to the South Vietnamese army (ARVN). Yet the ARVN proved grossly unprepared for the guerrilla warfare that began in the late 1950s. With help from Ho Chi Minh's government in Hanoi, Vietminh rebels in the south stepped up their attacks on the Diem government. The insurgents gained support from the largely Buddhist peasants, who were outraged by the repressive regime of the Catholic, Westernized Diem. Unwilling to abandon containment, Eisenhower left his successor with a deteriorating situation and a firm commitment to defend South Vietnam against communism.

Interventions in Latin America and the Middle East. While supporting friendly governments in Asia, the Eisenhower administration sought to topple unfriendly ones in Latin America and the Middle East. Officials saw internal civil wars in terms of the Cold War conflict between the superpowers and often viewed nationalist movements as Communist challenges to democracy. They also acted against governments that threatened U.S. economic interests. The Eisenhower administration took this course of action out of sight of Congress and the public, making the CIA an important arm of foreign policy.

Guatemala's government, under the popularly elected president Jacobo Arbenz, was not Soviet controlled, but it accepted support from the small local Communist Party. In 1953, Arbenz moved to help landless, poverty-stricken peasants by nationalizing land owned, but not cultivated, by the United Fruit Company, a U.S. corporation whose annual profits were twice the size of Guatemala's budget. United Fruit refused Arbenz's offer to compensate the company at the value of the land it had declared for tax purposes. Then, equating Arbenz's reformist government with the spread of communism, the CIA provided pilots and other support to an opposition army that overthrew the elected government and installed a military dictatorship in 1954. United Fruit kept its land, and Guatemala succumbed to destructive civil wars that lasted through the 1990s.

In 1959, when Cubans' desire for political and economic autonomy erupted into a revolution led by Fidel Castro, a CIA agent promised "to take care of Castro just like we took care of Arbenz." American companies controlled major Cuban resources, and decisions made in Washington directly influenced the lives of the Cuban people.

The 1959 **Cuban revolution** drove out the U.S.-supported dictator Fulgencio Batista and led the CIA to warn Eisenhower that "Communists and other extreme radicals appear to have penetrated the Castro movement." When the United States denied Castro's requests for loans, he turned to the Soviet Union. And when U.S. companies refused Castro's offer to purchase their Cuban holdings at their assessed value, he began to nationalize their property. Many anti-Castro Cubans fled to the United States and reported his atrocities. Before leaving office, Eisenhower broke off diplomatic relations with Cuba and authorized the CIA to train Cuban exiles for an invasion to overthrow the Castro government.

In the Middle East, the CIA intervened in Iran to oust an elected government, support an unpopular dictatorship, and maintain Western access to Iranian oil (Map 30.3). In 1951, the Iranian parliament, led by Prime Minister Mohammed Mossadegh, nationalized the country's oil fields and refineries, which had been held primarily by a British company and from which Iran received less than 20 percent of profits. Britain strongly objected to the takeover and eventually sought help from the United States.

Advisers convinced Eisenhower that Mossadegh, whom *Time* magazine had called "the Iranian George Washington," left Iran vulnerable to communism, and the president wanted to keep oil-rich areas "under the control of people who are friendly." With Eisenhower's authorization, CIA agents instigated a coup, bribing army officers and financing demonstrations in the streets. In August 1953, Iranian army officers captured Mossadegh and reestablished the authority of the shah, Mohammad Reza Pahlavi, known for favoring Western interests and the Iranian wealthy classes. U.S. companies received a 40 percent share of Iran's oil concessions. But resentment over the intervention would poison U.S.-Iranian relations into the twenty-first century.

Elsewhere in the Middle East, Eisenhower continued Truman's support of Israel but also pursued friendships with Arab nations to secure access to oil and build a bulwark against communism. U.S. officials demanded that smaller nations take the American side in the Cold War, even when those nations preferred neutrality. In 1955, as part of this effort to win Arab allies, Secretary of State Dulles began talks with Egypt about American support to build the Aswan Dam on the Nile River. The following year, Egypt's leader, Gamal Abdel Nasser, sought arms from Communist Czechoslovakia, formed a military alliance with other Arab nations, and recognized the People's Republic of China. In retaliation, Dulles called off the deal for the dam.

In July 1956, Nasser responded by seizing the Suez Canal, then owned by Britain and France but scheduled to revert to Egypt within seven years. In response to the seizure, Israel, whose forces had been skirmishing with Egyptian troops along their common border since 1948, attacked Egypt, with help from Britain and France. Eisenhower opposed the intervention, recognizing that the Egyptians had claimed their own territory and that Nasser "embodie[d] the emotional demands of the people . . . for independence." Calling on the United Nations to arrange a truce, he pressured Britain and France to pull back, forcing Israel to retreat.

Despite staying out of the Suez crisis, Eisenhower made it clear in a January 1957 speech that the United States would actively combat communism in the

Cuban revolution
Uprising led by Fidel Castro that drove out U.S.-supported dictator Fulgencio Batista and eventually allied Cuba with the Soviet Union.

THE SUEZ CRISIS, 1956

Middle East. In March, Congress approved aid to any Middle Eastern nation "request-ing assistance against armed aggression from any country controlled by international communism." The president invoked this **Eisenhower Doctrine** to send aid to Jor-dan in 1957 and troops to Lebanon in 1958 to counter anti-Western pressures on those governments.

Eisenhower Doctrine
President Eisenhower's 1957 declaration that the United States would actively combat communism in the Middle East. Following this doctrine, Congress approved the policy, and Eisenhower sent aid to Jordan in 1957 and troops to Lebanon in 1958.

The Nuclear Arms Race.
While Eisenhower moved against perceived Com-munist inroads abroad, he also sought to reduce superpower tensions. After Stalin's death in 1953, Nikita Khrushchev emerged as a more moderate leader. Like Eisen-hower, who remarked privately that the arms race would lead "at worst to atomic warfare, at best to robbing every people and nation on earth of the fruits of their own toil," Khrushchev wanted to reduce defense spending and the threat of nuclear dev-astation. Eisenhower and Khrushchev met in Geneva in 1955 at the first summit conference since the end of World War II. Although the meeting produced no new agreements, it symbolized what Eisenhower called "a new spirit of conciliation and cooperation."

In August 1957, the Soviets test-fired their first intercontinental ballistic missile (ICBM) and, two months later, beat the United States into space by launching *Sputnik*, the first man-made satellite to circle the earth. The United States launched a successful satellite of its own in January 1958, but *Sputnik* raised fears that the Soviets led not only in missile development and space exploration but also in science and education. In response, Eisenhower established the National Aeronautics and Space Administration (NASA) with a huge budget increase for space exploration. He also signed the National Defense Education Act, providing support for students in math, foreign languages, and science and technology.

Eisenhower assured the public that the United States possessed nuclear superi-ority. In fact, during his presidency, the stockpile of nuclear weapons more than quadrupled. With ICBMs at home and in Britain, the United States was prepared to deploy more in Italy and Turkey. In 1960, the United States launched the first Polaris submarine carrying nuclear missiles. Yet nuclear weapons could not guarantee secu-rity for either superpower because they both possessed sufficient capacity to devastate each other. Most Americans did not follow Civil Defense Administration recommen-dations to construct home bomb shelters, but they did realize how precarious their lives had become. A new organization, the Committee for a Sane Nuclear Policy, called the nuclear arms race "a danger unlike any danger that has ever existed."

In the midst of the arms race, the superpowers continued to talk, and by 1960 the two sides were close to a ban on nuclear testing. But just before a planned sum-mit in Paris, a Soviet missile shot down an American U-2 spy plane over Soviet ter-ritory. The State Department first denied that U.S. planes had been violating Soviet airspace, but the Soviets produced the pilot and the photos taken on his flight. Eisen-hower and Khrushchev met briefly, but the U-2 incident dashed all prospects for a nuclear arms agreement.

As Eisenhower left office, he warned about the growing influence of the **military-industrial complex**. Eisenhower had struggled against persistent pres-sures from defense contractors who, in tandem with the military, sought more dol-lars for newer, more powerful weapons systems. In his farewell address, he warned

military-industrial complex
A term President Eisenhower used to refer to the military establishment and defense contractors who, he warned, exercised undue influence in city, state, and federal government.

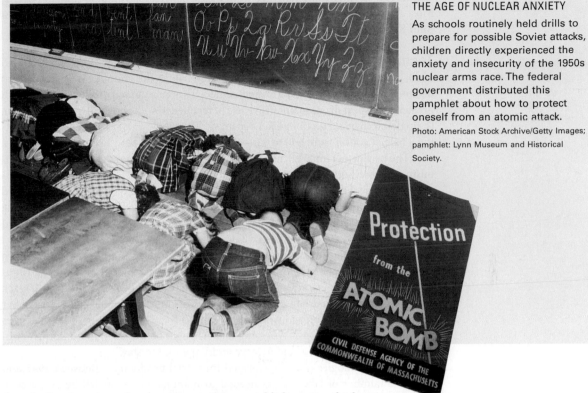

THE AGE OF NUCLEAR ANXIETY
As schools routinely held drills to prepare for possible Soviet attacks, children directly experienced the anxiety and insecurity of the 1950s nuclear arms race. The federal government distributed this pamphlet about how to protect oneself from an atomic attack. Photo: American Stock Archive/Getty Images; pamphlet: Lynn Museum and Historical Society.

that the "conjunction of an immense military establishment and a large arms industry . . . exercised a total influence . . . in every city, every state house, every office of the federal government," but his administration had done little to curtail the defense industry's power. The Cold War had created a warfare state.

REVIEW Where and how did Eisenhower practice containment?

New Work and Living Patterns in an Economy of Abundance

Stimulated by Cold War spending and technological advances, economic productivity increased enormously in the 1950s. A multitude of new items came on the market, and consumption became the order of the day. Millions of Americans enjoyed new homes in the suburbs, and higher education enrollments skyrocketed. Although every section of the nation enjoyed the new abundance, the Southwest and South — the Sun Belt — especially boomed in production, commerce, and population.

Work itself was changing. Fewer people labored on farms, service sector employment overtook manufacturing jobs, women's employment grew, and union membership soared. Not all Americans benefited from these changes; forty million lived in poverty. Most Americans, however, enjoyed a higher standard of living, prompting economist John Kenneth Galbraith to call the United States "the affluent society."

Technology Transforms Agriculture and Industry.

Between 1940 and 1960, agricultural output mushroomed even while the number of farmworkers declined by almost one-third. Farmers achieved unprecedented productivity through greater crop specialization, intensive use of fertilizers, and, above all, mechanization. A single mechanical cotton picker replaced fifty people and cut the cost of harvesting a bale of cotton from $40 to $5.

The decline of family farms and the growth of large commercial farming, or agribusiness, were both causes and consequences of mechanization. Benefiting handsomely from federal price supports begun in the New Deal, larger farmers could afford technological improvements, while smaller producers lacked capital to purchase the machinery necessary to compete. Consequently, average farm size more than doubled between 1940 and 1964, and the number of farms fell by more than 40 percent.

Many small farmers who hung on constituted a core of rural poverty. Southern landowners replaced sharecroppers and tenants with machines. Hundreds of thousands of African Americans moved to cities, where racial discrimination and a lack of jobs mired many in urban poverty. A Mississippi mother reported that most of her relatives headed for Chicago when they realized that "it was going to be machines now that harvest the crops." Worrying that "it might be worse up there" for her children, she agonized, "I'm afraid to leave and I'm afraid to stay."

New technologies also transformed industrial production. Between 1945 and 1960 the number of labor-hours needed to manufacture a car fell by 50 percent. Technology revolutionized industries such as electronics, chemicals, and air transportation. It also promoted the growth of television, plastics, computers, and other newer industries. American businesses enjoyed access to cheap oil, ample markets abroad, and little foreign competition. Even with Eisenhower's conservative fiscal policies, government spending reached $80 billion annually and created new jobs.

TECHNOLOGY TRANSFORMS AGRICULTURE

The years from 1945 to 1970 saw a second agricultural revolution in the United States. In 1940, one farmer could feed 10.7 people; by 1970, the ratio was one to 75.8. This photo of a Minnesota grain field in 1949 illustrates both the mechanization of agriculture and the rise of large commercial farming. Jack Fletcher/National Geographic Creative/Corbis.

The strength of labor unions contributed to prosperity by putting money into the hands of people who would spend it. Real earnings for production workers shot up 40 percent. A steelworker's son remembered, "In 1946, we did not have a car, a television set, or a refrigerator. By 1952 we had all those things." In most industrial nations, government programs underwrote their citizens' security, but the United States developed a mixed system in which company-funded programs won by unions provided for retirement, health care, paid vacations, supplementary unemployment benefits, and more. This system, often called a private welfare state, resulted in wide disparities among workers, disadvantaging those who did not belong to strong unions and those with irregular employment.

While the number of organized workers continued to grow, union membership peaked at 27.4 percent of all workers in 1957. Technological advances eliminated jobs in heavy industry. "You are going to have trouble collecting union dues from all of these machines," commented a Ford manager to union leader Walter Reuther. Moreover, the economy as a whole was shifting from production to service. Beginning in 1957, white-collar jobs outnumbered blue-collar jobs, as more workers distributed goods, performed services, provided education, and carried out government work. Unions made some headway in these fields, especially among government employees, but most service industries resisted unionization.

The growing clerical and service occupations swelled the demand for female workers, who held nearly one-third of all jobs by the end of the 1950s. The vast majority of them worked in offices, light manufacturing, domestic service, teaching, and nursing; because these occupations engaged primarily women, wages were relatively low. In 1960, the average female full-time worker earned just 60 percent of the average male worker's wages. At the bottom of the employment ladder, black women took home only 42 percent of what white men earned.

THE NEW SUBURBS

William J. Levitt adapted the factory assembly-line process to home building, planning nearly identical units so that individual workers could move from house to house performing the same single operation. This photograph reflects a typical Levittown street in 1954. Bettmann/Corbis.

Now—Enjoy 5-Way Air Conditioning!

Hotpoint 'Jet-Stream'
AIR CONDITIONERS

Give you cool, clean, comfortable, refreshing air...quietly...automatically

AIR-CONDITIONING

The first air-conditioning system was installed in factories, but room air-conditioning began to appear in homes in the 1930s and spread rapidly in the 1950s. Fewer than one million homes had room air conditioners in 1950, but nearly eight million did in 1960, and more than half of all homes had some form of air-conditioning by 1975, as its status changed from a luxury to a necessity. Picture Research Consultants & Archives.

Burgeoning Suburbs and Declining Cities. Although suburbs had existed since the nineteenth century, nothing symbolized the affluent society more than their tremendous expansion in the 1950s. Eleven million new homes went up in the suburbs, and by 1960 one in four Americans lived there. As Nixon boasted to Khrushchev during the kitchen debate, the suburban homes were accessible to families with modest incomes. Builder William J. Levitt adapted the factory assembly line to home construction, erecting nearly identical units so that workers moved from house to house performing one specific job. In 1949, families could purchase mass-produced houses in his 17,000-home development, called Levittown, on Long Island, New York, for just under $8,000 each ($80,000 in 2016 dollars). Similar developments, as well as more luxurious ones, quickly went up throughout the country. The government subsidized home ownership by guaranteeing low-interest mortgages and by making interest on mortgages tax deductible. Government-funded interstate highways running through metropolitan areas also encouraged suburban development.

By the 1960s, suburbs came under attack for bulldozing the natural environment, creating groundwater contamination, and disrupting wildlife patterns. Social critic Lewis Mumford disparaged suburbia as "a multitude of uniform, unidentifiable houses in a treeless communal wasteland, inhabited by people of the same class, the same income, the same age group." Yet most families were thrilled to be able to own new homes. "It was a miracle to them," one man said of his working-class parents who moved to Levittown.

The suburbs did help polarize society, especially along racial lines. Each Levittown homeowner signed a contract pledging not to rent or sell to a non-Caucasian. The Supreme Court declared such covenants unenforceable in 1948, but suburban America remained severely segregated. Although some African Americans joined the suburban migration, most moved to cities in search of economic opportunity, doubling their numbers in major cities during the 1950s. But those cities were already in decline, losing not only population but also commerce, industry, and jobs to the suburbs or to southern and western states. "Detroit is in the doldrums," commented social worker Mary Jorgensen in 1952.

The Rise of the Sun Belt. No regions experienced the postwar economic and population booms more intensely than the South and Southwest (Map 27.2). California overtook New York as the most populous state. Sports franchises followed fans: In 1958, the Brooklyn Dodgers moved to Los Angeles, joined by the Minneapolis Lakers three years later.

A pleasant natural environment attracted new residents to the **Sun Belt**, but no magnet proved stronger than economic opportunity. As railroads had fueled western

Sun Belt
Name applied to the Southwest and South, which grew rapidly after World War II as a center of defense industries and non-unionized labor.

growth in the nineteenth century, so the automobile and airplane spurred the post–World War II surge. Air-conditioning cooled nearly eight million homes by 1960, and it facilitated industrial development and tourism. "Can you conceive a Walt Disney World in central Florida without its air-conditioned hotels?" asked a journalist.

So important was the defense industry to the South and Southwest that the area was later referred to as the "Gun Belt." The aerospace industry boomed in such cities as Los Angeles and Dallas–Fort Worth, and military bases helped underwrite prosperity in San Diego and San Antonio. Although defense dollars benefited other regions — military bases and aerospace plants were numerous in the Northwest — the Sun Belt captured the lion's share of Cold War spending. By the 1960s, nearly one of every three California workers held a defense-related job.

The surging populations and industries soon threatened the environment. Providing sufficient water and power to cities and to agribusiness meant building dams and reservoirs on free-flowing rivers. Native Americans lost fishing sites on the Columbia River, and dams on the Upper Missouri displaced nine hundred Indian families. Sprawling suburban settlement without efficient public transportation contributed to blankets of smog over Los Angeles and other cities.

The high-technology basis of economic development drew well-educated, highly skilled workers to the West, but economic promise also attracted the poor. "We see opportunity all around us here. . . . We smell freedom here, and maybe soon

Map Activity

MAP 27.2   THE RISE OF THE SUN BELT, 1940–1980

The growth of defense industries, a non-unionized labor force, and the spread of air-conditioning all helped spur economic development and population growth in the Southwest and the South. This made the Sun Belt the fastest-growing region of the country between 1940 and 1980.

READING THE MAP: Which states experienced population growth of more than 20 percent? Which states experienced the largest population growth?

CONNECTIONS: What stimulated the population boom in the Southwest? What role did the Cold War play in this expansion? What developments made the Southwest diverse in the composition of its population?

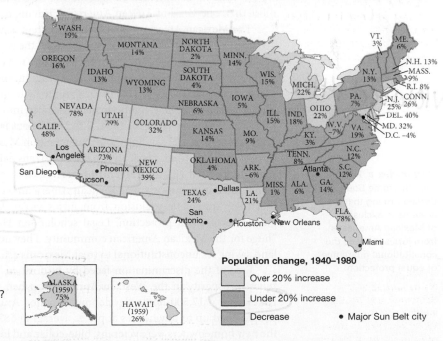

Population change, 1940–1980

- Over 20% increase
- Under 20% increase
- Decrease
- ● Major Sun Belt city

ROUNDING UP UNDOCUMENTED MIGRANTS

Not all Mexican Americans who wanted to work in the United States were accommodated by the *bracero* program. In 1953, Los Angeles police arrested these men who did not have legal documents and were hiding in a freight train.
Bettmann/Corbis.

we can taste it," commented a black mother in California. Between 1945 and 1960, more than one-third of African Americans leaving the South moved west.

The Mexican American population also grew, especially in California and Texas. To supply California's vast agribusiness industry, the government continued the *bracero* program begun in 1942, under which Mexicans were permitted to enter the United States to work for a limited period. Until the program ended in 1964, more than 100,000 Mexicans entered the United States each year to labor in the fields — and many of them stayed, legally or illegally. But permanent Mexican immigration was not as welcome as Mexicans' low-wage labor. In 1954, the government launched a series of raids called "Operation Wetback," sending more than a million Mexicans back across the border.

At the same time, Mexican American citizens gained a victory in their ongoing struggle for civil rights in ***Hernandez v. Texas***. In this 1954 case, the Supreme Court ruled unanimously that Mexican Americans constituted a distinct group and that their systematic exclusion from juries violated the Fourteenth Amendment guarantee of equal protection. Legal scholar Ian Haney-Lopez called *Hernandez* "huge for the Mexican American community. They now had the highest court in the land saying it's unconstitutional to treat Mexicans as if they're an inferior race."

Free of the discrimination faced by minorities, white Americans enjoyed the fullest prosperity in the West. In April 1950, when California developers opened Lakewood, a 17,500-home development in Los Angeles County, thirty thousand people lined up to buy houses at prices averaging $87,500 in 2016 dollars. Many of the new homeowners were veterans, blue-collar and lower-level white-collar workers whose defense-based jobs at aerospace corporations enabled them to fulfill the

violated 14th

Hernandez v. Texas
1954 Supreme Court decision ruling that the systematic exclusion of Mexican Americans from juries violated the constitutional guarantee of equal protection.

American dream of the 1950s. A huge shopping mall, Lakewood Center, offered myriad products of the consumer culture, and the workers' children lived within commuting distance from community colleges and six state universities.

The Democratization of Higher Education.
California's university system exemplified a spectacular transformation of higher education. Between 1940 and 1960, college enrollments in the United States more than doubled, and more than 40 percent of young Americans attended college by the mid-1960s. The federal government subsidized the education of more than two million veterans, and the Cold War sent millions of federal dollars to universities for defense-related research. State governments vastly expanded the number of public colleges and universities, while municipalities began to build two-year community colleges.

All Americans did not benefit equally from the democratization of higher education. Although their college enrollments surged from 37,000 in 1941 to 90,000 in 1961, African Americans constituted only about 5 percent of all college students. For a time the educational gap between white men and women grew, even though women's enrollments increased. In 1940, women had earned 40 percent of undergraduate degrees, but as veterans flocked to college campuses, women's proportion fell to 25 percent, rising to just 33 percent by 1960. Women were more likely than men to drop out of college after marriage, taking jobs to keep their husbands in school. Reflecting gender norms of the 1950s, most white college women agreed that "it is natural for a woman to be satisfied with her husband's success and not crave personal achievement."

> **REVIEW** What fueled the prosperity of the 1950s?

The Culture of Abundance

Prosperity in the 1950s intensified the transformation of the nation into a consumer society, changing the way Americans lived and shifting the traditional work ethic toward an ethic of consumption. The new medium of television both reflected and stimulated a consumer culture. People married at earlier ages, the birthrate soared, and dominant values celebrated family life and traditional gender roles. Undercurrents of rebellion, especially among young people, and women's increasing employment defied some of the dominant norms but did not greatly disrupt the complacency of the 1950s.

Consumption Rules the Day.
Scorned by Khrushchev during the kitchen debate as unnecessary gadgets, consumer items flooded American society in the 1950s. Although the purchase and display of consumer goods was not new (see chapter 23), at midcentury consumption had become a reigning value, vital for economic prosperity and essential to individuals' identity and status. In place of the traditional emphasis on work and savings, the consumer culture encouraged satisfaction and happiness through the acquisition of new products.

The consumer culture rested on a firm material base. Between 1950 and 1960, both the gross national product (the value of all goods and services produced) and median

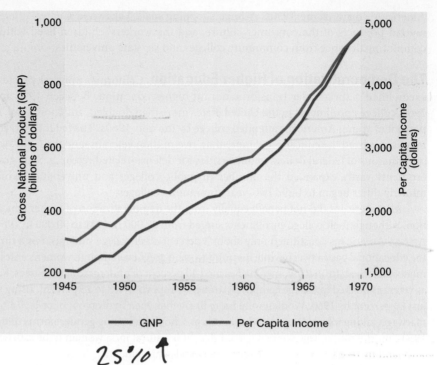

FIGURE 27.1 THE POSTWAR ECONOMIC BOOM: GNP AND PER CAPITA INCOME, 1945–1970

American dominance of the worldwide market, innovative technologies that led to new industries such as computers and plastics, population growth, and increases in worker productivity all contributed to the enormous economic growth of the United States after World War II.

[handwritten: 5% Black]

[handwritten: 25% ↑]

[handwritten: 60% middle class]

family income grew by 25 percent in constant dollars (Figure 27.1). Economists claimed that 60 percent of Americans enjoyed middle-class incomes in 1960. By then, four-fifths of all families owned a television set, nearly all had a refrigerator, and most owned at least one car. The number of shopping centers quadrupled between 1957 and 1963.

Several forces spurred this unparalleled abundance. A population surge — from 152 million to 180 million during the 1950s — expanded demand for products and boosted industries ranging from housing to baby goods. Consumer borrowing also fueled the economic boom, as people made purchases on installment plans and began to use credit cards. Increasingly Americans enjoyed their possessions while they paid for them instead of saving their money for future purchases.

Although the sheer need to support themselves and their families motivated most women's employment, a desire to secure some of the new abundance sent growing numbers of women to work. As one woman remarked, "My Joe can't put five kids through college . . . and the washer had to be replaced, and Ann was ashamed to bring friends home because the living room furniture was such a mess, so I went to work." The standards for family happiness imposed by the consumer culture increasingly required a second income.

The Revival of Domesticity and Religion. Despite married women's growing employment, a dominant ideology celebrated traditional family life and conventional gender roles. Both popular culture and public figures defined the ideal family as a male breadwinner, a full-time homemaker, and three or four children.

Writer and feminist Betty Friedan gave a name to the idealization of women's domestic roles in her 1963 book *The Feminine Mystique*. Friedan criticized health professionals, scholars, advertisers, and public officials for assuming that biological differences dictated different roles for men and women. According to this feminine
mystique that they promulgated, women should find fulfillment in devotion to their
homes, families, and serving others. Not many women directly challenged these
ideas, but writer Edith Stern maintained that "many arguments about the joys of
housewifery have been advanced, largely by those who have never had to work at it."

Although the glorification of domesticity clashed with women's increasing
employment, many Americans' lives did embody the family ideal. Postwar prosperity enabled people to marry earlier and to have more children. In the midst of a
general downward trend over the century, the American birthrate soared between
1945 and 1965, peaking in 1957 with 4.3 million births and producing the baby
boom generation. Experts like Dr. Benjamin Spock encouraged mothers to devote
even more attention to child rearing, while they also urged fathers to cultivate family
"togetherness" by spending more time with their children.

Interest in religion also surged in the 1950s. From 1940 to 1960, membership in
churches and synagogues rose from 50 to 63 percent of all Americans. Polls reported
that 95 percent of the population believed in God. Evangelism took on new life, most
notably in the nationwide crusades of Baptist minister Billy Graham. Congress
linked religion more closely to the state by adding "under God" to the pledge of allegiance and by requiring that "In God We Trust" be printed on all currency.

Religion helped to calm anxieties in the nuclear age, while ministers such as
Graham made the Cold War a holy war, labeling communism "a great sinister anti-
Christian movement masterminded by Satan." Some critics questioned the depth of
the religious revival, attributing the growth in church membership to a desire for
conformity and a need for social outlets. One commentator noted that 53 percent of
Americans could not name a single book of the Christian New Testament.

Television Transforms Culture and Politics. Just as family life and religion
offered a respite from Cold War anxieties, so too did the new medium of television. By
1960, nearly 90 percent of American homes boasted a television set, and the average viewer
spent more than five hours each day watching it. Audiences were especially attracted to
situation comedies, which projected the family ideal and the feminine mystique into millions of homes. On TV, married women did not have paying jobs and they deferred to
their husbands, though they often got the upper hand through subtle manipulation.

Television also began to affect politics. Eisenhower's 1952 presidential campaign used TV ads for the first time, although he was not happy that "an old soldier
should come to this." By 1960, television played a key role in election campaigns.
Reflecting on his narrow victory, president-elect John F. Kennedy remarked, "We
wouldn't have had a prayer without that gadget." In addition, money played a much
larger role in elections because candidates needed to pay for expensive TV ads.
The ability to appeal directly to voters in their living rooms put a premium on
personal attractiveness and encouraged candidates to build their own campaign
organizations, relying less on political parties. The declining strength of parties

baby boom
The surge in the American
birthrate between 1945 and
1965, which peaked in 1957
with 4.3 million births. The
baby boom both reflected
and promoted Americans'
postwar prosperity.

and the growing power of money in elections were not new trends, but TV accelerated them.

Unlike government-financed television in Europe, private enterprise paid for American TV. What NBC called a "selling machine in every living room" became the major vehicle for fostering consumption, and advertisers did not hesitate to interfere with shows that might jeopardize the sale of their products. In 1961, Newton Minow, chairman of the Federal Communications Commission, called television a "vast wasteland." While acknowledging some of TV's achievements, particularly documentaries and drama, Minow depicted it as "a procession of game shows, . . . formula comedies about totally unbelievable families, blood and thunder, mayhem, violence, sadism, murder, . . . and cartoons." But viewers kept tuning in. In little more than a decade, television came to dominate Americans' leisure time, influence their consumption patterns, and shape their perceptions of the nation's leadership.

Countercurrents. Pockets of dissent underlay the conventionality of the 1950s. Some intellectuals took exception to the materialism and conformity of the era. In *The Lonely Crowd* (1950), sociologist David Riesman lamented a shift from the "inner-directed" to the "other-directed" individual, as Americans replaced independent thinking with an eagerness to adapt to external standards of behavior and belief. Sharing that distaste for the importance of "belonging," William H. Whyte Jr., in his popular book *The Organization Man* (1956), blamed the modern corporation for making employees tailor themselves to the group. Vance Packard's 1959 best seller, *The Status Seekers*, decried "the vigorous merchandising of goods as status-symbols."

Implicit in much of the critique of consumer culture was concern about the loss of traditional masculinity. Consumption was associated with women and their presumed greater susceptibility to manipulation. Men, required to conform to get ahead, moved further away from the masculine ideals of individualism and aggressiveness. Moreover, the increase in married women's employment compromised the male ideal of breadwinner. Into this gender confusion came *Playboy*, which began publication in 1953 and quickly gained a circulation of one million. The new magazine idealized masculine independence in the form of bachelorhood and assaulted the middle-class norms of domesticity and respectability. By associating the sophisticated bachelor with good wine, music, furnishings, and the like, the magazine made consumption more masculine while promoting sexual freedom, at least for men.

In fact, two books published by Alfred Kinsey and other researchers at Indiana University — *Sexual Behavior in the Human Male* (1948) and *Sexual Behavior in the Human Female* (1953) — disclosed that Americans' sexual behavior often departed from the postwar family ideal. Large numbers of men and women reported that they had engaged in premarital sex and adultery; one-third of the men and one-seventh of the women reported homosexual experiences. Although Kinsey's sampling procedures later cast doubt on his ability to generalize across the population, the books became best sellers.

Less direct challenges to mainstream standards appeared in the everyday behavior of young Americans. "Roll over Beethoven and tell Tchaikovsky the news!" belted out Chuck Berry in his 1956 hit record celebrating **rock and roll**, a new form of music that combined country with black rhythm and blues. White teenagers lionized Elvis Presley, who shocked their parents with his tight pants, hip-rolling gestures, and sensuous rock-and-roll music. "Before there was Elvis . . . I started going crazy for 'race music,'" recalled a white man of his teenage years. His recollection underscored African Americans' contributions to rock and roll, as well as the rebelliousness expressed by white youths' attraction to black music.

The most blatant revolt against conventionality came from the self-proclaimed Beat generation, a small group of mostly male literary figures based in New York City and San Francisco. Rejecting nearly everything in mainstream culture — patriotism, consumerism, technology, conventional family life, discipline — writers such as Allen Ginsberg and Jack Kerouac celebrated spontaneity and absolute personal freedom, including drug consumption and freewheeling sex. The Beats shocked "square" Americans, but both they and their lifestyles would provide a model for a new movement of youthful dissidents in the 1960s.

Bold new styles in the visual arts also showed the 1950s to be more than a decade of bland conformity. In New York City, "action painting" or "abstract expressionism" flowered, rejecting the idea that painting should represent recognizable forms. Jackson Pollock and other abstract expressionists poured, dripped, and threw paint on canvases or substituted sticks and other implements for brushes. The new form of painting so captivated and redirected the Western art world that New York replaced Paris as its center.

JACKSON POLLOCK'S ABSTRACT EXPRESSIONISM

One of the leading artists of the post–World War II revolution in painting, Jackson Pollock often worked with the canvas on the floor, dripping paint onto it with sticks, turkey basters, and hard brushes, prompting *Time* magazine to dub him "Jack the Dripper." He struggled with alcohol and died in 1956, at the age of forty-four, crashing his car while drunk and speeding near his Long Island home. Hans Namuth/Science Source.

rock and roll

A music genre created from country music and black rhythm and blues that emerged in the 1950s and captivated American youth.

> **REVIEW** Why did American consumption expand so dramatically in the 1950s, and what aspects of society and culture did it influence?

The Emergence of a Civil Rights Movement

Building on the civil rights initiatives begun during World War II, African Americans posed the most dramatic challenge to the status quo of the 1950s as they sought to overcome discrimination and segregation. Every southern state mandated rigid segregation in public settings ranging from schools to cemeteries. Voting laws and practices in the South disfranchised the vast majority of African Americans. Employment discrimination kept blacks at the bottom throughout the country. Schools, restaurants, and other public spaces were often as segregated, though usually not by law, in the North as in the South.

Although black protest was as old as American racism, in the 1950s grassroots movements arose that attracted national attention and the support of white liberals. Pressed by civil rights groups, the Supreme Court delivered significant institutional reforms, but the most important changes occurred among blacks themselves. Ordinary African Americans in substantial numbers sought their own liberation, building a movement that would transform race relations in the United States.

African Americans Challenge the Supreme Court and the President.

Several factors spurred black protest in the 1950s. Between 1940 and 1960, more than three million African Americans moved from the South into areas where they had a political voice. Black leaders emphasized how racist practices at home tarnished the U.S. image abroad and handicapped the United States in its competition with the Soviet Union. The very system of segregation meant that African Americans controlled certain organizational resources, such as churches, colleges, and newspapers, where leadership skills could be honed and networks developed.

The legal strategy of the major civil rights organization, the National Association for the Advancement of Colored People (NAACP), reached its crowning achievement with the Supreme Court decision *Brown v. Board of Education* in 1954, which consolidated five separate suits. Oliver Brown, a World War II veteran in Topeka, Kansas, filed suit because his daughter had to pass by a white school near their home to attend a black school more than a mile away. In Virginia, sixteen-year-old Barbara Johns initiated a student strike over wretched conditions in her black high school, leading to another of the suits joined in *Brown*. The NAACP's lead lawyer, future Supreme Court justice Thurgood Marshall, urged the Court to overturn the "separate but equal" precedent established in *Plessy v. Ferguson* in 1896 (see chapter 21). A unanimous Court, headed by Chief Justice Earl Warren, agreed, declaring that "Separate educational facilities are inherently unequal" and thus violated the Fourteenth Amendment.

Ultimate responsibility for enforcement of the decision lay with President Eisenhower, but he refused to endorse *Brown*. He also kept silent in 1955 when whites murdered Emmett Till, a fourteen-year-old black boy who had allegedly whistled at a white woman in Mississippi. Reflecting his own prejudice, his preference for limited federal intervention in the states, and a leadership style that favored consensus and gradual progress, Eisenhower kept his distance from civil rights issues. Such inaction fortified southern resistance.

In September 1957, Governor Orval Faubus sent Arkansas National Guard troops to block the enrollment of nine black students in Little Rock's Central High School. Later, he allowed them to enter but withdrew the National Guard, leaving the students to face an angry white mob. "During those years when we desperately needed approval from our peers," Melba Patillo Beals remembered, "we were victims

Brown v. Board of Education
1954 Supreme Court ruling that overturned the "separate but equal" precedent established in *Plessy v. Ferguson* in 1896. The Court declared that separate educational facilities were inherently unequal and thus violated the Fourteenth Amendment.

of the most harsh rejection imaginable." As television cameras transmitted the ugly scene, Eisenhower was forced to send regular army troops to Little Rock, the first federal military intervention in the South since Reconstruction. Paratroopers escorted the "Little Rock Nine" into the school, but resistance to integration continued across the South. (See "Analyzing Historical Evidence," page 822.)

School segregation outside the South was not usually sanctioned by law, but northern school districts separated black and white students by manipulating neighborhood boundaries and with other devices. Even before *Brown*, black parents in dozens of northern cities challenged the assignment of their children to inferior "colored" schools. While these protests reaped some successes, the structure of residential segregation, often supported by official action, made school segregation a reality for African Americans in both the North and South.

Eisenhower ordered the integration of public facilities in Washington, D.C., and on military bases, and he supported the first federal civil rights legislation since Reconstruction. Yet the Civil Rights Acts of 1957 and 1960 were little more than symbolic. Baseball star Jackie Robinson spoke for many African Americans when he wired Eisenhower in 1957, "We disagree that half a loaf is better than none. Have waited this long for a bill with meaning — can wait a little longer." Eisenhower appointed the first black professional to his White House staff, but E. Frederick Morrow confided in his diary, "I feel ridiculous . . . trying to defend the administration's record on civil rights."

Montgomery and Mass Protest.

What set the civil rights movement of the 1950s and 1960s apart from earlier acts of black protest was its widespread presence in the South, the large number of people involved, their willingness to confront white institutions directly, and the use of nonviolent protest and civil disobedience to bring about change. The Congress of Racial Equality and other groups had experimented with these tactics in the 1940s, organizing to integrate movie theaters, restaurants, and swimming pools in northern cities. In the South, the first sustained protest to claim national attention began in Montgomery, Alabama, on December 1, 1955.

That day, police arrested Rosa Parks for violating a local segregation ordinance. Riding a crowded bus home from work, she refused to give up her seat in the white section so that a man could sit down. She resisted not because she was physically tired, she recalled; rather she was "tired of giving in." The bus driver called the police, who promptly arrested her. Parks had long been active in the local NAACP, headed by E. D. Nixon. They had already talked about challenging bus segregation. So had the Women's Political Council (WPC), led by Jo Ann Robinson, an English professor at Alabama State, who had once been humiliated by a bus driver when she accidentally sat in the white section.

When word came that Parks would fight her arrest, WPC leaders mobilized teachers and students to distribute fliers urging blacks to boycott the buses. E. D. Nixon called a mass meeting at a black church, where those assembled founded the Montgomery Improvement Association (MIA). The MIA arranged volunteer car pools and marshaled most of the black community to sustain the yearlong **Montgomery bus boycott**.

Montgomery bus boycott Yearlong boycott of Montgomery's segregated bus system in 1955–1956 by the city's African American population. The boycott brought Martin Luther King Jr. to national prominence and ended in victory when the Supreme Court declared segregated transportation unconstitutional.

Analyzing Historical Evidence

The *Brown* Decision

R esponding to lawsuits argued by NAACP lawyers, *Brown v. Board of Education* was the culmination of a series of Supreme Court rulings that chipped away at an earlier Court's decision in *Plessy v. Ferguson* (1896) permitting "separate but equal" public facilities.

DOCUMENT 1

Brown v. Board of Education, May 1954

In 1954, Chief Justice Earl Warren delivered the unanimous opinion of the Supreme Court, declaring racial segregation in public education unconstitutional and explaining why.

I t is doubtful that any child may reasonably be expected to succeed in life if he is denied the opportunity of an education. Such an opportunity, if the state has undertaken to provide it, is a right that must be made available to all on equal terms. . . .

We come then to the question presented: Does segregation of children in public schools solely on the basis of race, even though the physical facilities and other "tangible" factors may be equal, deprive the children of the minority group of equal educational opportunities?

We believe that it does. . . . In *McLaurin* [a 1950 case], the Court, in requiring that a Negro admitted to a white graduate school be treated like all other students, again resorted to intangible considerations: ". . . his ability to study, to engage in discussions and exchange views with other students, and, in general, to learn his profession." Such considerations apply with added force to children in grade and high schools. To separate them from others of similar age and qualifications solely because of their race generates a feeling of inferiority as to their status in the community that may affect their hearts and minds in a way unlikely ever to be undone.

We conclude that in the field of public education the doctrine of "separate but equal" has no place. Separate educational facilities are inherently unequal.

SOURCE: *Brown v. Board of Education*, 347 U.S. 483 (1954).

DOCUMENT 2

Southern Manifesto on Integration, March 1956

The Brown *decision outraged many southern whites. In 1956, more than one hundred members of Congress signed a manifesto pledging resistance to the ruling.*

W e regard the decision of the Supreme Court in the school cases as a clear abuse of judicial power. It climaxes a trend in the Federal judiciary undertaking to legislate . . . and to encroach upon the reserved rights of the states and the people.

The original Constitution does not mention education. Neither does the Fourteenth Amendment nor any amendment. . . . The Supreme Court of the United States, with no legal basis for such action, undertook to exercise their naked judicial power and substituted their personal political and social ideas for the established law of the land.

This unwarranted exercise of power by the court, contrary to the Constitution, is creating chaos and confusion in the states principally affected. It is destroying the amicable relations between the white and negro races that have been created through ninety years of patient effort by the good people of both races. . . .

We pledge ourselves to use all lawful means to bring about a reversal of this decision which is contrary to the Constitution and to prevent the use of force in its implementation.

SOURCE: "Southern Manifesto on Integration," *Congressional Record*, 84th Congress, 2nd Session, vol. 102, pt. 4 (Washington, D.C. Governmental Printing Office, 1956), 4459–60.

In the face of white hostility, black children carried the burden of implementing the Brown *decision, as these accounts testify.*

DOCUMENT 3

A High School Boy in Oak Ridge, Tennessee, 1957

I like it a whole lot better than the colored school. You have a chance to learn more and you have more sports. I play forward or guard on the basketball team, only I don't get to participate in all games. Some teams don't mind my playing. Some teams object not because of the fellows on the team, but because of the people in their community. Mostly it's the fans or the board of education that decides against me. . . . The same situation occurs in baseball. I'm catcher, but the first game I didn't get to participate in. A farm club of the major league wrote the coach that they were interested in seeing me play so maybe I'll get to play the next time.

SOURCE: Dorothy Sterling, *Tender Warriors* (New York: Hill and Wang, 1958), 83. Copyright © 1958 by Hill and Wang.

DOCUMENT 4

A High School Girl in the Deep South, May 1966

The first day a news reporter rode the bus with us. All around us were state troopers. In front of them were federal marshals. When we got to town there were lines of people and cars all along the road. A man without a badge or anything got on the bus and started beating up the newspaper reporter. . . . When we got to the school the students were all around looking through the windows. The mayor said we couldn't come there because the school was already filled to capacity. We turned around and the students started yelling and clapping. When we went back [after obtaining a court order] there were no students there at all. [The white students did not return, so the six black students finished the year by themselves.] The shocking thing was during the graduation ceremonies. All six of the students got together to make a speech. After we finished, I looked around and saw three teachers crying. The principal had tears in his eyes and he got up to make a little speech about us. He said at first he didn't think he would enjoy being around us. You could see in his face that he was really touched.

SOURCE: *In Their Own Words: A Student Appraisal of What Happened after School Desegregation* (Washington, D.C. Department of Health, Education, and Welfare, Office of Education, 1966), 17–18.

DOCUMENT 5

A High School Girl in the Deep South, May 1966

I chose to go because I felt that I could get a better education here. I knew that the [black] school that I was then attending wasn't giving me exactly what I should have had. . . . As far as the Science Department was concerned, it just didn't have the chemicals we needed and I just decided to change. When I went over the students there weren't very friendly and when I graduated they still weren't. They didn't want us there and they made that plain, but we went there anyway and we stuck it out.

SOURCE: *In Their Own Words: A Student Appraisal of What Happened after School Desegregation* (Washington, DC: Department of Health, Education, and Welfare, Office of Education, 1966), 44.

QUESTIONS FOR ANALYSIS

Recognize Viewpoints   What reasons did the Supreme Court give in favor of desegregation? What reasons did black students give for wanting to attend integrated schools? How do these reasons differ?

Analyze the Evidence   On what grounds did signers of the "Southern Manifesto" argue that the Supreme Court decision violated the Constitution?

Consider the Context   Why did President Eisenhower initially resist desegregation, and what steps did he eventually take to support integration?

Elected to head the MIA was twenty-six-year-old Martin Luther King Jr., a young Baptist pastor with a doctorate in theology from Boston University. A captivating speaker, King addressed mass meetings at churches throughout the bus boycott, inspiring blacks' courage and commitment by linking racial justice to Christianity. He promised, "If you will protest courageously and yet with dignity and

Visual Activity

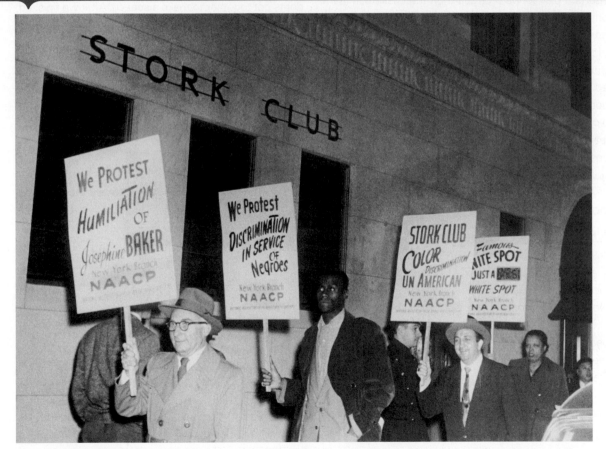

CIVIL RIGHTS ACTIVISM IN THE NORTH

While southern civil rights activism gained national attention in the 1950s, black protest had a long history in the North. African Americans and their allies battled job discrimination and segregation in schools, housing, and public accommodations. Here demonstrators march outside the Stork Club in New York City in 1951, protesting its refusal to serve the world-famous dancer, singer, and actress Josephine Baker. FPG/Getty Images.

READING THE IMAGE: Who sponsored this demonstration? What do the people in the photo tell you about the racial makeup of protest? How does one of the signs capitalize on Cold War rhetoric?

CONNECTIONS: How did this kind of protest in the North differ from that in the South?

Christian love . . . historians will have to pause and say, 'There lived a great people — a black people — who injected a new meaning and dignity into the veins of civilization.'"

Montgomery blacks summoned their courage and determination in abundance. An older woman insisted, "I'm not walking for myself, I'm walking for my children and my grandchildren." Boycotters walked miles or carpooled to get to work, contributed their meager financial resources, and stood up to intimidation and police harassment. Authorities arrested several leaders, and whites firebombed King's house. Yet the movement persisted until November 1956, when the Supreme Court declared unconstitutional Alabama's laws requiring bus segregation.

King's face on the cover of *Time* magazine in February 1957 marked his rapid rise to national and international fame. In January, black clergy from across the South had chosen King to head the Southern Christian Leadership Conference (SCLC), newly established to coordinate local protests against segregation and disfranchisement. The prominence of King and other ministers obscured the substantial numbers and critical importance of black women in the movement. King's fame and the media's focus on the South also hid the national scope of racial injustice and the struggles for racial equality in the North that both encouraged and benefited from the black freedom struggle in the South.

> **REVIEW** What were the goals and strategies of civil rights activists in the 1950s?

Conclusion: Peace and Prosperity Mask Unmet Challenges

At the American exhibit in Moscow in 1959, the consumer goods that Nixon proudly displayed to Khrushchev and the Cold War competition that crackled through their dialogue reflected two dominant themes of the 1950s: American prosperity and the superpowers' success in keeping their antagonism within the bounds of peace. The tremendous economic growth of the 1950s, which raised the standard of living for most Americans, resulted in part from Cold War defense spending.

Prosperity changed the very landscape of the United States. Suburban housing developments sprang up, interstate highways cut up cities and connected the country, farms declined in number but grew in size, and population and industry moved south and west. Daily habits and even values shifted as the economy became more service oriented and the appearance of television and a host of new products intensified the growth of a consumer culture.

The prosperity, however, masked a number of developments and problems that Americans would soon face head-on: rising resistance to racial injustice, a 20 percent poverty rate, married women's movement into the labor force, and the emergence of a youth rebellion. Although defense spending and housing, highway, and education subsidies helped to sustain the economic boom, in general Eisenhower tried to curb domestic programs and let private enterprise have its way. His administration maintained the welfare state inherited from the New Deal but resisted the expansion of federal programs.

In global affairs, Eisenhower exercised restraint on large issues, recognizing the limits of U.S. power. In the name of deterrence, he promoted the development of more destructive atomic weapons, but he withstood pressures for even larger defense budgets. Still, Eisenhower shared Truman's assumption that the United States must fight communism everywhere, and when movements in Iran, Guatemala, Cuba, and Vietnam seemed too radical, too friendly to communism, or too inimical to American economic interests, he tried to undermine them, often with secret operations. Eisenhower presided over eight years of peace and prosperity, but his foreign policy inspired anti-Americanism and forged commitments and interventions that plagued future generations. As Eisenhower's successors took on the struggle against communism and grappled with the domestic challenges of race, poverty, and urban decay that he had avoided, the tranquility and consensus of the 1950s would give way to turbulence and conflict in the 1960s.

Chapter Review

KEY TERMS

Interstate Highway and Defense System Act of 1956 (p. 801)

mutually assured destruction (MAD) (p. 804)

domino theory (p. 805)

Cuban revolution (p. 807)

Eisenhower Doctrine (p. 808)

military-industrial complex (p. 808)

Sun Belt (p. 812)

Hernandez v. Texas (p. 814)

baby boom (p. 817)

rock and roll (p. 819)

Brown v. Board of Education (p. 820)

Montgomery bus boycott (p. 821)

REVIEW QUESTIONS

❶ How did Eisenhower's domestic policies reflect his moderate political vision? (pp. 800–804)

❷ Where and how did Eisenhower practice containment? (pp. 804–9)

❸ What fueled the prosperity of the 1950s? (pp. 809–15)

❹ Why did American consumption expand so dramatically in the 1950s, and what aspects of society and culture did it influence? (pp. 815–19)

❺ What were the goals and strategies of civil rights activists in the 1950s? (pp. 819–25)

MAKING CONNECTIONS

❶ How did Eisenhower's "modern Republicanism" address the New Deal legacy?

❷ What economic and demographic changes contributed to the growth of suburbs and the Sun Belt? Consider both Americans who participated in these trends and those who did not.

❸ What developments in American society in the 1950s were at odds with prevailing norms and values?

❹ Explain how new policies and court decisions regarding minorities came about and their impact, for better and for worse.

LINKING TO THE PAST

❶ How did the policies of termination and relocation differ from the New Deal's policy toward Indians? (See chapter 24.)

❷ What developments stemming from World War II influenced U.S. foreign policy in such areas as Vietnam and Latin America? (See chapter 25.)

28

Reform, Rebellion, and Reaction, 1960–1974

CONTENT LEARNING OBJECTIVES

After reading and studying this chapter, you should be able to:

- Identify the ways in which liberalism was manifested in President Johnson's Great Society.

- Identify the strategies civil rights activists used during the 1960s and describe Washington's response. Explain the rise of the black power movement and its influence on American society.

- Explain how the civil rights movement inspired protest movements among other groups, including Native Americans, Chicanos, students, and gays and lesbians.

- Define the origins of the feminist movement and identify its various strategies and criticisms of society. Explain feminism's achievements and the backlash it provoked.

- Describe the ways in which liberalism persisted during the Nixon administration.

O n August 31, 1962, forty-five-year-old Fannie Lou Hamer boarded a bus carrying eighteen African Americans to the county seat in Indianola, Mississippi, where they intended to register to vote. Blacks constituted a majority of Sunflower County's population but only 1.2 percent of registered voters. Before civil rights activists arrived in Ruleville to start a voter registration drive, Hamer recalled, "I didn't know that a Negro could register and vote." The poverty, exploitation, and political disfranchisement she experienced typified the lives of most blacks in the rural South. The daughter of sharecroppers, Hamer began work in the cotton fields at age six, attending school in a one-room

PROTEST BANNER

In the 1960s, Americans carried banners to broadcast a variety of political positions. This pennant represents the black freedom struggle, which inspired a host of other movements. Collection of Mark Hooper.

shack from December to March and only until she was twelve. After marrying Perry Hamer, she moved onto a plantation where she worked in the fields, did domestic work for the owner, and recorded the cotton that sharecroppers harvested.

At the Indianola County courthouse, Hamer passed through a hostile, white, gun-carrying crowd. Refusing to be intimidated, she registered to vote on her third attempt, attended a civil rights leadership workshop, and began to mobilize others to vote. In 1963, she and other activists were arrested in Winona, Mississippi, and beaten so brutally that Hamer went from jail to the hospital.

Fannie Lou Hamer's courage and determination made her a prominent figure in the black freedom struggle, which shook the nation's conscience, provided a protest model for other groups, and pressured the government. After John F. Kennedy was assassinated in November 1963, Lyndon B. Johnson launched the Great Society — a multitude of efforts to promote racial justice, education, medical care, urban development, environmental and economic health, and more. Those who struggled for racial justice made great sacrifices, but by the end of the decade American law had caught up with the American ideal of equality.

Yet strong civil rights legislation and pathbreaking Supreme Court decisions could not alone mitigate the deplorable economic conditions of African Americans nationwide, on which Hamer and others increasingly focused after 1965. Nor were liberal politicians reliable supporters, as Hamer found out in 1964 when President Johnson's allies rebuffed black Mississippi Democrats' efforts to be represented at the Democratic National Convention. By 1966, a minority of African American activists were demanding black power; the movement soon splintered, while white support sharply declined. The war in Vietnam stifled liberal reform, while a growing conservative movement denounced the challenge to American traditions and institutions mounted by blacks, students, and others.

Though disillusioned and often frustrated, Fannie Lou Hamer remained an activist until her death in 1977, participating in new social movements stimulated by the black freedom struggle. In 1969, she supported students at Mississippi Valley State College who demanded black studies courses and a voice in campus decisions. In 1972, she attended the first conference of the National Women's Political Caucus, established to challenge sex discrimination in politics and government.

1960	John F. Kennedy elected president. Student Nonviolent Coordinating Committee (SNCC) founded. Students for a Democratic Society (SDS) established.
1961	Freedom Rides challenge segregation.
1962	United Farm Workers founded.
1963	President's Commission on the Status of Women issues report. Equal Pay Act passes. *Baker v. Carr* decided. *Abington School District v. Schempp* decided. March on Washington draws 250,000 participants. President Kennedy assassinated; Lyndon B. Johnson becomes president.
1964	Civil Rights Act passes. Mississippi Freedom Summer Project conducts voter drives.
1964–1966	Congress passes most of Johnson's Great Society domestic programs
1965	Voting Rights Act passes.
1965–1968	Riots erupt in major cities.
1966	Black Panther Party for Self-Defense founded. *Miranda v. Arizona* decided. National Organization for Women (NOW) founded.
1967	*Loving v. Virginia* decision strikes down state laws against interracial marriages.
1968	Martin Luther King Jr. assassinated. American Indian Movement (AIM) launched. Richard M. Nixon elected president.
1969	Stonewall riots erupt.
1970	Environmental Protection Agency (EPA) established. Clean Air Act passed.
1972	Title IX bans sex discrimination in education. "Trail of Broken Treaties" caravan protests in Washington, D.C.
1973	*Roe v. Wade* decided.

MISSISSIPPI FREEDOM DEMOCRATIC PARTY RALLY

Fannie Lou Hamer (left) and other activists rally at the 1964 Democratic National Convention, supporting the Mississippi Freedom Democratic Party (MFDP) in its challenge to the all-white delegation sent by the state party. Next to Hamer is civil rights lawyer Eleanor Holmes Norton, and Ella Baker (far right), who helped organize the Southern Christian Leadership Conference. In the straw hat is Stokely Carmichael, leader of the Student Nonviolent Coordinating Committee.
© George Ballis/Take Stock/The Image Works.

Feminists and other groups, including ethnic minorities, environmentalists, and gays and lesbians, carried the tide of reform into the 1970s. They pushed Richard M. Nixon's Republican administration to sustain the liberalism of the 1960s, with its emphasis on a strong government role in regulating the economy, guaranteeing the welfare and rights of all individuals, and improving the quality of life. Despite its conservative rhetoric, the Nixon administration implemented affirmative action and adopted innovative measures in environmental regulation, equality for women, and justice for Native Americans. The years between 1960 and 1974 witnessed the greatest efforts to reconcile America's promise with reality since the New Deal.

Liberalism at High Tide

At the Democratic National Convention in 1960, John F. Kennedy proclaimed "a New Frontier" that would confront "unsolved problems of peace and war, unconquered pockets of ignorance and prejudice, unanswered questions of poverty and surplus." Four years later, Lyndon B. Johnson invoked the ideal of a "Great Society, [which] rests on abundance and liberty for all [and] demands an end to poverty and racial injustice." Acting under the liberal faith that government should use its power to solve social and economic problems, end injustice, and promote the welfare of all citizens, the Democratic administrations of the 1960s won legislation on civil rights, poverty, education, medical care, housing, consumer safeguards, and environmental protection. These measures, along with momentous Supreme Court decisions, responded to demands for rights from African Americans and other groups and addressed problems arising from rapid economic growth.

The Unrealized Promise of Kennedy's New Frontier.

John F. Kennedy grew up in privilege, the child of an Irish Catholic businessman who became a New Deal official and the U.S. ambassador to Britain. Helped by a distinguished World War II navy record, Kennedy won election to the House of Representatives in 1946 and the Senate in 1952. With a powerful political machine, his family's fortune, and a dynamic personal appeal, Kennedy won the Democratic presidential nomination in 1960. He stunned many Democrats by choosing as his running mate Lyndon B. Johnson of Texas, whom liberals disparaged as a typical southern conservative.

In the general election, Kennedy narrowly defeated his Republican opponent, Vice President Richard M. Nixon, by a 118,550-vote margin (Map 28.1). African American voters contributed to his victory, Johnson helped carry the South, and Kennedy also benefited from the nation's first televised presidential debates, at which he appeared cool and confident beside a nervous and pale Nixon.

At forty-three, Kennedy was the youngest man ever to be elected president and the first Roman Catholic. His administration projected energy, idealism, and glamour, while the press kept from the public his serious health problems and extramarital affairs. At his inauguration, Kennedy called on Americans to serve the common good. "Ask not what your country can do for you," he implored, "ask what you can do for your country." That idealism inspired many, but Kennedy failed to persuade Congress to expand the welfare state with federal education and health care programs. Moreover, he resisted leadership on behalf of racial justice until civil rights activists gave him no choice.

Moved by the desperate conditions he observed while campaigning in Appalachia, Kennedy pushed poverty onto the national agenda. In 1962, he read Michael Harrington's *The Other America*, which identified more than one in five Americans "maimed in body and spirit, existing at levels beneath those necessary for human decency." By 1962, Kennedy had won support for a $2 billion urban renewal program, providing incentives to businesses to locate in economically depressed areas and job training for the unemployed. In the summer of 1963, he asked aides to plan a full-scale attack on poverty.

With economic growth a key objective, Kennedy called for an enormous tax cut in 1963, which he promised would increase demand and create jobs. Passed in February 1964, the law contributed to an economic boom, as unemployment fell to 4.1 percent and the gross national product shot up. Some liberal critics of the tax cut, however, noted that it favored the well-off and argued instead for increased spending on social programs.

Kennedy's domestic efforts were in their infancy when an assassin's bullets struck him down on November 22, 1963. Within minutes of the shooting — which

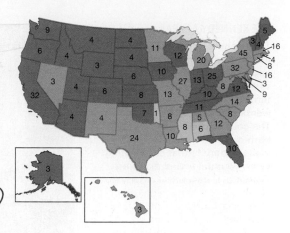

Candidate	Electoral Vote	Popular Vote	Percent of Popular Vote
John F. Kennedy (Democrat)	303	34,227,096	49.9
Richard M. Nixon (Republican)	219	34,108,546	49.6
Harry F. Byrd (Independent)	15	501,643	0

MAP 28.1 THE ELECTION OF 1960

THE KENNEDY APPEAL
The freshness and glamour of the Kennedy administration are apparent in this photo of the candidate and his wife riding through New York City a few weeks before his election in 1960. The couple's second child was born between his election and inauguration, further contributing to his youthful image. Frank Hurley/ New York Daily News Archive via Getty Images.

occurred as Kennedy's motorcade passed through Dallas, Texas — radio and television broadcast the unfolding horror to the nation. Stunned Americans struggled to understand what had happened. Soon after the assassination, police arrested Lee Harvey Oswald and concluded that he had fired the shots from a nearby building. Two days later, while officers were transferring Oswald from one jail to another, a local nightclub operator killed him. Suspicions arose that Oswald was murdered to cover up a conspiracy by ultraconservatives who hated Kennedy or by Communists who supported Castro's Cuba (as discussed in chapter 29). To get at the truth, President Johnson appointed a commission headed by Chief Justice Earl Warren, which concluded that both Oswald and his assassin had acted alone.

Kennedy's domestic record had been unremarkable in his first two years, but his attention to taxes, civil rights, and poverty in 1963 suggested an important shift. Whether Kennedy could have persuaded Congress to enact his proposals remained in question. Journalist James Reston commented, "What was killed was not only the president but the promise. . . . We saw him only as a rising sun."

Johnson Fulfills the Kennedy Promise. Lyndon B. Johnson assumed the presidency with a wealth of political experience. A self-made man from the Texas Hill Country, he had won election in 1937 to the House of Representatives and in 1948 to the Senate, where he served skillfully as Senate majority leader. His modest upbringing,

THE "JOHNSON TREATMENT"

Abe Fortas, a distinguished lawyer who had argued a major criminal rights case, *Gideon v. Wainwright* (1963), before the Supreme Court, was a close friend of and adviser to President Johnson. This photograph of the president and Fortas taken in July 1965 illustrates how Johnson used his body as well as his voice to bend people to his will. LBJ Library photo by Yoichi Okamoto.

his admiration for Franklin Roosevelt, and his ambition to outdo the New Deal president all spurred his commitment to reform. Equally compelling were external pressures generated by the black freedom struggle and the host of movements it helped inspire.

Lacking Kennedy's sophistication, Johnson excelled behind the scenes, where he could entice, maneuver, or threaten legislators to support his objectives. His persuasive power, the famous "Johnson treatment," became legendary. In his ability to achieve his legislative goals, Johnson had few peers in American history.

Johnson entreated Congress to act so that "John Fitzgerald Kennedy did not live or die in vain." He pushed through Kennedy's tax cut bill by February 1964. More remarkable was passage of the **Civil Rights Act of 1964**, which made discrimination in employment, education, and public accommodations illegal. The strongest such measure since Reconstruction required every ounce of Johnson's political skill to pry sufficient votes from Republicans to overcome opposition by southern Democrats. Republican senator Everett Dirksen's aide reported that Johnson "never left him alone for thirty minutes." In proportion to their numbers in Congress, more Republicans voted for the measure than Democrats.

Antipoverty legislation followed fast on the heels of the Civil Rights Act. Johnson announced "an unconditional war on poverty" in his January 1964 State of the Union message, and in August Congress passed the Economic Opportunity Act. The law authorized ten new programs, allocating $800 million — about 1 percent of the federal budget — for the first year. Many provisions targeted children and youths, including Head Start for preschoolers, work-study grants for college students, and the Job Corps for unemployed young people. The Volunteers in Service to America (VISTA) program paid modest wages to those working with the disadvantaged, and a legal services program provided lawyers for the poor.

The most novel and controversial part of the law, the Community Action Program (CAP), required "maximum feasible participation" of the poor themselves in antipoverty projects. Poor people began to organize to make welfare agencies, school boards, police departments, and housing authorities more accountable to the people they served. When local Democratic officials complained, Johnson backed off from pushing genuine representation for the poor. Still, CAP gave people usually excluded from government an opportunity to act on their own behalf and develop leadership skills. A Mississippi sharecropper was elated to attend a CAP literacy program that enabled him "to help my younger children when they start school."

Civil Rights Act of 1964
Law that responded to demands of the civil rights movement by making discrimination in employment, education, and public accommodations illegal. It was the strongest such measure since Reconstruction and included a ban on sex discrimination in employment.

Policymaking for a Great Society.
As the 1964 election approached, Johnson projected stability and security in the midst of a booming economy. Few

voters wanted to risk the dramatic change promised by his Republican opponent, Arizona senator Barry M. Goldwater, who attacked the welfare state and entertained the use of nuclear weapons in Vietnam. Johnson achieved a record-breaking 61 percent of the popular vote, and Democrats won resounding majorities in the House (295–140) and Senate (68–32). Still, Goldwater's considerable grassroots support marked a growing movement on the right (as discussed in chapter 30) and a threat to Democratic control of the South.

"I want to see a whole bunch of coonskins on the wall," Johnson told his aides, using a hunting analogy to stress his ambitious legislative goals for what he called the "Great Society." The large Democratic majorities in Congress, his own political skills, and pressure from the black freedom struggle and other movements enabled Johnson to obtain legislation on discrimination, poverty, education, medical care, housing, consumer and environmental protection, and more. Reporters called the legislation of the Eighty-ninth Congress (1965–1966) "a political miracle."

The Economic Opportunity Act of 1964 was the opening shot in the **War on Poverty**. Congress doubled the program's funding in 1965, enacted new economic development measures for depressed regions, and authorized more than $1 billion to improve the nation's slums. Direct aid included a new food stamp program, giving poor people greater choice in obtaining food, and rent supplements that provided alternatives to public housing. Moreover, a movement of welfare mothers, the National Welfare Rights Organization, assisted by antipoverty lawyers, pushed administrators of Aid to Families with Dependent Children (AFDC) to ease restrictions on welfare recipients. The number of families receiving assistance jumped from less than one million in 1960 to three million by 1972, benefiting 90 percent of those eligible.

Central to Johnson's War on Poverty were efforts to equip the poor with the skills necessary to find jobs. His Elementary and Secondary Education Act of 1965 marked a turning point by involving the federal government in K–12 education. The measure sent federal dollars to local school districts and provided equipment and supplies to private and parochial schools serving the poor. That same year, Congress passed the Higher Education Act, vastly expanding federal assistance to colleges and universities for buildings, programs, scholarships, and loans.

The federal government's responsibility for health care marked an even greater watershed. Faced with a powerful medical lobby that opposed national health insurance as "socialized medicine," Johnson focused on the elderly, who constituted a large portion of the nation's poor. Congress responded with the **Medicare** program, providing the elderly with universal medical insurance financed largely through Social Security taxes. A separate program, **Medicaid**, authorized federal grants to supplement state-paid medical care for poor people. By the twenty-first century, these two programs covered 87 million Americans, nearly 30 percent of the population.

Whereas programs such as Medicare fulfilled New Deal promises, the Great Society's civil rights legislation represented a break with the past. Racial minorities were neglected or discriminated against in many New Deal programs; by contrast, the Civil Rights Act of 1964 made discrimination in employment, education, and public accommodations illegal. The **Voting Rights Act of 1965** banned literacy tests and other practices used to disqualify black voters and authorized federal intervention to ensure access to the voting booth.

War on Poverty
President Lyndon Johnson's efforts, organized through the Office of Economic Opportunity, to ameliorate poverty primarily through education and training as well as by including the poor in decision making.

Medicare and Medicaid
Social programs enacted as part of Lyndon Johnson's Great Society. Medicare provided the elderly with universal compulsory medical insurance financed primarily through Social Security taxes. Medicaid authorized federal grants to supplement state-paid medical care for poor people of all ages.

Voting Rights Act of 1965
Law passed during Lyndon Johnson's administration that empowered the federal government to intervene to ensure minorities access to the voting booth. As a result of the act, black voting and officeholding in the South shot up, initiating a major transformation in southern politics.

MEDICARE BECOMES LAW
President Lyndon Johnson traveled to the Truman Presidential Library in Independence, Missouri, to sign the law establishing Medicare and Medicaid, recognizing that President Harry Truman had first tried to enact universal health care two decades earlier. Here, Lady Bird Johnson, Vice President Hubert Humphrey, and Bess Truman look on while Johnson presents Truman with a pen he used to sign the bill. LBJ Library photo.

Another form of bias fell with the **Immigration and Nationality Act of 1965**, which abolished quotas based on national origins that discriminated against non–Western European immigrants. The law maintained caps on the total number of immigrants and, for the first time, included the Western Hemisphere in those limits; preference was now given to immediate relatives of U.S. citizens and to those with desirable skills. The measure's unanticipated consequences triggered a surge of immigration in the 1980s and thereafter (as discussed in chapter 31).

Great Society benefits reached well beyond victims of discrimination and the poor. Medicare covered the elderly, regardless of income. A groundswell of consumer activism won legislation making cars safer and raising standards for the food, drug, and cosmetics industries. Johnson insisted that the Great Society meet "not just the needs of the body but the desire for beauty and hunger for community." In 1965, he sent Congress the first presidential message on the environment, obtaining measures to control water and air pollution and to preserve the natural beauty of the American landscape. In addition, the National Arts and Humanities Act of 1965 funded artists, musicians, writers, and scholars and brought their work to public audiences.

The flood of reform legislation dwindled after 1966, when Democratic majorities in Congress diminished and a backlash against government programs arose. The Vietnam War dealt the largest blow to Johnson's ambitions, diverting his attention, spawning an antiwar movement that crippled his leadership, and devouring tax dollars that might have been used for reform (as discussed in chapter 29).

In 1968, Johnson pried out of Congress one more civil rights law, which banned discrimination in housing and jury service. He also signed the National Housing Act of 1968, which authorized an enormous increase in low-income housing — 1.7 million units over three years — and put construction and ownership in private hands.

Immigration and Nationality Act of 1965
Legislation passed during Lyndon Johnson's administration abolishing discriminatory immigration quotas based on national origins. Although it did limit the number of immigrants, including those from Latin America for the first time, it facilitated a surge in immigration later in the century.

20% – 13%

Assessing the Great Society. The reduction in poverty in the 1960s was considerable. The number of poor Americans fell from more than <u>20 percent of</u> the population in 1959 to around <u>13 percent in</u> 1968. Those who in Johnson's words "live on the outskirts of hope" saw new opportunities. <u>To Rosemary Bray</u>, what turned her family of longtime welfare recipients into taxpaying workers "was the promise of the civil rights movement and the war on poverty." A Mexican American who learned to be a sheet metal worker through a jobs program reported, "[My children] will finish high school and maybe go to college. . . . I see my family and I know the chains are broken."

Certain groups, especially the aged, fared better than others. Many male-headed families rose out of poverty, but impoverishment among female-headed families actually increased. Whites escaped poverty faster than racial and ethnic minorities. Great Society programs contributed to a burgeoning black middle class, yet one in three African Americans remained poverty-stricken (Figure 28.1).

<u>Conservative critics</u> charged that Great Society programs <u>discouraged initiative</u> by giving the poor "handouts." Liberal critics claimed that focusing on training and education wrongly blamed the poor themselves rather than an economic system that could not provide enough adequately paying jobs. In contrast to the New Deal, the Great Society avoided structural reform of the economy and spurned public works projects as a means of providing jobs for the disadvantaged.

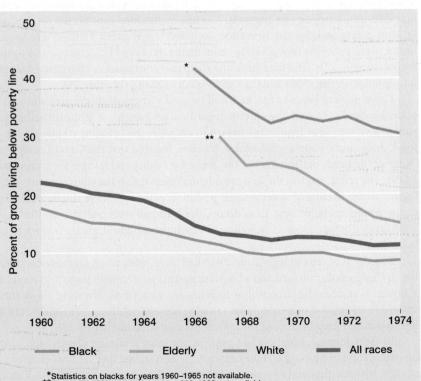

FIGURE 28.1 POVERTY IN THE UNITED STATES, 1960–1974

The short-term effects of economic growth and the Great Society's attack on poverty are seen here. Which groups experienced the sharpest decline in poverty, and what might account for the differences?

*Statistics on blacks for years 1960–1965 not available.
**Statistics on the elderly for years 1960–1966 not available.

Some critics insisted that ending poverty required raising taxes in order to create jobs, overhaul welfare systems, and rebuild slums. Great Society programs did invest more heavily in the public sector, but the Great Society was funded from economic growth rather than from new taxes on the rich or middle class. There was no significant redistribution of income, despite large increases in subsidies for food, housing, and medical care. Economic prosperity allowed spending for the poor to rise and improved the lives of millions, but that spending never approached the amounts necessary to claim victory in the War on Poverty.

The Judicial Revolution.

A key element of liberalism's ascendancy emerged in the Supreme Court under Chief Justice Earl Warren (1953–1969). In contrast to the federal courts of the Progressive Era and New Deal, which blocked reform, the **Warren Court** often moved ahead of Congress and public opinion. Expanding the Constitution's promise of equality and individual rights, the Court's decisions supported an activist government to prevent injustice and provided new protections to disadvantaged groups and accused criminals.

Following the pathbreaking *Brown v. Board of Education* school desegregation decision of 1954 (see chapter 27), the Court struck down southern states' maneuvers to avoid integration and defended protesters' rights to freedom of assembly and speech. In addition, a unanimous Court in *Loving v. Virginia* (1967) invalidated state laws banning interracial marriage, calling marriage one of the "basic civil rights of man."

Chief Justice Warren considered *Baker v. Carr* (1963) his most important decision. The case grew out of a complaint that inequitably drawn Tennessee electoral districts gave sparsely populated rural districts far more representatives than densely populated urban areas. Using the Fourteenth Amendment guarantee of "equal protection of the laws," the Court established the principle of "one person, one vote" for state legislatures and for the House of Representatives. As states redrew electoral districts, legislatures became more responsive to metropolitan interests.

The Warren Court also reformed the criminal justice system, overturning a series of convictions on the grounds that the accused had been deprived of "life, liberty, or property, without due process of law," guaranteed in the Fourteenth Amendment. In decisions that dramatically altered law enforcement practices, the Court declared that states, as well as the federal government, were subject to the Bill of Rights. *Gideon v. Wainwright* (1963) ruled that when an accused criminal could not afford to hire a lawyer, the state had to provide one. *Miranda v. Arizona* (1966) required police officers to inform suspects of their rights upon arrest. The Court also overturned convictions based on evidence obtained by unlawful arrest, by electronic surveillance, or without a search warrant. Critics accused the justices of "handcuffing the police" and letting criminals go free; liberals argued that these rulings promoted equal treatment in the criminal justice system.

The Court's decisions on religion provoked even greater outrage. *Abington School District v. Schempp* (1963) ruled that requiring Bible-reading and prayer in public schools violated the First Amendment principle of separation of church and state. Later judgments banned official prayer in public schools even if students were not required to participate. The Court's supporters declared that these decisions protected the rights of non-Christians and atheists and left students perfectly free to

Warren Court
The Supreme Court under Chief Justice Earl Warren (1953–1969), which expanded the Constitution's promise of equality and civil rights. It issued landmark decisions in the areas of civil rights, criminal rights, reproductive freedom, and separation of church and state.

pray on their own, but the decisions infuriated many Christians. Billboards demanding "Impeach Earl Warren" spoke for critics of the Court, who joined a larger backlash mounting against Great Society liberalism.

> **REVIEW** How did the Kennedy and Johnson administrations exemplify a liberal vision of the federal government?

The Second Reconstruction

As much as Supreme Court decisions, the black freedom struggle distinguished the liberalism of the 1960s from that of the New Deal. Before the Great Society reforms — and, in fact, contributing to them — African Americans had mobilized a movement that struck down legal separation and discrimination in the South and secured their voting rights. Whereas the first Reconstruction reflected the power of northern Republicans in the aftermath of the Civil War, the second Reconstruction depended heavily on the courage and determination of black people themselves to stand up to racist violence.

Civil rights activism that focused on the South and on legal rights won widespread acceptance in most of the country. But when African Americans stepped up protests against racial injustice outside the South and challenged the economic deprivation that equal rights left untouched, a strong backlash developed as the movement itself lost cohesion.

The Flowering of the Black Freedom Struggle. The Montgomery bus boycott of 1955–1956 gave racial issues national visibility and produced a leader in Martin Luther King Jr. In the 1960s, protest expanded dramatically, as blacks directly confronted the people and institutions that segregated and discriminated against them: retail establishments, public parks and libraries, buses and depots, voting registrars, and police forces.

Massive direct action in the South began in February 1960, when four African American college students in Greensboro, North Carolina, requested service at the whites-only Woolworth's lunch counter. Within days, hundreds of young people joined them, and others launched sit-ins in thirty-one southern cities. From Southern Christian Leadership Conference headquarters, Ella Baker telephoned her young contacts at black colleges: "What are you going to do? It's time to move."

In April, Baker helped protesters form a new organization, the Student Nonviolent Coordinating Committee (SNCC). Embracing King's civil disobedience and nonviolence principles, activists would confront their oppressors and stand up for their rights, but they would not respond if attacked. In the words of SNCC leader James Lawson, "Nonviolence nurtures the atmosphere in which reconciliation and justice become actual possibilities." SNCC, however, rejected the top-down leadership of King and the established civil rights organizations, adopting a structure that fostered decision making and leadership development at the grassroots level.

The activists' optimism and commitment to nonviolence soon underwent severe tests. Although some cities quietly met student demands, more typically activists encountered violence. Hostile whites poured food over demonstrators, burned them with cigarettes, called them "niggers," and pelted them with rocks.

LUNCH COUNTER SIT-IN

Tougaloo College professor John Salter Jr. and students Joan Trumpauer and Anne Moody take part in a 1963 sit-in at the Woolworth's lunch counter in Jackson, Mississippi. Shortly before this photograph was taken, whites had thrown two students to the floor, and police had arrested one student. In 1968, Moody published *Coming of Age in Mississippi*, a book about her experiences in the black freedom struggle. The Granger Collection, New York.

Local police attacked protesters with dogs, clubs, fire hoses, and tear gas, and they arrested thousands of demonstrators.

Another wave of protest occurred in May 1961, when the Congress of Racial Equality (CORE) organized Freedom Rides to implement Court orders for integrated transportation. When a group of six whites and seven blacks reached Alabama, whites bombed their bus and beat them with baseball bats so fiercely that an observer "couldn't see their faces through the blood." CORE leader James Farmer rebuffed President Kennedy's pleas for a cooling-off period, noting that blacks had been "cooling off for 150 years. If we cool off anymore, we'll be in a deep freeze." Finally, after a huge mob attacked the riders in Montgomery, Alabama, Attorney General Robert Kennedy dispatched federal marshals to restore order. Nonetheless, Freedom Riders arriving in Jackson, Mississippi, were promptly arrested, and several hundred spent weeks in jail. All told, more than four hundred blacks and whites participated in the Freedom Rides.

In the summer of 1962, SNCC and other groups began the Voter Education Project to register black voters in southern states. They, too, met violence. Whites bombed black churches, threw tenant farmers out of their homes, and beat and jailed activists like Fannie Lou Hamer. In June 1963, a white man gunned down Mississippi NAACP leader Medgar Evers in front of his house. Similar violence met King's 1963 campaign in Birmingham, Alabama, to integrate public facilities and open jobs to blacks. The police attacked demonstrators, including children, with dogs, cattle prods, and fire hoses — brutalities that television broadcast around the world.

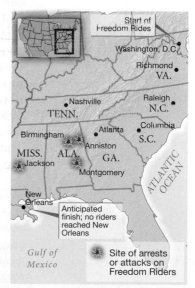

CIVIL RIGHTS FREEDOM RIDES, MAY 1961

The largest demonstration drew 250,000 blacks and whites to the nation's capital in August 1963 in the March on Washington for Jobs and Freedom, inspired by the strategy of A. Philip Randolph in 1941 (see chapter 25). Speaking from the Lincoln Memorial, King put his indelible stamp on the day. "I have a dream," he repeated again and again, imagining the day "when all of God's children . . . will be able to join hands and sing . . . 'Free at last, free at last; thank God Almighty, we are free at last.'"

The euphoria of the March on Washington faded as activists returned to face continued violence in the South. In 1964, the Mississippi Freedom Summer Project mobilized more than a thousand northern black and white college students to conduct voter registration drives. Resistance was fierce, and by the end of the summer, only twelve hundred new voters had been allowed to register. Southern whites had killed several activists, beaten eighty, arrested more than a thousand, and burned thirty-five black churches. Hidden resistance came from the federal government itself, as the Federal Bureau of Investigation (FBI) spied on King and expanded its activities to "expose, disrupt, misdirect, discredit, or otherwise neutralize" black protest.

Still, the movement persisted. In March 1965, Alabama state troopers used such violent force to turn back a voting rights march from Selma to the state capital, Montgomery, that the incident earned the name "Bloody Sunday" and compelled President Johnson to call up the Alabama National Guard to protect the marchers. Battered and hospitalized on Bloody Sunday, John Lewis, chairman of SNCC (and later a congressman from Georgia), called the Voting Rights Act, which passed that October, "every bit as momentous as the Emancipation Proclamation." Referring to the Selma march, he said, "we all felt we'd had a part in it."

The Response in Washington.

Civil rights leaders would have to wear sneakers, Lyndon Johnson said, if they were going to keep up with him. But both Kennedy and Johnson, reluctant to alienate southern voters and their congressional representatives, tended to move only when events gave them little choice. In June 1963, Kennedy finally made good on his promise to seek strong antidiscrimination legislation. Pointing to the injustice suffered by blacks, Kennedy asked white Americans, "Who among us would then be content with the counsels of patience and delay?" Johnson took up Kennedy's commitment with passion, as scenes of violence against peaceful demonstrators appalled television viewers across the world. The resulting public support, the "Johnson treatment," and the president's appeal to memories of the martyred Kennedy all produced the most important civil rights law since Reconstruction.

The Civil Rights Act of 1964 guaranteed access for all Americans to public accommodations, public education, employment, and voting, and it extended constitutional protections to Indians on reservations. Title VII of the measure, banning discrimination in employment, not only attacked racial discrimination but also outlawed discrimination against women. Because Title VII applied to every aspect of employment, including wages, hiring, and promotion, it represented a giant step toward equal employment opportunity for white women as well as for racial minorities.

Responding to voter registration drives in the South, Johnson demanded legislation to remove "every remaining obstacle to the right and the opportunity to vote." In August 1965, he signed the Voting Rights Act, empowering the federal government to intervene directly to enable African Americans to register and vote, thereby launching a major transformation in southern politics. Black voting rates shot up dramatically (Map 28.2). In turn, the number of African Americans holding political office in the South increased from a handful in 1964 to more than a thousand by 1972. Such gains translated into tangible benefits as black officials upgraded public facilities, police protection, and other basic services for their constituents.

Johnson also declared the need to realize "not just equality as a right and theory, but equality as fact and result." To this end, he issued an executive order in 1965 requiring employers holding government contracts (affecting about one-third of the labor force) to take affirmative action to ensure equal opportunity. Extended to cover women in 1967, the affirmative action program aimed to counter the effects of centuries of discrimination by requiring employers to act vigorously to align their labor forces with the available pool of qualified candidates. Most corporations came

Visual Activity

SELMA MARCH

The fifty-four-mile voting rights march from Selma, Alabama, to the state capital, Montgomery, gained national attention because of the violent reaction to the marchers from onlookers and state officials. The protest helped get the 1965 Voting Rights Act through Congress, a measure that eventually rewrote politics in the South. © Bruce Davidson/Magnum Photos.

READING THE IMAGE: Why do you think the young boy lowered the flag to cover his body? What do the presence of the priest in the background and the signs behind him reflect about the breadth of the black freedom struggle?

CONNECTIONS: How was this protest like and different from other civil rights protests during the 1960s?

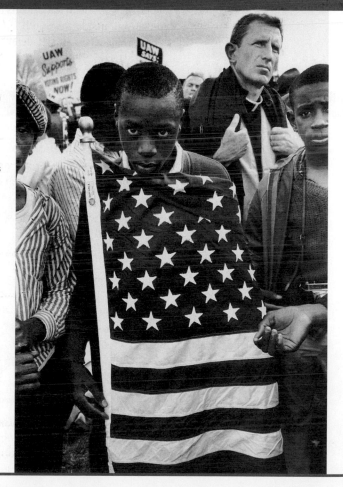

to see affirmative action as a good employment practice that could make them more successful in "today's increasingly global marketplace."

In 1968, Johnson maneuvered one final bill through Congress. While those in other regions often applauded the gains made by the black freedom struggle in the South, whites were just as likely to resist claims for racial justice in their own locations. In 1963, California voters rejected a law passed by the legislature banning discrimination in housing. And when Martin Luther King Jr. launched a campaign against de facto segregation in Chicago in 1966, thousands of whites jeered and threw stones at demonstrators. Johnson's efforts to get a federal open-housing law succeeded only in the wake of King's assassination in 1968. The Civil Rights Act of 1968 banned racial discrimination in housing and jury selection, and it authorized federal intervention when states failed to protect civil rights workers from violence.

Black Power and Urban Rebellions. By 1966, black protest engulfed the entire nation, demanding not just legal equality but also economic justice and abandoning passive resistance as a basic principle. These developments were not completely new. African Americans had waged campaigns for decent jobs, housing, and education outside the South since the 1930s. Some African Americans had always armed themselves in self-defense, and many protesters doubted that their passive

Map Activity

MAP 28.2 THE RISE OF THE AFRICAN AMERICAN VOTE, 1940–1976

Voting rates of southern blacks increased gradually in the 1940s and 1950s but shot up dramatically in the deep South after the Voting Rights Act of 1965 provided for federal agents to enforce African Americans' right to vote.

READING THE MAP: When did the biggest change in African American voter registration occur in the South? In 1968, which states had the highest and which had the lowest voter registration rates?

CONNECTIONS: What role did African American voters play in the 1960 election? What were the targets of two major voting drives in the 1960s?

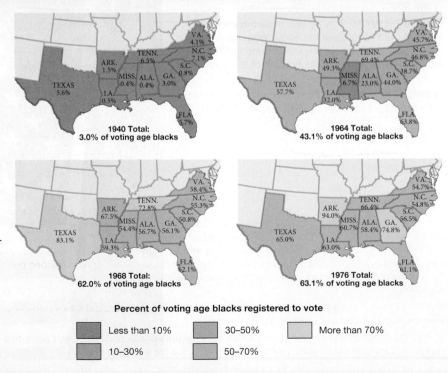

1940 Total: 3.0% of voting age blacks

1964 Total: 43.1% of voting age blacks

1968 Total: 62.0% of voting age blacks

1976 Total: 63.1% of voting age blacks

Percent of voting age blacks registered to vote

Less than 10%   30–50%   More than 70%

10–30%   50–70%

response to violent attacks would change the hearts of racists. Still, the black freedom struggle began to appear more threatening to the white majority.

The new emphases resulted from a combination of heightened activism and unrealized promise. Legal equality could not quickly ameliorate African American poverty, and black rage at oppressive conditions erupted in waves of urban uprisings from 1965 to 1968 (Map 28.3). In a situation where virtually all-white police forces patrolled black neighborhoods, incidents between police and local blacks typically

Map Activity

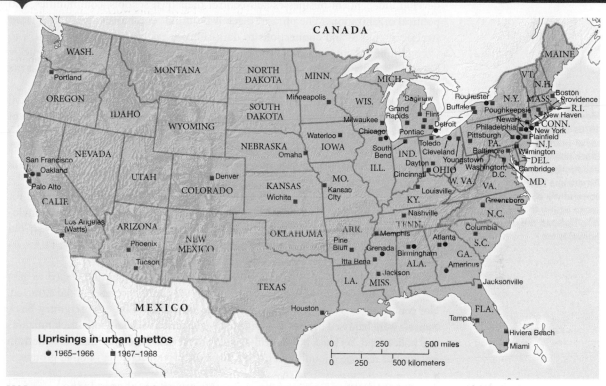

MAP 28.3 URBAN UPRISINGS, 1965–1968

When a white police officer in the Watts district of Los Angeles struck a twenty-one-year-old African American, whom he had just pulled over for driving drunk, one onlooker shouted, "We've got no rights at all — it's just like Selma." The altercation sparked a five-day uprising, during which young blacks set fires, looted, and attacked police and firefighters. When the riot ended, 34 people were dead, more than 3,000 were arrested, and scores of businesses had been wiped out. Similar but smaller-scale violence erupted in dozens of cities across the nation during the next three summers.

READING THE MAP: In what regions and cities of the United States were the 1960s uprisings concentrated? What years saw the greatest unrest?

CONNECTIONS: What were some of the causes of racial unrest in America's cities during this period? Whom did whites generally hold responsible for the violence, and why?

sparked the riots and resulted in looting, destruction of property, injuries, and deaths. The worst riots occurred in Watts (Los Angeles) in August 1965, Newark and Detroit in July 1967, and the nation's capital in April 1968, but violence visited hundreds of cities, and African Americans suffered most of the casualties.

In the North, Malcolm X posed a powerful challenge to the ethos of nonviolence. Calling for black pride and autonomy, separation from the "corrupt [white] society," and self-defense against white violence, Malcolm X attracted a large following, especially in urban ghettos. At a June 1966 rally in Greenwood, Mississippi, SNCC chairman Stokely Carmichael gave the ideas espoused by Malcolm X a new name when he shouted, "We want black power." Carmichael rejected integration and assimilation because they implied white superiority. African Americans were encouraged to develop independent businesses and control their own schools, communities, and political organizations. The phrase "Black is beautiful" emphasized pride in African American culture and connections to dark-skinned people around the world who were claiming their independence from colonial domination. Black power quickly became the rallying cry in SNCC and CORE as well as other organizations such as the Black Panther Party for Self-Defense, organized to combat police brutality.

black power movement
Movement of the 1960s and 1970s that emphasized black racial pride and autonomy. Black power advocates encouraged African Americans to assert community control, and some within the movement also rejected the ethos of nonviolence.

The press paid inordinate attention to the **black power movement**, and civil rights activism met with a severe backlash from whites. Although the urban riots of the mid-1960s erupted spontaneously, triggered by specific incidents of alleged police mistreatment, horrified whites blamed black power militants. By 1966, 85 percent of the white population — up from 34 percent two years earlier — thought that African Americans were pressing for too much too quickly.

Martin Luther King Jr. agreed with black power advocates about the need for economic justice and "a radical reconstruction of society," yet he clung to nonviolence and integration as the means to this end. In 1968, the thirty-nine-year-old leader went to Memphis to support striking municipal sanitation workers. There, on April 4, he was murdered by an escaped white convict.

Although black power organizations captured the headlines, they failed to gain the massive support from African Americans that King and other leaders had attracted. Nor could they alleviate the poverty and racism entrenched in the entire country. Black radicals were harassed by the FBI and jailed; some encounters left both black militants and police dead. Yet black power's emphasis on racial pride and its critique of American institutions resonated loudly and helped shape the protest activities of other groups.

REVIEW How and why did the civil rights movement change in the mid-1960s?

A Multitude of Movements

The civil rights movement's undeniable moral claims helped make protest more respectable, while its successes encouraged other groups with grievances. Native Americans, Latinos, college students, women, gay men and lesbians, and others drew on the black freedom struggle for inspiration and models of activism. Many of these groups engaged in direct-action protests, expressed their own cultural nationalism, and challenged dominant institutions and values. Their grievances gained attention in the political arena, and they expanded justice and opportunity for many of their constituents.

Native American Protest.

The cry "red power" reflected the influence of black radicalism on young Native Americans, whose activism took on fresh militancy and goals in the 1960s. The termination and relocation programs of the 1950s, contrary to their intent, stirred a sense of Indian identity across tribal lines and a determination to preserve traditional culture. Native Americans demonstrated and occupied land and public buildings, claiming rights to natural resources and territory they had owned collectively before European settlement.

In 1969, Native American militants captured world attention when several dozen seized Alcatraz Island, an abandoned federal prison in San Francisco Bay, claiming their right of "first discovery" of this land. For nineteen months, they used the occupation to publicize injustices against Indians, promote pan-Indian cooperation, and celebrate traditional cultures. One of the organizers, Dr. LaNada Boyer, the first Native American to attend the University of California, Berkeley, said of Alcatraz, "We were able to reestablish our identity as Indian people, as a culture, as political entities."

In Minneapolis in 1968, two Chippewa Indians, Dennis Banks and George Mitchell, founded the **American Indian Movement (AIM)** to attack problems in cities, where about 300,000 Indians lived. AIM sought to protect Indians from police harassment, secure antipoverty funds, and establish "survival schools" to teach Indian history and values. The movement's appeal quickly spread and filled many Indians with a new sense of purpose. Lakota activist and author Mary Crow Dog wrote that AIM's visit to her South Dakota reservation "loosened a sort of earthquake inside me." AIM leaders helped organize the "Trail of Broken Treaties" caravan to the nation's capital in 1972, when activists occupied the Bureau of Indian Affairs to express their outrage at the bureau's policies and interference in Indians' lives. In 1973, a much longer siege occurred on the Lakota Sioux reservation in South Dakota. Conflicts there between AIM militants and older tribal leaders led AIM to take over for seventy-two days the village of Wounded Knee, where U.S. troops had massacred more than one hundred Sioux Indians in 1890 (see chapter 17).

American Indian Movement (AIM) Organization established in 1968 to address the problems Indians faced in American cities, including poverty and police harassment. AIM organized Indians to end relocation and termination policies and to win greater control over their cultures and communities.

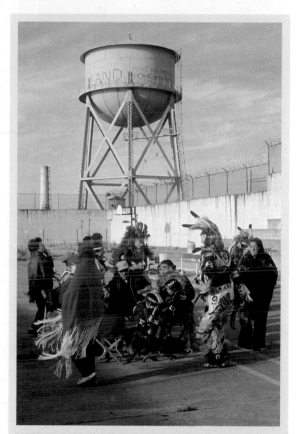

NATIVE AMERICANS OCCUPY ALCATRAZ ISLAND

From November 1969 to June 1971, groups of Native Americans occupied Alcatraz Island in San Francisco Bay. Calling themselves "Indians of All Tribes" to reflect their diversity, they demanded the deed to the island and the creation of an Indian university, museum, and cultural center. Although failing to achieve their goals, they brought attention to the Native American cause and spurred further activism.
Ralph Crane/Getty Images.

Although these dramatic occupations failed to achieve their specific goals, Indians won the end of relocation and termination policies, greater tribal sovereignty and control over community services, protection of Indian religious practices, and a measure of respect and pride. A number of laws and court decisions restored rights to ancestral lands and compensated tribes for land seized in violation of treaties.

Latino Struggles for Justice.

The fastest-growing minority group in the 1960s was Latino, or Hispanic American, an extraordinarily varied population encompassing people of Mexican, Puerto Rican, Caribbean, and other Latin American origins. (The term *Latino* stresses their common bonds as a minority group in the United States. The older, less political term *Hispanic* also includes people with origins in Spain.) People of Puerto Rican and Caribbean descent populated East Coast cities, but more than half of the nation's Latino population — including some six million Mexican Americans — lived in the Southwest. In addition, thousands illegally crossed the border between Mexico and the United States yearly in search of economic opportunity and security from violence.

Political organization of Mexican Americans dated back to the League of United Latin American Citizens (LULAC), founded in 1929, which fought segregation and discrimination through litigation (see chapter 26). In the 1960s, however, young Mexican Americans increasingly rejected traditional politics in favor of direct action. One symbol of this generational challenge was young activists' adoption of the term *Chicano* (from *mejicano*, the Spanish word for "Mexican").

The **Chicano movement** drew national attention to California, where Cesar Chavez and Dolores Huerta organized a movement to overcome the exploitation of migrant agricultural workers. As the child of migrant farmworkers, Chavez lived in soggy tents, saw his parents cheated by labor contractors, changed schools frequently, and encountered indifference and discrimination. One teacher, he recalled, "hung a sign on me that said, 'I am a clown, I speak Spanish.'" After serving in World War II, Chavez began to organize voter registration drives among Mexican Americans.

In contrast to Chavez, Dolores Huerta grew up in an integrated neighborhood and avoided the farmworkers' grinding poverty but witnessed subtle forms of discrimination. Once, a high school teacher challenged her authorship of an essay because it was so well written. Believing that collective action was the key to progress, she and

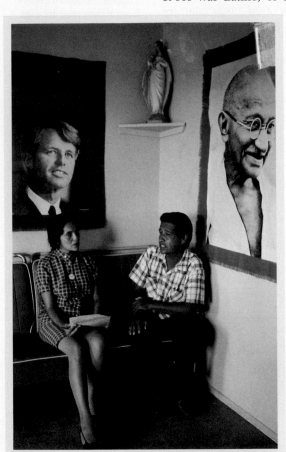

CESAR CHAVEZ AND DOLORES HUERTA
Under posters showing Senator Robert Kennedy and Mahatma Gandhi, Chavez and Huerta confer in 1968 during the United Farm Workers' struggle with grape growers for better wages and working conditions. Chavez, like Martin Luther King Jr., had studied the ideas of Gandhi, who used civil disobedience and nonviolence to gain independence for India. People across the country, including Robert Kennedy, supported the UFW's grape boycott. Arthur Schatz/Getty Images.

Chavez founded the United Farm Workers (UFW) union in 1962. To gain leverage for striking workers, the UFW mounted a nationwide boycott of California grapes, winning support from millions of Americans and gaining a wage increase for the workers in 1970. Although the UFW struggled and lost membership during the 1970s, it helped politicize Mexican Americans and improve farmworkers' lives.

Other Chicanos pressed the Equal Employment Opportunity Commission (EEOC) to act against job discrimination against Mexican Americans. After LULAC, the American GI Forum (see chapter 26), and other groups picketed government offices, President Johnson responded in 1967 by appointing Vicente T. Ximenes as the first Mexican American EEOC commissioner and creating a special committee on Mexican American issues.

Claiming "brown power," Chicanos organized to end discrimination in education, gain political power, and combat police brutality. In Denver, Rodolfo "Corky" Gonzales set up "freedom schools" where Chicano children learned Spanish and Mexican American history. The nationalist strains of Chicano protest were evident in La Raza Unida (the United Race), a political party founded in 1970 based on cultural pride and brotherhood. Along with blacks and Native Americans, Chicanos continued to be disproportionately impoverished, but they gradually won more political offices, more effective enforcement of antidiscrimination legislation, and greater respect for their culture.

Chicano movement
Mobilization of Mexican Americans in the 1960s and 1970s to fight for civil rights, economic justice, and political power and to combat police brutality. Most notably, the movement worked to improve the lives of migrant farmworkers and to end discrimination in employment and education.

Student Rebellion, the New Left, and the Counterculture.
Although materially and legally more secure than their African American, Indian, and Latino counterparts, white youths also expressed dissent, participating in the black freedom struggle, student protests, the antiwar movement, and the new feminist movement. Challenging establishment institutions, young activists were part of a larger international phenomenon of student movements around the globe.

The central organization of white student protest was Students for a Democratic Society (SDS), whose 1962 statement of purpose asserted, "We are people of this generation, bred in at least modest comfort, housed now in universities, looking uncomfortably at the world we inherit." The idealistic students criticized the complacency of their elders, the remoteness of decision makers, and the powerlessness and alienation generated by a bureaucratic society. SDS aimed to mobilize a "New Left" around the goals of civil rights, peace, and universal economic security. Other forms of student activism soon followed.

The first large-scale white student protest arose at the University of California, Berkeley, in 1964, when university officials banned students from setting up tables to recruit support for various causes. Led by whites returning from civil rights work in the South, the "free speech" movement occupied the administration building, and more than seven hundred students were arrested before the California Board of Regents overturned the new restrictions. Hundreds of student rallies and building occupations followed on campuses across the country, especially after 1965, when opposition to the Vietnam War mounted and students protested against universities' ties with the military (as discussed in chapter 29). Students also challenged the collegiate environment. Women at the University of Chicago, for example, charged in 1969 that all universities "discriminate against women, impede their full

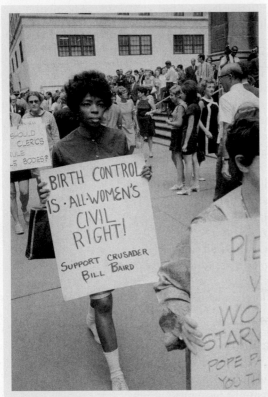

BIRTH CONTROL

In the 1960s, the advent of the birth control pill, court decisions lifting restrictions on contraception, the rise of feminism, and demands for greater sexual freedom all threw birth control into the political spotlight. In July 1968, Pope Paul VI issued an encyclical condemning artificial birth control, which prompted this demonstration in front of New York's St. Patrick's Cathedral.
Bettmann/Corbis.

intellectual development, deny them places on the faculty, exploit talented women and mistreat women students." At Howard University, African American students called for a "Black Awareness Research Institute," demanding that academic departments "place more emphasis on how these disciplines may be used to effect the liberation of black people." Across the country, students won curricular reforms such as black studies and women's studies programs, more financial aid for minority and poor students, independence from paternalistic rules, and a larger voice in campus decision making.

Student protest sometimes blended into a cultural revolution against nearly every conventional standard of behavior. Drawing on the ideas of the Beats of the 1950s (see chapter 27), the so-called hippies rejected mainstream values such as consumerism, order, and sexual restraint. Seeking personal rather than political change, they advocated "Do your own thing" and drew attention with their long hair, wildly colorful clothing, and drug use. Across the country, thousands of radicals established communes in cities or on farms, where they renounced private property and shared everything.

Rock and folk music defined both the counterculture and the political left. Music during the 1960s often carried insurgent political and social messages that reflected radical youth culture. "Eve of Destruction," a top hit of 1965, reminded young men of draft age at a time when the voting age was twenty-one, "You're old enough to kill but not for votin'." The 1969 Woodstock Music Festival, attended by 400,000 young people, epitomized the centrality of music to the youth rebellion. Hippies faded away in the 1970s, but many elements of the counterculture — rock music, jeans, and long hair, as well as new social attitudes — filtered into the mainstream. More tolerant approaches to sexual behaviors spawned what came to be called the "sexual revolution," with help from the birth control pill, which became available in the 1960s. Self-fulfillment became a dominant concern of many Americans, and questioning of authority became more widespread.

Gay Men and Lesbians Organize. More permissive sexual norms did not stretch easily to include tolerance of homosexuality. Gay men and lesbians escaped discrimination and ridicule only by concealing their very identities. Those who couldn't or wouldn't found themselves fired from jobs, arrested for their sexual activities, deprived of their children, or accused of being "perverted." Despite this, some gays and lesbians began to organize.

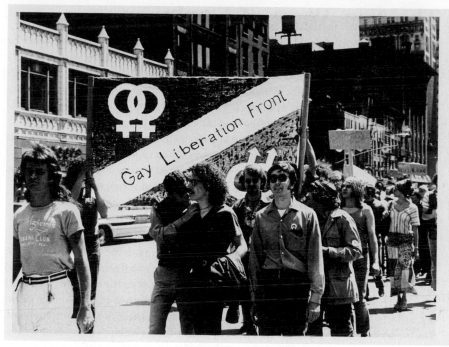

An early expression of gay activism challenged the government's aggressive efforts to keep homosexuals out of civil service. In October 1965, picketers outside the White House held signs calling discrimination against homosexuals "as immoral as discrimination against Negroes and Jews." Not until ten years later, however, did the Civil Service Commission formally end its antigay policy.

A turning point in gay activism came in 1969 when police raided a gay bar, the Stonewall Inn, in New York City's Greenwich Village, and gay men and lesbians fought back. "Suddenly, they were not submissive anymore," a police officer remarked. Energized by the defiance shown at the Stonewall riots, gay men and lesbians organized a host of new groups, such as the Gay Liberation Front and the National Gay and Lesbian Task Force.

In 1972, Ann Arbor, Michigan, passed the first antidiscrimination ordinance, and two years later Elaine Noble's election to the Massachusetts legislature marked the first time an openly gay candidate won state office. In 1973, gay activists persuaded the American Psychiatric Association to withdraw its designation of homosexuality as a mental disease. It would take decades for these initial gains to improve conditions for most homosexuals, but by the mid-1970s gay men and lesbians had a movement through which they could claim equal rights and express pride in their identities.

REVIEW What other movements emerged in the 1960s, and how were they influenced by the black freedom struggle?

The New Wave of Feminism

On August 26, 1970, the fiftieth anniversary of woman an suffrage, tens of thousands of women across the country — from radical women in jeans to conservatively dressed suburbanites, peace activists, and politicians — took to the streets. They carried signs reading "Sisterhood Is Powerful" and "Don't Cook Dinner — Starve a Rat Today." Some of the banners opposed the war in Vietnam, others demanded racial justice, but women's own liberation stood at the forefront.

Becoming visible by the late 1960s, a multifaceted women's movement reached its high tide in the 1970s and persisted into the twenty-first century. By that time, despite a powerful countermovement, women had experienced tremendous transformations in their legal status, public opportunities, and personal and sexual relationships, while popular expectations about appropriate gender roles had shifted dramatically.

A Multifaceted Movement Emerges.
Beginning in the 1940s, large demographic changes laid the preconditions for a resurgence of feminism. As more and more women took jobs, the importance of their paid work to the economy and their families challenged traditional views of women and awakened many women workers, especially labor union women, to the inferior conditions of their employment. The democratization of higher education brought more women to college campuses, where their aspirations exceeded the confines of domesticity and of routine, subordinate jobs.

Policy initiatives in the early 1960s reflected both these larger transformations and the efforts of women's rights activists. In 1961, Assistant Secretary of Labor Esther Peterson persuaded President Kennedy to create the President's Commission on the Status of Women (PCSW). Its 1963 report documented widespread discrimination against women and recommended remedies, although it did not challenge women's domestic roles. One of the commission's concerns was addressed even before its report came out, when Congress passed the Equal Pay Act of 1963, making it illegal to pay women less than men for the same work.

Like other movements, the rise of feminism owed much to the black freedom struggle. Women gained protection from employment discrimination through Title VII of the Civil Rights Act of 1964 and the extension of affirmative action to women by piggybacking onto civil rights measures. They soon grew impatient when the government failed to take these new policies seriously. Determining the need for "an NAACP for women" to put pressure on the government and other institutions, Betty Friedan, civil rights activist Pauli Murray, several union women, and others founded the **National Organization for Women (NOW)** in 1966.

Simultaneously, a more radical feminism grew among mostly white young women active in the black freedom struggle and the New Left. Frustrated when male leaders dismissed and ridiculed their claims of sex discrimination, many women walked out of New Left organizations and created independent women's liberation groups throughout the nation.

Women's liberation began to gain public attention, especially when dozens of women picketed the Miss America beauty pageant in 1968, protesting against being

National Organization for Women (NOW)
Women's civil rights organization formed in 1966. Initially, NOW focused on eliminating gender discrimination in public institutions and the workplace, but by the 1970s it also embraced many of the issues raised by more radical feminists.

forced "to compete for male approval [and] enslaved by ludicrous 'beauty' standards." Women began to speak publicly about personal experiences that had always been shrouded in secrecy, such as rape and abortion. Throughout the country, women joined consciousness-raising groups, where they discovered that what they had considered "personal" problems reflected an entrenched system of discrimination against and devaluation of women.

Radical feminists, who called their movement "women's liberation," differed from feminists in NOW and other more mainstream groups in several ways. NOW focused on equal treatment for women in the public sphere; women's liberation emphasized ending women's subordination in family and other personal relationships. Groups such as NOW wanted to integrate women into existing institutions; radical groups insisted that women's liberation required a total transformation of economic, political, and social institutions. Differences between these two strands of feminism blurred in the 1970s, as NOW and other mainstream groups embraced many of the issues raised by radicals.

Although NOW elected a black president, Aileen Hernandez, in 1970, the new feminism's leadership and constituency were predominantly white and middle-class. Women of color criticized white feminists for their inadequate attention to the disproportionate poverty experienced by minority women and to the particular forms of oppression women of color experienced when gender combined with race or ethnicity. To black women, who were much more frequently compelled to work in the lowest-paying jobs for their families' survival, employment did not necessarily look like liberation.

In addition to struggling with vast differences among women, feminism also contended with the media's refusal to take women's grievances seriously. For instance, when the House of Representatives passed an equal rights amendment to the U.S. Constitution in 1970, the *New York Times* criticized it in an editorial titled "The Henpecked House." After Gloria Steinem founded *Ms.: The New Magazine for Women* in 1972, feminists had their own mass-circulation periodical controlled by women and featuring articles on a broad range of feminist issues. *Ms.* reported on a multifaceted movement that reflected the tremendously diverse experiences, backgrounds, and goals of American women. New women's organizations represented ethnic and racial minorities, labor union women, religious women, welfare mothers, lesbians, and more. Other new groups focused on single issues such as health, education, abortion rights, and violence against women. In addition, U.S. women connected with women abroad, joining a movement that crossed national boundaries. (See "Beyond America's Borders," page 852.)

Common threads underlay the great diversity of organizations, issues, and activities. Feminism represented the belief that women were barred from, unequally treated in, or poorly served by the entire male-dominated public arena, including politics, medicine, law, education, culture, and religion. Many feminists also sought equality in the private sphere, challenging traditional norms that identified women primarily as wives and mothers or sex objects who accommodated themselves to men's needs and interests.

Feminist Gains Spark a Countermovement.
Although more an effect than a cause of women's rising employment, feminism lifted female aspirations and

helped lower barriers to occupations monopolized by men. By 2010, women's share of law and medical degrees had shot up from 5 percent and 10 percent, respectively, to around 50 percent, though they earned much less than men in those fields. Women gained political offices very slowly; yet by 2016, they constituted about 20 percent of Congress and nearly 25 percent of all state legislators.

Despite outnumbering men in college enrollments and making some inroads into male-dominated occupations, women still concentrated in low-paying, traditionally female jobs, and an earnings gap between men and women persisted into the twenty-first century. Employed women continued to bear primary responsibility for taking care of their homes and families, thereby working a "double day." Unlike in other advanced countries, women in the United States were not entitled to paid maternity leave, and government provisions for child care lagged far behind.

Beyond America's Borders

Transnational Feminisms

International organizations of women originated in the nineteenth century, but global connections among women increased dramatically in 1945 with the creation of the United Nations, whose charter affirmed "the equal rights of men and women." In 1947, the UN established a Commission on the Status of Women, creating a forum for women from around the globe to meet and be heard; in 1948, it adopted a Universal Declaration of Human Rights, which explicitly condemned sex discrimination. These commitments to justice for women went far beyond any rights guaranteed to women in the United States or most other nations, thereby setting standards and raising expectations.

The UN helped launch a global feminist movement of unparalleled size and diversity when it declared 1975 International Women's Year and sponsored a conference in Mexico City. In addition to official delegates from 125 nations, six thousand women came to Mexico City on their own. The assembly approved the World Plan of Action for Women and prompted the UN to declare 1976 to 1985 the UN Decade for Women.

In response to the call for action in individual countries, the U.S. government funded the National Women's

Conference in Houston, Texas, in 1977. More than two thousand state delegates attended, representing a cross section of American womanhood. They adopted the National Plan of Action, not only supporting ratification of the ERA and reproductive freedom but also addressing the needs of specific groups of women, including the elderly, lesbians, racial minorities, women with disabilities, rural women, and homemakers. For the first time, the U.S. women's movement had a comprehensive national agenda setting goals for decades to come.

The three themes of the UN Decade for Women — equality, development, and peace — reflected an effort to address the enormously diverse needs of women throughout the world. Feminists from Western nations who focused on equal rights met criticism from women who represented colonized, impoverished third world countries and insisted that "to talk feminism to a woman who has no water, no food, and no home is to talk nonsense." Ever-larger UN-sponsored meetings followed Mexico City — Copenhagen in 1980, Nairobi in 1985, and Beijing in 1995, where twenty thousand women gathered. These global exchanges taught American

By the mid-1970s feminism faced a powerful countermovement, organized around opposition to an Equal Rights Amendment (ERA) to the Constitution that would outlaw differential treatment of men and women under all state and federal laws. After Congress passed the ERA in 1972, Phyllis Schlafly, a conservative activist in the Republican Party, mobilized thousands of antifeminist women who feared that the ERA would devalue what they believed were their God-given roles as wives and mothers. These women, marching on state capitols, persuaded enough male legislators to block ratification so that when the time limit ran out in 1982, only thirty-five states had ratified it, three short of the necessary three-fourths majority. (As discussed in chapter 30, "Making Historical Arguments," page 914.)

Powerful opposition likewise arose to feminists' quest for abortion rights. "Without the full capacity to limit her own reproduction," abortion rights activist

feminists that to participate in a truly international movement, they would have to revise their Western-centered perspective on women's needs and understand that women's issues must include economic development and anticolonialism.

American feminists also learned that theirs was not always the most advanced nation when it came to women's welfare and status. Employed women in most industrialized countries had access to paid maternity leave and publicly subsidized child care. By 2015, women had headed governments in more than thirty countries, including India, Israel, Britain, and Germany. Many nations, such as Argentina, Egypt, and members of the European Union, had some form of affirmative action to increase the numbers of women in government. And whereas American women held just 20 percent of the seats in Congress, women constituted more than 35 percent of national legislatures in such countries as Sweden, South Africa, Costa Rica, and Belgium.

Despite enormous differences among women around the world, internationally minded feminists continued to seek common ground. As Gertrude Mongella, secretary general of the Beijing conference, insisted in 1995, "A revolution has begun and there is no going back. . . . This revolution is too just, too important, and too long overdue."

QUESTIONS FOR ANALYSIS

Analyze the Evidence   What were the three themes of the UN Decade for Women? How were these three themes related to women's status and well-being?

Recognize Viewpoints   How and why did the agendas of women from richer countries differ from those of women from the developing world?

Consider the Context   What goals did women's movements in the United States and abroad have in common with other protest movements of the 1960s?

Roe v. Wade
1973 Supreme Court ruling
that the Constitution
protects the right to
abortion, which states
cannot prohibit in the early
stages of pregnancy. The
decision galvanized social
conservatives and made
abortion a controversial
policy issue for decades to
come.

Lucinda Cisler insisted, "a woman's other 'freedoms' are tantalizing mockeries that cannot be exercised." In 1973, the Supreme Court ruled in the landmark ***Roe v. Wade*** decision that the Constitution protects the right to abortion, which states cannot prohibit in the early stages of pregnancy. This decision galvanized many Americans who believed that abortion constituted murder. Like ERA opponents, with whom they often overlapped, right-to-life activists believed that abortion disparaged motherhood and that feminism threatened their traditional roles. Beginning in 1977, abortion foes pressured Congress to restrict the right to abortion by prohibiting coverage under all government-financed health programs, and the Supreme Court allowed states to impose additional obstacles.

Despite resistance, feminists won other lasting gains. Title IX of the Education Amendments Act of 1972 banned sex discrimination in all aspects of education, such as admissions, athletics, and hiring. Congress also outlawed sex discrimination in credit in 1974, opened U.S. military academies to women in 1976, and prohibited discrimination against pregnant workers in 1978. Moreover, the Supreme Court struck down laws that treated men and women differently in Social Security, welfare and military benefits, and workers' compensation.

At the state and local levels, women saw reforms in areas that radical feminists had first introduced. They won laws forcing police departments and the legal system to treat rape victims more justly and humanely. Activists also pushed domestic violence onto the public agenda, obtaining government financing for shelters for battered women as well as laws ensuring both greater protection for victims of domestic violence and more effective prosecution of abusers.

REVIEW What were the key goals of feminist reformers, and why did a countermovement arise to resist them?

Liberal Reform in the Nixon Administration

Opposition to civil rights measures, Great Society reforms, and protest groups — along with frustrations over the war in Vietnam (as discussed in chapter 29)— delivered the White House to Republican Richard M. Nixon in 1968. Nixon attacked the Great Society for "pouring billions of dollars into programs that have failed" and promised to represent the "forgotten Americans, the non-shouters, the non-demonstrators." Yet his administration either promoted or accepted important elements of the liberal reform agenda, including greater federal assistance to the poor, new protections for women and minorities, and environmental reforms.

Extending the Welfare State and Regulating the Economy. A number of factors shaped the liberal policies of the Nixon administration. Democrats continued to control Congress, the Republican Party contained many liberals and moderates, and Nixon saw political advantages in accepting some liberal programs, especially those promoted by grassroots movements that persisted into the 1970s.

Serious economic problems also compelled new approaches, and although Nixon's real passion lay in foreign policy, he was eager to establish a domestic legacy.

Under Nixon, government assistance programs such as Social Security, housing, and food stamps grew, and Congress enacted a new billion-dollar program that provided Pell grants for low-income students to attend college. Noting the disparity between what Nixon said and what he did, his speechwriter, the archconservative Pat Buchanan, grumbled, "Vigorously did we inveigh against the Great Society, enthusiastically did we fund it."

Nixon also acted contrary to his antigovernment rhetoric when economic crises and energy shortages induced him to increase the federal government's power in the marketplace. By 1970, both inflation and unemployment had surpassed 6 percent, an unprecedented combination dubbed "stagflation." Domestic troubles were compounded by the decline of American dominance in the international economy. With Japan and Western Europe fully recovered from the devastation of World War II, foreign cars, electronic equipment, and other products now competed favorably with American goods. In 1971, for the first time in decades, the United States imported more than it exported. Because the amount of dollars in foreign hands exceeded U.S. gold reserves, the nation could no longer back up its currency with gold.

In 1971, Nixon abandoned the convertibility of dollars into gold and devalued the dollar to increase exports by making them cheaper. To protect domestic manufacturers, he imposed a 10 percent surcharge on most imports, and he froze wages and prices, thus enabling the government to stimulate the economy without fueling inflation. In the short run, these policies worked, and Nixon was resoundingly reelected in 1972. Yet by 1974, unemployment had crept back up and inflation soared.

Skyrocketing energy prices intensified stagflation. Throughout the post–World War II economic boom, abundant domestic oil deposits and access to cheap Middle Eastern oil had encouraged the building of large cars and skyscrapers with no concern for fuel efficiency. By the 1970s, the United States was consuming one-third of the world's fuel resources.

In the fall of 1973, the United States faced its first energy crisis. Arab nations, furious at the administration's support of Israel during the Yom Kippur War (as discussed in chapter 29), cut off oil shipments to the United States. Long lines formed at gas stations, where prices had nearly doubled, and many homes were cold. In response, Nixon authorized temporary emergency measures allocating petroleum and establishing a national 55-mile-per-hour speed limit to save gasoline. The energy crisis eased, but the nation had yet to come to grips with its seemingly unquenchable demand for fuel and dependence on foreign oil.

Responding to Environmental Concerns.
The oil crisis dovetailed with a rising environmental movement, which was pushing the government to conserve energy and protect nature and human beings from the hazards of rapid economic growth. Like the conservation movement born in the Progressive Era (see chapter 21), the new environmentalists sought to preserve natural areas for recreational and aesthetic purposes and to conserve natural resources for future use. Especially in the West, the post–World War II explosion of economic and population growth, with

the resulting demands for electricity and water, made such efforts seem even more critical. Already in the 1950s, environmental groups mobilized to stop construction of dams that would disrupt national parks and wilderness.

The new environmentalists, however, went beyond conservationism to attack the ravaging effects of industrial and technological advances on human life and health. The polluted air and water and spread of deadly chemicals attending economic growth threatened wildlife, plants, and the ecological balance that sustained human life. Biologist Rachel Carson drew national attention in 1962 with her best seller *Silent Spring*, which described the harmful effects of toxic chemicals such as the pesticide DDT. The Sierra Club and other older conservation organizations expanded their agendas, and a host of new groups arose. Millions of Americans expressed environmental concerns on the first observation of Earth Day in April 1970. The locally organized, grassroots events addressed a host of topics, including oil spills, water pollution, recycling, industrial waste, automobile emissions, and many more.

Responding to these concerns, Nixon built on efforts begun under Johnson. He called "clean air, clean water, open spaces . . . the birthright of every American" and urged Congress to "end the plunder of America's natural heritage." In 1970, he created the **Environmental Protection Agency (EPA)** to enforce environmental laws, conduct research, and reduce human health and environmental risks from pollutants. He also signed the landmark Occupational Safety and Health Act (OSHA), protecting workers against job-related accidents and disease; the Clean Air Act of 1970, restricting factory and automobile emissions of carbon dioxide and other pollutants; and the Endangered Species Act of 1973. Although environmentalists claimed that Nixon failed to do enough, pointing particularly to his veto of the Clean Water Act of 1972, which Congress overrode, his environmental initiatives far surpassed those of previous administrations.

Environmental Protection Agency (EPA)

Federal agency created by President Nixon in 1970 to enforce environmental laws, conduct environmental research, and reduce human health and environmental risks from pollutants.

Expanding Social Justice.
Nixon's 1968 campaign had appealed to southern Democrats and white workers by exploiting hostility to black protest and new civil rights policies, but his administration had to answer to the courts and to Congress. In 1968, fourteen years after the *Brown* decision, school desegregation had barely touched the South. Like Eisenhower, Nixon was reluctant to use federal power to compel integration, but the Supreme Court overruled the administration's efforts to delay court-ordered desegregation. By 1974, fewer than one in ten southern black children attended totally segregated schools.

Nixon also began to implement affirmative action among federal contractors and unions, and his administration awarded more government contracts and loans to minority businesses. Congress took the initiative in other areas. In 1970, it extended the Voting Rights Act of 1965, and in 1972 it strengthened the Civil Rights Act of 1964 by enlarging the powers of the Equal Employment Opportunity Commission. In 1971, Congress also responded to the massive youth movement with the Twenty-sixth Amendment to the Constitution, reducing the voting age to eighteen. And in 1973, Nixon signed legislation outlawing discrimination against people with disabilities in all programs receiving federal funds.

Several measures of the Nixon administration also specifically attacked sex discrimination, as the president confronted a growing feminist movement that included Republican women. Nixon vetoed a comprehensive child care bill and publicly opposed abortion, but he signed the landmark Title IX, guaranteeing equality in all aspects of education, and allowed his Labor Department to push affirmative action.

President Nixon advocated for Native Americans more than for any other protest group. He told Congress that Indians were "the most deprived and most isolated minority group . . . the heritage of centuries of injustice." While not bowing to radical demands, his administration dealt cautiously with extreme protests such as the occupations of Alcatraz and the Bureau of Indian Affairs. Nixon signed measures recognizing claims of Alaskan and New Mexican Indians, returned tribal status to groups that had undergone termination, and set in motion legislation restoring tribal lands and granting Indians more control over their schools and other service institutions.

REVIEW   How did liberal reform fare under President Nixon?

Conclusion: Achievements and Limitations of Liberalism

Senate majority leader Mike Mansfield was not alone in concluding that Lyndon Johnson "has done more than FDR ever did, or ever thought of doing." Taking up goals of John F. Kennedy's New Frontier, the Great Society expanded the New Deal's focus on economic security, refashioning liberalism to embrace individual rights and to extend material well-being to groups left out of or discriminated against in New Deal programs. Yet opposition to Johnson's leadership grew so strong that by 1968 his liberal vision lay in ruins. "How," he asked, "was it possible that all these people could be so ungrateful to me after I have given them so much?"

Fannie Lou Hamer could have pointed out how slowly the government acted when efforts to win civil rights met with violence. In addition, Hamer's failed attempts to use Johnson's antipoverty programs to help poor blacks in Mississippi reflected, in part, some of the more general shortcomings of the War on Poverty. Hastily planned and inadequately funded, antipoverty programs focused more on remediating individual shortcomings than on structural reforms that would ensure adequately paying jobs for all. Because Johnson launched an all-out war in Vietnam and refused to ask for sacrifices from prosperous Americans, the Great Society never commanded the resources necessary for victory over poverty.

Furthermore, black aspirations exceeded white Americans' commitment to genuine equality. Most whites supported overturning the crude and blatant forms of racism in the South, but when the civil rights movement attacked racial barriers long entrenched throughout the nation and sought equality in fact as well as in law, it faced a powerful backlash. By the end of the 1960s, the revolution in the legal status of African Americans was complete, but the black freedom struggle had lost momentum, and African Americans remained, with Native Americans and Latinos, at the bottom of the economic ladder.

Johnson's critics overlooked the Great Society's more successful and lasting elements. Medicare and Medicaid continue to provide access to health care for the elderly and the poor. Federal aid for education and housing became permanent elements of national policy. Moreover, Richard Nixon's otherwise conservative administration implemented school desegregation in the South and affirmative action, initiated environmental reforms, and secured new rights for Native Americans and women. Women benefited from the decline of discrimination, and significant numbers of African Americans and other minority groups began to enter the middle class.

Yet the perceived shortcomings of government programs contributed to social turmoil and fueled the resurgence of conservative politics. Young radicals launched direct confrontations with the government and universities that, together with racial conflict, escalated into political discord and social disorder. The Vietnam War polarized American society as much as did domestic change; it devoured resources that might have been used for social reform and undermined faith in government.

Chapter Review

KEY TERMS

Civil Rights Act of 1964 (p. 833)

War on Poverty (p. 834)

Medicare and Medicaid (p. 834)

Voting Rights Act of 1965 (p. 834)

Immigration and Nationality Act of 1965 (p. 835)

Warren Court (p. 837)

black power movement (p. 844)

American Indian Movement (AIM) (p. 845)

Chicano movement (p. 846)

National Organization for Women (NOW) (p. 850)

Roe v. Wade (p. 854)

Environmental Protection Agency (EPA) (p. 856)

REVIEW QUESTIONS

❶ How did the Kennedy and Johnson administrations exemplify a liberal vision of the federal government?   (pp. 830–38)

❷ How and why did the civil rights movement change in the mid-1960s? (pp. 838–44)

❸ What other movements emerged in the 1960s, and how were they influenced by the black freedom struggle?   (pp. 844–49)

❹ What were the key goals of feminist reformers, and why did a countermovement arise to resist them?   (pp. 850–54)

❺ How did liberal reform fare under President Nixon?   (pp. 854–57)

MAKING CONNECTIONS

❶ Why were Lyndon Johnson's reforms so much more far-reaching than John F. Kennedy's?

❷ What specific gains did the civil rights movement achieve in the 1960s, and how were those gains limited?

❸ What characteristics did all reform movements of the 1960s share?

LINKING TO THE PAST

❶ How was Lyndon Johnson's approach to poverty different from Franklin Roosevelt's? Which was more successful? (See chapter 24.)

❷ What changes that had been taking place in the United States since 1940 laid a foundation for the rise of a feminist movement in the 1960s? (See chapters 25 and 26.)

Vietnam and the End of the Cold War Consensus, 1961–1975

CONTENT LEARNING OBJECTIVES

After reading and studying this chapter, you should be able to:

- Describe President Kennedy's more aggressive implementation of the containment policy. Identify his approach to the third world, and explain U.S. involvement in Cuba and Vietnam.
- Explain why Johnson escalated involvement in Vietnam, and evaluate the effectiveness of this strategy.
- Explain how the war polarized the nation and contributed to a year of upheaval in 1968.
- Describe Nixon's approach to communism, including his pursuit of détente with the Soviet Union and China and anticommunism efforts in the third world. Explain how Nixon ended the war in Vietnam and the legacies of the war.

L ieutenant Frederick Downs Jr. grew up on an Indiana farm and enlisted in the army after three years of college. Leaving a ten-month-old daughter behind, he completed officer training and arrived in Vietnam in September 1967. The infantry platoon leader and his men went to Vietnam "cocky and sure of our destiny, gung ho, invincible."

That confidence was tempered by what they found in Vietnam. Unlike most of America's previous wars, there was no fixed battlefront; helicopters ferried fighting units all over South Vietnam, as U.S. and South Vietnamese troops attempted to defeat the South Vietnamese insurgents and their North Vietnamese allies. In a civil war characterized by guerrilla tactics, Downs and his men struggled to distinguish civilians

CAMOUFLAGE HELMET

The antiwar buttons on this military helmet reflect the bitter divisions that the Vietnam War produced in the United States, even among some of the soldiers themselves. Doug Steley B/Alamy.

from combatants and destroyed villages just because they might be used by the enemy. He had faith that his country could win the war, but he found the South Vietnamese army to be lazy and ineffective. "Maybe the people in Nam are worth saving, but their army isn't worth shit," he wrote in his memoir. Downs won several medals for bravery, but his one-year stint in Vietnam ended when a land mine blew off his left arm and wedged shrapnel into his legs and back.

Downs served in Vietnam at the height of a U.S. engagement that began with the Cold War commitments made by Presidents Harry S. Truman and Dwight D. Eisenhower. John F. Kennedy wholeheartedly took on those commitments, promising more flexible and vigorous efforts to thwart communism, declaring that the United States would "pay any price, bear any burden, meet any hardship, support any friend, oppose any foe to assure the survival and the success of liberty."

Kennedy sent increasing amounts of American arms and personnel to sustain the South Vietnamese government, and Lyndon B. Johnson dramatically escalated that commitment in 1965, turning a civil war among the Vietnamese into America's war. At peak strength in 1968, 543,000 U.S. military personnel served in Vietnam; all told, some 2.6 million saw duty there. Yet this massive intervention failed to defeat North Vietnam and created intense discord at home, "poisoning the soul of America," in Downs's words. Some Americans supported the government's goal in Vietnam and decried only the failure to pursue it effectively. Others believed that preserving a non-Communist South Vietnam was neither a vital interest of the United States nor within its capacity or moral right to achieve. Back home in college after months of surgery, Downs encountered a man who asked about the hook descending from his sleeve. When he said that he had lost his arm in Vietnam, the man shot back, "Serves you right."

This internal conflict was just one of the war's great costs. Like Downs, more than 150,000 soldiers suffered severe wounds, and more than 58,000 lost their lives. The war derailed domestic reform, depleted the federal budget, disrupted the economy, kindled domestic discord, and led to the violation of protesters' rights, leaving a lasting mark on the nation.

Even while fighting communism in Vietnam and in other third world countries, American leaders moved to ease Cold War tensions.

CHRONOLOGY

1961	Bay of Pigs invaded. Berlin Wall erected. Kennedy increases military aid to South Vietnam. Peace Corps created.
1962	Cuban missile crisis occurs.
1963	President Kennedy assassinated; Lyndon B. Johnson becomes president.
1964	Gulf of Tonkin Resolution passed.
1965	Operation Rolling Thunder begins. First combat troops sent to Vietnam. U.S. troops invade Dominican Republic.
1967	Arab-Israeli Six-Day War fought.
1968	Demonstrations against Vietnam War increase. Tet Offensive launched. Johnson decides not to seek second term. Violence erupts near Democratic convention in Chicago. Richard M. Nixon elected president.
1969	American astronauts land on moon.
1970	Nixon orders invasion of Cambodia. Students killed at Kent State and Jackson State.
1971	Portions of *Pentagon Papers* published.
1972	Nixon becomes first U.S. president to visit China. Nixon signs arms limitation treaties with Soviets.
1973	Paris Peace Accords end U.S. fighting in Vietnam. CIA backs military coup in Chile. Arab oil embargo follows Yom Kippur War.
1975	North Vietnam takes over South Vietnam, ending war. Helsinki accords signed.

After a tense standoff with the Soviet Union during the Cuban missile crisis, the United States began to cooperate with its Cold War enemy to limit the spread of nuclear weapons. In addition, Richard M. Nixon made a historic visit to China in 1972, abandoning the policy of isolating China and paving the way for normal diplomatic relations by the end of the 1970s.

New Frontiers in Foreign Policy

John F. Kennedy moved quickly to pursue containment more aggressively and with more flexible means. In contrast to the Eisenhower administration's emphasis on nuclear weapons, Kennedy expanded both the nation's nuclear capacity and its ability to fight conventional battles and engage in guerrilla warfare. Kennedy also accelerated the nation's space exploration program and increased engagement with the third world. When the Soviets tried to establish a nuclear outpost in Cuba in 1962, Kennedy took the United States to the brink of war. Less dramatically, Kennedy sent increasing amounts of American arms and personnel to save the South Vietnamese government from Communist insurgents.

Meeting the "Hour of Maximum Danger." Underlying Kennedy's foreign policy was an assumption that the United States had "gone soft — physically, mentally, spiritually soft," as he put it in 1960. Calling the Eisenhower era "years of drift and impotency," Kennedy warned in his inaugural address that the nation faced a grave peril: "Each day the crises multiply. . . . Each day we draw nearer the hour of maximum danger."

Although the president exaggerated the threat to national security, several developments in 1961 heightened the sense of crisis and provided a rationalization for his military buildup. Shortly before Kennedy's inauguration, Soviet premier Nikita Khrushchev publicly encouraged "wars of national liberation," thereby aligning the Soviet Union with independence movements in the third world that were often anti-Western. His statement reflected in part the Soviet competition with China for the allegiance of emerging nations, but U.S. officials saw it as a threat to the status quo of containment.

Cuba, just ninety miles off the Florida coast, posed the first crisis for Kennedy. The revolution led by Fidel Castro had moved Cuba into the Soviet orbit, and Eisenhower's Central Intelligence Agency (CIA) had planned an invasion of the island by Cuban exiles living in Florida. Kennedy ordered the invasion to proceed even though his military advisers deemed its success uncertain.

In April 1961, about 1,400 anti-Castro exiles trained and armed by the CIA landed at the **Bay of Pigs** on the south shore of Cuba (Map 29.1). Contrary to U.S. expectations, no popular uprising materialized to support the anti-Castro brigade. Kennedy refused to provide direct military support, and the invaders quickly fell to

Bay of Pigs
Failed U.S.-sponsored invasion of Cuba in 1961 by anti-Castro forces who planned to overthrow Fidel Castro's government. The disaster humiliated Kennedy and the United States. It alienated Latin Americans who saw the invasion as another example of Yankee imperialism.

Castro's forces. The disaster humiliated Kennedy and the United States, posing a stark contrast to the president's inaugural promise of a new, more effective foreign policy. And it alienated Latin Americans who saw it as another example of Yankee imperialism.

Days before the Bay of Pigs invasion, the Soviet Union dealt a psychological blow when a Soviet astronaut became the first human to orbit the earth. Kennedy then called for a huge new commitment to the space program, with the goal of sending a man to the moon by 1970. Congress authorized the **Apollo program** and

Apollo program
Project initiated by John F. Kennedy in 1961 to surpass the Soviet Union in space exploration and send a man to the moon.

Map Activity

MAP 29.1   U.S. INVOLVEMENT IN LATIN AMERICA AND THE CARIBBEAN, 1954–1994

During the Cold War, the United States frequently intervened in Central American and Caribbean countries to suppress Communist or leftist movements.

READING THE MAP: How many and which Latin American countries did the United States invade directly? What was the extent of indirect U.S. involvement in other upheavals in the region?

CONNECTIONS: What role, if any, did geographic proximity play in U.S. policy toward the region? What was the significance of the Cuban missile crisis for U.S. foreign policy?

boosted appropriations for space exploration. John H. Glenn orbited the earth in 1962, and the United States beat the Soviets to the moon, landing two astronauts there in 1969.

Kennedy was determined to show American toughness to Khrushchev, but when the two met in June 1961 in Vienna, Austria, Khrushchev took the offensive. The stunned Kennedy reported privately, "He just beat [the] hell out of me. . . . If he thinks I'm inexperienced and have no guts . . . we won't get anywhere with him." Khrushchev demanded an agreement recognizing the existence of two Germanys, and he threatened U.S. occupation rights in and access to West Berlin.

The Soviet premier was concerned about the massive exodus of East Germans into West Berlin, a major embarrassment for the Communists. To stop this flow, in August 1961 East Germany erected a wall between the sectors. With the **Berlin Wall** stemming the tide of escapees and Kennedy declaring West Berlin "the great testing place of Western courage and will," Khrushchev backed off from his threats. A decade later the superpowers recognized East and West Germany as separate nations and guaranteed Western access to West Berlin.

Kennedy used the Berlin crisis to add $3.2 billion to the defense budget. He increased draft calls and mobilized the reserves and National Guard, adding 300,000 troops to the military. This buildup of conventional forces provided for a "flexible response," offering "a wider choice than humiliation or all-out nuclear action," yet Kennedy also more than doubled the nation's nuclear force within three years.

New Approaches to the Third World.
Complementing Kennedy's hard-line policy toward the Soviet Union were fresh approaches to the nationalist movements that had multiplied since the end of World War II. In 1960 alone, seventeen African nations gained their independence. Much more than his predecessors, Kennedy publicly supported third world aspirations, believing that the United States could win the hearts and minds of people in developing nations by helping to fulfill hopes for autonomy and material well-being.

Kennedy launched his most popular third world initiative in 1961 with an idea borrowed from Senator Hubert H. Humphrey: the **Peace Corps**. The program recruited young people to work in developing countries, attracting many who had been moved by Kennedy's inaugural address appeal for idealism and sacrifice. One volunteer spoke of having been "born between clean sheets when others were issued into the dust with a birthright of hunger." Peace Corps volunteers worked directly with local people, opening schools, providing basic health care, and assisting with agriculture and small businesses. By the mid-1970s, more than 60,000 volunteers had served in Latin America, Africa, and Asia. Peace Corps projects were generally welcomed, but they did not address the receiving countries' larger economic and political challenges.

Kennedy also used military means to bring political stability to the third world. He rapidly expanded the elite special forces corps established under Eisenhower to aid groups fighting against Communist-leaning movements. These counterinsurgency forces, including the army's Green Berets and the navy's SEALs, were trained to wage guerrilla warfare and equipped with the latest technology. They would get their first test in Vietnam.

Berlin Wall
Structure erected by East Germany in 1961 to stop the massive exodus of East Germans into West Berlin, which was an embarrassment to the Communists.

Peace Corps
Program launched by President Kennedy in 1961 through which young American volunteers helped with education, health, and other projects in developing countries around the world. More than 60,000 volunteers had served by the mid-1970s.

The Arms Race and the Nuclear Brink.

The final piece of Kennedy's foreign policy was to strengthen American nuclear dominance. He tripled the number of nuclear weapons based in Europe to 7,200 and multiplied fivefold the supply of intercontinental ballistic missiles (ICBMs). Concerned that this buildup would enable the United States to launch a first strike and wipe out Soviet missile sites before they could respond, the Soviet Union stepped up its own ICBM program. Thus began the most intense arms race in history.

The superpowers came perilously close to using their weapons during the **Cuban missile crisis** in 1962. Khrushchev decided to install nuclear missiles in Cuba to protect Castro's regime from further U.S. attempts at invasion and to balance the U.S. missiles aimed at the Soviet Union from Europe. On October 22, after the CIA showed Kennedy aerial photographs of missile launching sites under construction in Cuba, Kennedy announced that the military was on full alert and that the navy would turn back any Soviet vessel suspected of carrying missiles to Cuba. He warned that any attack launched from Cuba would trigger a full nuclear assault against the Soviet Union.

With the superpowers on the brink of nuclear war, both Kennedy and Khrushchev also exercised caution. Kennedy refused advice from the military to bomb the missile sites. On October 24, Russian ships carrying nuclear warheads toward Cuba suddenly turned back. When one ship crossed the blockade line, Kennedy ordered the navy to follow it rather than confront it.

U.S. blockade zone

— Range of Soviet missiles

⚑ Soviet missile and jet bomber base

CUBAN MISSILE CRISIS, 1962

CUBAN MISSILE CRISIS

During the Cuban missile crisis, while many Americans prepared for the worst possible outcome, U.S. Navy pilots dodged antiaircraft fire to conduct low-altitude reconnaissance. This photo, taken on October 23, 1962, shows details of the missile site in Cuba. Bettmann/Corbis.

While Americans experienced the Cold War's most dangerous days, Kennedy and Khrushchev negotiated an agreement. The Soviets removed the missiles and pledged not to introduce new offensive weapons into Cuba. The United States promised not to invade the island. Secretly, Kennedy also agreed to remove U.S. missiles from Turkey. The Cuban crisis contributed to Khrushchev's fall from power two years later, while Kennedy emerged triumphant. The image of an inexperienced president fumbling the Bay of Pigs invasion gave way to that of a strong leader.

Having proved his toughness, Kennedy worked to ease superpower hostilities. In June 1963, Kennedy called for a reexamination of Cold War assumptions, asking Americans "not to see conflict as inevitable." Acknowledging the superpowers' differences, Kennedy stressed what they had in common: "We all breathe the same air. We all cherish our children's future and we are all mortal." In August 1963, the United States, the Soviet Union, and Great Britain signed a limited nuclear test ban treaty, reducing the threat of radioactive fallout and raising hopes for further superpower accord.

A Growing War in Vietnam. In 1963, Kennedy criticized the idea of "a Pax Americana enforced on the world by American weapons of war," but he had already increased the flow of those weapons into South Vietnam. Kennedy's strong anticommunism and attachment to a vigorous foreign policy prepared him to expand the commitment that he had inherited from Eisenhower.

By the time Kennedy took office, more than $1 billion in aid and seven hundred U.S. military advisers had failed to stabilize South Vietnam. Two major obstacles stood in the way. First, the South Vietnamese insurgents — whom Americans derisively called Vietcong — were an indigenous force whose initiative came from within. Because the Saigon government refused to hold elections, the rebels saw no choice but to take up arms. Increasingly, Ho Chi Minh's Communist government in North Vietnam supplied them with weapons and soldiers, aiming eventually to unify all of Vietnam.

Second, the South Vietnamese government refused to satisfy insurgents' demands, but the Army of the Republic of Vietnam (ARVN) could not defeat them militarily. Ngo Dinh Diem, South Vietnam's premier from 1954 to 1963, chose self-serving military leaders for their personal loyalty rather than for their effectiveness. Many South Vietnamese, the majority of whom were Buddhists, saw the Catholic Diem as a corrupt and brutal tool of the West. In contrast, Ho Chi Minh and his associates consolidated their power through land reform and their anticolonialist credentials on the one hand and imprisonment and mass executions on the other.

Stability and popular support enabled the Hanoi government in the North to wage war in the South. In 1960, it established the National Liberation Front (NLF), composed of South Vietnamese rebels but directed by the northern army. In addition, Hanoi constructed a network of infiltration routes, called the Ho Chi Minh Trail, in neighboring Laos and Cambodia, through which it sent people and supplies to help liberate the South (Map 29.2). Violence escalated between 1960 and 1963, bringing the Saigon government close to collapse.

In response, Kennedy gradually escalated the U.S. commitment. By spring 1963, military aid had doubled, and 9,000 Americans served in Vietnam as military advisers, occasionally participating in actual combat. The South Vietnamese government promised reform but never made good on its promises.

American officials assumed that technology and sheer power could win in Vietnam. Yet advanced weapons were ill suited to the guerrilla warfare practiced by the enemy, whose surprise attacks were designed to weaken support for the South Vietnamese government. Moreover, U.S. weapons and strategy harmed the very people they were

Map Activity

MAP 29.2   THE VIETNAM WAR, 1964–1975

The United States sent 2.6 million soldiers to Vietnam and spent more than $150 billion on the longest war in American history, but it was unable to prevent the unification of Vietnam under a Communist government.

READING THE MAP: What accords divided Vietnam into two nations? When were these accords signed, and where was the line of division drawn? Through what countries did the Ho Chi Minh Trail go?

CONNECTIONS: What was the Gulf of Tonkin incident, and how did the United States respond? What was the Tet Offensive, and how did it affect the war?

intended to save. Thousands of peasants were uprooted or fell victim to bombs — containing the highly flammable substance napalm — dropped by the South Vietnamese air force to quell the Vietcong. In 1962, U.S. planes began to spray herbicides such as **Agent Orange** to destroy the Vietcong's jungle hideouts and food supply.

Agent Orange
Herbicide used extensively during the Vietnam War to destroy the Vietcong's jungle hideouts and food supply. Its use was later linked to a wide range of illnesses that veterans and the Vietnamese suffered after the war, including birth defects, cancer, and skin disorders.

With tacit permission from Washington, in November 1963 South Vietnamese military leaders executed a coup against Diem and his brother, who headed the secret police. Kennedy expressed shock at the murders but indicated no change in policy. In a speech to be given on the day he was assassinated, Kennedy referred specifically to Southeast Asia and warned, "We dare not weary of the task." At his death, 16,700 Americans were stationed in Vietnam, and 100 had died there.

> **REVIEW** Why did Kennedy believe that engagement in Vietnam was crucial to his foreign policy?

Lyndon Johnson's War against Communism

Lyndon B. Johnson shared the Cold War assumptions underlying Kennedy's foreign policy. Retaining Kennedy's key advisers — Secretary of State Dean Rusk, Secretary of Defense Robert McNamara, and National Security Adviser McGeorge Bundy — Johnson continued the massive buildup of nuclear weapons as well as conventional and counterinsurgency forces. In 1965, he made the fateful decisions to order U.S. troops into combat in Vietnam and to initiate sustained bombing of the North. That same year, Johnson sent U.S. Marines to crush a leftist rebellion in the Dominican Republic.

An All-Out Commitment in Vietnam. The president, who wanted to make his mark on domestic policy, was compelled to deal with the commitments his predecessors had made in Vietnam. Some advisers, politicians, and international leaders questioned the wisdom of greater intervention there, recognizing the situation as a civil war rather than Communist aggression. Most U.S. allies did not consider Vietnam crucial to containing communism and were not prepared to share the military burden. Senate majority leader Mike Mansfield wondered, "What national interests in Asia would steel the American people for the massive costs of an ever-deepening involvement?" Disregarding the opportunity for disengagement that these critics saw in 1964, Johnson expressed his own doubt privately: "I don't think it's worth fighting for and I don't think we can get out."

Like Kennedy, Johnson remembered the political blows that Truman had taken when the Communists took over China, and he determined not "to be the president who saw Southeast Asia go the way China did." Like most of his advisers, he saw American credibility as a bulwark against the threat of communism, and he believed that abandoning Vietnam would undermine his ability to achieve his Great Society.

Johnson understood the ineffectiveness of his South Vietnamese allies and agonized over sending young men into combat. Yet he continued to dispatch more military advisers, weapons, and economic aid and, in August 1964, seized an opportunity to increase the pressure on North Vietnam. While spying in the Gulf of Tonkin, off the coast of North Vietnam, two U.S. destroyers reported that North Vietnamese gunboats had fired on them (Map 29.2). Johnson quickly ordered air strikes on North Vietnamese torpedo bases and oil storage facilities. Concealing the uncertainty about whether the second attack had even occurred, he won from Congress the **Gulf of Tonkin Resolution**, authorizing him to take "all necessary measures to repel any armed attacks against the forces of the United States and to prevent further aggression."

Soon after winning the election of 1964, Johnson widened the war. He dismissed reservations expressed by prominent Democrats and rejected peace overtures from North Vietnam, which insisted on American withdrawal and a coalition government in South Vietnam as steps toward unification of the country. In February 1965, Johnson authorized Operation Rolling Thunder, a gradually intensified bombing of North Vietnam. Less than a month later, Johnson ordered the first combat troops to South Vietnam, and in July he shifted U.S. troops from defensive to offensive operations, dispatching 50,000 more soldiers (Figure 29.1). Although the administration downplayed the import of these decisions, they marked a critical turning point. Now it was genuinely America's war.

Preventing Another Castro in Latin America. Johnson also faced persistent problems closer to home. Thirteen times during the 1960s, military coups toppled Latin American governments, and local insurgencies grew apace. The administration's response varied from case to case but centered on the determination to prevent any more Castro-type revolutions.

Gulf of Tonkin Resolution
Resolution passed by Congress in 1964 in the wake of a naval confrontation in the Gulf of Tonkin. It gave the president virtually unlimited authority in conducting the Vietnam War. The Senate terminated the resolution following outrage over the U.S. invasion of Cambodia in 1970.

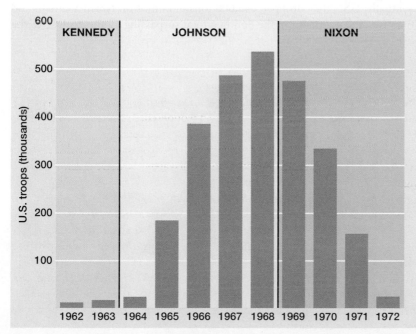

FIGURE 29.1 U.S. TROOPS IN VIETNAM, 1962–1972

The steepest increases in the American military presence in Vietnam came with Johnson's escalation of the war in 1965 and 1966. Although Nixon reduced troop levels significantly in 1971 and 1972, the United States continued massive bombing attacks.

In 1964, riots erupted in the Panama Canal Zone, instigated by Panamanians who viewed the United States as a colonial power because it had held the territory since early in the century (see chapter 21). Johnson sent troops to quell the disturbance, but he also initiated negotiations that eventually returned the canal to Panamanian authority in 2000.

Elsewhere, Johnson's Latin American policy generated new cries of "Yankee imperialism." In 1961, voters in the Dominican Republic ousted a longtime dictator and elected a constitutional government headed by reformist Juan Bosch, who was overthrown by a military coup two years later. In 1965, when Bosch supporters launched an uprising against the military government, Johnson sent more than 20,000 soldiers to suppress what he perceived to be a leftist revolt and to take control of the island.

This first outright show of Yankee force in Latin America in four decades damaged the administration. Although Johnson had justified intervention as necessary to prevent "another Cuba," no Communists were found among the rebels, and U.S. force kept the reform-oriented Boschists from returning to power. Moreover, the president had not consulted the Dominicans or the Organization of American States (OAS), to which the United States had pledged it would respect national sovereignty in Latin America.

The Americanized War. Military success in the Dominican Republic no doubt encouraged the president to press on in Vietnam. From 1965 to early 1968, the U.S. military presence grew to more than 500,000 troops as it escalated attacks on North Vietnam and on its ally, the National Liberation Front, in South Vietnam. To minimize protest at home and avoid provoking Chinese or Soviet involvement, Johnson expanded the war slowly. "I'm going up old Ho Chi Minh's leg an inch at a time," he gloated.

Eventually, U.S. pilots dropped 643,000 tons of bombs on North Vietnam and more than twice that amount in the South, a total surpassing all the explosives the

THE TOLL ON VIETNAMESE CIVILIANS
The guerrilla nature of the Vietnam War made it especially devastating on civilians. Here, in 1965, a Vietnamese woman tries to protect a child while U.S. Marines storm the village of My Son. The soldiers were searching for Vietcong insurgents, who had slipped away before the attack, but were able to get little information from the villagers. Bettmann/Corbis.

United States dropped in World War II. The North Vietnamese withstood monthly death tolls of more than 2,000 from the bombing. "They turned their hatred into activity," said one North Vietnamese about his comrades, whose ingenuity and sheer effort helped compensate for the destruction of transportation lines, industry sites, and power plants. In South Vietnam, the massive U.S. bombing campaign destroyed villages and fields, alienating the very population that the Americans had come to save and turning the former leading rice producer into a rice importer.

On the ground, General William Westmoreland's strategy of attrition was designed to seek out and kill the Vietcong and North Vietnamese regular army. Because there was no fixed battlefront, helicopters carried troops to conduct offensives all over South Vietnam, and officials calculated progress not in territory seized but in "body counts" and "kill ratios" — the number of enemies killed relative to the cost in American and ARVN lives. "To win a battle, we had to kill them," explained Lieutenant Frederick Downs Jr. "For them to win, all they had to do was survive." After U.S. troops fought and bled to take ground, the enemy would withdraw, only to come back whenever they liked. The Americans "never owned anything except the ground they stood on." And even though U.S.-ARVN forces achieved high kill ratios, North Vietnam sent in or recruited new Communist forces faster than they could be eliminated.

Those Who Served. Teenagers fought the Vietnam War, in contrast to World War II, when the average soldier was twenty-six years old. All the men in Frederick Downs's platoon were between the ages of eighteen and twenty-one, and the average age for all soldiers was nineteen. One eighteen-year-old reflected, "I should have been home getting ready to take a pretty girl to the prom." Until the Twenty-sixth Amendment to the Constitution dropped the voting age from twenty-one to eighteen in 1971, most soldiers could not even vote for the officials who sent them to war. Men of all classes had fought in World War II, but in Vietnam the poor and working class constituted about 80 percent of the troops. More privileged youths avoided the draft with college deferments or family connections to get into the National Guard. Sent from Plainville, Kansas, to Vietnam in 1965, Mike Clodfelter could not recall "a single middle-class son of the town's businessmen, lawyers, doctors, or ranchers from my high school graduating class who experienced the Armageddon of our generation."

More than World War II, Vietnam was a men's war. Because the United States did not undergo full mobilization for Vietnam, officials did not seek women's sacrifices for the war effort. Still, between 7,500 and 11,000 women served in Vietnam, the vast majority of them nurses. Some women were exposed to enemy fire, and eight died. Many more struggled with their helplessness to repair the maimed and dead bodies they attended.

Early in the war, African Americans constituted 31 percent of combat troops, often choosing the military over the meager opportunities in the civilian economy. Special forces ranger Arthur E. Woodley Jr. recalled, "The only way I could possibly make it out of the ghetto was to be the best soldier I possibly could." Death rates among black soldiers were disproportionately high until 1966, when the military adjusted personnel assignments to achieve a better racial balance.

The young troops faced extremely difficult conditions. Frederick Downs's platoon fought in thick leech-ridden jungles, in rain and oppressive heat, always

COUNTING THE DAYS IN VIETNAM

Unlike soldiers in previous wars, most soldiers in Vietnam served tours of duty lasting just one year. The soldier who carried this calendar expressed a common obsession with time "in country." Soldiers considered themselves "short" when they had fewer than 100 days left. Bobby McMaster was thinking either of his wife or of the woman he would marry when, and if, he returned home. Nathan Benn/Corbis.

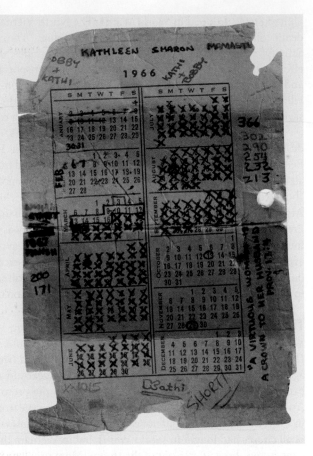

vulnerable to sniper bullets and land mines. Soldiers in previous wars had served "for the duration," but in Vietnam a soldier served a one-year tour of duty. A commander called it "the worst personnel policy in history," because men had less incentive to fight near the end of their tours, wanting merely to stay alive and whole. American soldiers inflicted great losses on the enemy, yet the war remained a stalemate.

Many Vietnamese saw the South Vietnamese government as a tool of Western imperialism, full of graft and corruption. Moreover, with the difficulty of distinguishing friend from foe, ARVN and American troops killed and wounded thousands of South Vietnamese civilians and destroyed their villages. By 1968, nearly 30 percent of the population had become refugees. According to Downs, "All Vietnamese had a common desire — to see us go home." The failure to stabilize South Vietnam even as the U.S. military presence expanded enormously created grave challenges for the administration at home.

> **REVIEW** Why did massive amounts of airpower and ground troops fail to bring U.S. victory in Vietnam?

A Nation Polarized

Soon President Johnson was fighting a war on two fronts, as domestic opposition to the war swelled after 1965. In March 1968, torn between his domestic critics and the military's clamor for more troops, Johnson announced a halt to the bombing, a new effort at negotiations, and his decision not to pursue reelection. Throughout 1968, demonstrations, violence, and assassinations convulsed the increasingly polarized nation. Vietnam took center stage in the election, and voters narrowly favored the Republican candidate, former vice president Richard Nixon, who promised to achieve "peace with honor."

The Widening War at Home. Johnson's authorization of Operation Rolling Thunder expanded the previously quiet doubts and criticism into a mass movement against the war. In April 1965, Students for a Democratic Society (SDS) recruited 20,000 people for the first major antiwar protest in Washington, D.C. Thousands of students protested against Reserve Officers Training Corps (ROTC) programs, CIA and defense industry recruiters, and military research projects on their campuses. Environmentalists attacked the use of chemical weapons, such as the deadly Agent Orange.

Antiwar sentiment entered society's mainstream, including, by 1968, the *New York Times*, the *Wall Street Journal*, *Life* magazine, and popular TV anchorman Walter Cronkite. Clergy, businesspeople, scientists, and physicians formed their own groups to pressure Johnson to stop the bombing and start negotiations. Prominent Democratic senators urged Johnson to substitute negotiation for force.

Opposition to the war took diverse forms, including letter writing, public demonstrations, draft card burnings, and attempts to stop troop trains. Although the peace movement never claimed a majority of the population, it focused media attention on the war and severely limited the administration's options. The twenty-year-old consensus around Cold War foreign policy had shattered.

Many refused to serve. The World Boxing Association stripped Muhammad Ali of his heavyweight title when he refused to "drop bombs and bullets on brown people in Vietnam while so-called negro people in Louisville are treated like dogs." More than 170,000 men gained conscientious objector status and performed nonmilitary duties at home or in Vietnam. About 60,000 fled the country to escape the draft, and more than 200,000 were accused of failing to register or of committing other draft offenses.

Opponents of the war held diverse views. Those who saw the conflict in moral terms wanted total withdrawal, claiming that their country had no right to interfere in a civil war and stressing the suffering of the Vietnamese people. A larger segment of antiwar sentiment reflected practical considerations — the belief that the war could not be won at a bearable cost. Those activists wanted Johnson to stop bombing North Vietnam and seek negotiations. Working-class people were no more antiwar than other groups, but they recognized the class dimensions of the war and the antiwar movement. A firefighter whose son had died in Vietnam said bitterly, "It's people like us who give up our sons for the country."

The antiwar movement outraged millions of Americans who supported the war. Some members of the generation who had fought against Hitler could not understand younger men's refusal to support their government. They expressed their anger at war protesters with bumper stickers that read "America: Love It or Leave It."

By 1967, the administration realized that "discontent with the war is now wide and deep." President Johnson used various means to silence critics. He equated opposition to the war with communism and assistance to the enemy. His administration deceived the public by making optimistic statements and concealing officials' doubts about the possibility of success. Johnson ordered the CIA to spy on peace advocates, and without the president's specific authorization, the FBI infiltrated the

Visual Activity

MOTHERS AGAINST THE WAR

Founded in 1961 to work for nuclear disarmament, Women Strike for Peace (WSP) began to protest the Vietnam War in 1963. As "concerned housewives" and mothers, members mobilized around the slogan "Not Our Sons, Not Your Sons, Not Their Sons." In February 1967, more than 2,000 women, some shown here, protested at the Pentagon, banging on doors, which were locked as they approached. Bettmann/Corbis.

READING THE IMAGE: Notice how these women look. Do they appear threatening to you? Why do you think Pentagon officials locked them out? How do their signs draw on their roles as mothers?

CONNECTIONS: How are the antiwar arguments made by WSP similar to and different from those of other opponents of the Vietnam War?

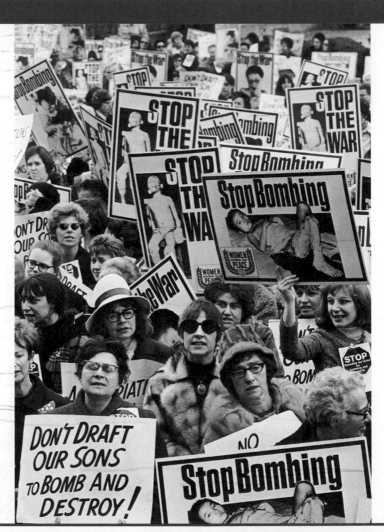

peace movement, disrupted its work, and spread false information about activists. Even the resort to illegal measures failed to subdue the opposition.

The Tet Offensive and Johnson's Move toward Peace.
The year 1968 was marked by violent confrontations around the world. Protests against governments erupted from Mexico City to Paris to Tokyo, usually led by students in collaboration with workers. (See "Beyond America's Borders," page 876.) American society became increasingly polarized. The so-called hawks charged that the United States was fighting with one hand tied behind its back and called for intensification of the war. The doves wanted de-escalation or withdrawal. As U.S. troop strength neared half a million and military deaths approached 20,000 by the end of 1967, most people were torn between weariness with the war and a desire to fulfill the U.S. commitment. As one woman said, "I want to get out but I don't want to give up."

Grave doubts penetrated the administration itself. Secretary of Defense Robert McNamara, a principal architect of U.S. involvement, now believed that the North Vietnamese "won't quit no matter how much bombing we do." He feared for the image of the United States, "the world's greatest superpower, killing or seriously injuring 1,000 noncombatants a week, while trying to pound a tiny, backward nation into submission on an issue whose merits are hotly disputed." McNamara left the administration in early 1968, but he kept his concerns private and did not publicly oppose the war.

A critical turning point came with the **Tet Offensive.** On January 30, 1968, the North Vietnamese and Vietcong launched a campaign of attacks on key cities, every major American base, and the U.S. Embassy in Saigon during Tet, the Vietnamese

Tet Offensive
Major campaign of attacks launched throughout South Vietnam in early 1968 by the North Vietnamese and Vietcong. A major turning point in the war, it exposed the credibility gap between official statements and the war's reality, and it shook Americans' confidence in the government.

THE BATTLE FOR HUE
During the Tet Offensive in early 1968, North Vietnamese troops captured the city of Hue, the ancient capital of Vietnam, rich with the country's history and culture. It took nearly a month of brutal house-to-house fighting for U.S. and ARVN troops to retake the city, 80 percent of which had by then been destroyed. Here U.S. Marines are pinned down near the center of Hue. Bettmann/Corbis.

Beyond America's Borders

1968: A Year of Protest

To many people living through it, 1968 looked like the start of a worldwide political revolution. A surge of protests against the U.S. war in Vietnam and demands for greater democracy and economic justice jumped over borders and challenged authorities in many countries around the world. Although local grievances ignited much of the unrest, a common feature was the central role played by university students. The protests of 1968 unfolded rapidly, giving rise to excitement and apprehension. From February to December, demonstrations erupted in North and South America, Europe, and Asia. Many demonstrators expressed transnational solidarity by carrying the flag of Vietnam's National Liberation Front or placards bearing the image of Ernesto "Che" Guevara, a Latin American radical killed by the Bolivian military in 1967. And yet there was little international coordination of events or any shared plan for remaking the world.

One of the first large-scale protests occurred in February at West Berlin's Free University, where some 10,000 participants from ten countries at the "Vietnam Congress" called for "an international manifestation of solidarity" with the people of Vietnam. Protests continued throughout the spring, prompting the West German government to pass emergency laws to stifle disorder. In February and March, demonstrations flared up in Madrid, Warsaw, Rome, São Paulo, and London, met by police with clubs. Charges of police brutality, disseminated in television and newspaper reports, further fed the cycle of protest.

In April and May, violence erupted in the United States. The assassination of Martin Luther King Jr. on April 4 ignited riots in many U.S. cities. Less than a month later, students at Columbia University in New York City seized buildings and shut down the campus, leading to a bloody showdown between police and protesters.

In May, rebellion paralyzed France. It began with students' complaints about services at a university north of Paris and spread to the Sorbonne in the capital city. Police tear-gassed a small rally, only to face tens of thousands of students streaming into Paris over the next few days. Violence escalated as protesters barricaded streets. Independent radio stations broadcast live interviews with demonstrators, and soon a million people were in the streets. Workers joined the rebellion, shutting down factories across France. Students proclaimed that "exceptional domestic and international conditions" had brought powerless students and workers together around the world. By late May, France was in deep crisis.

Prague, the capital of Communist Czechoslovakia, also stirred in May. A liberal president, Alexander Dubček, pushed for reforms against heavy-handed Soviet control, giving rise to hopes for greater freedom. Students demonstrated, and thousands signed manifestos. But this "Prague Spring" was cut short in August when Soviet tanks rumbled into the country and Dubček was arrested. Throughout Europe, students marched on Soviet embassies to protest the crackdown. At the same moment in the United States, Chicago police battled young protesters near the Democratic National Convention.

In July, Mexican police attacked marchers carrying posters of Fidel Castro and Che Guevara. When thousands rallied against the violence, police fired into the crowd, killing several students. Violent clashes continued into August and September, as activists protested the Olympic Games, scheduled to open in Mexico City in October. Insisting that the money spent on the Olympics should instead have been used to alleviate the country's widespread poverty, protesters chanted, "We don't want Olympic Games; we want revolution." The upcoming Olympics created pressure for the authorities to clear the city of dissidents. When some 10,000 students assembled for a rally on October 2,

PRAGUE SPRING
Czech students march
in the capital of Czech-
oslovakia in support of
proposals introduced in the
spring of 1968 that would
loosen Soviet control of
the Communist satellite
and promote freedom of
speech and economic
reform. Their banner reads
"Never Again with the
Soviet Union," mocking an
earlier Czech-Stalinist
slogan, "Forever with the
Soviet Union." Bettmann/
Corbis.

jeeps with machine guns arrived. More than 100 protesters were killed, and another several hundred were
wounded. The Olympic Games went on as scheduled
ten days later.

In the wake of the massacre, protesters staged
demonstrations and attacks on Mexican embassies in
Latin America and Europe. By December, more episodes of violence against protesters occurred in Spain,
Pakistan, and Northern Ireland. In the United States, violence diminished generally, but not in urban ghettos.

By year's end, a kind of stunned exhaustion set in. The
Soviets had shut down the Prague Spring, the student-led
protests in France and Germany had reached a stalemate,
and Republican Richard Nixon had won the U.S. presidential election with promises to maintain law and order at
home and to end the war in Vietnam. The year of global
protest ended with despair and fear on all sides. Student
protest did not disappear, but the excitement of worldwide revolutionary solidarity was blunted by the very real
threat of fatal consequences faced by protesters.

QUESTIONS FOR ANALYSIS

Analyze the Evidence What were some of the specific aims of protesters across the world in
1968?

Ask Historical Questions What did the global protests of 1968 have in common? In what
ways were they different?

Consider the Context What international events prompted many of the protests?

New Year holiday. Although the enemy was eventually pushed back and lost ten times as many soldiers as ARVN and U.S. forces, Tet was psychologically devastating to the United States because it exposed the credibility gap between official statements and the war's reality. The attacks created a million more South Vietnamese refugees as well as widespread destruction. Public approval of Johnson's handling of the war dropped to 26 percent.

In the aftermath of Tet, Johnson conferred with advisers in the Defense Department and an unofficial group of foreign policy experts who had been key architects of Cold War policy since the 1940s. Dean Acheson, who had been Truman's secretary of state, summarized their conclusion: "We can no longer do the job we set out to do in the time we have left and we must begin to take steps to disengage."

On March 31, 1968, Johnson announced a sharp reduction in the bombing of North Vietnam and an offer to begin peace talks. He added the stunning declaration that he would not run for reelection. The gradual escalation of the war was over, and military strategy shifted from "Americanization" to "Vietnamization" of the war. But this was not a shift in policy. The goal remained a non-Communist South Vietnam; the United States would simply rely more heavily on the South Vietnamese to achieve it.

Negotiations began in Paris in May 1968. The United States would not agree to recognize the Hanoi government's National Liberation Front, to allow a coalition government in the South, or to withdraw. The North Vietnamese would agree to nothing less. Although the talks continued, so did the fighting.

Meanwhile, violence escalated at home. Protests struck two hundred college campuses in the spring of 1968. In the bloodiest action, students occupied buildings at Columbia University in New York City, condemning the university's war-related research and its treatment of African Americans. When negotiations failed, university officials called in the city police, who cleared the buildings, injuring scores of demonstrators and arresting hundreds. An ensuing student strike prematurely ended the academic year.

The Tumultuous Election of 1968.
Disorder and violence also entered the election process. In June, two months after the murder of Martin Luther King Jr. and the riots that followed, antiwar candidate Senator Robert F. Kennedy, campaigning for the Democratic Party's presidential nomination, was killed by a Palestinian Arab refugee because of his support for Israel.

In August, protesters battled the police in Chicago, site of the Democratic National Convention. Several thousand demonstrators came to the city, some to support peace candidate Senator Eugene McCarthy, others to cause disruption. On August 25, when demonstrators jeered at orders to disperse, police attacked them with tear gas and clubs. Street battles continued for three days, culminating in a police riot on the night of August 28. Taunted by the crowd, the police sprayed Mace and clubbed not only those who had come to provoke violence but also reporters, peaceful demonstrators, and convention delegates.

The bloodshed in Chicago had little effect on the convention's outcome. Vice President Hubert H. Humphrey believed that the nation was "throwing lives and money down a corrupt rat hole" in Vietnam, but he kept his views to himself and trounced the remaining antiwar candidate, McCarthy, by nearly three to one for the Democratic nomination.

In contrast to the turmoil in Chicago, the Republican convention met peacefully and nominated former vice president Richard Nixon. In a bid for southern support, Nixon chose Maryland governor Spiro T. Agnew for his running mate. A strong third candidate entered the race when the American Independent Party nominated staunch segregationist George C. Wallace. The former Alabama governor appealed to Americans' dissatisfaction with the reforms and rebellions of the 1960s and their outrage at the assaults on traditional values. Nixon guardedly played on resentments that fueled the Wallace campaign, calling for "law and order" and attacking liberal Supreme Court decisions, busing for school desegregation, and protesters.

The candidates differed little on the central issue of Vietnam. Nixon promised "an honorable end" to the war but did not indicate how to achieve it. Humphrey had reservations about U.S. policy in Vietnam, yet as vice president he was tied to Johnson's policies. Nixon edged out Humphrey by just half a million popular votes but won 301 electoral college votes to Humphrey's 191 and Wallace's 46 (Map 29.3). The Democrats maintained control of Congress.

Candidate	Electoral Vote	Popular Vote	Percent of Popular Vote
Richard M. Nixon (Republican)	301	31,770,237	43.4
Hubert H. Humphrey (Democrat)	191	31,270,533	42.7
George C. Wallace (American Independent)	46	9,906,141	13.5

Note: North Carolina split its vote, with one elector voting for Wallace.

MAP 29.3 THE ELECTION OF 1968

The 1968 election revealed deep cracks in the coalition that had maintained Democratic dominance in Washington since the 1930s. Johnson's liberal policies on race shattered a century of Democratic Party rule in the South, which delivered all its electoral votes to Wallace and Nixon. Elsewhere, large numbers of blue-collar workers broke their traditional alliance with the Democrats to vote for Wallace or Nixon, as did other groups that associated the Democrats with racial turmoil, poverty programs, changing sexual mores, and failure to turn the tide in Vietnam. Autoworker Dewey Burton voted for Wallace, objecting to paying "high taxes and more for a home so that somebody can [bus] my son 30 miles away to get an inferior education." These resentments would soon be mobilized into a resurging right in American politics (as discussed in chapter 30).

REVIEW How did the war in Vietnam polarize the nation?

Nixon, Détente, and the Search for Peace in Vietnam

Richard M. Nixon hoped to make his mark on history by applying his broad understanding of international relations to a changing world. Diverging from Republican orthodoxy, he made dramatic overtures to the Soviet Union and China. Yet anticommunism remained central to U.S. policy. Nixon backed repressive regimes around the world and aggressively pursued the war in Vietnam, despite mounting opposition. He expanded the conflict into Cambodia and Laos and ferociously bombed North Vietnam. In the end, however, he was forced to settle for peace without victory.

Moving toward Détente with the Soviet Union and China.

Nixon perceived that the "rigid and bipolar world of the 1940s and 1950s" was changing, and America's European allies were seeking to ease East-West tensions. Moreover, Nixon and his national security adviser Henry A. Kissinger believed they could exploit the increasing discord between the Soviet Union and China. In addition, these two nations might be used to help the United States extricate itself from Vietnam.

Following two years of secret negotiations, in February 1972 Nixon became the nation's first president to set foot on Chinese soil, an astonishing move by one who had built his career on anticommunism. Although his visit was largely symbolic, cultural and scientific exchanges followed, and American manufacturers began to find markets in China — small steps in the process of globalization that would take giant strides in the 1990s (as discussed in chapter 31). In 1979, the United States and China established formal diplomatic relations.

As Nixon and Kissinger had hoped, the warming of U.S.-Chinese relations furthered their strategy of **détente**, their term for easing conflict with the Soviet Union. Détente did not mean abandoning containment; instead it focused on issues of common concern, such as arms control and trade. Containment now would be achieved not just by military threat but also by ensuring that the Soviets and Chinese had stakes in a stable international order. Nixon's goal was "a stronger, healthy United States, Europe, Soviet Union, China, Japan, each balancing the other."

Arms control, trade, and stability in Europe were three areas where the United States and the Soviet Union had common interests. In May 1972, Nixon visited

détente

Term (from the French for "loosening") given to the easing of conflict between the United States and the Soviet Union during the Nixon administration by focusing on issues of common concern, such as arms control and trade.

Strategic Arms Limitation Treaty (SALT)

A 1972 agreement between the United States and the Soviet Union limiting antiballistic missiles (ABMs) to two each. The treaty prevented either nation from building an ABM system defense so secure against a nuclear attack that it would risk a first strike.

NIXON IN CHINA

During his surprise visit to China in February 1972, Nixon, alluding to his anti-Communist credentials, remarked to Chinese leader Mao Zedong, "Those on the right can do what those on the left only talk about." Here, Mao, Nixon, and Kissinger meet at Mao's residence in Beijing. In the preceding months, Kissinger had traveled secretly to China to lay the groundwork for the visit. Bettmann/Corbis.

Moscow, signing agreements on trade and cooperation in science and space. Most significantly, the two superpowers concluded the **Strategic Arms Limitation Treaty (SALT)** in 1972, agreeing to limit antiballistic missiles (ABMs) to two each. Giving up pursuit of a defense against nuclear weapons was a crucial move because it denied both nations an ABM defense so secure against a nuclear attack that they would risk a first strike.

Although détente made little progress after 1974, U.S., Canadian, Soviet, and European leaders signed a historic agreement in 1975 in Helsinki, Finland, that formally recognized the post–World War II boundaries in Europe. Conservatives excoriated the **Helsinki accords** because they acknowledged the status quo: Soviet domination over Eastern Europe. Yet the agreement also committed the signing countries to recognize "the universal significance of human rights and fundamental freedoms." Dissidents in the Soviet Union and its Eastern European satellites used this official promise of rights to challenge the Soviet dictatorship and help force its overthrow fifteen years later.

Shoring Up U.S. Interests around the World.

Despite the thaw in U.S. relations with the Soviet Union and China, in other parts of the world Nixon and Kissinger continued to view left-wing movements as threats to U.S. interests and actively resisted social revolutions that might lead to communism. For example, the Nixon administration helped overthrow Salvador Allende, a self-proclaimed Marxist who was elected president of Chile in 1970. Since 1964, the CIA and U.S. corporations concerned about nationalization of their Chilean properties had assisted Allende's opponents. After Allende's election, Nixon ordered the CIA director to destabilize Allende's government and the economy, and in 1973 the CIA helped the Chilean military engineer a coup, resulting in Allende's death and a brutal dictatorship under General Augusto Pinochet.

In other parts of the world, too, the Nixon administration backed repressive regimes. In southern Africa, it eased pressures on white minority governments that tyrannized blacks. In the Middle East, the United States sent massive arms shipments to support the shah of Iran's harsh regime because Iran had enormous petroleum reserves and seemed a stable anti-Communist ally.

Like his predecessors, Nixon pursued a delicate balance between defending Israel's security and seeking the goodwill of Arab nations strategically and economically important to the United States. Conflict between Israel and the Arab nations had escalated into the **Six-Day War** in 1967, when Israel attacked Egypt after Egypt had massed troops on the Israeli border and cut off sea passage to Israel's southern port. Although Syria and Jordan joined the war on Egypt's side, Israel won a stunning victory, seizing the Sinai Peninsula and Gaza Strip from Egypt, the Golan Heights from Syria, and the West Bank, where hundreds of thousands of Palestinians lived, from Jordan.

That decisive victory did not quell Middle Eastern turmoil. In October 1973, on the Jewish holiday Yom Kippur, Egypt and Syria surprised Israel with a full-scale attack. When the Nixon administration sided with Israel, Arab nations retaliated with an oil embargo that created severe shortages in the United States. After Israel repulsed the attack, tensions remained high. The Arab countries refused to

Helsinki accords

1975 agreement signed by U.S., Canadian, Soviet, and European leaders, recognizing the post–World War II borders in Europe and pledging the signatories to respect human rights and fundamental freedoms.

CHILE

Six-Day War

1967 conflict between Israel and the Arab nations of Egypt, Syria, and Jordan. Israel attacked Egypt after Egypt had massed troops on its border and cut off the sea passage to Israel's southern port. Israel won a stunning victory, seizing territory that amounted to twice its original size.

**ISRAELI TERRITORIAL GAINS
IN THE SIX-DAY WAR, 1967**

recognize Israel's right to exist, Israel began to settle its citizens in the West Bank and other territories it had seized during the Six-Day War, and no solution could be found for the Palestinian refugees who had been displaced by the creation of Israel in 1948. The simmering conflict contributed to anti-American sentiment among Arabs who viewed the United States as Israel's supporter.

Vietnam Becomes Nixon's War. "I'm going to stop that war. Fast," Nixon asserted. He gradually withdrew ground troops, but he was no more willing than his predecessors to be the president who let South Vietnam fall to the Communists. That goal was tied to the larger objective of maintaining American credibility. Regardless of the wisdom of the initial intervention, Kissinger asserted, "the commitment of 500,000 Americans has settled the importance of Vietnam. For what is involved now is confidence in American promises."

From 1969 to 1972, Nixon and Kissinger pursued a three-pronged approach. First, they tried to strengthen the South Vietnamese military and government. ARVN forces grew to more than a million, and the South Vietnamese air force became the fourth largest in the world. The United States also promoted land reform, village elections, and the building of schools, hospitals, and transportation facilities. Second, Nixon gradually reduced the U.S. presence in Vietnam, a move that somewhat disarmed the antiwar movement at home. American forces decreased from 543,000 in 1968 to 140,000 by the end of 1971, although casualties remained high. Third, the United States replaced U.S. forces with intensive bombing. In the spring of 1969, Nixon began a ferocious air war in Cambodia, hiding it from Congress and the public for more than a year. Seeking to knock out North Vietnamese sanctuaries in Cambodia, Americans dropped more than 100,000 tons of bombs but succeeded only in sending the enemy to other hiding places. Echoing Johnson, Kissinger believed that a "fourth-rate power like North Vietnam" had to have a "breaking point," but the massive bombing failed to find it.

To support a new, pro-Western Cambodian government installed through a military coup and "to show the enemy that we were still serious about our commitment in Vietnam," Nixon ordered a joint U.S.-ARVN invasion of Cambodia in April 1970. He accompanied that action with a belligerent speech emphasizing the importance of U.S. credibility: "If when the chips are down, the world's most powerful nation acts like a pitiful helpless giant, the forces of totalitarianism and anarchy will threaten free nations" everywhere.

In response to this escalation of the war, more than 100,000 people protested in Washington, D.C., and students boycotted classes on hundreds of campuses. At a rally on May 4 at Kent State University in Ohio, National Guard troops opened fire, killing four and wounding ten others. "They're starting to treat their own children like they treat us," commented a black woman in Harlem. In a confrontation at Jackson State College in Mississippi on May 14, police shot into a dormitory, killing two black students.

**U.S. INVASION OF
CAMBODIA, 1970**

Congressional reaction to the invasion of Cambodia revealed increasing concern about abuses of presidential power. In the name of national security, presidents since Franklin Roosevelt had conducted foreign policy without the consent or sometimes even the knowledge of Congress — for example, Eisenhower in Iran and Kennedy in Cuba. But in their determination to win the war in Vietnam, Johnson and Nixon had taken extreme measures to deceive the public and silence their critics. The aggression into Cambodia infuriated enough legislators that the Senate voted to terminate the Gulf of Tonkin Resolution and to cut off funds for the Cambodian operation. The House refused to go along, but by the end of June 1970 Nixon had pulled all U.S. troops out of Cambodia.

In 1971, Vietnam veterans became a visible part of the peace movement, the first men in U.S. history to protest a war in which they had fought. They held a public investigation of "war crimes" in Vietnam, rallied in front of the Capitol, and cast away their war medals. In May 1971, veterans numbered among the 40,000 protesters who engaged in civil disobedience in an effort to shut down Washington. Officials made more than 12,000 arrests, which courts later ruled violations of protesters' rights.

After the spring of 1971, there were fewer massive antiwar demonstrations, but opposition to the war continued. Public attention focused on the court-martial of Lieutenant William Calley, which began in November 1970. During the trial, Americans learned that in March 1968 Calley's company had killed every inhabitant of the

PRO-WAR DEMONSTRATORS

Supporters as well as opponents of the war in Vietnam took to the streets, as these New Yorkers did in support of the U.S. invasion of Cambodia in May 1970. Construction workers — called "hard hats" — and other union members marched with American flags and posters championing President Nixon's policies and blasting New York mayor John Lindsay for his antiwar position. Paul Fusco/ Magnum Photos.

hamlet of My Lai, even though it had encountered no enemy forces and the four hundred villagers were nearly all old men, women, and children. The military covered up the massacre for more than a year before a journalist exposed it. Eventually, twelve officers and enlisted men were charged with murder or assault, but only Calley was convicted.

Administration policy suffered another blow in June 1971 when the *New York Times* published portions of the ***Pentagon Papers***, a secret internal study of the war begun in 1967. Nixon sent government lawyers to court to stop further publication, in part out of fear that other information would be leaked. The Supreme Court, however, ruled that suppression of the publication violated the First Amendment. Subsequent circulation of the *Pentagon Papers*, which revealed pessimism among officials even as they made rosy promises, heightened disillusionment with the war by casting doubts on the government's credibility. More than 60 percent of Americans polled in 1971 considered it a mistake to have sent American troops to Vietnam; 58 percent believed the war to be immoral.

Military morale sank in the last years of the war. Having been exposed to the antiwar movement at home, many soldiers had less faith in the war than their predecessors had had. Racial tensions among the troops mounted, many soldiers sought escape in illegal drugs, and enlisted men committed hundreds of "fraggings," attacks on officers. In a 1971 report, *The Collapse of the Armed Forces*, a retired Marine colonel described the lack of discipline: "Our army that now remains in Vietnam [is] near mutinous."

The Peace Accords.
Nixon and Kissinger continued to believe that intensive firepower could bring the North Vietnamese to their knees. In March 1972, responding to a North Vietnamese offensive, the United States resumed sustained bombing of the North, mined Haiphong and other harbors for the first time, and announced a naval blockade. With peace talks stalled, in December Nixon ordered the most devastating bombing yet. Though costly to both sides, it brought renewed negotiations. On January 27, 1973, representatives of the United States, North Vietnam, South Vietnam, and the Vietcong (now called the Provisional Revolutionary Government) signed a formal peace accord in Paris. The agreement required removal of all U.S. troops and military advisers from South Vietnam but allowed North Vietnamese forces to remain. Both sides agreed to return prisoners of war. Nixon called the agreement "peace with honor," but in fact it allowed only a face-saving withdrawal. Unlike the ending of World War II, "There's nothing to celebrate," said an American Legion commander.

Fighting resumed immediately among the Vietnamese. Nixon's efforts to support the South Vietnamese government, and indeed his ability to govern at all, were increasingly eroded by what came to be known as the Watergate scandal, which forced him to resign in 1974 (as discussed in chapter 30). In 1975, North Vietnam launched a new offensive, seizing Saigon on April 30. The Americans remaining in the U.S. Embassy and their Marine guard hastily evacuated, along with 150,000 of their South Vietnamese allies. Confusion, humiliation, and tragedy marked the rushed departure. The United States lacked sufficient transportation capacity and time to evacuate all those who had supported the South Vietnamese government

Pentagon Papers
Secret government documents published in 1971 containing an internal study of the Vietnam War. The documents further disillusioned the public by revealing that officials harbored pessimism about the war even as they made rosy public pronouncements about its progress.

and were desperate to leave. A U.S. diplomat who escaped Saigon commented, "The rest of our lives we will be haunted by how we betrayed those people." Eventually more than 600,000 Vietnamese fled to the United States, but others lost their lives trying to escape, and many who could not get out suffered from political repression or poverty.

During the four years it took Nixon to end the war, he had expanded the conflict into Cambodia and Laos and launched massive bombing campaigns. Although increasing numbers of legislators criticized the war, Congress never denied the funds to fight it. Only after the peace accords did the legislative branch try to reassert its constitutional authority in the making of war. The War Powers Act of 1973 required the president to secure congressional approval for any substantial, long-term deployment of troops abroad. The new law, however, did little to dispel the distrust of government that resulted from Americans' realization that their leaders had not told the truth about Vietnam.

The war produced widespread criticism of the draft from both the left and right. As the United States withdrew from Vietnam, Nixon and Congress agreed to abandon conscription, which had been part of the Cold War since its beginning. Replacing the principle of obligation with the offer of opportunity, military leaders predicted that an all-volunteer army would make a more disciplined and professional fighting force. At the same time, ending service as a common sacrifice distanced most Americans from the horrors of warfare and from the military, whose ranks would be disproportionately filled by poorer Americans and people of color.

The Legacy of Defeat. Four presidents had declared that the survival of South Vietnam was critical to U.S. containment policy. Yet their predictions that a Communist victory in South Vietnam would set the dominoes cascading did not materialize. Although Vietnam, Laos, and Cambodia all fell within the Communist camp in the spring of 1975, the rest of Southeast Asia did not. When China and Vietnam reverted to their historically hostile relationship, the myth of a monolithic Communist power overrunning Asia evaporated.

Antigovernment sentiment was just one of the war's legacies. Vietnam also left bitter divisions among Americans and diverted money from domestic programs. The war created federal budget deficits and triggered inflation that contributed to ongoing economic crises throughout the 1970s (as discussed in chapter 30).

EVACUATING SOUTH VIETNAM

As Communist troops approached Saigon in the spring of 1975, desperate South Vietnamese attempted to flee along with the departing Americans. Here they attempt to scale the wall of the U.S. Embassy to reach evacuation helicopters. Thousands were left behind, while South Vietnamese president Nguyen Van Thieu fled with fifteen tons of baggage on a U.S. plane.
AP Images/Neal Ulevich

TABLE 29.1 VIETNAM WAR CASUALTIES	
United States	
Battle deaths	47,434
Other deaths	10,786
Wounded	153,303
South Vietnam	
Killed in action	110,357
Military wounded	499,026
Civilians killed	415,000
Civilians wounded	913,000
Communist Regulars and Guerrillas	
Killed in action	66,000

Source: U.S. Department of Defense.

The long pursuit of victory in Vietnam complicated the United States' relations with other nations, as even its staunchest ally, Britain, doubted the wisdom of the war. The use of terrifying American power against a small Asian country alienated many in the third world and compromised efforts to win the hearts and minds of people in developing nations.

The cruelest legacy of Vietnam fell on those who had served. "The general public just wanted to ignore us," remembered Frederick Downs, while opponents of the war "wanted to argue with us until we felt guilty about what we had done over there." Many veterans believed in the war's purposes and felt betrayed by the government for not letting them win it. Others blamed the government for sacrificing the nation's youth in an immoral, unnecessary war, expressing their sense of the war's futility by referring to their dead comrades as having been "wasted." Veterans of color had more reason to doubt the nobility of their purpose. A Native American soldier assigned to resettle Vietnamese civilians found it to be "just like when they moved us to the rez [reservation]. We shouldn't have done that."

Because the Vietnam War was a civil war involving guerrilla tactics, combat was especially brutal (Table 29.1). The terrors of conventional warfare were multiplied, and so were the motivations to commit atrocities. The 1968 massacre at My Lai was only the most widely publicized war crime. To demonstrate the immorality of the war, peace advocates stressed the atrocities, contributing to a distorted image of the Vietnam veteran as dehumanized and violent.

Most veterans came home to public neglect. Government benefits were less generous to Vietnam veterans than they had been to those of previous wars. While two-thirds of Vietnam veterans said that they would serve again, and while most veterans readjusted well to civilian life, some suffered long after the war ended. The Veterans Administration estimated that nearly one-sixth of the veterans suffered from post-traumatic stress disorder, experiencing recurring nightmares, feelings of guilt and shame, violence, substance abuse, and suicidal tendencies. Thirty years after performing army intelligence work in Saigon, Doris Allen "still hit the floor sometimes when [she heard] loud bangs." Some who had served in Vietnam began to report birth defects, cancer, severe skin disorders, and other ailments. Veterans claimed a link between those illnesses and Agent Orange, which had exposed many to the deadly poison dioxin in Vietnam. In 1991, Congress began to provide assistance to veterans with diseases linked to the poison.

By then, the climate had changed. The war began to enter the realm of popular culture, with novels, TV shows, and hit movies depicting a broad range of military experience — from soldiers reduced to brutality, to men and women serving with courage and integrity. The incorporation of the Vietnam War into the collective experience was symbolized most dramatically in the Vietnam Veterans Memorial unveiled in Washington, D.C., in November 1982. Designed by Yale architecture student Maya Lin, the black, V-shaped wall inscribed with the names of 58,200 men and women lost in the war became one of the most popular sites in the nation's capital. In an article describing the memorial's dedication, a Vietnam combat veteran spoke to and for his former comrades: "Welcome home. The war is over."

> **REVIEW** What strategies did Nixon implement to bring American involvement in Vietnam to a close?

Conclusion: An Unwinnable War

Lieutenant Frederick Downs Jr. fought in America's longest war. The United States spent $111 billion (more than $600 billion in 2014 dollars) and sent 2.6 million men and women to Vietnam. Of those, 58,200 never returned, and 150,000, like Downs, suffered serious injury. The war shattered consensus at home, increased presidential power at the expense of congressional authority and public accountability, weakened the economy, diminished trust in government, and contributed to the downfall of two presidents.

Even as Nixon and Kissinger took steps to ease Cold War tensions with the major Communist powers — the Soviet Union and China — they also acted vigorously throughout the third world to install or prop up anti-Communist governments. They embraced their predecessors' commitment to South Vietnam as a necessary Cold War engagement: To do otherwise would threaten American credibility and make the United States appear weak. Defeat in Vietnam did not make the United States the "pitiful helpless giant" predicted by Nixon, but it did signify a relative decline of U.S. power and the impossibility of containment on a global scale.

One of the constraints on U.S. power was the tenacity of revolutionary movements determined to achieve national independence. Overestimating the effectiveness of American technological superiority, U.S. officials badly underestimated the sacrifices that the enemy was willing to make and failed to realize how easily the United States could be perceived as a colonial intruder. A second constraint on Eisenhower, Kennedy, Johnson, and Nixon was their resolve to avoid a major confrontation with the Soviet Union or China. For Johnson, who conducted the largest escalation of the war, caution was critical so as not to provoke direct intervention by the Communist superpowers. After China exploded its first atomic bomb in 1964, the potential heightened for the Vietnam conflict to escalate into worldwide disaster.

Third, in Vietnam the United States sought to prop up an extremely weak ally engaged in a civil war. The South Vietnamese government failed to win the support of its people, and the intense devastation the war brought to civilians only made things worse. Short of taking over the South Vietnamese government and military, the United States could do little to strengthen South Vietnam's ability to resist communism.

Finally, domestic opposition to the war, which by 1968 had spread to mainstream America, constrained the options of Johnson and Nixon. As the war dragged on, with increasing American casualties and growing evidence of the damage being inflicted on innocent Vietnamese, more and more civilians wearied of the conflict. Even some who had fought in the war joined the peace movement, sending their military ribbons and bitter letters of protest to the White House. In 1973, Nixon and Kissinger bowed to the resoluteness of the enemy and the limitations of U.S. power. As the war wound down, passions surrounding it contributed to a rising conservative movement that would substantially alter the post–World War II political order.

Chapter Review

KEY TERMS

Bay of Pigs (p. 862)
Apollo program (p. 863)
Berlin Wall (p. 864)
Peace Corps (p. 864)
Cuban missile crisis (p. 865)
Agent Orange (p. 868)
Gulf of Tonkin Resolution (p. 869)

Tet Offensive (p. 875)
détente (p. 880)
Strategic Arms Limitation Treaty (SALT) (p. 881)
Helsinki accords (p. 881)
Six-Day War (p. 881)
Pentagon Papers (p. 884)

REVIEW QUESTIONS

❶ Why did Kennedy believe that engagement in Vietnam was crucial to his foreign policy? (pp. 862–68)

❷ Why did massive amounts of airpower and ground troops fail to bring U.S. victory in Vietnam? (pp. 868–72)

❸ How did the war in Vietnam polarize the nation? (pp. 873–79)

❹ What strategies did Nixon implement to bring American involvement in Vietnam to a close? (pp. 879–87)

MAKING CONNECTIONS

① How did Cuba figure into President Kennedy's Cold War policies?

② Explain the Gulf of Tonkin incident and its significance to American foreign policy. How did President Johnson respond to the incident, and why?

③ Discuss the range of American responses to the war in Vietnam. How did they change over time?

LINKING TO THE PAST

① What commitments were made in the Truman and Eisenhower administrations that resulted in the United States' full-scale involvement in Vietnam? (See chapters 26 and 27.)

② Compare American public sentiment during World War II to that during the Vietnam War. What policies, events, attitudes, and technological advancements contributed to the differences? (See chapter 25.)

America Moves to the Right,
1969–1989

CONTENT LEARNING OBJECTIVES

After reading and studying this chapter, you should be able to:

• Explain the emergence of a grassroots conservative movement and how Nixon courted the right. Identify the events that led to Nixon's resignation.

• Describe the "outsider" presidency of Jimmy Carter and explain his approach to energy and environmental regulation, human rights, and the Cold War.

• Explain how Ronald Reagan's presidency represented ascendant conservatism and the factors behind Reagan's broad appeal.

• Explain how minority groups, feminists, gays and lesbians, and lower-income Americans struggled during the 1980s.

• Describe Reagan's foreign policies, including increased militarization and interventions in the Middle East, Latin America, and Asia. Explain what led to a thaw in Soviet-American relations.

O ne of the "most exciting days" of Phyllis Schlafly's life was hearing Republican Barry Goldwater address the Federation of Republican Women in 1963. Schlafly wanted the United States to do more than just contain communism; like Goldwater, she wanted to eliminate that threat entirely. She also wanted to cut back the federal government, especially its role in providing social welfare and enforcing civil rights. Goldwater's loss to Lyndon Johnson in 1964 did not diminish Schlafly's conservative commitment. She added new issues to the conservative agenda, cultivating a grass-roots movement that would redefine the Republican Party and American politics well into the twenty-first century.

Phyllis Stewart was born in St. Louis in 1924, attended Catholic schools, and worked her way through Washington University

MAKING AMERICA "REAGAN COUNTRY"
This delegate badge from the 1980 Republican National Convention displayed key themes of Ronald Reagan's presidency and politics in the 1980s — patriotism and the rugged individualism of the West. Division of Political History, National Museum of American History, Smithsonian Institution.

testing ammunition at a World War II defense plant. After earning a master's degree in government from Radcliffe College, she worked at the American Enterprise Institute, where she imbibed the think tank's conservatism. Returning to the Midwest, she married Fred Schlafly, an Alton, Illinois, attorney, and bore six children. "I don't think there's anything as much fun as taking care of a baby," Schlafly claimed.

Yet while insisting that caring for home and family was women's most important career, Schlafly spent much of her time writing or on the road, speaking, leading Republican women's organizations, and testifying before legislative committees. She ran twice for Congress but lost in her heavily Democratic district in Illinois. Her 1964 book, *A Choice Not an Echo*, pushed Barry Goldwater for president and sold more than three million copies. In 1967, she began publishing the *Phyllis Schlafly Report*, a monthly newsletter about current political issues. Throughout the 1950s and 1960s, Schlafly advocated stronger efforts to combat communism, a more powerful military, and limited government action in domestic affairs.

In the 1970s, Schlafly expanded the agenda of conservatism to address new issues such as feminism, abortion, gay rights, busing for racial integration, and religion in the schools. Her ideas resonated with Americans who were fed up with the expansion of government, liberal Supreme Court decisions, protest movements, and the loosening of moral standards that seemed to define the 1960s. Although Richard Nixon did not embrace the entire conservative agenda, he won the presidency in 1968 on a platform that sought to make the Republicans the dominant party by appealing to disaffected blue-collar and southern white Democrats. The Watergate revelations forced Nixon to resign the presidency in 1974, and his Republican successor, Gerald Ford, served only two years; but the political spectrum continued to shift right even when Democrat Jimmy Carter captured the White House in 1976. Carter advanced environmental and energy legislation, but an economy beset by both inflation and unemployment and a crisis in U.S.-Iranian relations burdened his campaign for reelection.

Consequently, Schlafly's call for "a choice not an echo" was realized when Ronald Reagan won the presidency in 1980. Cutting taxes, government regulations, and social programs; expanding the nation's military capacity; and pressuring the Soviet Union and communism in the third world, Reagan addressed the hopes of the

CHRONOLOGY

1968   Richard Nixon elected president.

1969   Warren E. Burger appointed chief justice of Supreme Court.

1971   Nixon vetoes child care bill.

1972   Watergate scandal begins. Nixon reelected president.

1974   Nixon resigns; Vice President Gerald Ford becomes president. Ford pardons Nixon.

1976   Jimmy Carter elected president.

1977   United States signs Panama Canal treaty.

1978   *Regents of University of California v. Bakke* decided. Congress deregulates airlines.

1979   Carter facilitates Camp David accords. Carter establishes formal diplomatic relations with China. Soviet Union invades Afghanistan. Iranian hostage crisis begins. Moral Majority founded.

1980   Congress deregulates banking, trucking, and railroad industries. Congress passes Superfund legislation. Ronald Reagan elected president.

1981   AIDS virus discovered. Economic Recovery Tax Act passes.

1983   Terrorist bomb kills 241 U.S. Marines in Beirut, Lebanon. Family Research Council founded.

1984   Reagan reelected president.

1986   Iran-Contra scandal uncovered.

1987   Intermediate-range nuclear forces agreement signed.

1988   Civil Rights Restoration Act passes.

The Phyllis Schlafly Report

VOL. 5, NO. 10, SECTION 2   Box 618, ALTON, ILLINOIS 62002   MAY, 1972

The Fraud Called The Equal Rights Amendment

If there ever was an example of how a tiny minority can cram its views down the throats of the majority, it is the Equal Rights Amendment, called ERA. A noisy claque of women's lib agitators rammed ERA through Congress, intimidating the men into voting for it so they would not be labeled "anti-woman."

The ERA passed Congress with big majorities on March 22, 1972 and was sent to the states for ratification. When it is ratified by 38 states, it will become the law of the land. Within two hours of Senate passage, Hawaii ratified it. New Hampshire and Nebraska, both anxious to be second, rushed their approval the next day. Then in steady succession came Iowa, Idaho, Delaware, Kansas, Texas, Maryland, Tennessee, Alaska, Rhode Island, and New Jersey. As this goes to press, 13 states have ratified it and others are on the verge of doing so.

Three states have rejected it: Oklahoma, Vermont and Connecticut.

What is ERA? The Amendment reads: "Equality of rights under the law shall not be denied or abridged by the United States or by any state on account of sex." Does that sound good? Don't kid yourself. This innocuous-sounding amendment will take away far more important rights than it will ever give. This was made abundantly clear by the debate in Congress. Senator Sam Ervin (D., N.C.) called it "the most drastic measure in Senate history." He proved this by putting into the *Congressional Record* an article from the *Yale Law Journal* of April 1971.

The importance of this *Yale Law Journal* article is that both the proponents and the opponents of ERA agree that it is an accurate analysis of the consequences of ERA. Congresswoman Martha Griffiths, a leading proponent of ERA, sent a copy of this article to every member of Congress, stating that "It w... understand the purposes and effe... Rights Amendment.... The art... ERA will work in m...

the most important of all women's rights.

"In all states husbands are primarily liable for the support of their wives and children.... The child support sections of the criminal nonsupport laws ... could not be sustained where only the male is liable for support." (YLJ, pp. 944-945)

"The Equal Rights Amendment would bar a state from imposing greater liability for support on a husband than on a wife merely because of his sex." (YLJ, p. 945)

"Like the duty of support during marriage and the obligation to pay alimony in the case of separation or divorce, nonsupport would have to be eliminated as a ground for divorce against husbands only...." (YLJ, p. 951)

"The Equal Rights Amendment would not require that alimony be abolished but only that it be available equally to husbands and wives." (YLJ, p. 952)

2. ERA will wipe out the laws which protect only women against sex crimes such as rape.

"Courts faced with criminal laws which do not apply equally to men and women would be likely to invalidate the laws rather than extending or rewriting them to apply to women and men alike." (YLJ, p. 966)

"Seduction laws, statutory rape laws, laws prohibiting obscene language in the presence of women, prostitution and 'manifest danger' laws ... The Equal Rights Amendment would not permit such laws, which base their sex discriminatory classification on social stereotypes." (YLJ, p. 954)

"The statutory rape laws, which punish men for having sexual intercourse with any wom... under an age specified by law ... suffer from a... fect under the Equal Rights Amendmen...

traditional right. Like Schlafly, he also championed the concerns of Christian conservatives, opposing abortion and sexual permissiveness and favoring a larger role for religion in public life.

In the face of resistance from feminists, civil rights groups, environmentalists, and others, Reagan failed to enact the entire conservative agenda. Although he enormously increased the national debt, and his aides engaged in illegal activities to thwart communism in Latin America, his popularity boosted the Republican Party. And Reagan's optimism and spirited leadership contributed to a revival in national pride and confidence.

Nixon, Conservatism, and Constitutional Crisis

Richard Nixon acquiesced in continuing most Great Society programs and even approved pathbreaking environmental, minority, and women's rights measures (see chapter 28), prompting Phyllis Schlafly to call him "too liberal." Yet his public rhetoric and some of his actions signaled the country's rightward move. Whereas John F.

Kennedy had summoned Americans to contribute to the common good, Nixon invited Americans to "ask — not just what will government do for me, but what can I do for myself?" invoking individualism and reliance on private enterprise, not on government. These preferences would grow stronger in the nation during the 1970s and beyond, as a new strand of conservatism joined the older movement that focused on anticommunism, a strong national defense, and limited government. New conservatives wanted to restore what they considered traditional moral values.

Just two years after Nixon won reelection by a huge margin, his abuse of power and efforts to cover up crimes committed by subordinates, revealed in the so-called Watergate scandal, forced the first presidential resignation in history. His successor, Gerald Ford, faced the aftermath of Watergate and severe economic problems, which returned the White House to the Democrats in 1976.

Emergence of a Grassroots Movement.
Hidden beneath Lyndon B. Johnson's landslide victory over Arizona senator Barry Goldwater in 1964 lay a rising conservative movement. Defining his purpose as "enlarging freedom at home and safeguarding it from the forces of tyranny abroad," Goldwater argued that government intrusions into economic life hindered prosperity, stifled personal responsibility, and interfered with citizens' rights to determine their own values. Conservatives assailed big government in domestic affairs but demanded a strong military to eradicate "Godless communism."

The grassroots movement supporting Goldwater's nomination was especially vigorous in the South and West, and it included middle-class suburban women and men, members of the rabidly anti-Communist John Birch Society, and college students in the new Young Americans for Freedom (YAF). In 1966, California conservatives helped Ronald Reagan defeat the liberal incumbent governor, whom Reagan linked to the Watts riot, student disruptions at California universities, and rising taxes.

A number of Sun Belt characteristics made conservatism strong in places such as Orange County, California; Dallas, Texas; and Scottsdale, Arizona. These predominantly white areas contained relatively homogeneous, skilled, and economically comfortable populations, as well as military bases and defense plants. The West harbored a long-standing tradition of Protestant morality, individualism, and opposition to interference by a remote federal government, although that tradition was hardly consistent with the Sun Belt's economic dependence on defense spending and on huge federal projects providing water and power for the burgeoning region. The South, which also benefited from military bases and the space program, shared the West's antipathy toward the federal government, but hostility to racial change was much more central to the South's conservatism. After signing the Civil Rights Act of 1964, President Johnson remarked privately, "I think we just delivered the South to the Republican Party."

Grassroots movements proliferated around what conservatives believed marked the "moral decline" of their nation. For example, in 1962 Mel and Norma Gabler got the Texas Board of Education to drop books that they believed undermined "the Christian-Judeo morals, values, and standards as given to us by God through . . . the Bible." Sex education roused the ire of Eleanor Howe in Anaheim, California, who felt that "nothing [in the sex education curriculum] depicted my values." The U.S. Supreme Court's liberal decisions on school prayer, obscenity, and abortion also galvanized conservatives to restore "traditional values."

In the 1970s, grassroots protests against taxes grew alongside concerns about morality. As Americans struggled with inflation and unemployment, many found themselves paying higher taxes, especially higher property taxes as the value of their homes increased. Some were incensed to see their taxes fund government programs for people they considered undeserving. In 1978, Californians revolted in a popular referendum, slashing property taxes and limiting the state legislature's ability to raise other taxes. What a newspaper called a "primal scream by the People against Big Government" spread to other states.

Law and order was yet another rallying cry of the right, reflecting concerns about rising rates of crime, which were due in part to baby boomers maturing into the age group most prone to crime. Conservatives lumped common crime with civil disobedience and antiwar protest into a cry for law and order, and blamed liberals for Great Society programs that had failed to reduce crime, permissive attitudes

Visual Activity

THE TAX REVOLT

Neighbors gather in Los Angeles to rally for Proposition 13, an initiative launched by conservative Howard Jarvis in 1978. Many homeowners rallied to Jarvis's antitax movement because rising land values had increased their property taxes sharply. After Californians passed Proposition 13, some thirty-seven states cut property taxes, and twenty-eight reduced income taxes. The tax issue helped the Republican Party end decades of Democratic dominance. Tony Korody/The LIFE Images Collection/Getty Images.

READING THE IMAGE: Considering the signs, what is the main concern of the people pictured here? What kinds of people are pictured here, and what are their stakes in the property tax issue?

CONNECTIONS: What other issues did Republicans capitalize on in the 1970s and 1980s?

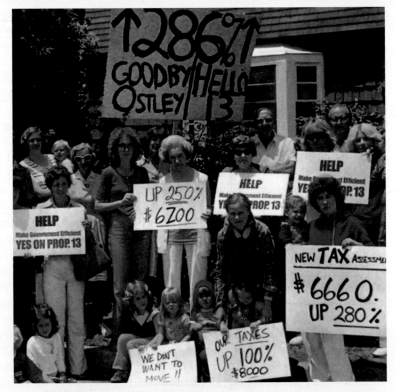

toward protesters, and Supreme Court decisions that coddled criminals. A Pennsylvania man called "crime, the streets being unsafe, strikes, the trouble with the colored, all this dope-taking . . . a breakdown of the American way of life."

Nixon Courts the Right.
Highlighting law and order in his 1968 presidential campaign, Nixon appealed to "forgotten Americans, those who did not indulge in violence, those who did not break the law." He also exploited hostility to black protest and new civil rights policies to woo white southerners and a considerable number of northern voters away from the Democratic Party. As president, he used this "southern strategy" to make further inroads into traditional Democratic strongholds in the 1972 election.

Nixon reluctantly enforced court orders to achieve high degrees of integration in southern schools, but he resisted efforts to deal with segregation outside the South. In northern and western cities, where segregation resulted from discrimination in housing and in the drawing of school district boundaries, half of all African American children attended nearly all-black schools. After courts began to order the transfer of students between schools in white and black neighborhoods to achieve desegregation, busing became a hot-button issue. "We've had all we can take of judicial interference with local schools," Phyllis Schlafly railed in 1972.

Children had been riding buses to school for decades, but busing for racial integration provoked fury. Violence erupted in Boston in 1974 when a district judge found that school officials had maintained what amounted to a dual system based on race and ordered busing "if necessary to achieve a unitary school system." The whites most affected by busing came from working-class families. Left in cities abandoned by the more affluent, their children often rode buses to predominantly black, overcrowded schools with deficient facilities. Clarence McDonough denounced the liberal officials who bused his "kid half way around Boston so that a bunch of politicians can end up their careers with a clear conscience." African Americans themselves

Percent of black students statewide attending schools more than 50% white

60% or more	30–40%
50–60%	20–30%
40–50%	20% or less

INTEGRATION OF PUBLIC SCHOOLS, 1968

SCHOOL BUSING

Controversy over busing as a means of integration erupted in Boston in 1974 after a federal judge ruled that Boston officials had deliberately constructed a segregated school system. Antibusing outrage was especially virulent at historically white South Boston High School, where one black student recalled that "it was like a war zone." Here Tactical Patrol Force officers protect black students at the high school. Jack O'Connell/The *Boston Globe* via Getty Images.

were conflicted about sending their children on long rides to schools where white teachers might not welcome or respect them.

Whites eventually became more accepting of integration, especially after the creation of schools with specialized programs and other new mechanisms for desegregation offered greater choice. Nonetheless, integration propelled white flight to the suburbs. Nixon failed to persuade Congress to end court-ordered busing, but after he had appointed four new justices, the Supreme Court imposed strict limits on the use of that tool to achieve racial balance.

Nixon's judicial appointments also reflected the southern strategy. He criticized the Supreme Court under Chief Justice Earl Warren for being "unprecedentedly politically active . . . using their interpretation of the law to remake American society according to their own social, political, and ideological precepts." When Warren resigned in 1969, Nixon replaced him with Warren E. Burger, a federal appeals court judge who was a strict constructionist, inclined to interpret the Constitution narrowly and to limit government intervention on behalf of individual rights. The Burger Court curbed somewhat the protections of individual rights established by its predecessor, but it upheld many of the liberal programs of the 1960s. For example, *Regents of the University of California v. Bakke* (1978) limited the range of affirmative action but allowed universities to attack the results of past discrimination as long as they did not use strict quotas and racial classifications to do so.

Nixon's southern strategy and other repercussions of the civil rights revolution ended the Democratic hold on the "solid South." Beginning in 1964, a number of conservative southern Democrats changed their party affiliation; by 2015, Republicans controlled every southern state legislature, every governorship, and every Senate seat.

In addition to exploiting racial fears, Nixon appealed to anxieties about women's changing roles and new demands. In 1971, he vetoed a bill providing federal funds for day care centers with a message that combined the old and new conservatism. Parents should purchase child care services "in the private, open market," he insisted, not rely on government. He appealed to social conservatives by warning about the measure's "family-weakening implications." In response to the movement to liberalize abortion laws, Nixon sided with "defenders of the right to life of the unborn," anticipating the Republican Party's eventual embrace of the issue.

The Election of 1972.

Nixon's ability to attract Democrats and appeal to concerns about Vietnam, race, law and order, and traditional morality heightened his prospects for reelection in 1972. Although the war in Vietnam continued, antiwar protests ebbed with the decrease in American ground forces and casualties. Nixon's economic initiatives had temporarily checked inflation and unemployment (see chapter 28), and his attacks on busing and antiwar protesters had won increasing support from the right.

South Dakota senator George S. McGovern came to the Democratic convention as the clear leader and was easily nominated by the delegates, who included unprecedented numbers of women, minorities, and youth. But McGovern struggled as Republicans portrayed him as a left-wing extremist, while his support for busing, a generous welfare program, and immediate withdrawal from Vietnam alienated some Democrats.

Nixon achieved a landslide victory, winning 60.7 percent of the popular vote and every state except Massachusetts. Although the Democrats held on to Congress, Nixon won majorities among traditional Democrats — southerners, Catholics, urbanites, and blue-collar workers. The president, however, had little time to savor his triumph, as revelations began to emerge about crimes committed to ensure the victory.

Watergate. During the early-morning hours of June 17, 1972, five men working for Nixon's reelection crept into Democratic Party headquarters in the Watergate complex in Washington, D.C. Intending to repair a bugging device installed in an earlier break-in, they were discovered and arrested. Nixon and his aides then tried to cover up the burglars' connection to administration officials, setting in motion the scandal reporters dubbed **Watergate**.

Nixon was not the first president to lie to the public or misuse power. Every president since Franklin D. Roosevelt had enlarged the powers of his office in the name of national security. This expansion of executive powers, often called the "imperial presidency," weakened traditional checks and balances on the executive branch and opened the door to abuses. No president, however, had dared go as far as Nixon, who saw opposition to his policies as a personal attack and was willing to violate the Constitution to stop it.

Upon learning of the Watergate arrests, Nixon plotted to manipulate the Central Intelligence Agency (CIA) and Federal Bureau of Investigation (FBI) to conceal links between the burglars and the White House, while publicly denying any connection. In April 1973, after investigations by a grand jury and the Senate suggested that White House aides had been involved in the cover-up effort, Nixon accepted official responsibility for Watergate but denied any knowledge of the break-in or cover-up. He also announced the resignations of three White House aides and the attorney general. In May, he authorized the appointment of an independent special prosecutor, Archibald Cox, to conduct an investigation.

Meanwhile, speaking before a Senate investigating committee headed by Democrat Samuel J. Ervin of North Carolina, White House counsel John Dean described projects to harass "enemies" through tax audits and other illegal means and implicated the president in efforts to cover up the Watergate break-in. Another White House aide struck the decisive blow when he disclosed that all conversations in the Oval Office were taped. Both Cox and Ervin immediately asked for the tapes related to Watergate. When Nixon refused, citing executive privilege and separation of powers, they won a unanimous decision from the Supreme Court ordering him to release the recordings.

Additional disclosures exposed Nixon's misuse of federal funds and tax evasion. In August 1973, Vice President Spiro Agnew resigned after an investigation uncovered his acceptance of bribes while governor of Maryland. Nixon's choice of House minority leader Gerald Ford of Michigan to succeed Agnew won widespread

Watergate
Term referring to the 1972 break-in at Democratic Party headquarters in the Watergate complex in Washington, D.C., by men working for President Nixon's reelection, along with Nixon's efforts to cover it up. The Watergate scandal led to President Nixon's resignation.

WATERGATE

In this drawing, famed political cartoonist Herbert Lawrence Block, known as Herblock, cleverly combined two elements of the Watergate scandal that felled Nixon. During the investigation, the president declared, "I am not a crook," and the tapes of conversations in the Oval Office that he was forced to turn over to investigators showed an eighteen-minute gap at a critical moment. © The Herb Block Foundation.

approval, but Agnew's resignation further tarnished the administration, and Nixon's popular support plummeted.

In February 1974, the House of Representatives began an impeachment investigation. In April, Nixon began to release edited transcripts of the tapes. The transcripts revealed Nixon's orders to aides in March 1973: "I don't give a shit what happens. I want you all to stonewall it, let them plead the Fifth Amendment, cover up or anything else, if it'll save it — save the plan." House Republican leader Hugh Scott of Pennsylvania called the documents a "deplorable, shabby, disgusting, and immoral performance by all."

In July 1974, the House Judiciary Committee voted to impeach the president on three counts: obstruction of justice, abuse of power, and contempt of Congress. Seven or eight Republicans on the committee sided with the majority, and it seemed certain that the House would follow suit. Georgia state legislator and civil rights activist Julian Bond commented, "The prisons of Georgia are full of people who stole $5 or $10, and this man tried to steal the Constitution."

To avoid impeachment, Nixon announced his resignation to a national television audience on August 8, 1974. Acknowledging some incorrect judgments, he insisted that he had always tried to do what was best for the nation. The next morning, Nixon ended a rambling, emotional farewell to his staff with some advice: "Always give your best, never get discouraged, never get petty; always remember, others may hate you, but those who hate you don't win unless you hate them, and then you destroy yourself." Had he followed his own advice, he might have saved his presidency.

The Ford Presidency and the 1976 Election.
Upon taking office, Gerald R. Ford announced, "Our long national nightmare is over." But he shocked many Americans one month later by granting Nixon a pardon "for all offenses against the United States which he . . . has committed or may have committed or taken part in" during his presidency. Prompted by Ford's concern for Nixon's health and by his hope to get the country beyond Watergate, this sweeping pardon saved Nixon from nearly certain indictment and trial, and it provoked a tremendous outcry from Congress and the public. Democrats made impressive gains in the November congressional elections, while Ford's action gave Nixon a new political life. Without having to admit that he had violated the law, Nixon rebuilt his image over the next two decades into that of an elder statesman. Thirty of his associates ultimately pleaded guilty to or were convicted of crimes related to Watergate.

Congress's efforts to guard against the types of abuses revealed in the Watergate investigations had only limited effects. The Federal Election Campaign Act of 1974 established public financing of presidential campaigns and imposed some restrictions on contributions to curtail the selling of political favors. Yet politicians found other ways of raising money — for example, through political action committees (PACs), to which individuals could contribute more than they could to candidates. Moreover, the Supreme Court struck down limitations on campaign spending as violations of freedom of speech. Ever-larger campaign donations flowed to candidates from interest groups, corporations, labor unions, and wealthy individuals.

Congressional investigating committees discovered a host of illegal FBI and CIA activities stretching back to the 1950s, including surveillance of American citizens such as Martin Luther King Jr., harassment of political dissenters, and plots to assassinate Fidel Castro and other foreign leaders. In response to these revelations, President Ford placed new controls on covert operations, and Congress created permanent committees to oversee the intelligence agencies. Yet these measures did little to diminish the public's cynicism about their government or to curtail massive government surveillance of private communications that accompanied terrorist threats to the United States in the twenty-first century.

Disillusionment grew as the Ford administration struggled with serious economic problems: a low growth rate, high unemployment, a foreign trade deficit, and soaring energy prices. Ford carried these burdens into the election campaign of 1976, while contending with a major challenge from the Republican right. Blasting Nixon's and Ford's foreign policy of détente for causing the "loss of U.S. military supremacy," California governor Reagan came close to capturing the nomination.

The Democrats nominated James Earl "Jimmy" Carter Jr., former governor of Georgia. A graduate of the U.S. Naval Academy, Carter spent seven years as a nuclear engineer in the navy before returning to Plains, Georgia, to run the family peanut farming business. Carter stressed his faith as a "born-again Christian" and his distance from the government in Washington. Although he selected liberal senator Walter F. Mondale of Minnesota as his running mate, Carter's nomination nonetheless marked a rightward turn in the party.

Carter had considerable appeal as a candidate who carried his own bags, lived modestly, and taught a Bible class at his Baptist church. He also benefited from Ford's failure to solve the country's economic problems, which helped him win the traditional Democratic coalition of blacks, organized labor, and ethnic groups and even recapture some of the white southerners who had voted for Nixon in 1972. Still, Carter received just 50 percent of the popular vote to Ford's 48 percent, while Democrats retained substantial margins in Congress (Map 30.1).

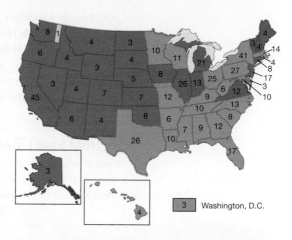

Candidate	Electoral Vote	Popular Vote	Percent of Popular Vote
Jimmy Carter (Democrat)	297	40,830,763	50.1
Gerald R. Ford (Republican)	240	39,147,793	48.0
Ronald Reagan (Independent Republican)	1	n/a	n/a

MAP 30.1   THE ELECTION OF 1976

> **REVIEW** How did Nixon's policies reflect the increasing influence of conservatives on the Republican Party?

The "Outsider" Presidency of Jimmy Carter

Jimmy Carter promised a government that was "competent" as well as "decent, open, fair, and compassionate." He also warned Americans "that even our great Nation has its recognized limits, and that we can neither answer all questions nor solve all problems." Carter's humility and personal integrity helped revive trust in the presidency, but he faltered in the face of domestic and foreign crises.

Energy shortages and stagflation worsened, exposing Carter's deficiencies in working with Congress and rallying public opinion. He achieved notable advances in environmental and energy policies, and he oversaw foreign policy successes concerning the Panama Canal, China, and the Middle East. Yet near the end of his term, Soviet-American relations deteriorated, new crises emerged in the Middle East, and the economy plummeted.

Retreat from Liberalism.
Carter vowed "to help the poor and aged, to improve education, and to provide jobs," but at the same time "not to waste money." When these goals conflicted, budget balancing took priority over reform. Carter's approach pleased Americans unhappy about their tax dollars being used to benefit the disadvantaged while stagflation eroded their own standard of living. But his fiscal stringency frustrated liberal Democrats pushing for major welfare reform and a national health insurance program. Carter himself said, "In many cases I feel more at home with the conservative Democratic and Republican members of Congress than I do with the others."

Although Carter did fulfill liberals' desire to make government more inclusive by appointing unprecedented numbers of women and minorities to cabinet, judicial, and diplomatic posts, a number of factors thwarted Carter's policy goals. His outsider status helped him win the election but left him without strong ties to party leaders in Congress. Democrats complained that Carter flooded them with comprehensive proposals without consultation or a strategy to get them enacted. Even if he had possessed Lyndon Johnson's political skills, Carter might not have done much better. The economic problems he inherited — unemployment, inflation, and sluggish economic growth — confounded economic doctrine. Usually, rising prices accompanied a humming economy with a strong demand for labor. Now, however, stagflation burdened the economy with both steep inflation and high unemployment, enlarging the federal budget deficit.

Carter first targeted unemployment, signing bills that pumped $14 billion into the economy through public works and public service jobs programs and cutting taxes by $34 billion. Unemployment receded, but then inflation surged. Working people, wrote one journalist, "winced and ached" as their paychecks bought less and less, "hollowing their hopes and dreams, their plans for a house or their children's college education." To curb inflation, Carter curtailed federal spending, and the Federal Reserve Board tightened the money supply. Not only did these measures fail to halt inflation, which surpassed 13 percent in 1980, but they also contributed to rising unemployment, reversing the gains made in Carter's first two years.

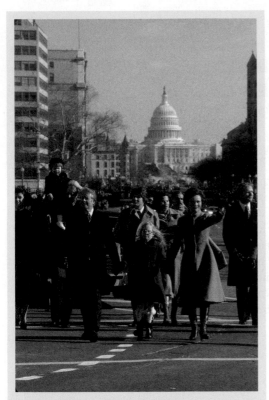

JIMMY CARTER'S INAUGURATION

At the close of his inauguration in January 1977, Carter was the first president to walk from the Capitol to the White House, to symbolize his connection with ordinary people. As he said subsequently, "Government officials can't be sensitive to your problems if we are living like royalty here." Here he is shown hand in hand with his daughter Amy and wife Rosalynn.
Bernard Gotfryd/Getty Images.

Carter's commitment to restraining the federal budget frustrated Democrats pushing for comprehensive welfare reform, national health insurance, and a substantial jobs program that would make government the employer of the last resort. His refusal to propose a comprehensive national health insurance plan, long a key Democratic Party objective, led to a bitter split with Massachusetts senator Ted Kennedy, who fought Carter for the 1980 presidential nomination. Carter's agreement to legislation to ensure solvency in the Social Security system resulted in higher payroll taxes on lower- and middle-income Americans.

By contrast, corporations and wealthy individuals gained from new legislation, such as a sharp cut in the capital gains tax. When the Chrysler Corporation approached bankruptcy, Congress provided $1.5 billion in loan guarantees to bail out the auto giant. Congress also acted on Carter's proposals to deregulate airlines in 1978 and the banking, trucking, and railroad industries in 1980, beginning a policy turn toward implementing conservatives' insistence on a free market and unfettered private enterprise.

Energy and Environmental Reform.

Complicating the government's battle with stagflation was the nation's enormous energy consumption and dependence on foreign sources for one-third of its energy demands. Consequently, Carter proposed a comprehensive program to conserve energy, and he elevated its importance by establishing the Department of Energy. Beset with competing demands among energy producers and consumers, Congress picked Carter's program apart. The **National Energy Act of 1978** penalized manufacturers of gas-guzzling automobiles and provided other incentives for conservation and development of alternative fuels, such as wind and solar power, but the act fell far short of a long-term, comprehensive program.

National Energy Act of 1978
Legislation that penalized manufacturers of gas-guzzling automobiles and provided additional incentives for energy conservation and development of alternative fuels, such as wind and solar power. The act fell short of the long-term, comprehensive program that President Carter advocated.

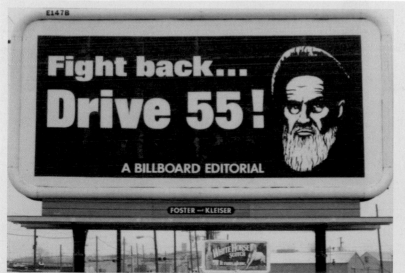

THE FUEL SHORTAGE
This billboard appeared in 1980 while Iran held Americans hostage in Tehran (see page 906). The Iranian revolution brought to power Ayatollah Ruholla Khomeini, pictured on the billboard, and created gasoline shortages and rising gas prices, vexing motorists all over the United States. The ad urges drivers to observe the fuel-saving 55-mile-per-hour speed limit imposed in 1974 during the first oil crisis. Outdoor Advertising Association of America (OAAA) Archives, David M. Rubenstein Rare Book & Manuscript Library, Duke University.

In 1979, a new upheaval in the Middle East, the Iranian revolution, created the most severe energy crisis yet. In midsummer, shortages caused 60 percent of gasoline stations to close down, resulting in long lines and high prices. In response, Congress reduced controls on the oil and gas industry to stimulate American production and imposed a windfall profits tax on producers to redistribute some of the profits they would reap from deregulation.

European nations were no less dependent on foreign oil than the United States, but they more successfully controlled consumption. They levied high taxes on gasoline, encouraging people to use public transportation and manufacturers to produce more energy-efficient cars. In the automobile-dependent United States, however, with inadequate public transit, a sprawling population, and an aversion to taxes, politicians dismissed that approach. By the end of the century, the United States, with 6 percent of the world's population, would consume more than 25 percent of global oil production (Figure 30.1 and Map 30.2).

A vigorous environmental movement opposed nuclear energy as an alternative fuel, warning of radiation leakage, potential accidents, and the hazards of radioactive wastes. In 1976, hundreds of members of the Clamshell Alliance went to jail for attempting to block construction of a nuclear power plant in Seabrook, New Hampshire; other groups sprang up across the country to demand an environment safe from nuclear radiation and waste. The perils of nuclear energy claimed

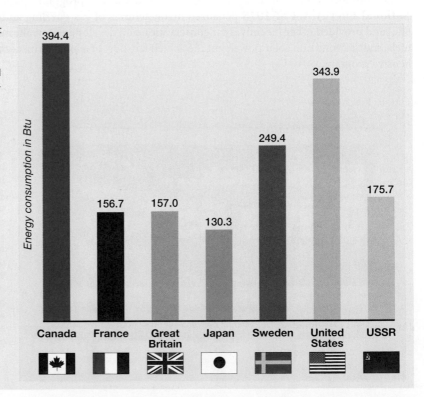

FIGURE 30.1 GLOBAL COMPARISON: ENERGY CONSUMPTION PER CAPITA, 1980

By 1980, the United States consumed more energy than most other industrialized nations, with a per capita rate of consumption that was more than double that of Britain, France, and Japan and nearly twice as high as that of the Soviet Union. A number of factors influence a nation's energy consumption, including standard of living, climate, size of landmass, population distribution, availability and price of energy, and government policies.

Energy consumption in Btu

Canada 394.4
France 156.7
Great Britain 157.0
Japan 130.3
Sweden 249.4
United States 343.9
USSR 175.7

international attention in March 1979, when a meltdown of the reactor core was narrowly averted at the nuclear facility near Harrisburg, Pennsylvania. Popular opposition and the great expense of building nuclear power plants limited development of the industry, which provided 20 percent of the nation's electricity in 2015.

A disaster at Love Canal in Niagara Falls, New York, advanced other environmental goals by underscoring the human costs of unregulated development. Residents suffering high rates of serious illness discovered that their homes sat atop highly toxic waste products from a nearby chemical company. Finally responding to the residents' claims in 1978, the state of New York agreed to help families relocate, and the Carter administration sponsored legislation in 1980 that created the so-called Superfund, $1.6 billion for cleanup of hazardous wastes left by the chemical industry around the country.

Carter also signed bills to improve clean air and water programs; to expand the Arctic National Wildlife Refuge (ANWR) preserve in Alaska; and to control strip mining, which left destructive scars on the land. During the 1979 gasoline crisis,

Map Activity

MAP 30.2 WORLDWIDE OIL RESERVES, 1980

Geologists and engineers can estimate the size of "proved oil reserves," quantities recoverable with existing technology and prices. In 1980, worldwide reserves were estimated at 645 billion barrels. Recovery of reserves depends on many factors, including the location of the oil. Large portions of U.S. reserves, for example, lie under the Gulf of Mexico, where it is expensive to drill and where hurricanes can disrupt operations.

READING THE MAP: Where did the United States rank in 1980 in the possession of oil reserves? About what portion of the total oil reserves were located in the Middle East?

CONNECTIONS: When during the 1970s did the United States experience oil shortages? What caused these shortages?

Oil Reserves	Billions of Barrels
1. Saudi Arabia	166.5
2. Kuwait	68.5
3. Soviet Union	67.0
4. Iran	58.0
5. Mexico	31.3
6. Iraq	31.0
7. United States	29.8
8. U.A.E.	29.4
9. Libya	23.5
10. China	20.0

Carter attempted to balance the development of domestic fuel sources with environmental concerns, winning legislation to conserve energy and to provide incentives for the development of solar energy and environmentally friendly alternative fuels.

Promoting Human Rights Abroad. "We're ashamed of what our government is as we deal with other nations around the world," Jimmy Carter charged, promising to reverse U.S. support of dictators, secret diplomacy, interference in the internal affairs of other countries, and excessive reliance on military solutions. Human rights formed the cornerstone of his approach. The Carter administration applied economic pressure on governments that denied their citizens basic rights, refusing aid or trading privileges to nations such as Chile and El Salvador, as well as to the white minority governments of Rhodesia and South Africa. Yet in other instances, Carter sacrificed human rights ideals to strategic and security considerations, invoking no sanctions against repressive governments in Iran, South Korea, and the Philippines.

Carter's human rights principles faced another test when a popular movement overthrew an oppressive dictatorship in Nicaragua. U.S. officials were uneasy about the leftist Sandinistas who led the rebellion and had ties to Cuba. Once the Sandinistas assumed power in 1979, however, Carter recognized the new government and sent economic aid, signaling that how a government treated its citizens was as important as how anti-Communist and friendly to American interests it was.

Applying moral principles to relations with Panama, Carter sped up negotiations over control of the Panama Canal and in 1977 signed a treaty providing for Panama's takeover of the canal in 2000. Supporters viewed the treaty as restitution for the use of U.S. power to gain control of the territory in 1903. Opponents insisted on retaining the vital waterway. "We bought it, we paid for it, it's ours," claimed Ronald Reagan during the presidential primaries of 1976. It took a massive effort by the administration to get Senate ratification of the **Panama Canal treaty**.

Seeking to promote peace in the Middle East, Carter seized on the courage of Egyptian president Anwar Sadat, the first Arab leader to risk his political career by talking directly with Israeli officials. In 1979, Carter invited Sadat and Israeli prime minister Menachem Begin to Camp David, Maryland, where he applied his tenacious diplomacy for thirteen days. These talks led to the **Camp David accords**, whereby Egypt became the first Arab state to recognize Israel, and Israel agreed to gradual withdrawal from the Sinai Peninsula, which it had seized in the 1967 Six-Day War (Map 30.3). Although Israel maintained control of other Palestinian land (the West Bank and Gaza) and continued to settle Israelis there, Carter had nurtured the first meaningful steps toward peace in the Middle East (see chapter 29).

The Cold War Intensifies. Consistent with his human rights approach, Carter preferred to pursue national security through nonmilitary means and initially sought accommodation with the nation's Cold War enemies. Following up on Nixon's initiatives, in 1979 he opened formal diplomatic relations with the People's Republic of China and signed a second strategic arms reduction treaty with Soviet premier Leonid Brezhnev.

Panama Canal treaty
1977 agreement that returned control of the Panama Canal from the United States to Panama in 2000. To pass the treaty President Carter overcame stiff opposition in the Senate from conservatives who regarded control of the canal as vital to America's interests.

Camp David accords
Agreements between Egypt and Israel reached at the 1979 talks hosted by President Carter at Camp David. In the accords, Egypt became the first Arab state to recognize Israel, and Israel agreed to gradual withdrawal from the Sinai Peninsula.

Yet that same year, Carter decided to pursue a military buildup when the Soviet Union invaded neighboring Afghanistan, whose recently installed Communist government was threatened by Muslim opposition (Map 30.3). Carter imposed economic sanctions on the Soviet Union, barred U.S. participation in the 1980 Summer Olympic Games in Moscow, and obtained legislation requiring all nineteen-year-old men to register for the draft.

Map Activity

MAP 30.3   THE MIDDLE EAST, 1948–1989

Determination to preserve access to the rich oil reserves of the Middle East and commitment to the security of Israel were fundamental — and often conflicting — principles of U.S. foreign policy in that region.

READING THE MAP: Where did the United States become involved diplomatically or militarily in the Middle East between 1948 and 1989?

CONNECTIONS: What role did U.S. foreign policy regarding the Middle East and events in Israel play in provoking the 1973 Arab oil embargo against the United States? What precipitated the taking of U.S. hostages in Iran in 1979?

Claiming that Soviet actions jeopardized oil supplies from the Middle East, the president announced the "Carter Doctrine," threatening the use of any means necessary to prevent an outside force from gaining control of the Persian Gulf. His human rights policy fell by the wayside as the United States stepped up aid to the military dictatorship in Afghanistan's neighbor, Pakistan, and the CIA funneled secret aid through Pakistan to the Afghan rebels. Finally, Carter called for hefty increases in defense spending.

Events in Iran also encouraged this hard-line approach. Generous U.S. arms and aid had not enabled the shah to crush Iranian dissidents who still resented the CIA's role in the overthrow of the Mossadegh government in 1953 (see chapter 27), condemned the shah's brutal attempts to silence opposition, and detested his adoption of Western culture and values. These grievances erupted into a revolution in 1979 that forced out the shah and brought to power Shiite Islamic fundamentalists led by Ayatollah Ruholla Khomeini, whom the shah had exiled in 1964.

Carter's decision to allow the shah into the United States for medical treatment enraged Iranians, who believed that the United States would restore him to power as it had done in 1953. On November 4, 1979, a crowd broke into the U.S. Embassy in Iran's capital, Tehran, and seized sixty-six U.S. diplomats, CIA officers, citizens, and military attachés. Refusing the captors' demands to return the shah to Iran for trial, Carter froze Iranian assets in U.S. banks and placed an embargo on Iranian oil. In April 1980, he sent a small military operation into Iran, but the rescue mission failed.

Iran hostage crisis
Crisis that began in 1979 after the deposed shah of Iran was allowed into the United States following the Iranian revolution. Iranians broke into the U.S. Embassy in Tehran and took sixty-six Americans hostage. The hostage crisis contributed to Carter's reelection defeat.

The disastrous rescue attempt and scenes of blindfolded U.S. citizens paraded before TV cameras fed Americans' feelings of impotence, simmering since the defeat in Vietnam. These frustrations in turn increased support for a more militaristic foreign policy. Opposition to Soviet-American détente, combined with the Soviet invasion of Afghanistan, nullified the thaw in superpower relations that had begun in the 1960s. Iran released a handful of the captives (primarily women and African Americans), but the **Iran hostage crisis** dominated the news during the 1980 presidential campaign and contributed to Carter's defeat. Iran freed the remaining fifty-two hostages the day Carter left office, but relations with the United States remained tense.

> **REVIEW** How did Carter implement his commitment to human rights, and why did human rights give way to other priorities?

Ronald Reagan and the Conservative Ascendancy

The election of Ronald Reagan in 1980 marked the most important turning point in politics since Franklin D. Roosevelt's election in 1932. Reagan's victory established conservatism's dominance in the Republican Party, while Democrats searched for votes by moving toward the right. The United States was not alone in this political shift. Conservatives rose to power in Britain with the election of Prime Minister Margaret Thatcher, and they led governments in Germany, Canada, and Sweden, while social democratic governments elsewhere trimmed their welfare states.

The Reagan administration embraced the values of the New Christian Right, but it left its most important mark on the economy: victory over inflation, deregulation of industry, enormous tax cuts, and a staggering federal budget deficit. Popular culture celebrated financial success, but poverty increased and economic inequality grew. Although the Reagan era did not see a policy revolution comparable to that of the New Deal, it dealt a sharp blow to the liberalism that had informed American politics since the 1930s.

Appealing to the New Right and Beyond.

Sixty-nine-year-old Ronald Reagan was the oldest candidate ever nominated for the presidency. Gaining national attention first as a movie actor, he initially shared the politics of his staunchly Democratic father but moved to the right in the 1940s and 1950s and campaigned for Barry Goldwater in 1964.

Reagan's political career took off when he was elected governor of California in 1966. He ran as a conservative, but in office he displayed flexibility, approving a major tax increase, a strong water pollution bill, and a liberal abortion law. Displaying similar agility in the 1980 presidential campaign, he softened earlier attacks on programs such as Social Security and chose the moderate George H. W. Bush as his running mate.

Some Republicans balked at his nomination and the party platform, which reflected the concerns of the party's right wing. For example, after Phyllis Schlafly persuaded the party to reverse its forty-year support for the Equal Rights Amendment, moderate and liberal Republicans protested outside the convention hall. Moderate John B. Anderson, congressman from Illinois, deserted his party to run as an independent.

Reagan's campaign capitalized on the economic recession and the international challenges symbolized by the American hostages in Iran. Repeatedly, Reagan asked voters, "Are you better off now than you were four years ago?" He promised to "take government off the backs of the people" and to restore Americans' morale and other nations' respect. Reagan won the election, and Republicans took control of the Senate for the first time since the 1950s.

While the economy and the Iran hostage crisis sealed Reagan's victory, he also benefited from the burgeoning grassroots conservative movement that had pushed Goldwater's candidacy in 1964. That movement grew with the politicization of religious conservatives, predominantly Protestants who had traditionally refrained from partisan politics and who came to be known as the **New Christian Right**. During the 1970s, evangelical and fundamentalist Christianity claimed thousands of new adherents. Evangelical ministers such as Pat Robertson preached to huge television audiences, attacking feminism, abortion, and homosexuality. They called for the restoration of old-fashioned "family values." A considerable number of Catholics, such as Phyllis Schlafly, shared the fundamentalists' goal of a return to "Christian values."

Conservatives created political organizations such as the Moral Majority, founded by the Reverend Jerry Falwell in 1979, to fight "left-wing, social welfare bills, . . . pornography, homosexuality, [and] the advocacy of immorality in school textbooks." Dr. James Dobson, a psychologist with a popular Christian talk show,

New Christian Right
Politically active religious conservatives who became particularly vocal in the 1980s. Religious conservatives criticized feminism, opposed abortion and homosexuality, and promoted "family values" and military preparedness.

founded the Family Research Council in 1983 to lobby Congress for measures to curb abortion, divorce, homosexuality, and single motherhood. The instruments of more traditional conservatives, who stressed limited government at home and militant anticommunism abroad, likewise flourished, while Schlafly's newsletter merged the sentiments of the old and new right.

Reagan spoke for the Christian Right on such issues as abortion and school prayer, but he did not push hard for so-called moral policies. Instead, his major achievements fulfilled goals of the older right — strengthening the nation's anti-Communist posture and reducing taxes and government restraints on free enterprise. "In the present crisis," Reagan declared, "government is not the solution to our problem, government is the problem."

Reagan was extraordinarily popular, appealing even to Americans who opposed his policies but warmed to his optimism, confidence, and easygoing humor. Ignoring the darker moments of the American past, he presented a version of history that Americans could feel good about. Declaring that it was "morning in America," he promised an even more glorious future.

Unleashing Free Enterprise.
Reagan's first domestic objective was a massive tax cut. To justify tax cuts in the face of a large budget deficit, Reagan relied on a new theory called **supply-side economics**, which held that cutting taxes would actually increase revenue by enabling businesses to expand, encouraging individuals to work harder because they could keep more of their earnings (especially the wealthy, who enjoyed the greatest tax savings), and increase the production of goods and services — the supply — which in turn would boost demand. Reagan promised that

---

supply-side economics
Economic theory that claims tax cuts for individuals (especially the wealthy) and businesses encourage investment and production (supply) and stimulate consumption (demand) because individuals can keep more of their earnings. Despite promises to the contrary, under President Reagan supply-side economics created a massive federal budget deficit.

RONALD REAGAN ADDRESSES RELIGIOUS CONSERVATIVES

Reagan's victory in 1980 helped to reshape the Republican Party by attracting millions of evangelical Christians. In his 1983 address to the National Association of Evangelicals, Reagan called the Soviet Union an "evil empire" and appealed to religious conservatives with strong words about abortion and prayer in the schools, rejoicing that "America is in the midst of a spiritual awakening and a moral renewal." Ronald Reagan Presidential Library.

the economy would grow so much that the government would recoup the lost taxes, but instead it incurred a galloping deficit.

In the summer of 1981, Congress passed the **Economic Recovery Tax Act**, the largest tax reduction in U.S. history. Rates were cut from 14 percent to 11 percent for the lowest-income individuals and from 70 percent to 50 percent for the wealthiest, who also benefited from reduced levies on corporations, capital gains, gifts, and inheritances. A second measure, the Tax Reform Act of 1986, cut taxes still further. Although the 1986 law narrowed loopholes used primarily by the wealthy, affluent Americans saved far more on their tax bills than did average taxpayers, and the distribution of wealth tipped further in favor of the rich.

Carter had confined deregulation to particular industries, such as air transportation and banking, while increasing health, safety, and environmental regulations. The Reagan administration, by contrast, pursued across-the-board deregulation. It declined to enforce the Sherman Antitrust Act (see chapter 18), which limited monopolies, against an unprecedented number of business mergers and takeovers. Reagan also loosened regulations protecting employee health and safety, and he weakened labor unions. When members of the Professional Air Traffic Controllers Organization — one of the few unions to support Reagan in 1980 — struck in 1981, the president fired them, destroying the union and intimidating organized labor.

Reagan blamed environmental laws for the nation's sluggish economic growth and targeted them for deregulation. His first secretary of the interior, James Watt, declared, "We will mine more, drill more, cut more timber," and released federal lands to private exploitation. Meanwhile, the head of the Environmental Protection Agency relaxed enforcement of air and water pollution standards. Of environmentalists, Reagan wisecracked, "I don't think they'll be happy until the White House looks like a bird's nest," but their numbers grew in opposition to his policies. Popular support for environmental protection forced several officials to resign and blocked full realization of Reagan's deregulatory goals.

Deregulation of the banking industry, begun under Carter with bipartisan support, created a crisis in the savings and loan (S&L) industry. Some of the newly deregulated S&L institutions extended enormous loans to real estate developers and invested in other high-yield but risky ventures. The lenders reaped lavish profits, and their depositors enjoyed high interest rates, but when real estate values plunged, hundreds of S&Ls went bankrupt, creating the largest financial scandal in U.S. history thus far. The government bailout of the industry in 1989 cost American taxpayers more than $100 billion.

The S&L crisis deepened the federal deficit. Reagan cut funds for food stamps, job training, student aid, and other social welfare programs, and hundreds of thousands of people lost benefits. Yet increases in defense spending far exceeded the budget cuts and, along with the tax cuts, caused the deficit to soar. The nation's debt tripled to $2.3 trillion, consuming one-seventh of all federal expenditures. Despite Reagan's antigovernment rhetoric, the number of federal employees increased from 2.9 million to 3.1 million during his presidency.

It took the severest recession since the 1930s to squeeze inflation out of the U.S. economy. Unemployment approached 11 percent late in 1982, and record numbers of banks and businesses closed. The threat of unemployment further undermined

Economic Recovery Tax Act
Legislation passed by Congress in 1981 that authorized the largest reduction in taxes in the nation's history. The tax cuts benefited affluent Americans disproportionately and widened the distribution of American wealth in favor of the rich.

organized labor, forcing unions to make concessions that management insisted were necessary for industry's survival. In 1983, the economy recovered and entered a period of unprecedented growth.

That economic upswing and Reagan's own popularity posed a formidable challenge to the Democrats in the 1984 election. They nominated Carter's vice president, Walter F. Mondale, to head the ticket, but even his precedent-breaking choice of a woman as his running mate — New York representative Geraldine A. Ferraro — did not save the Democrats from a humiliating defeat. Reagan charged his opponents with concentrating on America's failures, while he emphasized success and possibility. Democrats, he claimed, "see an America where every day is April 15th [the deadline for income tax returns] . . . we see an America where every day is the Fourth of July." Reagan was reelected in a landslide victory, winning 59 percent of the popular vote and every state but Mondale's Minnesota.

Winners and Losers in a Flourishing Economy. After the economy took off in 1983, some Americans won great fortunes. Popular culture celebrated making money and displaying wealth. Books by business wizards topped best seller lists, the press described lavish million-dollar parties, and a new television show, *Lifestyles of the Rich and Famous,* drew large audiences. College students listed making money as their primary ambition.

Many of the newly wealthy got rich from moving assets around rather than from producing goods, making money by manipulating debt and restructuring corporations through mergers and takeovers. Notable exceptions included Steven Jobs, who invented the Apple computer in his garage; Bill Gates, who transformed the software industry; and Liz Claiborne, who created a billion-dollar fashion enterprise. Most financial wizards operated within the law, but greed sometimes led to criminal convictions.

Older industries faced increasing international pressures, as German and Japanese corporations overtook U.S. manufacturing in steel, automobiles, and electronics. International competition forced the collapse of some companies, while others moved factories and jobs abroad to be closer to foreign markets or to benefit from the low wages in countries such as Mexico and Korea. Service industries expanded and created new jobs at home, but at substantially lower wages. The number of full-time workers earning wages below the poverty level ($12,195 for a family of four in 1990) rose from 12 percent to 18 percent of all workers in the 1980s.

The weakening of organized labor combined with the decline in manufacturing to erode the position of blue-collar workers. Chicago steelworker Ike Mazo, who contemplated the $6-an-hour jobs available to him, fumed, "It's an attack on the living standards of workers." Increasingly, a second income was needed to stave off economic decline. By 1990, nearly 60 percent of married women with young children worked outside the home. Yet even with two incomes, families struggled. Speaking of her children, Mazo's wife confessed, "I worry about their future every day. Will we be able to put them through college?" The average $10,000 gap between men's and women's annual earnings made things even harder for the nearly 20 percent of families headed by women.

In keeping with conservative philosophy, Reagan adhered to trickle-down economics, insisting that the benefits of a booming economy would trickle down to everyone. Average personal income did rise during his tenure, but the trend toward greater economic inequality that had begun in the 1970s intensified in the 1980s, encouraged in part by his tax policies. During Reagan's presidency, the percentage of Americans living in poverty increased from 11.7 to 13.5, the highest poverty rate in the industrialized world. Social Security and Medicare helped to stave off destitution among the elderly. Less fortunate were other groups that the economic boom had bypassed: racial minorities, female-headed families, and children. One child in five lived in poverty.

REVIEW What conservative goals were realized in the Reagan administration?

Continuing Struggles over Rights

The rise of conservatism put liberal social movements on the defensive, as the government abandoned the commitment to equal opportunity undertaken in the 1960s and the president's federal court appointments reflected that shift. Feminists and minority groups fought to keep protections they had recently won, and the newer gay and lesbian rights movement made some gains.

Battles in the Courts and Congress. Ronald Reagan agreed with conservatives that the nation had moved too far in guaranteeing rights to minority groups. Crying "reverse discrimination," conservatives maintained that affirmative action unfairly hurt whites, ignoring statistics showing that minorities and white women still lagged far behind white men in opportunities and income. Black labor leader Cleveland Robinson pointed to the difficulty of achieving equal opportunity in a faltering economy, calling full employment "the basic ingredient of successful affirmative action." Without it, "you will have both blacks and whites fighting for the same job." Intense mobilization by civil rights groups, educational leaders, labor, and even corporate America prevented the administration from abandoning affirmative action, and the Supreme Court upheld important antidiscrimination policies. Moreover, against Reagan's wishes, Congress extended the Voting Rights Act with veto-proof majorities. The administration did, however, limit civil rights enforcement by appointing conservatives to the Justice Department, the Civil Rights Commission, and other agencies as well as by slashing their budgets.

Congress stepped in to defend antidiscrimination programs after the Justice Department, in the case of *Grove City v. Bell* (1984), persuaded the Supreme Court to severely weaken Title IX of the Education Amendments Act of 1972, a key law promoting equal opportunity in education. In 1988, Congress passed the Civil Rights Restoration Act over Reagan's veto, reversing the administration's victory in *Grove City* and banning government funding of any organization that practiced discrimination on the basis of race, color, national origin, sex, disability, or age.

The *Grove City* decision reflected a rightward movement in the federal judiciary, on which liberals had counted as a powerful ally. With the opportunity to

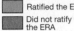

■ Ratified the ERA	■ Ratified and then voted to rescind ratification
■ Did not ratify the ERA	

THE FIGHT FOR THE EQUAL
RIGHTS AMENDMENT

**Equal Rights
Amendment (ERA)**

Constitutional amendment
passed by Congress in 1972
that would require equal
treatment of men and
women under federal and
state law. Facing fierce
opposition from the New
Right and the Republican
Party, the ERA was defeated
as time ran out for state
ratification in 1982.

appoint half of the 761 federal court judges and three new Supreme Court justices, President Reagan encouraged the rightward trend by carefully selecting conservative candidates. The full impact of these appointments became clear after Reagan left office, as the Court allowed states to impose restrictions that weakened access to abortion for poor and rural women, reduced protections against employment discrimination, and whittled down legal safeguards against the death penalty.

Feminism on the Defensive. A signal achievement of the New Right was capturing the Republican Party's position on women's rights. For the first time in its history, the party took an explicitly antifeminist tone, opposing both the **Equal Rights Amendment (ERA)** and abortion rights, key goals of women's rights activists. When the time limit for ratification of the ERA ran out in 1982, Phyllis Schlafly and her followers celebrated the defeat of a central feminist objective. (See "Making Historical Arguments," page 914.)

Cast on the defensive, feminists focused more on women's economic and family problems, where they found some common ground with the Reagan administration. The Child Support Enforcement Amendments Act helped single and divorced mothers collect court-ordered child support payments from absent fathers. The Retirement Equity Act of 1984 benefited divorced and older women by strengthening their claims to their husbands' pensions and enabling women to qualify more easily for private retirement pensions.

Reagan's advisers had their own concerns about women, specifically about the gender gap in voting — women's tendency to support liberal and Democratic candidates in larger numbers than men did. Reagan appointed three women to cabinet posts and, in 1981, selected the first woman, Sandra Day O'Connor, a moderate conservative, for the Supreme Court, despite the Christian Right's objection to her support of abortion. But these actions accompanied a general decline in the number of women and minorities in high-level government positions. And with higher poverty rates than men, women suffered most from Reagan's cuts in social programs.

Although Supreme Court decisions allowed increasing restrictions on women's ability to obtain abortions, feminists fought successfully to retain the basic principles of *Roe v. Wade*. Moreover, they won a key decision from the Supreme Court ruling that sexual harassment in the workplace constituted sex discrimination. Feminists also made some gains at the state level on such issues as pay equity, rape, and domestic violence.

The Gay and Lesbian Rights Movement. In contrast to feminism and other social movements, gay and lesbian rights activism grew during the 1980s, galvanized in part by the discovery in 1981 of a devastating disease, acquired immune deficiency syndrome (AIDS). Because initially the disease disproportionately affected male homosexuals in the United States, activists mobilized to promote public funding for AIDS education, prevention, and treatment.

The gay and lesbian rights movement encouraged closeted homosexuals to "come out," and their visibility increased awareness, if not always acceptance, of homosexuality among the larger population. Beginning with the election of Elaine

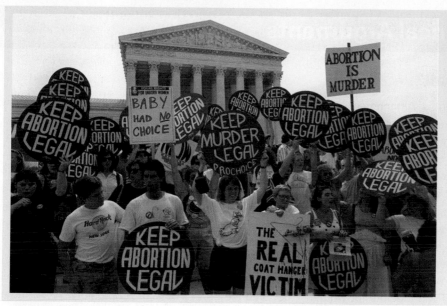

THE ABORTION DEBATE

After the *Roe v. Wade* decision in 1973, several states enacted restrictions on abortion. In 1989, the Supreme Court upheld a Missouri law prohibiting public employees from performing abortions except to save a woman's life. It also banned abortions in public buildings and required physicians to perform viability tests on the fetus after twenty weeks. Here, activists on both sides rally before the Supreme Court. AP Photo/ Ron Edmonds.

Noble to the Massachusetts legislature in 1974, several openly gay politicians won offices ranging from mayor to member of Congress, and the Democrats began to include gay rights in their party platforms. Activists organized gay rights marches throughout the country, turning out half a million people in New York City in 1987.

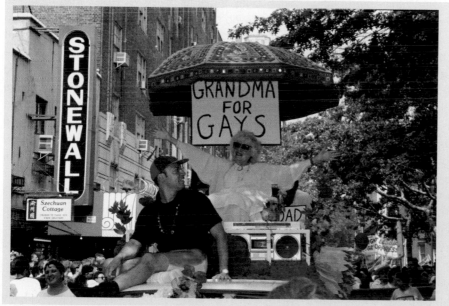

GAY RIGHTS PARADE

Annual gay rights parades in the United States began in June 1970, the first anniversary of Stonewall (see chapter 28). More than 150,000 people marched in this parade in New York City in 1989, including many friends and relatives of homosexuals. Here, E. G. Smith wears the "rainbow" colors of the movement, while his grandmother, Norma Isaacs, demonstrates her support. AP Photo/ Sergio Florez.

Making Historical Arguments

Why Did the ERA Fail?

The proposed Equal Rights Amendment to the U.S. Constitution guaranteed that "equality of rights under the law shall not be denied or abridged by the United States or by any State on account of sex." Two more short sections gave Congress enforcement powers and provided that the ERA would take effect two years after ratification. By the 1970s, it had become the symbol of the women's movement, and the controversy it sparked revealed profound differences in beliefs and values among Americans.

The National Woman's Party, a militant suffrage organization that had helped win the vote for women in 1920, first proposed an equal rights amendment to the Constitution in 1923. It won little support, however, before the resurgence of feminism in the late 1960s, when the National Organization for Women and other women's groups made the ERA a key objective.

Both houses of Congress passed the ERA in March 1972 by overwhelming margins, 354–23 in the House and 84–8 in the Senate. Within three hours, Hawaii; rushed to become the first state to ratify, and twenty-three states quickly followed. Public opinion heavily favored ratification, peaking at 74 percent in favor in 1974 and never falling below 52 percent, while opposition never topped 31 percent. Yet even after Congress extended the ratification period until 1982, the ERA fell three short of the three-fourths of the states required by the Constitution (see The Fight for the Equal Rights Amendment spot map on page 912). Why did a measure with so much congressional and popular support fail?

The ERA encountered well-organized and passionate opposition linked to the growing conservative forces in the 1970s. Conservatives' opposition to the ERA reflected in part their distaste for big government, but even more it signaled the Christian Right's determination to preserve traditional gender roles and "family values." What feminists saw as a simple measure to ensure equal rights for all citizens, ERA opponents saw as a threat to women's God-given and natural right to be protected and supported by men. They raised fears by suggesting extravagant ways in which courts might interpret the amendment. Phyllis Schlafly claimed that the ERA would put abortion rights and gay rights into the Constitution, deprive women of alimony and child support, and send them into combat.

Anti-ERA arguments drew on conservative Christian beliefs. Evangelical minister and politician Jerry Falwell declared the ERA "a definite violation of holy Scripture [and its] mandate that 'the husband is the head of the wife.'" Anti-ERA rhetoric also appealed to some women's understanding of their own self-interest. Many ERA opponents were full-time housewives who had no stake in equal treatment in the marketplace and who feared that the amendment would eliminate the duty of men to support their families.

Schlafly and other conservatives skillfully mobilized women who saw their traditional roles threatened. In October 1972, she established a national movement called STOP (Stop Taking Our Privileges) ERA, whose members deluged legislators with letters and lobbied them personally in state capitols. In Illinois, they gave lawmakers apple pies with notes that read, "My heart and my hand went into this dough / For the sake of the family please vote 'no.'" Opponents also brought baby girls to the legislature wearing signs that pleaded, "Please don't draft me."

ERA opponents had an easier task than supporters because the framers of the Constitution had stacked the odds against revision. All opponents had to do was convince a minority of legislators in a minority of states to preserve the status quo. In addition, unlike their suffragist predecessors, pro-ERA forces had concentrated on winning Congress and were not prepared for the state campaigns.

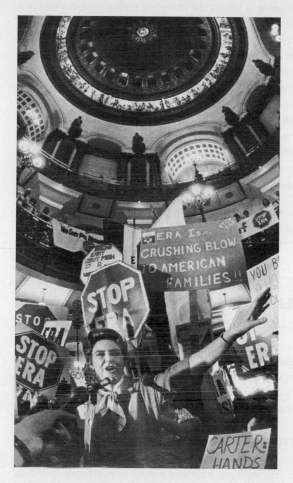

PHYLLIS SCHLAFLY DERAILS THE ERA IN ILLINOIS
Illinois was one of the most hotly contested states in the battle over ratification of the ERA. Here Schlafly rallies ERA opponents in the state capitol in 1975. Schlafly's STOP ERA movement succeeded in Illinois, her home state and the only northern state that failed to ratify. Despite political activities that required extensive traveling and speaking, Schlafly insisted on calling herself a housewife. Bettmann/Corbis.

tion, and other areas, and the Supreme Court had struck down several discriminatory laws, thus making it harder for ERA advocates to demonstrate the urgency of constitutional revision.

The ERA failed because a handful of men in a handful of state legislatures voted against it. The shift of only a few votes in states such as Illinois and North Carolina would have meant ratification. Schlafly's forces played a key role in the defeat because men could vote no and take cover behind the many women who opposed it. And those women proved willing to commit time, energy, and money to block ratification because they were convinced that the ERA threatened their very way of life.

Feminists did not leave the ERA battle empty-handed, however. Thousands of women were mobilized on both sides of the issue, participating in the public arena for the first time. Fourteen states passed their own equal rights amendments after 1970. And feminists continued to fight legislative and judicial battles for the expansion of women's rights into the twenty-first century.

The very gains that feminists made in the 1960s and 1970s also worked against ratification. Congress had banned sex discrimination in employment, educa-

QUESTIONS FOR ANALYSIS

Summarize the Argument   What different values were expressed by opponents and supporters of the ERA? What did both sides gain from the campaigns?

Analyze the Evidence   What structural features of the U.S. Constitution made ratification difficult for ERA advocates? What other specific obstacles prevented ERA's passage?

Consider the Context   Why were woman suffrage supporters more successful than ERA advocates in gaining a constitutional amendment?

Popular attitudes about homosexuality moved toward greater tolerance but remained complex, leading to uneven changes in policies. Dozens of cities banned job discrimination against homosexuals, and beginning with Wisconsin in 1982, some states made sexual orientation a protected category under civil rights laws. Local governments and large corporations began to offer health insurance and other benefits to same-sex domestic partners.

Yet a strong countermovement challenged the drive for gay rights. The Christian Right targeted gays and lesbians as symbols of national immorality, and when the AIDS epidemic appeared, some fundamentalists believed that it represented "the wrath of God upon homosexuals." Conservatives succeeded in overturning some homosexual rights measures, which already lagged far behind protections for women and minorities. Many states removed antisodomy laws from the books, but in 1986 the Supreme Court upheld the constitutionality of such laws. Until the Court reversed that opinion in 2003, more than a dozen states retained statutes that left homosexuals vulnerable to criminal charges for private consensual behavior.

> **REVIEW** What gains and setbacks did minorities, feminists, and gays and lesbians experience during the Reagan years?

Ronald Reagan Confronts an "Evil Empire"

Reagan accelerated Carter's arms buildup and harshly censured the Soviet Union, calling it "an evil empire." Yet despite the new aggressiveness — or, as some argued, because of it — Reagan presided over the most impressive thaw in superpower conflict since the Cold War had begun. On the periphery of the Cold War, Reagan practiced militant anticommunism, assisting anti-leftist movements in Asia, Africa, and Central America and dispatching troops to the Middle East and the Caribbean.

Militarization and Interventions Abroad. Reagan expanded the military with new bombers and missiles, an enhanced nuclear force in Europe, a larger navy, and a rapid-deployment force. Throughout Reagan's presidency, defense spending averaged $216 billion a year, up from $158 billion in the Carter years and higher even than in the Vietnam era.

Reagan justified the military buildup as a means to negotiate with the Soviets from a position of strength, but he provoked an outburst of pleas to halt the arms race. In 1982, 700,000 people marched in New York City, demanding a freeze on additional nuclear weapons. That same year the National Conference of Catholic Bishops issued a strong call for nuclear disarmament. Hundreds of thousands demonstrated across Europe, stimulated by fears of new U.S. missiles scheduled for deployment there in 1983.

The U.S. military buildup was powerless before the growing threat of terrorism by nonstate organizations seeking to gain political objectives by attacking civilian populations. Terrorism had a long history throughout the world, but in the 1970s and 1980s Americans saw it escalate among groups hostile to Israel and Western policies. In 1972, for example, after the Israeli occupation of the West Bank, Palestinian terrorists murdered eleven Israeli athletes at the Munich Olympics. The terrorist organization Hezbollah, composed of Shiite Muslims and backed by Iran and Syria, arose in Lebanon in 1982 after Israeli forces invaded that country to stop the Palestine Liberation Organization from using sanctuaries in Lebanon to launch attacks on Israel.

Reagan's effort to stabilize Lebanon by sending 2,000 Marines to join an international peacekeeping mission failed. In April 1983, a suicide attack on the U.S. Embassy in Beirut killed 63 people, and in October a Hezbollah fighter drove a bomb-filled truck into a U.S. barracks there, killing 241 Marines. The attack prompted the withdrawal of U.S. troops, signaling that political violence could affect U.S. policy. Lebanon remained in chaos, while incidents of murder, kidnapping, and hijacking by various Middle Eastern extremist groups continued.

Following a Cold War pattern begun under Dwight D. Eisenhower, the Reagan administration sought to contain leftist movements across the globe. In October 1983, 5,000 U.S. troops invaded Grenada, a small Caribbean nation where Marxists had staged a successful coup. In Asia, the United States covertly aided the Afghan rebels' war against Afghanistan's Soviet-backed government. In the African nation of Angola, the United States armed rebel forces against the government supported by the Soviet Union and Cuba. Reagan also sided with the South African government, which was brutally suppressing black protest against apartheid, forcing Congress to override his veto to impose economic sanctions against South Africa.

Administration officials were most fearful of left-wing movements in Central America, which Reagan claimed could "destabilize the entire region from the Panama Canal to Mexico." When a leftist uprising occurred in El Salvador in 1981, the United States sent money and military advisers to prop up the authoritarian government. In neighboring Nicaragua, the administration secretly aided the Contras, an armed coalition seeking to unseat the left-wing Sandinistas, who had toppled a long-standing dictatorship.

The Iran-Contra Scandal.
Fearing being drawn into another Vietnam, many Americans opposed aligning the United States with reactionary forces not supported by the majority of Nicaraguans. Congress repeatedly instructed the president to stop aiding the Contras, but the administration continued to secretly provide them with weapons and training. It also helped wreck the Nicaraguan economy. With support for his government undermined, Nicaragua's president, Daniel Ortega, agreed to a political settlement, and when he was defeated by a coalition of all the opposition groups, he stepped aside.

Secret aid to the Contras was part of a larger project that came to be known as the **Iran-Contra scandal**. It began in 1985 when officials of the National Security Council and the CIA covertly arranged to sell arms to Iran, then in the midst of an eight-year war with neighboring Iraq, even while the United States openly supplied Iraq with funds and weapons. The purpose was to get Iran to pressure Hezbollah to release American hostages being held in Lebanon. Profits from the arms sales were then channeled through Swiss bank accounts to aid the Nicaraguan Contras. Over the objections of his secretaries of state and defense, Reagan approved the arms sales

EL SALVADOR AND NICARAGUA

Iran-Contra scandal
Reagan administration scandal that involved the sale of arms to Iran in exchange for its efforts to secure the release of hostages held in Lebanon and the redirection of the proceeds of those sales to the Nicaraguan Contras.

to Iran, but the three subsequently denied knowing that the proceeds were diverted to the Contras.

When news of the affair surfaced in November 1986, the Reagan administration faced serious charges. The president's aides had defied Congress's express ban on military aid to the Contras. Investigations by an independent prosecutor led to a trial in which seven individuals pleaded guilty or were convicted of lying to Congress and destroying evidence. One felony conviction was later overturned on a technicality, and President George H. W. Bush pardoned the other six officials in December 1992. The independent prosecutor's final report found no evidence that Reagan had broken the law, but it concluded that he had known about the diversion of funds to the Contras and had "knowingly participated or at least acquiesced" in covering up the scandal.

A Thaw in Soviet-American Relations. A momentous reduction in Cold War tensions soon overshadowed the Iran-Contra scandal. The new Soviet-American accord depended both on Reagan's flexibility and profound desire to end the possibility of nuclear war and on an innovative Soviet head of state who recognized that his country's domestic problems demanded an easing of Cold War antagonism. Mikhail Gorbachev assumed power in 1985 determined to revitalize an economy incapable of satisfying basic consumer needs. Hoping to stimulate production and streamline distribution of consumer goods, Gorbachev lifted some economic regulations and proclaimed a new era of *glasnost* (greater freedom of expression), eventually allowing contested elections and challenges to Communist rule.

Concerns about immense defense budgets moved both Reagan and Gorbachev to the negotiating table. Enormous military expenditures stood between the Soviet

THE FIRESIDE SUMMIT
This photograph captures the warmth that developed between President Ronald Reagan and Soviet leader Mikhail Gorbachev, shown here at their first meeting at Geneva in November 1985. Although the meeting did not produce any key agreements, the two men began to appreciate each other's concerns and to build trust, launching a relationship that would lead to nuclear arms reductions and the end of the Cold War. Ronald Reagan Presidential Library.

premier and his goal of economic revival. With growing popular support for arms reductions, Reagan made disarmament a major goal in his last years in office and readily responded when Gorbachev took the initiative. A positive personal chemistry developed between them, and the two leaders met four times between 1985 and 1988. Reagan had to fend off criticism from the hard anti-Communist right, but by December 1987 the superpowers had completed an **intermediate-range nuclear forces (INF) agreement,** marking a major turning point in U.S.-Soviet relations. The treaty eliminated all short- and medium-range missiles from Europe and provided for on-site inspection for the first time. This was also the first time that either nation had agreed to eliminate weapons already in place.

In 1988, Gorbachev further reduced tensions by announcing a gradual withdrawal from Afghanistan, which had become the Soviet equivalent of America's Vietnam. In addition, the Soviet Union, the United States, and Cuba agreed on a political settlement of the civil war in Angola. In the Middle East, both superpowers supported a cease-fire and peace talks in the eight-year war between Iran and Iraq. Within three years, the Cold War that had defined the world for nearly half a century would be history.

> **intermediate-range nuclear forces (INF) agreement**
> Nuclear disarmament agreement reached between the United States and the Soviet Union in 1987, signifying a major thaw in the Cold War. The treaty eliminated all short- and medium-range missiles from Europe and provided for on-site inspection for the first time.

REVIEW How did anticommunism shape Reagan's foreign policy?

Conclusion: Reversing the Course of Government

"Ours was the first revolution in the history of mankind that truly reversed the course of government," boasted Ronald Reagan in his farewell address in 1989. The word *revolution* exaggerated the change, but his administration did mark the slowdown or reversal of expanding federal budgets for domestic programs and regulations that had taken off in the 1930s. Although he did not deliver on the social or moral issues dear to the heart of the New Right, Reagan represented the "choice not an echo" that Phyllis Schlafly had called for in 1964, using his skills as "the Great Communicator" to cultivate antigovernment sentiment and undermine the liberal assumptions of the New Deal.

Antigovernment sentiment grew along with the backlash against the reforms and cultural changes of the 1960s and the conduct of the Vietnam War. Watergate and other lawbreaking by Nixon administration officials further disillusioned Americans. Presidents Ford and Carter restored morality to the White House, but neither could solve the gravest economic problems since the Great Depression — slow economic growth, stagflation, and an increasing trade deficit. Even the Democrat Carter gave higher priority to fiscal austerity than to social reform, stressed the limitations of what government could or should do, and began the government's retreat from regulation of key industries.

A new conservative movement helped Reagan win the presidency and flourished during his administration. Reagan's tax cuts, combined with hefty increases in defense spending, created a federal deficit crisis that justified cuts in social welfare spending, made new federal initiatives unthinkable, and burdened the country for years to come. These policies also contributed to a widening income gap between the rich and poor, weighing especially heavily on minorities, female-headed families, and children. Many Americans continued to support specific federal programs — especially those, such as Social Security and Medicare, that reached beyond the poor — but public sentiment about the government in general had taken a U-turn from the Roosevelt era. Instead of seeing the government as a helpful and problem-solving institution, many believed that it was ineffective at solving national problems and often made things worse. As Reagan appointed new justices, the Supreme Court retreated from liberalism, curbing the government's authority to protect individual rights and regulate the economy.

With the economic recovery that set in after 1982 and his optimistic rhetoric, Reagan lifted the confidence of Americans about their nation and its promise — confidence that had eroded with the economic and foreign policy blows of the 1970s. Beginning his presidency with harsh rhetoric against the Soviet Union and a huge military buildup, he left office having helped move the two superpowers to the highest level of cooperation since the Cold War began. Although that accord was not welcomed by strong anti-Communist conservatives like Phyllis Schlafly, it signaled developments that would transform American-Soviet relations — and the world — in the next decade.

Chapter Review

KEY TERMS

Watergate (p. 897)

National Energy Act of 1978 (p. 901)

Panama Canal treaty (p. 904)

Camp David accords (p. 904)

Iran hostage crisis (p. 906)

New Christian Right (p. 907)

supply-side economics (p. 908)

Economic Recovery Tax Act (p. 909)

Equal Rights Amendment (ERA) (p. 912)

Iran-Contra scandal (p. 917)

intermediate-range nuclear forces (INF) agreement (p. 919)

REVIEW QUESTIONS

❶ How did Nixon's policies reflect the increasing influence of conservatives on the Republican Party? (pp. 892–99)

❷ How did Carter implement his commitment to human rights, and why did human rights give way to other priorities? (pp. 899–906)

❸ What conservative goals were realized in the Reagan administration? (pp. 906–11)

❹ What gains and setbacks did minorities, feminists, and gays and lesbians experience during the Reagan years? (pp. 911–16)

❺ How did anticommunism shape Reagan's foreign policy? (pp. 916–19)

MAKING CONNECTIONS

❶ What was Watergate's legacy for American politics in the following decade? In your answer, explain what led to Nixon's resignation.

❷ How did the Republican and Democratic parties change in the 1970s and 1980s? Discuss how those changes shaped American politics.

❸ How did Americans' memory of the Vietnam War affect foreign policy in the 1970s and 1980s?

❹ Why was grassroots conservatism particularly strong in the Sun Belt in the 1970s and 1980s?

LINKING TO THE PAST

❶ How were the conservatives of the 1980s similar to and different from the conservatives who opposed the New Deal in the 1930s? (See chapter 24.)

❷ Presidents Jimmy Carter and Woodrow Wilson both claimed human rights as a central principle of their foreign policies. Which one was more successful in advancing human rights? Explain your answer. (See chapter 22.)

31

The Promises and Challenges of Globalization, Since 1989

CONTENT LEARNING OBJECTIVES

After reading and studying this chapter, you should be able to:

- Explain the limited domestic initiatives of George H. W. Bush's presidency, and explain U.S. interventions in Central America and the Persian Gulf.
- Explain the Clinton administration's search for a middle ground in domestic policy, and outline the factors that guided the administration's military interventions around the world.
- Describe the debates over globalization and its effects on the United States.
- Explain George W. Bush's key domestic initiatives and his foreign policy of preemption and unilateralism, including the invasion of Iraq in 2003.
- Describe the historic 2008 presidential election and President Obama's response to domestic and foreign challenges.

In his Moscow hotel room in April 1988, Ronald Reagan's national security adviser, Colin L. Powell, contemplated Soviet premier Mikhail Gorbachev's reforms that would dramatically alter the Soviet Union's government and economy. Powell recalled, "I realized that one phase of my life had ended, and another was about to begin. Up until now, as a soldier, my mission had been to confront, contain, and, if necessary, combat communism. Now I had to think about a world without a Cold War."

Colin Powell was born in Harlem in 1937, the son of Jamaican immigrants who worked in a garment factory. At the City College of New York, he joined

CONTAINER BOX

Using truck-size boxes to move goods without loading and unloading individual items became the norm by the 1980s. The container box's efficiency stimulated global industrial development and increased Americans' access to cheaper goods. Oleksiy Mark/Shutterstock.

the army's Reserve Officers Training Corps (ROTC) program and, on graduation in 1958, began a lifelong career in military and public service, rising to the highest rank of four-star general. He stayed in the army because "I loved what I was doing," but he also knew that "for a black, no other avenue in American society offered so much opportunity." Powell's service in Vietnam taught him that "you do not squander courage and lives without clear purpose, without the country's backing, and without full commitment." In his subsequent positions as national security adviser to Ronald Reagan, chairman of the Joint Chiefs of Staff under George H. W. Bush and William Jefferson (Bill) Clinton, and secretary of state under George W. Bush, Powell endeavored to keep his country out of "halfhearted warfare for half-baked reasons that the American people could not understand or support."

Powell's sense that Gorbachev's reforms would transform the Cold War became a reality more quickly than anyone anticipated. Eastern Europe threw off communism in 1989, and the Soviet Union disintegrated in 1991. Throughout the 1990s, as the lone superpower, the United States deployed military and diplomatic power during episodes of instability in Latin America, the Middle East, Eastern Europe, and Asia, almost always in concert with other major nations. In 1991, the United States led a United Nations–authorized force of twenty-eight nations to repel Iraq's invasion of Kuwait.

In the 1990s, Powell remarked that "neither of the two major parties fits me comfortably." Many Americans seemed to agree: From 1988 to 2016, they elected two Republicans — George H. W. Bush and George W. Bush — and two Democrats — Bill Clinton and Barack Obama — as president, and each faced Congresses where the opposing party controlled at least one house. Bipartisan cooperation produced a few initiatives, including disability rights legislation, welfare reform, drug benefits under Medicare, and expanded federal involvement in public education. But the most far-reaching law — expansion and reform of health care — passed without one Republican vote. In the face of congressional stalemate, Obama used executive powers to achieve modest reforms in the areas of immigration, environmental protection, minimum wage, and gay and transgender rights.

All four presidents supported globalization. As capital, products, information, and people crossed national boundaries in greater

CHRONOLOGY

1988	George H. W. Bush elected president.
1989	Communism collapses in Eastern Europe.
1990	Americans with Disabilities Act passes.
1991	Persian Gulf War fought.
1992	William Jefferson "Bill" Clinton elected president.
1993	Israel and PLO sign peace accords. North American Free Trade Agreement signed.
1994	World Trade Organization established.
1995	Federal building in Oklahoma City bombed.
1996	Temporary Assistance for Needy Families program established. President Clinton reelected.
1998–2000	United States bombs Iraq.
1999	Senate trial rejects impeachment of Clinton.
2000	George W. Bush elected president.
2001	Terrorists attack World Trade Center and Pentagon. U.S.-led coalition drives Taliban government out of Afghanistan. USA Patriot Act passes. Federal taxes cut by $1.35 trillion.
2002	No Child Left Behind Act passes.
2003	United States attacks Iraq.
2004	President Bush reelected.
2005	Hurricane Katrina devastates Gulf states.
2008	Financial crisis leads to Great Recession. Barack Obama elected president.
2009	American Recovery and Reinvestment Act passes.
2010	Patient Protection and Affordable Care Act passes. Wall Street Reform and Consumer Protection Act passes. United States ends combat operations in Iraq, increases troops in Afghanistan. Citizens United v. FEC guts regulations on campaign financing.

2011   Osama bin Laden
        killed.
        Arab Spring
        uprisings begin.

2012   President Obama
        reelected.

2015   U.S. Supreme Court
        declares that
        same-sex couples
        have constitutional
        right to marriage.
        Iran nuclear deal
        signed.
        United States restores
        diplomatic relations
        with Cuba.

numbers and at greater speed, a surge of immigration rivaled the stream that had brought Powell's parents to the United States. Powell shared the worldwide shock when in September 2001 terrorist attacks in New York City and Washington, D.C., exposed American vulnerability to horrifying threats. The United States sent soldiers into Afghanistan to overthrow the government that had harbored the attackers. The administration's response to terrorism overwhelmed Secretary of State Powell's commitments to internationalism, multilateralism, and military restraint when, in 2003, George W. Bush began a second war against Iraq. The unpopularity of that war and a severe financial crisis helped the Democrats regain power and elect Barack Obama as the first African American president in 2008. Obama pursued a more multilateral approach and improved the U.S. image abroad. Nonetheless, although the Iraq War ended, the Middle East grew more unstable and terrorism remained a threat around the world.

Domestic Stalemate and Global Upheaval: The Presidency of George H. W. Bush

Vice President George H. W. Bush announced his bid for the presidency in 1988, declaring, "We don't need radical new directions." As president, Bush proposed few domestic initiatives, but he signed key environmental and disability rights legislation. More dramatic changes swept through the world, shattering the free-world-versus-communism framework of the Cold War years. Most Americans approved of Bush's handling of the disintegration of the Soviet Union and its hold over Eastern Europe and of his response to Iraq's invasion of Kuwait. But voters' concern over a sluggish economy limited him to one term as president.

Gridlock in Government. The son of a wealthy U.S. senator from New England, George Herbert Walker Bush fought in World War II, served in Congress, and headed the Central Intelligence Agency under Richard Nixon. When Ronald Reagan tapped him for second place on the Republican ticket in 1980, Bush tailored his more moderate positions to Reagan's conservative agenda. At the end of Reagan's second term, Republicans rewarded him with the presidential nomination.

In the Democratic primaries in 1988, civil rights leader Reverend Jesse Jackson — whose Rainbow Coalition campaign centered on the needs of minorities, women, the working class, and the poor — won several primaries and seven million votes. But the centrist candidate, Massachusetts governor Michael Dukakis, won the nomination. On election day, Bush won 54 percent of the vote while the Democrats gained seats in Congress.

Promising "a kinder, gentler nation," President Bush was more inclined than Reagan to approve government activity in the private sphere. For example, Bush approved the **Clean Air Act of 1990**, the strongest, most comprehensive environmental law in history. Some forty million Americans benefited when Bush signed another regulatory measure in 1990, the **Americans with Disabilities Act (ADA),** banning discrimination against people with disabilities and requiring that private businesses and public facilities be accessible to them. As a breeze rippled over the White House lawn at the signing ceremony, disability advocate Cynthia Jones said, "It was kind of like a new breath of air was sweeping across America. . . . People knew they had rights. That was wonderful."

Yet Bush also needed to satisfy party conservatives to whom he had pledged "Read my lips: No new taxes." Bush vetoed thirty-six bills, including those extending unemployment benefits, raising taxes, and mandating family and medical leave for workers. Press reports increasingly used the words *stalemate* and *divided government*.

Continuing a trend begun during the Reagan years, some states compensated for this paralysis with their own innovations. State legislatures enacted laws to establish parental leave policies, improve food labeling, and protect the environment. Dozens of cities passed ordinances requiring businesses receiving tax abatements or other benefits to pay wages well above the federal minimum. In 1999, California passed a much tougher gun control bill than reformers had been able to get through Congress.

The huge federal budget deficit inherited from Reagan impelled Bush in 1990 to abandon his "no new taxes" pledge, outraging conservatives. The new law modestly raised taxes on high-income Americans and increased levies on gasoline, cigarettes, alcohol, and luxury items, while leaving intact most of Reagan's massive tax cuts. Neither the new revenues nor controls on spending curbed the deficit, however, which was boosted by rising costs for Social Security, Medicare, Medicaid, and natural disaster relief.

Like Reagan, Bush created a more conservative Supreme Court. His first nominee was a moderate, but in 1991, when the only African American on the Court, Thurgood Marshall, retired, Bush nominated Clarence Thomas, a conservative black appeals court judge who had opposed affirmative action when he headed the Equal Employment Opportunity Commission (EEOC) under Reagan. Charging that Thomas would not protect minority rights, civil rights groups and other liberal organizations fought the nomination. Then Anita Hill, a black law professor and former EEOC employee, accused Thomas of sexual harassment. Thomas angrily denied the charges, and the Senate voted narrowly to confirm him. The hearings angered many women, who noted that only two women sat in the Senate and denounced the male senators for not taking sexual harassment seriously.

The Cold War Ends.

While domestic policy remained fairly constant during Bush's presidency, the world experienced enormous changes. In 1989, the progressive forces that Gorbachev had encouraged in the Communist world (see chapter 30) swept through Eastern Europe, where popular uprisings demanded an end to state repression and inefficient economic bureaucracies. Communist governments toppled like dominoes (Map 31.1), virtually without bloodshed, because Gorbachev refused to prop them up with Soviet armies. East Germany opened its border with West Germany, and in November 1989 ecstatic Germans danced on the Berlin Wall.

Unification of East and West Germany sped to completion in 1990. Soon Poland, Hungary, and other former iron curtain countries lined up to join the North

Clean Air Act of 1990
Environmental legislation signed by President George H. W. Bush. The legislation was the strongest and most comprehensive environmental law in the nation's history.

Americans with Disabilities Act (ADA)
Legislation signed by President George H. W. Bush in 1990 that banned discrimination against the disabled. The law also required handicapped accessibility in public facilities and private businesses.

Atlantic Treaty Organization (NATO), a development that Russia found threatening. Eight former Soviet satellites joined the European Union and the common economic market it had established in 1992. Inspired by the liberation of Eastern Europe, republics within the Soviet Union soon established their own independence. With nothing left to govern, Gorbachev resigned. The Soviet Union had dissolved, and with it the Cold War conflict that had defined U.S. foreign policy for decades.

Democracy also prevailed in South Africa, which began to dismantle apartheid; this process led in 1994 to the election of the country's first black president, Nelson Mandela. Colin Powell joked that he was "running out of villains. I'm down to Castro and Kim Il-sung," the North Korean dictator who, along with China's leaders,

Map Activity

MAP 31.1 EVENTS IN EASTERN EUROPE, 1989–2002

The overthrow of Communist governments throughout Eastern Europe and the splintering of the Soviet Union into more than a dozen separate nations were among the most momentous changes in world history since World War II.

READING THE MAP: Which country was the first to overthrow its Communist government? Which was the last? In which nations did elections usher in a change in government?

CONNECTIONS: What problems did Mikhail Gorbachev try to solve, and how did he try to solve them? What made President Reagan ready to reach an accommodation with Gorbachev? (See chapter 30.)

FALL OF THE BERLIN WALL
After 1961, the Berlin Wall became the prime symbol of the Cold War and the iron grip of communism over Eastern Europe and the Soviet Union. When Communist authorities opened the wall on November 9, 1989, Berliners on both sides rushed to the gate to celebrate. Here thousands gather at the Brandenburg Gate, Berlin's most famous landmark.
AP Photo.

resisted the liberalizing tides sweeping the world. In 1989, Chinese soldiers killed hundreds of pro-democracy demonstrators in Beijing, and the Communist government arrested some ten thousand reformers. North Korea remained a Communist dictatorship, committed to developing nuclear weapons.

"The post–Cold War world is decidedly not post-nuclear," declared one U.S. official. In 1990, the United States and the Soviet Union signed the Strategic Arms Reduction Talks (START) treaty, which cut about 30 percent of each superpower's nuclear arsenal. And in 1996, the United Nations General Assembly overwhelmingly approved a total nuclear test ban treaty. Yet India and Pakistan, hostile neighbors, refused to sign the treaty, and both exploded atomic devices in 1998. Moreover, the Republican-controlled U.S. Senate defeated ratification of the treaty. The potential for rogue nations and terrorist groups to develop nuclear weapons posed an ongoing threat.

Going to War in Central America and the Persian Gulf.
Near its borders, the United States continued to exercise its military power. In Central America, U.S. officials had supported Panamanian dictator Manuel Noriega, whom they valued for his anticommunism. But in 1989, after an American grand jury indicted Noriega for drug trafficking and after his troops killed an American Marine, Bush ordered 25,000 military personnel into Panama to capture him. U.S. forces quickly

overcame Noriega's troops, sustaining 23 deaths, while hundreds of Panamanians, including many civilians, died. Colin Powell noted that "our euphoria over our victory was not universal." Both the United Nations and the Organization of American States condemned the unilateral action by the United States.

By contrast, Bush's second military engagement rested solidly on international approval. Viewing Iran as America's major enemy in the Middle East, U.S. officials had quietly assisted the Iraqi dictator Saddam Hussein in the Iran-Iraq war, which began in 1980 and ended inconclusively in 1988. Struggling with an enormous war debt, in August 1990 Hussein invaded the small country of Kuwait (Map 31.2), and his troops soon neared the Saudi Arabian border. Faced with this threat to the world's largest oil reserves, President Bush quickly ordered a massive military mobilization and assembled an international coalition to stand up to Iraq. He invoked principles of national self-determination and international law, but access to Middle Eastern oil was also a key concern.

Reflecting the easing of Cold War tensions, the Soviet Union supported a UN embargo on Iraqi oil and authorization for using force if Iraq did not withdraw from Kuwait by January 15, 1991. By then, the United States had deployed more than 400,000 soldiers to Saudi Arabia, joined by 265,000 troops from two dozen other nations, including several Arab states. "The community of nations has resolutely gathered to condemn and repel lawless aggression," Bush announced. "With few exceptions, the world now stands as one."

When the UN-imposed deadline for Iraqi withdrawal expired, Bush asked Congress to approve war. Many legislators favored waiting to see whether the embargo would force Hussein to back down, a position quietly urged within the administration by Colin Powell. Congress debated for three days and then authorized war by a margin of five votes in the Senate and sixty-seven in the House, with most Democrats opposed. On January 17, 1991, U.S. forces led a forty-day bombing campaign against Iraqi military targets, power plants, oil refineries, and transportation networks. Having severely crippled Iraq by air, the coalition then stormed into Kuwait, forcing Iraqi troops to withdraw (Map 31.2).

"By God, we've kicked the Vietnam syndrome once and for all," President Bush exulted on March 1. Most Americans found no moral ambiguity in the **Persian Gulf War** and took pride in the display of military prowess. The United States stood at the apex of global leadership, steering a coalition in which Arab nations fought beside their former colonial rulers.

Some Americans wondered why Bush ended the war without deposing Hussein. Bush pointed to the limited UN mandate and to Middle Eastern leaders' concerns that invading Iraq would destabilize the region. His secretary of defense, Richard Cheney, doubted that a stable government could be created to replace Hussein and considered the price of a long occupation too high. Instead, administration officials counted on Hussein's pledge not to rearm or develop weapons of mass destruction, secured by a system of UN inspections, to contain him.

After the war, Israel, which had endured Iraqi missile attacks, was more secure, but the Israeli-Palestinian conflict seethed. Despite military losses, Hussein remained

Persian Gulf War
1991 war between Iraq and a U.S.-led international coalition. The war was sparked by the 1990 Iraqi invasion of Kuwait. A forty-day bombing campaign against Iraq, followed by coalition troops storming into Kuwait, brought a quick coalition victory.

Map Activity

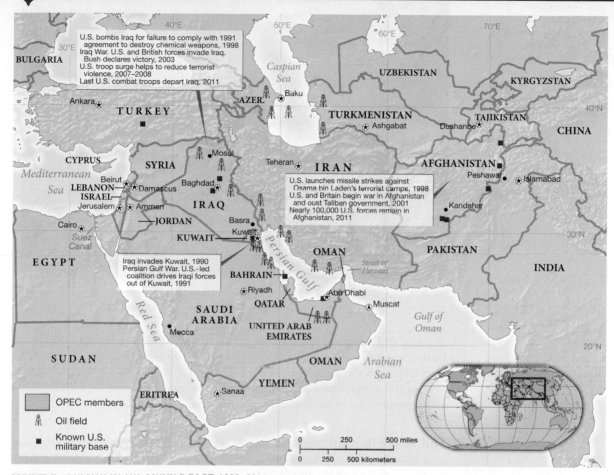

U.S. bombs Iraq for failure to comply with 1991 agreement to destroy chemical weapons, 1998 Iraq War. U.S. and British forces invade Iraq. Bush declares victory, 2003 U.S. troop surge helps to reduce terrorist violence, 2007–2008 Last U.S. combat troops depart Iraq, 2011

U.S. launches missile strikes against Osama bin Laden's terrorist camps, 1998 U.S. and Britain begin war in Afghanistan and oust Taliban government, 2001 Nearly 100,000 U.S. forces remain in Afghanistan, 2011

Iraq invades Kuwait, 1990 Persian Gulf War. U.S.-led coalition drives Iraqi forces out of Kuwait, 1991

OPEC members

Oil field

Known U.S. military base

MAP 31.2   EVENTS IN THE MIDDLE EAST, 1989–2011

The Arab League supported the war to liberate Kuwait in 1991, and after September 11, 2001, it also approved of U.S. military operations in Afghanistan. Yet only the countries where the United States had military bases supported the American invasion of Iraq in 2003. Arab hostility toward the United States also reflected the deterioration of Israeli-Palestinian relations after 1999.

READING THE MAP: In what countries are the sources of oil located? In what countries does the United States have military bases?

CONNECTIONS: What conditions prompted the U.S. military interventions in Iraq and Afghanistan in 1991, 2001, and 2003? What were the U.S. goals in each of these interventions? To what extent were those goals realized?

THE GULF WAR

On Thanksgiving 1990, during the buildup to the Gulf War, President George H. W. Bush visited U.S. troops deployed to Saudi Arabia. Here he talks with one of the 33,000 women stationed throughout the area. For the first time, women served in combat support positions, piloting planes and helicopters, directing artillery, and fighting fires. Diana Walker/Time Life Pictures/ Getty Images.

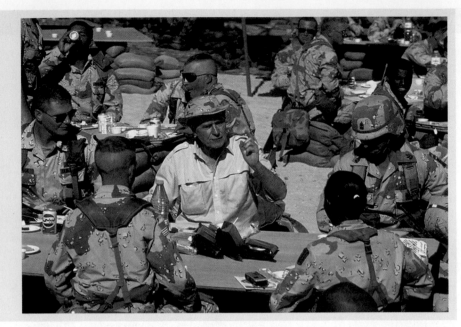

in power and turned his war machine on Iraqi Kurds and Shiite Muslims, whom the United States had encouraged to rebel. Hussein also found ways to conceal arms from UN inspectors before he threw the inspectors out in 1998. Finally, the decision to keep U.S. troops based in Saudi Arabia, the holy land of Islam, fueled the hatred and determination of Muslim extremists like Osama bin Laden.

The 1992 Election. Bush's popularity after the Gulf War caused the most prominent Democrats to opt out of the presidential race of 1992. But that did not deter William Jefferson "Bill" Clinton, who at age forty-five had served as governor of Arkansas for twelve years. Like Carter in 1976, Clinton and his running mate, Tennessee senator Albert Gore Jr., presented themselves as "New Democrats" and sought to rid the party of its liberal image.

Clinton cultivated the "forgotten middle class," who "do the work, pay the taxes, raise the kids, and play by the rules." He promised a tax cut for the middle class, pledged to reinvigorate government and the economy, and vowed "to put an end to welfare as we know it." Bush was vulnerable to an unemployment rate of 7 percent and to a challenge from self-made Texas billionaire H. Ross Perot, whose third-party organization revealed Americans' frustrations with government and the major parties. Clinton won 43 percent of the popular vote, Bush 38 percent, and Perot 19 percent — the strongest third-party finish in eighty years.

REVIEW How did George H. W. Bush respond to threats to U.S. interests as the Cold War came to an end?

The Clinton Administration's Search for the Middle Ground

Bill Clinton's assertion that "the era of big government is over" reflected the Democratic Party's move to the right that had begun with Jimmy Carter, but Clinton did not completely abandon liberal principles. He extended benefits for the working poor; delivered incremental reforms to feminists, environmentalists, and other groups; and spoke out for affirmative action and gay rights. Yet his administration restricted welfare benefits and attended more to the concerns of middle-class Americans than to the needs of the disadvantaged.

Clinton's two-term presidency witnessed the longest economic boom in history and ended with a budget surplus. Although various factors generated the prosperity, many Americans identified Clinton with the buoyant economy, elected him to a second term, and supported him even when his reckless sexual behavior led to impeachment, which crippled his leadership in his last years in office.

Clinton's Reforms. Clinton wanted to restore confidence in government as a force for good while not alienating antigovernment voters. Yet he inherited a huge budget deficit — $4.4 trillion in 1993 — that precluded substantial federal initiatives. Moreover, Clinton never won a majority of the popular vote, and the Republicans controlled Congress after 1994. Throughout his presidency, Clinton was burdened by investigations into past financial activities and private indiscretions.

Despite these obstacles, Clinton achieved a number of reforms. He issued executive orders easing restrictions on abortion and signed several bills that Republicans had previously blocked. In 1993, Congress enacted gun control legislation and the Family and Medical Leave Act, which mandated unpaid leave for childbirth, adoption, and family medical emergencies for workers in larger companies. The Violence against Women Act of 1994 authorized $1.6 billion and new remedies for combating sexual assault and domestic violence. Clinton won stricter air pollution controls and greater protection for national forests and parks. Other liberal measures included a minimum-wage increase and a large expansion of aid for college students. Most significantly, Clinton pushed through a substantial increase in the **Earned Income Tax Credit (EITC)**. Begun in 1975, EITC gave tax breaks to people who worked full-time at meager wages or, if they owed no taxes, a subsidy to lift their family income above the poverty line. By 2003, some fifteen million low-income families were benefiting from the EITC, almost half of them minorities. One expert called it "the largest antipoverty program since the Great Society." The program implicitly recognized the inability of the free market to secure a living wage for all workers.

Shortly before Clinton took office, the economy had begun to rebound. Economic expansion, along with spending cuts, tax increases, and declining unemployment, produced in 1998 the first budget surplus since 1969. Clinton failed, however, in his major domestic initiative to provide universal health insurance and to curb skyrocketing medical costs. Congress enacted important smaller reforms, such as underwriting health care for five million uninsured children, yet forty million Americans remained uninsured.

Earned Income Tax Credit (EITC)
Federal antipoverty program initiated in 1975 that assisted the working poor by giving tax breaks to low-income, full-time workers or a subsidy to those who owed no taxes. President Bill Clinton pushed through a significant increase in the program in 1993.

Pledging to make the face of government "look like America," Clinton built on the gradual progress women and minorities had made since the 1960s. For example, African Americans and women had become mayors in major cities from New York to San Francisco. Virginia had elected the first black governor since Reconstruction, and Florida the first Latino. Clinton's cabinet appointments included six women, three African Americans, two Latinos, and an Asian American. His judicial appointments had a similar cast, and in 1993 he named the second woman to the Supreme Court, Ruth Bader Ginsburg, whose arguments as an attorney had won key women's rights rulings from that Court.

Accommodating the Right.
The 1994 midterm elections swept away the Democratic majorities in Congress and helped push Clinton to the right. Republicans claimed the 1994 election as a mandate for their conservative platform to end "government that is too big, too intrusive, and too easy with the public's money" and for "a Congress that respects the values and shares the faith of the American family."

The most extreme antigovernment sentiment developed far from Washington in the form of grassroots armed militias that celebrated white Christian supremacy and reflected conservatives' hostility to such diverse institutions as taxes and the United Nations. The militia movement grew after passage of new gun control legislation and after government agents stormed the headquarters of an armed religious cult in Waco, Texas, in April 1993, killing more than 80. On the second anniversary of that event, two militia sympathizers bombed a federal building in Oklahoma City, taking 168 lives in the worst terrorist attack in the nation's history up to that point.

Bowing to conservative views on gay and lesbian rights and following the advice of military leaders, Clinton backed away from his promise to lift the ban on gays in the military. Cathleen Glover, an army specialist in Arabic who lost her position along with thousands of other soldiers, lamented, "The army preaches integrity, but asks you to lie to everyone around you." In addition, in 1996, Clinton signed the Defense of Marriage Act (DOMA), prohibiting the federal government from recognizing state-licensed marriages between same-sex couples.

Yet attitudes and practices relating to homosexuality were changing rapidly, and the years following Clinton's presidency would witness a number of significant victories for gay rights. By 2006, a majority of the largest companies provided health benefits to same-sex domestic partners and included sexual orientation in their nondiscrimination policies. A majority of states banned discrimination in public employment, and many of those laws extended to private employment, housing, and education. In 2015, the Supreme Court in *Obergefell v. Hodges* declared by a vote of five to four that same-sex couples had a constitutional right to marry, making gay marriage legal in all fifty states. The gay rights movement continued to fight other forms of discrimination, including job bias, which was still legal in many states, and worked for the rights of transgender people.

In the 1990s, hardening attitudes about poverty were reflected in Clinton's handling of the New Deal program Aid to Families with Dependent Children (AFDC), popularly called welfare. Using the term *welfare queen* to stigmatize AFDC recipients, critics encouraged voters to blame poverty on the poor themselves and on welfare programs that fostered dependency, rather than on external circumstances such as lack of adequate jobs and child care. Many questioned why they should subsidize poor mothers when so many women worked outside the home. Defenders of AFDC doubted that the economy could provide sufficient jobs at decent wages and pointed to the much greater subsidies the government provided to other groups, such as large farmers, corporations, and homeowners. After vetoing two welfare bills, Clinton signed a less punitive measure as the 1996 election approached. The **Temporary Assistance for Needy Families (TANF) program** replaced AFDC and limited welfare payments to two consecutive years, with a lifetime maximum of five years.

Clinton's signature on the new law denied Republicans a partisan issue in the 1996 presidential campaign. The Republican Party also moved to the center,

Temporary Assistance for Needy Families (TANF) program
Program established by the Personal Responsibility and Work Opportunity Reconciliation Act of 1996. Replacing Aid to Families with Dependent Children, TANF provided grants to the states to assist the poor and limited welfare payments to two consecutive years, with a lifetime maximum of five years.

Visual Activity

THE END OF WELFARE

After signing the bill that sharply curtailed government support for poor mothers and their children, Bill Clinton made it a part of his 1996 campaign for reelection. He highlighted the issue especially when campaigning in more conservative regions, as this photo from a campaign stop in Daytona, Florida, shows. Paul J. Richards/AFP/Getty Images.

READING THE IMAGE: What does the poster behind Clinton say about the importance of welfare as an issue in 1996? What American "values" do you think it refers to?

CONNECTIONS: What other programs that addressed the issue of poverty did Clinton advance?

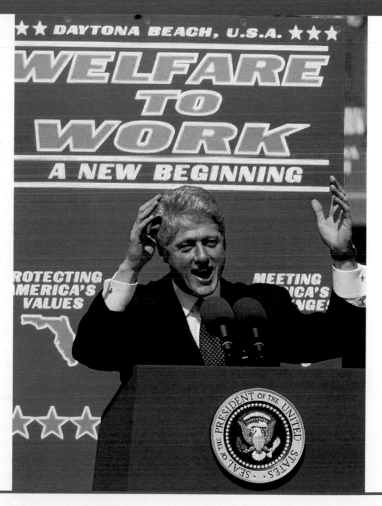

nominating Kansan Robert Dole, a World War II hero and former Senate majority leader. Clinton won 49 percent of the votes; 41 percent went to Dole and 9 percent to third-party candidate Ross Perot. Voters sent a Republican majority back to Congress.

In 1999, Clinton and Congress further deregulated the financial industry by repealing key aspects of the Glass-Steagall Act, passed during the New Deal to avoid another Great Depression. The Financial Services Modernization Act ended the separation between banking, securities, and insurance services, allowing financial institutions to engage in all three areas, practices that contributed to the severe financial meltdown of 2008.

Impeaching the President.
Clinton's magnetism, his ability to capture the middle ground, and the nation's economic resurgence enabled him to survive scandals and impeachment. Early in his presidency, charges related to firings of White House staff, political use of FBI records, and the Clintons' real estate investments in Arkansas led to an official investigation by an independent prosecutor.

In January 1998, the independent prosecutor, Kenneth Starr, began to investigate a charge that Clinton had had sexual relations with a twenty-one-year-old White House intern and then lied about it to a federal grand jury. Starr prepared a case for the House of Representatives, which in December 1998 voted to impeach the president for perjury and obstruction of justice. Clinton became the second president (after Andrew Johnson, in 1868) to be impeached by the House and tried by the Senate.

Most Americans condemned the president's behavior but approved of the job he was doing and opposed his removal from office. One man said, "Let him get a divorce. . . . Don't take him out of office and disrupt the country." Some saw Starr as a fanatic invading individuals' privacy. Those favoring removal insisted that the president must set a high moral standard and that lying to a grand jury, even over a private matter, was a serious offense. The Senate votes fell far short of the two-thirds majority needed for conviction on either count. A majority, including some Republicans, seemed to agree with a Clinton supporter that the president's behavior, though "indefensible, outrageous, unforgivable, shameless," did not warrant his removal from office.

The Booming Economy of the 1990s.
Clinton's ability to weather impeachment owed much to the prosperous economy, which in 1991 began a period of tremendous expansion. During the 1990s, the gross domestic product grew by more than one-third, thirteen million new jobs were created, inflation remained in check, unemployment reached 4 percent — its lowest point in twenty-five years — and the stock market soared.

Clinton's policies contributed to the boom. He made deficit reduction a priority, and in exchange the Federal Reserve Board and bond market traders encouraged economic expansion by lowering interest rates. Businesses also prospered because they had lowered their costs through corporate restructuring and employee layoffs. Economic problems in Europe and Asia helped American firms become more competitive in the international market. And the computer revolution and the application of information technology boosted productivity.

People at all income levels benefited from the economic boom, but income inequality, rising since the 1970s, endured (Figure 31.1). The growing use of computer technology increased demand for highly skilled workers, while the movement of manufacturing jobs abroad diminished opportunities and wages for the less skilled. Moreover, deregulation and the continuing decline of unions hurt lower-skilled workers, tax cuts favored the better-off, and the minimum wage failed to keep up with inflation.

Although more minorities than ever attained middle-class status, people of color overall remained lowest on the economic ladder. For instance, in 1999 the median income for white households surpassed $45,000, but it stood at only $29,423 and $33,676 for African American and Latino households, respectively. In 2000, poverty afflicted more than 20 percent of African Americans and Latinos, in contrast to 7.5 percent of whites.

FIGURE 31.1 THE GROWTH OF INEQUALITY: CHANGES IN FAMILY INCOME, 1969–1998

For most of the post–World War II period, income increased for all groups on the economic ladder. But after 1969, the income of the poorest families actually declined, while the income of the richest 20 percent of the population grew substantially. Adapted from the *New York Times*, 1989.

> **REVIEW** How did President Clinton seek a middle ground in American politics?

The United States in a Globalizing World

America's economic success in the 1990s was linked to its dominance in a world economy that was undergoing tremendous transformations in a process called globalization — the growing integration and interdependence of national citizens and economies. President Clinton lowered a number of trade barriers, despite heated arguments about whether that was in the country's best interest. Debates likewise arose over the large numbers of immigrants entering the United States.

Clinton agreed with Bush that the United States must retain its supreme position in the world. He used military force in Somalia, the Middle East, and Eastern Europe, and he pushed hard to ease the conflict between Israelis and Palestinians. Clinton also strove to safeguard American interests from terrorist attacks around the world, a challenge in some ways more difficult than combating communism.

Defining America's Place in a New World Order. In 1991, President George H. W. Bush declared a "new world order" emerging from the ashes of the Cold War. As the sole superpower, the United States was determined to let no nation challenge its military superiority or global leadership: It spent ten times more on defense than its nearest competitor, United Kingdom (Figure 31.2). Defining principles for the use of that power in a post–Cold War world remained a challenge.

FIGURE 31.2 GLOBAL COMPARISON: COUNTRIES WITH THE HIGHEST MILITARY EXPENDITURES, 2005

During the Cold War, the military budgets of the United States and the Soviet Union were relatively even. Even before the Iraq War began in 2003, the U.S. military budget constituted 47 percent of total world military expenditures. Massive defense budgets reflected the determination of Democratic and Republican administrations alike to maintain dominance in the world, even while the capacities of traditional enemies shrunk.

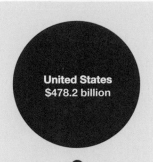

United States
$478.2 billion

United Kingdom
$48.3 billion

France
$46.2 billion

Japan
$42.1 billion

China
$41.0 billion

Germany
$33.2 billion

Italy
$27.2 billion

Saudi Arabia
$25.2 billion

Russia
$21.0 billion

India
$20.4 billion

Africa, where civil wars and extreme human suffering rarely evoked a strong U.S. response, was a case in point. In 1992, President Bush had attached U.S. forces to a UN operation in the northern African country of Somalia, where famine and civil war raged. In 1993, President Clinton allowed that humanitarian mission to turn into "nation building" — an effort to establish a stable government — and eighteen U.S. soldiers were killed. The outcry after Americans saw film of a soldier's corpse dragged through the streets suggested that most citizens were unwilling to sacrifice lives when no vital interest was threatened. Indeed, both the United States and the UN stood by in 1994 when more than half a million people were massacred in a brutal civil war in Rwanda.

In Eastern Europe, the collapse of communism ignited a severe crisis when, after the Communists were swept out of power in Yugoslavia in 1989, ruthless leaders exploited ethnic differences to bolster their power. Yugoslavia splintered into separate states and fell into civil war. The Serbian aggression under President Slobodan Milosevic against Bosnian Muslims, which included rape, torture, and mass killings, horrified much of the world, but European and U.S. leaders hesitated to use military force. Finally, in 1995, Clinton ordered U.S. fliers to join NATO forces in intensive bombing of Serbian military concentrations. That effort and successful offensives by the Croatian and Bosnian armies forced Milosevic to the bargaining table, where representatives from Serbia, Croatia, and Bosnia hammered out a peace treaty.

In 1998, new fighting broke out in the southern Serbian province of Kosovo, where ethnic Albanians, who constituted 90 percent of the population, demanded independence. When the Serbian army retaliated, in 1999, NATO launched a U.S.-led bombing attack on Serbian military and government targets that, after three months, forced Milosevic to agree to a settlement. Serbians voted Milosevic out of office in 2000, and he died in 2006 while on trial for genocide by a UN war crimes tribunal.

Elsewhere, Clinton deployed U.S. power when he could send missiles rather than soldiers, and he was prepared to act without international support or UN sanction. In August 1998, bombings at the U.S. embassies in Kenya and Tanzania killed 12 Americans and more than 250 Africans. Clinton retaliated with missile attacks on training camps in Afghanistan and facilities in Sudan controlled by Osama bin Laden, a Saudi-born millionaire who financed Al Qaeda, the Islamic-extremist terrorist network linked to the embassy attacks. Clinton also bombed Iraq in 1993 when a plot to assassinate former president Bush was uncovered, in 1996 after Saddam Hussein attacked the Kurds in northern Iraq, and repeatedly between 1998 and 2000 after Hussein expelled UN weapons inspectors. Whereas Bush had acted in the Gulf War with the support of an international force that included Arab states, Clinton acted unilaterally and in the face of Arab opposition.

To defuse the Israeli-Palestinian conflict, Clinton applied diplomatic rather than military power. In 1993, Norwegian diplomats had brokered an agreement between Yasir Arafat, head of the Palestine Liberation Organization (PLO), and Yitzhak Rabin, Israeli prime minister, to recognize the existence of each other's states. Israel agreed to withdraw from the Gaza Strip and Jericho, allowing for Palestinian self-government there. In July 1994, Clinton presided over another turning point as Israel and Jordan signed a declaration of peace. Yet difficult issues remained, especially control of Jerusalem and the presence of more than 200,000 Israeli settlers in the West Bank, the land seized by Israel in 1967, where three million Palestinians were determined to establish their own state.

BREAKUP OF YUGOSLAVIA

Debates over Globalization.

Building on efforts by Reagan and Bush, Clinton sought to speed up the growth of a "global marketplace" with new measures to ease restrictions on international commerce. Although the process of globalization was centuries old, new communications technologies such as the Internet and cell phones connected nations, corporations, and individuals at much faster speeds and much lower costs. To advance globalization and the U.S. economy, in 1993 Clinton won congressional approval of the **North American Free Trade Agreement (NAFTA)**, which eliminated all tariffs and trade barriers among the United States, Canada, and Mexico. Fearing loss of jobs and industries to Mexico, a majority of Democrats opposed NAFTA, but Republican support ensured approval. In 1994, the Senate ratified the General Agreement on Tariffs and Trade, establishing the **World Trade Organization (WTO)** to enforce substantial tariff and import quota reductions among some 135 member nations. In 2005, Clinton's successor, George W. Bush, lowered more trade barriers with the Central American–Dominican Republic Free Trade Agreement. The Obama administration negotiated the largest trade pact ever, the Trans-Pacific Partnership, but struggled to obtain Congressional approval.

The free trade issue was intensely contested. Much of corporate America welcomed the elimination of trade barriers and opportunities to lower their taxes. "Ideally, you'd have every plant you own on a barge," remarked Jack Welch, CEO of General Electric. Critics, including many Democrats, linked globalization to the loss of good jobs, the weakening of unions, and the growing gap between rich and poor. Demanding "fair trade" rather than simply free trade, critics wanted treaties to require decent wage and labor standards. Environmentalists wanted countries seeking increased commerce with the United States to reduce pollution and prevent the destruction of endangered species.

Globalization controversies often centered on relationships between the United States, which dominated the world's industrial core, and developing nations on the periphery, whose cheap labor and lax environmental standards attracted investors. United Students against Sweatshops, for example, attacked Nike, which paid Chinese workers $1.50 per hour to produce shoes selling for

First Persian Gulf War, 1991
Israel and PLO sign accords, 1993
Israel and Jordan sign peace treaty, 1994
Progress of Israeli-Palestinian negotiations
   halts and violence escalates, 2000
Israel withdraws from Gaza, 2005
Israel at war with Hezbollah in Lebanon, 2006
Israel invades Gaza, 2008

EVENTS IN ISRAEL
SINCE 1989

North American Free Trade Agreement (NAFTA)

1993 treaty that eliminated all tariffs and trade barriers among the United States, Canada, and Mexico. NAFTA was supported by President Clinton, a minority of Democrats, and a majority of Republicans.

World Trade Organization (WTO)

International economic body established in 1994 through the General Agreement on Tariffs and Trade to enforce substantial tariff and import quota reductions. Many corporations welcomed these trade barrier reductions, but critics linked them to job loss and the weakening of unions.

more than $100 in the United States. Yet leaders of developing nations actively sought foreign investment because wages deemed pitiful by Americans often provided their impoverished people a higher standard of living. At the same time, developing countries often pointed to American hypocrisy in advocating free trade in industry while heavily subsidizing the U.S. agricultural sector. "When countries like America, Britain and France subsidize their farmers," complained a grower in Uganda, "we get hurt."

While globalization's cheerleaders pointed to the cheap consumer goods available to Americans and argued that everyone would benefit in the long run, critics focused on the short-term victims. American businessman George Soros recognized that international trade and investments generated wealth but could not meet other needs, "such as the preservation of peace, alleviation of poverty, protection of the environment, labor conditions, or human rights." According to World Bank president James D. Wolfensohn, "Our challenge is to make globalization an instrument of opportunity and inclusion — not fear."

The Internationalization of the United States. The United States experienced the dynamic forces of globalization in many ways. Already in the 1980s, Japanese, European, and Middle Eastern investors had purchased U.S. stocks and bonds, real estate, and corporations. Local communities welcomed foreign capital, and states competed to recruit foreign automobile plants. By 2002, the paychecks of nearly four million American workers came from foreign-owned companies such as Honda and BMW.

Visual Activity

THE INTERNET

In 1958, in response to the Soviet launch of *Sputnik*, President Eisenhower created the Advanced Research Projects Agency (ARPA), which produced a system that routed digitized messages between computers to facilitate military communications. The technology spread beyond the military; by 2000, even the poorest countries had some access to what became the Internet. By 2011, Internet-enabled smartphones were abundant. Activists used digital networks to organize protests and broadcast their stories and images during the Arab Spring of 2011. Ron Haviv/VII/Corbis.

READING THE IMAGE: What forms of technology do you see among these Egyptian protesters? What are some pros and cons of using these technologies for political activism?

CONNECTIONS: How did the Obama administration respond to the Arab Spring revolutions?

Globalization was also transforming American society, as the United States experienced a tremendous surge of immigration, part of a worldwide movement of some 214 million immigrants in 2010 alone. By 2014, the United States' 42.2 million immigrants constituted 13.2 percent of the population. In contrast to earlier immigrants, who had come largely from Europe, by the 1980s the vast majority came from Asia, Latin America, and the Caribbean. Consequently, immigration changed the racial and ethnic composition of the nation. By 2014, 55 million Latinos constituted the largest U.S. minority group, at 17 percent of the population. But since 2010, more immigrants have come from Asia than from Latin America.

The promise of economic opportunity, as always, lured immigrants to America, and the Immigration and Nationality Act of 1965 enabled them to come. The law allowed close relatives of U.S. citizens to enter above the annual ceiling of 270,000 immigrants, thus creating family migration chains. Moreover, during the Cold War, U.S. immigration policy was generous to refugees from communism, welcoming more than 800,000 Cubans and more than 600,000 Vietnamese, Laotians, and Cambodians.

The racial composition of the new immigration heightened the long-standing wariness of native-born Americans toward newcomers. Pressure for more restrictive policies stemmed from beliefs that immigrants took jobs from the native-born, suppressed wages by accepting low pay, strained social services, or eroded the dominant culture and language. Americans expressed particular hostility toward immigrants who were in the country illegally, estimated at 11.3 million in 2014, even though the economy depended on their cheap labor.

The new immigration was making America an international, interracial society. The largest numbers of immigrants flocked to California, New York, Texas, Florida, New Jersey, and Illinois, but new immigrants dispersed throughout the country. Taquerias, sushi bars, and Vietnamese restaurants appeared in southeastern and midwestern towns; cable TV companies added Spanish-language stations; and the international sport of soccer soared in popularity. Mixed marriages displayed the growing fusion of cultures, recognized in 2000 on Census Bureau forms, where Americans could check more than one racial category. Like their predecessors, the majority of post-1965 immigrants were unskilled and poor. They took the lowest-paying jobs, constituting nearly half of all farmworkers and housekeepers. Yet a significant number of immigrants were highly skilled workers, sought after by burgeoning high-tech industries. By 2006, nearly one-third of all software developers were foreign-born, as were 28 percent of all physicians.

MIGRANT WORKERS

Mexican immigrants constituted more than two-thirds of crop workers in 2015 and a sizable share of tobacco workers. These migrant workers labor in a tobacco curing barn in Finchville, Kentucky, where tobacco hangs from rafters. The labor not only was long and arduous but also exposed workers to nicotine and other poisons that could be absorbed directly through the skin. Luke Sharrett/Bloomberg via Getty Images.

REVIEW What were the costs and benefits to the United States of globalization in the 1990s and early 2000s?

President George W. Bush: Conservatism at Home and Radical Initiatives Abroad

Although losing the popular vote in 2000, George W. Bush made his mark in domestic policy with key legislation to improve public school education, subsidize prescription drugs for elderly citizens, and greatly reduce taxes for the wealthy. The tax cuts, along with spending on new crises, created the largest budget deficit in the nation's history, and a financial crisis near the end of his presidency sent the economy into a recession.

As Islamist terrorism replaced communism as the primary threat to U.S. security, the Bush administration invaded Afghanistan in 2001 and Iraq in 2003. Bush won reelection in 2004, but stability in Iraq and Afghanistan remained elusive, and he confronted serious foreign and domestic crises in his second term. Democrats capitalized on widespread dissatisfaction with his administration to gain control of Congress in 2006 and the White House in 2008.

The Disputed Election of 2000. The oldest son of former president George H. W. Bush, George W. Bush was the governor of Texas when he won the Republican presidential nomination. Inexperienced in national and international affairs, Bush chose for his running mate a seasoned official, Richard B. Cheney, who had served in three previous Republican administrations. Many observers predicted that the thriving economy would benefit the Democratic contender, Vice President Al Gore, and he did surpass Bush by more than half a million votes. But Florida's 25 electoral college votes would decide the presidency. Bush's tiny margin in Florida prompted an automatic recount of the votes, which eventually gave him an edge of 537 votes in that state.

The Democrats asked for hand-counting of Florida ballots in several heavily Democratic counties where machine errors and confusing ballots may have left thousands of Gore votes unrecorded. The Republicans, in turn, went to court to try to stop the hand-counts. The outcome of the 2000 election hung in the balance for weeks as cases went up to the Supreme Court. Finally, the sharply divided justices ruled five to four against allowing the state to conduct further recounts. While critics charged partisanship, noting that the conservative justices had abandoned their principle of favoring state over federal authority, Gore conceded to Bush. For the first time since 1888, a president who failed to win the popular vote took office (Map 31.3).

The Domestic Policies of a "Compassionate Conservative." Bush had promised to govern as a "compassionate conservative." Embracing the nation's diversity and following in Clinton's footsteps, he appointed African

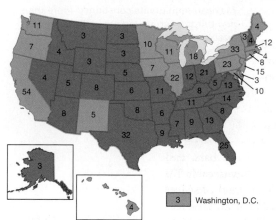

Candidate	Electoral Vote	Popular Vote	Percent of Popular Vote
George W. Bush (Republican)	271	50,456,062	47.8
Al Gore (Democrat)	267	50,996,862	48.4
Ralph Nader (Green Party)	0	2,858,843	2.7
Patrick J. Buchanan (Reform Party)	0	438,760	0.4

MAP 31.3 THE ELECTION OF 2000

Americans, Latinos, and Asian Americans to his cabinet. A devout born-again Christian, he immediately established the White House Office of Faith-Based and Community Initiatives, funding religious groups to run programs for prison inmates, the unemployed, and others. Conservatives praised the initiatives, which encouraged private institutions to replace government as the provider of welfare, but others charged that they violated the constitutional separation of church and state. Federal courts ruled in several dozen cases that faith ministries were using government funds to indoctrinate the people they served. More substantial was Bush's achievement of legislation authorizing a $15 billion anti-AIDS program in Africa that eventually saved millions of lives.

By contrast, Bush's fiscal policies were more compassionate toward the rich. In 2001, he signed a bill reducing taxes over the next ten years by $1.35 trillion. A 2003 tax law slashed another $320 billion. The laws heavily favored the wealthy by reducing income taxes, phasing out estate taxes, and cutting tax rates on capital gains and dividends. They also provided benefits for married couples and families with children and offered tax deductions for college expenses.

The tax cuts helped turn the budget surplus that Bush had inherited into a mushrooming federal deficit — the highest in U.S. history. In 2009, the deficit surpassed $1 trillion as the government struggled to combat a recession. By then, the national debt had risen to $9.6 trillion, making the United States increasingly dependent on China and other foreign investors, who held more than half of the debt.

Bush used executive powers to weaken environmental protection as part of his larger agenda to reduce government regulation, promote economic growth, and increase energy production. The administration opened millions of wilderness acres to mining, oil, and timber industries and relaxed standards under the Clean Air and Clean Water Acts. To worldwide dismay, the administration withdrew from the Kyoto Protocol, signed in 1997 by 178 nations to reduce greenhouse gas emissions that cause global warming.

Conservatives hailed Bush's two appointments to the Supreme Court. In 2005, John Roberts, who had served in the Reagan and George H. W. Bush administrations, was named chief justice. When the moderate Sandra Day O'Connor resigned, Bush nominated Samuel A. Alito, a staunch conservative who was narrowly confirmed. While the Court upheld the rights of homosexuals and stood up to the administration on the rights of accused terrorists, it also upheld increasing restrictions on abortion and struck down regulations in the areas of voting rights, gun control, sex discrimination in employment, and business practices. Its five-to-four ruling in *Citizens United v. FEC* (2010) gutted regulation of election campaign financing by holding that such spending was a form of speech protected by the First Amendment.

In contrast to the partisan conflict over judicial appointments and tax and environmental policy, Bush won bipartisan support for the **No Child Left Behind Act** of 2002, a substantial expansion of the federal government into public education. Promising to end, in Bush's words, "the story of children being just shuffled through the system," the law set national standards and imposed penalties on failing schools. But the law was never adequately funded; school officials criticized the one-size-fits-all approach and pointed to poverty as a source of student deficiencies, which schools alone could not overcome. In 2015, Congress returned considerable control to the states and local districts.

President Bush's second effort to co-opt Democratic Party issues constituted what he hailed as "the greatest advance in health care coverage for America's

No Child Left Behind Act
2002 legislation championed by President George W. Bush that expanded the role of the federal government in public education. The law required every school to meet annual testing standards, penalized failing schools, and allowed parents to transfer their children out of such schools.

seniors" since Medicare began in 1965. In 2003, Bush signed a bill providing prescription drug benefits for the elderly and also expanding the role of private insurers in the Medicare system. Most Democrats opposed the legislation because it subsidized private insurers with federal funds, banned imports of low-priced drugs, and prohibited the government from negotiating with drug companies to reduce prices. The law was a boon to the elderly, but medical costs overall continued to soar, and 40 million Americans remained uninsured.

One domestic undertaking of the Bush administration found little approval anywhere: its response to Hurricane Katrina, which in August 2005 devastated the coasts of Alabama, Louisiana, and Mississippi and ultimately took some fifteen hundred lives. The catastrophe that ensued when the levees broke, flooding 80 percent of New Orleans, shook many Americans' deeply rooted assumption that government would protect citizens from natural disasters. New Orleans residents who were too old, too poor, or too sick to evacuate spent days waiting on rooftops for help; wading in filthy, toxic water; and enduring the heat and disorder at the centers where they had been told to go for help. "How can we save the world if we can't save our own people?" wondered one Louisianan. Since so many of Katrina's hardest-hit victims were poor and black, the disaster also highlighted racial injustices and deprivations remaining in American society.

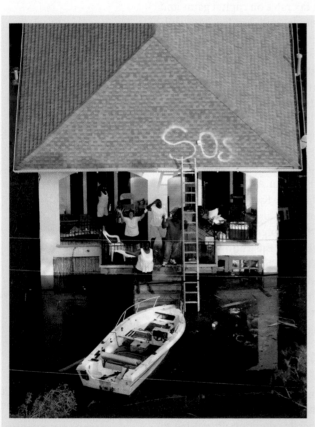

HURRICANE KATRINA
Residents of the poverty-stricken Lower Ninth Ward of New Orleans pleaded for help in the flooding that followed Hurricane Katrina in August 2005. The boat was useless because it had lost its motor. Some residents waited as long as five days to be rescued. A historian of the disaster wrote, "Americans were not used to seeing their country in ruins, their people in want." AP Photo/David J. Phillip.

The Globalization of Terrorism.
The response to Hurricane Katrina contrasted sharply with the government's decisive reaction to the horror that had unfolded four years earlier on the morning of September 11, 2001. Nineteen terrorists hijacked four planes and flew two of them into the twin towers of New York City's World Trade Center and one into the Pentagon in Washington, D.C.; the fourth crashed in a field in Pennsylvania. The attacks took nearly 2,800 lives, including people from ninety different countries.

The hijackers belonged to Osama bin Laden's Al Qaeda international terrorist network. Organized in Afghanistan then ruled by the radical Muslim Taliban government, the attacks expressed Islamic extremists' rage at the spread of Western culture and values into the Muslim world, as well as their opposition to the 1991 Persian Gulf War against Iraq and the stationing of American troops in Saudi Arabia. Bin Laden sought to rid the Middle East of Western influence and install puritanical Muslim control.

The 9/11 terrorists and others who came after them ranged from poor to well-off; many lived in

Middle Eastern homelands governed by undemocratic and corrupt governments, others in Western cities where they felt alienated and despised. All saw the West, especially the United States, as the evil source of their humiliation and the supporter of Israel's oppression of Palestinian Muslims.

In the wake of the September 11 attacks, President Bush sought a global alliance against terrorism and won at least verbal support from most governments. On October 11, with NATO support, the United States and Britain began bombing Afghanistan, and American forces aided the Northern Alliance, the Taliban government's main opposition. By December, the Taliban government was destroyed, but bin Laden eluded capture until U.S. special forces killed him in Pakistan in 2011. Afghans elected a new national government, but the Taliban remained strong in large parts of the country and contributed to ongoing economic instability and insecurity. When the Taliban retook the city of Kunduz in 2015, a U.S. soldier who had fought there wrote, "You wonder what all that effort and sacrifice was for."

After the September 11 attacks, anti-immigrant sentiment revived throughout the United States, and residents appearing to be Middle Eastern or practicing Islam often aroused suspicion. Authorities arrested more than a thousand Arabs and Muslims; a Justice Department study later found that many people with no connection to terrorism spent months in jail, denied their rights. "I think America overreacted . . . by singling out Arab-named men like myself," said Shanaz Mohammed, who was jailed for eight months for an immigration violation.

In October 2001, Congress passed the **USA Patriot Act**, giving the government new powers to monitor suspected terrorists, including the ability to access all Americans' personal information. It soon provoked calls for revision from both conservatives and liberals. Kathleen MacKenzie, a councilwoman in Ann Arbor, Michigan, explained why the council opposed the Patriot Act: "As concerned as we were about national safety, we felt that giving up [rights] was too high a price to pay." A security official countered, "If you don't violate someone's human rights some of the time, you probably aren't doing your job." A decade past 9/11, the government continued to gather personal information on individual citizens, seeming to some to have sacrificed too much liberty for security.

Insisting that presidential powers were virtually limitless in times of national crisis, Bush stretched his authority until he met resistance from the courts and Congress. The United States detained more than 700 prisoners captured in Afghanistan and taken to the U.S. military base at Guantánamo, Cuba, where, until the courts acted, they had no rights and were sometimes tortured. Although President Barack Obama

9/11

The magnitude of the destruction and loss of lives in the 9/11 attacks made Americans feel more vulnerable than they had since the Cold War ended. The attacks also affected people around the world, who streamed to U.S. embassies or expressed their shock and sympathy in other ways. Steve Ludlum/The *New York Times*/Redux.

USA Patriot Act
2001 law that gave the government new powers to monitor suspected terrorists and their associates, including the ability to access personal information. Critics charged that it represented an unwarranted abridgment of civil rights.

AFGHANISTAN

Iraq War

War launched by the United States, Britain, and several smaller countries in March 2003 against the government of Iraqi dictator Saddam Hussein. The decision to go to war was based on claims (subsequently refuted) that Hussein's government had links to Al Qaeda, harbored terrorists, and possessed weapons of mass destruction.

IRAQ

promised to close the detention camp, he met resistance from Congress, and more than fifty prisoners remained there in 2015.

The government also sought to protect Americans from future terrorist attacks through the greatest reorganization of the executive branch since 1948. In November 2002, Congress authorized the new Department of Homeland Security, combining 170,000 federal employees from twenty-two agencies responsible for various aspects of domestic security. Chief among the department's duties were intelligence analysis; immigration and border security; chemical, biological, and nuclear countermeasures; and emergency preparedness and response.

Unilateralism, Preemption, and the Iraq War. The Bush administration sought collective action against the Taliban, but on most international issues it adopted a go-it-alone approach. In addition to withdrawing from the Kyoto Protocol on global warming and violating international rules about the treatment of military prisoners, it withdrew from the UN's International Criminal Court and rejected an agreement to enforce bans on biological weapons that all of America's European allies had signed.

Nowhere was the policy of unilateralism more striking than in a new war against Iraq, a war pushed by Vice President Dick Cheney and Secretary of Defense Donald H. Rumsfeld, but not by Secretary of State Colin Powell. Addressing West Point graduates in June 2002, President Bush proclaimed a new strategy based not on containment but on preemption: "Traditional concepts of deterrence will not work against a terrorist enemy whose avowed tactics are wanton destruction and the targeting of innocents; whose so-called soldiers seek martyrdom in death and whose most potent protection is statelessness." Because even weak countries and small groups could strike devastating blows at the United States, as Al Qaeda had done on 9/11, the nation had to "be ready for preemptive action." The president's claim that the United States had the right to start a war was at odds with international law and with many Americans' understanding of their nation's ideals. It distressed most of America's great-power allies.

Nonetheless, the Bush administration soon applied the doctrine of preemption to Iraq, whose dictator, Saddam Hussein, appeared to be violating UN restrictions on Iraqi development of nuclear, chemical, and biological weapons. In November 2002, the United States obtained a UN Security Council resolution demanding that Iraq disarm or face "serious consequences." When Iraq failed to comply fully with UN inspections, the Bush administration decided on war. Making claims — later proved false — that Hussein had links to Al Qaeda and held weapons of mass destruction, the president insisted that the threat was immediate and great enough to justify preemptive action. Despite the absence of UN approval and opposition from the Arab world and most major nations — including France, Germany, China, and Russia — the United States and Britain invaded Iraq on March 19, 2003, supported by some thirty nations (Map 31.2). Coalition forces won an easy victory, and Bush declared the end of the **Iraq War** on May 1. Saddam Hussein was captured in December 2003, tried by an Iraqi court, and executed.

Chaos followed the quick victory. Damage from U.S. bombing and widespread looting resulting from the failure of U.S. troops to secure order and provide basic necessities left Iraqis wondering how much they had gained. "With Saddam there was tyranny, but at least you had a salary to put food on your family's table," said a young father. A Baghdad hospital worker complained, "They can take our oil, but at least they should let us have electricity and water." Five years after the invasion, continuing violence had caused 2 million to flee their country and displaced 1.9 million within Iraq.

The administration had not planned adequately for the occupation and failed to send sufficient troops to Iraq. The 140,000 American forces there came under attack almost daily from remnants of the former Hussein regime, religious extremists, and hundreds of foreign terrorists now entering the chaotic country. Seeking to divide Iraqis and undermine the occupation, terrorists launched assaults that killed tens of thousands of Iraqis. By the end of the Iraq War, nearly 4,500 U.S. soldiers had lost their lives, and many returned home grievously wounded.

The war became an issue in the presidential campaign of 2004. U.S. senator John Kerry, the Democratic nominee, criticized Bush's unilateralist foreign policy and the administration's conduct of the war. A slim majority of voters, however, indicated their belief that Bush would better protect American security than Kerry, giving the president a 286 to 252 victory in the electoral college, 50.7 percent of the popular vote, and Republican majorities in Congress.

In June 2004, the United States transferred sovereignty to a Shiite-dominated Iraqi government, which failed to satisfy Iraq's other major groups — Sunnis and Kurds. Violence escalated against government officials, Iraqi civilians, and occupation forces. A nineteen-year-old Iraqi confined to his house by his parents, who feared he could be killed or lured into terrorist activities, said, "If I'm killed, it doesn't even matter because I'm dead right now." By 2006, a majority of Americans believed that the Iraq War was a mistake.

Criticism of the war crossed party lines and included military leaders. Critics acknowledged that the United States had felled a brutal dictator, but coalition forces were not adequately prepared for the turmoil that followed. Nor did they find the weapons of mass destruction or links to Osama bin Laden that administration officials had insisted made the war necessary. Rather, in the chaos induced by the invasion, more than a thousand terrorists entered Iraq — the place, according to one expert, "for fundamentalists to go . . . to stick it to the West."

The war and occupation exacted a steep price in American and Iraqi lives, dollars (more than $750 billion), U.S. relations with other great powers, and the nation's reputation in the world, especially among Arab nations. Revelations of prisoner abuse in the Abu Ghraib prison in Iraq and in the Guantánamo detention camp housing captives from the Afghan war further tarnished the image of the United States, as anti-Americanism rose around the world. The budget deficit swelled, and resources were diverted to Iraq from other national security challenges, including the stabilization of Afghanistan, the elimination of Al Qaeda, and the threats posed by North Korea's and Iran's pursuit of nuclear weapons.

Voters registered their dissatisfaction in 2006, giving Democrats control of Congress for the first time since 1994. A temporary troop surge in Iraq in 2007, along with actions by Iraqi leaders, contributed to a significant reduction in violence, and the administration began planning for the withdrawal of U.S. forces, which was completed at the end of 2011. Peace eluded the Iraqis, however, who continued to live amid sectarian violence. Unrest was exacerbated by the rise of the Islamic State in Iraq and Syria (ISIS), a more brutal and effective offspring of

Al Qaeda. By 2016, ISIS controlled key areas of Iraq and Syria and was linked to or inspired terrorist attacks on civilians in Egypt; Turkey; Paris, France; San Bernardino, California; Orlando, Florida; Brussels, Belgium; and elsewhere.

> **REVIEW** What impact did the terrorist attacks on September 11, 2001, have on U.S. foreign and domestic policies?

The Obama Presidency: Reform and Backlash

Bush's successor, Barack Hussein Obama, aimed to turn the page in both domestic and foreign policy. He achieved major health care reform and some antirecession measures, but a determined grassroots movement on the Republican right pushed the party to oppose the president at every turn. In foreign policy, Obama generally sought a less aggressive, more multilateral approach to challenges around the world. His administration reopened diplomatic relations with Cuba in 2015 and negotiated a treaty with five major powers and Iran to keep that nation from developing nuclear weapons. But most of the Middle East remained an unstable and dangerous place, and the United States seemed increasingly vulnerable to terrorist threats.

Governing during Economic Crisis and Political Polarization.

Obama won an election that represented momentous changes in American politics. The Republican nominee, Senator John McCain of Arizona, a Vietnam War hero, chose as his running mate Alaska governor Sarah Palin, the first Republican woman vice presidential candidate. In the Democratic Party, for the first time, an African American and a woman were the top two contenders. (See "Analyzing Historical Evidence," page 948.) In a hard-fought primary battle, Obama edged out New York senator and former First Lady Hillary Clinton for the nomination.

Born to a white mother and a Kenyan father and raised in Hawai'i and Indonesia, Obama was the first African American to head the *Harvard Law Review*. He settled in Chicago, taught law, served in the Illinois Senate, and won election to the U.S. Senate in 2004. At the age of forty-seven, he won the Democratic presidential nomination with brilliant grassroots and Internet organizing and by promising a new kind of politics and racial reconciliation. Obama won 53 percent of the popular vote and defeated McCain 365 to 173 in the electoral college, while Democrats increased their majorities in the House and Senate.

Defining "individual responsibility and mutual responsibility" as "the essence of the American promise," Obama hoped to work across party lines to enact reforms in health care, education, the environment, and immigration policy, but he confronted a severe economic crisis. A recession had struck in late 2007, fueled by a breakdown in financial institutions that had accumulated trillions of dollars of bad debt, much of it from risky home mortgages. As the recession spread to other parts of the economy and the world, mortgage foreclosures skyrocketed, major companies went bankrupt, and unemployment rose to 9.8 percent in late 2010.

The Great Recession was so severe that Congress passed the Bush administration's $700 billion Troubled Asset Relief Program in 2008 to inject credit into the economy and shore up banks and other businesses. Obama followed with the American Recovery and Reinvestment Act of 2009, $787 billion worth of spending and tax cuts to stimulate the economy and relieve unemployment. He also arranged a federal bailout of General Motors and Chrysler, saving some one million jobs related to the automobile industry. Finally, to address the sources of the financial crisis, Congress expanded governmental regulation with the Wall Street Reform and Consumer Protection Act in 2010. Nonetheless, the recovery was agonizingly slow, and income inequality reached its highest level since the 1920s.

With a Democrat-controlled Congress for only the first two years of his presidency, Obama's domestic achievements fell short of his promises. His judicial appointments increased the number of women on the Supreme Court to three and included the first-ever Latina justice, and he signed legislation that strengthened women's right to equal pay. In addition, Congress ended discrimination against gays in the military and rolled back some of the Bush tax cuts that had disproportionately favored the wealthy.

Obama's paramount achievement was passage of health care reform, putting the United States in step with the other advanced nations that subsidized some kind of health care for all citizens. The **Patient Protection and Affordable Care Act** of 2010 required that nearly everyone carry health insurance, and to that end, it provided subsidies and compelled larger businesses to cover their employees. The law also included protections for health care consumers and contained provisions to limit medical costs. Although liberals failed to get a public option to allow government-managed programs to compete with private insurance plans, the law represented the largest expansion of government since the Great Society. Even though Republicans had previously endorsed key elements of the measure, and it resembled Massachusetts's health care program established under Republican governor Mitt Romney, not a single Republican voted for it. Most Republican governors impeded its implementation in their states.

"Obamacare" (a derisive label later embraced by its supporters), along with the government bailouts of big corporations, helped fuel a grassroots movement of mostly white, middle-class, and older voters funded by billionaire conservatives and encouraged by conservative media. These Americans, self-identified as members of the Tea Party movement, raged at what they considered an overreaching government and the sense that they and their values were being displaced. As one Tea Party supporter put it, "The government is taking over everything — I want my freedom back." Most Tea Party activists defended Social Security and Medicare as programs they had "earned" but resisted any new federal entitlement programs.

The intensely polarized political environment posed a roadblock to reducing unemployment and thwarted Obama's efforts to reform environmental and immigration policy. Obama carried the burden of a nearly 8 percent unemployment rate into the 2012 election, where he faced Republican Mitt Romney. With the electorate deeply divided over the role of the federal government, Obama won easily in the electoral college, with 332 votes to Romney's 206, and he captured 51 percent of the popular vote to Romney's 47 percent (Map 31.4). Yet, following the 2014 midterm elections, Republicans took over both houses of Congress.

With Republicans in Congress blocking him at every turn, Obama used his executive authority to raise the minimum wage for federal workers, protect younger undocumented immigrants from deportation, and chip away at some of the racial injustices in the criminal justice system. He stiffened curbs on motor vehicle and power plant

Patient Protection and Affordable Care Act
Sweeping 2010 health care reform bill that established nearly universal health insurance by providing subsidies and compelling larger businesses to offer coverage to employees. Championed by President Barack Obama, the act also imposed new regulations on insurance companies and contained provisions to limit health care costs.

Analyzing Historical Evidence

Caricaturing the Candidates: Clinton and Obama in 2008

In the Democratic presidential primaries of 2008, political cartoonists faced an unfamiliar challenge. As usual, cartoonists had to draw a recognizable image of a subject but exaggerate or enhance it to make it humorous. For the first time in a U.S. presidential primary campaign, a woman and an African American squared off as major rivals, upsetting centuries-old notions of who a president should be. Political cartoonists now faced the challenge of caricaturing a woman and a black man without opening themselves to charges of sexism or racism.

Hillary Clinton had a long history in political cartoons as First Lady and then as senator from New York. A favorite theme of cartoonists who commented on her active involvement in policy during her husband's presidency suggested that she was exerting too much power rather than playing the traditional supporting role of First Lady. During her own campaign in 2008, cartoonists continued to exaggerate her hips, and they took advantage of the lines on the sixty-year-old's face.

Political cartoonists drawing Barack Obama faced the challenge of avoiding obvious racial stereotypes. In contrast to Clinton, long in the public eye, Obama was a relative newcomer to the national scene, having spent just two years in the U.S. Senate before announcing his candidacy. Forty-seven years old, with a long, lean face and body and closely clipped hair, he provided fewer opportunities for caricature than did Clinton. Obama had already described himself as "a skinny kid with big ears and a funny name," and cartoonists pounced on that image.

In the first cartoon, from February 2008, Hillary Clinton is in the driver's seat of "The Clinton Machine," which is about to crush Barack Obama. Note who is

"THE CLINTON MACHINE" Pat Bagley, The *Salt Lake Tribune*, Cagle Cartoons.

providing the power for the steamroller and how his appearance contrasts with that of Obama. Although Obama had won two of the four earliest primaries, the cartoonist suggests that Hillary Clinton's campaign was about to clobber Obama. Consider what the cartoon suggests about Bill Clinton's role in his wife's campaign and about Hillary Clinton's ambition.

Political cartoonists sometimes use animal images that have certain associations for their viewers. The second cartoon, showing Hillary Clinton as a wasp who will not let go of Obama, reflects the view of Obama supporters that Clinton should have pulled out of the race earlier. By May 2008, Obama had won the most delegates through state primaries. Yet Clinton hung on, claiming that she had won more of the overall popular vote and that she led Obama in support from the so-called superdelegates, including elected officials and party leaders, whose votes were not tied to primary election results. Even after her concession in early June 2008, some cartoons showed her threatening Obama as he contemplated choosing a running mate. This cartoon may have tapped into stereotypes of nagging women and into anxieties about an ambi-

"IT'S NOT MY PLACE" Daryl Cagle, Cagle Cartoons.

tious black man by making him appear weak and deferential.

Although cartoonists tended to portray Clinton and Obama as bitter enemies throughout the primaries, the two politicians began an effective partnership when president-elect Obama selected Clinton for the position of secretary of state in November 2008.

QUESTIONS FOR ANALYSIS

Analyze the Evidence　　What is the effect of portraying Obama as oblivious to the Clinton machine's power in the first cartoon and as unable to stand up to Clinton's determination in the second? What stereotypes about women are conveyed in the ways in which Clinton is drawn in each of the cartoons? Would a man have been portrayed as a wasp?

Recognize Viewpoints　　What attitude about Bill Clinton's role in his wife's campaign is conveyed in the first cartoon? What message does the second cartoon send about Obama in showing Clinton seeming to overpower him, even though he was ahead of her in the race for the nomination? Do you think that these cartoonists successfully avoided sexist or racist stereotypes?

Consider the Context　　In what ways was the election of 2008 groundbreaking?

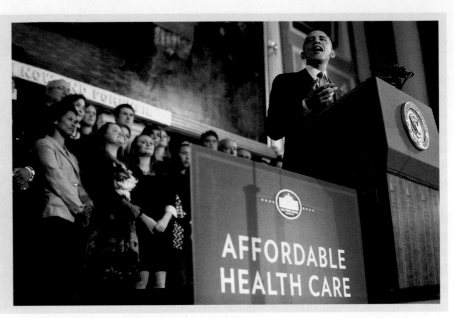

HEALTH CARE REFORM
Repeated breakdowns of the federal government's Web site when it opened for health insurance enrollment in October 2013 added fuel to the critics of the Patient Protection and Affordable Care Act. President Obama chose Faneuil Hall in Boston, where former governor Mitt Romney had signed a similar health reform measure for Massachusetts, to defend the law and promise that the Web site would be fixed. Yoon S. Byun/ The *Boston Globe* via Getty Images.

emissions, encouraged alternative energy development, and helped make possible a landmark climate change agreement signed in Paris in 2015 by 195 nations, which pledged action to reduce carbon emissions that threatened to devastate the earth.

Redefining the War on Terror. Obama criticized much of his predecessor's foreign policy, embodied in Bush's term "global war on terror." Obama believed that that concept exaggerated the threat, rationalized disastrous decisions like the invasion of Iraq, sacrificed American ideals in the pursuit of security, and distracted attention from serious problems at home. In office, however, Obama left some Bush initiatives in place. The Bush administration had ended its use of torture , but Obama failed to convince Congress to close Guantánamo, where sixty prisoners remained, without rights, in 2016. Obama greatly increased the use of unmanned drone strikes in other countries, killing hundreds of people, both terrorists and innocent citizens. Continuing Bush's surveillance programs, the Obama administration secretly collected data about millions of citizens' communications.

Obama followed the Bush administration's plan to withdraw from Iraq, and the last troops departed in 2011, whereupon terrorist violence and sectarian strife grew stronger. He dispatched 50,000 more military personnel to Afghanistan, nearly 10,000 of whom remained there in 2016. In May 2011, U.S. special forces killed Osama bin Laden, who was hiding in Pakistan, weakening but not destroying Al Qaeda and its offshoots.

Obama wanted to regain the trust of Muslim nations, but he sometimes floundered when confronted with difficult decisions about what the United States should do, such as when, in 2011, popular uprisings, collectively referred to as the "Arab Spring," sought reforms from entrenched dictators in Tunisia, Egypt, Libya, and Syria. Each country had experienced long-standing internal divisions, decades of official corruption, and neglect of its population's basic needs, such as water and food; moreover, terrorists operated in each country, hoping to exploit the situation to install a radical fundamentalist Islamic state. Although some rebellions toppled corrupt dictators, such as Libya's Muammar al-Gaddafi, little progress was made toward stability, constitutional government, equal rights, and economic security. Protests in Syria turned into a civil war that took more than 200,000 lives; sent four million Syrians into exile creating a refugee crisis in Europe; and provided an opening for the spread of the radical Islamist organization ISIS.

The calamity of the Iraq War and the desire to improve the nation's international reputation made Obama wary of intervention. Though reluctant to commit military force beyond air strikes and some special forces on the ground, Obama insisted that the United States must remain engaged in the Middle East. Preferring to attack problems with diplomacy, in 2015 Obama worked with China, Russia, France, the United Kingdom, and Germany to secure a treaty with Iran to keep that nation from developing nuclear weapons. The harsh condemnation of the Iran nuclear deal by most Republicans reflected how much Americans disagreed about where their nation's international interests lay and what the United States could and should do to protect those interests and national security.

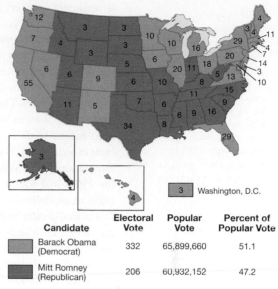

Candidate	Electoral Vote	Popular Vote	Percent of Popular Vote
Barack Obama (Democrat)	332	65,899,660	51.1
Mitt Romney (Republican)	206	60,932,152	47.2

MAP 31.4   THE ELECTION OF 2012

REVIEW What obstacles stood in the way of Obama's reform agenda?

Conclusion: Defining the Government's Role at Home and Abroad

More than two hundred years after the birth of the United States, Colin Powell referred to the unfinished nature of the American promise when he declared that the question of America's role in the world "isn't answered yet." In fact, the end of the Cold War, the rise of international terrorism, and the George W. Bush administration's doctrines of preemption and unilateralism sparked new debates over the long-standing question of how the United States should act beyond its borders.

Nor had Americans set to rest questions about the role of government at home. In a population greatly composed of people fleeing oppressive governments, Americans had always debated what responsibilities the government should shoulder and what was best left to private enterprise, families, churches, and other voluntary institutions. Far more than other industrialized democracies, the United States had relied on private rather than public obligation, individual rather than collective solutions. In the twentieth century, Americans had significantly enlarged the federal government's powers and responsibilities, but the years since the 1960s had seen a decline of trust in government's ability to improve people's lives, even as a poverty rate of 20 percent among children continued and a growing gap between rich and poor intensified into the twenty-first century.

The shifting of control of the government back and forth between Republicans and Democrats from 1989 to 2016 revealed a dynamic debate over government's role in domestic affairs. The first Bush administration's civil rights measure for people with disabilities, Clinton's incremental reforms, and Obama's Affordable Care Act built on a deep-rooted tradition that sought to realize the American promise of justice and human well-being. Those who mobilized against the ravages of globalization worked internationally for what populists, progressives, New Deal reformers, and activists of the 1960s had sought for the domestic population: protection of individual rights, curbs on capitalism, assistance for victims of rapid economic change, and fiscal policies that placed greater responsibility on those best able to pay for the collective good. Even the second Bush administration, which sought to limit government's reach, supported the No Child Left Behind Act and the Medicare prescription drug program; it departed from traditional conservative policy in a gigantic program to bail out failing businesses when the Great Recession struck in 2008. The controversy surrounding Obama's efforts to stimulate the economy and reform health care and the financial industry replayed America's long-standing debate about the government's appropriate role.

The United States became more embedded in the global economy as products, information, and people crossed borders with amazing speed and frequency. New waves of immigration altered the face of the American population and the makeup of its culture. Although the end of the Cold War brought about unanticipated cooperation between the United States and its former enemies, globalization also contributed to the threat of deadly terrorism within America's own borders. In response to those dangers, the second Bush administration launched wars in Afghanistan and Iraq. Both Democratic and Republican presidents sought to maintain the preeminence in the world that the United States had held since World War II, but debate continued about how much it could accomplish in other parts of the world and where and how best to use American power.

Chapter Review

KEY TERMS

Clean Air Act of 1990 (p. 925)

Americans with Disabilities Act (ADA) (p. 925)

Persian Gulf War (p. 928)

Earned Income Tax Credit (EITC) (p. 931)

Temporary Assistance for Needy Families (TANF) program (p. 933)

North American Free Trade Agreement (NAFTA) (p. 937)

World Trade Organization (WTO) (p. 937)

No Child Left Behind Act (p. 941)

USA Patriot Act (p. 943)

Iraq War (p. 944)

Patient Protection and Affordable Care Act (p. 947)

REVIEW QUESTIONS

❶ How did George H. W. Bush respond to threats to U.S. interests as the Cold War came to an end?   (pp. 924–30)

❷ How did President Clinton seek a middle ground in American politics? (pp. 931–35)

❸ What were the costs and benefits to the United States of globalization in the 1990s and early 2000s?   (pp. 935–39)

❹ What impact did the terrorist attacks on September 11, 2001, have on U.S. foreign and domestic policies?   (pp. 940–46)

❺ What obstacles stood in the way of Obama's reform agenda? (pp. 946–51)

MAKING CONNECTIONS

❶ How did the fall of the Soviet Union influence the foreign policy of George H. W. Bush?

❷ How did Clinton's policies differ from those of Democrats in the past?

❸ Explain what economic globalization is, and describe how it affected the U.S. economy and population in the 1990s.

❹ What gave rise to the 9/11 attacks? How did the United States respond?

LINKING TO THE PAST

❶ How did George W. Bush's doctrine of preemption differ from the doctrine of containment? (See chapter 26.)

❷ What features did immigration after 1980 have in common with immigration between 1880 and 1920? What was different? (See chapter 19.)

Appendix Directory

APPENDIX I
Documents   *A-1*

The Declaration of Independence   *A-1*
The Constitution of the United States   *A-3*
Amendments to the Constitution with Annotations
   (including the six unratified amendments)   *A-10*

APPENDIX II
Government
and Demographics   *A-26*

Presidential Elections   *A-26*
Supreme Court Justices   *A-31*
Population Growth, 1630–2010   *A-33*
Major Trends in Immigration, 1820–2010   *A-34*

Documents

THE DECLARATION OF INDEPENDENCE

In Congress, July 4, 1776,

THE UNANIMOUS DECLARATION OF THE THIRTEEN UNITED STATES OF AMERICA

When in the course of human events, it becomes necessary for one people to dissolve the political bands which have connected them with another, and to assume, among the powers of the earth, the separate and equal station to which the laws of nature and of nature's God entitle them, a decent respect to the opinions of mankind requires that they should declare the causes which impel them to the separation.

We hold these truths to be self-evident, that all men are created equal; that they are endowed by their Creator with certain unalienable rights; that among these, are life, liberty, and the pursuit of happiness. That, to secure these rights, governments are instituted among men, deriving their just powers from the consent of the governed; that, whenever any form of government becomes destructive of these ends, it is the right of the people to alter or to abolish it, and to institute a new government, laying its foundation on such principles, and organizing its powers in such form, as to them shall seem most likely to effect their safety and happiness. Prudence, indeed, will dictate that governments long established, should not be changed for light and transient causes; and, accordingly, all experience hath shown, that mankind are more disposed to suffer, while evils are sufferable, than to right themselves by abolishing the forms to which they are accustomed. But, when a long train of abuses and usurpations, pursuing invariably the same object, evinces a design to reduce them under absolute despotism, it is their right, it is their duty, to throw off such government and to provide new guards for their future security. Such has been the patient sufferance of these colonies, and such is now the necessity which constrains them to alter their former systems of government. The history of the present King of Great Britain is a history of repeated injuries and usurpations, all having, in direct object, the establishment of an absolute tyranny over these States. To prove this, let facts be submitted to a candid world:

He has refused his assent to laws the most wholesome and necessary for the public good.

He has forbidden his governors to pass laws of immediate and pressing importance, unless suspended in their operation till his assent should be obtained; and, when so suspended, he has utterly neglected to attend to them.

He has refused to pass other laws for the accommodation of large districts of people, unless those people would relinquish the right of representation in the legislature; a right inestimable to them, and formidable to tyrants only.

He has called together legislative bodies at places unusual, uncomfortable, and distant from the depository of their public records, for the sole purpose of fatiguing them into compliance with his measures.

He has dissolved representative houses repeatedly for opposing, with manly firmness, his invasions on the rights of the people.

He has refused, for a long time after such dissolutions, to cause others to be elected; whereby the legislative powers, incapable of annihilation, have returned to the people at large for their exercise; the state remaining in the mean-time exposed to all the danger of invasion from without, and convulsions within.

He has endeavoured to prevent the population of these States; for that purpose, obstructing the laws for naturalization of foreigners, refusing to pass others to encourage their migration hither, and raising the conditions of new appropriations of lands.

He has obstructed the administration of justice, by refusing his assent to laws for establishing judiciary powers.

He has made judges dependent on his will alone, for the tenure of their offices, and the amount and payment of their salaries.

He has erected a multitude of new offices, and sent hither swarms of officers to harass our people, and eat out their substance.

He has kept among us, in times of peace, standing armies, without the consent of our legislature.

He has affected to render the military independent of, and superior to, the civil power.

He has combined, with others, to subject us to a jurisdiction foreign to our Constitution, and unacknowledged by our laws; giving his assent to their acts of pretended legislation:

For quartering large bodies of armed troops among us:

For protecting them by a mock trial, from punishment, for any murders which they should commit on the inhabitants of these States:

For cutting off our trade with all parts of the world:

For imposing taxes on us without our consent:

For depriving us, in many cases, of the benefit of trial by jury:

For transporting us beyond seas to be tried for pretended offences:

For abolishing the free system of English laws in a neighboring province, establishing therein an arbitrary government, and enlarging its boundaries, so as to render it at once an example and fit instrument for introducing the same absolute rule into these colonies:

For taking away our charters, abolishing our most valuable laws, and altering, fundamentally, the powers of our governments:

For suspending our own legislatures, and declaring themselves invested with power to legislate for us in all cases whatsoever.

He has abdicated government here, by declaring us out of his protection, and waging war against us.

He has plundered our seas, ravaged our coasts, burnt our towns, and destroyed the lives of our people.

He is, at this time, transporting large armies of foreign mercenaries to complete the works of death, desolation, and tyranny, already begun, with circumstances of cruelty and perfidy scarcely paralleled in the most barbarous ages, and totally unworthy the head of a civilized nation.

He has constrained our fellow citizens, taken captive on the high seas, to bear arms against their country, to become the executioners of their friends, and brethren, or to fall themselves by their hands.

He has excited domestic insurrections amongst us, and has endeavored to bring on the inhabitants of our frontiers, the merciless Indian savages, whose known rule of warfare is an undistinguished destruction of all ages, sexes, and conditions.

In every stage of these oppressions, we have petitioned for redress; in the most humble terms; our repeated petitions have been answered only by repeated injury. A prince, whose character is thus marked by every act which may define a tyrant, is unfit to be the ruler of a free people.

Nor have we been wanting in attention to our British brethren. We have warned them, from time to time, of attempts made by their legislature to extend an unwarrantable jurisdiction over us. We have reminded them of the circumstances of our emigration and settlement here. We have appealed to their native justice and magnanimity, and we have conjured them, by the ties of our common kindred, to disavow these usurpations, which would inevitably interrupt our connections and correspondence. They, too, have been deaf to the voice of justice and consanguinity. We must, therefore, acquiesce in the necessity which denounces our separation, and hold them as we hold the rest of mankind, enemies in war, in peace, friends.

We, therefore, the representatives of the United States of America, in general Congress assembled, appealing to the Supreme Judge of the world for the rectitude of our intentions, do, in the name, and by authority of the good people of these colonies, solemnly publish and declare, that these united colonies are, and of right ought to be, free and independent states: that they are absolved from all allegiance to the British Crown, and that all political connection between them and the state of Great Britain is, and ought to be, totally dissolved; and that, as free and independent states, they have full power to levy war, conclude peace, contract alliances, establish commerce, and to do all other acts and things which independent states may of right do. And, for the support of this declaration, with a firm reliance on the protection of Divine Providence, we mutually pledge to each other our lives, our fortunes, and our sacred honor.

The foregoing Declaration was, by order of Congress, engrossed, and signed by the following members:

JOHN HANCOCK

New Hampshire
Josiah Bartlett
William Whipple
Matthew Thornton

Massachusetts Bay
Samuel Adams
John Adams
Robert Treat Paine
Elbridge Gerry

Rhode Island
Stephen Hopkins
William Ellery

Connecticut
Roger Sherman
Samuel Huntington
William Williams
Oliver Wolcott

New York
William Floyd
Phillip Livingston
Francis Lewis
Lewis Morris

New Jersey
Richard Stockton
John Witherspoon
Francis Hopkinson
John Hart
Abraham Clark

Pennsylvania
Robert Morris
Benjamin Rush
Benjamin Franklin
John Morton
George Clymer
James Smith

George Taylor
James Wilson
George Ross

Delaware
Caesar Rodney
George Read
Thomas M'Kean

Maryland
Samuel Chase
William Paca
Thomas Stone
Charles Carroll, of
    Carrollton

North Carolina
William Hooper
Joseph Hewes
John Penn

South Carolina
Edward Rutledge
Thomas Heyward, Jr.
Thomas Lynch, Jr.
Arthur Middleton

Virginia
George Wythe
Richard Henry Lee
Thomas Jefferson
Benjamin Harrison
Thomas Nelson, Jr.
Francis Lightfoot Lee
Carter Braxton

Georgia
Button Gwinnett
Lyman Hall
George Walton

Resolved, That copies of the Declaration be sent to the several assemblies, conventions, and committees, or councils of safety, and to the several commanding officers of the continental troops; that it be proclaimed in each of the United States, at the head of the army.

THE CONSTITUTION OF THE UNITED STATES[1]

Agreed to by Philadelphia Convention, September 17, 1787. Implemented March 4, 1789.

Preamble

We the people of the United States, in order to form a more perfect union, establish justice, insure domestic tranquility, provide for the common defense, promote the general welfare, and secure the blessings of liberty to ourselves and our posterity, do ordain and establish this Constitution for the United States of America.

Article I

Section 1 All legislative powers herein granted shall be vested in a Congress of the United States, which shall consist of a Senate and a House of Representatives.

Section 2 The House of Representatives shall be composed of members chosen every second year by the people of the several States, and the electors in each State shall have the qualifications requisite for electors of the most numerous branch of the State Legislature.

No person shall be a Representative who shall not have attained to the age of twenty-five years, and been seven years a citizen of the United States, and who shall not, when elected, be an inhabitant of that State in which he shall be chosen.

Representatives and direct taxes shall be apportioned among the several States which may be included within this Union, according to their respective numbers, *which shall be determined by adding to the whole number of free persons, including those bound to service for a term of years and excluding Indians not taxed, three-fifths of all other persons.* The actual enumeration shall be made within three years after the first meeting of the

---

[1]Passages no longer in effect are in italic type.

Congress of the United States, and within every subsequent term of ten years, in such manner as they shall by law direct. The number of Representatives shall not exceed one for every thirty thousand, but each State shall have at least one Representative; *and until such enumeration shall be made, the State of New Hampshire shall be entitled to choose three, Massachusetts eight, Rhode Island and Providence Plantations one, Connecticut five, New York six, New Jersey four, Pennsylvania eight, Delaware one, Maryland six, Virginia ten, North Carolina five, South Carolina five, and Georgia three.*

When vacancies happen in the representation from any State, the Executive authority thereof shall issue writs of election to fill such vacancies.

The House of Representatives shall choose their Speaker and other officers; and shall have the sole power of impeachment.

Section 3 The Senate of the United States shall be composed of two Senators from each State, *chosen by the legislature thereof,* for six years; and each Senator shall have one vote.

Immediately after they shall be assembled in consequence of the first election, they shall be divided as equally as may be into three classes. The seats of the Senators of the first class shall be vacated at the expiration of the second year, of the second class at the expiration of the fourth year, and of the third class at the expiration of the sixth year, so that one-third may be chosen every second year; *and if vacancies happen by resignation or otherwise, during the recess of the legislature of any State, the Executive thereof may make temporary appointments until the next meeting of the legislature, which shall then fill such vacancies.*

No person shall be a Senator who shall not have attained to the age of thirty years, and been nine years a citizen of the United States, and who shall not, when elected, be an inhabitant of that State for which he shall be chosen.

The Vice-President of the United States shall be President of the Senate, but shall have no vote, unless they be equally divided.

The Senate shall choose their other officers, and also a President pro tempore, in the absence of the Vice-President, or when he shall exercise the office of President of the United States.

The Senate shall have the sole power to try all impeachments. When sitting for that purpose, they shall be on oath or affirmation. When the President of the United States is tried, the Chief Justice shall preside: and no person shall be convicted without the concurrence of two-thirds of the members present.

Judgment in cases of impeachment shall not extend further than to removal from the office, and disqualification to hold and enjoy any office of honor, trust or profit under the United States: but the party convicted shall nevertheless be liable and subject to indictment, trial, judgment and punishment, according to law.

Section 4 The times, places and manner of holding elections for Senators and Representatives shall be prescribed in each State by the legislature thereof; but the Congress may at any time by law make or alter such regulations, except as to the places of choosing Senators.

The Congress shall assemble at least once in every year, and such meeting *shall be on the first Monday in December, unless they shall by law appoint a different day.*

Section 5 Each house shall be the judge of the elections, returns and qualifications of its own members, and a majority of each shall constitute a quorum to do business; but a smaller number may adjourn from day to day, and may be authorized to compel the attendance of absent members, in such manner, and under such penalties, as each house may provide.

Each house may determine the rules of its proceedings, punish its members for disorderly behavior, and with the concurrence of two-thirds, expel a member.

Each house shall keep a journal of its proceedings, and from time to time publish the same, excepting such parts as may in their judgment require secrecy; and the yeas and nays of the members of either house on any question shall, at the desire of one-fifth of those present, be entered on the journal.

Neither house, during the session of Congress, shall, without the consent of the other, adjourn for more than three days, nor to any other place than that in which the two houses shall be sitting.

Section 6 The Senators and Representatives shall receive a compensation for their services, to be ascertained by law and paid out of the treasury of the

United States. They shall in all cases except treason, felony and breach of the peace, be privileged from arrest during their attendance at the session of their respective houses, and in going to and returning from the same; and for any speech or debate in either house, they shall not be questioned in any other place.

No Senator or Representative shall, during the time for which he was elected, be appointed to any civil office under the authority of the United States, which shall have been created, or the emoluments whereof shall have been increased, during such time; and no person holding any office under the United States shall be a member of either house during his continuance in office.

Section 7 All bills for raising revenue shall originate in the House of Representatives; but the Senate may propose or concur with amendments as on other bills.

Every bill which shall have passed the House of Representatives and the Senate, shall, before it become a law, be presented to the President of the United States; if he approve he shall sign it, but if not he shall return it with objections to that house in which it shall have originated, who shall enter the objections at large on their journal, and proceed to reconsider it. If after such reconsideration two-thirds of that house shall agree to pass the bill, it shall be sent, together with the objections, to the other house, by which it shall likewise be reconsidered, and, if approved by two-thirds of that house, it shall become a law. But in all such cases the votes of both houses shall be determined by yeas and nays, and the names of the persons voting for and against the bill shall be entered on the journal of each house respectively. If any bill shall not be returned by the President within ten days (Sundays excepted) after it shall have been presented to him, the same shall be a law, in like manner as if he had signed it, unless the Congress by their adjournment prevent its return, in which case it shall not be a law.

Every order, resolution, or vote to which the concurrence of the Senate and House of Representatives may be necessary (except on a question of adjournment) shall be presented to the President of the United States; and before the same shall take effect, shall be approved by him, or being disapproved by him, shall be repassed by two-thirds of the Senate and House of Representatives, according to the rules and limitations prescribed in the case of a bill.

Section 8 The Congress shall have power

To lay and collect taxes, duties, imposts, and excises, to pay the debts and provide for the common defense and general welfare of the United States; but all duties, imposts and excises shall be uniform throughout the United States;

To borrow money on the credit of the United States;

To regulate commerce with foreign nations, and among the several States, and with the Indian tribes;

To establish an uniform rule of naturalization, and uniform laws on the subject of bankruptcies throughout the United States;

To coin money, regulate the value thereof, and of foreign coin, and fix the standard of weights and measures;

To provide for the punishment of counterfeiting the securities and current coin of the United States;

To establish post offices and post roads;

To promote the progress of science and useful arts by securing for limited times to authors and inventors the exclusive right to their respective writings and discoveries;

To constitute tribunals inferior to the Supreme Court;

To define and punish piracies and felonies committed on the high seas and offences against the law of nations;

To declare war, grant letters of marque and reprisal, and make rules concerning captures on land and water;

To raise and support armies, but no appropriation of money to that use shall be for a longer term than two years;

To provide and maintain a navy;

To make rules for the government and regulation of the land and naval forces;

To provide for calling forth the militia to execute the laws of the Union, suppress insurrections and repel invasions;

To provide for organizing, arming, and disciplining the militia, and for governing such part of them as may be employed in the service of the United States, reserving to the States respectively the appointment of the officers, and the authority of training the militia according to the discipline prescribed by Congress;

To exercise exclusive legislation in all cases whatsoever, over such district (not exceeding ten miles square) as may, by cession of particular States, and the acceptance of Congress, become the seat of the government of the United States, and to exercise like authority over all places purchased by the consent of the legislature of the State, in which the same shall be, for erection of forts, magazines, arsenals, dock-yards, and other needful buildings;—and

To make all laws which shall be necessary and proper for carrying into execution the foregoing powers, and all other powers vested by this Constitution in the government of the United States, or in any department or officer thereof.

Section 9 *The migration or importation of such persons as any of the States now existing shall think proper to admit shall not be prohibited by the Congress prior to the year one thousand eight hundred and eight; but a tax or duty may be imposed on such importation, not exceeding ten dollars for each person.*

The privilege of the writ of habeas corpus shall not be suspended, unless when in cases of rebellion or invasion the public safety may require it.

No bill of attainder or ex post facto law shall be passed.

No capitation, or other direct, tax shall be laid, unless in proportion to the census or enumeration herein before directed to be taken.

No tax or duty shall be laid on articles exported from any State.

No preference shall be given by any regulation of commerce or revenue to the ports of one State over those of another; nor shall vessels bound to, or from, one State be obliged to enter, clear, or pay duties in another.

No money shall be drawn from the treasury, but in consequence of appropriations made by law; and a regular statement and account of the receipts and expenditures of all public money shall be published from time to time.

No title of nobility shall be granted by the United States: and no person holding any office of profit or trust under them, shall, without the consent of the Congress, accept of any present, emolument, office, or title, of any kind whatever, from any king, prince, or foreign state.

Section 10 No State shall enter into any treaty, alliance, or confederation; grant letters of marque and reprisal; coin money; emit bills of credit; make anything but gold and silver coin a tender in payment of debts; pass any bill of attainder, ex post facto law, or law impairing the obligation of contracts, or grant any title of nobility.

No State shall, without the consent of Congress, lay any imposts or duties on imports or exports, except what may be absolutely necessary for executing its inspection laws: and the net produce of all duties and imposts, laid by any State on imports or exports, shall be for the use of the treasury of the United States; and all such laws shall be subject to the revision and control of the Congress.

No State shall, without the consent of Congress, lay any duty of tonnage, keep troops, or ships of war in time of peace, enter into any agreement or compact with another State, or with a foreign power, or engage in war, unless actually invaded, or in such imminent danger as will not admit of delay.

Article II

Section 1 The executive power shall be vested in a President of the United States of America. He shall hold his office during the term of four years, and, together with the Vice-President, chosen for the same term, be elected as follows:

Each State shall appoint, in such manner as the legislature thereof may direct, a number of electors, equal to the whole number of Senators and Representatives to which the State may be entitled in the Congress; but no Senator or Representative, or person holding an office of trust or profit under the United States, shall be appointed an elector.

The electors shall meet in their respective States, and vote by ballot for two persons, of whom one at least shall not be an inhabitant of the same State with themselves. And they shall make a list of all the persons voted for, and of the number of votes for each; which list they shall sign and certify, and transmit sealed to the seat of government of the United States, directed to the President of the Senate. The President of the Senate shall, in the presence of the Senate and House of Representatives, open all the certificates, and the votes shall then be counted. The person having the greatest number of votes shall be the President, if such number be a majority of the whole number of electors appointed; and if there be more than one who have such majority, and have an equal number of votes, then the House of Representatives shall immediately choose by ballot one of them for President; and if no person have a majority, then from the five highest on the list said house shall in like manner choose the President. But in choosing the President the votes shall be taken by States, the representation from each State having one vote; a quorum for this purpose shall consist of a member or members from two-thirds of the States, and a majority of all the States shall be necessary to a choice. In every case, after the choice of the President, the person having the greatest number of votes of the electors shall be the Vice-President. But if there should remain two or more who have equal votes, the Senate shall choose from them by ballot the Vice-President.

The Congress may determine the time of choosing the electors, and the day on which they shall give their votes; which day shall be the same throughout the United States.

No person except a natural-born citizen, *or a citizen of the United States at the time of the adoption of this Constitution*, shall be eligible to the office of President; neither shall any person be eligible to that office who shall not have attained to the age of thirty-five years, and been fourteen years a resident within the United States.

In cases of the removal of the President from office or of his death, resignation, or inability to discharge the powers and duties of the said office, the same shall devolve on the Vice-President, and the Congress may by law provide for the case of removal, death, resignation, or inability, both of the President and Vice President, declaring what officer shall then act as President, and such officer shall act accordingly, until the disability be removed, or a President shall be elected.

The President shall, at stated times, receive for his services a compensation, which shall neither be increased nor diminished during the period for which he shall have been elected, and he shall not receive within that period any other emolument from the United States, or any of them.

Before he enter on the execution of his office, he shall take the following oath or affirmation:—"I do solemnly swear (or affirm) that I will faithfully execute the office of the President of the United States, and will to the best of my ability preserve, protect and defend the Constitution of the United States."

Section 2 The President shall be commander in chief of the army and navy of the United States, and of the militia of the several States, when called into the actual service of the United States; he may require the opinion, in writing, of the principal officer in each of the executive departments, upon any subject relating to the duties of their respective offices, and he shall have power to grant reprieves and pardons for offenses against the United States, except in cases of impeachment.

He shall have power, by and with the advice and consent of the Senate, to make treaties, provided two-thirds of the Senators present concur; and he shall nominate, and by and with the advice and consent of the Senate, shall appoint ambassadors, other public ministers and consuls, judges of the Supreme Court, and all other officers of the United States, whose appointments are not herein otherwise provided for, and which shall be established by law: but Congress may by law vest the appointment of such inferior officers, as they think proper, in the President alone, in the courts of law, or in the heads of departments.

The President shall have power to fill up all vacancies that may happen during the recess of the Senate, by granting commissions which shall expire at the end of their next session.

Section 3 He shall from time to time give to the Congress information of the state of the Union, and recommend to their consideration such measures as he shall judge necessary and expedient; he may, on extraordinary occasions, convene both houses, or either of them, and in case of disagreement between them, with respect to the time of adjournment, he may adjourn them to such time as he shall think proper; he shall receive ambassadors and other public ministers; he shall take care that the laws be faithfully executed, and shall commission all the officers of the United States.

Section 4 The President, Vice-President and all civil officers of the United States shall be removed from office on impeachment for, and on conviction of, treason, bribery, or other high crimes and misdemeanors.

Article III

Section 1 The judicial power of the United States shall be vested in one Supreme Court, and in such inferior courts as the Congress may from time to time ordain and establish. The judges, both of the Supreme and inferior courts, shall hold their offices during good behavior, and shall, at stated times, receive for their services a compensation which shall not be diminished during their continuance in office.

Section 2 The judicial power shall extend to all cases, in law and equity, arising under this Constitution, the laws of the United States, and treaties made, or which shall be made, under their authority; — to all cases affecting ambassadors, other public ministers and consuls; — to all cases of admiralty and maritime jurisdiction; — to controversies to which the United States shall be a party; — to controversies between two or more States; — *between a State and citizens of another State;* — between citizens of different States; — between citizens of the same State claiming lands under grants of different States, and between a State, or the citizens thereof, and foreign states, citizens or subjects.

In all cases affecting ambassadors, other public ministers and consuls, and those in which a State shall be party, the Supreme Court shall have original jurisdiction. In all the other cases before mentioned, the Supreme Court shall have appellate jurisdiction, both as to law and fact, with such exceptions, and under such regulations, as the Congress shall make.

The trial of all crimes, except in cases of impeachment, shall be by jury; and such trial shall be held in the State where said crimes shall have been committed; but when not committed within any State, the trial shall be at such place or places as the Congress may by Law have directed.

Section 3 Treason against the United States shall consist only in levying war against them, or in adhering to their enemies, giving them aid and comfort. No person shall be convicted of treason unless on the testimony of two witnesses to the same overt act, or on confession in open court.

The Congress shall have power to declare the punishment of treason, but no attainder of treason shall work corruption of blood, or forfeiture except during the life of the person attainted.

Article IV

Section 1 Full faith and credit shall be given in each State to the public acts, records, and judicial proceedings of every other State. And the Congress may by general laws prescribe the manner in which such acts, records, and proceedings shall be proved, and the effect thereof.

Section 2 The citizens of each State shall be entitled to all privileges and immunities of citizens in the several States.

A person charged in any State with treason, felony, or other crime, who shall flee from justice, and be found in another State, shall on demand of the executive authority of the State from which he fled, be delivered up, to be removed to the State having jurisdiction of the crime.

No Person held to service or labor in one State, under the laws thereof, escaping into another, shall, in consequence of any law or regulation therein, be discharged from such service or labor, but shall be delivered up on claim of the party to whom such service or labor may be due.

Section 3 New States may be admitted by the Congress into this Union; but no new State shall be formed or erected within the jurisdiction of any other State; nor any State be formed by the junction of two or more States, or parts of States, without the consent of the legislatures of the States concerned as well as of the Congress.

The Congress shall have power to dispose of and make all needful rules and regulations respecting the territory or other property belonging to the United States; and nothing in this Constitution shall be so construed as to prejudice any claims of the United States, or of any particular State.

Section 4 The United States shall guarantee to every State in this Union a republican form of government, and shall protect each of them against invasion; and on application of the legislature, or of the executive (when the legislature cannot be convened), against domestic violence.

Article V

The Congress, whenever two-thirds of both houses shall deem it necessary, shall propose amendments to this Constitution, or, on the application of the legislatures of two-thirds of the several States, shall call a convention for proposing amendments, which, in either case, shall be valid to all intents and purposes, as part of this Constitution, when ratified by the legislatures of three-fourths of the several States, or by conventions in three-fourths thereof, as the one or the other mode of ratification may be proposed by the Congress; provided *that no amendments which may be made prior to the year one thousand eight hundred and eight shall in any manner affect the first and fourth clauses in the ninth section of the first article*; and that no State, without its consent, shall be deprived of its equal suffrage in the Senate.

Article VI

All debts contracted and engagements entered into, before the adoption of this Constitution, shall be as valid against the United States under this Constitution, as under the Confederation.

This Constitution, and the laws of the United States which shall be made in pursuance thereof; and all treaties made, or which shall be made, under the authority of the United States, shall be the supreme law of the land; and the judges in every State shall be bound thereby, anything in the Constitution or laws of any State to the contrary notwithstanding.

The Senators and Representatives before mentioned, and the members of the several State legislatures, and all executive and judicial officers, both of the United States and of the several States, shall be bound by oath or affirmation to support this Constitution; but no religious test shall ever be required as a qualification to any office or public trust under the United States.

Article VII

The ratification of the conventions of nine States shall be sufficient for the establishment of this Constitution between the States so ratifying the same.

Done in convention by the unanimous consent of the States present, the seventeenth day of September in the year of our Lord one thousand seven hundred and eighty-seven and of the Independence of the United States of America the twelfth. In witness whereof we have hereunto subscribed our names.

GEORGE WASHINGTON
President and Deputy from Virginia

New Hampshire
John Langdon
Nicholas Gilman

Massachusetts
Nathaniel Gorham
Rufus King

Connecticut
William Samuel Johnson
Roger Sherman

New York
Alexander Hamilton

New Jersey
William Livingston
David Brearley
William Paterson
Jonathan Dayton

Pennsylvania
Benjamin Franklin
Thomas Mifflin
Robert Morris
George Clymer
Thomas FitzSimons
Jared Ingersoll
James Wilson
Gouverneur Morris

Delaware
George Read
Gunning Bedford, Jr.
John Dickinson
Richard Bassett
Jacob Broom

Maryland
James McHenry
Daniel of St. Thomas
   Jenifer
Daniel Carroll

Virginia
John Blair
James Madison, Jr.

North Carolina
William Blount
Richard Dobbs Spaight
Hugh Williamson

South Carolina
John Rutledge
Charles Cotesworth
   Pinckney
Charles Pinckney
Pierce Butler

Georgia
William Few
Abraham Baldwin

AMENDMENTS TO THE CONSTITUTION WITH ANNOTATIONS (including the six unratified amendments)

- *IN THEIR EFFORT TO GAIN Antifederalists' support for the Constitution, Federalists frequently pointed to the inclusion of Article 5, which provides an orderly method of amending the Constitution. In contrast, the Articles of Confederation, which were universally recognized as seriously flawed, offered no means of amendment. For their part, Antifederalists argued that the amendment process was so "intricate" that one might as easily roll "sixes an hundred times in succession" as change the Constitution.*

    The system for amendment laid out in the Constitution requires that two-thirds of both houses of Congress agree to a proposed amendment, which must then be ratified by three-quarters of the legislatures of the states. Alternatively, an amendment may be proposed by a convention called by the legislatures of two-thirds of the states. Since 1789, members of Congress have proposed thousands of amendments. Besides the seventeen amendments added since 1789, only the six "unratified" ones included here were approved by two-thirds of both houses and sent to the states for ratification.

    Among the many amendments that never made it out of Congress have been proposals to declare dueling, divorce, and interracial marriage unconstitutional as well as proposals to establish a national university, to acknowledge the sovereignty of Jesus Christ, and to prohibit any person from possessing wealth in excess of $10 million.[2]

    Among the issues facing Americans today that might lead to constitutional amendment are efforts to balance the federal budget, to limit the number of terms elected officials may serve, to limit access to or prohibit abortion, to establish English as the official language of the United States, and to prohibit flag burning. None of these proposed amendments has yet garnered enough support in Congress to be sent to the states for ratification.

    Although the first ten amendments to the Constitution are commonly known as the Bill of Rights, only Amendments 1–8 actually provide guarantees of individual rights. Amendments 9 and 10 deal with the structure of power within the constitutional system. The Bill of Rights was promised to appease Antifederalists who refused to ratify the Constitution without guarantees of individual liberties and limitations to federal power. After studying more than two hundred amendments recommended by the ratifying conventions of the states, Federalist James Madison presented a list of seventeen to Congress, which used Madison's list as the foundation for the twelve amendments that were sent to the states for ratification. Ten of the twelve were adopted in 1791. The first on the list of twelve, known as the Reapportionment Amendment, was never adopted (see page A-14). The second proposed amendment was adopted in 1992 as Amendment 27 (see page A-25).

Amendment I

Congress shall make no law respecting an establishment of religion, or prohibiting the free exercise thereof; or abridging the freedom of speech, or of the press; or the right of the people peaceably to assemble, and to petition the government for a redress of grievances.

• • •

- *The First Amendment is a potent symbol for many Americans. Most are well aware of their rights to free speech, freedom of the press, and freedom of religion and their rights to assemble and to petition, even if they cannot cite the exact words of this amendment.*

    The First Amendment guarantee of freedom of religion has two clauses: the "free exercise clause," which allows individuals to practice or not practice any religion, and the "establishment clause," which prevents the federal government from discriminating against or favoring any particular religion. This clause was designed to create what Thomas Jefferson referred to as "a wall of separation between church and state." In the 1960s, the Supreme Court ruled that the First Amendment prohibits prayer (see Engel v. Vitale, *online) and Bible reading in public schools.*

---

[2]Richard B. Bernstein, *Amending America* (New York: Times Books, 1993), 177–81.

Although the rights to free speech and freedom of the press are established in the First Amendment, it was not until the twentieth century that the Supreme Court began to explore the full meaning of these guarantees. In 1919, the Court ruled in Schenck v. United States *(online) that the government could suppress free expression only where it could cite a "clear and present danger." In a decision that continues to raise controversies, the Court ruled in 1990, in* Texas v. Johnson, *that flag burning is a form of symbolic speech protected by the First Amendment.*

Amendment II

A well-regulated militia being necessary to the security of a free State, the right of the people to keep and bear arms shall not be infringed.

• • •

- *Fear of a standing army under the control of a hostile government made the Second Amendment an important part of the Bill of Rights. Advocates of gun ownership claim that the amendment prevents the government from regulating firearms. Proponents of gun control argue that the amendment is designed only to protect the right of the states to maintain militia units.*

  In 1939, the Supreme Court ruled in United States v. Miller *that the Second Amendment did not protect the right of an individual to own a sawed-off shotgun, which it argued was not ordinary militia equipment. Since then, the Supreme Court has refused to hear Second Amendment cases, while lower courts have upheld firearms regulations. Several justices currently on the bench seem to favor a narrow interpretation of the Second Amendment, which would allow gun control legislation. The controversy over the impact of the Second Amendment on gun owners and gun control legislation will certainly continue.*

Amendment III

No soldier shall, in time of peace, be quartered in any house without the consent of the owner, nor in time of war, but in a manner to be prescribed by law.

• • •

- *The Third Amendment was extremely important to the framers of the Constitution, but today it is nearly forgotten. American colonists were especially outraged that they were forced to quarter British troops in the years before and during the American Revolution. The philosophy of the Third Amendment has been viewed by some justices and scholars as the foundation of the modern constitutional right to privacy. One example of this can be found in Justice William O. Douglas's opinion in* Griswold v. Connecticut *(online).*

Amendment IV

The right of the people to be secure in their persons, houses, papers, and effects, against unreasonable searches and seizures, shall not be violated, and no warrants shall issue but upon probable cause, supported by oath or affirmation, and particularly describing the place to be searched, and the persons or things to be seized.

• • •

- *In the years before the Revolution, the houses, barns, stores, and warehouses of American colonists were ransacked by British authorities under "writs of assistance" or general warrants. The British, thus empowered, searched for seditious material or smuggled goods that could then be used as evidence against colonists who were charged with a crime only after the items were found. The first part of the Fourth Amendment protects citizens from "unreasonable" searches and seizures.*

  The Supreme Court has interpreted this protection as well as the words search *and* seizure *in different ways at different times. At one time, the Court did not recognize electronic eavesdropping as a form of search and seizure, though it does today. At times, an "unreasonable" search has been almost any search carried out without a warrant, but in the two decades before 1969, the Court sometimes sanctioned warrantless searches that it considered reasonable based on "the total atmosphere of the case."*

  The second part of the Fourth Amendment defines the procedure for issuing a search warrant and states the requirement of "probable cause," which is generally viewed as evidence indicating that a suspect has committed an offense.

The Fourth Amendment has been controversial because the Court has sometimes excluded evidence that has been seized in violation of constitutional standards. The justification is that excluding such evidence deters violations of the amendment, but doing so may allow a guilty person to escape punishment.

Amendment V

No person shall be held to answer for a capital, or otherwise infamous crime, unless on a presentment or indictment of a grand jury, except in cases arising in the land or naval forces, or in the militia, when in actual service in time of war or public danger; nor shall any person be subject for the same offence to be twice put in jeopardy of life or limb; nor shall be compelled in any criminal case to be a witness against himself, nor be deprived of life, liberty, or property, without due process of law; nor shall private property be taken for public use without just compensation.

• • •

• *The Fifth Amendment protects people against government authority in the prosecution of criminal offenses. It prohibits the state, first, from charging a person with a serious crime without a grand jury hearing to decide whether there is sufficient evidence to support the charge and, second, from charging a person with the same crime twice. The best-known aspect of the Fifth Amendment is that it prevents a person from being "compelled . . . to be a witness against himself." The last clause, the "takings clause," limits the power of the government to seize property.*

  Although invoking the Fifth Amendment is popularly viewed as a confession of guilt, a person may be innocent yet still fear prosecution. For example, during the Red-baiting era of the late 1940s and 1950s, many people who had participated in legal activities that were associated with the Communist Party claimed the Fifth Amendment privilege rather than testify before the House Un-American Activities Committee because the mood of the times cast those activities in a negative light. Since "taking the Fifth" was viewed as an admission of guilt, those people often lost their jobs or became unemployable. (See chapter 26.) Nonetheless, the right to protect oneself against

self-incrimination plays an important role in guarding against the collective power of the state.

Amendment VI

In all criminal prosecutions, the accused shall enjoy the right to a speedy and public trial, by an impartial jury of the State and district wherein the crime shall have been committed, which district shall have been previously ascertained by law, and to be informed of the nature and cause of the accusation; to be confronted with the witnesses against him; to have compulsory process for obtaining witnesses in his favor, and to have the assistance of counsel for his defence.

• • •

• *The original Constitution put few limits on the government's power to investigate, prosecute, and punish crime. This process was of great concern to the early Americans, however, and of the twenty-eight rights specified in the first eight amendments, fifteen have to do with it. Seven rights are specified in the Sixth Amendment. These include the right to a speedy trial, a public trial, a jury trial, a notice of accusation, confrontation by opposing witnesses, testimony by favorable witnesses, and the assistance of counsel.*

  Although this amendment originally guaranteed these rights only in cases involving the federal government, the adoption of the Fourteenth Amendment began a process of applying the protections of the Bill of Rights to the states through court cases such as Gideon v. Wainwright (online).

Amendment VII

In suits at common law, where the value in controversy shall exceed twenty dollars, the right of trial by jury shall be preserved, and no fact tried by a jury shall be otherwise reexamined in any court of the United States, than according to the rules of the common law.

• • •

• *This amendment guarantees people the same right to a trial by jury as was guaranteed by English common law in 1791. Under common law, in civil trials (those involving money damages) the role of the judge was to settle questions of law and that of the jury was to settle questions of fact. The amendment does not specify the size of the jury or its role in a trial, however. The Supreme Court has generally held that those issues be determined by English common law of 1791, which stated that a jury consists of twelve people, that a trial must be conducted before a judge who instructs the jury on the law and advises it on facts, and that a verdict must be unanimous.*

Amendment VIII

Excessive bail shall not be required, nor excessive fines imposed, nor cruel and unusual punishments inflicted.

• • •

- *The language used to guarantee the three rights in this amendment was inspired by the English Bill of Rights of 1689. The Supreme Court has not had a lot to say about "excessive fines." In recent years, it has agreed that, despite the provision against "excessive bail," persons who are believed to be dangerous to others can be held without bail even before they have been convicted.*

   Although opponents of the death penalty have not succeeded in using the Eighth Amendment to achieve the end of capital punishment, the clause regarding "cruel and unusual punishments" has been used to prohibit capital punishment in certain cases (see Furman v. Georgia, *online) and to require improved conditions in prisons.*

Amendment IX

The enumeration in the Constitution, of certain rights, shall not be construed to deny or disparage others retained by the people.

• • •

- *Some Federalists feared that inclusion of the Bill of Rights in the Constitution would allow later generations of interpreters to claim that the people had surrendered any rights not specifically enumerated there. To guard against this, Madison added language that became the Ninth Amendment. Interest in this heretofore largely ignored amendment revived in 1965 when it was used in a concurring opinion in* Griswold v. Connecticut

(online). While Justice William O. Douglas called on the Third Amendment to support the right to privacy in deciding that case, Justice Arthur Goldberg, in the concurring opinion, argued that the right to privacy regarding contraception was an unenumerated right that was protected by the Ninth Amendment.

   In 1980, the Court ruled that the right of the press to attend a public trial was protected by the Ninth Amendment. While some scholars argue that modern judges cannot identify the unenumerated rights that the framers were trying to protect, others argue that the Ninth Amendment should be read as providing a constitutional "presumption of liberty" that allows people to act in any way that does not violate the rights of others.

Amendment X

The powers not delegated to the United States by the Constitution, nor prohibited by it to the States, are reserved to the States respectively, or to the people.

• • •

- *The Antifederalists were especially eager to see a "reserved powers clause" explicitly guaranteeing the states control over their internal affairs. Not surprisingly, the Tenth Amendment has been a frequent battleground in the struggle over states' rights and federal supremacy. Prior to the Civil War, the Democratic Republican Party and Jacksonian Democrats invoked the Tenth Amendment to prohibit the federal government from making decisions about whether people in individual states could own slaves. The Tenth Amendment was virtually suspended during Reconstruction following the Civil War. In 1883, however, the Supreme Court declared the Civil Rights Act of 1875 unconstitutional on the grounds that it violated the Tenth Amendment. Business interests also called on the amendment to block efforts at federal regulation.*

   The Court was inconsistent over the next several decades as it attempted to resolve the tension between the restrictions of the Tenth Amendment and the powers the Constitution granted to Congress to regulate interstate commerce and levy taxes. The Court upheld the Pure Food and Drug Act (1906), the Meat Inspection Acts (1906 and 1907), and the White Slave Traffic Act (1910), all of which affected the states, but struck down an act prohibiting inter-state shipment of goods produced through child labor. Between 1934 and 1935, a number of New Deal programs created by Franklin D. Roosevelt were declared unconstitutional on the grounds that they violated the Tenth Amendment. (See chapter 24.) As Roosevelt appointees changed the composition of the Court, the Tenth Amendment was declared to have no substantive meaning. Generally, the amendment is held to protect the rights of states to regulate inter-nal matters such as local government, education, commerce, labor, and business, as well as matters involving families such as marriage, divorce, and inheritance within the state.

Unratified Amendment
Reapportionment Amendment (proposed by Congress September 25, 1789, along with the Bill of Rights)

After the first enumeration required by the first article of the Constitution, there shall be one Representative for every thirty thousand, until the number shall amount to one hundred, after which the proportion shall be so regulated by Congress, that there shall be not less than one hundred Representatives, nor less than one Repre-sentative for every forty thousand persons, until the number of Representatives shall amount to two hun-dred; after which the proportion shall be so regulated by Congress, that there shall not be less than two hundred Representatives, nor more than one Representative for every fifty thousand persons.

• • •

- *If the Reapportionment Amendment had passed and remained in effect, the House of Representatives today would have more than 5,000 members rather than 435.*

Amendment XI
[Adopted 1798]

The judicial power of the United States shall not be con-strued to extend to any suit in law or equity, commenced or prosecuted against one of the United States by citizens of another State, or by citizens or subjects of any foreign state.

• • •

- *In 1793, the Supreme Court ruled in favor of Alexan-der Chisholm, executor of the estate of a deceased South Carolina merchant. Chisholm was suing the state of Georgia because the merchant had never been paid for provisions he had supplied during the Revolu-tion. Many regarded this Court decision as an error that violated the intent of the Constitution.*

  Antifederalists had long feared a federal court system with the power to overrule a state court.

  When the Constitution was being drafted, Feder-alists had assured worried Antifederalists that section 2 of Article 3, which allows federal courts to hear cases "between a State and citizens of another State," did not mean that the federal courts were authorized to hear suits against a state by citizens of another state or a foreign country. Antifederalists and many other Americans feared a powerful federal court system because they worried that it would become like the British courts of this period, which were accountable only to the monarch. Furthermore, Chisholm v. Georgia *prompted a series of suits against state gov-ernments by creditors and suppliers who had made loans during the war.*

  In addition, state legislators and Congress feared that the shaky economies of the new states, as well as the country as a whole, would be destroyed, especially if loyalists who had fled to other countries sought reim-bursement for land and property that had been seized. The day after the Supreme Court announced its deci-sion, a resolution proposing the Eleventh Amendment, which overturned the decision in Chisholm v. Georgia, *was introduced in the U.S. Senate.*

Amendment XII
[Adopted 1804]

The electors shall meet in their respective States, and vote by ballot for President and Vice-President, one of whom, at least, shall not be an inhabitant of the same State with themselves; they shall name in their ballots the person voted for as President, and in distinct ballots the person voted for as Vice-President, and they shall make distinct lists of all persons voted for as President, and of all persons voted for as Vice-President, and of the number of votes for each, which lists they shall sign and certify, and transmit sealed to the seat of government of the United States, directed to the President of the Senate;—the President of the Senate shall, in the presence of the Senate and House of Representatives, open all the certificates and the votes shall then be counted;—the person having the greatest number of votes for President shall be the President, if such number be a majority of the whole number of electors appointed; and if no person have such majority, then from the persons having the highest numbers not exceeding three on the list of those voted for as President, the House of Representatives shall choose immediately, by ballot, the President. But in choosing the President, the votes shall be taken by States, the representation from each State having one vote; a quorum for this purpose shall consist of a member or members from two-thirds of the States, and a majority of all the States shall be necessary to a choice. And if the House of Representatives shall not choose a President whenever the right of choice shall devolve upon them, before the fourth day of March next following, then the Vice-President shall act as President, as in the case of the death or other constitutional disability of the President.

The person having the greatest number of votes as Vice-President shall be the Vice-President, if such number be a majority of the whole number of electors appointed; and if no person have a majority, then from the two highest numbers on the list the Senate shall choose the Vice-President; a quorum for the purpose shall consist of two-thirds of the whole number of Senators, and a majority of the whole number shall be necessary to a choice. But no person constitutionally ineligible to the office of President shall be eligible to that of Vice-President of the United States.

• • •

- *The framers of the Constitution disliked political parties and assumed that none would ever form. Under the original system, electors chosen by the states would each vote for two candidates. The candidate who won the most votes would become president, while the person who won the second-highest number of votes would become vice president.*

Rivalries between Federalists and Antifederalists led to the formation of political parties, however, even before George Washington had left office. Though Washington was elected unanimously in 1789 and 1792, the elections of 1796 and 1800 were procedural disasters because of party maneuvering (see chapters 9 and 10). In 1796, Federalist John Adams was chosen as president, and his great rival, the Antifederalist Thomas Jefferson (whose party was called the Republican Party), became his vice president. In 1800, all the electors cast their two votes as one of two party blocs. Jefferson and his fellow Republican nominee, Aaron Burr, were tied with 73 votes each. The contest went to the House of Representatives, which finally elected Jefferson after 36 ballots. The Twelfth Amendment prevents these problems by requiring electors to vote separately for the president and vice president.

Unratified Amendment

Titles of Nobility Amendment (proposed by Congress May 1, 1810)

If any citizen of the United States shall accept, claim, receive or retain any title of nobility or honor or shall, without the consent of Congress, accept and retain any present, pension, office or emolument of any kind whatever, from any emperor, king, prince or foreign power, such person shall cease to be a citizen of the United States, and shall be incapable of holding any office of trust or profit under them or either of them.

• • •

- *This amendment would have extended Article 1, section 9, clause 8 of the Constitution, which prevents the awarding of titles by the United States and the acceptance of such awards from foreign powers without congressional consent. Historians speculate that general nervousness about the power of the emperor Napoleon, who was at that time extending France's empire throughout Europe, may have prompted the proposal. Though it fell one vote short of ratification, Congress and the American people thought the proposal had been ratified, and it was included in many nineteenth-century editions of the Constitution.*

The Civil War and Reconstruction Amendments
(Thirteenth, Fourteenth, and Fifteenth Amendments)

- *In the four months between the election of Abraham Lincoln and his inauguration, more than 200 proposed constitutional amendments were presented to Congress as part of a desperate attempt to hold the rapidly dissolving Union together. Most of these were efforts to appease the southern states by protecting the right to own slaves or by disfranchising African Americans through constitutional amendment. None were able to win the votes required from Congress to send them to the states. The relatively innocuous Corwin Amendment seemed to be the only hope for preserving the Union by amending the Constitution.*

  The northern victors in the Civil War tried to restructure the Constitution just as the war had restructured the nation. Yet they were often divided in their goals. Some wanted to end slavery; others hoped for social and economic equality regardless of race; others hoped that extending the power of the ballot box to former slaves would help create a new political order. The debates over the Thirteenth, Fourteenth, and Fifteenth Amendments were bitter. Few of those who fought for these changes were satisfied with the amendments themselves; fewer still were satisfied with their interpretation. Although the amendments put an end to the legal status of slavery, it took nearly a hundred years after the amendments' passage before most of the descendants of former slaves could begin to experience the economic, social, and political equality the amendments had been intended to provide.

Unratified Amendment
Corwin Amendment (proposed by Congress March 2, 1861)

No amendment shall be made to the Constitution which will authorize or give to Congress the power to abolish or interfere, within any State, with the domestic institutions thereof, including that of persons held to labor or service by the laws of said State.

• • •

- *Following the election of Abraham Lincoln, Congress scrambled to try to prevent the secession of the slaveholding states. House member Thomas Corwin of Ohio proposed the "unamendable" amendment in the hope that by protecting slavery where it existed, Congress would keep the southern states in the Union. Lincoln indicated his support for the proposed amendment in his first inaugural address. Only Ohio and Maryland ratified the Corwin Amendment before it was forgotten.*

Amendment XIII
[Adopted 1865]

Section 1 Neither slavery nor involuntary servitude, except as a punishment for crime whereof the party shall have been duly convicted, shall exist within the United States, or any place subject to their jurisdiction.

Section 2 Congress shall have power to enforce this article by appropriate legislation.

• • •

- *Although President Lincoln had abolished slavery in the Confederacy with the Emancipation Proclamation of 1863, abolitionists wanted to rid the entire country of slavery. The Thirteenth Amendment did this in a clear and straightforward manner. In February 1865, when the proposal was approved by the House, the gallery of the House was newly opened to black Americans who had a chance at last to see their government at work. Passage of the proposal was greeted by wild cheers from the gallery as well as tears on the House floor, where congressional representatives openly embraced one another.*

  The problem of ratification remained, however. The Union position was that the Confederate states were part of the country of thirty-six states. Therefore, twenty-seven states were needed to ratify the amendment. When Kentucky and Delaware rejected it, backers realized that without approval from at least four former Confederate states, the amendment would fail. Lincoln's successor, President Andrew Johnson, made ratification of the Thirteenth Amendment a condition for southern states to rejoin the

Union. Under those terms, all the former Confederate states except Mississippi accepted the Thirteenth Amendment, and by the end of 1865 the amendment had become part of the Constitution and slavery had been prohibited in the United States.

Amendment XIV
[Adopted 1868]

Section 1 All persons born or naturalized in the United States, and subject to the jurisdiction thereof, are citizens of the United States and of the State wherein they reside. No State shall make or enforce any law which shall abridge the privileges or immunities of citizens of the United States; nor shall any State deprive any person of life, liberty, or property, without due process of law; nor deny to any person within its jurisdiction the equal protection of the laws.

Section 2 Representatives shall be appointed among the several States according to their respective numbers, counting the whole number of persons in each State, excluding Indians not taxed. But when the right to vote at any election for the choice of Electors for President and Vice-President of the United States, Representatives in Congress, the executive and judicial officers of a State, or the members of the legislature thereof, is denied to any of the male inhabitants of such State, being twenty-one years of age and citizens of the United States, or in any way abridged, except for participation in rebellion, or other crime, the basis of representation therein shall be reduced in the proportion which the number of such male citizens shall bear to the whole number of male citizens twenty-one years of age in such State.

Section 3 No person shall be a Senator or Representative in Congress, or Elector of President and Vice-President, or hold any office, civil or military, under the United States, or under any State, who, having previously taken an oath, as a member of Congress, or as an officer of the United States, or as a member of any State legislature, or as an executive or judicial officer of any State, to support the Constitution of the United States, shall have engaged in insurrection or rebellion against the same, or given aid or comfort to the enemies thereof.

Congress may, by a vote of two-thirds of each house, remove such disability.

Section 4 The validity of the public debt of the United States, authorized by law, including debts incurred for payment of pensions and bounties for services in suppressing insurrection or rebellion, shall not be questioned. But neither the United States nor any State shall assume or pay any debt or obligation incurred in aid of insurrection or rebellion against the United States, or any claim for the loss or emancipation of any slave; but all such debts, obligations, and claims shall be held illegal and void.

Section 5 The Congress shall have power to enforce, by appropriate legislation, the provisions of this article.

• • •

- *Without Lincoln's leadership in the reconstruction of the nation following the Civil War, it soon became clear that the Thirteenth Amendment needed additional constitutional support. Less than a year after Lincoln's assassination, Andrew Johnson was ready to bring the former Confederate states back into the Union with few changes in their governments or politics. Anxious Republicans drafted the Fourteenth Amendment to prevent that from happening. The most important provisions of this complex amendment made all native-born or naturalized persons American citizens and prohibited states from abridging the "privileges or immunities" of citizens; depriving them of "life, liberty, or property, without due process of law"; and denying them "equal protection of the laws." In essence, it made all ex-slaves citizens and protected the rights of all citizens against violation by their own state governments.*

  As occurred in the case of the Thirteenth Amendment, former Confederate states were forced to ratify the amendment as a condition of representation in the House and the Senate. The intentions of the Fourteenth Amendment, and how those intentions should be enforced, have been the most debated point of constitutional history. The terms due process *and* equal protection *have been especially troublesome. Was the amendment designed to outlaw racial segregation? Or was the goal simply to prevent the leaders of the rebellious South from gaining political power?*

The framers of the Fourteenth Amendment hoped Article 2 would produce black voters who would increase the power of the Republican Party. The federal government, however, never used its power to punish states for denying blacks their right to vote. Although the Fourteenth Amendment had an immediate impact in giving black Americans citizenship, it did nothing to protect blacks from the vengeance of whites once Reconstruction ended. In the late nineteenth and early twentieth centuries, section 1 of the Fourteenth Amendment was often used to protect business interests and strike down laws protecting workers on the grounds that the rights of "persons," that is, corporations, were protected by "due process." More recently, the Fourteenth Amendment has been used to justify school desegregation and affirmative action programs, as well as to dismantle such programs.

Amendment XV
[Adopted 1870]

Section 1 The right of citizens of the United States to vote shall not be denied or abridged by the United States or by any State on account of race, color, or previous condition of servitude.

Section 2 The Congress shall have power to enforce this article by appropriate legislation.

• • •

- *The Fifteenth Amendment was the last major piece of Reconstruction legislation. While earlier Reconstruction acts had already required black suffrage in the South, the Fifteenth Amendment extended black voting rights to the entire nation. Some Republicans felt morally obligated to do away with the double standard between North and South since many northern states had stubbornly refused to enfranchise blacks. Others believed that the freedman's ballot required the extra protection of a constitutional amendment to shield it from white counterattack. But partisan advantage also played an important role in the amendment's passage, since Republicans hoped that by giving the ballot to northern blacks, they could lessen their political vulnerability.*

Many women's rights advocates had fought for the amendment. They had felt betrayed by the inclusion of the word "male" in section 2 of the Fourteenth Amendment and were further angered when the proposed Fifteenth Amendment failed to prohibit denial of the right to vote on the grounds of sex as well as "race, color, or previous condition of servitude." In this amendment, for the first time, the federal government claimed the power to regulate the franchise, or vote. It was also the first time the Constitution placed limits on the power of the states to regulate access to the franchise. Although ratified in 1870, the amendment was not enforced until the twentieth century.

The Progressive Amendments
(Sixteenth–Nineteenth Amendments)

- *No amendments were added to the Constitution between the Civil War and the Progressive Era. America was changing, however, in fundamental ways. The rapid industrialization of the United States after the Civil War led to many social and economic problems. Hundreds of amendments were proposed, but none received enough support in Congress to be sent to the states. Some scholars believe that regional differences and rivalries were so strong during this period that it was almost impossible to gain a consensus on a constitutional amendment. During the Progressive Era, however, the Constitution was amended four times in seven years.*

Amendment XVI
[Adopted 1913]

The Congress shall have power to lay and collect taxes on incomes, from whatever source derived, without apportionment among the several States, and without regard to any census or enumeration.

• • •

- *Until passage of the Sixteenth Amendment, most of the money used to run the federal government came from customs duties and taxes on specific items, such as liquor. During the Civil War, the federal government taxed incomes as an emergency measure. Pressure to enact an income tax came from those who* were concerned about the growing gap between rich and poor in the United States. The Populist Party began campaigning for a graduated income tax in 1892, and support continued to grow. By 1909, thirty-three proposed income tax amendments had been presented in Congress, but lobbying by corporate and other special interests had defeated them all. In June 1909, the growing pressure for an income tax, which had been endorsed by Presidents Roosevelt and Taft, finally pushed an amendment through the Senate. The required thirty-six states had ratified the amendment by February 1913.

Amendment XVII
[Adopted 1913]

Section 1 The Senate of the United States shall be composed of two Senators from each State, elected by the people thereof, for six years; and each Senator shall have one vote. The electors in each State shall have the qualifications requisite for electors of [voters for] the most numerous branch of the State legislatures.

Section 2 When vacancies happen in the representation of any State in the Senate, the executive authority of such State shall issue writs of election to fill such vacancies: Provided, that the Legislature of any State may empower the executive thereof to make temporary appointments until the people fill the vacancies by election as the Legislature may direct.

Section 3 This amendment shall not be so construed as to affect the election or term of any Senator chosen before it becomes valid as part of the Constitution.

• • •

• The framers of the Constitution saw the members of the House as the representatives of the people and the members of the Senate as the representatives of the states. Originally senators were to be chosen by the state legislators. According to reform advocates, however, the growth of private industry and transportation conglomerates during the Gilded Age had created a network of corruption in which wealth and power were exchanged for influence and votes in the Senate. Senator Nelson Aldrich, who represented Rhode Island

in the late nineteenth and early twentieth centuries, for example, was known as "the senator from Standard Oil" because of his open support of special business interests.

Efforts to amend the Constitution to allow direct election of senators had begun in 1826, but since any proposal had to be approved by the Senate, reform seemed impossible. Progressives tried to gain influence in the Senate by instituting party caucuses and primary elections, which gave citizens the chance to express their choice of a senator who could then be officially elected by the state legislature. By 1910, fourteen of the country's thirty senators received popular votes through a state primary before the state legislature made its selection. Despairing of getting a proposal through the Senate, supporters of a direct election amendment had begun in 1893 to seek a convention of representatives from two-thirds of the states to propose an amendment that could then be ratified. By 1905, thirty-one of forty-five states had endorsed such an amendment. Finally, in 1911, despite extraordinary opposition, a proposed amendment passed the Senate; by 1913, it had been ratified.

Amendment XVIII
[Adopted 1919; repealed 1933 by Amendment XXI]

Section 1 After one year from the ratification of this article the manufacture, sale, or transportation of intoxicating liquors within, the importation thereof into, or the exportation thereof from the United States and all territory subject to the jurisdiction thereof, for beverage purposes, is hereby prohibited.

Section 2 The Congress and the several States shall have concurrent power to enforce this article by appropriate legislation.

Section 3 This article shall be inoperative unless it shall have been ratified as an amendment to the Constitution by the legislatures of the several States, as provided by the Constitution, within seven years from the date of the submission thereof to the States by the Congress.

• • •

- *The Prohibition Party, formed in 1869, began calling for a constitutional amendment to outlaw alcoholic beverages in 1872. A prohibition amendment was first proposed in the Senate in 1876 and was revived eighteen times before 1913. Between 1913 and 1919, another thirty-nine attempts were made to prohibit liquor in the United States through a constitutional amendment. Prohibition became a key element of the progressive agenda as reformers linked alcohol and drunkenness to numerous social problems, including the corruption of immigrant voters. While opponents of such an amendment argued that it was undemocratic, supporters claimed that their efforts had widespread public support. The admission of twelve "dry" western states to the Union in the early twentieth century and the spirit of sacrifice during World War I laid the groundwork for passage and ratification of the Eighteenth Amendment in 1919. Opponents added a time limit to the amendment in the hope that they could thus block ratification, but this effort failed. (See also Amendment XXI.)*

Amendment XIX
[Adopted 1920]

Section 1 The right of citizens of the United States to vote shall not be denied or abridged by the United States or by any State on account of sex.

Section 2 Congress shall have the power to enforce this article by appropriate legislation.

• • •

- *Advocates of women's rights tried and failed to link woman suffrage to the Fourteenth and Fifteenth Amendments. Nonetheless, the effort for woman suffrage continued. Between 1878 and 1912, at least one and sometimes as many as four proposed amendments were introduced in Congress each year to grant women the right to vote. While over time women won very limited voting rights in some states, at both the state and federal levels opposition to an amendment for woman suffrage remained very strong. President Woodrow Wilson and other officials felt that the federal government should not interfere with the power of the states in this matter. Others worried that granting*

suffrage to women would encourage ethnic minorities to exercise their own right to vote. And many were concerned that giving women the vote would result in their abandoning traditional gender roles. In 1919, following a protracted and often bitter campaign of protest in which women went on hunger strikes and chained themselves to fences, an amendment was introduced with the backing of President Wilson. It narrowly passed the Senate (after efforts to limit the suffrage to white women failed) and was adopted in 1920 after Tennessee became the thirty-sixth state to ratify it.

Unratified Amendment
Child Labor Amendment (proposed by Congress June 2, 1924)

Section 1 The Congress shall have power to limit, regulate, and prohibit the labor of persons under eighteen years of age.

Section 2 The power of the several States is unimpaired by this article except that the operation of State laws shall be suspended to the extent necessary to give effect to legislation enacted by Congress.

• • •

- *Throughout the late nineteenth and early twentieth centuries, alarm over the condition of child workers grew. Opponents of child labor argued that children worked in dangerous and unhealthy conditions, that they took jobs from adult workers, that they depressed wages in certain industries, and that states that allowed child labor had an economic advantage over those that did not. Defenders of child labor claimed that children provided needed income in many families, that working at a young age developed character, and that the effort to prohibit the practice constituted an invasion of family privacy.*

  In 1916, Congress passed a law that made it illegal to sell goods made by children through interstate commerce. The Supreme Court, however, ruled that the law violated the limits on the power of Congress to regulate interstate commerce. Congress then tried to penalize industries that used child labor by taxing such goods. This measure was also thrown out by the courts. In response, reformers set out to amend the

Constitution. The proposed amendment was ratified by twenty-eight states, but by 1925, thirteen states had rejected it. Passage of the Fair Labor Standards Act in 1938, which was upheld by the Supreme Court in 1941, made the amendment irrelevant.

Amendment XX
[Adopted 1933]

Section 1 The terms of the President and Vice-President shall end at noon on the 20th day of January, and the terms of Senators and Representatives at noon on the 3rd day of January, of the years in which such terms would have ended if this article had not been ratified; and the terms of their successors shall then begin.

Section 2 The Congress shall assemble at least once in every year, and such meeting shall begin at noon on the 3rd day of January, unless they shall by law appoint a different day.

Section 3 If, at the time fixed for the beginning of the term of the President, the President-elect shall have died, the Vice-President-elect shall become President. If a President shall not have been chosen before the time fixed for the beginning of his term, or if the President-elect shall have failed to qualify, then the Vice-President-elect shall act as President until a President shall have qualified; and the Congress may by law provide for the case wherein neither a President-elect nor a Vice-President-elect shall have qualified, declaring who shall then act as President, or the manner in which one who is to act shall be selected, and such person shall act accordingly until a President or Vice-President shall have qualified.

Section 4 The Congress may by law provide for the case of the death of any of the persons from whom the House of Representatives may choose a President whenever the right of choice shall have devolved upon them, and for the case of the death of any of the persons from whom the Senate may choose a Vice-President whenever the right of choice shall have devolved upon them.

Section 5 Sections 1 and 2 shall take effect on the 15th day of October following the ratification of this article.

Section 6 This article shall be inoperative unless it shall have been ratified as an amendment to the Constitution by the Legislatures of three-fourths of the several States within seven years from the date of its submission.

• • •

- *Until 1933, presidents took office on March 4. Since elections are held in early November and electoral votes are counted in mid-December, this meant that more than three months passed between the time a new president was elected and when he took office. Moving the inauguration to January shortened the transition period and allowed Congress to begin its term closer to the time of the president's inauguration. Although this seems like a minor change, an amendment was required because the Constitution specifies terms of office. This amendment also deals with questions of succession in the event that a president- or vice president-elect dies before assuming office. Section 3 also clarifies a method for resolving a deadlock in the electoral college.*

Amendment XXI
[Adopted 1933]

Section 1 The eighteenth article of amendment to the Constitution of the United States is hereby repealed.

Section 2 The transportation or importation into any State, Territory, or Possession of the United States for delivery or use therein of intoxicating liquors, in violation of the laws thereof, is hereby prohibited.

Section 3 This article shall be inoperative unless it shall have been ratified as an amendment to the Constitution by conventions in the several States, as provided in the Constitution, within seven years from the date of the submission thereof to the States by the Congress.

• • •

- *Widespread violation of the Volstead Act, the law enacted to enforce prohibition, made the United States a nation of lawbreakers. Prohibition caused more problems than it solved by encouraging crime, bribery, and corruption. Further, a coalition of liquor and beer manufacturers, personal liberty advocates, and* constitutional scholars joined forces to challenge the amendment. By 1929, thirty proposed repeal amendments had been introduced in Congress, and the Democratic Party made repeal part of its platform in the 1932 presidential campaign. The Twenty-first Amendment was proposed in February 1933 and ratified less than a year later. The failure of the effort to enforce prohibition through a constitutional amendment has often been cited by opponents to subsequent efforts to shape public virtue and private morality.

Amendment XXII
[Adopted 1951]

Section 1 No person shall be elected to the office of the President more than twice, and no person who has held the office of President, or acted as President, for more than two years of a term to which some other person was elected President shall be elected to the office of President more than once. But this article shall not apply to any person holding the office of President when this Article was proposed by the Congress, and shall not prevent any person who may be holding the office of President, or acting as President, during the term within which this Article becomes operative from holding the office of President or acting as President during the remainder of such term.

Section 2 This article shall be inoperative unless it shall have been ratified as an amendment to the Constitution by the legislatures of three-fourths of the several States within seven years from the date of its submission to the States by the Congress.

• • •

- George Washington's refusal to seek a third term of office set a precedent that stood until 1912, when former president Theodore Roosevelt sought, without success, another term as an independent candidate. Democrat Franklin Roosevelt was the only president to seek and win a fourth term, though he did so amid great controversy. Roosevelt died in April 1945, a few months after the beginning of his fourth term. In 1946, Republicans won control of the House and the Senate, and early in 1947 a proposal for an amendment to limit future presidents to two four-year terms was offered to the states for ratification. Democratic critics of the Twenty-second Amendment charged that it was a partisan posthumous jab at Roosevelt.

  Since the Twenty-second Amendment was adopted, however, the only presidents who might have been able to seek a third term, had it not existed, were Republicans Dwight Eisenhower, Ronald Reagan, and George W. Bush and Democrat Bill Clinton. Since 1826, Congress has entertained 160 proposed amendments to limit the president to one six-year term. Such amendments have been backed by fifteen presidents, including Gerald Ford and Jimmy Carter.

Amendment XXIII
[Adopted 1961]

Section 1 The District constituting the seat of Government of the United States shall appoint in such manner as the Congress may direct: A number of electors of President and Vice-President equal to the whole number of Senators and Representatives in Congress to which the District would be entitled if it were a State, but in no event more than the least populous State; they shall be in addition to those appointed by the States, but they shall be considered for the purposes of the election of President and Vice-President, to be electors appointed by a State; and they shall meet in the District and perform such duties as provided by the twelfth article of amendment.

Section 2 The Congress shall have the power to enforce this article by appropriate legislation.

• • •

- When Washington, D.C., was established as a federal district, no one expected that a significant number of people would make it their permanent and primary residence. A proposal to allow citizens of the district to vote in presidential elections was approved by Congress in June 1960 and was ratified on March 29, 1961.

Amendment XXIV
[Adopted 1964]

Section 1 The right of citizens of the United States to vote in any primary or other election for President or

Vice-President, for electors for President or Vice-President, or for Senator or Representative in Congress, shall not be denied or abridged by the United States or any State by reason of failure to pay any poll tax or other tax.

Section 2 The Congress shall have the power to enforce this article by appropriate legislation.

• • •

- *In the colonial and Revolutionary eras, financial independence was seen as necessary to political independence, and the poll tax was used as a requirement for voting. By the twentieth century, however, the poll tax was used mostly to bar poor people, especially southern blacks, from voting. While conservatives complained that the amendment interfered with states' rights, liberals thought that the amendment did not go far enough because it barred the poll tax only in national elections and not in state or local elections. The amendment was ratified in 1964, however, and two years later, the Supreme Court ruled that poll taxes in state and local elections also violated the equal protection clause of the Fourteenth Amendment.*

Amendment XXV
[Adopted 1967]

Section 1 In case of the removal of the President from office or of his death or resignation, the Vice-President shall become President.

Section 2 Whenever there is a vacancy in the office of the Vice-President, the President shall nominate a Vice-President who shall take office upon confirmation by a majority vote of both Houses of Congress.

Section 3 Whenever the President transmits to the President pro tempore of the Senate and the Speaker of the House of Representatives his written declaration that he is unable to discharge the powers and duties of his office, and until he transmits to them a written declaration to the contrary, such powers and duties shall be discharged by the Vice-President as Acting President.

Section 4 Whenever the Vice-President and a majority of either the principal officers of the executive departments or of such other body as Congress may by law provide, transmit to the President pro tempore of the Senate and the Speaker of the House of Representatives their written declaration that the President is unable to discharge the powers and duties of his office, the Vice-President shall immediately assume the powers and duties of the office as Acting President.

Thereafter, when the President transmits to the President pro tempore of the Senate and the Speaker of the House of Representatives his written declaration that no inability exists, he shall resume the powers and duties of his office unless the Vice-President and a majority of either the principal officers of the executive department[s] or of such other body as Congress may by law provide, transmit within four days to the President pro tempore of the Senate and the Speaker of the House of Representatives their written declaration that the President is unable to discharge the powers and duties of his office. Thereupon Congress shall decide the issue, assembling within forty-eight hours for that purpose if not in session. If the Congress, within twenty-one days after receipt of the latter written declaration, or, if Congress is not in session, within twenty-one days after Congress is required to assemble, determines by two-thirds vote of both Houses that the President is unable to discharge the powers and duties of his office, the Vice-President shall continue to discharge the same as Acting President; otherwise, the President shall resume the powers and duties of his office.

• • •

- *The framers of the Constitution established the office of vice president because someone was needed to preside over the Senate. The first president to die in office was William Henry Harrison, in 1841. Vice President John Tyler had himself sworn in as president, setting a precedent that was followed when seven later presidents died in office. The assassination of President James A. Garfield in 1881 posed a new problem, however. After he was shot, the president was incapacitated for two months before he died; he was unable to lead the country, while his vice president, Chester A. Arthur, was unable to assume leadership. Efforts to resolve questions of succession in the event of a presidential disability thus began with the death of Garfield.*

In 1963, the assassination of President John F. Kennedy galvanized Congress to action. Vice President Lyndon Johnson was a chain smoker with a history of heart trouble. According to the 1947 Presidential Succession Act, the two men who stood in line to succeed him were the seventy-two-year-old Speaker of the House and the eighty-six-year-old president of the Senate. There were serious concerns that any of these men might become incapacitated while serving as chief executive. The first time the Twenty-fifth Amendment was used, however, was not in the case of presidential death or illness, but during the Watergate crisis. When Vice President Spiro T. Agnew was forced to resign following allegations of bribery and tax violations, President Richard M. Nixon appointed House Minority Leader Gerald R. Ford vice president. Ford became president following Nixon's resignation eight months later and named Nelson A. Rockefeller as his vice president. Thus, for more than two years, the two highest offices in the country were held by people who had not been elected to them.

Amendment XXVI
[Adopted 1971]

Section 1 The right of citizens of the United States, who are eighteen years of age or older, to vote shall not be denied or abridged by the United States or by any State on account of age.

Section 2 The Congress shall have power to enforce this article by appropriate legislation.

• • •

- *Efforts to lower the voting age from twenty-one to eighteen began during World War II. Recognizing that those who were old enough to fight a war should have some say in the government policies that involved them in the war, Presidents Eisenhower, Johnson, and Nixon endorsed the idea. In 1970, the combined pressure of the antiwar movement and the demographic pressure of the baby boom generation led to a Voting Rights Act lowering the voting age in federal, state, and local elections.*

    In Oregon v. Mitchell (1970), the state of Oregon challenged the right of Congress to determine the age

at which people could vote in state or local elections. The Supreme Court agreed with Oregon. Since the Voting Rights Act was ruled unconstitutional, the Constitution had to be amended to allow passage of a law that would lower the voting age. The amendment was ratified in a little more than three months, making it the most rapidly ratified amendment in U.S. history.

Unratified Amendment
Equal Rights Amendment (proposed by Congress March 22, 1972; seven-year deadline for ratification extended to June 30, 1982)

Section 1 Equality of rights under the law shall not be denied or abridged by the United States or by any State on account of sex.

Section 2 The Congress shall have the power to enforce, by appropriate legislation, the provisions of this article.

Section 3 This amendment shall take effect two years after the date of ratification.

• • •

- *In 1923, soon after women had won the right to vote, Alice Paul, a leading activist in the woman suffrage movement, proposed an amendment requiring equal treatment of men and women. Opponents of the proposal argued that such an amendment would invalidate laws that protected women and would make women subject to the military draft. After the 1964 Civil Rights Act was adopted, protective workplace legislation was removed anyway.*

    The renewal of the women's movement, as a by-product of the civil rights and antiwar movements, led to a revival of the Equal Rights Amendment (ERA) in Congress. Disagreements over language held up congressional passage of the proposed amendment, but on March 22, 1972, the Senate approved the ERA by a vote of 84 to 8, and it was sent to the states. Six states ratified the amendment within two days, and by the middle of 1973 the amendment seemed well on its way to adoption, with thirty of the needed thirty-eight states having ratified it. In the mid-1970s, however, a powerful "Stop ERA" campaign developed. The campaign portrayed the ERA as a threat to "family values" and traditional relationships between men and women. Although thirty-five states ultimately ratified the ERA, five of those state legislatures voted to rescind ratification, and the amendment was never adopted.

Unratified Amendment
D.C. Statehood Amendment (proposed by Congress August 22, 1978)

Section 1 For purposes of representation in the Congress, election of the President and Vice-President, and article V of this Constitution, the District constituting the seat of government of the United States shall be treated as though it were a State.

Section 2 The exercise of the rights and powers conferred under this article shall be by the people of the District constituting the seat of government, and as shall be provided by Congress.

Section 3 The twenty-third article of amendment to the Constitution of the United States is hereby repealed.

Section 4 This article shall be inoperative, unless it shall have been ratified as an amendment to the Constitution by the legislatures of three-fourths of the several states within seven years from the date of its submission.

• • •

• *The 1961 ratification of the Twenty-third Amendment, giving residents of the District of Columbia the right to vote for a president and vice president, inspired an effort to give residents of the district full voting rights. In 1966, President Lyndon Johnson appointed a mayor and city council; in 1971, D.C. residents were allowed to name a nonvoting delegate to the House; and in 1981, residents were allowed to elect the mayor and city council. Congress retained the right to overrule laws that might affect commuters, the height of federal buildings, and selection of judges and prosecutors. The district's nonvoting delegate to Congress, Walter Fauntroy, lobbied fiercely for a congressional amendment granting statehood to the district. In*

1978, a proposed amendment was approved and sent to the states. A number of states quickly ratified the amendment, but, like the ERA, the D.C. Statehood Amendment ran into trouble.

Opponents argued that section 2 created a separate category of "nominal" statehood. They argued that the federal district should be eliminated and that the territory should be reabsorbed into the state of Maryland. Although these theoretical arguments were strong, some scholars believe that racist attitudes toward the predominantly black population of the city were also a factor leading to the defeat of the amendment.

Amendment XXVII
[Adopted 1992]

No law, varying the compensation for the services of the Senators and Representatives, shall take effect, until an election of Representatives shall have intervened.

• • •

• *While the Twenty-sixth Amendment was the most rapidly ratified amendment in U.S. history, the Twenty-seventh Amendment had the longest journey to ratification. First proposed by James Madison in 1789 as part of the package that included the Bill of Rights, this amendment had been ratified by only six states by 1791. In 1873, however, it was ratified by Ohio to protest a massive retroactive salary increase by the federal government. Unlike later proposed amendments, this one came with no time limit on ratification.*

In the early 1980s, Gregory D. Watson, a University of Texas economics major, discovered the "lost" amendment and began a single-handed campaign to get state legislators to introduce it for ratification. In 1983, it was accepted by Maine. In 1984, it passed the Colorado legislature. Ratifications trickled in slowly until May 1992, when Michigan and New Jersey became the thirty-eighth and thirty-ninth states, respectively, to ratify. This amendment prevents members of Congress from raising their own salaries without giving voters a chance to vote them out of office before they can benefit from the raises.

Government and Demographics

PRESIDENTIAL ELECTIONS

Year	Candidates	Parties	Popular Vote	Percentage of Popular Vote	Electoral Vote	Percentage of Voter Participation
1789	**GEORGE WASHINGTON (Va.)***				69	
	John Adams				34	
	Others				35	
1792	**GEORGE WASHINGTON (Va.)**				132	
	John Adams				77	
	George Clinton				50	
	Others				5	
1796	**JOHN ADAMS (Mass.)**	Federalist			71	
	Thomas Jefferson	Democratic Republican			68	
	Thomas Pinckney	Federalist			59	
	Aaron Burr	Dem. Rep.			30	
	Others				48	
1800	**THOMAS JEFFERSON (Va.)**	Dem. Rep.			73	
	Aaron Burr	Dem. Rep.			73	
	John Adams	Federalist			65	
	C. C. Pinckney	Federalist			64	
	John Jay	Federalist			1	
1804	**THOMAS JEFFERSON (Va.)**	Dem. Rep.			162	
	C. C. Pinckney	Federalist			14	
1808	**JAMES MADISON (Va.)**	Dem. Rep.			122	
	C. C. Pinckney	Federalist			47	
	George Clinton	Dem. Rep.			6	
1812	**JAMES MADISON (Va.)**	Dem. Rep.			128	
	DeWitt Clinton	Federalist			89	
1816	**JAMES MONROE (Va.)**	Dem. Rep.			183	
	Rufus King	Federalist			34	
1820	**JAMES MONROE (Va.)**	Dem. Rep.			231	
	John Quincy Adams	Dem. Rep.			1	

*State of residence when elected president.

Year	Candidates	Parties	Popular Vote	Percentage of Popular Vote	Electoral Vote	Percentage of Voter Participation
1824	**JOHN Q. ADAMS (Mass.)**	Dem. Rep.	108,740	30.5	84	26.9
	Andrew Jackson	Dem. Rep.	153,544	43.1	99	
	William H. Crawford	Dem. Rep.	46,618	13.1	41	
	Henry Clay	Dem. Rep.	47,136	13.2	37	
1828	**ANDREW JACKSON (Tenn.)**	Democratic	647,286	56.0	178	57.6
	John Quincy Adams	National Republican	508,064	44.0	83	
1832	**ANDREW JACKSON (Tenn.)**	Democratic	687,502	55.0	219	55.4
	Henry Clay	National Republican	530,189	42.4	49	
	John Floyd	Independent			11	
	William Wirt	Anti-Mason	33,108	2.6	7	
1836	**MARTIN VAN BUREN (N.Y.)**	Democratic	765,483	50.9	170	57.8
	W. H. Harrison	Whig			73	
	Hugh L. White	Whig	739,795	49.1	26	
	Daniel Webster	Whig			14	
	W. P. Mangum	Independent			11	
1840	**WILLIAM H. HARRISON (Ohio)**	Whig	1,274,624	53.1	234	78.0
	Martin Van Buren	Democratic	1,127,781	46.9	60	
	J. G. Birney	Liberty	7,069		—	
1844	**JAMES K. POLK (Tenn.)**	Democratic	1,338,464	49.6	170	78.9
	Henry Clay	Whig	1,300,097	48.1	105	
	J. G. Birney	Liberty	62,300	2.3	—	
1848	**ZACHARY TAYLOR (La.)**	Whig	1,360,099	47.4	163	72.7
	Lewis Cass	Democratic	1,220,544	42.5	127	
	Martin Van Buren	Free-Soil	291,263	10.1	—	
1852	**FRANKLIN PIERCE (N.H.)**	Democratic	1,601,274	50.9	254	69.6
	Winfield Scott	Whig	1,386,580	44.1	42	
	John P. Hale	Free-Soil	155,825	5.0	5	
1856	**JAMES BUCHANAN (Pa.)**	Democratic	1,838,169	45.3	174	78.9
	John C. Frémont	Republican	1,341,264	33.1	114	
	Millard Fillmore	American	874,534	21.6	8	
1860	**ABRAHAM LINCOLN (Ill.)**	Republican	1,866,452	39.9	180	81.2
	Stephen A. Douglas	Democratic	1,375,157	29.4	12	
	John C. Breckinridge	Democratic	847,953	18.1	72	
	John Bell	Union	590,631	12.6	39	
1864	**ABRAHAM LINCOLN (Ill.)**	Republican	2,213,665	55.1	212	73.8
	George B. McClellan	Democratic	1,805,237	44.9	21	
1868	**ULYSSES S. GRANT (Ill.)**	Republican	3,012,833	52.7	214	78.1
	Horatio Seymour	Democratic	2,703,249	47.3	80	

Year	Candidates	Parties	Popular Vote	Percentage of Popular Vote	Electoral Vote	Percentage of Voter Participation
1872	ULYSSES S. GRANT (Ill.)	Republican	3,597,132	55.6	286	71.3
	Horace Greeley	Democratic; Liberal Republican	2,834,125	43.9	66	
1876	RUTHERFORD B. HAYES (Ohio)	Republican	4,036,298	47.9	185	81.8
	Samuel J. Tilden	Democratic	4,288,590	51.0	184	
1880	JAMES A. GARFIELD (Ohio)	Republican	4,454,416	48.5	214	79.4
	Winfield S. Hancock	Democratic	4,444,952	48.1	155	
1884	GROVER CLEVELAND (N.Y.)	Democratic	4,874,986	48.5	219	77.5
	James G. Blaine	Republican	4,851,981	48.3	182	
1888	BENJAMIN HARRISON (Ind.)	Republican	5,439,853	47.9	233	79.3
	Grover Cleveland	Democratic	5,540,309	48.6	168	
1892	GROVER CLEVELAND (N.Y.)	Democratic	5,555,426	46.1	277	74.7
	Benjamin Harrison	Republican	5,182,690	43.0	145	
	James B. Weaver	People's	1,029,846	8.5	22	
1896	WILLIAM McKINLEY (Ohio)	Republican	7,104,779	51.1	271	79.3
	William J. Bryan	Democratic-People's	6,502,925	47.7	176	
1900	WILLIAM McKINLEY (Ohio)	Republican	7,207,923	51.7	292	73.2
	William J. Bryan	Dem.-Populist	6,358,133	45.5	155	
1904	THEODORE ROOSEVELT (N.Y.)	Republican	7,623,486	57.9	336	65.2
	Alton B. Parker	Democratic	5,077,911	37.6	140	
	Eugene V. Debs	Socialist	402,283	3.0	—	
1908	WILLIAM H. TAFT (Ohio)	Republican	7,678,908	51.6	321	65.4
	William J. Bryan	Democratic	6,409,104	43.1	162	
	Eugene V. Debs	Socialist	420,793	2.8	—	
1912	WOODROW WILSON (N.J.)	Democratic	6,293,454	41.9	435	58.8
	Theodore Roosevelt	Progressive	4,119,538	27.4	88	
	William H. Taft	Republican	3,484,980	23.2	8	
	Eugene V. Debs	Socialist	900,672	6.1	—	
1916	WOODROW WILSON (N.J.)	Democratic	9,129,606	49.4	277	61.6
	Charles E. Hughes	Republican	8,538,221	46.2	254	
	A. L. Benson	Socialist	585,113	3.2	—	
1920	WARREN G. HARDING (Ohio)	Republican	16,143,407	60.5	404	49.2
	James M. Cox	Democratic	9,130,328	34.2	127	
	Eugene V. Debs	Socialist	919,799	3.4	—	
1924	CALVIN COOLIDGE (Mass.)	Republican	15,725,016	54.0	382	48.9
	John W. Davis	Democratic	8,386,503	28.8	136	
	Robert M. La Follette	Progressive	4,822,856	16.6	13	

Year	Candidates	Parties	Popular Vote	Percentage of Popular Vote	Electoral Vote	Percentage of Voter Participation
1928	HERBERT HOOVER (Calif.)	Republican	21,391,381	57.4	444	56.9
	Alfred E. Smith	Democratic	15,016,443	40.3	87	
	Norman Thomas	Socialist	881,951	2.3	—	
1932	FRANKLIN D. ROOSEVELT (N.Y.)	Democratic	22,821,857	57.4	472	56.9
	Herbert Hoover	Republican	15,761,841	39.7	59	
	Norman Thomas	Socialist	881,951	2.2	—	
	William Z. Foster	Communist	102,991	0.3	—	
1936	FRANKLIN D. ROOSEVELT (N.Y.)	Democratic	27,751,597	60.8	523	61.0
	Alfred M. Landon	Republican	16,679,583	36.5	8	
	William Lemke	Union	882,479	1.9	—	
1940	FRANKLIN D. ROOSEVELT (N.Y.)	Democratic	27,244,160	54.8	449	62.5
	Wendell Willkie	Republican	22,305,198	44.8	82	
1944	FRANKLIN D. ROOSEVELT (N.Y.)	Democratic	25,602,504	53.5	432	55.9
	Thomas E. Dewey	Republican	22,006,285	46.0	99	
1948	HARRY S. TRUMAN (Mo.)	Democratic	24,105,695	49.5	303	53.0
	Thomas F. Dewey	Republican	21,969,170	45.1	189	
	J. Strom Thurmond	States'-Rights Democratic	1,169,021	2.4	39	
	Henry A. Wallace	Progressive	1,156,103	2.4	—	
1952	DWIGHT D. EISENHOWER (N.Y.)	Republican	33,936,252	55.1	442	63.3
	Adlai Stevenson	Democratic	27,314,992	44.4	89	
1956	DWIGHT D. EISENHOWER (N.Y.)	Republican	35,575,420	57.6	457	60.6
	Adlai Stevenson	Democratic	26,033,066	42.1	73	
	Other	—	—		1	
1960	JOHN F. KENNEDY (Mass.)	Democratic	34,227,096	49.9	303	62.8
	Richard M. Nixon	Republican	34,108,546	49.6	219	
	Other	—	—		15	
1964	LYNDON B. JOHNSON (Texas)	Democratic	43,126,506	61.1	486	61.7
	Barry M. Goldwater	Republican	27,176,799	38.5	52	
1968	RICHARD M. NIXON (N.Y.)	Republican	31,770,237	43.4	301	60.9
	Hubert H. Humphrey	Democratic	31,270,533	42.7	191	
	George Wallace	American Indep.	9,906,141	13.5	46	

Year	Candidates	Parties	Popular Vote	Percentage of Popular Vote	Electoral Vote	Percentage of Voter Participation
1972	**RICHARD M. NIXON (N.Y.)**	Republican	47,169,911	60.7	520	55.2
	George S. McGovern	Democratic	29,170,383	37.5	17	
	Other	—	—		1	
1976	**JIMMY CARTER (Ga.)**	Democratic	40,830,763	50.1	297	53.5
	Gerald R. Ford	Republican	39,147,793	48.0	240	
	Other	—	1,575,459	2.1	—	
1980	**RONALD REAGAN (Calif.)**	Republican	43,901,812	51.0	489	54.0
	Jimmy Carter	Democratic	35,483,820	41.0	49	
	John B. Anderson	Independent	5,719,722	7.0	—	
	Ed Clark	Libertarian	921,188	1.1	—	
1984	**RONALD REAGAN (Calif.)**	Republican	54,455,075	59.0	525	53.1
	Walter Mondale	Democratic	37,577,185	41.0	13	
1988	**GEORGE H. W. BUSH (Texas)**	Republican	47,946,422	54.0	426	50.2
	Michael S. Dukakis	Democratic	41,016,429	46.0	112	
1992	**WILLIAM J. CLINTON (Ark.)**	Democratic	44,908,254	43.0	370	55.9
	George H. W. Bush	Republican	39,102,282	38.0	168	
	H. Ross Perot	Independent	19,721,433	19.0	—	
1996	**WILLIAM J. CLINTON (Ark.)**	Democratic	47,401,185	49.2	379	49.0
	Robert Dole	Republican	39,197,469	40.7	159	
	H. Ross Perot	Independent	8,085,294	8.4	—	
2000	**GEORGE W. BUSH (Texas)**	Republican	50,456,062	47.8	271	51.2
	Albert Gore	Democratic	50,996,862	48.4	267	
	Ralph Nader	Green Party	2,858,843	2.7	—	
	Patrick J. Buchanan	Reform Party	438,760	0.4	—	
2004	**GEORGE W. BUSH (Texas)**	Republican	61,872,711	50.7	286	60.3
	John F. Kerry	Democratic	58,894,584	48.3	252	
	Other	—	1,582,185	1.3	—	
2008	**BARACK OBAMA (Illinois)**	Democratic	69,456,897	52.9	365	56.8
	John McCain	Republican	59,934,314	45.7	173	
2012	**BARACK OBAMA (Illinois)**	Democratic	65,899,660	51.1	332	57.5
	Willard Mitt Romney	Republican	60,932,152	47.2	206	
2016*	**DONALD J. TRUMP (N.Y.)**	Republican	59,704,886	47.5	279	56.5
	Hillary Clinton	Democratic	59,938,290	47.7	228	
	Gary Johnson	Libertarian	4,072,835	3.3	—	
	Jill Stein	Green Party	1,218,065	1.0	—	

*As of 11/10/16

SUPREME COURT JUSTICES

Name	Service	Appointed by	Name	Service	Appointed by
John Jay*	1789–1795	Washington	**Roger B. Taney**	1836–1864	Jackson
James Wilson	1789–1798	Washington	Philip P. Barbour	1836–1841	Jackson
John Blair	1789–1796	Washington	John Catron	1837–1865	Van Buren
John Rutledge	1790–1791	Washington	John McKinley	1837–1852	Van Buren
William Cushing	1790–1810	Washington	Peter V. Daniel	1841–1860	Van Buren
James Iredell	1790–1799	Washington	Samuel Nelson	1845–1872	Tyler
Thomas Johnson	1791–1793	Washington	Levi Woodbury	1845–1851	Polk
William Paterson	1793–1806	Washington	Robert C. Grier	1846–1870	Polk
John Rutledge†	1795	Washington	Benjamin R. Curtis	1851–1857	Fillmore
Samuel Chase	1796–1811	Washington	John A. Campbell	1853–1861	Pierce
Oliver Ellsworth	1796–1799	Washington	Nathan Clifford	1858–1881	Buchanan
Bushrod Washington	1798–1829	J. Adams	Noah H. Swayne	1862–1881	Lincoln
Alfred Moore	1799–1804	J. Adams	Samuel F. Miller	1862–1890	Lincoln
John Marshall	1801–1835	J. Adams	David Davis	1862–1877	Lincoln
William Johnson	1804–1834	Jefferson	Stephen J. Field	1863–1897	Lincoln
Henry B. Livingston	1806–1823	Jefferson	**Salmon P. Chase**	1864–1873	Lincoln
Thomas Todd	1807–1826	Jefferson	William Strong	1870–1880	Grant
Gabriel Duval	1811–1836	Madison	Joseph P. Bradley	1870–1892	Grant
Joseph Story	1811–1845	Madison	Ward Hunt	1873–1882	Grant
Smith Thompson	1823–1843	Monroe	**Morrison R. Waite**	1874–1888	Grant
Robert Trimble	1826–1828	J. Q. Adams	John M. Harlan	1877–1911	Hayes
John McLean	1829–1861	Jackson	William B. Woods	1880–1887	Hayes
Henry Baldwin	1830–1844	Jackson	Stanley Matthews	1881–1889	Garfield
James M. Wayne	1835–1867	Jackson	Horace Gray	1882–1902	Arthur

*Chief Justices appear in bold type.
†Acting Chief Justice; Senate refused to confirm appointment.

Name	Service	Appointed by	Name	Service	Appointed by
Samuel Blatchford	1882–1893	Arthur	**Harlan F. Stone**	1941–1946	F. Roosevelt
Lucius Q. C. Lamar	1888–1893	Cleveland	James F. Byrnes	1941–1942	F. Roosevelt
Melville W. Fuller	1888–1910	Cleveland	Robert H. Jackson	1941–1954	F. Roosevelt
David J. Brewer	1889–1910	B. Harrison	Wiley B. Rutledge	1943–1949	F. Roosevelt
Henry B. Brown	1890–1906	B. Harrison	Harold H. Burton	1945–1958	Truman
George Shiras	1892–1903	B. Harrison	**Frederick M. Vinson**	1946–1953	Truman
Howell E. Jackson	1893–1895	B. Harrison	Tom C. Clark	1949–1967	Truman
Edward D. White	1894–1910	Cleveland	Sherman Minton	1949–1956	Truman
Rufus W. Peckham	1896–1909	Cleveland	**Earl Warren**	1953–1969	Eisenhower
Joseph McKenna	1898–1925	McKinley	John Marshall Harlan	1955–1971	Eisenhower
Oliver W. Holmes	1902–1932	T. Roosevelt	William J. Brennan Jr.	1956–1990	Eisenhower
William R. Day	1903–1922	T. Roosevelt	Charles E. Whittaker	1957–1962	Eisenhower
William H. Moody	1906–1910	T. Roosevelt	Potter Stewart	1958–1981	Eisenhower
Horace H. Lurton	1910–1914	Taft	Byron R. White	1962–1993	Kennedy
Charles E. Hughes	1910–1916	Taft	Arthur J. Goldberg	1962–1965	Kennedy
Willis Van Devanter	1910–1937	Taft	Abe Fortas	1965–1969	L. Johnson
Edward D. White	1910–1921	Taft	Thurgood Marshall	1967–1991	L. Johnson
Joseph R. Lamar	1911–1916	Taft	**Warren E. Burger**	1969–1986	Nixon
Mahlon Pitney	1912–1922	Taft	Harry A. Blackmun	1970–1994	Nixon
James C. McReynolds	1914–1941	Wilson	Lewis F. Powell Jr.	1972–1988	Nixon
Louis D. Brandeis	1916–1939	Wilson	William H. Rehnquist	1972–1986	Nixon
John H. Clarke	1916–1922	Wilson	John Paul Stevens	1975–	Ford
William H. Taft	1921–1930	Harding	Sandra Day O'Connor	1981–2006	Reagan
George Sutherland	1922–1938	Harding	**William H. Rehnquist**	1986–2005	Reagan
Pierce Butler	1923–1939	Harding	Antonin Scalia	1986–2016	Reagan
Edward T. Sanford	1923–1930	Harding	Anthony M. Kennedy	1988–	Reagan
Harlan F. Stone	1925–1941	Coolidge	David H. Souter	1990–2009	G. H. W. Bush
Charles E. Hughes	1930–1941	Hoover	Clarence Thomas	1991–	G. H. W. Bush
Owen J. Roberts	1930–1945	Hoover	Ruth Bader Ginsburg	1993–	Clinton
Benjamin N. Cardozo	1932–1938	Hoover	Stephen Breyer	1994–	Clinton
Hugo L. Black	1937–1971	F. Roosevelt	**John G. Roberts Jr.**	2005–	G. W. Bush
Stanley F. Reed	1938–1957	F. Roosevelt	Samuel Anthony Alito Jr.	2006–	G. W. Bush
Felix Frankfurter	1939–1962	F. Roosevelt			
William O. Douglas	1939–1975	F. Roosevelt	Sonia Sotomayor	2009–	Obama
Frank Murphy	1940–1949	F. Roosevelt	Elena Kagan	2010–	Obama

POPULATION GROWTH, 1630–2010

Year	Population	Percent Increase	Year	Population	Percent Increase
1630	4,600	—	1830	12,866,020	33.5
1640	26,600	473.3	1840	17,069,453	32.7
1650	50,400	89.1	1850	23,191,876	35.9
1660	75,100	49.0	1860	31,443,321	35.6
1670	111,900	49.1	1870	39,818,449	26.6
1680	151,500	35.4	1880	50,155,783	26.0
1690	210,400	38.9	1890	62,947,714	25.5
1700	250,900	19.3	1900	75,994,575	20.7
1710	331,700	32.2	1910	91,972,266	21.0
1720	466,200	40.5	1920	105,710,620	14.9
1730	629,400	35.0	1930	122,775,046	16.1
1740	905,600	43.9	1940	131,669,275	7.2
1750	1,170,800	30.0	1950	150,697,361	14.5
1760	1,593,600	36.1	1960	179,323,175	19.0
1770	2,148,100	34.8	1970	203,302,031	13.4
1780	2,780,400	29.4	1980	226,542,199	11.4
1790	3,929,214	41.3	1990	248,718,302	9.8
1800	5,308,483	35.1	2000	281,422,509	13.1
1810	7,239,881	36.4	2010	308,745,538	9.7
1820	9,638,453	33.1			

SOURCE: *Historical Statistics of the U.S.* (1960), *Historical Statistics of the U.S., Colonial Times to 1970* (1975), *Statistical Abstract of the U.S., 1996* (1996), *Statistical Abstract of the U.S., 2000* (2003), and United States Census (2010).

MAJOR TRENDS IN IMMIGRATION, 1820–2010

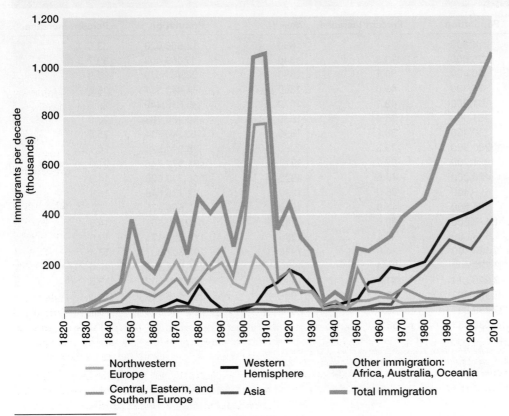

Northwestern Europe

Central, Eastern, and Southern Europe

Western Hemisphere

Asia

Other immigration: Africa, Australia, Oceania

Total immigration

SOURCE: Data from *Historical Statistics of the U.S., Colonial Times to 1970* (1975),
Statistical Abstract of the U.S., 1999 (1999), and *Statistical Abstract of the U.S., 2011* (2011).

Glossary

A Note to Students: For definitions and discussions of words not included here, consult a dictionary and the book's index, which will point you to topics covered at greater length in the book.

Agent Orange Herbicide used extensively during the Vietnam War to destroy the Vietcong's jungle hideouts and food supply. Its use was later linked to a wide range of illnesses that veterans and the Vietnamese suffered after the war, including birth defects, cancer, and skin disorders.

Agricultural Adjustment Act (AAA) New Deal legislation passed in May 1933 aimed at cutting agricultural production and raising crop prices and, consequently, farmers' income. Through the "domestic allotment plan," the AAA paid farmers to not grow crops.

American Expeditionary Force (AEF) American armed forces under the command of General John Pershing who fought under a separate American command in Europe during World War I. They helped defeat Germany when they entered the conflict in full force in 1918.

American Federation of Labor (AFL) Organization created by Samuel Gompers in 1886 that coordinated the activities of craft unions throughout the United States. The AFL worked to achieve immediate benefits for skilled workers. Its narrow goals for unionism became popular after the Haymarket bombing.

American Indian Movement (AIM) Organization established in 1968 to address the problems Indians faced in American cities, including poverty and police harassment. AIM organized Indians to end relocation and termination policies and to win greater control over their cultures and communities.

Americans with Disabilities Act (ADA) Legislation signed by President George H. W. Bush in 1990 that banned discrimination against the disabled. The law also required handicapped accessibility in public facilities and private businesses.

Apollo program Project initiated by John F. Kennedy in 1961 to surpass the Soviet Union in space exploration and send a man to the moon.

appeasement British strategy aimed at avoiding a war with Germany in the late 1930s by not objecting to Hitler's policy of territorial expansion.

baby boom The surge in the American birthrate between 1945 and 1965, which peaked in 1957 with 4.3 million births. The baby boom both reflected and promoted Americans' postwar prosperity.

Battle of the Little Big Horn 1876 battle begun when American cavalry under George Armstrong Custer attacked an encampment of Indians who refused to remove to a reservation. Indian warriors led by Crazy Horse and Sitting Bull annihilated the American soldiers, but their victory was short-lived.

Battle of Midway June 3–6, 1942, naval battle in the Central Pacific in which American forces surprised and defeated the Japanese who had been massing an invasion force aimed at Midway Island. The battle put the Japanese at a disadvantage for the rest of the war.

Bay of Pigs Failed U.S.-sponsored invasion of Cuba in 1961 by anti-Castro forces who planned to overthrow Fidel Castro's government. The disaster humiliated Kennedy and the United States. It alienated Latin Americans who saw the invasion as another example of Yankee imperialism.

Berlin Wall Structure erected by East Germany in 1961 to stop the massive exodus of East Germans into West Berlin, which was an embarrassment to the Communists.

birth control movement Movement launched in 1915 by Margaret Sanger in New York's Lower East Side. Birth control advocates hoped contraception would alter social and political power relationships by reducing the numbers of the working class to induce higher wages and by limiting the supply of soldiers to end wars.

black codes Laws passed by state governments in the South in 1865 and 1866 that sought to keep ex-slaves subordinate to whites. At the core of the black codes lay the desire to force freedmen back to the plantations.

Black Hills Mountains in western South Dakota and northeast Wyoming that are sacred to the Lakota Sioux. In the 1868 Treaty of Fort Laramie, the United States guaranteed Indians control of the Black Hills, but it broke its promise after gold was discovered there in 1874.

black power movement Movement of the 1960s and 1970s that emphasized black racial pride and autonomy. Black power advocates encouraged African Americans to assert community control, and some within the movement also rejected the ethos of nonviolence.

Bolshevik Russian revolutionary. Bolsheviks forced Czar Nicholas II to abdicate and seized power in Russia in 1917. In a separate peace with Germany, the Bolshevik government withdrew Russia from World War I.

Bonus Marchers World War I veterans who marched on Washington, D.C., in 1932 to lobby for immediate payment of the pension ("bonus") promised them in 1924. President Herbert Hoover believed the bonuses would bankrupt the government and sent the U.S. Army to evict the veterans from the city.

bossism Pattern of urban political organization that arose in the late nineteenth century in which an often corrupt "boss" maintains an inordinate level of power through command of a political machine that distributes services to its constituents.

Boxer uprising Uprising in China led by the Boxers, an antiforeign society, in which 30,000 Chinese converts and 250 foreign Christians were killed. An international force rescued foreigners in Beijing, and European powers imposed the humiliating Boxer Protocol on China in 1901.

Brown v. Board of Education 1954 Supreme Court ruling that overturned the "separate but equal" precedent established in *Plessy v. Ferguson* in 1896. The Court declared that separate educational facilities were inherently unequal and thus violated the Fourteenth Amendment.

Camp David accords Agreements between Egypt and Israel reached at the 1979 talks hosted by President Carter at Camp David. In the accords, Egypt became the first Arab state to recognize Israel, and Israel agreed to gradual withdrawal from the Sinai Peninsula.

Carlisle Indian School Institution established in Pennsylvania in 1879 to educate and assimilate American Indians. It pioneered the "outing system," in which Indian students were sent to live with white families in order to accelerate acculturation.

carpetbaggers Southerners' pejorative term for northern migrants who sought opportunity in the South after the Civil War. Northern migrants formed an important part of the southern Republican Party.

Central Intelligence Agency (CIA) Agency created by the National Security Act of 1947 to expand the government's espionage capacities and ability to thwart communism through covert activities, including propaganda, sabotage, economic warfare, and support for anti-Communist forces around the world.

Chicano movement Mobilization of Mexican Americans in the 1960s and 1970s to fight for civil rights, economic justice, and political power and to combat police brutality. Most notably, the movement worked to improve the lives of migrant farmworkers and to end discrimination in employment and education.

Chinese Exclusion Act 1882 law that effectively barred Chinese immigration and set a precedent for further immigration restrictions. The Chinese population in America dropped sharply as a result of the passage of the act, which was fueled by racial and cultural animosities.

Civil Rights Act of 1866 Legislation passed by Congress in 1866 that nullified the black codes and affirmed that black Americans should have equal benefit of the law. This expansion of black rights and federal authority drew a veto from President Johnson, which Congress later overrode.

Civil Rights Act of 1964 Law that responded to demands of the civil rights movement by making discrimination in employment, education, and public accommodations illegal. It was the strongest such measure since Reconstruction and included a ban on sex discrimination in employment.

civil service reform Effort in the 1880s to end the spoils system and reduce government corruption. The Pendleton Civil Service Act of 1883 created the Civil Service Commission to award government jobs under a merit system that required examinations for office and made it impossible to remove jobholders for political reasons.

Civilian Conservation Corps (CCC) Federal relief program established in March 1933 that provided assistance in the form of jobs to millions of unemployed young men and a handful of women. CCC workers worked on conservation projects throughout the nation.

Clean Air Act of 1990 Environmental legislation signed by President George H. W. Bush. The legislation was the strongest and most comprehensive environmental law in the nation's history.

Cold War Term given to the tense and hostile relationship between the United States and the Soviet Union from 1947 to 1989. The term *cold* was apt because the hostility stopped short of direct armed conflict.

Comanchería Indian empire based on trade in horses, hides, guns, and captives that stretched from the Canadian plains to Mexico in the eighteenth century. By 1865, fewer than five thousand Comanches lived in the empire, which ranged from west Texas north to Oklahoma.

Committee for Industrial Organization (CIO) Coalition (later called the Congress of Industrial Organizations) of mostly unskilled workers formed in 1935 that mobilized massive union organizing drives in major industries. By 1941, through the CIO-affiliated United Auto Workers, organizers had overcome violent resistance to unionize the entire automobile industry.

Compromise of 1877 Informal agreement in which Democrats agreed not to block Rutherford Hayes's inauguration and to deal fairly with freedmen, and Hayes vowed not to use the army to uphold the remaining Republican regimes in the South and to provide the South with substantial federal subsidies for railroads. The compromise brought the Reconstruction era to an end.

Comstock Lode Silver ore deposit discovered in 1859 in Nevada. Discovery of the Comstock Lode touched off a mining rush that brought a diverse population into the region and led to the establishment of a number of boomtowns, including Virginia City, Nevada.

containment The post–World War II foreign policy strategy that committed the United States to resisting the influence and expansion of the Soviet Union and communism. The strategy of containment shaped American foreign policy throughout the Cold War.

court-packing plan Law proposed by Franklin Roosevelt to add one new Supreme Court justice for each existing judge who had served for ten years and who was over the age of seventy. Roosevelt wanted to pack the Court with up to six New Dealers who could protect New Deal legislation, but the Senate defeated the bill in 1937.

Coxey's army Unemployed men who marched to Washington, D.C., in 1894 to urge Congress to enact a public works program to end unemployment. Jacob S. Coxey of Ohio led the most publicized contingent. The movement failed to force federal relief legislation.

Cripple Creek miners' strike of 1894 Strike led by the Western Federation of Miners in response to an attempt to lengthen their workday to ten hours. With the support of local businessmen and the Populist governor of Colorado, the miners successfully maintained an eight-hour day.

Cuban missile crisis 1962 nuclear standoff between the Soviet Union and the United States when the Soviets attempted to deploy nuclear missiles in Cuba. In a negotiated settlement, the Soviet Union agreed to remove its missiles from Cuba, and the United States agreed to remove its missiles from Turkey.

Cuban revolution Uprising led by Fidel Castro that drove out U.S.-supported dictator Fulgencio Batista and eventually allied Cuba with the Soviet Union.

cult of domesticity Nineteenth-century belief that women's place was in the home, where they should create havens for their families. This sentimentalized ideal led to an increase in the hiring of domestic servants and freed white middle-class women to spend time in pursuits outside the home.

D Day June 6, 1944, the date of the Allied invasion of northern France. D Day was the largest amphibious assault in world history. The invasion opened a second front against the Germans and moved the Allies closer to victory in Europe.

Dawes Allotment Act 1887 law that divided up reservations and allotted parcels of land to individual Indians as private property. In the end, the American government sold almost two-thirds of "surplus" Indian land to white settlers. The Dawes Act dealt a crippling blow to traditional tribal culture.

détente Term given to the easing of conflict between the United States and the Soviet Union during the Nixon administration by focusing on issues of common concern, such as arms control and trade.

domino theory Theory of containment articulated by President Eisenhower in the context of Vietnam. He warned that the fall of a non-Communist government to communism would trigger the spread of communism to neighboring countries.

Double V campaign World War II campaign in America to attack racism at home and abroad. The campaign pushed the federal government to require defense contractors to integrate their workforces. In response, Franklin Roosevelt authorized a committee to investigate and prevent racial discrimination in employment.

Earned Income Tax Credit (EITC) Federal antipoverty program initiated in 1975 that assisted the working poor by giving tax breaks to low-income, full-time workers or a subsidy to those who owed no taxes. President Clinton pushed through a significant increase in the program in 1993.

Economic Recovery Tax Act Legislation passed by Congress in 1981 that authorized the largest reduction in taxes in the nation's history. The tax cuts benefited affluent Americans disproportionately and widened the distribution of American wealth in favor of the rich.

Eighteenth Amendment (prohibition) Amendment banning the manufacture, transportation, and sale of alcohol. Congress passed the amendment in December 1917, and it was ratified in January 1920. World War I provided a huge boost to the crusade to ban alcohol.

Eisenhower Doctrine President Eisenhower's 1957 declaration that the United States would actively combat communism in the Middle East. Following this doctrine, Congress approved the policy, and Eisenhower sent aid to Jordan in 1957 and troops to Lebanon in 1958.

Ellis Island Immigration facility opened in 1892 in New York harbor that processed new immigrants coming into New York City. In the late nineteenth century, some 75 percent of European immigrants to America came through New York.

Environmental Protection Agency (EPA) Federal agency created by President Nixon in 1970 to enforce environmental laws, conduct environmental research, and reduce human health and environmental risks from pollutants.

Equal Rights Amendment (ERA) Constitutional amendment passed by Congress in 1972 that would require equal treatment of men and women under federal and state law. Facing fierce opposition from the New Right and the Republican Party, the ERA was defeated as time ran out for state ratification in 1982.

family economy Economic contributions of multiple members of a household that were necessary to the survival of the family. From the late nineteenth century into the twentieth, many working-class families depended on the wages of all family members, regardless of sex or age.

Farmers' Alliance Movement to form local organizations to advance farmers' collective interests that gained wide popularity in the 1880s. Over time, farmers' groups consolidated into the Northwestern Farmers' Alliance and the Southern Farmers' Alliance. In 1892, the Farmers' Alliance gave birth to the People's Party.

Federal Deposit Insurance Corporation (FDIC) Regulatory body established by the Glass-Steagall Banking Act that guaranteed the federal government would reimburse bank depositors if their banks failed. This key feature of the New Deal restored depositors' confidence in the banking system during the Great Depression.

finance capitalism Investment sponsored by banks and bankers that typified the American business scene at the end of the nineteenth century. After the panic of 1893, bankers stepped in and reorganized major industries to stabilize them, leaving power concentrated in the hands of a few influential capitalists.

fireside chats Series of informal radio addresses Franklin Roosevelt made to the nation in which he explained New Deal initiatives. The chats helped bolster Roosevelt's popularity and secured popular support for his reforms.

first transcontinental railroad Railroad completed in 1869 that was the first to span the North American continent. Built in large part by Chinese laborers, this railroad and others opened access to new areas, which fueled land speculation and actively recruited settlers.

Five-Power Naval Treaty of 1922 Treaty that committed Britain, France, Japan, Italy, and the United States to a proportional reduction of naval forces, producing the world's greatest success in disarmament up to that time. Republicans orchestrated its development at the 1921 Washington Disarmament Conference.

Fourteen Points Woodrow Wilson's plan, proposed in 1918, to create a new democratic world order with lasting peace. Wilson's plan affirmed basic liberal ideals, supported the right to self-determination, and called for the creation of a League of Nations. Wilson compromised on his plan at the 1919 Paris peace conference, and the U.S. Senate refused to ratify the resulting treaty.

Fourteenth Amendment Constitutional amendment passed in 1866 that made all native-born or naturalized persons U.S. citizens and prohibited states from abridging the rights of national citizens. The amendment hoped to provide a guarantee of equality before the law for black citizens.

free silver Term used in the late nineteenth century by those who advocated minting silver dollars in addition to supporting the gold standard and the paper currency backed by gold. Western silver barons wanted the government to buy silver and mint silver dollars, thereby raising the price of silver.

Freedmen's Bureau Government organization created in March 1865 to distribute food and clothing to destitute Southerners and to ease the transition of slaves to free persons. Early efforts by the Freedmen's Bureau to distribute land to the newly freed blacks were later overturned by President Johnson.

Ghost Dance Religion founded in 1889 by Paiute shaman Wovoka that combined elements of Christianity and traditional Indian religion and served as a nonviolent form of resistance for Indians in the late nineteenth century. The Ghost Dance frightened whites and was violently suppressed.

GI Bill of Rights Legislation passed in 1944 authorizing the government to provide World War II veterans with funds for education, housing, and health care, as well as loans to start businesses and buy homes.

Gilded Age A period of enormous economic growth and ostentatious displays of wealth during the last quarter of the nineteenth century. Industrialization dramatically changed U.S. society and created a newly dominant group of rich entrepreneurs and an impoverished working class.

global migration Movement of populations across large distances such as oceans and continents. In the late nineteenth century, large-scale immigration from southern and eastern Europe into the United States contributed to the growth of cities and changes in American demographics.

good neighbor policy Foreign policy announced by Franklin Roosevelt in 1933 that promised the United States would not interfere in the internal or external affairs of another country, thereby ending U.S. military interventions in Latin America.

gospel of wealth The idea that the financially successful should use their wisdom, experience, and wealth to help the poor. Andrew Carnegie promoted this view in an 1889 essay in which he maintained that the wealthy should serve as stewards of society as a whole.

Great Railroad Strike A violent multicity strike that began in 1877 with West Virginia railroad brakemen who protested against sharp wage reductions and quickly spread to include roughly 600,000 workers. President Rutherford B. Hayes used federal troops to break the strike. Following the strike's failure, union membership surged.

Gulf of Tonkin Resolution Resolution passed by Congress in 1964 in the wake of a naval confrontation in the Gulf of Tonkin. It gave the president virtually unlimited authority in conducting the Vietnam War.

The Senate terminated the resolution following outrage over the U.S. invasion of Cambodia in 1970.

Haymarket bombing May 4, 1886, conflict in which both workers and policemen were killed or wounded during a labor demonstration in Chicago. The violence began when someone threw a bomb into the ranks of police at the gathering. The incident created a backlash against labor activism.

Helsinki accords 1975 agreement signed by U.S., Canadian, Soviet, and European leaders, recognizing the post–World War II borders in Europe and pledging the signatories to respect human rights and fundamental freedoms.

Hernandez v. Texas 1954 Supreme Court decision that found that the systematic exclusion of Mexican Americans from juries violated the constitutional guarantee of equal protection.

Holocaust German effort during World War II to murder Europe's Jews, along with other groups the Nazis deemed "undesirable." Despite reports of the ongoing genocide, the Allies did almost nothing to interfere. In all, some 11 million people were killed in the Holocaust, most of them Jews.

Homestead Act of 1862 Act that promised 160 acres in the trans-Mississippi West free to any citizen or prospective citizen who settled on the land for five years. The act spurred American settlement of the West. Altogether, nearly one-tenth of the United States was granted to settlers.

Homestead lockout 1892 lockout of workers at the Homestead, Pennsylvania, steel mill after Andrew Carnegie refused to renew the union contract and workers prepared to strike. Union supporters attacked the Pinkerton National Detective Agency guards hired to protect the mill, but the National Guard soon broke the strike.

House Un-American Activities Committee (HUAC) Congressional committee especially prominent during the early years of the Cold War that investigated Americans who might be disloyal to the government or might have associated with Communists or other radicals. It was one of the key institutions that promoted the second Red scare.

Housing Act of 1949 Law authorizing the construction of 810,000 units of government housing. This landmark effort marked the first significant commitment of the federal government to meet the housing needs of the poor.

Immigration and Nationality Act of 1965 Legislation passed during Lyndon Johnson's administration abolishing discriminatory immigration quotas based on national origins. Although it did limit the number of immigrants, including those from Latin America for the first time, it facilitated a surge in immigration later in the century.

Industrial Workers of the World (IWW) Umbrella union and radical political group founded in 1905 that was dedicated to organizing unskilled workers to oppose capitalism. Nicknamed the Wobblies, it advocated direct action by workers, including sabotage and general strikes, in hopes of triggering a widespread workers' uprising.

intermediate-range nuclear forces (INF) agreement Nuclear disarmament agreement reached between the United States and the Soviet Union in 1987, signifying a major thaw in the Cold War. The treaty eliminated all short- and medium-range missiles from Europe and provided for on-site inspection for the first time.

internment camps Makeshift prison camps, to which Americans of Japanese descent were sent as a result of Roosevelt's Executive Order 9066, issued in February 1942. In 1944, the Supreme Court upheld this blatant violation of constitutional rights as a "military necessity."

Interstate Commerce Commission (ICC) Federal regulatory agency designed to oversee the railroad industry. Congress created it through the 1887 Interstate Commerce Act after the Supreme Court decision in *Wabash v. Illinois* (1886) effectively denied states the right to regulate railroads. The ICC proved weak and did not immediately pose a threat to the industry.

Interstate Highway and Defense System Act of 1956 Law authorizing the construction of a national highway system. Promoted as essential to national defense and an impetus to economic growth, the national highway system accelerated the movement of people and goods and changed the nature of American communities.

Iran hostage crisis Crisis that began in 1979 after the deposed shah of Iran was allowed into the United States following the Iranian revolution. Iranians broke into the U.S. Embassy in Teheran and took sixty-six Americans hostage. The hostage crisis contributed to Carter's reelection defeat.

Iran-Contra scandal Reagan administration scandal that involved the sale of arms to Iran in exchange for its efforts to secure the release of hostages held in Lebanon and the redirection of the proceeds of those sales to the Nicaraguan Contras.

Iraq War War launched by the United States, Britain, and several smaller countries in March 2003 against the government of Iraqi dictator Saddam Hussein. It was based on claims (subsequently refuted) that Hussein's government had links to Al Qaeda, harbored terrorists, and possessed weapons of mass destruction.

iron curtain Metaphor coined by Winston Churchill in 1946 to demark the line dividing Soviet-controlled countries in Eastern Europe from democratic nations in Western Europe following World War II.

Jim Crow System of racial segregation in the South lasting from after the Civil War into the twentieth century. Jim Crow laws segregated African Americans in public facilities such as trains and streetcars, curtailed their voting rights, and denied other basic civil rights.

Johnson-Reed Act 1924 law that severely restricted immigration to the United States to no more than 161,000 a year, with quotas for each European nation. The racist restrictions were designed to staunch the flow of immigrants from southern and eastern Europe and from Asia.

Knights of Labor The first mass organization of America's working class. Founded in 1869, the Knights of Labor attempted to bridge the boundaries of ethnicity, gender, ideology, race, and occupation to build a "universal brotherhood" of all workers.

Korean War Conflict between North Korean forces supported by China and the Soviet Union and South Korean and U.S.-led United Nations forces over control of South Korea. Lasting from 1950 to 1953, the war represented the first time that the United States went to war to implement containment.

Ku Klux Klan Secret society that first thwarted black freedom after the Civil War as a paramilitary organization supporting Democrats. It was reborn in 1915 to fight against perceived threats posed by blacks, immigrants, radicals, feminists, Catholics, and Jews. The new Klan spread well beyond the South in the 1920s.

League of Nations International organization proposed in Woodrow Wilson's Fourteen Points that was designed to secure political independence and territorial integrity for all states and thus ensure enduring peace. The U.S. Senate refused to ratify the Treaty of Versailles, and the United States never became a member.

Lend-Lease Act Legislation in 1941 that enabled Britain to obtain arms from the United States without cash but with the promise to reimburse the United States when the war ended. The act reflected Roosevelt's desire to assist the British in any way possible, short of war.

Lusitania British passenger liner torpedoed by a German U-boat on May 7, 1915. The attack killed 1,198 passengers, including 128 Americans. The incident challenged American neutrality during World War I and moved the United States on a path toward entering the war.

Manhattan Project Top-secret project authorized by Franklin Roosevelt in 1942 to develop an atomic bomb ahead of the Germans. The thousands of Americans who worked on the project at Los Alamos, New Mexico, succeeded in producing a successful atomic bomb by July 1945.

Marshall Plan Aid program begun in 1948 to help European economies recover from World War II. Between 1948 and 1953, the United States provided $13 billion to seventeen Western European nations in a project that helped its own economy as well.

Medicare and Medicaid Social programs enacted as part of Lyndon Johnson's Great Society. Medicare provided the elderly with universal compulsory medical insurance financed primarily through Social Security taxes. Medicaid authorized federal grants to supplement state-paid medical care for poor people of all ages.

Military Reconstruction Act Congressional act of March 1867 that initiated military rule of the South. Congressional reconstruction divided the ten unreconstructed Confederate states into five military districts, each under the direction of a Union general. It also established the procedure by which unreconstructed states could reenter the Union.

military-industrial complex A term President Eisenhower used to refer to the military establishment and defense contractors who, he warned, exercised undue influence in city, state, and federal government.

Monroe Doctrine President James Monroe's 1823 declaration that the Western Hemisphere was closed to further colonization or interference by European powers. In exchange, Monroe pledged that the United States would not become involved in European struggles. The United States strengthened the doctrine during the late nineteenth century.

Montgomery bus boycott Yearlong boycott of Montgomery's segregated bus system in 1955–1956 by the city's African American population. The boycott brought Martin Luther King Jr. to national prominence and ended in victory when the Supreme Court declared segregated transportation unconstitutional.

muckraking Early-twentieth-century style of journalism that exposed the corruption of big business and government. Theodore Roosevelt coined the term after a character in *Pilgrim's Progress* who was too busy raking muck to notice higher things.

mutually assured destruction (MAD) Term for the standoff between the United States and Soviet Union based on the assumption that a nuclear first strike by either nation would result in massive retaliation and mutual destruction for each. Despite this, both countries pursued an ever-escalating arms race.

National American Woman Suffrage Association (NAWSA) Organization formed in 1890 that united the National Woman Suffrage Association and the American Woman Suffrage Association. The NAWSA pursued state-level campaigns to gain the vote for women. With successes in Idaho, Colorado, and Utah, woman suffrage had become more accepted by the 1890s.

National Energy Act of 1978 Legislation that penalized manufacturers of gas-guzzling automobiles and provided additional incentives for energy conservation and development of alternative fuels, such as wind and solar power. The act fell short of the long-term, comprehensive program that President Carter advocated.

National Organization for Women (NOW) Women's civil rights organization formed in 1966. Initially, NOW focused on eliminating gender discrimination in public institutions and the workplace, but by the 1970s it also embraced many of the issues raised by more radical feminists.

National Recovery Administration (NRA) Federal agency established in June 1933 to promote industrial recovery. It encouraged industrialists to voluntarily adopt codes that defined fair working conditions, set prices, and minimized competition. In practice, large corporations developed codes that served primarily their own interests rather than those of workers or the economy.

neutrality acts Legislation passed in 1935 and 1937 that sought to avoid entanglement in foreign wars while protecting trade. It prohibited selling arms to nations at war and required nations to pay cash for nonmilitary goods and to transport them in their own ships.

New Christian Right Politically active religious conservatives who became particularly vocal in the 1980s.

The New Right religious conservatives criticized feminism, opposed abortion and homosexuality, and promoted "family values" and military preparedness.

New Deal coalition Political coalition that supported Franklin D. Roosevelt's New Deal and the Democratic Party, including farmers, factory workers, immigrants, city folk, women, African Americans, and progressive intellectuals. The coalition dominated American politics during and long after Roosevelt's presidency.

"The New Freedom" Woodrow Wilson's 1912 campaign slogan, which reflected his belief in limited government and states' rights. Wilson promised to use antitrust legislation to eliminate big corporations and to improve opportunities for small businesses and farmers.

"The New Nationalism" Theodore Roosevelt's 1912 campaign slogan, which reflected his commitment to federal planning and regulation. Roosevelt wanted to use the federal government to act as a "steward of the people" to regulate giant corporations.

New Negro Term referring to African Americans who challenged American racial hierarchy through the arts. The New Negro emerged in New York City in the 1920s in what became known as the Harlem Renaissance, which produced dazzling literary, musical, and artistic talent.

new woman Alternative image of womanhood that came into the American mainstream in the 1920s. The mass media frequently portrayed young, college-educated women who drank, smoked, and wore skimpy dresses. New women also challenged American convictions about separate spheres for women and men and the sexual double standard.

Nineteenth Amendment (woman suffrage) Amendment granting women the vote. Congress passed the amendment in 1919, and it was ratified in August 1920. Like proponents of prohibition, the advocates of woman suffrage triumphed by linking their cause to the war.

No Child Left Behind Act 2002 legislation championed by President George W. Bush that expanded the role of the federal government in public education. The law required every school to meet annual testing standards, penalized failing schools, and allowed parents to transfer their children out of such schools.

North American Free Trade Agreement (NAFTA) 1993 treaty that eliminated all tariffs and trade barriers among the United States, Canada, and Mexico. NAFTA was supported by President Clinton, a minority of Democrats, and a majority of Republicans.

North Atlantic Treaty Organization (NATO) Military alliance formed in 1949 among the United States, Canada, and Western European nations to counter any possible Soviet threat. It represented an unprecedented commitment by the United States to go to war if any of its allies were attacked.

NSC 68 Top-secret government report of April 1950 warning that national survival required a massive military buildup. The Korean War brought nearly all of the expansion called for in the report, and by 1952 defense spending claimed nearly 70 percent of the federal budget.

Open Door policy Policy successfully insisted upon by Secretary of State John Hay in 1899–1900 recommending that the major powers of the United States, Britain, Japan, Germany, France, and Russia all have access to trade with China and that Chinese sovereignty be maintained.

Panama Canal treaty 1977 agreement that returned control of the Panama Canal from the United States to Panama in 2000. To pass the treaty, President Carter overcame stiff opposition in the Senate from conservatives who regarded control of the canal as vital to America's interests.

Patient Protection and Affordable Care Act Sweeping 2010 health care reform bill that established nearly universal health insurance by providing subsidies and compelling larger businesses to offer coverage to employees. Championed by President Obama, it also imposed new regulations on insurance companies and contained provisions to limit health care costs.

Peace Corps Program launched by President Kennedy in 1961 through which young American volunteers helped with education, health, and other projects in developing countries around the world. More than 60,000 volunteers had served by the mid-1970s.

Pentagon Papers Secret government documents published in 1971 containing an internal study of the Vietnam War. The documents further disillusioned the public by revealing that officials harbored pessimism about the war even as they made rosy public pronouncements about its progress.

People's Party (Populist Party) Political party formed in 1892 by the Farmers' Alliance to advance the goals of the Populist movement. Populists sought economic democracy, promoting land, electoral, banking, and monetary reform. Republican victory in the presidential election of 1896 effectively destroyed the People's Party.

Persian Gulf War 1991 war between Iraq and a U.S.-led international coalition. The war was sparked by the 1990 Iraqi invasion of Kuwait. A forty-day bombing campaign against Iraq followed by coalition troops storming into Kuwait brought a quick coalition victory.

Plessy v. Ferguson 1896 Supreme Court ruling that upheld the legality of racial segregation. According to the ruling, blacks could be segregated in separate schools, restrooms, and other facilities as long as the facilities were "equal" to those provided for whites.

progressivism A reform movement that often advocated government activism to mitigate the problems created by urban industrialism. Progressivism reached its peak in 1912 with the creation of the Progressive Party. The term *progressivism* has come to mean any general effort advocating for social welfare programs.

prohibition The ban on the manufacture and sale of alcohol that went into effect in January 1920 with the Eighteenth Amendment. Prohibition proved almost impossible to enforce. By the end of the 1920s, most Americans wished it to end, and it was finally repealed in 1933.

Pullman boycott Nationwide railroad workers' boycott of trains carrying Pullman cars in 1894 after Pullman workers, suffering radically reduced wages, joined the American Railway Union (ARU) and union leaders were fired in response. The boycott ended after the U.S. Army fired on strikers and ARU leader Eugene Debs was jailed.

Reconstruction Finance Corporation (RFC) Federal agency established by Herbert Hoover in 1932 to help American industry by lending government funds to endangered banks and corporations, which Hoover hoped would benefit people at the bottom through trickle-down economics. In practice, this provided little help to the poor.

Redeemers Name taken by southern Democrats who harnessed white rage in order to overthrow Republican rule and black political power and thus, they believed, save southern civilization.

Red scare The widespread fear of internal subversion and Communist revolution that swept the United States in 1919 and resulted in suppression of dissent. Labor unrest, postwar recession, the difficult peacetime readjustment, and the Soviet establishment of the Comintern all contributed to the scare.

reform Darwinism Sociological theory developed in the 1880s that argued humans could speed up evolution by altering their environment. A challenge to the laissez-faire approach of social Darwinism, reform Darwinism insisted the liberal state should play an active role in solving social problems.

reservations Land assigned by the federal government to American Indians beginning in the 1860s in an attempt to reduce tensions between Indians and western settlers. On reservations, Indians subsisted on meager government rations and faced a life of poverty and starvation.

rock and roll A music genre created from country music and black rhythm and blues that emerged in the 1950s and captivated American youth.

Roe v. Wade 1973 Supreme Court ruling that the Constitution protects the right to abortion, which states cannot prohibit in the early stages of pregnancy. The decision galvanized social conservatives and made abortion a controversial policy issue for decades to come.

Roosevelt Corollary Theodore Roosevelt's 1904 follow-up to the Monroe Doctrine in which he declared the United States had the right to intervene in Latin America to stop "brutal wrongdoing" and protect American interests. The corollary warned European powers to keep out of the Western Hemisphere.

scalawag A derogatory term that Southerners applied to southern white Republicans, who were seen as traitors to the South. Most were yeoman farmers.

Schenck v. United States 1919 Supreme Court decision that established a "clear and present danger" test for restricting free speech. The Court upheld the conviction of socialist Charles Schenck for urging resistance to the draft during wartime.

Scopes trial 1925 trial of John Scopes, a biology teacher in Dayton, Tennessee, for violating his state's ban on teaching evolution. The trial created a nationwide media frenzy and came to be seen as a showdown between urban and rural values.

Scottsboro Boys Nine African American youths who were arrested for the alleged rape of two white women in Scottsboro, Alabama, in 1931. After an all-white jury sentenced the young men to death, the Communist Party took action that saved them from the electric chair.

Selective Service Act Law enacted in 1940 requiring all men who would be eligible for a military draft to register in preparation for the possibility of a future conflict. The act also prohibited discrimination based on "race or color."

settlement houses Settlements established in poor neighborhoods beginning in the 1880s. Reformers like Jane Addams and Lillian Wald believed that only by living among the poor could they help bridge the growing class divide. College-educated women formed the backbone of the settlement house movement.

sharecropping Labor system that emerged in the South during Reconstruction. Under this system, planters divided their plantations into small farms that freedmen rented, paying with a share of each year's crop. Sharecropping gave blacks some freedom, but they remained dependent on white landlords and country merchants.

Sherman Antitrust Act 1890 act that outlawed pools and trusts, ruling that businesses could no longer enter into agreements to restrict competition. Government inaction, combined with the Supreme Court's narrow reading of the act in the *United States v. E. C. Knight Company* decision, undermined the law's effectiveness.

Six-Day War 1967 conflict between Israel and the Arab nations of Egypt, Syria, and Jordan. Israel attacked Egypt after Egypt had massed troops on its border and cut off the sea passage to Israel's southern port. Israel won a stunning victory, seizing territory that amounted to twice its original size.

social Darwinism A social theory popularized in the late nineteenth century by Herbert Spencer and William Graham Sumner. Proponents believed that only relentless competition could produce social progress and that wealth was a sign of "fitness" and poverty a sign of "unfitness" for survival.

social gospel A vision of Christianity that saw its mission as not simply to reform individuals but to reform society. Emerging in the early twentieth century, it offered a powerful corrective to social Darwinism and the gospel of wealth, which fostered the belief that riches signaled divine favor.

Social Security A New Deal program created in August 1935 that was designed to provide a modest income for elderly people. The act also created unemployment insurance with modest benefits. Social Security provoked sharp opposition from conservatives and the wealthy.

Socialist Party Political party formed in 1900 that advocated cooperation over competition and promoted the breakdown of capitalism. Its members, who were largely middle-class and native-born, saw both the Republican and the Democratic parties as hopelessly beholden to capitalism.

Spanish-American War 1898 war between Spain and the United States that began as an effort to free Cuba from Spain's colonial rule. This popular war left the United States an imperial power in control of Cuba and colonies in Puerto Rico, Guam, and the Philippines.

spoils system System in which politicians doled out government positions to their loyal supporters. This patronage system led to widespread corruption during the Gilded Age.

Strategic Arms Limitation Treaty (SALT) A 1972 agreement between the United States and the Soviet Union limiting antiballistic missiles (ABMs) to two each. The treaty prevented either nation from building an ABM system defense so secure against a nuclear attack that it would risk a first strike.

Sun Belt Name applied to the Southwest and South, which grew rapidly after World War II as a center of defense industries and non-unionized labor.

supply-side economics Economic theory that claims tax cuts for individuals (especially the wealthy) and businesses encourage investment and production (supply) and stimulate consumption (demand) because individuals can keep more of their earnings. Despite promises to the contrary, under President Reagan supply-side economics created a massive federal budget deficit.

sweatshop A small room used for clothing piecework beginning in the late nineteenth century. As mechanization transformed the garment industry with the introduction of foot-pedaled sewing machines and mechanical cloth-cutting knives, independent tailors were replaced with sweatshop workers hired by contractors to sew pieces into clothing.

Taft-Hartley Act Law passed by the Republican-controlled Congress in 1947 that amended the Wagner Act and placed restrictions on organized labor that made it more difficult for unions to organize workers.

Teapot Dome Nickname for the scandal in which Interior Secretary Albert Fall accepted $400,000 in bribes for leasing oil reserves on public land in Teapot

Dome, Wyoming. It was part of a larger pattern of corruption that marred Warren G. Harding's presidency.

Temporary Assistance for Needy Families (TANF) program Program established by the Personal Responsibility and Work Opportunity Reconciliation Act of 1996. Replacing Aid to Families with Dependent Children, TANF provided grants to the states to assist the poor and limited welfare payments to two consecutive years, with a lifetime maximum of five years.

Tet Offensive Major campaign of attacks launched throughout South Vietnam in early 1968 by the North Vietnamese and Vietcong. A major turning point in the war, it exposed the credibility gap between official statements and the war's reality, and it shook Americans' confidence in the government.

Triple Alliance Early-twentieth-century alliance among Germany, Austria-Hungary, and Italy, formed as part of a complex network of military and diplomatic agreements intended to prevent war in Europe by balancing power. In actuality, such alliances made large-scale conflict more likely.

Triple Entente Early-twentieth-century alliance among Great Britain, France, and Russia, which was formed as part of a complex network of military and diplomatic agreements intended to prevent war in Europe by balancing power. In actuality, such alliances made large-scale conflict more likely.

Truman Doctrine President Harry S. Truman's commitment to "support free peoples who are resisting attempted subjugation by armed minorities or by outside pressures." First applied to Greece and Turkey in 1947, it became the justification for U.S. intervention into many countries during the Cold War.

trust A system in which corporations give shares of their stock to trustees who hold the stocks "in trust" for their stockholders, thereby coordinating the industry to ensure profits to the participating corporations and curb competition.

"typewriters" Women who were hired by businesses in the decades after the Civil War to keep records and conduct correspondence, often using equipment such as typewriters. Secretarial work constituted one of the very few areas where middle-class women could use their literacy for wages.

Uncle Tom's Cabin Enormously popular antislavery novel written by Harriet Beecher Stowe and published in 1852. It helped to solidify northern sentiment against slavery and to confirm white Southerners' sense that no sympathy remained for them in the free states.

underconsumption New Dealers' belief that the root cause of the country's economic paralysis was that factories and farms produced more than they could sell, causing factories to lay off workers and farmers to lose money. The only way to increase consumption, they believed, was to provide jobs that put wages in consumers' pockets.

Union blockade The United States' use of its navy to patrol the southern coastline to restrict Confederate access to supplies. Over time, the blockade became increasingly effective and succeeded in depriving the Confederacy of vital supplies.

United States Constitution The document written in 1787 and subsequently ratified by the original thirteen states that laid out the governing structure of the United States in separate legislative, executive, and judicial branches.

USA Patriot Act 2001 law that gave the government new powers to monitor suspected terrorists and their associates, including the ability to access personal information. Critics charged that it represented an unwarranted abridgment of civil rights.

Versailles treaty Treaty signed on June 28, 1919, that ended World War I. The agreement redrew the map of the world and assigned Germany sole responsibility for the war, saddling it with a debt of $33 billion in war damages. Many Germans felt betrayed by the treaty.

Voting Rights Act of 1965 Law passed during Lyndon Johnson's administration that empowered the federal government to intervene to ensure minorities access to the voting booth. As a result of the act, black voting and officeholding in the South shot up, initiating a major transformation in southern politics.

Wagner Act 1935 law that guaranteed industrial workers the right to organize into unions; also known as the National Labor Relations Act. Following passage of the act, union membership skyrocketed to 30 percent of the workforce, the highest in American history.

War on Poverty President Lyndon Johnson's efforts, organized through the Office of Economic Opportunity, to ameliorate poverty primarily through education and training as well as by including the poor in decision making.

Warren Court The Supreme Court under Chief Justice Earl Warren (1953–1969), which expanded the Constitution's promise of equality and civil rights. It issued landmark decisions in the areas of civil rights, criminal rights, reproductive freedom, and separation of church and state.

Watergate Term referring to the 1972 break-in at Democratic Party headquarters in the Watergate complex in Washington, D.C., by men working for President Nixon's reelection, along with Nixon's efforts to cover it up. The Watergate scandal led to President Nixon's resignation.

welfare capitalism Industrial programs for workers that became popular in the 1920s. Some businesses improved safety and sanitation inside factories. They also instituted paid vacations and pension plans. This encouraged loyalty to companies rather than to independent labor unions.

Woman's Christian Temperance Union (WCTU) All-women organization founded in 1874 to advocate total abstinence from alcohol. The WCTU provided important political training for women, which many used in the suffrage movement.

Works Progress Administration (WPA) Federal New Deal program established in 1935 that provided government-funded public works jobs to millions of unemployed Americans during the Great Depression, in areas ranging from construction to the arts.

World Trade Organization (WTO) International economic body established in 1994 through the General Agreement on Tariffs and Trade to enforce substantial tariff and import quota reductions. Many corporations welcomed these trade barrier reductions, but critics linked them to job loss and the weakening of unions.

World's Columbian Exposition World's fair held in Chicago in 1893 that attracted millions of visitors. The elaborately designed pavilions of the "White City" included exhibits of technological innovation and of cultural exoticism. They embodied an urban ideal that contrasted with the realities of Chicago life.

Wounded Knee 1890 massacre of Sioux Indians by American cavalry at Wounded Knee Creek, South Dakota. Sent to suppress the Ghost Dance, the soldiers opened fire on the Sioux as they attempted to surrender. More than two hundred Sioux men, women, and children were killed.

yellow journalism Term first given to sensationalistic newspaper reporting and cartoon images rendered in yellow. A circulation war between two New York City papers provoked the tactics of yellow journalism that fueled popular support for the Spanish-American War in 1898.

Index

A NOTE ABOUT THE INDEX:
Names of individuals appear in boldface.
Key terms are in boldface and italics.
Letters in parentheses following pages refer to:
(b)   boxed features
(f)   figures, including charts and graphs
(i)   illustrations, including photographs and artifacts
(m)   maps
(t)   tables

Abington School District v. Schempp
      (1963), 837
ABMs. *See* Antiballistic missiles
Abolition and abolitionism, Lincoln
      and, 461
Abortion and abortion rights, 941
      debate over, 853–854, 913–916
      Roe v. Wade and, 854, 913(i)
Abu Ghraib prison abuse, 945
Abundance. *See also* Consumers;
      Prosperity; Wealth
      culture of, 815–819
      work and living patterns with,
      809–815
Accommodation
      by Indians, 494
      Washington, Booker T., and, 639
Acheson, Dean, 777, 878
Acquired immune deficiency
      syndrome (AIDS), 912
      Bush, G. W., and, 941
Activism. *See also* Protest(s);
      Revolts and rebellions
      civil rights movement and,
      820–825, 824(i)
      Latino, 846–847
      Native American, 845–846
      progressivism and, 611–612
      in Vietnam War, 873–875,
      876–877(b), 878
      women's, 533–536, 536–537,
      590–593, 850–853
ADA. *See* Americans with Disabilities
      Act

Adaptation, 530
      Native American, 503
Addams, Jane, 612(i), 613
      Hull House and, 610–611, 612(i)
      woman suffrage and, 616
      World War I and, 657
Adding machine, 563
Advanced Research Projects Agency
      (ARPA), 938(i)
Adventures of Huckleberry Finn,
      The (Twain), 519
Advertising, in 1920s, 680–681
AEF. *See* American Expeditionary
      Force
Aerospace industry, 813, 814
AFDC. *See* Aid to Families with
      Dependent Children
Affirmative action. *See also* African
      Americans
      Johnson, L. B., executive order for
      (1965), 841–842
      Nixon and, 830, 856
      Thomas, Clarence, and, 925
      for women, 853
Affluent society, 810. *See also* Wealth
      in 1950s, 810, 812
      Galbraith on, 810
Afghanistan, 944(m)
      missile attacks on, 936
      Obama and, 950
      prisoners detained from, 943
      Soviets and, 905, 919
      Taliban in, 942, 943
      U.S. and, 917, 929(m)

AFL. *See* American Federation of
      Labor
Africa. *See also* African Americans;
      North Africa; Slavery
      anti-AIDS program in, 941
      Italy and, 740, 742–743
      in World War II, 755, 755(i), 763
African Americans. *See also* Africa;
      Civil rights; Civil rights
      movement; Freedmen; Race
      and racism; Race riots; Rights;
      Slavery; Voting and voting rights
      in 1950s, 800
      in armed forces, 504
      black codes and, 465–466
      as buffalo soldiers, 504
      in cities, 556, 559
      civil rights movement and,
      819–825, 838–844
      civil rights of, 786–787
      in Clinton cabinet, 932
      Colored Farmers' Alliance and,
      583–584
      as cowboys, 512
      discrimination against, 482, 504
      as Exodusters, 512–513
      Farmers' Alliance and, 583
      in government, 459, 474,
      474(f), 932
      in Great Depression, 719
      in higher education, 815
      Jim Crow laws and, 475, 533, 556
      labor unions and, 566
      lynchings of, 533–536, 534–535(b)

African Americans *(continued)*
median income for (1999), 935
migration by, 556, 668–670, 668*(i)*, 786, 810
in New Deal, 728–729, 735
opportunities for, 923
People's Party and, 595
as president, 946–951
progressives and, 612
protests by, 842–844, 843*(m)*
in Republican Party, 472, 483–484
rights of, 637
segregation of, 475, 482, 533, 556, 559
sharecropping and, 478–479, 478*(i)*
in South, 483–484, 532
in southern congressional delegations (1865–1877), 474, 474*(f)*
urban uprisings by, 843–844, 843*(m)*
voting and, 684, 828–829, 834, 839–841, 841*(i)*, 842*(m)*
Washington, Booker T., and, 638, 638*(i)*
in West, 504, 814
women and, 478*(i)*, 536, 562, 811
in World War I, 651
in World War II, 750, 751*(i)*, 757–758
African Methodist Episcopal Church, 464
Age. *See* Elderly
Agencies of government.
See Government (U.S.)
Agent Orange, 868, 873, 886
Agnew, Spiro T., 879, 897–898
Agrarianism, transformation of, 489, 514
Agribusiness, 813
Agricultural Adjustment Act (AAA), 716
first (1933), 716
second (1938), 733–734
Agricultural Marketing Act (1929), 698
Agricultural rural domain (global economic region), 551, 552*(m)*
Agriculture. *See also* Farms and farming; Rural areas
in 1920s, 677
commercial, 507, 513, 514
industrialism and, 514
in New Deal, 715–717, 719–720, 733–734

railroads and, 512
sharecropping system of, 478–479, 513
in South, 532
technology and, 513–514, 810, 810*(i)*
in World War I, 654
Aguinaldo, Emilio, 607
AIDS. *See* Acquired immune deficiency syndrome
Aid to Families with Dependent Children (AFDC), 834, 932–933
AIM. *See* American Indian Movement
Air-conditioning, 812
Sun Belt and, 813
Air force, in World War II, 763
Airplane, Lindbergh and, 690
Air pollution. *See also* Clean Air Act; Environment
Carter and, 903
Clinton, Bill, and, 931
environmentalists and, 856
Johnson, L. B., and, 835
Alabama, 459, 484. *See also* Birmingham; Montgomery
civil rights march in, 840
Indians in, 499
Albanians, ethnic, 936
Alcatraz, Indian seizure of, 845, 845*(i)*, 857
Alcohol and alcoholism. *See also* Temperance
prohibition and, 682–683
social purity movement and, 613
after World War I, 655
Algeciras, Spain, conference in (1905), 628
Ali, Muhammad (boxer), 873
Alien Land Law (California, 1913), 637
Aliens. *See* Illegal immigrants; Immigrants and immigration
Alito, Samuel A., 941
Allen, Doris, 886
Allende, Salvador, 881
Alliance(s). *See also* specific alliances
peacetime military, 781, 782
Vietnam and, 806
in World War I, 646, 647*(m)*
in World War II, 748
Allies (World War I). *See also* World War I
at Paris peace conference, 660–662

Allies (World War II), 765, 767*(i)*.
See also World War II
in UN, 765
after war, 774, 775
weapons comparison with Axis, 752*(f)*
Allotment policy, 497–498, 716
Al Qaeda, 936, 942, 944, 944*(m),* 945
ISIS and, 945–946
Altgeld, John Peter, 590
Amalgamated Association of Iron and Steel Workers, 566, 585–586, 587
Amalgamated Clothing Workers, 725
America(s). *See also* Central America; North America; South America
Wilson and, 645–646
American Bell (telephone company), 527
American Civil Liberties Union (ACLU), 668
American Communist Party.
See Communist Party
American Equal Rights Association, 468
American Expeditionary Force (AEF), 642, ***651,*** 653, 653*(m)*
American Federation of Labor (AFL), 564, ***566***–567, 569, 581, 585, 587.
See also Labor unions; Strikes
general strike and (1919), 664
in Great Depression, 702, 724–725
American GI Forum. *See* GI Forum
American Historical Association, 488
American Independent Party, 879
American Indian Movement (AIM), 845
American Indians. *See* Native Americans
Americanization
immigrants and, 556
of Vietnam War, 870–871
American Liberty League, 719
American Medical Association
African Americans in, 787
birth control and, 684
American National Exhibition (Moscow, 1959), 798–799
American Psychiatric Association, on gays and lesbians, 849
American Railway Union (ARU), Pullman strike and, 589
American Recovery and Reinvestment Act (2009), 947
American Sugar Refining Company, 543

Americans with Disabilities Act
    (*ADA,* 1990), **925**
American Telephone and Telegraph
    (AT&T), 527
American Tobacco Company, 532
American Woman Suffrage
    Association (AWSA), 592
Ames, Adelbert, 484
Amusement parks, 570(*i*), 571
Anarchism
    Sacco and Vanzetti trial and, 693
    unionism and, 587
Anderson, John B., 907
Angel Island immigration station, 557
Anglo-American alliance
    (World War II), 746
Anglo-Americans
    in Southwest, 504, 505
    in West, 489
Angola, 919
    U.S. arms to, 917
Annexation(s)
    Hawai'i and, 598, 605
    of Texas, 504
Anthony, Susan B., 468, 469(*i*)
    on "Negro first" strategy, 471–472
    woman suffrage and, 536,
        592–593
Anti-Americanism
    in Arab world, 882
    in Caribbean, 630
    Eisenhower's foreign policy and, 826
    Iraq War and, 945
Antiballistic missiles (ABMs), 880
Anticommunism
    Eisenhower and, 800–801
    Nixon and, 794, 880
    Reagan and, 908, 916
Antidiscrimination programs
    for gays and lesbians, 849
    Reagan, affirmative action, and, 911
Antifeminism, 892(*i*)
Antiforeign hysteria, in 1920s, 693
Antigay policies, 849
Anti-German sentiment, during
    World War I, 657–658
Antigovernment sentiment, 919
Anti-immigrant sentiment, 506, 553,
    557, 943
Anti-imperialism, 607
Antilynching laws, 685–688, 729(*i*), 735
Antilynching movement, 533–536,
    534–535(*b*)

Antin, Mary, 555
Antipoverty programs. *See also* Great
    Society
    of Clinton, 931
    of Johnson, L. B., 833
Anti-Saloon League, 613
Anti-Semitism. *See also* Jews and
    Judaism
    atomic bomb scientists and,
        760–761(*b*)
    of Coughlin, 721
    of Hitler, 742
Antisodomy laws, 916
Antitrust activities
    legislation and, 526, 542–543
    Roosevelt, Theodore, and,
        619–620, 631
    Taft and, 631
Antiwar movement, in Vietnam War,
    873–878, 882, 883
Antwerp, in World War II, 763
Apache Indians, 499
Apollo program, 863–864
Appeasement, 743–744
Apple computer, 910
Appliances, in 1950s, 815
Apprenticeship, laws in black codes,
    466
Arab-Israeli wars
    Six-Day War (1967), 881–882
    Yom Kippur War (1973), 855, 881
Arab League, Middle East events
    (1989–2001) and, 929(*m*)
Arab Spring (2011), 950–951
Arab world. *See also* Arab-Israeli wars;
    Iraq War; Middle East
    Clinton, Bill, and, 936
    Eisenhower and, 807
    energy crisis and, 855
    Israel and, 881–882
    Persian Gulf War and, 928
    Truman and, 783
    after World War I, 660
Arafat, Yasir, 937
Arapaho Indians, 493, 500, 500(*i*)
Arbenz, Jacobo, 806
Arbitration
    in strikes, 588
    treaties, Taft and, 631
Architecture
    Chicago school of, 571–572
    skyscrapers and, 525, 571
    of White City, 574(*b*)

Arctic National Wildlife Refuge
    (ANWR), Carter and, 903
Arizona, 491, 499, 515
Arkansas, 462, 484
Armed forces. *See* Military; specific
    battles and wars
Armenian immigrants, 552
Armistice
    in Korean War, 795
    in World War I, 652, 660
Arms and armaments. *See* Weapons
Arms limitation treaties, 880
Arms race. *See* Disarmament; Nuclear
    arms race; Nuclear weapons
Army of the Republic of Vietnam
    (ARVN), 806, 866, 871, 875(*i*)
ARPA. *See* Advanced Research
    Projects Agency
"Arsenal of democracy," U.S. as, 746
Art(s). *See also* Literature; Painting;
    specific arts and artists
    in 1950s, 819, 819(*i*)
    in Harlem Renaissance, 688
    Johnson, L. B., and, 835
    New Deal support for, 723(*i*), 724
Arthur, Chester A., 538
Article 231 (World War I peace treaty),
    660
Artisans, 560
ARVN. *See* Army of the Republic of
    Vietnam
Aryans, Nazi ideology of, 742,
    757–758, 760(*b*)
Asia. *See also* specific locations
    immigrants from, 551, 556,
        693, 939
    Japan and, 740, 747–748
    Open Door policy in, 601, 601(*i*)
    trade with, 597
    World War II and, 765–768
Asian Americans
    in Clinton cabinet, 932
    in New Deal, 730
    rights of, 637
Assassinations
    of Garfield, 538–539
    of Kennedy, J. F., 831, 832
    of King, Martin Luther, Jr., 842,
        844, 876(*b*)
    of Lincoln, 464
    of Long, 722(*i*)
    of McKinley, 618
Assembly lines, 675, 680

Assimilation
    immigrants and, 556
    of Indians, 496–498, 730, 801–802
Aswan Dam, 807
Atlanta, race riot in, 639
Atlanta Compromise, 638
Atlanta Constitution, 532
Atlantic Charter (1941), 746
Atlantic Ocean region, in World
    War II, 754
Atomic bomb. *See also* Nuclear
    weapons
    Jewish scientists and, 760–761(b)
    Soviet, 780
    in World War II, 739, 762–763,
        768–769, 768(i)
Audiotapes, Watergate, 897
Auschwitz, Poland, concentration
    camp in, 759–762
Australia
    migration to, 551
    in World War II, 753
Austria
    Hitler annexation of, 743, 744(m)
    after World War I, 660
Austria-Hungary, World War I and,
    646, 660
Authors. *See* Literature; specific
    authors and works
Automobiles and automobile industry,
    676(m), 679–680. *See also*
    Suburbs
    in 1950s, 798(i)
    Detroit and, 679(m)
    energy consumption and, 902
    Ford and, 674–675, 674(i)
    Sun Belt and, 813
Axis powers. *See also* World War II
    aggression through 1941, 744(m)
    unconditional surrender and, 755
    weapons comparison with Allies,
        752(f)

B-17 Flying Fortress (bomber),
    739, 763
B-29 Super Fortress (bomber), 739
Babbitt (Lewis), 691
Baby boom, 817
"Back to Africa" movement, 688
Baer, George, 620, 621
Baker, Ella, 830(i), 838
Baker, Josephine, 824(i)
Bakke case, 896

Balance of power, Algeciras conference
    (1905) and, 628
Balch, Emily Greene, 657
Baldwin, Roger, 668
Balkan region, after World War I, 660
Ballistic missiles, 805(i)
Ballparks, 570
Baltimore and Ohio Railroad, 564
"Banana republics," 600
Banking, 528. *See also* Federal Reserve
    Board; Panic(s)
    in 1920s, 697
    failure of, 697
    Federal Reserve and, 633–634
    finance capitalism and, 528,
        529–530
    Financial Services Modernization
        Act and, 934
    government deregulation of, 901
    in Great Depression, 713–714
    Morgan and, 529
    in South, 475
    U.S., in Latin America, 645
    Wilson and, 633
Banknotes, 544
Bankruptcies
    in depression of 1890s, 528, 544
    of farmers (1920s), 677
Banky, Vilma, 687(i)
Bannock Shoshoni Indians, 503
Baptists, 464
Barbed wire
    for cattle ranches, 512
    in World War I, 643
Barboncito (Navajo leader), 491
Barrow plantation (1860 and 1881),
    479(m)
Barry, Leonora, 566
Baruch, Bernard, 654
Baseball, 570–571, 689
    integration of, 787, 821
Bastogne, in World War II, 765
Bataan Death March, 753
Battle of Britain (1940), 745
Battle of the Bulge, 763–765
Battles. *See* specific battles and wars
Bay of Pigs invasion (1961), **862**–863
Bayonet rule, in South, 483, 485
Beals, Melba Patillo, 820–821
Bear Paw Mountains, siege against
    Nez Percé in, 498
Beat generation, 819, 848
Begin, Menachem, 904

Beijing, Boxers in, 599
Belgium, in World War II, 745
Bell, Alexander Graham, 527, 528(i)
Belleau Wood, battle at, 651
Bentley, Elizabeth, 790
Benton, Thomas Hart (artist), 723
Berger, Victor, 668
Berkeley, California, free speech
    movement in, 847
Berkman, Alexander, 587
Berlin, Germany
    Allied occupation of, 775, 777(m)
    division of, 780
    Soviet capture of, 765
Berlin, Treaty of (1899), 600
Berlin airlift, 780, 780(i)
Berliner, Emile, 574(b)
Berlin Wall, **864,** 925, 927(i)
Bessemer, Henry, 524
Bethune, Mary McLeod, 729
Bevin, Ernest, 778
Bible reading, 837
"Big Bonanza," 503
Big business. *See also* Business;
    Economy
    in New Deal, 713
    railroads as, 520–524
    Roosevelt, T., and, 632
    steel as, 524
Big-city boss. *See* Bosses (political)
"Big stick" foreign policy, of Roosevelt,
    Theodore, 625–628
Big Three (World War II), 765
"Billion Dollar Congress," 542
Bill of Rights (U.S.). *See also*
    Constitution (U.S.)
    equal protection in, 814, 837
Bimetallism system, 544
Bin Laden, Osama, 930, 936, 942,
    945, 950
"Birds of passage" (immigrants), 555
Birmingham, Alabama, 839
Birth control and ***birth control
    movement,* 635,** 684
    feminism and, 848(i)
Birth control pill, 848
Birthrate. *See also* Baby boom
    in 19th century, 636
    in baby boom, 817
    after World War II, 785
Bison (buffalo), slaughter of, 491,
    493–494, 493(i)
***Black codes,* 465**–466

Black Elk (Oglala holy man), 496
Black Hills, Indians and, *495*–496,
    509*(b)*
"Black is beautiful" movement, 844
Black Kettle (Cheyenne leader), 493
Blacklist
    McCarthyism and, 791
    of union members, 587, 588
Black nationalism, 688
Black Panther Party for Self-Defense,
    844
Black power movement, 844
Blacks. *See* Africa; African Americans;
    Freedmen; Slavery
Black studies, 848
Black Thursday (October 24, 1929),
    697
Black Tuesday (October 29, 1929), 697
Blaine, James G., 538, 539–540,
    540*(m)*, 541, 600
Blitzkrieg ("lightning war"), 745
Blizzards, "Great Die Up" and, 512
Block, Herbert Lawrence (Herblock),
    897*(i)*
Blockades
    in Cuban missile crisis, 865–866
    in World War I, 648, 649
"Bloody Sunday," in Montgomery, 840
Blue-collar workers, in 1950s, 811
BMW, 938
Boarding schools, for Indians, 496–497
Board of Indian Commissioners, 497
Bolsheviks and Bolshevism, *650*.
    See also Communism; Russia;
        Soviet Union
    Bolshevik Revolution and, 650
    fears of, after World War I,
        665–668, 666–667*(b)*
Bombs and bombings. *See also* Atomic
    bomb; Nuclear weapons
    of Cambodia, 882
    of England, 745
    Haymarket, 567–569
    hydrogen bomb, 781
    of Vietnam, 869, 870–871, 884
    in World War II, 739, 762–763,
        768–769
Bonanza farms, 514
Bonds, railroad, 522
Bonfield, John ("Blackjack"), 568
Bonus Marchers, in Great Depression,
    703, 723
Books. *See* Literature; specific works

Boom and bust cycles, 523
Booth, John Wilkes, 464
Bootlegging, 683, 683*(i)*
Borah, William, 666*(b)*
Border(s). *See also* Frontier
    Venezuela–British Guiana dispute
        and, 600
Borrowing. *See* Credit
Bosch, Juan, 870
Bosnia, peacekeeping in, 936
Bosque Redondo Reservation, 491
Bosses (political), 538, 573–576
Bossism, 573
Boston, 572
    immigrants in, 555
    police strike in (1919), 664–665
    school busing in, 895
Boston Public Library, 562
Bow, Clara, 689
Boxer Protocol (1901), 599
Boxer uprising (China), 597,
    599–600
Boxing, 689–690
Boycotts
    grape, 846*(i),* 847
    Montgomery bus boycott,
        821–825, 838
    of Pullman cars, 588–590
Boyer, LaNada, 845
Boys. *See also* Men
    in workforce, 562
Bozeman Trail, 495
Bracero program, 814, 814*(i)*
Brains Trust, of Roosevelt, Franklin D.,
    712
Brandeis, Louis, 634
Brandenburg Gate, 927*(i)*
Bray, Rosemary, 836
Brazil
    slavery in, 477*(b)*
    southern planters' migration to,
        476–477*(b)*
Brezhnev, Leonid, 904
Briand, Aristide, 679
Bridges, 525
    Brooklyn, 548–549, 548*(i),* 571
Briggs, Laura, 775
Brinksmanship, 804
Britain. *See* England
    battle of, 745 (*See also* England)
British Guiana, Venezuela and, 600
Brooklyn Bridge, 548–549, 548*(i),* 560
Brooklyn Dodgers, move by, 812

Brooks, Gwendolyn, 787
Brotherhood of Sleeping Car Porters,
    758
Brown, Oliver, 820
Browne, George ("Brownie"),
    642–644, 644*(i),* 651
Brown v. Board of Education (1954),
    820, 822–823*(b),* 837
Brunauer, Esther, 790
Bryan, William Jennings
    election of 1896 and, 595–597,
        596*(m),* 597*(i),* 607–608
    election of 1904 and, 621
    Scopes trial and, 694
    as secretary of state, 645, 648
    on U.S. expansionism, 607
Bryce, James, 573
Buchanan, Patrick J., 855, 940*(m)*
Budget. *See* Federal budget
Buffalo. *See* Bison (buffalo)
Buffalo soldiers, 504
Buffalo Telegraph, 540
Bulge, battle of the, 763–765
Bull Moose Party. *See* Progressive
    Party, of 1912
Bunche, Ralph J., 787
Bundy, McGeorge, 868
Bureau of Animal Husbandry, 509*(b)*
Bureau of Indian Affairs, 494, 500
    Indian occupation of, 845, 857
Bureau of Refugees, Freedmen, and
    Abandoned Lands. *See*
        Freedmen's Bureau
Burger, Warren E., 896
Burleson, Albert, 658
Burma
    Japan and, 747
    in World War II, 765
Burnham, Daniel, 576, 577
Burton, Dewey, 879
Bush, George H. W., 924–930
    Central America and, 927–928
    election of 1980 and, 907
    election of 1988 and, 924
    foreign policy of, 935–936
    Iran-Contra scandal pardons by, 918
    Persian Gulf War and, 928–930,
        930*(i)*
Bush, George W. *See also* September 11,
    2001, attacks
    cabinet of, 941
    domestic policy of, 940–942
    election of 2000 and, 940, 940*(m)*

Bush, George W. *(continued)*
　election of 2004 and, 945
　foreign policy and, 942–946
　Hurricane Katrina and, 942
　Iraq War and, 944–946
　September 11, 2001, attacks and, 943
　Supreme Court and, 941
　taxation and, 940, 941
　trade and, 937
　war on terror and, 950
Business. *See also* Big business;
　　Corporations; Finance
　　capitalism
　in 1920s, 676, 677–678
　in 1990s, 934–935
　campaign contributions and, 539
　Cuba and, 604
　foreign policy and, 598
　in Gilded Age, 520–527, 545–546
　government and, 677
　Hoover and, 696
　labor unions and, 566
　management changes in, 562
　mechanization in, 563
　monopolies in, 524, 526
　in New Deal, 713
　regulation of trusts and, 526,
　　542–543
　resistance to New Deal reforms,
　　718–719
　unregulated, 677, 678
　in World War I, 654–655
Business organization. *See also*
　　Corporations
　horizontal integration as, 526
　trusts and, 526
　vertical integration as, 525
Busing, school integration and, 895
Butler, Nicholas Murray, 657
Buxton, Myron, New Deal and, 726*(b)*
Byrd, Harry F., 831*(m)*

California, 514. *See also* Los Angeles
　Asians in, 505–506
　Chinese in, 505–506, 557
　defense industry in, 813
　gold rush in, 501
　gun control in, 925
　manifest destiny and, 491
　Mexican Americans in, 513
　progressivism in, 617–618, 637
　Reagan as governor of, 893, 907
　woman suffrage and, 593

California gold rush, 501, 508*(b)*
Californios, 504–505
Calley, William, 883–884
Cambodia, 866, 885
　bombing of, 882
　immigrants from, 939
　U.S. invasion of (1970), 882,
　　882*(m)*, 883
Campaigns (political). *See also*
　　Elections
　of 1884, 539–540
　federal employees and, 539
　financing of, 539, 898, 941
　TV use for, 817
Camp David accords, **904**
Canada
　immigrants from, 501, 551
　Indian movement to, 498
　NAFTA and, 937
Canals. *See* Panama Canal and Panama
　　Canal region
Cannon, Joseph, 625
Cantigny, battle at, 651
CAP. *See* Community Action Program
Capitalism
　corporate, 543, 560
　finance, 528, 529–530
　in Great Depression, 703
　industrial, 520, 574*(b)*
　in New Deal, 712
　social gospel and, 613
　welfare, 680
Capone, Alphonse ("Big Al"), 683
Caribbean region. *See also* specific
　　locations
　immigrants from, 939
　U.S. involvement in, 600, 863*(m)*
Carlisle Indian School, **497**
Carmichael, Stokely, 830*(i)*, 844
Carnegie, Andrew, 520, 532, 562
　and gospel of wealth, 530
　Homestead lockout and, 585–586
　Morgan, J. P., and, 529–530
　social Darwinism and, 530
　steel industry and, 524–525, 551
Carpetbaggers, 458*(i)*, **472**–473
Cars. *See* Automobiles and automobile
　　industry
Carson, Rachel, 856
Carter, James Earl, Jr. ("Jimmy"),
　　899–906
　deregulation by, 901
　domestic policy of, 900–904

economy and, 900–901
　election of 1976 and, 899, 899*(m)*
　energy, environment, and, 901–904
　foreign policy of, 904–906
　human rights and, 904
　inauguration of, 900
Carter Doctrine, 906
Casablanca meeting (1943), 755
Cash-and-carry foreign trade policy,
　　742, 745–746
Cash register, 563
Castro, Fidel, 806–807, 927
　Bay of Pigs invasion and, 862–863
　CIA illegal activities against,
　　806–807, 899
　protests of 1968 and, 876*(b)*
Casualties. *See also* specific wars
　during Brooklyn Bridge
　　construction, 549
　in Filipino guerrilla warfare, 607
　in mining accidents, 503
Catholicism. *See also* Missions and
　　missionaries; Religion(s)
　of immigrants, 692
　of Kennedy, 831
　of Smith, Alfred, 695
Cattell, James McKeen, 657
Cattle. *See* Ranching
Census, racial categories in, 939
Central America. *See also* Latin
　　America; specific locations
　Bush, G. H. W., and, 927–928
　immigrants from, 501
　Reagan and, 917
　U.S. intervention in, 600, 645
Central American–Dominican
　　Republic Free Trade Agreement
　　(2005), 937
Central High School, Little Rock, 820
Central Intelligence Agency (CIA),
　　781
　Afghanistan secret aid by, 906
　Chile and, 881
　Cuba and, 806–807, 862
　Guatemala and, 806
　illegal activities by, 898–899
　intelligence gathering and, 782*(i)*
　Iran and, 807
　Nixon and, 897
　Vietnam and, 806
Central Pacific Railroad, 506, 506*(i)*
Central Park (New York City),
　　572–573

Century of Dishonor, A (Jackson), 497
Chamberlain, Neville, 743
Chamber of Commerce, 719
Chambers, Whittaker, 790
Chaplin, Charlie, 689
Chase, Salmon P., 464, 471
Château-Thierry, battle at (1918), 651
Chavez, Cesar, 846, 846*(i)*
Cheney, Richard B.
   Iraq War and, 944
   Persian Gulf War and, 928
   as vice president, 940
Cherokee Indians, 491
Cherokee strip, land rush in, 512
Cheyenne Indians, 493, 495, 500
Chiang Kai-shek. *See* Jiang Jieshi
   (Chiang Kai-shek)
Chicago
   African Americans in, 556,
      669*(i)*, 670
   de facto segregation in, 835
   Democratic National Convention
      in (1968), 876*(b)*, 878–879
   Great Fire of 1871 in, 571
   Haymarket bombing in, 567–569
   Hull House in, 610–611, 612*(i)*
   immigrants in, 555
   population in, 550
   protests in (1968), 876*(b)*
   skyscrapers in, 571
   World's Columbian Exposition in,
      488, 489–490, 574–575*(b)*,
      576–577
Chicago Bears (football team), 690
"Chicago school" of architecture,
   571–572
Chicago Tribune, 466
   on Pullman strike, 590
Chicano movement and Chicanos, **846**
Chickasaw Indians, 491
Chief Joseph (Nez Percé chief),
   498–499
Chief justice. *See* Supreme Court
   (U.S.); Warren, Earl, and Warren
   Court; specific justices
Childbirth, in 1930s, 701
Child care
   Nixon and, 857
   women's employment and, 852
Child labor, 560
   in coal mines, 620
   in late 19th century, 562
· in New Deal, 735

in textile mills, 532, 560
   Wilson and, 634
Children
   black codes, apprenticeship laws,
      and, 466
   of freedmen, 475*(i)*, 478
   of immigrants, 506
   middle class, 570
   Native American, 493, 496–497
   in New Deal, 728
   in textile mills, 532
   working-class, 562
Children's Bureau, in Labor
   Department, 630
Child Support Enforcement
   Amendments Act, 912
Chile, 881*(m)*
   Carter and, 904
   CIA and, 881
   immigrants from, 501
China
   Boxer uprising in, 597, 599–600
   civil war in, 782–783
   Egypt and, 807
   Japan and, 743, 747
   Korea and, 792
   Korean War and, 794
   missionaries in, 599–600
   Nationalists in, 742
   Nixon and, 862, 879, 880–881,
      880*(i)*
   Open Door policy in, 601, 601*(i)*
   People's Republic of, 783, 807, 904
   pro-democracy demonstrators in,
      927
   Soviet treaty with, 783
   United Nations and, 765
   Vietnam and, 885
   World War I and, 646
   in World War II, 765
   after World War II, 765, 770
Chinese Americans, in World War II,
   750
Chinese Exclusion Act (1882, 1902),
   506, 508*(b)*, 513, 557, 637, 670
Chinese immigrants, 489, 693
   in California, 505–506
   in cities, 557
   in mining, 501, 503, 505–506
   railroads and, 506, 506*(i)*
Chirachua Apache Indians, 499
Chivington, John M., 493
Choctaw Indians, 491

Choice Not an Echo, A (Schlafly), 891
Christian fundamentalism, 907, 916
Christianity
   in China, 599, 600
   Indians and, 500
   social gospel and, 613
Christian Right. *See* New Christian
   Right
Chrysler Corporation, bailout of
   (1976), 901, 947
Churches. *See also* Religion(s)
   black, 463–464
   membership in, 817
Churchill, Winston. *See also*
   World War II
   Atlantic Charter and, 746
   on Bolshevism, 666*(b)*
   at Casablanca, 755
   iron curtain speech of, 775, 776*(m)*
   Nazi Germany and, 745
   at Teheran, 763
   in World War II, 755
   at Yalta, 765
Church of Jesus Christ of Latter-Day
   Saints. *See* Mormons
CIA. *See* Central Intelligence Agency
Cigarettes, 532. *See also* Tobacco and
   tobacco industry
Cincinnati, Ohio, 570–571
CIO. *See* Committee for Industrial
   Organization; Congress of
   Industrial Organizations
Cisler, Lucinda, 854
Cities and towns. *See also* Urban areas
   in 1920s, 691, 692*(m)*
   in 1950s, 812
   African Americans in, 556,
      669*(i)*, 670
   architecture of, 571–572
   automobiles and, 679–680
   bosses (political) in, 538, 573–576
   child labor in, 562
   electric lights in, 528
   in Gilded Age, 531, 546, 558–559,
      571–577, 577–578
   global migration and, 551–555
   growth of, 550–555
   immigrants in, 554–555, 558–559
   leisure in, 570–571
   mass transit in, 558
   mining towns, 503–504
   movement to, 551
   neighborhoods in, 558–559

Cities and towns *(continued)*
  parks in, 572
  population in, 513*(f)*, 550
  poverty in, 555, 559
  progressive government in, 617–618
  public libraries in, 572–573
  public works in, 572–573
  segregation in, 558
  social geography of, 558–559
  urban renewal and, 831
Citizens and citizenship
  Asians and, 506
  for Californios, 504
  Fourteenth Amendment and, 468
  gender and, 533
  Native Americans and, 498, 693
  Supreme Court and, 482
Citizens United v. FEC (2010), 941
Civil disobedience, 838, 846*(i)*, 883
Civilian Conservation Corps (CCC),
  715
Civil liberties
  Red scare and, 664, 668
  World War I and, 644
Civil rights. *See also* Civil rights
    movement
  of African Americans, 467, 481,
    786–787
  Eisenhower and, 801
  Johnson, L. B., and, 834, 840–842
  Kennedy, J. F., and, 831
  for Mexican Americans, 846–847
  New Left and, 847
  Nixon and, 856
  in North, 824*(i)*
  southern Republican governments
    and, 475
  Truman and, 787
Civil Rights Act
  of 1866, 467
  of 1875, 482
  of 1964, 833, 840, 850, 856, 893
Civil Rights Commission, 911
Civil rights movement, 486, 838–844.
    See also King, Martin Luther, Jr.
  emergence of, 819–825
  Freedom Rides during, 839, 839*(m)*
Civil service, 538
  exams, 539, 539*(i)*
  gays and lesbians in, 849
  McCarthyism and, 790
Civil Service Commission, 539
Civil service reform, 538, **539**

Civil war(s)
  in China, 782–783
  in Guatemala, 806
  in Rwanda, 936
  in Spain, 743, 743*(m)*
  in Syria, 951
  in Yugoslavia (former), 936
Civil War (U.S., 1861–1865). *See*
    Reconstruction
Civil Works Administration (CWA),
    715
Claiborne, Liz, 910
Clamshell Alliance, 902–903
Class conflict, tariff debate and, 542
Classes. *See* Hierarchy; specific classes
Clayton Antitrust Act (1914), 634
Clean Air Act
  of 1970, 856
  of 1990, **925**
  weakening under Bush, G. W., 941
Clean Water Act (1972), 856
  weakening under Bush, G. W., 941
"Clear and present danger" test, 668
Clemenceau, Georges, 651, 660, 662*(i)*
Clemens, Samuel Langhorne. *See*
    Twain, Mark
Clergy. *See also* Religion(s)
  Anti-Saloon League and, 613
Clerical jobs, by 1890s, 563
Cleveland, Grover, 600
  depression of 1890s and, 544–545
  election of 1884 and, 539–540,
    540*(m)*
  election of 1888 and, 540, 541
  election of 1892 and, 541, 542
  election of 1896 and, 596
  gold standard and, 544
  Hawai'i and, 598
  on immigration restriction, 558
  Pullman strike and, 590
  tariff reform and, 541
Cleveland, Ohio, 558
  progressive government in,
    617, 618*(i)*
Climate and climate change. *See also*
    Environment
  Paris agreement about (2015), 950
Clinton, Hillary Rodham, election of
    2008 and, 946, 948–949*(b)*, 948*(i)*
Clinton, William Jefferson ("Bill")
  cabinet of, 932
  Clinton, Hillary, campaign of 2008
    and, 948–949*(b)*, 948*(i)*

  economy and, 931–932
  election of 1992 and, 930
  election of 1996 and, 933–934
  foreign policy of, 935, 936–937
  gays in military and, 932
  globalization and, 935–937
  impeachment of, 934
  presidency of, 931–935
  reforms by, 931–932
  Supreme Court and, 932
Closed shop, 678
Clothing. *See also* Cotton and cotton
    industry; Textiles and textile
    industry
  in Indian boarding schools, 497
Coal and coal industry
  child labor in, 620
  in Great Depression, 724
  strikes against, 620–621
Coalitions
  in New Deal, 711, 712, 879
  reform, 591
Cockran, Bourke, 607
Codes, National Recovery
    Administration and, 718
Cody, William F. ("Buffalo Bill"),
    488, 489*(i)*
Coins. *See* Currency
Cold War, 770, **775**–776. *See also*
    Soviet Union; Vietnam War
  1945–1953, 772–796
  beginning of, 774–776
  Carter and, 904–906
  comic book during, 772*(i)*
  costs and consequences of,
    795–796
  easing of, 861–862
  end of, 922, 923, 925–926
  Johnson, L. B., and, 868–872
  Kennedy, J. F., and, 862–868
  Korean War and, 791–795
  spying during, 782*(i)*
  Truman Doctrine and, 777
  Vietnam War and, 861
Cole, Jim, New Deal and, 726–727*(b)*
Colfax, Schuyler, 480
Colfax massacre, 483–484
"Collapse of the Armed Forces, The"
    (1971 report), 884
Collective security
  in national security state, 781
  after World War I, 661, 678
Colleges. *See* Universities and colleges

Collier, John, 730
Colombia, Panama Canal and, 625
Colonies and colonization
    in third world, 551
    by U.S. in Panama Canal Zone, 870
    after World War I, 660
Colorado, 491, 515
    voting by women in, 593
Color barrier, breaking of, 787
Colored Farmers' Alliance, 583–584
Colt firearms factory, 574(b)
Columbia University, student protests
    at (1968), 878
Columbus, Christopher, 574(b)
Comanche Indians, 493, 494–495, 498
Comanchería, 494
Combine (farm machine), 514
Coming of Age in Mississippi (Moody),
    839
Comintern, 665
Commerce. *See* Taxation; Trade
Commercial agriculture, 507, 513, 514
Commercialization, of leisure,
    570–571
Commission on the Status of Women
    (UN), 852
Committee for a Sane Nuclear Policy,
    808
***Committee for Industrial
    Organization*** (CIO), **725**
Committee on Civil Rights (1946). *See*
    President's Committee on Civil
    Rights (1946)
Committee on Fair Employment
    Practices (1941), 758
Committee on Public Information
    (Creel committee), 657
Commodity credit, 585
Commodity Credit Corporation, 716
Common laborers, 560
Communes, hippie, 848
Communication(s)
    railroads and, 523
    telegraph and, 523
    telephone and, 527, 528(i)
Communism. *See also* Cold War;
    Red scare; Russia; Soviet Union
    in China, 783
    Cold War and, 773–774, 925–926
    Eastern Europe and, 925–926, 926(m)
    in East Germany, 775
    Eisenhower foreign policy and,
    804–806, 807–808

Goldwater on, 893
    in Greece, 777
    in Guatemala, 806
    Johnson, L. B., and, 868–872
    Kennedy, J. F., and, 862–868
    Marshall Plan and, 780(b)
    McCarthy and, 789–791
    New Deal and, 730–731
    in postwar Eastern Europe, 770
    refugees from, 939
    in Southeast Asia, 805
    Vietnam War and, 861, 866
    after World War I, 665
Communist Party, 666(b). *See also*
    Communism
    in Great Depression, 703, 720–721
    McCarthyism and, 791
Communities, African American, 504
Community Action Program (CAP),
    833
Community colleges, 815
Compassionate conservatism, of Bush,
    G. W., 940–942
Compensation, to Indians, 802
Competition
    antitrust laws and, 543
    in cattle industry, 509(b)
    Morgan and, 529
    in petroleum industry, 526, 530
    in railroad industry, 523
    social Darwinism and, 530, 531
    tariffs and, 541
Compromise of 1877, 485
Computers, income inequality and, 935
Comstock, Anthony, 636
Comstock, Henry, 501
Comstock Lode (Nevada), *501*–504,
    502(m), 508(b)
Concentration camps
    in Cuba, 601
    in Holocaust, 759
    Japanese, 753
Condren, Dan, 785
Coney Island, New York, 570(i),
    571, 577
Confederate Congress, 466
Confiscation Act(s), 462
Conger, Sarah, 599
Congress (U.S.). *See also*
    Congressional reconstruction;
    Elections; House of
    Representatives; Senate
    "Billion Dollar," 542

election of 1876 and, 485
    elections of 1918 and, 658–659
    ex-Confederates in, 466, 467, 482
    in Gilded Age, 542
    investigating committees in, 898–899
    Obama and, 947
    override of presidential vetoes, 467
    Reagan and, 911–912
    Reconstruction and, 461–462, 464,
    481–482
    southern delegations in
    (1865–1877), 474(f)
    Vietnam War and, 883
Congressional reconstruction,
    467–472
Congress of Industrial Organizations
    (CIO), 725
Congress of Racial Equality (CORE),
    758, 821, 839, 844
Conkling, Roscoe, 533
Conscientious objectors, in Vietnam
    War, 873
Conscription. *See* Draft (military)
Conservation. *See also* Environment
    of energy, 901
    in New Deal, 715
    Nixon and, 855
    Roosevelt, T., and, 624–625
    Taft and, 630
Conservatives and conservatism,
    890–892
    Eisenhower and, 800, 801, 810
    New Deal and, 725–728
    Nixon and, 830, 892–896
    Reagan and, 906–911, 919–920
    religious, 907–908
    in Sun Belt, 893
Consolidation
    of business, 528, 530, 545
    in mining, ranching, and agricul-
    ture, 507
Constitution(s). *See also* Constitution
    (U.S.)
    Cuban, 605
    Reconstruction, in South, 461, 465,
    470, 473–474
Constitution (U.S.). *See also* Bill of
    Rights; Supreme Court (U.S.)
    strict construction of, 896
Consumer culture
    in 1920s, 680–682
    Columbian Exposition and, 575(b)
    in Gilded Age, 563

Consumer goods
  capitalism and, 799
  production of (1921–1929), 681(*f*)
  in World War II, 756–757
Consumer prices, and farm income
  (1865–1910), 583(*f*)
Consumers
  tariffs and, 541
  after World War II, 785, 786(*i*)
Consumption
  in 1920s, 681, 697
  in 1950s, 809, 815–818
  gender roles and, 818
Container (box), 922(*i*)
Containment policy, **775**–776, 777, 781
  global, 782–783
  in Korean War, 793–794
  military implementation of, 791–793
  in Vietnam, 805–806
Contraception. *See* Birth control and
  birth control movement; Birth
  control pill
Contract labor
  Asian immigrants and, 557
  freedmen and, 462
Contracts, labor, 678
Conventions. *See also* Democratic
  National Convention
  state constitutional, in
  Reconstruction, 470, 473
Coolidge, Calvin, 665, 677–678
  foreign policy of, 678–679
  taxation cut by, 697
"Coolie labor," 557
Cooperatives, farmers', 584
Coral Sea, battle of (1942), 753, 765
CORE. *See* Congress of Racial Equality
Corporate capitalism, 543, 560
Corporate consolidation. *See*
  Consolidation
Corporations. *See also* Business
  in New Deal, 713
  Supreme Court and, 531
  taxation of, 728
Corruption
  in city government, 573, 576
  Crédit Mobilier scandal, 524, 538
  in Gilded Age, 524
  under Grant, 480, 481(*i*), 538
  in southern Republican
  governments, 476
  in territorial government, 515
Costa Rica, 600

Cotton and cotton industry. *See also*
  Textiles and textile industry
  sharecropping and, 478–479, 510
  in Texas, 513
Cotton Club, 688, 689(*i*)
Coughlin, Charles, 721
Council of Economic Advisers, 784
Counterculture, 848
Countermovement, to feminism,
  853–854
Coups
  in Iran, 807
  in Vietnam, 868
Court-packing plan, of Roosevelt, F. D.,
  731–732
Courts. *See also* Supreme Court (U.S.)
  Reagan and, 911–912
Covenants, in housing, 812
Covert operations. *See also* Central
  Intelligence Agency
  of CIA, 899
Cowboys, 489, 512, 513
  industrial, 514
Cox, Archibald, 897
Cox, James M., 671, 671(*i*), 709
Coxey, Jacob S., 594
Coxey's army, **594**–595, 594(*i*)
Craft unions, 566
Crane, Stephen, 620
Crashes (financial). *See also*
  Depressions (financial);
  Great Depression; Panic(s)
  of 1929, 697, 714
Crazy Horse (Sioux chief), 495, 496
Credit. *See also* National debt
  farmers and, 583, 584, 585
  installment buying and, 697
  railroad boom and, 521
Crédit Mobilier scandal, 524, 538
Creek Indians, removal of, 491
Creel, George, 657
Crime and criminals
  in 1930s, 701
  law-and-order movement and, 894
  in prohibition, 683
Crimes against humanity, by Nazis, 762
Criminal justice system, reforms of,
  837, 947–948
Cripple Creek, 503
  miners' strike of 1894, **587**–588
Croatia, 936
Crocker, Charles, 506
Crogman, William, 639

Croly, Jane Cunningham
  (Jennie June), 536
Cronkite, Walter, 873
Crook, George, 495, 499
Crop lien system, 478, 583
Crops. *See also* Agriculture; Farms and
  farming
  in New Deal, 715–717
"Cross of gold" speech, of Bryan, 596
Crow Dog, Mary, 845
Crow Indians, 498
Crusade for Justice (Wells), 536
Cuba. *See also* Cuban missile crisis
  dictator in, 742
  Obama and, 946
  Platt Amendment and, 605–606
  refugees from, 939
  revolution in, 741, 806–807
  Spain and, 601
  Spanish-American War and, 601,
  604–605, 605(*m*), 645(*m*)
  United States and, 741, 742
Cuban missile crisis, 862–863,
  865–866, 865(*i*)
Cuban revolution (1959), **807**
Cullen, Countee, 688
Cult of domesticity, **569,** 570, 591
Culture(s)
  of abundance, 798–800, 815
  consumer, 680–682
  dissent in, 818–819
  Lost Generation and, 690–691
  Mexican American, 671
  Native American, 496–497, 498
  and politics in Gilded Age, 531–540
Currency. *See also* Money
  Federal Reserve Act and, 633–634
  "In God We Trust" on, 817
Curriculum, in Indian schools, 497
Cushman, Belle, 563
Custer, George Armstrong, 493, 495
"Custer's Last Stand," 495–496
Czechoslovakia
  Communists in, 779(*b*)
  Nazi invasion of, 743
  Prague Spring in, 876(*b*)
  after World War I, 660
Czolgosz, Leon, 618

Dakota Sioux Indians, 494
Dakota territory, 515
Dams, in wilderness, 856
Dana, Charles, 524

Dance halls, 570
Darrow, Clarence, 694
Darwin, Charles, 530. *See also* Reform Darwinism; Social Darwinism
Davis, Henry Winter, 461, 462
Davis, James J., 560
Davis, John W., 678
Dawes, Henry, 498
Dawes Allotment Act (1887), *498,* 730, 803
Dawes Plan, 679
D Day invasion (June 6, 1944), *763*
DDT, 856
Dean, John, 897
Death camps, Nazi, 759
Death rate. *See* Mortality rate
Debates, presidential (1960), 831
Debs, Eugene V.
  election of 1912 and, 632, 633, 633(*m*), 635
  election of 1920 and, 671(*m*)
  Espionage Act and, 658
  Pullman strike and, 588, 589, 590
  Socialist Party and, 590, 632, 635
Debt. *See also* National debt
  Confederate, 465
  farm, 514, 532, 543
  in Reconstruction South, 475
  tariffs and, 541
De facto segregation, in Chicago, 842
Defender (Chicago newspaper), 556
Defense. *See* Defense spending; National security
Defense of Marriage Act (DOMA, 1996), 932
Defense spending
  countries with highest military expenditures (2005), 936(*f*)
  in higher education, 815
  Kennedy, J. F., and, 864
  NSC 68 and, 795
  Reagan and, 909, 916
  in Sun Belt, 813, 893
  after World War II, 785
Deficit, in federal budget, 909, 925, 931, 934, 941
Deflation, 595
Demilitarized zone, in Korea, 795
Democracy, after World War I, 660, 664–671
Democratic National Convention
  of 1896, 595–596
  of 1960, 830

of 1964, 829
of 1968, 876(*b*), 878–879
Democratic Party. *See* Democrats (Democratic Party)
Democratization, of higher education, 814–815
Democrats (Democratic Party).
  See also Elections
  election of 1876 and, 485
  free silver issue and, 544, 595, 596
  in Gilded Age, 531, 539–540
  Populists and, 596
  as Redeemers, 483, 484
  sectionalism in, 595
  South and, 473, 483–484, 532, 597
  southern Republican state governments and, 474, 483
  tariffs and, 541, 542
  Tweed and, 573
  white supremacy and, 483, 484
Demonstration(s). *See* Protest(s); Resistance; Revolts and rebellions
Dempsey, Jack, 689–690
Denby, Charles, 600
Denmark, in World War II, 745
Department stores, 563
Depressions (financial). *See also* Great Depression; Panic(s); Recessions
  in 1870s, 481, 519, 543, 553, 564
  in 1890s, 514, 519, 528, 541, 544–545, 553, 577, 588, 593, 595, 598, 607–608
Deregulation
  by Carter, 901, 909
  by Reagan, 909
  workers and, 935
Desegregation. *See also* Integration; Segregation
  of military, 787
Détente policy, *880*
Detention camp, at Guantánamo, 943–944, 945
Deterrence policy, in Cold War, 781, 826
Detroit
  automobile industry and (1920s), 679(*m*)
  drinking in, 683
  race riot in (1943), 758
  race riot in (1967), 844
Developing nations, United States and, 782, 937, 938

Dewey, Thomas E., 759, 788, 789(*i*), 789(*m*)
Díaz, Porfirio, 670
Dickens, Charles, 536
Diem, Ngo Dinh, 806, 866, 868
Dien Bien Phu, 805, 806
Dioxin, Agent Orange and, 886
Diplomacy. *See also* Foreign policy
  dollar diplomacy, 630–631, 630(*m*)
  Monroe Doctrine and, 600
  of Wilson, 648
Direct election of senators, 538, 585, 630
Direct primary, 618
Dirksen, Everett, 833
Disabled people, discrimination outlawed against, 856
Disarmament
  calls for, 916
  naval, 679
  Reagan, Gorbachev, and, 919
Discrimination. *See also* Affirmative action; Civil rights; Civil rights movement; Integration; Race and racism; Segregation
  against African Americans, 482, 504, 533, 820–825, 824(*i*)
  against Asians, 503, 505–506
  black codes and, 465–466
  against gays and lesbians, 849, 947
  gender, 850
  against Hispanics, 504–505
  in housing, 835, 842
  in jury selection, 835, 842
  legislation against, 840
  against Mexican Americans, 787, 847
  in military, 750
  against people with disabilities, 856
  during Reconstruction, 475
  Supreme Court on, 482
  during World War II, 758
  after World War II, 785–786
Diseases. *See also* Medicine; specific conditions
  epidemics in 1918, 665
  Indians and, 491
  from Vietnam War, 886
Disfranchisement. *See also* Voting and voting rights
  of African Americans, 729
  of ex-Confederates, 473

Dissent and dissenters. *See also* Civil
    rights movement; Protest(s)
    in 1950s, 818–819
    World War I and, 657–658
Dissidents, in Soviet Union and
    Eastern Europe, 881
Distribution of wealth
    in 1920s, 697
    in New Deal, 713
District of Columbia. *See* Washington,
    D.C.
Diversity
    in West, 504–506
    of workforce, 560–561
Division of labor, sexual, 555
Dixiecrats, 788
Dobson, James, 907–908
Doctors. *See* Medicine
Dodge, Richard, 493(*i*)
Dole, Robert, 934
Dollar diplomacy (Taft), 630–631,
    630(*m*)
Domesticity
    in 1950s, 816–817
    cult of, 569, 591
Domestics (domestic servants).
    See also Servants
    black women as, 562, 668–669
    women as, 569
Domestic violence, 854
Dominican Republic, 627
    U.S. intervention in, 645, 868, 870
Dominis, Lydia Kamakaeha.
    See Lili'uokalani
Domino theory, 805
Dom Pedro II (Brazil), 476(*b*)
Donnelly, Ignatius, 581, 595
Double V campaign, 757–**758**
"Doughboys," 642, 644(*i*)
Douglas, Aaron, 688
Douglas, Helen Gahagan, 772–774, 788
    containment and, 795
    economy and, 784
    "Hollywood Ten" and, 791
    Nixon and, 794
    Truman Doctrine and, 777
Douglas, Melvyn, 772
Douglass, Frederick, 468
Downs, Frederick Jr., 860–861,
    871–872, 886, 887
Draft (military)
    Carter and, 905
    peacetime, 781

    in Vietnam War, 873
    in World War I, 650–651
    in World War II, 750
Drift and Mastery (Lippmann), 617
Drone strikes, 950
Drought. *See also* Dust Bowl
    on Great Plains (1880s–1890s), 512
Drugs (legal). *See* Prescription
    medication
Drugs (illegal), Noriega and, 928
Dry states, 613
Dubček, Alexander, 876(*b*)
Du Bois, W. E. B., 536, 639, 685–688
Due process, 468. *See also* Fourteenth
    Amendment
Dukas, Helen, 761(*i*)
Duke family, 532
Dulles, John Foster, 804, 806, 807
Dunkirk, withdrawal from, 745
Du Pont, 620
Durant, Thomas, 524
Dust Bowl, in Great Depression, 707,
    719–720, 719(*m*)
Dutch East Indies. *See* East Indies;
    Indonesia
Dynamic Sociology (Ward), 616–617

Earned Income Tax Credit (EITC), **931**
Earth Day (1970), 856
East (U.S. region), immigrants in, 551,
    555, 557
East Berlin, 780
    Berlin Wall and, 864
Eastern Europe. *See also* Europe and
    Europeans
    1989–2002, 926(*m*)
    Clinton, Bill, and, 935
    Cold War and, 774–776, 926
    dissidents in, 881
    Marshall Plan and, 777
    in World War II, 763
    after World War II, 765, 770
Eastern front, in World War II,
    754–755
Eastern Hemisphere, competition for
    trade in, 600–601
East Germany
    end of communism in, 925
    Khrushchev and, 864
East Indies
    Japan and, 747
    in World War II, 753
East River, 548, 550(*i*)

East St. Louis, Illinois, race riot in, 670
Ecology, 856
    of Great Plains, 493
Economic cycles. *See* Boom and bust
    cycles
Economic democracy, Populists and,
    585
Economic inequality, social
    Darwinism and, 530
Economic Opportunity Act (1964),
    833, 834
Economic Recovery Tax Act (1981),
    909
Economics
    laissez-faire and, 531
    supply-side, 908–909
Economy. *See also* Depressions;
        Globalization; Great Depression;
        New Deal; Panic(s); Tariffs;
        Trade; Wealth
    in 1920s, 697
    in 1929, 696–697
    in 1950s, 809–815
    automobile industry and, 679
    boom and bust cycles in, 523
    boom in (1945–1970), 816(*f*)
    boom in (1990s), 934–935
    Carter and, 900–901
    Clinton, Bill, and, 931–932,
        934–935
    in Cold War, 799–800
    consumer culture and, 680
    crash of 1929 and, 697
    Eisenhower and, 803–804
    family, 561–562
    free market, 545
    in Gilded Age, 520, 540–545
    global, 952
    Great Society and, 834–837
    Kennedy, J. F., and, 831–832
    Marshall Plan and, 780
    Nixon and, 854–855
    Obama and, 946–950
    plantation, 512
    Reagan and, 908–911
    recession of 1937–1938 and,
        732–733
    in Reconstruction South, 475
    Roosevelt, F. D., and, 710, 712–718
    in South, 532
    Sun Belt development and,
        813–814
    in West, 514

during World War I, 654–655
after World War I, 664–665
during World War II, 750–752,
    756–757
after World War II, 778–779(b),
    784–786
Edison, Thomas Alva, 527–528, 574(b)
Edison General Electric, 528
Education. *See also* Higher education;
    School(s)
Brown v. Board of Education and, 820
equal opportunity in, 911
equal rights to, 787
freedmen and, 463, 475(i), 478
for Indians, 496–497
Johnson, L. B., and, 834
for Mexican Americans, 788
public, in South, 474–475
for women, 683, 852
Education Amendments Act (1972),
    Title IX of, 854, 911
EEOC. *See* Equal Employment
    Opportunity Commission
Efficiency, 612, 617
assembly lines and, 680
Egypt
    Arab Spring and, 951
    Eisenhower administration and, 807
    recognition of Israel by, 904
    Six-Day War and, 881
    Yom Kippur War and, 855, 881
Eighteenth Amendment, **655,** 683
Eight-hour workday, 567, 569, 585,
    634, 655
Eighty-ninth Congress, 834
Einstein, Albert, 760(b), 761(i)
Einstein, Margot, 761(i)
Eisenhower, Dwight D.
    Advanced Research Projects
        Agency and, 938
    CIA and, 862
    civil rights and, 820
    Cold War pattern of, 917
    Cuba and, 807, 862
    election of 1952 and, 794
    election of 1956 and, 803
    foreign policy of, 804–809
    Israel and, 807
    Latin America and, 806–807
    Middle East and, 807–808
    "middle way" of, 800–804
    on military-industrial complex,
        808–809

Soviet Union and, 799
Vietnam and, 805–806
in World War II, 755
Eisenhower Doctrine (1957), **808**
EITC. *See* Earned Income Tax Credit
El-Alamein, battle of (1942), 755
Elderly. *See also* Pensions
in 1960s, 836
in New Deal, 728
prescription drugs for, 940, 942
Elections. *See also* Campaigns (politi-
    cal); Voting and voting rights
of 1865, 466
of 1866, 469
of 1868, 459, 480, 480(m)
of 1872, 459, 480–481
of 1874, 482
of 1876, 484–485, 485(m)
of 1878, 543
of 1880, 538
of 1884, 539–540, 540(m)
of 1888, 540, 541
of 1890, 542
of 1892, 541, 542, 595, 595(m)
of 1896, 581, 595–597, 596(m)
of 1904, 621
of 1908, 629
of 1910, 630
of 1912, 610(l), 631–633, 635
of 1916, 634, 648
of 1918, 652–659
of 1920, 671, 671(m), 709
of 1924, 678
of 1928, 694–695, 695(m)
of 1932, 709(i), 710–712, 711(m)
of 1934, 722
of 1936, 731
of 1940, 746
of 1944, 758–759
of 1948, 787, 788, 789(i), 789(m)
of 1950, 794
of 1952, 794–795
of 1956, 803
of 1960, 831, 831(m)
of 1964, 833–834, 869
of 1968, 854, 873, 877(b), 878–879,
    879(m)
of 1972, 855, 896–897
of 1976, 893, 899, 899(m)
of 1980, 907
of 1984, 910
of 1988, 924
of 1992, 930

of 1996, 933–934
of 2000, 940, 940(m)
of 2004, 945
of 2008, 946
of 2012, 947, 951(m)
of 2014, 947
of senators, 538, 585
television and, 817–818
Electoral commission, for 1876
    election, 485
Electorate, shift in (1928–1932),
    711(m)
Electric industry, 527, 528
Electricity
    in cities, 528
    hydroelectricity and, 715
    in rural areas, 715
Electric streetcar, 558, 558(i)
Electric trolleys, 528
Elementary and Secondary Education
    Act (ESEA, 1965), 834
Elevated trains, 525, 572
Elkins Act (1903), 620, 621
Ellington, Duke, 689(i)
Ellis, Havelock, 687
Ellis Island, 557
El Paso, Texas, Mexican immigrants to,
    670(t)
El Salvador, Carter and, 904
Embargo
    Neutrality Acts and, 742
    in World War II, 748
Embassies
    in Saigon, 875
    terrorist attacks on U.S., 917
Emergency Banking Act (1933), 713
Emerging nations, 782
Emigration. *See* Immigrants and
    immigration; Migration
Emmons, Glenn, 802
Empire(s)
    Comanchería, 494
    of United States, 489, 597,
        605–607, 606(m)
Employment. *See also* Unemployment;
    Women; Work; Workforce
    Committee on Fair Employment
        Practices (1941), 758
    equal rights to, 787
    of women, 560, 562, 562(f),
        816, 852
    in World War II, 751
    after World War II, 784

Employment Act (1946), 784
Endangered Species Act (1973), 856
Energy. *See also* Steam power
  Carter and, 900–903
  consumption of, 902(*f*)
  electricity as, 528
  fuel shortage and, 901(*i*)
  Nixon and, 855
  nuclear, 801
Energy crisis, in 1973, 855
Energy Department, 901
England (Britain). *See also* World
    War I; World War II
  American war materiel and,
    745–746
  German blockade of, 648, 649
  immigrants from, 501, 551, 552
  United Nations and, 765
  Venezuelan–British Guiana borders
    and, 600
  World War I and, 650
  World War II and, 745, 746
Enola Gay (airplane), 739, 740(*i*), 768(*i*)
Entertainment. *See also* Leisure
  in 1920s, 688–690
  television as, 817–818
Environment. *See also* Air pollution
  Agent Orange and, 873
  Bush, G. H. W., and, 925
  Bush, G. W., and, 941
  Carter and, 902–904
  global, 937
  Johnson, L. B., and, 835
  Native Americans and, 489
  Nixon and, 855–856
  nuclear energy and, 902–903
  Obama and, 947
  Reagan and, 909
  of Sun Belt, 813–814
  Superfund for cleanup of, 903
Environmental movement
  nuclear energy and, 902–903
  trade and, 937
Environmental Protection Agency
  (EPA, 1970), ***856***
Epidemics. *See also* Diseases
  in 1918, 665
Equal Employment Opportunity
  Commission (EEOC), 847,
  856, 925
Equality. *See also* Civil rights movement;
    Gender and gender issues; Slavery
  racial, 460, 482

Equal Pay Act (1963), 850
Equal pay for equal work principle,
  784
Equal protection, in Fourteenth
  Amendment, 468, 814, 837
Equal rights, Truman on, 787
Equal Rights Amendment (ERA)
  of 1923, 684
  of 1972, 851, 853, 907, ***912,*** 912(*m*)
  reasons for failure of, 914–915(*b*),
    915(*i*)
Ervin, Samuel J., 897
Espionage. *See* Spies and spying
Espionage Act (1917), 658
Ethiopia, Italian invasion of, 742
"Ethnic cleansing" against Comanche,
  494
Ethnic groups
  in cities, 555, 558–559
  immigration and, 555
  politics and, 531
  racism and, 555–558
  after World War I, 663
Eugenics, birth control and, 636, 684
Europe and Europeans. *See also*
    Colonies and colonization;
    World War I; World War II
  division after World War II,
    775–776, 776(*m*)
  emigration from (1870–1910), 554(*f*)
  global comparison of emigration
    from (1870–1890), 554(*f*)
  Hitler and, 743–746
  immigrants from, 551, 557
  recession of 1937–1938 and, 732
  before World War I, 646
  after World War I, 659–662, 661(*m*)
  World War I casualties in, 653–654
  in World War II, 754–755, 764(*m*)
  after World War II, 769–770
European Recovery Program (ERP).
    See Marshall Plan
European Union (EU), 778
  former Soviet satellites in, 926
Evangelicals and evangelicalism,
  907, 908(*i*)
Evangelism, in 1950s, 817
"Eve of Destruction," 848
Everett, Wesley, 668
Evers, Medgar, 787, 839
"Evil empire," Reagan on, 916–919
Evolution, 530
Examinations, civil service, 539, 539(*i*)

Exceptionalism, 489
Executive authority, Obama and,
  947–950
Executive branch, reorganization after
  September 11, 2001, 944
Executive Orders
  8802, 758
  9066, 750
  for affirmative action (1965),
    841–842
  by Clinton, Bill, 931
Exodusters, 512–513
Expansion and expansionism. *See also*
    Imperialism; Monroe Doctrine;
    Open door policy
  as foreign policy, 597–607
  Japanese, 628
  missionaries and, 599–600
  of railroads, 520–521, 521(*m*)
  Spanish-American War and, 604
  trade and, 601, 604
  U.S. overseas through 1900, 606(*m*)
Expatriates, in 1920s, 690–691
Expertise, 617
Exploration. *See* Space exploration
Exports
  business and, 598
  colonial, 551
  imports and, 855
  to Latin America, 742

Factionalism, 476, 537, 538, 539
Factions. *See* Political parties
Factories
  assembly lines in, 680
  in Great Depression, 699
  in New Deal, 713
  women in, 756
Fair Deal, 783–789
Fair Labor Standards Act (1938),
  734–735
Fair trade, 937
Fall, Albert, 677
Falwell, Jerry, 907
Families
  in 1930s, 701
  in 1950s, 816–817
  birth control movement and,
    635–636
  female-headed, 836
  of freedmen, 463, 464(*i*)
  sharecropping and, 478
  in working class, 560, 561–562

Family economy, **561**–562
Family Research Council, 908
Family values, 907
Farm Board, 698
Farm Credit Act (FCA, 1933), 716
Farmers' Alliance, 581, **582**–584,
    584*(i)*
Farms and farming. *See also*
    Agriculture; *Bracero* program;
    Rural areas; Tenant farmers
    in 1920s, 677, 691
    commercial, 507, 513, 514
    consumer prices and farm income
        (1865–1910), 583*(f)*
    cooperatives and, 584
    droughts and, 512
    free silver issue and, 543, 544
    on Great American Desert,
        510–511
    in Great Depression, 715–717,
        719–720
    income decline and, 582
    mechanization and, 513–514, 810,
        810*(i)*
    Mexican workers and, 846, 847
    militancy in, 702–703
    protests by, 542, 582–584
    railroads and, 512, 513, 542,
        582–583
    sharecropping and, 478–479, 510
    in South, 483
    surplus and, 733*(i)*
    tariffs and, 541
    tenant, 513
    in West, 508*(b)*, 509*(b)*, 513–514,
        582–583
    Wilson and, 634
Farm Security Administration
    (FSA, 1937), 733
Fascism. *See also* Mussolini, Benito;
    Nazi Germany
    in Europe, 742, 743
Fathers. *See* Families; Men
Faubus, Orval, 820–821
Faulkner, William, 691
FBI. *See* Federal Bureau of
    Investigation
FDIC. *See* Federal Deposit Insurance
    Corporation
Federal budget. *See also* National debt
    Carter and, 901
    Clinton, Bill, and surplus in, 931
    deficit in, 909, 925, 931, 934, 941

Federal Bureau of Investigation (FBI)
    black harassment by, 844
    illegal activities by, 898–899
    King, Martin Luther, Jr., and,
        840, 899
    Nixon and, 897
Federal Deposit Insurance
    Corporation (FDIC), **713**
Federal Election Campaign Act (1974),
    898
Federal Emergency Relief
    Administration (FERA, 1933),
    715
Federal government. *See* Government
    (U.S.)
Federal Republic of Germany. *See* West
    Germany
Federal Reserve Act (1913), 633–634
Federal Reserve Board, 633–634, 934
Federal Trade Commission (FTC), 678
Federal Writers' Project, 726–727*(b)*
Female suffrage. *See* Woman suffrage
Feminine Mystique, The (Friedan), 817
Feminism and feminists, 850–853.
        See also Women
    birth control and, 848*(i)*
    countermovement to, 851–854
    Fifteenth Amendment and, 472
    Reagan and, 912
    transnational, 852–853
    voting and, 684
Fences, ranching and, 505, 512
Ferraro, Geraldine A., 919
Ferris wheel, 574*(b),* 576
Fetterman, William, 495
Fifteenth Amendment, 459–460,
    471–472
Filipinos. *See also* Philippines
    as migratory labor, 513
Films. *See* Movies
"Final Report on Removing the Wreck
    of Battleship *Maine* from the
    Harbor of Habana, Cuba,"
    604*(b)*
Finance capitalism, **528,** 529–530
Finances. *See also* Economy; Federal
    budget; Taxation
    aid to college students, 931
    of Comstock Lode operations, 501
    government spending in 1950s and,
        810
    of homesteaders, 507
    in New Deal, 713

Nixon's misuse of funds and, 897
    of railroads, 522–523
    in Reconstruction South, 483
    S&L scandal and, 909
    tariffs and, 541
    of television, 818
Financial institutions
    2008 economic collapse and dereg-
        ulation of, 934
    Glass-Steagall Act repeals and, 934
Financial Services Modernization Act
    (1999), 934
Fire
    Great Fire of 1871 (Chicago), 571
    at Triangle Shirtwaist Company,
        614–615, 615*(i)*
Fireside chats, of Roosevelt, Franklin
    D., **713,** 746
First Amendment, Bible reading,
    school prayer, and, 837
First hundred days. *See* Hundred Days
First transcontinental railroad, **507,**
    522. *See also* Transcontinental
    railroad
First World War. *See* World War I
Fishing and fishing industry, Sun Belt
    development and, 813
Fitzgerald, F. Scott, 684, 691, 697
Five Civilized Tribes, 491
Five-Power Naval Treaty (1922), **679**
Flaming Youth, 677
Flappers, 684, 685, 685*(i)*, 686*(b)*
Flexible response, 864
Florida
    election of 1876 and, 485
    election of 2000 and, 940
    Indians in, 499
Floyd, Pretty Boy, 701–702
Flu, after World War I, 665
Flying Fortress. *See* B-17 Flying
    Fortress
Folk music, counterculture, left,
    and, 848
Food(s). *See also* Agriculture; Hunters
    and hunting
    at Columbian Exposition, 574*(b)*
Food Administration, in World War I,
    654
Food stamp program, 834, 909
Football, 690
Ford, Gerald, 893, 897–898,
    899, 899*(m)*
Ford, Henry, 674–675, 679, 681–682

Ford Motor Company, 675, 702
Foreclosures, on farms, 582
Foreign aid
    Marshall Plan and, 777
    to Nationalist China, 783
    Truman Doctrine and, 777
    after World War II, 777–780
Foreigners. See Immigrants and
        immigration
Foreign markets, 512, 514, 681
Foreign policy. See also Cold War;
        Diplomacy; specific presidents
    of Coolidge, 678–679
    Eisenhower's "New Look" in,
        804–805
    isolationism and expansionism in,
        597–607
    militarization of, 791
    Monroe Doctrine and, 600
    Open Door policy and, 601, 601(i)
    Washington Disarmament
        Conference and, 679
    before World War II, 742–743
    after World War II, 774–776
Forests
    conservation of, 624–625
    national, 626(m), 931
Forrestal, James V., 775
Fortas, Abe, 833(i)
Fort Laramie
    Treaty of (1851), 491
    Treaty of (1868), 495
Fort Sill reservation, 499
Foster, William Z., 711(m)
"Four-Minute Men," 657
Fourteen Points, 659, 663
Fourteenth Amendment, 459–460,
        467–469, 482
    equal protection in, 468, 814, 837
    Mexican American rights and, 814
    ratification by southern states, 469,
        470, 474
    schools and, 820
    voting rights and, 468–469, 837
"Fraggings," in Vietnam War, 884
France. See also World War I
    American war materiel and,
        745–746
    immigrants from, 501
    Indochina and, 747
    Ruhr occupation by, 679
    student rebellions in (1968), 876(b)
    United Nations and, 765

Vietnamese independence from,
    805
World War I and, 650, 651–652
after World War I, 660
in World War II, 745, 763
Franchise. See Voting and voting rights
Franz Ferdinand (Archduke, Austria-
    Hungary), 646
Freedmen, 489
    black codes and, 465–466
    education and, 463, 475(i)
    as Exodusters, 512–513
    freedom and, 463–464
    labor code and, 462
    land for, 462–463, 465, 470
    in Republican Party, 472
    search for families by, 463
    sharecropping by, 478–479
    taxes and, 483
    voting rights for, 462, 470, 472
    women's labor and, 478
Freedmen's Bureau, 463, 465
Freedmen's Bureau Acts (1865 and
    1866), 463, 467
Freedom(s). See also Rights; specific
        rights and freedoms
    for freedmen, 463–464
    McCarthyism and, 791
Freedom fighters, in Hungary,
    804–805
Freedom Rides, 839, 839(m)
"Freedom schools," for Chicano chil-
    dren, 847
Free enterprise, Reagan and, 908–910
Free market, Carter and, 901
Free silver, 543–544, 585, 595, 596
"Free speech" movement, 847
Free trade
    agreements for, 937
    in New Deal, 742
Fremont, John C., 515
Freud, Sigmund, 687(b)
Frick, Henry Clay, 586, 587
Friedan, Betty, 816–817, 892(i)
Frontier, women on, 507–510, 510(i)
Frontier thesis (Turner), 488, 489, 516
Frowne, Sadie, 560
FTC. See Federal Trade Commission
Fuel. See also Energy; Gasoline; Oil
        and oil industry
    of homesteaders, 510
Fuel Administration (World War I),
    654

Fundamentalism
    Christian, 907, 916
    Islamic in Iran, 906
Fusco, Charles, New Deal and, 726(b)

Gabler, Mel and Norma, 893–894
al-Gaddafi, Muammar (Libya), 951
Gadsden Purchase (1853), 491
Galbraith, John Kenneth, 810
Gandhi, Mohandas (Mahatma)
    Chavez, Cesar, and, 846(i)
    King, Martin Luther, Jr., and, 846(i)
Gangsters, in prohibition, 683
García, Héctor Peréz, 787
Garfield, James A., 469–470, 480,
    538–539
Garland, Hamlin, 576
Garrison, William Lloyd, 485
Garvey, Marcus, 688
Gary, Martin, 483
Gas. See Poison gas
Gasoline. See also Energy; Oil and oil
        industry
    for automobiles, 679
    energy crisis and, 855
    fuel shortage and, 901(i)
Gates, Bill, 910
Gates, Merrill, 497
Gay Liberation Front, 849, 849(i)
Gays and lesbians
    activism of, 844, 848–849
    antidiscrimination policy and, 849
    in civil service, 849
    gay rights protests and (1960s),
        848–849, 913(i)
    Holocaust and, 759
    job discrimination against, 916
    McCarthyism and, 790
    in military, 750, 932, 947
    rights movement, 912–916
    rights of, 932
Gaza Strip, 881, 904, 937
Gender and gender issues. See also
        Gays and lesbians; Men; Women
    in 1950s, 816–817, 818
    equality and, 460
    higher education and, 815
    lynching of black men and, 533
    politics and, 533–536
    separate spheres idea and, 533
General Agreement on Tariffs and
    Trade, 937
General Electric, 528, 529

General Federation of Women's Clubs (GFWC), 536
General Land Office, 508(b)
General Managers Association, 589
General Motors (GM), 798(i), 947
General strike, in 1919, 664
Geneva accords (1954), 806, 806(m)
Geneva summit (1955), 808
Genocide
    Holocaust as, 759–762
    by Milosevic, 936
"Gentlemen's Agreement" (1907), 628
Geographic regions, global, 551, 552(m)
Georgia, Redeemers in, 484
German Americans, World War I and, 657–658
Germany. See also East Germany; Nazi Germany; West Germany; World War I; World War II
    colonies of, 660
    division after World War II, 775
    economic recovery in, 778(b)
    fascism in, 742
    immigrants from, 501, 551, 552, 613
    reparations after World War I, 660, 679
    U.S. navy and, 600
    U.S. industry and, 910
    Venezuela confrontation and, 627
    World War I and, 646, 647, 660
    after World War I, 660, 663
    World War II Allies in, 765
Geronimo (Apache shaman), 499
Ghettos, urban, 551
Ghost Dance, 500, 500(i)
Gibbon, John, 495
GI Bill of Rights (1944), 758–759, 785
Gideon v. Wainwright (1963), 833(i), 837
GI Forum, 787
Gilded Age, 518–520
    business in, 520–527, 545–546
    cities in, 531, 546, 558–559, 571–577
    consolidation in, 528, 530
    depression of 1890s in, 514, 519, 528
    economy during, 520, 540–545
    finance capitalism and, 528, 529–530
    free silver issue in, 543–544

gender, race, and politics in, 533–536
industry during, 520, 532
labor in, 560–569
materialism of, 574(b)
New South during, 532
politics in, 531
poverty in, 555, 559, 561
presidency during, 537–538
presidential politics in, 537–540
social Darwinism and, 530
Supreme Court during, 531
wealthy in, 520, 523, 559
West in, 515–516
women in, 533–536, 536–537
Gilded Age, The (Twain and Warner), 515, 518–519
Gilman, Charlotte Perkins, 686
Ginsberg, Allen, 819
Ginsburg, Ruth Bader, 932
Girls. See Women
Glasnost, 918
Glass-Steagall Banking Act (1933), 713, 934
Glenn, John H., 864
Global issues. See Economy; Globalization; Immigrants and immigration; Imperialism; Migration
Globalization
    in 1990s, 935–939
    debates over, 937–938
    Nixon in China and, 880
    societal impact of, 939
    of terrorism, 942–944
    U.S. and, 952
Global market economy, 574(b)
Global migration, growth of cities and, 551–555
Global warming, 941
Glover, Cathleen, 932
God's Trombones (Johnson), 688
Golan Heights, 881
Gold. See also Gold standard
    discoveries of, 509(b)
    Indians and discoveries of, 495
    U.S. reserves of, 543, 544
Goldman, Emma, 665–668
Gold rush (California), 501, 508(b)
Gold standard, 544
    election of 1896 and, 595
    vs. free silver, 543–544, 595
    Nixon and, 855

Goldwater, Barry M., 834, 890, 891, 893–895, 907
Gompers, Samuel, 566, 567, 569, 665
Gonzales, Rodolfo ("Corky"), 847
Goode, G. Brown, 575(b)
Good neighbor policy, 741–742
Goods and services. See Consumer culture
"Goo goos" (good government proponents), 573
Gorbachev, Mikhail
    end of Cold War and, 922, 923, 925–926
    Reagan and, 918–919, 918(i)
Gore, Albert, Jr., 940
Gospel of wealth, 530
"Gospel of Wealth, The" (Carnegie), 530
Gould, Jay, 520, 521–522, 522(i), 523, 545
Gould and Curry mine, 503
Government. See also Government (U.S.), Legislation; State(s)
    aid to railroads by, 522
    city, 572, 573–576
    of military districts in South, 470, 470(m)
    progressive, 617–618
    territorial, 508(b), 515
Government (U.S.). See also Constitution (U.S.); Federal budget; Legislation
    business and, 545–546, 598, 677
    in depression of 1890s, 544–545, 593
    Eisenhower and, 800
    railroads and, 521, 522, 523, 542
    under Reagan, 909
    role of, 951–952
    Tea Party on, 947
    wealth imbalance and, 713
    western settlement and, 508–509(b)
    World War I agencies and, 654
Government assistance programs, under Nixon, 855
Governors
    African Americans and Latinos as, 932
    progressive, 617–618
    territorial, 508(b), 515
Graduated tax
    on corporations, 728
    on income, 630

Grady, Henry, 532
Graham, Billy, 817
Grain, western, 514
Gramophone, 574(b)
Grand Alliance. See Allies
    (World War II)
Grange, 542, 583
Grange, Harold ("Red"), 690
Grant, Ulysses S.
    corruption and, 480, 481(i), 538
    election of 1868 and, 480, 480(m)
    election of 1872 and, 480–481
    peace policy for Indians, 494
Grape boycott, 846(i), 847
Grapes of Wrath, The (Steinbeck), 720
Grassroots conservatism, 893–895
Great American Desert, farmers in,
    510–511
Great Britain. See England (Britain)
Great Crash, 695
Great Depression (1930s), 695,
    697–698. See also New Deal;
    Roosevelt, Franklin Delano
    agriculture in, 713, 715–717,
        733–734
    crash of 1929 and, 697
    Hoover and, 697–698
    human toll of, 699–701
    industrial recovery in, 717–718
    labor in, 702–703
    lifestyle in, 699–703
    migrant labor during, 706–707,
        707(i)
    rural areas in, 719–720
    underconsumption and, 713
    U.S. productivity during, 734(f)
"Great Die Up," 512
Greater East Asia Co-Prosperity
    Sphere, 747
Great Fire (Chicago, 1871), 571
Great Gatsby, The (Fitzgerald), 697
Great migration
    of African Americans, 668–670,
        669(i)
    of Mexican Americans, 670–671,
        670(i)
Great Plains. See also Plains Indians
    bison hunters in, 493
    drought on, 512
    ecology of, 493
    Indians of, 491, 495
Great Railroad Strike (1877), 564–566,
    564(m), 565(i), 588–590

Great Recession (2008), 946–947
Great Sioux Uprising (1862), 494
Great Society, 830, 833–837
    civil rights legislation and, 833,
        834, 835
    Vietnam War and, 868
Great War. See World War I
Great White Fleet, 628
Greece
    immigrants from, 501
    military assistance to, 777
    Truman Doctrine and, 777
    Turkey and, 660
Greeley, Horace, 481, 550
Green, William, 702
Greenback Labor Party, 543–544,
    543(i), 583
Greenbacks (paper money), 543
Green Berets, 864
Greenfield Village, 675
Greenhouse gases, 941
Greensboro, North Carolina,
    sit-in in, 838
Greenwich Village, gays and lesbians
    in, 849
Grenada, U.S. invasion of, 917
Griffith, D. W., Hearts of the World,
    658(i)
Grinnell, Julius S., 568
Gross domestic product, in 1990s, 934
Gross national product (GNP)
    in 1937, 732
    1945–1970, 816(f)
    in 1960s, 831
Grove City v. Bell (1984), 911
Guadalcanal, battle of, 765
Guadalupe Hidalgo, Treaty of (1848),
    504
Guam, 605, 606, 753
Guantánamo, Cuba
    detention camp in, 943–944, 945, 950
    U.S. base at, 606
Guatemala, 600
    civil wars in, 806
    revolution in, 741
Guerrilla warfare
    by Apaches, 499
    with Filipino nationalists, 601, 607
    in Vietnam, 860–861, 864, 886
Guevara, Ernesto (Che), 876(b)
Guiteau, Charles Julius, 539
Gulf of Tonkin Resolution (1964),
    868–869, 883

Gulf War. See Persian Gulf War
Gun control
    in California, 925
    legislation (1993), 932
    Supreme Court and, 941
Gunter, Charles G., 476–477(b)
Guthrie, Woody, 701, 730
Gypsies, Holocaust and, 759

Haiti
    Marine withdrawal from, 741–742
    U.S. intervention in, 645
Half Breeds, 538
Hall of Mirrors, Versailles treaty
    signed in (1919), 662(i)
Halvorsen, Gail S., 780(i)
Hamer, Fannie Lou, 828–829,
    830(i), 839
Hampton Institute (Indian boarding
    school), 496
Hancock, Winfield Scott, 538
Haney-López, Ian, 814
Hanna, Mark, 596, 604
Hanoi. See Vietnam; Vietnam War
Harassment. See Sexual harassment
Harding, Warren Gamaliel,
    671, 671(m)
Hard money, 543
Harlem, 670, 688
Harlem Renaissance, 688
Harper's Weekly, 493(i)
Harrington, Michael, 831
Harris, Frank, 549
Harrison, Benjamin, 500, 540, 541, 542
Harrison, Carter, 568
Harrison, William Henry, 540
Hawai'i. See also Pearl Harbor
    annexation and, 598, 605
Hawley-Smoot tariff (1930), 698
Hay, John, 601
Hayes, Rutherford B.
    election of 1876 and, 485, 485(m)
    Great Railroad Strike and, 565–566
    presidency of, 537–538
Haymarket bombing, 567–569,
    568, 568(i)
Haywood, William Dudley
    ("Big Bill"), 635
Head Start, 833
Health and health care. See also
    Disease; Medicine
    Bush, G. W., and, 941–942
    Clinton, Bill, and, 931

national health insurance and, 931
Obama and, 947, 950(i)
Health insurance
Eisenhower and, 801
Johnson, L. B., and, 834
Patient Protection and Affordable
Care Act and, 947, 950(i)
Health programs, 854
Hearst, William Randolph,
602(b), 604
Hearts of the World (Griffith movie),
658(i)
Hegemony, of U.S., 600
Helsinki accords (1975), **881**
Hemingway, Ernest, 690
Hendricks, Thomas A., 482
Hepburn Act (1906), 621
Herbicide, Agent Orange as, 868
Herblock, 897(i)
Hernandez, Aileen, 851
Hernandez v. Texas (1954), **814**
Hester Street (New York City),
555, 573
Hezbollah, 917
Hierarchy, labor, 560
Higher education. *See also* Universities
and colleges
in 1950s, 809
democratization of, 814–815
Higher Education Act (1965), 834
High-technology industries
economy and, 814
immigrants in, 936
Highways. *See* Roads and highways
Hill, Anita, 925
Hillman, Sidney, 725
Hippies, 848
Hiroshima, bombing of, 739, 763,
768, 768(i)
Hispanics and Hispanic Americans.
See also Latinos/Latinas
in New Deal, 729–730
in Southwest, 504–505
use of term, 846
in West, 489, 508(b)
Hitler, Adolf, 740. *See also* Nazi
Germany
anti-Semitism of, 742
in World War II, 754–755
Hoboes, in 1920s, 700(i)
Ho Chi Minh, 805, 866
Ho Chi Minh Trail, 866
Holding companies, 526, 543

Holland. *See* Netherlands
Hollywood, and movies in 1920s, 689
"Hollywood Ten," 791
Holmes, Oliver Wendell (Supreme
Court justice), 668
Holocaust (1933–1945), **759**–762,
759(m), 762(i)
Home front
in World War I, 654–655
in World War II, 749–750,
756–762
Homeland Security, Department of,
944
Homelessness
in 1890s depression, 577
in 1930s, 699–700
of children, 562
Home protection, woman suffrage
and, 591, 592
Home rule, for South, 480, 483
Homestead Act (1862), **507,** 508(b)
Homesteaders, 507–512
Homestead lockout, 585–**587,**
586(i), 594
Homestead steelworks, 529(i)
Homosexuals and homosexuality.
See Gays and lesbians
Honda, 938
Honduras, 600
Hoover, Herbert, 695–696, 696(i)
as commerce secretary, 678, 695
crash of 1929 and, 697–698
election of 1928 and, 694
election of 1932 and, 710, 711(m)
as Food Administration head,
654, 695
Great Depression and, 697–698,
704
Hoovervilles and, 701
Hoover, J. Edgar, Red scare (1919)
and, 668
Hoovervilles, 701
Horizontal integration, 526
Horse car, 558
Hostages, in Iran, 906
Hotchkiss rapid-fire guns, 500
House Judiciary Committee, 898
House of Representatives (U.S.), 459.
See also Congress (U.S.)
presidential impeachment by, 471
House Un-American Activities
Committee (HUAC), **791,** 794
Housewives. *See* Domesticity

Housing
in cities, 551, 558, 559
discrimination in, 835, 842
equal rights to, 787
of homesteaders, 510
Johnson, L. B., and, 834
in New Deal, 734
open-housing laws and, 842
in Pullman, 588
racism in, 812
segregation in, 842
slums and, 551, 559
sod houses, 507, 510, 510(i)
of wealthy, 559
for whites, 814
Housing Act (1949), **789**
Howard University, "Black Awareness
Research Institute" and, 848
Howe, Eleanor, 893–894
How the Other Half Lives (Riis),
559, 624(b)
HUAC. *See* House Un-American
Activities Committee
Huerta, Dolores, 846–847, 846(i)
Huerta, Victoriano, 645–646
Hughes, Charles Evans, 648, 679
Hughes, Langston, 688
Hull, Charles, 610
Hull House, 610–611, 612(i), 613
Humanitarian missions, as nation
building, 936
Human rights, Carter and, 904, 906
Humphrey, Hubert H., 835(i),
878–879, 879(m)
Hundred Days (F. D. Roosevelt),
712, 722
Hungary
immigrants from, 501, 551, 552
in NATO, 925–926
revolt in 1956, 804–805
after World War I, 660
Huns, in World War I, 657
Hunters and hunting, of bison, 493
Hurricane Katrina, 942, 942(i)
Hurston, Zora Neale, 688
Hussein, Saddam
Clinton, Bill, and, 936
Iraq War and, 944
Persian Gulf War and, 928–930
Hydroelectricity
New Deal programs for, 715, 716(m)
Taft and, 630
Hydrogen bomb, 781

ICBMs. *See* Intercontinental ballistic missiles
Idaho, 515
  voting rights for women in, 593
"I have a dream" speech (King), 840
Illegal immigrants, 814(*i*), 939
Illness. *See* Disease
Immigrants and immigration. *See also* Migration
  in 1920s, 691–693
  anti-immigrant sentiment and, 506, 553, 557, 943
  Asian, 505–506
  birth control movement and, 636
  as bridge labor, 549
  to California, 505–506
  in cities, 554–555, 573, 577
  Comstock Lode and, 501–503
  as domestic servants, 569
  global migration, urbanization, and, 551–555
  impact to 1910, 553(*m*)
  Japanese, 628
  as migratory labor, 513
  in mining, 501–503
  old and new immigration, 552–553
  political parties and, 531
  racism and, 555–558, 939
  restrictions on, 506, 557
  skills and poverty of, 939
  sources of, 939
  in textile industry, 560
Immigration and Nationality Act (1965), **835**
Impeachment
  of Clinton, 934
  of Johnson, Andrew, 470–471, 934
  of Nixon, 898
Imperialism
  debate over, 607
  Indians and, 601
  by United States, 601, 872
  in West, 601
  after World War I, 660
  "Yankee," 870
Imperial presidency, 897
Imports, in 1971, 855
Inauguration
  of Carter, 900(*i*)
  of Kennedy, J. F., 862
  of Roosevelt, T., 499
Incandescent lightbulb, 528

Income. *See also* Wage(s)
  in 1920s, 697
  1920–1940, 699(*f*)
  1945–1970, 816(*f*)
  in 1950s, 815–816
  1969–1998, 935(*f*)
  of black families, 758
  consumerism and, 682
  of farm families, 582
  inequality of, 935, 935(*f*)
  Native American, 802
  Reagan and, 910, 911
  for women, 684
Income gap, 920
Income tax, 630, 633
  in New Deal, 728
Independence
  in Cuba, 601
  of Vietnam, 805
  after World War II, 782
Independence movements, Soviet Union and, 862
Independent magazine, 560, 562, 565
India
  Japan and, 747
  nuclear test ban treaty and, 927
Indian(s). *See* Native Americans
Indian Citizenship Act (1924), 693
Indian Claims Commission (1946), 802
Indian country. *See* Indian Territory; Oklahoma; West
Indian policy. *See also* Native Americans
  allotment as, 497–498
  assimilation as, 496–497
  peace policy as, 494
  removal as, 491–493
  reservations and, 489, 491–492, 492(*m*), 494
Indian Relocation Program (1948), 803, 803(*m*)
Indian Reorganization Act (IRA, 1934), 730
Indian Rights Association, 497–498
Indian Territory, 512
Indian wars, in West, 489, 491, 494–495, 597, 601
Indies. *See* East Indies
Indigenous people. *See* Native Americans
Indochina. *See also* Cambodia; Laos; Vietnam
  Japan and, 747

Indonesia. *See also* East Indies
  Dutch in, 747
Industrial capitalism, 520, 574(*b*)
Industrial core (global economic region), 551, 552(*m*)
Industrialism
  urban, 501, 569, 577–578, 591
  western commercial farming and, 514
Industrialization, agrarianism and, 514
Industrial Workers of the World (IWW), **635,** 664, 668
Industry
  buffalo slaughter and, 493
  defense, 813
  environmentalists and, 856
  federal control of, 621
  in Germany, 778(*b*)
  in Gilded Age, 520, 545
  globalization and, 937
  Great Depression and, 717–718
  international pressure on, 910
  in Japan, 783
  in Reagan era, 910
  seasonal labor in, 560
  in South, 475, 532
  technology and, 810–811
  wages in (1912–1920), 655(*f*)
  women in, 756
  in World War I, 654
Inequality. *See also* Equality
  social Darwinism and, 530
  wealth and, 935, 935(*f*)
Infant mortality, 684
Inflation. *See also* Economy; Stagflation
  in 1990s, 934
  Carter and, 900
  Nixon and, 855
  during World War II, 756
Influenza. *See* Flu
"In God We Trust," on currency, 817
In His Steps (Sheldon), 613
Initiative, 585, 618
Injunctions, in Pullman strike, 590
Insider trading, 714
Installment buying, 697
Insurance
  Financial Services Modernization Act and, 934
  health, 801, 931, 947
  private, 942

Integration. *See also* Segregation
    busing for, 895
    Eisenhower and, 820–821
    in Little Rock, 821
    of military, 787, 788(i)
    of public schools, 820–821, 823(b),
        895(m)
    white flight from, 896
Intellectual thought. *See also* Art(s);
        Education; Harlem Renaissance;
        Literature
    after World War I, 690–691
Intelligence (information), 753,
        781, 782(i)
Intercontinental ballistic missiles
        (ICBMs), 808
***Intermediate-range nuclear
    forces (INF) agreement*** (1987),
    919
Internationalization, of United States,
        938–939
International Ladies' Garment
        Workers Union (ILGWU), 614
Internet, 938(i)
    globalization and, 937
Internment camps, for Japanese
        Americans, **750**
Interracial marriage, Supreme Court
        on, 837
Interstate Commerce Act (1887),
        542, 621
***Interstate Commerce Commission
    (ICC), 542,*** 543
***Interstate Highway and Defense
    System Act*** (1956), **801,** 802(m).
        See also Roads and highways
Inventions and inventors. *See also*
        Electricity
    telegraph and, 523, 527
    telephone and, 527–528, 528(i)
Investment
    finance capitalism and, 528,
        529–530
    foreign, in U.S., 938–939
Iran
    Carter and, 904
    CIA and, 807
    hostage crisis in, 906
    nuclear weapons and, 951
    revolution in, 906
Iran-Contra scandal, 917
    Reagan and, 917–918, 917(m)
Iran hostage crisis, 906

Iraq. *See also* Iraq War (2003–2011)
    ISIS and, 945–946
    occupation of, 928
    Persian Gulf War and, 928
    troop withdrawal from, 950
    U.S. invasion of (2003), 929
    after World War I, 660
Iraq War (2003–2011), **944**–946,
        944(m)
    casualties in, 945
Ireland
    immigrants from, 552, 555, 560, 613
    after World War I, 663
Irish immigrants
    in domestic service, 569
    in mining, 501, 502–503
Iron and iron industry, 520, 524, 532
    and steel production (1870–1900),
        525(f)
Iron curtain, 775, 776(m), 779(b), 782.
        See also Soviet Union
Irreconcilables, in Congress, 663
ISIS. *See* Islamic State in Iraq and Syria
Islam. *See* Muslims
Islamic State in Iraq and Syria (ISIS),
        945–946
Islamic terrorism, 940
    Al Qaeda and, 936, 942–943
Isolationism
    in 1930s, 741, 742, 743
    foreign policy and, 597–607
    World War II in Europe and, 743
Israel. *See also* Arab world; Middle East
    in 1948, 783, 783(m)
    since 1989, 937(m)
    Camp David accords and, 904
    Clinton, Bill, and, 935, 937
    Eisenhower and, 807
    Palestine and, 929(m)
    after Persian Gulf War, 928–929
    Six-Day War and (1967), 881–882,
        882(m)
    Suez crisis and, 807, 807(m)
    terrorism against, 916–917
    Truman and, 783
    Yom Kippur War and, 855, 882
Italy. *See also* Mussolini, Benito
    Communist Party in, 781
    Ethiopian invasion by, 742
    fascism in, 742
    immigrants from, 501, 552,
        556(i), 613
    missiles and, 808

Tripartite Pact, 748
    in World War I, 660, 663, 740
Iwo Jima, War II, 755
IWW. *See* Industrial Workers of the
        World

Jackson, Helen Hu 497
Jackson, Jesse, 924
Jackson State College, Mississippi,
        killings at, 882
Japan
    atomic bombing of, 739, 762, 763
    China and, 743, 747
    expansionism of, 628, 747(m)
    "Gentlemen's Agreement" with
        (1907), 628
    immigrants from, 501, 506, 513,
        557, 693
    Manchuria and, 740, 742
    Pacific battles and, 753
    Pearl Harbor and, 738–739, 743,
        747–749, 747(m), 748(i),
        748(m), 753
    "Rape of Nanking" by, 743
    in Tripartite Pact, 748
    U.S. industry and, 910
    withdrawal from League, 741
    in World War I, 646
    after World War I, 661
    World War II and, 738–739, 742,
        747–749, 753, 761(b), 762–763,
        763(i), 765–768
    after World War II, 769–770, 783
Japanese Americans, during World
        War II, 749–750, 750(m)
Jarvis, Howard, 894(i)
Jazz, 688, 689(i)
Jazz Age, 677
Jericho, Israeli withdrawal from, 937
Jerusalem, 937
Jews and Judaism. *See also*
        Anti-Semitism
    Holocaust and, 759–762, 762(i)
    immigrants and, 552, 555, 692
    Israel and, 783
    in Nazi Germany, 742
    after World War I, 660
Jiang Jieshi (Chiang Kai-Shek), 742,
        765, 782, 783
Jim Crow laws, 475, **533,** 556, 637–638
"Jingoes," 602
Job Corps, 833

Migrant workers, 513, 514
  in Great Depression, 706–707,
    719–720
  Mexican immigrants as, 513, 939(i)
Migration. See also Immigrants and
    immigration
  African American, 556, 668–670,
    668(i), 669(i), 758, 786, 810
  global, 551–555
  to Sun Belt, 812–814, 813(m)
Miles, Dora, 757(i)
Miles, Nelson, 499
Militancy. See also Protest(s)
  black, 844
  Native American, 845
  of working class (1930s), 702–703
Militarism, before World War II,
    644, 742
Military. See also Defense; Defense
    spending; Soldiers
  African Americans in, 504
  Boxer uprising and, 599, 599(i)
  Clinton, Bill, use of, 935
  countries with highest expendi-
    tures, 2005, 936(f)
  gays and lesbians in, 750, 932, 947
  in Great Railroad Strike, 565
  Indians and, 494–495, 495–496,
    498, 500
  integration of, 787, 788(i)
  Kennedy, J. F., and, 864
  in Korean War, 793
  in Latin America, 600
  NSC 68 and, 795
  peacetime draft and, 781
  in Pullman strike, 590
  Reagan and, 916–917
  in South Vietnam, 882
  in Spanish-American War, 604
  in World War II, 750
Military districts, in South,
    470, 470(m)
Military-industrial complex,
  Eisenhower warning about,
    808–809
Military Reconstruction Act (1867),
    470, 470(m)
Militia. See also Military; National
    Guard
  in Great Railroad Strike, 564, 565
  Homestead lockout and, 587
  Indians and, 493
Militia movement, Clinton and, 932

Miller, Henry, 514
Miller & Lux (agribusiness), 514
Mills
  in mining, 503
  textile, 560
Milosevic, Slobodan, 936
Mines and mining. See also Coal and
    coal industry; Gold rush
  "Big Bonanza" and, 503
  Comstock Lode and, 501–504,
    503(i)
  government support for,
    508–509(b)
  in Great Depression, 703
  immigrants in, 501–503, 505–506
  Indians and, 491, 495, 503
  mining towns, 503–504
  safety and, 503, 509(b)
  silver and, 543, 544
  strikes and, 587–588
  strip mining and, 903
  technology for, 503
  in West, 501–504, 502(m), 505–506
Miniconjou Sioux Indians, 500
Minimum wage, 947
Minneapolis Lakers, move by, 812
Minnesota, 514
Minorities. See also Ethnic groups
  in feminist movement, 851
  income gap and, 920
  Latino, 939
  in middle class, 935
  New Deal and, 728–730
  reverse discrimination and, 911
Minow, Newton, 818
Miranda v. Arizona (1966), 837
Miscegenation, Garvey on, 688
Miss America pageant, 850–851
Missiles, 805(i). See also
    Intercontinental ballistic
    missiles
  Cuban missile crisis and, 862–863,
    865–866, 865(i)
  in Turkey, 808, 866
Missions and missionaries, in China,
    599–600
Mississippi, state elections in (1876),
    484
Mississippi Freedom Democratic Party
    (MFDP), 829, 830(i)
Mississippi Freedom Summer Project
    (1964), 840
Mississippi Valley State College, 829

Mobility, of global population, 551
Mobilization
  for World War I, 654–655
  for World War II, 749–752
Mob Rule in New Orleans (Wells),
    535(b)
Model T Ford, 674(i), 675
"Modern Republicanism"
    (Eisenhower), 800–801
Mondale, Walter F., 899, 910
Money
  in 1920s, 677
  gold standard and, 543
  paper, 543
Money supply. See also Banking
  contraction of, 544
  free silver and, 543, 544
"Money trust" of Morgan, 529, 633
Mongella, Gertrude, 853
"Monkey trial." See Scopes trial
Monongahela River, labor-Pinkerton
    violence at, 586, 586(i)
Monopolies. See also Sherman
    Antitrust Act
  business, 524, 526
  land, 513
  Reagan and, 909
Monroe Doctrine (1823), 600
  foreign policy and, 600
  Roosevelt, T., and, 625
  Spanish-American War and, 601
  Wilson and, 645
Montana, 515
Montgomery, Alabama
  Freedom Rides in, 839
  voting rights march to, 840, 841(i)
Montgomery bus boycott, 821–825, 838
Montgomery Improvement
    Association (MIA), 821–825
Moody, Anne, 839(i)
Moon landing (1969), 864
Morality
  in 1920s, 691
  conservatism and, 893–894
  Reagan and, 907
  sexual, 687(b)
Moral Majority, 907
Moral reform movement, 531
Morgan, Anne, 614
Morgan, J. P., 530, 620, 624, 630, 631
  depression of 1890s and, 544–545
  finance capitalism and, 529–530
  U.S. Steel and, 529–530

Morgan, J. P., and Company, 633
Mormons, 505, 508*(b)*
Morocco, 501
   in World War II, 755
Morrow, E. Frederick, 821
Morse, Samuel F. B., 523
Mortality rate, of infants, 684
Mortgages, 812
   farmers and, 514
Mosher, Clelia Duel, 686–687*(b)*
Mossadegh, Mohammed, 807, 906
Mothers. *See* Families; Women
Motion picture camera, 528
Moudy, Ross, 503
Movies
   in 1920s, 688, 689
   in 1930s, 701
Ms. magazine, 851
Muckraking, 624
Mugwumps, 538, 540
Muller v. Oregon (1908), 616
Mumford, Lewis, 812
Munich Olympics, terrorists at, 917
Munn v. Illinois (1877), 542
Murals, in New Deal, 723*(i)*
Murray, Pauli, 850
Music
   in 1950s, 818–819
   of counterculture and left, 848
   jazz, 688, 689*(i)*
   rhythm and blues music, 819
   rock and roll, 818–819
Music halls, 570
Muslims
   in Afghanistan, 905
   Bosnian, 936
   Obama and, 950–951
   Shiite, 917
   Sunni, 945
Mussolini, Benito, 740, 744*(m)*, 755.
   See also Italy; World War II
Mutually assured destruction (MAD),
   804
Mutual security pact, with Japan, 783
Myer, Dillon S., 802
My Lai massacre, 884, 886

NAACP. *See* National Association for
   the Advancement of Colored
   People
Nader, Ralph, 940*(m)*
NAFTA. *See* North American Free
   Trade Agreement

Nagasaki, bombing of, 739, 763, 769
Names, English, for Indian children,
   497
Nanjing (Nanking), China, Japanese
   capture of, 743
NASA. *See* National Aeronautics and
   Space Administration
Nasser, Gamal Abdel, 807
Nast, Thomas
   anti-Grant cartoon by, 481*(i)*
   on Democrats' white supremacy,
   469*(i)*
National Aeronautics and Space
   Administration (NASA, 1958),
   808
National American Woman Suffrage
   Association (NAWSA), 592,
   637, 656
National Arts and Humanities Act
   (1965), 835
National Association for the
   Advancement of Colored People
   (NAACP), 536*(i)*, 639, 758, 820
   Brown v. Board of Education and,
   820
   Montgomery bus boycott and, 821
   after World War II, 786, 787
National Association of Evangelicals,
   Reagan and, 908*(i)*
National Association of
   Manufacturers, 719
National Conference of Catholic
   Bishops, 916
National Consumers League (NCL),
   615–616
National Council of Negro Women, 729
National debt. *See also* Debt; Federal
   budget
   Reagan and, 909
National Defense Education Act
   (NDEA, 1958), 808
National Energy Act (1978), 901
National Farmers' Holiday Association
   (1932), 702
National forests, 626*(m)*, 931
National Gay and Lesbian Task Force,
   849
National Geographic, on *Maine*
   sinking, 605*(b)*
National Guard
   in Boston police strike, 665
   Homestead lockout and, 587
   at Kent State, 882

National health insurance. *See also*
   Health and health care; Health
   insurance
   Carter and, 901
   Eisenhower and, 801
   Johnson, L. B., and, 834
National Housing Act
   of 1937, 734
   of 1968, 835
Nationalism
   black, 688
   Chicano, 847
   after World War I, 660
Nationalist China, 742, 782
Nationalization
   in Cuba, 807
   in Guatemala, 806
National Labor Relations (Wagner)
   Act (NLRA, 1935), 724
National Liberation Front (NLF,
   Vietnam), 866, 870, 876*(b)*, 878
National liberation movements, after
   World War II, 770
National Miners Union, 703
National Organization for Women
   (NOW), 850
National parks and forests, 626
National Recovery Administration
   (NRA, 1933), 718, 719
National security
   Bush, George W., on, 943–944
   Carter and, 904–906
   Kennan on, 775–776
   Kennedy, J. F., and, 862
   Powell, Colin, and, 923
   after September 11, 2001, 943, 944
   and World War II home front,
   749–750
National Security Act (1947), 781
National Security Council (NSC)
   Iran-Contra and, 917–918
   NSC 68 and, 795
National security state, 780–782
National self-determination. *See*
   Self-determination
National Socialist Party. *See* Nazi
   Germany
National Union for Social Justice
   (Union Party), 721
National Union Party, 469
National War Labor Policies Board, 655
National Welfare Rights Organization,
   834

National Woman's Party (NWP), 637, 914
National Woman Suffrage Association (NWSA), 536, 581, 592
National Women's Conference (Houston, 1977), 852
National Women's Political Caucus, 829
National Youth Administration, Division of Negro Affairs, 729
Nation building, 936
Native Americans
    Alcatraz seizure by, 845, 845(i)
    assimilation of, 496–498, 730
    in Black Hills, 495–496, 509(b)
    buffalo and, 491, 493–494, 493(i)
    citizenship and, 498
    compensation of, 802
    Comstock Lode discovery and, 503
    Dawes Act and, 497–498
    diseases and, 492
    Ghost Dance of, 500, 500(i)
    loss of lands (1850–1890), 492(m)
    mass execution of, 494
    in New Deal, 730
    Nixon advocacy for, 857
    peace policy for, 494
    protests by, 844, 845–846
    removal and, 491–493
    reservations for, 489, 491–492, 492(m), 494, 495, 497–498, 499
    resistance by, 489, 494–495, 498–501
    rights of, 846
    Sand Creek massacre against, 493
    scorched-earth policy against, 494–495
    in Southwest, 491, 499
    termination and relocation of, 801–803
    treaties with, 491, 493, 495, 509(b)
    Vietnam War and, 886
    as wards of the state, 491, 494
    warfare and, 489, 494–495
    Washita River massacre of, 493
    in West, 488, 489, 490–496, 508(b)
    in World War II, 750
    Wounded Knee massacre against, 500
Nativism, 506, 613, 691
NATO. See North Atlantic Treaty Organization
Natural areas, preservation of, 855–856
Natural disasters, Hurricane Katrina as, 942, 942(i)
Naturalization. See Citizens and citizenship
Natural resources, in West, 508(b)
Natural selection, 530
Nature. See Environment
Navajo Indians, 491, 499
Navies. See also Navy (U.S.)
    British, 648
    limitations on, 679, 742
Navy (U.S.), 600
    Five-Power Naval Treaty (1922) and, 679
    Great White Fleet of, 628
    at Guantánamo, 606
    Maine sinking inquiry by, 604(b)
    in Manila, 604
    Panama Canal and, 627(m)
    Washington Disarmament Conference and, 679
    in World War II, 753
Nazi Germany, 742. See also Germany; Hitler, Adolf; World War II
    aggression by, 743–745, 744(m)
    Allied bombings of, 763
    anti-Semitism in, 742, 760–761(b)
    Austria and, 743, 744(m)
    Rhineland and, 742
    Soviet invasion by, 746
    Soviet treaty with, 745
    in Tripartite Pact, 748
Nazi-Soviet nonaggression treaty (1939), 745
Negro. See African Americans
"Negro domination," 471, 474
"Negro first" strategy, 468, 472
Negro national anthem, 688
"Negro rule," 532
Neighborhoods, 558–559
Nelson, Knute, 607
Netherlands, in World War II, 745
Neutrality
    in World War I, 643, 647–648, 649
    before World War II, 743, 745–746
Neutrality acts, of 1935–1937, 742, 745
Nevada, 515
    Comstock Lode in, 501–504, 502(m)
Newark, race riot in (1967), 844
New Christian Right, 907
    ERA and, 914
    gay rights and, 916
    Reagan and, 907–908
New Deal, 706(i), 707–708, 710–712. See also Economy; Fair Deal; Great Depression; Roosevelt, Franklin Delano
    African Americans in, 729
    agriculture in, 715–717, 719–720, 733–734
    Asian Americans in, 730
    banking in, 713–714
    business in, 713
    challenges to, 718–722
    citizen responses to, 726–727(b)
    conservation programs in, 715
    conservatism in, 725
    early period of, 712–718
    economy in, 712–718
    election of 1934 and, 722
    final reforms of, 733–735
    Hispanic Americans in, 729–730
    industrial recovery in, 717–718
    in mid-1930s, 730–735
    Native Americans in, 730
    neglected Americans and, 728–730
    politics in, 720–722
    relief programs in, 714–715
    rural areas in, 719–720
    welfare state in, 722–730
New Deal coalition, 711, 712, 879
New England, textile mills in, 532, 560
"New Era," 1920s as, 677–682
Newfoundland, Atlantic Charter and, 746
New Freedom, The, 632, 634
New Frontier (Kennedy), 830, 831–832
    in foreign policy, 862–868
New Guinea, 753, 767
New immigration, 552–553
"New Left," 847
    women and, 850
"New Look" (Eisenhower), 804–805
New Mexico
    Hispanics in, 504, 505
    Indians in, 491
    manifest destiny and, 491
    statehood and, 515
New Nationalism, The, 632
"New Negro," in 1920s, 676, 688
New Orleans
    Hurricane Katrina in, 942, 942(i)
    racial violence in, 469
New Right. See New Christian Right
New South, 532

Newspapers, 604. *See also* Journalism
    Pullman strike coverage in, 589, 590
New woman, 676, **683**–685, 685*(i),*
    686–687*(b)*
"New world order," of Bush, G. H. W.,
    935–936
New York (city), 548, 572
    African Americans in, 556
    Central Park in, 572–573
    immigrants in, 555, 556*(i),* 557, 559
    population in, 550
    public schools in, 572
    settlement houses in, 613
    Tammany Hall in, 573
New York (state), Roosevelt, Franklin
    D., as governor of, 709–710
New York Central Railroad, 559
New York Journal, 602*(b),* 604
New York Stock Exchange, 523
New York Sun, on Crédit Mobilier, 524
New York Times
    on "dangerous classes," 565
    on Indian policy, 497
New York Tribune, 481
New York World, 559, 604
New Zealand, in World War II, 753
Nez Percé Indians, 498–499
Nez Percé war (1877), 498
Niagara movement (1905), 639
Nicaragua
    dictator in, 742
    Reagan aid to Contras in, 917
    revolution in, 741
    Sandinistas in, 904
    U.S. intervention in, 645
Nicholas II (Russia), 650
Nicodemus, Kansas, 504
Night riders, 483
Nike, 937–938
Nimitz, Chester W., 753
Nineteenth Amendment (woman
    suffrage), **656,** 684. *See also*
    Woman suffrage
    women's voting rights before, 657*(m)*
Nixon, E. D., 821
Nixon, Isaac, lynching of, 787
Nixon, Richard M.
    China and, 862, 879, 880–881, 880*(i)*
    civil rights and, 830
    conservatism and, 892–893
    disabled people and, 856
    Douglas, Helen Gahagan, and,
      773–774

    election of 1950 and, 794
    election of 1952 and, 794
    election of 1960 and, 831, 831*(m)*
    election of 1968 and, 854, 873,
      877*(b),* 879
    election of 1972 and, 855, 896–897
    environment and, 855–856
    impeachment of, 898
    Khrushchev and, 798–799
    liberal reform under, 854–857
    Native Americans and, 857
    pardon of, 898
    resignation of, 898
    sex discrimination outlawed by, 857
    social justice under, 856–857
    Soviet Union and, 879, 881
    Supreme Court appointments by, 896
    Vietnam War and, 873, 882–885
    Watergate and, 897–898
Nobel Peace Prize
    for Bunche, Ralph J., 787
    for Roosevelt, T., 628
    to Wilson, 664
Noble, Elaine, 849, 913
Noble and Holy Order of the Knights
    of Labor. *See* Knights of Labor
No Child Left Behind (NCLB) *Act*
    (2002), **941**
Nonintervention policy, 742
Nonviolent resistance
    black resistance to, 844
    in civil rights movement, 838
    by United Farm Workers, 846
Noriega, Manuel, 927–928
"Normalcy," Harding on, 671
North (U.S. region)
    African American migration to,
      556, 669*(i),* 670, 758, 786
    domestics in, 569–570
    Reconstruction and, 466, 480,
      481–482
    southern Republican Party and,
      472–473
North Africa, in World War II, 755,
    755*(i),* 763
North American Free Trade
    Agreement (NAFTA), **937**
North Atlantic Treaty Organization
    (NATO), 776*(m),* **781**
    after Cold War, 925–926
    interventions by, 936
North Carolina, 484
Northern Alliance (Afghanistan), 943

Northern Pacific Railroad, 495
Northern Paiute Indians, 503
Northern Securities Company, 620, 621
North Korea, 792
    communism in, 927
North Vietnam, 860, 866, 870. *See also*
    Vietnam; Vietnam War
    bombings of, 869, 870–871
    CIA and, 806
    Saigon seized by, 884
Northwestern Farmers' Alliance, 583
Norton, Eleanor Holmes, 830*(i)*
Norway
    immigrants from, 510*(i)*
    in World War II, 745
No-strike pledge, in World War II, 751
NOW. *See* National Organization for
    Women
NSC 68, **795.** *See also* National
    Security Council
Nuclear arms race, 781, 808–809,
    865–866. *See also* Cuban missile
    crisis; Disarmament; Nuclear
    weapons
    anxiety during, 809*(i)*
    after Cold War, 927
    disarmament and, 919
    Eisenhower and, 808–809
    missiles and, 805*(i),* 808
    Reagan and, 916, 918*(l)*
Nuclear disarmament. *See*
    Disarmament
Nuclear energy. *See also* Atomic bomb
    accidents in, 903
    Clamshell Alliance and, 902–903
    Eisenhower and, 801
    environmental movement and,
      902–903
Nuclear test ban treaty
    limited (1963), 866
    total (1996), 927
Nuclear weapons. *See also* Atomic
    bomb; Nuclear arms race
    Eisenhower and, 804, 808–809
    hydrogen bomb and, 781
    Iran and, 951
    limited test ban treaty (1963), 866
Nye, Gerald, and Nye Committee, 742

Oak Ridge, Tennessee, school
    integration in, 822–823*(b)*
Oath of allegiance, in Lincoln's
    reconstruction plan, 461

Obama, Barack, 946–951
  economy and, 946–950
  election of 2008 and, 946,
    948–949(b), 949(i)
  election of 2012 and, 947
  foreign policy of, 950–951
  Guantánamo base and, 943–944
  Patient Protection and Affordable
    Care Act and, 947, 950(i)
  Supreme Court appointments by,
    947
  Trans-Pacific Partnership and, 937
  war on terror and, 950
"Obamacare," 947
Obergefell v. Hodges, 932
Occupation (military)
  of Berlin, 775, 777(m)
  of Germany, 775
  of Iraq, 928, 944–945
  of Korea, 792
Occupational Safety and Health Act
  (OSHA, 1970), 856
Occupations (jobs). *See* Employment;
  Work
O'Connor, Sandra Day, 912, 941
O'Dell, Jack, 791
O'Donnell, Hugh, 586
Officeholders
  African Americans as, 459,
    474, 474(f)
  ex-Confederate, 466, 467, 482
Ohio gang, of Harding, 677
Oil and oil industry. *See also* Energy
  crisis
  gasoline shortages and, 902
  Iran and, 807
  in Middle East, 928
  Nixon and, 855
  Rockefeller in, 525–527
Oil embargo (1973), 881
Okies, 707, 719–720
Okinawa, battle at, 767
Oklahoma, 494. *See also* Indian
  Territory
  as Indian Territory, 491
  land runs in, 512
Oklahoma City, terrorism in, 932
Oklahoma Tenant Farmers' Union, 717
Older Americans. *See* Elderly
Old immigration, 552–553
Olesdater, Beret, 510(i)
Oligopoly, in mining industry, 503
Olmsted, Frederick Law, 572, 576

Olney, Richard B., 590
Olympic Games
  protests at (1968), 876–877(b)
  terrorists at, 917
Oñate, Juan de, 504
"One person, one vote" principle, 837
On the Origin of Species (Darwin), 530
"On to Washington" movement, 594
Open Door policy, 601, 601(i)
Open-housing laws, 842
Open range, fencing of, 505, 512
Operation Rolling Thunder, 869, 873
Opper, Frederick Burr, 522(i)
Oregon, 491
Organization of American States
  (OAS), 870
  on U.S. invasion of Panama, 928
Organized labor. *See* Labor unions
Organized Trades and Labor Unions,
  566
Orpen, William, *Signing of Peace in
  the Hall of Mirrors . . . ,* 662(i)
Ortega, Daniel, 917
OSHA. *See* Occupational Safety and
  Health Act
Ostracism, by southern whites, 483
Oswald, Lee Harvey, 832
Other America, The (Harrington), 831
Ottoman empire, after World War I, 660
"Outing system," at Carlisle Indian
  School, 497
Overlord, second-front operation as,
  763
Owens, Florence, and family, in Great
  Depression, 706–707, 708(i)

P-51 Mustang (fighter), 763
Pacific Coast region. *See also* Pacific
  Ocean region
  Asian immigrants in, 557
  Hispanics in, 504
Pacific Islander immigrants, 501
Pacific Ocean region
  Japanese Americans in, 749
  U.S. involvement in, 600
  in World War II, 748, 753,
    765–768, 766(m)
Pago Pago, Samoa, 600
Pahlavi, Mohammad Reza (shah of
  Iran), 807, 906
Painting. *See also* Art(s)
  in 1950s, 819, 819(i)
  in Harlem Renaissance, 688

Paiute Indians, 499, 500, 503
Pakistan
  Carter and, 906
  nuclear test ban treaty and, 927
Palestine and Palestinians. *See also*
  Middle East
  Clinton, Bill, and, 935, 937
  Israel and, 881, 928, 929(m), 943
  refugees from, 882
  Truman and, 783
  after World War I, 660
Palestine Liberation Organization
  (PLO), 937
Palin, Sarah, 946
Palmer, A. Mitchell, 665, 666(b)
Panama
  intervention in, 928
  Noriega and, 927–928
  uprising in (1903), 625–627
Panama Canal and Panama Canal
  region
  Roosevelt, Theodore, and, 625, 627
  U.S. control of, 645(m)
Panama Canal treaty (1977), **904**
Panama Canal Zone, riots in, 870
Panic(s) (financial). *See also*
  Depressions (financial); Great
  Depression
  of 1873, 481, 519, 543, 553, 564
  of 1893, 514, 519, 528, 541, 544,
    553, 587
Pan-Indian movement, 497, 803
Paper money. *See* Money
Pardons
  for Confederates, 460, 465, 466
  for Nixon, 898
Parham, Adam, 751(i)
Paris
  liberation in World War II, 763
  student rebellion in (1968), 876(b)
  Vietnam peace talks in, 878
Paris, Treaty of, 1898, 606–607
Paris peace conference (1919),
  659–662
Parker, Alton B., 621
Parks
  national, 626(m)
  public, 572
Parks, Rosa, 821
Parsons, Albert, 567, 568
Party politics. *See* Political parties
PATCO. *See* Professional Air Traffic
  Controllers Organization

Patent, of Edison, 528
Patent medicines, regulation of, 624
Patient Protection and Affordable Care Act (2010), **947,** 950(*i*)
Patriarchy, 533
Patriot Act (2001). *See* USA Patriot Act
Patriotism
    Spanish-American War and, 608
    in World War I, 644, 654
    after World War I, 657
Patronage, 531, 538. *See also* Civil service
Patrons of Husbandry. *See* Grange
Patton, George, 750, 755
Paul, Alice, 637, 656
Pawnee Indians, 500
Payne-Aldrich bill, 630
Peace. *See also* Treaties
    in 1920s, 678–679
    Israel-Jordan, 937
    after Korean War, 794
    in Vietnam War, 878, 884–885
Peace Corps, **864**
Peace movement. *See also* Antiwar movement
    in Vietnam War, 873, 874–875, 882–883
    World War I and, 657
Pearl Harbor, Japanese attack on, 738–739, 743, 747–749, 747(*m*), 748(*i*), 748(*m*), 753
Pell grants, 855
Pendleton Civil Service Act (1883), 539
Pennsylvania, September 11, 2001, terrorist attack and, 942
Pennsylvania Railroad, 523, 524, 526
Pensions, 680
    bonus as, 703
    for Union soldiers, 541
Pentagon, terrorist attack on, 942
Pentagon Papers, **884**
People of color. *See also* Minorities
    as immigrants, 552
People's (Populist) Party, 578, 584(*i*), **585,** 591. *See also* Populist movement
    Debs and, 590
    election of 1892 and, 595, 595(*m*)
    election of 1896 and, 595–597, 596(*m*)
    launch of, 580–581, 584–585
    subtreasury plan of, 585

People's Republic of China (PRC). *See* China
People's Republic of North Korea. *See* North Korea
Per capita income, 1945–1970, 816(*f*)
Perot, H. Ross, 930, 934
Pershing, John J. ("Black Jack")
    in Mexico, 646
    in World War I, 651
Persian Gulf region, Carter Doctrine and, 906
Persian Gulf War (1991), **928**–930, 930(*i*)
Personal Responsibility and Work Opportunity Reconciliation Act (1996), 933
Pesticides, 856
Peterson, Esther, 850
Petroleum. *See* Oil and oil industry
Philadelphia, 550, 555, 556, 572
Philanthropy, of Carnegie, 524, 525, 530
Philippines
    Carter and, 904
    Japan and, 747
    Spanish-American War and, 604, 605(*m*)
    U.S. acquisition of, 605, 606
    warfare against U.S., 601, 607
    in World War II, 753, 766(*m*)
Phillips, Wendell, 461
Philosophy, social Darwinism as, 530
Phonograph, 528, 574(*b*)
Photojournalism, 559, 622(*i*), 624–625(*b*), 623(*i*)
Phyllis Schlafly Report, The, 891, 892(*i*)
Physicians. *See* Medicine
Piecework, 560, 561, 589
Pilgrim's Progress, 624
Pill, the. *See* birth control and birth control movement; Birth control pill
Pinchot, Gifford, 625, 630
Pine Ridge Reservation, 495, 500
Pinkerton Detective Agency
    Homestead lockout and, 586, 586(*i*)
    McCormick reaper works strike and, 567
Pittsburgh Courier, The, 757–758
Plains Indians. *See also* Great Plains
    buffalo decimation and, 493–494, 493(*i*)
    westward movement and, 491
Plantation economy, 512

Planters and plantations
    in 1860 and 1881, 479(*m*)
    after Civil War, 476–479, 512
    exodus to Brazil, 476–477(*b*)
    Johnson, Andrew, and, 465
    labor code and, 462
    sharecropping and, 478
Platt Amendment (1898), 605–606
Playboy magazine, 818
Pledge of allegiance, "under God" in, 817
Plenty Coups (Crow chief), 498
Plessy v. Ferguson (1896), **638,** 820
PLO. *See* Palestine Liberation Organization
Plow, steel, 513
Plural marriage (polygamy), 505, 508(*b*)
Pogroms, against Jews, 555
Poison gas (in World War I), 651
    masks for, 642(*i*), 643
Poland
    immigrants from, 501, 552, 555
    in NATO, 925–926
    Nazi Germany and, 743, 744(*m*), 745
    after World War I, 660
Polaris nuclear submarines, 808
Police
    Coxey's army and, 594
    Haymarket bombing and, 567, 568
Polio
    Roosevelt, Franklin, and, 709
    vaccine for, 801, 801(*i*)
Political action committees (PACs), 898
Political campaigns. *See* Campaigns (political)
Political cartoons
    on Bryan, William Jennings, 597(*i*)
    of Clinton and Obama (2008), 948–949(*b*), 948(*i*), 949(*i*)
    on Democrats' white supremacy, 469(*i*)
    on Gould, Jay, 522(*i*)
    on Grant and corruption, 481(*i*)
    by Nast, 469(*i*), 481(*i*)
    on Open Door policy, 601(*i*)
    Reconstruction, 468(*i*)
    on Rockefeller and government, 527(*i*)
    on temperance women, 537(*i*)
    on wartime Reconstruction, 461(*i*)
Political office. *See* Officeholders

Political parties. *See also* specific
    parties
    in 1928–1932, 711*(m)*
    in 1990–2000s, 923
    factionalism and, 476, 538
    in Gilded Age, 531
    realignment of, 541–545
    U.S. government control by, 952
Politics. *See also* Political parties
    of abundance, 798–800
    African Americans in, 459
    conservatism in, 890–892
    during depression of 1890s,
        593–597
    gender and, 533
    in Gilded Age, 521, 531–537
    Klan and, 693
    in New Deal, 720–722
    presidential, 537–540
    women and, 533, 580, 581, 656,
        684, 853
    during World War II, 758–759
Pollock, Jackson, 819*(i)*
Poll taxes, 637, 684
Pollution. *See also* Air pollution;
        Environment; Water pollution
    climate change agreement and, 950
    environmentalists and, 856
    Johnson, L. B., and, 835
Polygamy, 505, 508*(b)*
Pony Express, 523
Pools (business), 523, 542
Poor people. *See* Poverty
Popular culture, in 1920s, 688–690
Popular Front, 731
Population. *See also* Immigrants and
        immigration
    in 1950s, 816
    baby boom and, 817
    of Californios, 505
    changes in rural and urban
        (1870–1900), 513*(f)*
    of Chinese immigrants, 506
    of cities, 550
    Latinos in, 939
    Mexican American, 505
    Native American, 491
    shift of (1920–1930), 692*(m)*
    of Sun Belt, 813–814
    in Virginia City, 504
Populist movement, 581, 584–585.
        See also People's (Populist) Party
    Cripple Creek strike and, 588

    in election of 1896, 595–597,
        596*(m)*
    Homestead lockout and, 587
Pork barrel programs, 542
Port cities, immigrants in, 551, 555
Portugal, immigrants from, 501
Potatoes, famine in Ireland and, 555
Poverty
    in 1920s, 691
    in 1930s, 699–700
    in 1950s, 810
    1960–1974, 836*(f)*
    Addams, Jane, and, 610–611
    Chicano, 847
    in cities, 555, 559, 572–573
    Clinton policies and, 932–933
    in families, 836, 837
    Great Society and, 836–837
    Johnson, L. B., and, 833
    Kennedy, J. F., and, 831
    Native American, 491, 802
    under Reagan, 911
    on reservations, 491–492, 497
    social Darwinism and, 530
    of working-class families, 561
Powderly, Terence V., 557, 566,
        567, 581
Powell, Colin L., 922–924
    on American promise, 951
    on Central America, 928
    after Cold War, 927
    Iraq War and, 944
    Persian Gulf War and, 928
    as secretary of state, 944
Power (energy). *See* Energy;
        Energy crisis
Power (political), social Darwinism
        on, 530
Prager, Robert, lynching of, 658
Prague Spring, 876*(b),* 877*(i),* 877*(b)*
Preemption doctrine, of Bush, G. W.,
        944–945
Prejudice. *See* Discrimination
Presbyterians, 531
Prescription medication. *See also*
        Medicine
    for elderly, 940, 942
Preservationists, 625
Presidency, under Roosevelt,
        Franklin D., 733
President(s). *See* Elections; Executive;
        specific individuals
Presidential reconstruction, 464–467

President's Commission on the Status
        of Women (PCSW, 1961), 850
President's Committee on Civil Rights
        (1946), 787
Presley, Elvis, 819
Price(s)
    agricultural, 514
    farm income and consumer
        (1865–1910), 583*(f)*
Price freeze, 855
Primary elections, direct, 618
Prisoners of war (POWs)
    in Korean War, 795
    in Vietnam War, 884
    in World War II, 763
Private property
    Indians and, 498
    vs. workers' rights, 585
Proclamation of Amnesty and
        Reconstruction (1863), 460–461
Production, in World War II, 751, 756
Productivity
    in Great Depression, 734*(f)*
    in steel industry, 525
    Taylor and, 617
    technology and, 810–811
Professional Air Traffic Controllers
        Organization (PATCO),
        strike by, 909
Professions, women in, 852
Progressive Party
    of 1912, 610*(i),* 631–633, 633*(m)*
    of 1924, 678
    of 1948, 788
Progressivism, 611–625, **612,** 631–639
    Addams, Jane, and, 611
    African Americans and, 637–639
    in city and state government,
        617–618
    grassroots, 612–616
    limits of, 635–639
    Roosevelt, Theodore, and, 618–628
    for white men, 636–639
    Wilson and, 631–634
    working class and, 614–616
    World War I and, 644–650, 651,
        654–655
Prohibition, **682**–683. *See also* Alcohol
        and alcoholism; Temperance
    nativism and, 613
    after World War I, 655
Prohibition Party, 537, 591
Proletariat, Bolshevik, 666*(b)*

Promontory Point, Utah,
    transcontinental railroad at, 522
Propaganda, for national security, 781
Proposition 13 (California), 894
Prosperity
    in 1920s, 678–679, 696(i)
    in World War II, 757
Prostitution, 570
    poverty and, 613
    World War I and, 651
Protective legislation, for working
    women, 616
Protective tariffs, 541. See also Tariffs
Protest(s). See also Civil rights
    movement; Resistance;
    Revolts and rebellions
    in 1968, 875–878, 876–877(b)
    by African Americans, 729, 828(i),
        842–844, 843(m)
    by farmers, 542, 582–584
    by Native Americans, 845–846
    against taxation, 894
    against Vietnam War, 861,
        873–878, 874(i), 882–883
Protestantism, in 1920s, 691
Provisional Revolutionary
    Government (Vietnam), 884
Pro-war demonstrations, in Vietnam
    War, 883(i)
Pubic domain, land in, 508(b)
Public accommodations,
    discrimination in, 482
Public credit. See Credit
Public debt. See Debt; National debt
Public land. See Land
Public libraries, 525, 572–573
Public opinion, on Maine sinking, 604(b)
Public Opinion (journal), 557
Public schools. See also Education;
    School(s)
    in cities and towns, 572
    integration of, 820–821,
        823(b), 895(m)
Public sphere, access to, 533
Public transportation, gas shortage
    and, 902
Public works
    in 1930s, 698
    in cities, 572–573
    Coxey on, 594
Puerto Rico, 605, 606, 645(m)
Pulitzer, Joseph, 604
Pullman (town), 588–589

Pullman, George M., 588, 589, 590
Pullman boycott, 589–590
Pullman Palace cars, 589(i)
Pullman strike (1894), 588–590, 614
Pure Food and Drug Act (1906), 624

Quotas, on immigration, 692

Rabin, Yitzhak, 937
Race and racism. See also Abolition
    and abolitionism; African
    Americans; Civil rights move-
    ment; Segregation
    against African Americans, 556
    against Asians, 505–506
    civil rights movement and,
        828–829
    foreign policy and, 607
    Garvey and, 688
    in Great Depression, 703, 729
    in housing, 812
    immigrants and, 555–558, 939
    Johnson, L. B., legislation and, 834
    of Johnson, Andrew, 465
    in labor unions, 726–727(b)
    lynchings and, 556
    Native Americans and, 492–493
    New Deal and, 735
    Obama and, 947–948
    politics and, 533–536
    Populists and, 595
    Reconstruction and, 459
    in South, 459, 483–484
    of southern progressives, 637
    Wilson and, 638
    after World War I, 661
    during World War II, 750, 758
    after World War II, 786–788
Race riots
    in Atlanta, 639
    King's death and, 876(b), 878
    in Watts (1965), 843(m), 844
    after World War I, 670
    during World War II, 758
Racial segregation. See Segregation
Radical feminism, 850–851
Radical reconstruction, 469–470
Radical Republicans, 461, 470
Radicals and radicalism
    in Great Depression, 703
    IWW and, 635
    labor, 567
    in New Deal, 721

Socialist Party and, 635
    in suffrage movement, 637
    after World War I, 665–668
Radio, in 1920s, 688, 690
Radioactive fallout, from nuclear
    testing, 866
Railroad Administration
    (World War I), 654
Railroads
    as big business, 520–524
    buffalo hunting and, 493
    Chinese workers on, 506, 506(i)
    expansion of, 520–521, 521(m),
        545, 551
    farming and, 512, 513, 582–583
    financing of, 522–523
    Gould and, 521–522
    government deregulation of, 901
    land grants to, 510, 511(m), 521, 523
    Morgan and reorganization of, 529
    overbuilding of, 520, 523
    ranching and, 509(b), 513
    rebates from, 526, 582, 620, 621
    regulation of, 542, 621–624
    in South, 475, 532
    steel use by, 524
    strikes against, 564–566, 564(m),
        565(i), 584, 588–590
    telegraph communication and, 523
    transcontinental, 493, 522, 523
    in West, 507, 510, 511(m),
        520–521, 521(m)
    Wilson and, 634
    workers on, 523
Rainbow Coalition, 924
Ranching
    federal government and, 509(b)
    fencing and, 505, 512
    vaqueros in, 513
Ranchos, 504
Randolph, A. Philip, 758, 840
Rape
    lynching and, 533
    treatment of victims, 854
"Rape of Nanking," 743
Rapier, James T., 458–459, 460(i),
    474, 482
Rapier, John, 458
Ratification
    of 19th Amendment, 656
    of Versailles treaty, 663
Raw materials, Japan and, 747–748,
    747(m)

Raza Unida, La. *See* La Raza Unida
Reaction, in New Deal, 732
Reading, Pennsylvania, strike in, 564
Readjusters, 533
Reagan, Ronald, 890*(i)*, 908*(i)*
　as California governor, 893, 907
　conservatism and, 906–911
　deregulation and, 909
　election of 1976 and, 899, 899*(m)*
　election of 1980 and, 907
　election of 1984 and, 910
　foreign policy of, 916–919
　Iran-Contra scandal and, 917–918,
　　917*(m)*
　on Panama Canal, 904
　Soviet Union and, 918–919, 918*(i)*
　Supreme Court justices appointed
　　by, 912
Reapers, mechanical, 513
Rebates, railroad, 526, 582, 620, 621
Rebellions. *See* Protest(s); Revolts and
　rebellions
Recall, 618
　Populists on, 585
Recessions. *See also* Depressions;
　Economy; Panic(s)
　in 1937–1938, 732–733
　in 1957, 803
　in 2008, 934, 946–947
　under Reagan, 909–910
　after World War I, 665
Reconstruction (1863–1877),
　459–460
　carpetbaggers and, 458*(i)*, 472–473
　cartoon on, 468*(i)*
　collapse of, 480–485
　congressional, 467–472
　Johnson impeachment and,
　　470–471
　Ku Klux Klan and, 459, 482
　labor code and, 462
　military rule during, 470, 470*(m)*
　North and, 466, 480, 481–482
　politics in, 482
　presidential, 464–467
　radical, 469–470
　Redeemers and, 483, 484
　scalawags and, 473
　South and, 462, 465–466, 472–479,
　　482–484, 484*(m)*
　southern Republican Party and,
　　473–476, 480, 481–482, 483,
　　484, 484*(m)*

Supreme Court and, 482
　wartime, 460–463, 461*(i)*
　white supremacy and, 482–484
Reconstruction Acts (1867), 470, 473
***Reconstruction Finance Corporation
　(RFC,* 1932), 698**
Recovery
　in 1930s, 699*(f)*
　in New Deal, 717–718
　after World War II, 777–780,
　　778–779*(b)*
Recreation. *See* Leisure
Red Army (Soviet Union)
　in Berlin, 765
　in Eastern Europe, 765
　World War II and, 762, 775
Red-baiting, 789
Redbook magazine, "flappers" in,
　685*(i)*
Red Cloud (Sioux chief), 495
Red Cross
　in 1930s, 698
　women in World War I, 656
***Redeemers,* in South, *483,* 484, 486**
Red Record (Wells), 534–535*(b)*
Red River region, 514
***Red scare,* 665**
　in 1950s, 789–791
　after World War I, 664, 665–668,
　　666–667*(b)*
Red Stockings, 570–571
Referendum, 585, 618
Reform and reform movements.
　　See also Great Society;
　　specific movements
　in cities, 573
　civil service, 538, 539
　Clinton, Bill, and, 931–932
　Johnson, L. B., 833–837
　Kennedy, J. F., and, 831
　moral reform movement and, 531
　New Deal and, 718–722, 733–735
　political, 538
　Populist movement, 584–585
　progressive, 611, 613–616
　Red scare and, 667*(b)*
　Roosevelt, T., and, 619, 621–624
　southern Republican governments
　　and, 473–476
　temperance and, 537, 590–591
　women and, 536–537, 590–593
　after World War II, 664
***Reform Darwinism,* 616–617**

Refugees
　from communism, 939
　Jewish, 759, 760*(b)*
　Palestinian, 882
　Vietnam War and, 872
*Regents of the University of California
　v. Bakke* (1978), 896
Regulation
　of banking, 713
　by Bush, G. H. W., 925
　of business, 677–678
　Nixon and, 854–855
　of railroads, 542, 621–624
　of trusts, 526, 542–543, 619–620
Reid, Whitelaw, 466
Relief programs. *See also* Welfare and
　　welfare system
　in 1930s, 698
　in New Deal, 714–715, 726*(b)*
Religion(s). *See also* Churches;
　　Missions and missionaries
　in 1950s, 817
　of freedmen, 463–464
　Indians and, 500, 500*(i)*
　politics and, 531
　of Smith, Alfred, 695
Relocation. *See also* Removal policy
　of Indians, 803, 803*(i)*, 803*(m)*, 846
　of Japanese Americans, 749–750,
　　750*(m)*
Remington, Frederic, 604
Removal policy, for Indians, 491–493
Rent controls, 784
Reparations
　after World War I, 660, 679
　after World War II, 775
Repeal, of prohibition, 683
Republic(s), independence of Soviet,
　926
Republican Party. *See also* Elections
　business and, 523, 538
　Eisenhower and, 800–801
　ex-Confederates in Congress and,
　　466, 467
　factionalism in, 476, 537, 538, 539
　Fourteenth Amendment and, 468
　Fifteenth Amendment and, 471
　freedmen in, 472
　free silver issue and, 544
　during Gilded Age, 523, 531
　Klan and political violence against,
　　481–482
　Liberal Party and, 480–481

presidential reconstruction and, 466–467

radical reconstruction and, 470–471

in South, 473–476, 480, 481, 482, 483–484

tariffs and, 541–542

women and, 592

after World War I, 663

Reservationists, in Congress, 663

Reservations (Indian), 489, *491,* 492(*m*), 494, 495, 497–498, 499

Reserve Officers Training Corps (ROTC), 873, 923

Residential segregation, 559

Resistance. *See also* Revolts and rebellions

by Indians, 489, 494–495, 498–501

Resources. *See* Conservation; Natural resources

Reston, James, 832

Retirement Equity Act (1984), 912

Reuther, Walter, 811

Revenues. *See* Finances

Reverse discrimination, 911

Revolts and rebellions. *See also* Resistance

in Hungary (1956), 804–805

Revolution(s)

Bolshevism and, 650, 665, 666–667(*b*)

in Cuba, 601, 806–807

in Iran, 906

in Mexico (1911), 631

Rhee, Syngman, 792

Rhett, Robert Barnwell, Sr., 476(*b*)

Rhineland

Nazis in, 742

after World War I, 660

Rhodesia, Carter and, 904

Rhythm and blues music, 819

Rickover, Hyman, 602–603(*b*)

Ridgway, Matthew B., 795

Riesman, David, 818

Rifles, 493

Rights. *See also* Bill of Rights (U.S.)

for African Americans, 758

Burger Court and, 896

Native American, 845

private property *vs.* workers', 585, 587

Reagan and, 911–916

of same-sex couples, 932

state *vs.* federal, 482

for women, 656

of workers, 585

Right wing (political), 879. *See also* Conservatives and conservatism

Reagan and, 891–892

Riis, Jacob, 559, 562, 624–625(*b*)

Riots. *See also* Protest(s); Race riots

in Panama Canal Zone, 870

River Rouge factory (Ford), 675, 702

Roads and highways, interstate system and, 801, 802(*m*), 812

Roaring Twenties, 677, 682–691

"Robber barons," 528, 675

Roberts, John, 941

Robertson, Pat, 907

Robinson, Jackie, 787, 821

Robinson, Jo Ann, 821

Rock and roll music, 818–*819,* 848

Rockefeller, John D., 520, 527(*i*), 558, 598

criticism of, 526–527

oil industry and, 525–527

Roosevelt, Theodore, and, 619

Rockefeller, John D., Jr., 530

Rockne, Knute, 690

Roebling family

Emily Warren, 549

John, 549

Washington, 549

Roe v. Wade (1973), *854,* 912, 913(*i*)

Roman Catholicism. *See* Catholicism

Romania, after World War I, 660

Rommel, Erwin, 755

Romney, Mitt, 947

Roosevelt, Eleanor, 708, 712

African American women and, 729

women in CCC and, 715

Roosevelt, Franklin Delano, 706(*i*). *See also* Great Depression; New Deal

African American protests and, 729

Atlantic Charter and, 746

Brains Trust of, 712

at Casablanca, 755

court-packing plan of, 731–732

death of, 765

economy and, 712–718

election of 1920 and, 671, 709

election of 1932 and, 709(*i*), 710–712, 711(*m*)

election of 1936 and, 731

election of 1940 and, 746

election of 1944 and, 758–759

fireside chats of, 713

good neighbor policy and, 741–742

isolationism and, 741

New Deal coalition of, 711

as New York governor, 709–710

recession of 1937–1938 and, 732–733

at Tehran, 763

in World War II, 755

at Yalta, 765

Roosevelt, Theodore, 619(*i*)

"big stick" foreign policy of, 625–628

conservation and, 624–625

election of 1904 and, 621

election of 1912 and, 610(*i*), 631–633, 633(*m*)

foreign policy of, 625–628

on *Maine* sinking, 604(*b*)

muckraking and, 624

Nobel Peace Prize to, 628

progressivism and, 618–628

as reformer, 619, 621–624

Roosevelt Corollary and, 627, 628(*i*)

Spanish-American War and, 604–605

Square Deal of, 621

Taft and, 630

trusts and, 619–620, 631

Washington, Booker T., and, 638(*i*)

Roosevelt Corollary, 627

Root-Takahira agreement (1908), 628

Rosebud, battle of (1876), 495

Rosenberg, Ethel and **Julius,** 790

"Rosie the Riveter," 756, 757(*i*)

ROTC. *See* Reserve Officers Training Corps

Roughing It (Twain), 515

Rough Riders, 604–605, 619

Royal Air Force (England), 745

Royal Navy. *See* Navies, British

Ruhr Valley region, France and, 679

Rumsfeld, Donald, 944

Rural areas. *See also* Agriculture; Farms and farming

in 1920s, 691, 692(*m*)

in 1930s, 700

electricity and, 528

Klan in, 693

in New Deal, 719–720

population in, 513(*f*)

population movement from, 551, 692(*m*)

Rural Electrification Administration (REA), 715, 717(i)
Rusk, Dean, 868
Russell, Harold, 774
Russia. *See also* Soviet Union
    Bolshevism in, 650, 666–667(b)
    immigrants from, 501, 552, 555
    revolution of 1917 in, 650
    World War I and, 646, 650
Ruth, George Herman ("Babe"), 689
Rwanda, civil war in, 936

Sacco, Nicola, 693
Sadat, Anwar, 904
Saddam Hussein. *See* Hussein, Saddam
Safety legislation. *See* Occupational Safety and Health Act (OSHA, 1970)
Saigon. *See* Vietnam War
Sailors. *See* Navies; Ships and shipping
St. Louis, Missouri, 580, 581
St. Louis Exposition (1904), 499
St.-Mihiel, battle at, 643
Salesclerks, 560, 563
Salk, Jonas, 801(i)
SALT. *See* Strategic Arms Limitation Talks
Salter, John, Jr., 839(i)
Saltonstall, Nora, 656
Same-sex couples, rights of, 932
Samoan Islands, 600, 600(m)
San Carlos Reservation, 499
Sand Creek massacre (1864), 493
San Diego, 504
Sandinistas, 904, 917
S&L scandal, 909
Sandoz, Jules, 500
San Francisco, 557
    Native Americans at Alcatraz and, 845, 845(i)
Sanger, Margaret, 635–636, 684
Sanitation, in factories, 680
San Juan Hill, battle of, 605
Santee (Dakota) Indians, 494
Santee Uprising (1862), 494
Satellites (space), 808
Saturday Evening Post, 683
Saudi Arabia
    Bush, G. H. W., in, 930(i)
    Hussein and, 928
    U.S. soldiers in, 930
Savings and loan (S&L) crisis, 909

"Scabs" (strikebreakers), 565, 567
Scalawags, 473
Scandinavia, immigrants from, 501, 552
Scapegoats, in 1930s, 701
Schenck, Charles, 668
Schenck v. United States (1919), *668*
Schlafly, Fred, 891
Schlafly, Phyllis, 853, 890–892, 892(i), 895, 907, 908, 912, 914, 915(i), 915(b)
Schneiderman, Rose, 615
School(s). *See also* Education; Higher education; Public schools
    freedmen's, 475(i)
    Indian, 496–497
    integration of, 820–821, 822–823(b)
    public, 474–475
    segregation in, 475
School prayer, 837
Schurz, Carl, 459, 485, 486
Sciences, Eisenhower and, 808
SCLC. *See* Southern Christian Leadership Conference
Scopes, John, 694
Scopes trial, 694
Scorched-earth policy, against Indians, 494–495
Scotland. *See also* Scots-Irish
    immigrants from, 501
Scots-Irish, 560
Scott, Tom, 524
Scottsboro Boys, 702(i), 703
SDS. *See* Students for a Democratic Society
Seabrook, N.H., nuclear power plant in, 902
SEALS (Navy), 864
Seaports. *See* Port cities
Sea routes. *See* Trade
Seasonal laborers. *See also* Migrant workers
    in manufacturing and industry, 560
Seattle, strike in (1919), 664
SEC. *See* Securities and Exchange Commission
Secession, repudiation of, 461, 465
Secondary schools, 572. *See also* Education; School(s)
Second front, in World War II, 755, 763, 774
Second Reconstruction, 838–844. *See also* Reconstruction
Second World War. *See* World War II

Secretarial work, women in, 563
Secret ballot, Populists on, 585
Sectionalism
    New South and, 532
    People's Party and, 595
    in politics, 538
Securities and Exchange Commission (SEC, 1934), 714
Securities services, Financial Services Modernization Act and, 934
Security. *See* Defense; National security; National security state
Sedition Act, of 1918, 658
Segregation. *See also* Desegregation; Integration
    of African Americans in military, 750
    of buses, 821–825
    in California, 505
    in cities, 558
    of housing, 812
    Jim Crow and, 475, 533, 556, 637
    Plessy v. Ferguson (1896) and, 638
    of public transportation, 475, 482
    residential, 559
    of schools, 475
    social, 558
    in South, 475, 482, 533, 556
    Wilson and, 638–639
    after World War II, 787
Selective Service Act
    of 1917, 650–651
    of 1940, *750*
Self-determination
    Atlantic Charter and, 746
    Roosevelt, Franklin D., and, 742
    after World War I, 659
    after World War II, 765, 782
Selma, Alabama, voting rights march in, 840, 841(i)
Seminole Indians, 491
Senate (U.S.). *See also* Congress (U.S.)
    election to, 538, 585, 630
    Foreign Relations Committee in, 663
    Johnson, Andrew, impeachment and, 471
Seniors. *See* Elderly
"Separate but equal" doctrine, 638, 820
Separate spheres idea, 533, 683
Separation of church and state, Bible reading, school prayer, and, 837
September 11, 2001, attacks, 924, 942–943, 943(i)

Serbs and Serbia
  in former Yugoslavia, 936
  World War I and, 646
Servants. *See also* Domestics (domestic
    servants); Slavery
  women as, 502–503, 562
Service industries, 910
Servicemen's Readjustment Act (1944).
    See GI Bill of Rights (1944)
Settlement(s). *See also* Colonies and
    colonization; Land
  midwestern before 1862, 510(*m*)
Settlement houses, 612(*i*), **613**
Settler(s). *See also* Homesteaders
  on Great Plains, 491
  recruitment of, 510, 511
  western diversity and, 504
Seventeenth Amendment, 630
Sewall, Arthur M., 596
Sewing machine, 561
Sex and sexuality. *See also* Gays and
    lesbians
  in 1920s, 686–687(*b*)
  in 1950s, 818
  birth control and, 848(*i*)
  working-class women and, 570
Sex discrimination, outlawing of,
    854, 857
Sex education, 893–894
Sexual Behavior in the Human Female
    (Kinsey), 818
Sexual Behavior in the Human Male
    (Kinsey), 818
Sexual division of labor. *See also*
    Gender and gender issues
  female immigrants and, 555
Sexual harassment, in workplace, 925
Sexual revolution
  in 1920s, 686–687(*b*)
  in 1960s, 848
Seymour, Horatio, 480, 480(*m*)
Shafter, William, 605
Shah of Iran. *See* Pahlavi, Mohammad
    Reza
"Shame of the Cities, The" (Steffens),
    576
Shandong (Shan-tung) Province,
    Boxers in, 599
Sharecropping, 478–479, 513, 719, 720(*i*)
"Share Our Wealth" plan (Long),
    721–722, 722(*i*)
Sheldon, Charles M., 613
Sheppard-Towner Act (1921), 684

Sherman, William Tecumseh, 462, 465
Sherman Antitrust Act (1890),
    542–543, 619–620, 909
"Sherman land," 463
Sherman Silver Purchase Act (1890),
    544
Shiite Muslims, Hezbollah and, 917
Ships and shipping. *See also* Navies;
    Navy (U.S.); Submarines
  Panama Canal and, 627, 627(*m*)
  in World War I, 648–649,
    648(*m*), 649
Shoshoni Indians, 498, 500, 503
Sicily, 755
Sierra Club, 625, 856
Sierra Madre, 499
Sierra Nevada, railroads in, 506, 506(*i*)
"Significance of the Frontier in
    American History, The"
    (Turner), 488
*Signing of Peace in the Hall of
    Mirrors . . .* (Orpen), 662(*i*)
Sigsbee, Charles Dwight, 602(*b*)
Silent Spring (Carson), 856
Silver
  Comstock Lode and, 501–504,
    502(*m*)
  free silver issue, 543–544, 585,
    595, 596
Sin, social gospel and, 613
Sinai Peninsula, 881, 904
Sinatra, Frank, 791
Sinclair, Upton, 624, 720
Sioux Indians, 493, 498
  Black Hills and, 495–496, 509(*b*)
  Wounded Knee and, 500, 845
Sit-ins
  at Woolworth's, 838, 839(*i*)
  during World War II, 758
Sitting Bull (Sioux leader), 493, 495,
    496, 500
Six-Day War (1967), **881**–882, 882(*m*)
Sixteenth Amendment, 630, 633
Skilled workers, 555, 559, 560, 563,
    566, 586
Skin color, 556
  "Black is beautiful" movement and,
    844
Skyscrapers, 525, 571
Slaughterhouse cases (1873), 482
Slaveholders. *See also* Planters and
    plantations
  labor code and, 462

Slavery. See also Abolition and aboli-
    tionism; African Americans;
    Revolts and rebellions
  Johnson, Andrew, and, 465
Slavic immigrants, 551, 553
Slum clearance, 789
Slums, 551
Smartphones, 938(*i*)
Smith, Alfred E. (Al), 694–695
Smith, E. G., 913(*i*)
Smith, Joseph, Jr., 505
Smithsonian Institution, *Maine* study
    by, 605(*b*)
Smog, 814
Smoking. *See* Tobacco and tobacco
    industry
SNCC. *See* Student Nonviolent
    Coordinating Committee
Snelling, Fort, mass execution at, 494
Social Darwinism, 520, **530**
  depression of 1890s and, 593
  racism and, 556
  social gospel and, 530
Social Democratic Party. *See* Socialist
    Party
Social geography, of cities, 558–559
Social gospel, **613**
Socialism and socialists, 567, 635
  New Deal and, 720, 730–731
  after World War I, 668
Socialist Party, **635**
  in 1912, 632
  in 1930s, 703
  Debs and, 590, 632
Social programs, Eisenhower and, 801
Social purity movement, 613
Social Security, 723, **725**–728
  Carter and, 901
  Eisenhower and, 801
Social segregation, 558
Social welfare. *See* Welfare and welfare
    system
Society. *See also* Culture(s); Great
    Society; Progressivism; Reform
    and reform movements
  in Gilded Age, 569–571
  globalization and, 939
  in Great Depression, 699–701
  immigration and, 939
  separate spheres and, 533
  after World War II, 784
"Sodbusters," 507
Sod houses, 507, 510, 510(*i*)

Software developers, foreign-born, 939
Software industry, Gates in, 910
Soldiers. *See also* Military; Veterans;
    specific battles and wars
    African American, 651, 787
    black, 504
    in Korean War, 793
    in Vietnam War, 869, 869(*f*),
        871–872, 872(*i*)
    in World War I, 650–651
    in World War II, 750
    after World War II, 769
Solid South, 532, 896
Solomon Islands, 751, 754(*i*), 767
Somalia, 935
Somme, battle of (1916), 651
Sonoran Desert, 499
Soros, George, 938
Sorosis Club, 536
Souls of Black Folk, The (Du Bois), 639
Sousa, John Philip, 601
South (U.S. region). *See also* Civil
    rights movement; New South;
    Reconstruction; Slavery;
    Sun Belt
    in 1950s, 809
    African American migration from,
        556, 668–670, 758
    African Americans and, 476–479,
        478(*i*), 532, 729
    black codes in, 465–466
    civil rights movement and, 838
    congressional delegations from
        (1865–1877), 474(*f*)
    crop lien system in, 478, 583
    economy in, 475, 532
    Fourteenth Amendment and, 468,
        469, 474
    free silver and, 595
    home rule for, 480, 483
    Indian removal in, 491
    Jim Crow laws in, 475, 533, 556
    Klan in, 459, 473, 481–482
    lynching in, 533
    migration of planters from,
        476–477(*b*)
    migration to, 812
    military rule in, 470, 470(*m*)
    Populists in, 595
    public education in, 474–475
    racial violence in, 469, 483–484
    racism of progressives in, 637
    railroads in, 475, 532

Reconstruction and, 462, 465–466,
    472–479, 482–484, 484(*m*)
Redeemers in, 483, 484, 486
Republican governments in, 473–476,
    480, 483, 484, 484(*m*), 485
Republican Party in, 472–473,
    481–482, 483–484
segregation in, 475, 482, 533
sharecropping in, 478–479
tariffs and, 541
textile industry in, 532
voting in, 459, 470, 474, 684
white supremacy and, 480
South Africa
    apartheid ended in, 926–927
    Carter and, 904
    Reagan's support of, 917
South America. *See also* Latin
    America; North America;
    specific locations
    immigrants from, 501
    immigrants to, 551
    U.S. intervention in, 645
South Carolina, election of 1876 and,
    485
South Dakota, Lakota Sioux siege in,
    845
Southeast Asia. *See also* Vietnam War
    communism in, 805–806, 868
    Japan and, 747–748
    after Vietnam War, 885
Southern Africa, Nixon and, 881
Southern Arapaho Indians, 493
Southern Christian Leadership
    Conference (SCLC), 825, 830(*i*),
    838, 840
Southern Farmers' Alliance, 583
Southern Horrors: . . .(Wells), 534(*b*)
Southern Manifesto on Integration,
    822(*b*)
Southern strategy, of Nixon, 896
Southern Unionists. *See* Unionists,
    in South
South Korea, 792
    Carter and, 904
South Vietnam, 860. *See also* Vietnam
    War
    ARVN in, 806
    U.S. evacuation, 884–885, 885(*i*)
    Vietcong from, 866
Southwest (U.S. region)
    in 1950s, 809
    Hispanics in, 504–505

Indians in, 491, 499
Latinos in, 846
Mexican Americans in, 513,
    670–671, 670(*i*), 787, 814
Sovereignty. *See* State(s)
Soviet Union. *See also* Bolsheviks and
    Bolshevism; Cold War; Russia;
    Stalin, Joseph
    in 1930s, 741
    Afghanistan and, 905
    Bolshevism in, 666–667(*b*)
    Chinese treaty with, 783
    in Cold War, 773, 774–776
    Cuba and, 807
    dissidents in, 881
    Eisenhower and, 799
    emerging nations and, 782
    end of, 925–926
    Korean War and, 792–793
    Lend-Lease to, 746
    MAD policy and, 804–805
    Marshall Plan and, 780
    Nazis and, 745, 746
    Nixon and, 879, 881
    Popular Front and, 731
    Reagan and, 908(*i*), 918–919, 918(*i*)
    Red scare and, 666–667(*b*)
    Truman Doctrine and, 777
    U-2 spy plane and, 808
    United Nations and, 765
    after World War II, 770
Space exploration
    Sputnik and, 808, 863
    by United States, 863–864
Spain. *See also* Colonies and colonization;
    Spanish-American War
    Cuba and, 601, 604
    immigrants from, 501
Spanish-American War (1898),
    601–606, 602–603(*b*), 605(*m*)
    Puerto Rico and, 645(*m*)
    treaty ending, 606–607
Spanish civil war (1936–1939),
    743, 743(*m*)
Spanish influenza, after World War I,
    665
Spanish-language TV stations, 939
Speakeasies, 683
Speculation
    in land, 510
    in mining, 501
    in railroads, 520, 521, 521(*m*),
        522, 524

Spencer, Herbert, 530
Spending. *See also* Defense spending;
  Finances
  government, in Reconstruction
    South, 483
  on political campaigns, 898
Spheres of influence
  in China, 601
  in third world, 551
  of U.S., 597, 600
Spies, August, 567, 568
Spies and spying
  in Cold War, 782(*i*)
  McCarthy and, 790
  U-2 incident and, 808
Spock, Benjamin, 817
Spoils system, 531, 538, 539
Sports, team movement to Sun Belt, 812
Sputnik, 808, 938(*i*)
Square Deal, 621
Squatters, 504
Stagflation
  Carter and, 900, 901
  Nixon and, 855
Stalin, Joseph
  Cold War and, 774
  death of, 808
  Marshall Plan and, 779
  Nazi agreement with, 745
  at Tehran, 763
  in World War II, 746, 754
  at Yalta, 765
Stalingrad, battle at (1942–1943),
  762, 764(*m*)
Stalwarts, 538
Standard of living. *See* Lifestyle; Wealth
Standard Oil Company, 526–527, 530,
  538, 543, 598, 619, 620
Standing Bear, Luther, 494, 497
Standing Rock Reservation, 500
Stanton, Edwin M., 471
Stanton, Elizabeth Cady, 469(*i*)
  on "Negro first" strategy, 471–472
  woman suffrage movement and,
    468, 536, 592–593
  on word *male* in Constitution, 469
Starr, Kenneth, 934
START treaty. *See* Strategic Arms
  Reduction Talks treaty
Starvation
  in 1930s, 700
  during depression of 1893, 593
  on reservations, 491

State(s)
  in 1990s, 925
  Bill of Rights (U.S.) and, 837
  business regulation by, 678
  Eisenhower and, 801
  federal rights *vs.*, 482
  progressive government in,
    617–618
  during Reconstruction, 465–466,
    473–476
  restoration to Union, 461, 462,
    465, 474
  strikes and, 588
Statehood
  for territories, 509(*b*), 515
  voting and, 505
State legislatures, 538
States' rights, Johnson, Andrew, on,
  465, 466, 467
States' Rights Party. *See* Dixiecrats
Statue of Liberty, 557
Steam power, 514
  steam engine and, 503
  steamships, global migration, and,
    551, 553
Steel and steel industry
  Bessemer and, 524
  Carnegie in, 524–525, 587
  and iron production (1870–1900),
    525(*f*)
  Morgan, J. P., in, 529–530
  in New South, 532
  strikes against, 585–587, 665
  structural steel and, 571
Steeplechase Park, 571
Steffens, Lincoln, 576, 617
Stein, Gertrude, 690
Steinbacher, Joseph, 767
Steinbeck, John, 720
Steinem, Gloria, 851
Stephens, Alexander, 466
Stephens, Harry, and family,
  464(*i*)
Stephenson, David, 693
Stern, Edith, 817
Stevens, Thaddeus, 470
Stevenson, Adlai E., 794–795, 803
Stock(s)
  crash of 1929 and, 697
  Gould and, 521, 523
  mining, 501
  of railroads, 521, 522, 524, 564
  speculation in, 523

Stock market
  crash of (1929), 697–698
  in San Francisco, 501
Stonewall riots (1969), 849, 849(*i*)
Strategic Arms Limitation Talks
  (***SALT,*** 1972), **880**
Strategic Arms Reduction Talks
  (START) treaty (1990), 927
Strategic arms reduction treaty (1979),
  second, 904
Streetcars, 558, 558(*i*)
Strict construction, 896
Strikebreakers, 565, 567, 587, 589
Strikes. *See also* Labor; Labor unions
  by Boston police (1919), 664–665
  by bridge workers, 549
  by coal miners, 620–621
  by Cripple Creek miners, 587–588
  Gompers and, 566
  Great Railroad Strike (1877),
    564–566, 564(*m*), 565(*i*), 588
  Homestead lockout, 585–587,
    586(*i*)
  at McCormick reaper works, 567
  PATCO, 909
  Pullman, 588–590
  against railroads, 584
  steel (1919), 665
  at Triangle Shirtwaist Company, 614
  after World War I, 664
  in World War II, 751
Strip mining, 903
Student Nonviolent Coordinating
  Committee (SNCC), 838, 844
Students. *See also* Young people
  financial aid for colleges, 931
  protests by, 847–848, 873–875
Students for a Democratic Society
  (SDS), 847, 873
Submarines
  Polaris nuclear submarine, 808
  in World War I, 648, 653
  in World War II, 746, 748(*i*), 754
Subsidies
  for business, 520
  for home ownership, 812
  for transportation, 521, 523
Subtreasury plan, of Populists, 585
Suburbs
  in 1950s, 809, 811, 812
  growth of, 799
  interstate highways and, 812
  in Sun Belt, 814

Subversion
    fear of in 1919, 665–668
    fear of in 1940s–1950s, 665–668
Subway system, 572
Sudan, Clinton and, 936
Sudetenland, 743
Suez Canal, 755, 807
Suez crisis (1956), 807, 807(m)
Suffrage. See also Voting and voting
        rights; Woman suffrage
    black, 462, 470, 472
    Fourteenth Amendment and,
        468–469
    for Indians, 693
    for men, 474
    World War I and, 655–656
Suffragettes, 593, 593(i), 637(i)
Sugar and sugar industry
    in Hawai'i, 598
    monopoly and, 543
Sullivan, Louis, 574(b)
Sultzer, William, 602(b)
Summit meetings, at Geneva (1955),
    808
Sumner, Charles, 462, 468, 470
Sumner, William Graham, 530
Sun Also Rises, The (Hemingway),
    690
Sun Belt, 799, 809, 812–815, *813,*
    813(m)
    conservatism in, 893
Sunni Muslims, 945
Super Fortress. See B-29 Super Fortress
Superfund, 903
Superpowers. See also Cold War
    in arms race, 808–809
    global rivalry of, 782–783
    Kennedy, J. F., and, 866
    U.S. as, 769
Supply-side economics, 908–909
Supreme Court (U.S.)
    antitrust law and, 543
    Burger Court and, 896
    Bush, G. H. W., and, 925
    Bush, G. W., and, 941
    business and, 528
    on business regulation, 678
    on bus segregation, 825
    Californio land claims and, 504
    on campaign spending, 898
    civil rights and, 820–821
    Clinton and, 932
    on Colfax massacre attackers, 484

corporations as "persons," 531
    on election of 2000, 940
    on equal opportunity, 911
    on housing covenants, 812
    on Mexican Americans on juries,
        814
    Nixon and, 896
    Obama and, 947
    on railroad regulation, 542
    Reconstruction and, 482
    on "separate but equal" doctrine,
        638
    on separation of church and state,
        837
    Sherman Act and, 620
    on Sioux claim to Black Hills, 496
    on Social Security, 728
    on voting rights, 837
    Warren Court and, 837–838
    women on, 912, 932
Surplus (financial), 541, 542
    under Clinton, 931
    in New Deal, 733(i)
"Survival of the fittest," 520, 530, 531
"Survival schools," Native American,
    845
Sweatshops, 560, *561,* 561(i)
Switzerland, immigrants from, 501
Syria, 951
    ISIS and, 945–946
    Six-Day War and, 881
"Systematized shop management"
    (Taylor), 617
Szilard, Leo, 761(b)

Taft, Robert A., 794
Taft, William Howard, 629–631,
    629(i)
    dollar diplomacy of, 630–631,
        630(m)
    election of 1908 and, 629
    election of 1912 and, 631, 633(m)
    tariffs and, 629–630
Taft-Hartley Act (1947), *788*
Taiwan, Nationalist Chinese on, 783
Takeovers, Reagan and, 909
Taliban (Afghanistan), 942, 943
Tammany Hall, 573, 694
Tanks, in World War II, 755(i)
Tanzania, embassy attack in, 936
Tarbell, Ida M., 526–527, 629
Tariffs
    in 1920s, 677, 697

Hawley-Smoot, 698
    McKinley, 541–542, 598
    NAFTA and, 937
    Payne-Aldrich, 630
    reduction of (1934), 742
    Taft and, 629
    Underwood (1913), 633
    Wilson and, 633
Taxation. *See also* Income tax
    in black codes, 466
    Bush, G. H. W., and, 925
    Bush, G. W., and, 940, 941
    Clinton, Bill, and, 931
    Coolidge and, 697
    of corporations, 728
    Eisenhower and, 801
    income, 630
    Johnson, L. B., and, 833
    Kennedy, J. F., and, 831
    in New Deal, 725–728
    protests against, 893
    Reagan on, 908–909
    in South, 475, 483
Tax Reform Act (1986), 909
Taylor, Frederick Winslow, 617
Tea Party movement, 947
Teapot Dome scandal, *677,* 678(i)
Technocrats, 617
Technology. *See also* Automobiles;
        Weapons
    agriculture, industry, and, 810–811,
        810(i)
    at Columbian Exposition, 574(b)
    environmentalists and, 856
    for farming, 513
    Ford and, 675
    Internet and, 938
    for mining, 503
Teenagers. See Young people
Tehran, U.S. hostages in, 906
Tehran conference (1943), 763
Tejanos, 505, 513
Telegraph, 523, 527
Telephone, 527–528, 528(i)
Television
    in 1950s, 817–818
    private financing of, 818
Temperance, 613. *See also* Alcohol and
        alcoholism; Prohibition
    women and, 536–537, 537(i), 570,
        581, 590–591
*Temporary Assistance for Needy
    Families (TANF) program, 933*

Tenant farmers
    New Deal and, 719
    in West, 513
Tenements, 573
Ten-hour workday, for women, 616
Tennessee, 462, 469, 484
Tennessee Coal and Iron Company,
    624, 631
Tennessee Valley Authority (TVA),
    715, 716(m), 717(i)
Tenure of Office Act (1867), 471
Termination program, for Indians,
    802–803, 846, 857
Territorial Enterprise, 501
Territories
    government in, 508(b), 515
    statehood for, 509(b)
Terrorism
    in 1970s and 1980s, 916–917
    globalization of, 942–944
    in Iraq, 945
    ISIS and, 946
    Islamic, 940
    by Klan, 473, 481–482
    Maine sinking and, 604(b), 605(b)
    at Munich Olympics, 917
    protection from, 944
    September 11, 2001, attacks, and,
        923, 942–943, 943(i)
    southern Democratic Party and,
        483–484
    after World War I, 665
Tet Offensive (1968), **875**–878,
    875(i)
Texas, 484
    Hispanics in, 504, 505
    manifest destiny and, 491
    Native Americans in, 494
    Tejanos in, 505, 505(i), 513
Texas and Pacific Railroad, 584
Texas Rangers, 505
Textiles and textile industry. *See also*
    Clothing; Cotton and cotton
    industry
    employment in, 523, 591
    mechanization in, 560
    in South, 532
Thatcher, Margaret, 906
Their Eyes Were Watching God
    (Hurston), 688
Thieu, Nguyen Van, 885(i)
Third parties, 532
    Perot and, 930, 934

Third world, 551, 552(m), 782
    Kennedy, J. F., and, 864
Thirteenth Amendment, 465
This Side of Paradise (Fitzgerald),
    684, 691
Thomas, Clarence, 925
Thomas, Elmer, 779(b)
Thomas, Norman, 703, 711(m)
Thor ballistic missile, 805(i)
Threshers, 514
Thurber, James, 691
Thurmond, J. Strom, 788
Thygeson, Sylvie, 563
Tianjin (Tientsin) treaty (1858), 599
Tibbets, Paul, 738–740, 740(i), 761(b),
    763, 768
Tiffany, Louis Comfort, 574(b)
Tilden, Samuel J., 485, 485(m)
Till, Emmett, 820
Tillman, Benjamin, 595
Tilyou, George, 571
Tinian Island, 739
Title VII, of Civil Rights Act (1964),
    840, 850
Title IX, of Education Amendments
    Act (1972), 854, 857, 911
Tobacco and tobacco industry, in
    South, 532
Tojo, Hideki (Japan), 748
Torture, Bush, G. W., and, 950
Toxic chemicals, 856
Toxic wastes
    Love Canal disaster and, 903
    Superfund for cleanup of, 903
Trade. *See also* Free trade; Market(s);
    Ships and shipping;
    Transportation
    with Asia, 597, 600, 601
    with China, 601
    with Cuba, 604
    expansion of (1870–1910), 598(f)
    free trade agreements, 937
    NAFTA and, 937
Trade unions, 566, 567. *See also* Labor
    unions
Trading with the Enemy Act (1917),
    658
Trail(s), to West, 495
"Trail of Broken Treaties" caravan, 845
Transcontinental railroad, 493, 523
    first, 507, 522
Transit system, in Cleveland, 617,
    618(i)

Trans-Mississippi West
    expansion in, 490
    land rush in, 507
Trans-Pacific Partnership, 937
Transportation. *See also* Railroads;
        Roads and highways
    container boxes and, 922(i)
    federal government support for,
        508(b)
    mass transit, 558
    segregation of public, 475, 482
Treasury Department, 541
    prohibition and, 682
Treaties. *See also* specific treaties
    with Indians, 491, 493, 495, 509(b)
    after World War II, 783
Trench warfare, in World War I, 643,
    651, 652(i)
Triangle Shirtwaist Company
    fire at, 614–615, 615(i)
    strike at, 614
Tribes. *See* Native Americans
Trickle-down economics, 698,
    910–911
Tripartite Pact (1940), 748
Triple Alliance, **646**
Triple Entente, **646**
Trolleys, 528
Troops. *See* Military; Soldiers
Troubled Assets Relief Program
    (2008), 946–947
Trucking, government deregulation of,
    901
Truman, Bess, 835(i)
Truman, Harry S.
    assumption of presidency, 765, 773
    civil rights and, 787
    Cold War and, 775
    developing nations and, 782
    economy and, 784–786
    election of 1944 and, 759
    election of 1948 and, 787, 788,
        789(i), 789(m)
    election of 1952 and, 794
    Fair Deal and, 783–789
    Israel, Palestine, and, 783
    Korean War and, 792, 794
    Marshall Plan and, 778
    Medicare, Medicaid, and, 835(i)
    national security state and,
        780–782
    after World War II, 774–775
Truman Doctrine, **777**

Trumbull, Lyman, 467
Trumpauer, Joan, 839*(i)*
Trust(s), **526,** 542–543
Tunisia, 951
Tunney, Gene, 690
Turkey
    Greece and, 660
    immigrants from, 501, 552
    missiles and, 808, 866
    Truman Doctrine and, 777
Turner, Frederick Jackson, 488, 489,
    515, 516
Tuskegee Institute, 638, 639
TVA. *See* Tennessee Valley Authority
Twain, Mark (Samuel Langhorne
    Clemens), 515
    on baseball, 571
    on Comstock Lode, 501
    on Gilded Age, 518–519, 545
Tweed, William Marcy ("Boss"), 573
Twenty-sixth Amendment, 856, 871
Two Moons (Cheyenne chief), 495
Tycoons, in Gilded Age, 520
"Typewriters" (secretarial workers),
    563

U-2 spy plane incident, 808
U-boats. *See* Submarines
UFW. *See* United Farm Workers
Ukraine, Holocaust and, 762*(i)*
UN. *See* United Nations
Underconsumption, Great Depression
    and, **713,** 718
Underwood tariff (1913), 633
Undocumented immigrants. *See* Illegal
    immigrants
Unemployment
    in 1920s, 677
    in 1930s, 699–700
    in 1937–1940, 732
    of African Americans, 728–729
    Carter and, 900
    Clinton, Bill, and, 934
    in depression of 1870s, 481, 560
    in depression of 1890s, 544, 560,
        577, 593, 594
    in Great Recession, 947
    industrial recovery and, 717–718
    Kennedy, J. F., and, 831
    Nixon and, 855
    Reagan and, 909–910
    after World War I, 664
Unification, of Germany, 925

Unilateralism, in foreign policy of
    Bush, G. W., 944, 945
Union (labor). *See* Labor unions
Unionists, in South, 465, 473
Union Pacific Railroad, 524
Union Party, 721
Union Signal, 591
United Farm Workers (UFW),
    846*(i),* 847
United Fruit Company, 600, 806
United Mine Workers (UMW), 620,
    621, 724
    strike by (1943), 751
United Nations (UN), 765
    Charter of, 765
    Commission on the Status of
        Women (UN), 852
    Iraq War (2003–2011) and, 944
    Korean War and, 793
    Persian Gulf War and, 928–930,
        929*(m)*
    Rwanda civil war and, 936
    total nuclear test ban treaty of, 927
    on U.S. invasion of Panama, 928
    women's meetings sponsored by,
        852–853
UN Decade for Women, 852
United States. *See also* Constitution
    (U.S.); Government (U.S.)
    internationalization of, 938–939
    League of Nations and, 664
    role of, 951–952
    as superpower, 769–770
    United Nations and, 765
U.S. Biological Survey, 509*(b)*
U.S. Communist Party. *See*
    Communist Party
U.S. Congress. *See* Congress (U.S.)
United States Constitution. *See*
    Constitution (U.S.)
U.S. Forest Service, 509*(b)*
U.S. Geological Survey, West and,
    508*(b)*
U.S. Government. *See* Government
    (U.S.)
U.S. Steel (USX), 520, 529–530, 624
U.S. Supreme Court. *See* Supreme
    Court (U.S.)
United States v. Cruikshank (1876), 482
United States v. E. C. Knight Company
    (1895), 543
Universal Declaration of Human Rights
    (UN, 1948), women and, 852

Universal health insurance, 931
Universal male suffrage, 473
Universal Negro Improvement
    Association (UNIA), 688
Universities and colleges. *See also*
        Higher education
    black studies and, 848
    funding for, 834
    Pell grants and, 855
    protests in, 878
    sexual revolution (1920s) and, 686*(b)*
    student financial aid for, 931
    women in, 815, 847–848
    after World War II, 785–786,
        814–815
University of California, free speech
    movement at Berkeley, 847
University of Chicago, women at,
    847–848
Unskilled workers, 553, 555, 560,
    563, 586
Uprisings. *See* Protest(s); Revolts and
    rebellions
Urban areas. *See also* Cities and towns
    electricity in, 528
    in Great Depression, 700
    housing in, 551
    population in, 513*(f)*
    population shift to (1920–1930),
        692*(m)*
    progressivism and, 612–613
    uprisings in (1965–1968), 843–844,
        843*(m)*
Urban industrialism
    commercialized leisure and, 569
    social problems of, 577–578
    in West, 501
    women activists and, 591
Urbanization. *See also* Cities and
        towns
    global migration, immigration,
        and, 551–555
    produce markets and, 513
Urban renewal, 831
USA Patriot Act (2001), **943**
Utah, 491, 515
    Mormons in, 505
    women's voting rights in, 505, 593

Vacations, paid, 680
Vaccines, polio, 801
Vagrancy, black codes and, 466
Valentino, Rudolph, 689

Values
  of hippies, 848
  traditional *vs.* modern, 676
Vandenberg, Arthur, 777, 779(*b*)
Vanderbilt family
  Alice, 559
  Alva, 559
  Cornelius ("Commodore"), 523, 559
  William K., 559
Vanzetti, Bartolomeo, 693
Vaqueros, 513
Vaqueros in a Horse Corral (Walker), 505(*i*)
Vaux, Calvert, 572
Venereal disease, 613
Venezuela, 600, 627
Veracruz, Marines in, 645–646
Versailles, Paris peace conference at, 659
Versailles treaty (1919), **662,** 662(*i*), 742
Vertical integration, 525
Veterans
  African American, 786, 787
  in colleges and universities, 815
  GI Bill and, 785–786
  in Great Depression, 723
  of Vietnam War, 883, 886
  after World War I, 664, 691
Vetoes
  by Cleveland, 558
  by Johnson, Andrew, 467, 470
Vice
  birth control movement and, 636
  social purity movement and, 613
Vice president. *See* Elections
Vichy France, 745
Victorians, sexuality and, 686–687(*b*)
Vietcong, 866, 870(*i*), 884
Vietminh, 805
Vietnam. *See also* Indochina
  containment in, 805–806
  immigrants from, 939
  independence from France, 805
  Kennedy, J. F., and, 862
Vietnamization policy, in Vietnam War, 878
Vietnam Veterans Memorial (1982), 886
Vietnam War (1964–1975), 860–861, 860(*i*), 867(*m*). *See also* Vietnam
  Americanization of, 870–871
  atrocities in, 886
  bombings in, 869, 870–871
  casualties in, 861, 886(*t*)

costs and effects of, 887–888
Johnson, L. B., and, 835
Kennedy, J. F., and, 866–868, 867(*m*)
legacy of, 885–886
mothers against, 874(*i*)
Nixon and, 882–885
peace accords in, 884–885
protests against, 873–878, 882–883
pro-war demonstrations during, 883(*i*)
soldiers in, 869, 869(*f*), 871–872, 872(*i*)
Tet Offensive in, 875–878, 875(*i*)
U.S. troops in, 869(*f*)
veterans of, 883, 886
Vietnamese civilians during, 870(*i*)
Villa, Francisco ("Pancho"), 646
Violence. *See also* Race riots; Riots; Strikes
  in 1968, 878
  against African Americans, 787, 839–840
  against southerns blacks, 469, 483–484
  in United States (1968), 876(*b*)
Violence against Women Act (1994), 931
Virginia, 462, 484. *See also* Tobacco and tobacco industry
  Readjusters in, 533
Virginia City, 501, 502, 503, 504
VISTA. *See* Volunteers in Service to America
Visual arts, in 1950s, 819, 819(*i*)
Voice of America, 781
Volunteers in Service to America (VISTA), 833
Voter Education Project (1961), 839
Voting and voting rights. *See also* Elections; Woman suffrage
  African Americans and, 828–829, 834, 839–841, 841(*i*), 842(*m*)
  age for voting and (1971), 856
  equal, 787
  Fourteenth Amendment and, 468–469
  Fifteenth Amendment and, 471–472
  for freedmen, 462, 470, 472
  interference with, 482
  "one person, one vote" principle and, 837
  during Reconstruction, 459, 474

in South, 459, 470, 474
Twenty-sixth Amendment and, 856, 871
voter turnout and, 531, 596
for women, 468–469, 471–472, 505, 636–637, 684
Voting Rights Act (1965), **834,** 840–841, 841(*i*)
  extensions of, 856, 911

Wabash v. Illinois (1886), 542
Waco, Texas, religious cult in, 932
Wade, Benjamin, 461, 462
Wade-Davis bill (1864), 461–462
Wage(s)
  in 1950s, 811
  in Comstock, 503
  Fair Labor Standards Act and, 734
  at Ford, 682
  in Gilded Age, 561, 562, 563
  of immigrants, 555
  industrial, 655(*f*)
  of management, 562
  for migrant laborers, 514
  minimum, 947
  in Pullman, 588
  of railroad workers, 564
  for women, 561, 563
  workers and, 560, 935
Wage freeze, 855
Wage labor. *See also* Labor
  in ranching, 512
Wagner, Robert, 724, 734
Wagner Act (NLRA, 1935), **723**–724, 788
Waite, Davis H., 588
Wald, Lillian, 613
Walker, James, 505(*i*)
Walking city, 558
Wallace, George C., 879, 879(*m*)
Wallace, Henry A., 788
Wall Street
  crash of 1929 and, 697, 714
  Main Street and, 520
  Roosevelt, T., and, 620
War(s) and warfare. *See* Guerrilla war; Nuclear arms race; specific battles and wars
War crimes. *See also* Holocaust; Milosevic, Slobodan
  in Vietnam War, 883
Ward, Lester Frank, 616
Wards of the state, Indians as, 491, 494

Ware, Isaac, 584(*i*)
War Industries Board (WIB), 654
Warm Springs, Georgia, 709
Warner, Charles Dudley, 518,
    522–523
War on Poverty, 833, **834,** 837
War on terror, Obama and, 950–951
Warren, Earl, and *Warren Court,*
    837–838
    Brown decision and, 820
    report on Kennedy, John F., assassi-
        nation and, 832
Wars of national liberation,
    Khrushchev and, 862
Wartime reconstruction (Civil War),
    460–463, 461(*i*)
Washington (state), 515
Washington, Booker T., 475(*i*), 638,
    638(*i*), 639
Washington, D.C., Coxey's army in,
    594–595
Washington Disarmament Conference
    (1921), 679
Washington Monument, 525
Washington Post, on U.S. empire, 607
Washita River, massacre at, 493
Water
    on plains, 507–510
    TVA and, 715, 717(*i*)
Watergate scandal, **897**–898, 897(*i*)
Water pollution. *See also* Clean Air
    Act; Environment
    Carter and, 903
    environmentalists and, 856
    Johnson, L. B., and, 835
Watson, Henry, 476(*b*), 584
Watson, Tom, 595, 596
Watt, James, 909
Watts riots (1965), 843(*m*), 844
"Waving the bloody shirt," 480
WCTU. *See* Woman's Christian
    Temperance Union
We (Lindbergh), 690
Wealth
    in 1920s, 697
    Bush, G. W., and, 941
    distribution of, 697, 713
    in Gilded Age, 520, 523, 559
    under Reagan, 910–911
    social Darwinism on, 530
Wealth gap, 523, 530, 549–550, 559, 920
    in 1990s, 935
    Reagan and, 910–911

Weapons. *See also* Nuclear weapons
    Agent Orange as, 868
    Eisenhower and, 808
    global production comparison in
        World War II, 752(*f*)
    inspections in Iraq, 936
    nuclear, 780–781, 808–809
    in World War II, 754(*i*)
Weapons of mass destruction,
    Iraq War and, 944, 945
Wehrmacht (German army), 746, 762
Welfare and welfare system
    AFDC and, 834, 932–933
    Bush, G. W., and, 941
    Clinton, Bill, and, 933, 933(*i*)
    Johnson, L. B., and, 834
    in New Deal, 722–730
    TANF and, 933
    "welfare queens" and, 932–933
    after World War II, 785
Welfare capitalism, 680
Welfare state
    in New Deal, 722–730
    Nixon extension of, 854–855
    private, in 1950s, 811
Wells, Ida B., antilynching
        campaign of, 533–536,
        534–535(*b*), 536(*i*)
Welsh immigrants, 501
West (U.S. region). *See also* Pacific
    Ocean region; Sun Belt
    African Americans in, 814
    cowboys in, 489, 512, 513, 514
    diversity in, 504–506
    economy in, 514
    environmental preservation in,
        855–856
    farming in, 508(*b*), 509(*b*), 512,
        513–514, 582–583
    federal government and,
        508–509(*b*)
    free silver and, 543, 544, 595
    in Gilded Age, 515–516
    Homestead Act and, 507
    Indians and, 488, 489, 490–496,
        492(*m*)
    land in, 507–514
    Mexican Americans in, 814
    migration to, 812
    mining in, 501–504, 502(*m*),
        505–506
    movement to, 507–514
    natural resources in, 508(*b*)

    railroads in, 507, 510, 511(*m*),
        520–521, 521(*m*), 522, 582–583
    ranching in, 505, 509(*b*), 512, 513
    Roosevelt, Theodore, and, 625
    territorial government in, 515
    Turner on, 488, 489
    woman suffrage in, 505, 591, 593
West Bank, 881, 882, 904, 917, 937
West Berlin, 780
    Berlin Wall and, 864
    protests in (1968), 876(*b*)
West Coast. *See* Pacific Ocean region
Western Europe. *See also* Europe and
    Europeans
    foreign aid to, 777–780
Western Federation of Miners (WFM),
    587–588
Western Hemisphere. *See also*
    America(s); Latin America
    Monroe Doctrine and, 600,
        625, 645
    U.S. sphere of influence in, 597
Western Union, 523
West Germany, 775
    end of Cold War and, 925
Westinghouse, George W., 528
Westmoreland, William, 871
West Virginia, 564
West Virginia (battleship), 748(*i*)
Weyler, Valeriano ("Butcher"), 601,
    602(*b*), 603(*b*), 604
What Social Classes Owe to Each Other
    (Sumner), 530
Wheat, 514
Whippings, of blacks, 462
White, William Allen, 604
White City (World's Columbian
    Exposition), 488, 574(*b*),
    576, 577
White-collar workers, 562–563
    in 1950s, 811
    women as, 684
White flight, integration and, 896
White House, use of name, 619
Whites
    emancipation and, 463
    in feminist movement, 851
    as immigrants, 556
    in Indian lands, 491, 500
    median income for (1999), 935
    progressivism for, 636–639
    social Darwinism and, 556
    in South, 459, 482, 483, 533

in southern Africa, 881
in southern Republican Party, 473
student protest by, 847–848
in West, 814
White supremacy
Ku Klux Klan and, 473, 693–694
Reconstruction and, 466, 482–484
in South, 480, 483
"White terror," 473
Wilderness
mining allowed in, 941
preservation of, 624–625, 856
Wild West show, 489, 490(i)
Wilhelm II (Germany), 646, 649(i), 652
Willard, Frances, 580–581, 582(i)
Woman's Christian Temperance
Union and, 537, 590–591
Williamsburg Bridge, 571
Willkie, Wendell, 746
Wilson, Edith, 656, 658(i)
Wilson, Woodrow, 630, 632(i)
election of 1912 and, 631–633
election of 1916 and, 634, 648
election of 1920 and, 671
foreign policy of, 644–654
Fourteen Points of, 659
League of Nations and, 659–662,
663(i)
neutrality in World War I and, 643,
647–648
progressivism and, 631–634
reforms and, 633–634
segregation and, 638–639
Versailles treaty and, 662–664,
662(i)
on women's rights, 656
World War I and, 643–644,
658–659
Winnemucca, Sarah, 494
Wisconsin, La Follette in, 617
Witch-hunts, against radicalism,
667(b)
Wobblies. *See* Industrial Workers of
the World
Wolfensohn, James D., 938
Woman Rebel (newspaper), 636
***Woman's Christian Temperance
Union (WCTU),* 537,** 580, 581,
590–591
postcard of, 592(i)
Woman's Crusade, 537
Woman's rights. *See* Feminism and
feminists; Women

Woman suffrage, 570, 637(i), **672**
14th Amendment and, 468–469
15th Amendment and, 471–472
19th Amendment and, 656,
657(m), 684
movement for, 536, 592–593, 593(i)
progressivism and, 616
in West, 505, 591, 593
Willard and, 581
Wilson and, 634
World War I and, 655–656
Women. *See also* Feminism; Gender
and gender issues; Slavery;
Voting and voting rights
in 1950s, 816–817
activism of, 533–536, 536–537,
590–593, 844
affirmative action for, 853
in CCC, 715
in Clinton cabinet, 932
in combat, 930(i)
on Comstock, 502–503, 504
cult of domesticity and, 569
as domestic servants, 569
education for, 683, 852
employment of, 816
equality and, 830
Farmers' Alliance and, 583, 584
in feminist movement, 850–851
Fourteenth Amendment and, 468
in garment industry, 561
in higher education, 815
as homesteaders, 507–510, 510(i)
as immigrants, 506, 555
Irish American, 502–503, 569
labor movement and, 566, 614–616
in middle class, 569, 570
in military, 750
Native American, 499, 500(i)
in New Deal, 728
new woman and, 676, 683–685
occupations for, 684
politics and, 533, 580, 581
separate spheres doctrine and, 533
sexual revolution (1920s) and,
686–687(b)
in South, 478(i), 533, 668–669
on Supreme Court, 912
in temperance movement, 536–537,
537(i), 570, 581, 590–591
in textile industry, 532, 560, 591
University of Chicago protests by,
847–848

in Vietnam War, 871
voting rights for, 468–469,
471–472, 505, 636–637, 684
in workforce, 560, 561, 561(i), 562,
562(f), 563, 701, 784, 785(f),
811, 816
World War I and, 655–656
in World War II, 750, 756–757
after World War II, 786(i)
Women's clubs, 536, 570
Women's liberation, 850–851
Women's movement. *See also*
Feminism and feminists;
Women
feminism and, 850–853
Women's Political Council (WPC), 821
Women's rights
activism for, 850
voting before 19th Amendment,
657(m)
Women's Trade Union League
(WTUL), 614, 615
Women Strike for Peace (WSP), 874(i)
Wood, Leonard, 499
Woodland peoples, 491
Woodstock Music Festival, 848
Woolworth's, lunch counter sit-in at,
838, 839(i)
Work. *See also* Labor; Workers;
Workplace
women and (1870–1890), 562(f)
Workday
in coal mines, 621
eight-hour, 567, 569, 585, 634, 655
Fair Labor Standards Act and, 734
in mining industry, 587
in steel industry, 525, 562
ten-hours, for women, 616
Workers. *See also* Factories; Labor;
Labor unions; Strikes; Women;
Workforce; Working class
in 1930s, 698, 699
African American, 462, 669
on Brooklyn Bridge, 548–549,
550(i)
Carnegie and, 525, 562, 585–586
Chinese immigrants as, 506, 506(i)
Farmers' Alliance and, 583, 584
in France, 876(b)
in Gilded Age, 551, 560–563,
563–569
homes for, 812
industrial, 551, 560

Workers *(continued)*
    in Pullman, 588–589, 589(*i*), 590
    on railroads, 523
    regulation and, 678
    skilled, 555, 559, 563, 566
    Social Security and, 725–728
    tariffs and, 542
    unskilled, 553, 555, 560, 563
    wages of, 514, 555, 560
    white-collar, 562–563
    women as, 562, 562(*f*), 563, 756
    after World War I, 666–667(*b*)
Workforce. *See also* Workers
    in 1950s, 809–810
    African Americans in, 758
    of Carnegie, 551
    diversity of, 560–561
    women in, 503, 560, 561, 561(*i*), 562,
        562(*f*), 784, 785(*f*), 811, 816
    after World War II, 784
Working class. *See also* Workers
    birth control movement and, 636
    in cities, 577
    families in, 560, 561–562
    leisure of, 569, 570–571
    militancy in 1930s, 702–703
    politics and, 531
    progressivism and, 614–616
    school busing and, 895
Workingmen's Party, 506
Workplace, women in, 591
Works Progress Administration
    (WPA), **723**–724, 726(*b*)
World Bank, on globalization, 938
World Boxing Association, 873
World Jewish Congress, 759
World's Columbian Exposition
    (Chicago, 1893), 488, 489–490,
    574–575(*b*), **576**–577
World Trade Center, September 11,
    2001, destruction of, 942, 943(*i*)
World Trade Organization (WTO),
    937
World War I (1914–1918), 659–662.
    See also Allies (World War I)
    AEF in, 642, 653(*m*)
    African Americans and, 651,
        669–670

alliances in, 646, 647(*m*)
armistice in, 652
Asia and, 661
casualties in, 643, 651, 652,
    653–654, 672
democracy after, 664–671
Europe before, 646
Europe after, 659–662, 661(*m*)
France and, 650, 651–652, 660
Germany and, 646, 647, 660
home front in, 654–655
industry during, 654
Japan after, 661
legacy of, 740
Ottoman empire after, 660
patriotism and, 644, 654, 657
peace settlement after, 659–664
Red scare after, 665–668
soldiers in, 650–651
submarine warfare in, 648
trench warfare in, 643, 651, 652(*i*)
U.S. entry into, 649–650
U.S. neutrality in, 643, 647–648
women in, 655–656
World War II (1939–1945). *See also*
    Allies (World War II); Nazi
    Germany
    alliances in, 748
    Atlantic, battle of the, 754
    casualties in, 748, 763, 765,
        767–768
    economy during, 750–752,
        756–757
    Europe divided after, 775–776,
        776(*m*)
    Europe in, 754–755, 764(*m*)
    events leading to, 745–746
    GI mail during, 738(*i*)
    home front in, 756–762
    Japan after, 769–770
    Japanese Americans during,
        749–750, 750(*m*)
    labor during, 758
    mobilization for, 749–752
    Nazi aggression in, 743–745, 744(*m*)
    opening of, 743–745, 743–749,
        744(*m*)
    Pacific battles in, 753

politics during, 758–759
poster from, 741(*i*)
second front in, 763, 774
Tibbets in, 738–740, 740(*i*)
U.S. entry into, 748–749
Wounded Knee
    Indian takeover at, 845
    massacre at (1890), **500**
Wovoka (Paiute shaman), 500
WPA. *See* Works Progress
    Administration
Wright, Frank Lloyd, 574(*b*)
WTO. *See* World Trade Organization
Wyoming, 515
    voting by women in, 505, 591

Ximenes, Vicente T., 847

Yalta Conference (1945), 765
Yamamoto, Isoroku (Japan), 753
Yankee imperialism, in Latin America,
    870
Yellow journalism, 602(*b*), **604**
Yellow Wolf (Nez Percé), 498
Yeomen
    Reconstruction and, 483
    in southern Republican Party, 473
YMCA, 651, 655
Yom Kippur War (1973), 855, 881
Young, Brigham, 505
Young Americans for Freedom (YAF),
    893
Young people. *See also* Students
    activism of, 844, 847–848
    as immigrants, 555
    working class, 570
Youth movement
    Beats and, 819
    voting and, 856
Yugoslavia, breakup of, 937(*m*)
    fighting in former, 936
    after World War I, 660

Zimmermann, Arthur, and
    Zimmermann telegram, 650
Zitkala-Sa, 497
Zones of occupation, in postwar
    Germany, 775